The Official History of t
Intelligence Committee

CW01499959

Volume I of *The Official History of the Joint Intelligence Committee* draws upon a range of released and classified papers to produce the first, authoritative account of the way in which intelligence was used to inform policy.

For almost 80 years the Joint Intelligence Committee (JIC) has been a central player in the secret machinery of the British Government, providing a co-ordinated intelligence service to policy makers and drawing upon the work of the intelligence agencies and Whitehall departments. Since its creation, reports from the JIC have contributed to almost every key foreign policy decision taken by the British Government. This volume covers the evolution of the JIC since 1936 and culminates with its role in the events of Suez in 1956.

This book will be of much interest to students of intelligence studies, British politics, international diplomacy, security studies and international relations in general.

Michael S. Goodman is Reader in Intelligence and International Affairs in the Department of War Studies, King's College London. He is the author or editor of five previous books, including the *Routledge Companion to Intelligence Studies* (2013).

Whitehall histories: government official history series
ISSN: 1474-8398

The Government Official History series began in 1919 with wartime histories, and the peacetime series was inaugurated in 1966 by Harold Wilson. The aim of the series is to produce major histories in their own right, compiled by historians eminent in the field, who are afforded free access to all relevant material in the official archives. The Histories also provide a trusted secondary source for other historians and researchers while the official records are not in the public domain. The main criteria for selection of topics are that the histories should record important episodes or themes of British history while the official records can still be supplemented by the recollections of key players; and that they should be of general interest, and, preferably, involve the records of more than one government department.

The United Kingdom and the European Community
Vol. I: The Rise and Fall of a National Strategy, 1945–1963
Alan S. Milward

Secret Flotillas
Vol. I: Clandestine Sea Operations to Brittany, 1940–1944
Vol. II: Clandestine Sea Operations in the Mediterranean, North Africa and the Adriatic 1940–1944
Sir Brooks Richards

SOE in France
M. R. D. Foot

The Official History of the Falklands Campaign
Vol. I: The Origins of the Falklands War
Vol. II: War and Diplomacy
Sir Lawrence Freedman

The Official History of Britain and the Channel Tunnel
Terry Gourvish

Churchill's Mystery Man: Desmond Morton and the World of Intelligence
Gill Bennett

The Official History of Privatisation
Vol. I: The Formative Years 1970–1987
Vol. II: Popular Capitalism 1987–1997
David Parker

Secrecy and the Media: The Official History of the D-Notice System
Nicholas Wilkinson

The Official History of the Civil Service: Reforming the Civil Service
Vol. I: The Fulton Years, 1966–1981
Rodney Lowe

The Official History of North Sea Oil and Gas
Vol. I: The Growing Dominance of the State
Vol. II: Moderating the State's Role
Alex Kemp

The Official History of Britain and the European Community
Vol. II: From Rejection to Referendum, 1963–1975
Stephen Wall

The Official History of the Joint Intelligence Committee
Volume I: From the Approach of the Second World War to the Suez Crisis
Michael S. Goodman

The Official History of the Joint Intelligence Committee

Volume I: From the Approach
of the Second World War to
the Suez Crisis

Michael S. Goodman

Routledge
Taylor & Francis Group

LONDON AND NEW YORK

First published in paperback in 2016

First published 2014
by Routledge
2 Park Square, Milton Park, Abingdon, Oxon OX14 4RN

and by Routledge
711 Third Avenue, New York, NY 10017

Routledge is an imprint of the Taylor & Francis Group, an informa business

British Library Cataloguing in Publication Data
A catalogue record for this book is available from the British Library

Library of Congress Cataloging in Publication Data
Goodman, Michael S.
The official history of the Joint Intelligence Committee / Michael
S. Goodman.
    pages cm.—(Whitehall histories : government official history series)
  Includes bibliographical references and index.
  1. Great Britain. Joint Intelligence Committee—History. 2. Great
Britain—Foreign relations—20th century. 3. Intelligence service—
Great Britain—History—20th century. I. Title.
  JN329.I6G67 2014
  327.1241—dc23   2013050458

ISBN: 978-0-415-84104-7 (hbk)
ISBN: 978-1-138-92500-7 (pbk)
ISBN: 978-1-315-88156-0 (ebk)

Typeset in Baskerville
by Keystroke, Station Road, Codsall, Wolverhampton

This book is dedicated to my lovely family.

Contents

List of Illustrations

Foreword by the Chairman of the Joint Intelligence Committee

As the current Chairman of the Joint Intelligence Committee (JIC) I have been invited to provide a few words about this book, which is the first in the series of Official Histories to address post-war intelligence history.

In recent years several books have appeared which tell the story of British Intelligence, notably Christopher Andrew's work on the Security Service and Keith Jeffrey's book on the Secret Intelligence Service. It is hoped that this volume on the history of the JIC will go some way towards completing the picture as the Committee sits at the centre of the intelligence community, acting as the interface between the worlds of intelligence and policy.

The genesis of this book lies in the Butler report, which examined the intelligence effort prior to the start of the Iraq War of 2003. Before it, little had been published or was known outside Whitehall and a few academic institutions about the workings of the JIC, although the publication of *Know Your Enemy*, by one of my esteemed predecessors, Sir Percy Cradock, is a notable exception. Public interest in this organisation emerged following the publication of the Butler report and in a time of greater transparency over public activity it is hoped that this history will provide a record of the contribution made by the Committee to the formulation of foreign policy since its inception in 1936.

Another reason for writing this history is to provide the academic world and independent researchers with a sound basis upon which to draw, from records available in The National Archives (TNA) and those yet to be released. In particular, this account draws upon a range of retained files and offers an authoritative account of the evolution of the JIC.

It is also intended to help present day practitioners working within the intelligence community to understand something of their own history and the tradition within which they work and the lessons which can be learned from past experience.

Dr Michael Goodman, a Reader in the Department of War Studies, King's College London, has had the advantage of being able to interview a significant number of former civil servants who worked on the Committee. In addition to the papers in TNA, he has had unrestricted access to the closed files of the Cabinet Office and those of several other departments, including the Foreign Office and Ministry of Defence. Dr Goodman has formed his views on the performance of the JIC on the basis of his extensive researches. The present volume covers the period to the end of the 1950s, and a second volume is in preparation which will take the story up to the end of the Cold War. For those historians who have long awaited a definitive history of the JIC, this volume should fill that gap.

Jon Day, CBE
Chairman of the Joint Intelligence Committee

List of abbreviations

ACAS(I)	Assistant Chief of the Air Staff (Intelligence)
AEIC	Atomic Energy Intelligence Committee
AIOC	Anglo-Iranian Oil Company
APS	Axis Planning Section
AUS	Assistant Under Secretary of State, Foreign Office
BIOS	British Intelligence Objectives Sub-Committee
BJSM	British Joint Services Mission
'C'	Chief of SIS
CAS	Chief of the Air Staff
CBW	Chemical and Biological (Bacteriological) Warfare
CIA	Central Intelligence Agency
CID	Committee of Imperial Defence
CIG	Central Intelligence Group, US
CIGS	Chief of the Imperial General Staff
CIOS	Combined Intelligence Objectives Sub-Committee
CNS	Chief of the Naval Staff
COS	Chiefs of Staff
COSSAC	Chief of Staff to Supreme Allied Commander
CRO	Commonwealth Relations Office
CX	SIS Reporting
DCOS	Deputy Chiefs of Staff
D-G	Director-General
DIS	Defence Intelligence Staff
DMI	Director of Military Intelligence
DMO&I	Director of Military Operations and Intelligence
DNI	Director of Naval Intelligence
DUS	Deputy Under Secretary of State, Foreign Office
FCI	Industrial Intelligence in Foreign Countries Sub-Committee
FO	Foreign Office
FO(E)S	Future Operations (Enemy) Section
GC&CS	Government Code and Cypher School
GCHQ	Government Communication Headquarters
GSO	General Staff Officer

ICBM	Inter-Continental Ballistic Missile
IIC	Industrial Intelligence Centre
IRD	Information Research Department
IS(O)	Intelligence Section (Operations)
ISIC	Inter-Service Intelligence Committee
ISSB	Inter-Service Security Board
ISTD	Inter-Service Topographical Department
JCS	US Joint Chiefs of Staff
JIB	Joint Intelligence Bureau
JIC	Joint Intelligence Committee
JIC(ACA)	Joint Intelligence Committee (Allied Commission for Austria)
JIC(AF)	Joint Intelligence Committee (Allied Force)
JIC(CCG)	Joint Intelligence Committee (Control Commission Germany)
JIC(FE)	Joint Intelligence Committee (Far East)
JIC(G)	Joint Intelligence Committee (Germany)
JIC(ME)	Joint Intelligence Committee (Middle East)
JIC(SEAC)	Joint Intelligence Committee (South East Asia Command)
JIC(W)	Joint Intelligence Committee (Washington)
JIS	Joint Intelligence Staff
JPC	Joint Planning Committee
JPS	Joint Planning Staff
JSIC	Joint Scientific Intelligence Committee
JSTIC	Joint Scientific and Technical Intelligence Committee
JTIC	Joint Technical Intelligence Committee
JSM	Joint Staff Mission
LIC	Local Intelligence Committee
LSIB	London Signals Intelligence Board
MEW	Ministry of Economic Warfare
MI5	Security Service
MI6	Secret Intelligence Service
MoD	Ministry of Defence
MSC	Military Sub-Committee
NARA II	US National Archives and Records Administration II Archive, College Park, MD, USA.
NSC	National Security Council, US
ONE	Office of National Estimates
OSS	Office of Strategic Services
PHP	Post-Hostilities Planning
PHPS	Post-Hostilities Planning Staff
PIG	Political Intelligence Group
PRC	People's Republic of China
PSIS	Committee of Permanent Secretaries on Intelligence Services
PUS	Permanent Under Secretary
PUSC	Permanent Under Secretary's Committee
PUSD	Permanent Under Secretary's Department

SAC	Strategical Appreciation Committee
SAF	Soviet Air Force
SCUA	Suez Canal User's Association
SEAC	South-East Asia Command
SHAEF	Supreme Headquarters Allied Expeditionary Force
SHAPE	Supreme Headquarters Allied Powers Europe
SIS	Secret Intelligence Service
SRC	Situation Report Centre
SSB	Secret Service Bureau
SSU	Strategic Services Unit
STIB	Scientific and Technical Intelligence Branch (Germany)
TNA	The National Archives, Kew
UKUSA	UK-US Sigint agreement
USAF	United States Air Force
WMD	Weapons of Mass Destruction
WRCI	Weekly Review of Current Intelligence
WSI	Weekly Survey of Intelligence

Introduction

I think all my colleagues would agree that it will be in the future quite impossible for anybody to unravel with any accuracy from the archives the detailed history of events . . .

Lord Greenhill of Harrow
Chairman of the Joint Intelligence Committee, 1966–8[1]

The Joint Intelligence Committee (JIC) has often been regarded as a secret organisation on a par with the other intelligence agencies, yet in many ways it has acquired a greater mystique because it is less well known or understood. Indeed, until members of the JIC were called to account for their 2002 dossier on Iraqi weapons of mass destruction, prepared for the Blair government, the JIC was one of the less talked about and least understood of Whitehall committees. This volume, in charting the JIC's first twenty years, from its origins in 1936 to the events at Suez in 1956, seeks to throw some light on this enigmatic Whitehall organisation and to assess how effective it was. In doing so it sets out how successful the JIC system has been in providing a coherent voice on intelligence for policymakers and in becoming an indispensable element of central government.

Created in 1936 to remedy the lack of co-ordination in the British intelligence community, the JIC has since then been involved in every single defining moment of British diplomatic and military history in the twentieth and twenty-first centuries. A 1944 paper nicely summarised its wartime functions:

> The Joint Intelligence Committee in addition to its responsibility for co-ordinating the product of the various collectors of intelligence into the form of agreed advice on enemy intentions, has the additional responsibility of watching, directing and to some extent controlling the British intelligence organisation throughout the world, so as to ensure that intelligence is received at the most economical cost in time, effort and manpower, so as to prevent overlapping.[2]

The Committee had nine Chairmen during the period covered in this volume.[3] After a slow start, the JIC rapidly rose to prominence during the Second World War, firmly establishing itself as a central and integral component of the British governmental machinery. Towards the end of the war its Chairman and Secretary produced a forward looking report on the 'Intelligence Machine', and in a notable phrase they captured the precise ethos of the JIC: 'we believe that no Department, however experienced and well staffed, has anything to lose by bringing the intelligence directly available to it to the *anvil of discussion*.'[4] The JIC has worked best when it has been used as a forum for debate and where its assessments have been relevant to decision making.

Throughout its first two decades the JIC was a sub-committee of the Chiefs of Staff but its remit extended far beyond simple military boundaries: in that twenty-year period the JIC had to deal with the rise and fall of several dictatorships, the onset of the Cold War, the start of Britain's retreat from Empire, and the peaks and troughs of the Anglo-American relationship.

The chapters in this volume have been arranged largely chronologically, and there are four key issues that are central to the history:

1)   how the JIC has developed (in terms of organisation and membership)
2)   how the process of all-source assessment supports the JIC's work (by examining, in detail, certain significant episodes)
3)   the impact of JIC assessments on policy (by examining the use made of the JIC's products in these case-studies; here I have taken 'policy' in its widest sense)
4)   the management by the JIC of the intelligence community (i.e. the setting of requirements and priorities, agency co-ordination).

The volume is arranged into three chronological sections. The first covers the origins of the JIC, 1936–9, when the JIC was established and needed to prove its value. The second focuses on the wartime years, when the JIC was able to demonstrate to military planners and policymakers the advantages of having an integrated intelligence assessment process. The third looks at the post-war years, up to the aftermath of the Suez affair. During this time the JIC faced a series of new threats, in particular from the Soviet Union with the onset of the Cold War, but also with more diverse threats elsewhere, including the rise of nationalism and challenges to the West in the Middle and Far East. Along the way the JIC had to be flexible to adapt to the new threats and the several crises that they posed; it also had to handle the changing intelligence relationship with the United States; and come to terms with the growing technological threat from atomic warfare. In addition, thematic chapters cover the JIC's post-war reorganisation and its relations with other intelligence communities, principally those of the United States, Canada, Australia, and New Zealand.

Reviewing the preparation of a publication on special operations in 1949 the JIC concluded by 'maintaining their view that they were always averse to the publication of secret matters'.[5] A similar discussion had taken place a year earlier on the thorny issue of whether historians working on the vast Official History series for the Second World War should be indoctrinated into 'special intelligence', or ULTRA, as it was called. The solution was to allow historians access to the material, but the writing was to be done in such a way that 'it will be impossible for anyone to deduce from reading the nature and value of intelligence obtained from this source'.[6] For the JIC, secret intelligence was just that. It was privileged information that should remain forever hidden. The idea of an Official History of the JIC would have been anathema to many of its illustrious members. Yet, seventy years after its first meeting that is precisely what happened, when the then Prime Minister, Tony Blair, announced my appointment as Official Historian of the JIC.[7]

An Official Historian is perhaps one of the strangest of academic creatures. On the one hand he can be the envy of colleagues, being provided with an historian's Valhalla: high level clearances, access to sensitive documents, and a free run in the archives. On the other hand the sword of Damocles is constantly hanging overhead: papers have to be reviewed for sensitivity and cleared in advance and, particularly, having to abide by official guidelines on what can be disclosed as authoritative regardless of what non-official papers (such as memoirs) might say. Clearly, given such a dichotomous position, the Official Historian needs to be sure that what is published is not only what he or she had in mind, but that the historical judgment has been reached objectively and free from governmental interference. This is a serious concern and some academics have regarded officialdom with scepticism. The nineteenth century Regius Professor of Modern History, Lord Acton, famously declared that 'there is an enmity between the truth of history and the reason of state, between sincere quest and official secrecy'.[8] Similarly, Sir Herbert Butterfield, another Cambridge historian, stated that 'we must never lose sight of the separate interests of officialdom on the one hand and the academic historian on the other, never allow the situation to be blurred or the tension and conflict between the two to be quietened.'[9]

The issue is mainly one of sources: Official Historians have unparalleled and unlimited access to files which have not yet been released. The problem was eloquently summarised by Hugh Trevor-Roper (later Lord Dacre), who said 'when a historian relies mainly on primary sources, which we cannot easily check, he challenges our confidence and forces us to ask critical questions. How reliable is his historical method? How sound is his judgment?'[10] Unlike the archives on which the recent MI5 and SIS authorised histories were based, most JIC records are routinely transferred to The National Archives (TNA) at their 30-year point, and are therefore far more accessible and well-organised in TNA.

The JIC records that are now released cover the Committee's various roles:

Assessments: The majority of the minutes and memoranda for the period covered by this volume have been released, and these provide a very good overview of how assessments changed over time. Some of the JIC Secretariat files have been released, though a great number have not. None of the Confidential Annex volumes have been released. Some of the Weekly Reviews of Current Intelligence have been released, but none of the more sensitive Weekly Surveys of Intelligence. A comparison of released and retained material reveals that the conclusions of the assessments generally are not affected, but there is, unsurprisingly, more specific information in the retained volumes. Furthermore there are some topics which are covered by retained files which are not revealed in the released files.

The result is that whilst the JIC's more strategic role is clear from the released record, its rather more tactical role in supporting decision making in operations and in crises has remained hidden. This conclusion is especially borne out by the Second World War records, where the JIC's memoranda have been preserved but, apart from a small handful of examples, none of the various daily summaries survive.

Management: From the released files the management function of the JIC remains virtually invisible. This role, historically, has been three-fold: setting requirements and priorities for the intelligence community; assessing the performance of the agencies themselves; and looking at methods of improving Britain's intelligence capability. It is in these areas, in addition to the JIC's tactical role, that this Official History hopes in particular to shed new light.

Any historical account would not be complete without accessing other governmental departments' files. It is perhaps in this category – access to sources – that this account differs from Sir Percy Cradock's book *Know Your Enemy*.[11] Not only is this history longer and broader, but the position of Official Historian permits access to a wider range of sources. Furthermore, it builds upon the important precedent set by the Sir Harry Hinsley volumes covering the Official History of *British Intelligence in the Second World War,* but includes far more detail on the role of personalities.[12]

There is a wealth of relevant papers in the PREM (Prime Ministerial) and CAB (Cabinet Office) group of records, as well as FO (Foreign Office), but above all else it is the records of the Foreign Office's Permanent Under Secretary's Department (PUSD) that often hold the key to understanding the JIC's successes and failures. Following Lord Franks' report on the Falklands War, the chairmanship of the JIC became a Cabinet Office appointment, having been historically a role reserved for a FO diplomat. Yet chairing the JIC was never a full-time position, and from 1939 onwards it was routinely combined with heading PUSD – the department in the FO responsible for liaising with the intelligence community, particularly SIS and GCHQ, but also the COS and the JIC. This ensured that during this period the JIC Chairman not only was the highest placed individual in the intelligence machine involved in the process of assessment, but was also centrally located and involved in operational and policy matters within the FO and, at times, 10 Downing Street. Today we might be concerned over the danger of politicisation of intelligence assessment by policy considerations, but in this period this was a crucial combination. PUSD records provide a wealth of JIC material and include papers which are often missing from the regular Cabinet Office series. So, typically, drafts of JIC reports can be found in PUSD records, whereas only the final version is preserved in the JIC series. Similarly, and often of the most value, are the notes and memoranda sent from the JIC Chairman, wearing his FO hat, to the Permanent Under Secretary (PUS). These invaluable records are slowly being reviewed and released in the FO 1093 series.

Another value of having an Official Historian's status is that former civil servants, diplomats and military personnel are prepared to be interviewed, usually without the restrictions of classification. I have had the great fortune to interview a fascinating mix of people. The great value of interviews, as many contemporary historians will attest, is that they fill in the gaps left in the official, documented record. For the JIC this is crucial for three reasons: oral history provides something of the colour and atmosphere of the JIC; as this is a history of a committee personalities are absolutely crucial, yet their contribution is all but missing from the archival record; and JIC records alone do not tell the whole story. This latter point needs some explanation.

Brian Stewart, the Secretary in the late 1960s, wrote about the science of minute writing. He noted that the minutes produced would not necessarily reflect the discussions in the Committee: '. . . it was an interesting challenge requiring us to invent an introduction and summing up to put in the mouth of the Chairman, to catch the sense of the meeting. Sometimes after particularly turbulent debate, we were forced to minute what we thought the members intended to say, rather than what they actually said'.[13] One of Stewart's predecessors in the early 1950s had a similar tale to tell:

> After a week in the job I got called into Searight's [Colonel Eric Searight, JIC Secretary] office and who said [discussing Alldis' draft minutes of a JIC meeting] "you can't make so and so say that". I said "but he did say it" and Searight said "but it's absolute tripe. You can't send that around Whitehall over his name". I said "well, what can I do about it?" "Oh no", he said, "your job is to make the minutes readable and correct and not to send out absolute nonsense". We didn't alter them factually, we just made them sound like they were uttered by intelligent and gifted and knowledgeable people. Sometimes you had to change them if they said something against the policies of their Department. Very rarely did Committee members want them [the resulting minutes] changing.[14]

Admiral John Godfrey, the DNI in the early part of the war, recorded that 'the personality of Secretary is very important. He must avoid the pitfalls of being entirely objective, merely recording the words of members and trying not to project his own views into the JIC papers'.[15] Thus it is clear that records alone cannot tell the whole story. They are incomplete so it is essential to fill the gaps through a combination of interviews with the few surviving participants and research in other departments' files.

Of the JIC members themselves, many of the FO Chairmen produced memoirs. It is interesting to compare what they say about their time serving on the JIC. The amount of material covering the activities of the JIC varies. Some were clearly disinclined to write about their experience, including Sir William Hayter (Chairman, 1946–9) and Sir Bernard Burrows (Chairman, 1963–6).[16] Burrows justifies the decision to omit four years of FO work on the basis that 'a good deal has been written . . . about the functioning of the Intelligence Services. I do not propose to add to this.'[17] Some former Chairmen, however, have written about their experiences, but these are often lacking in any great detail about the work or the nature of the Committee itself. Thus, for instance, Lord Greenhill (Chairman, 1966–8) does mention the JIC, as does Sir Percy Cradock (Chairman, 1985–92) in his quasi-memoir, devoting a whole chapter on its relationship to policy; while Sir Edward Peck, (Chairman, 1968–70) mentions that one of the most rewarding aspects was the regular lunch he had with 'C' atop Century House.[18]

In addition to the nature of the records themselves, there have been other difficulties and problems to overcome, and four other complicating factors are worth mentioning here:

The **first** is the range of topics. Anyone who has studied the JIC's records will have noted just how broad its remit has been. The Committee has produced assessments, both long term and immediate; has had a management function; has set collection requirements and priorities; has dealt with security matters; the clearance of books; allocation of codewords, and many more related subjects. Even considering the assessment side of the JIC's task alone, the range of topics covered is vast. The difficulty has been in conveying this worldwide coverage by the JIC in chapters that, generally speaking, focus on specific topics. By concentrating solely on assessments of Suez in 1956, for instance, the JIC's performance on that topic alone cannot be divorced from the fact that it was also involved in providing daily updates on events in Hungary at the same time. This is a problem which recurs throughout. Although for most of this period the Cold War was the JIC's main concern, it was not its only one. Statistically it is impossible to categorise JIC papers which often covered several subjects and from a variety of angles. Even where a paper focussed on a Third World country, for example, the role of Moscow was an important aspect to be assessed. A glimpse of any of the Committee's minutes reveals the global remit it was designed to fill.

A **second** difficulty is to know what exactly to include under the JIC umbrella. The full Committee had, at various points, a large number of sub-committees that were subordinate to it; furthermore, there were a number of regional and local JIC's that reported back to London. In addition, the role of the JIC Secretary sometimes took him beyond strictly-JIC work: Brian Stewart, for instance, also served as an investigator for the Intelligence Co-ordinator, a senior central official who was also a member of the JIC. How should the FO Chairman's role be considered when not strictly related to the JIC and how relevant were his other tasks to his JIC work? Suez is a classic example of this.

A **third** issue, and perhaps the most crucial, is demonstrating where intelligence made an impact on policy or a military decision. For the period covered by this volume it is somewhat easier than post-1957, when the JIC moved to the Cabinet Office, for the simple reason that many of the JIC papers were discussed, commented upon and approved by members of the COS Committee; they were therefore clearly read, if not necessarily acted on, by them. More difficult is trying to quantify the difference that the JIC made: we can examine events that happened and check whether the JIC was correct in its predictions; but when a JIC report relates to an event or circumstance when nothing happened, it is impossible to know the JIC's impact. Another of the JIC's more useful roles was the provision of regular updates on an evolving situation. The function, after all, was to keep readers as informed as possible, to reduce ignorance, and to provide context for decision making to take place. For the sake of space, this volume is largely restricted to coverage of those events that have been selected for their historical significance. However, there is a wide range of JIC assessments in the archives that pertain to regular updating on issues which never developed into a serious policy matter. The JIC provided justified reassurance at times as well as sounding the alarm.

A **fourth** and final problem has been trying to gauge who exactly this book is for. Official Histories are 'intended to provide authoritative histories in their own right; a reliable secondary source for historians until all the records are available in The National Archives'.[19] Balancing the level of historical context with the specific JIC content has not been an easy task, and this intentionally varies slightly from chapter to chapter, depending on the JIC's precise role and involvement. I hope it will satisfy a wide readership of academics, practitioners, and the general public alike.

Writing the Official History of the Joint Intelligence Committee has been and is an honour and a privilege. There are a great number of people to thank, without whom this book would not have possible, including: the team in the Cabinet Office, my advisory board, the reviewers and archivists across HMG, archivists in other repositories, and those with whom I have corresponded and interviewed. In particular I would like to thank Ian Beesley, John Gray, Matthew Jones, Ron Lawrence and Nick Weekes. I am especially indebted to the tireless work of my 'research assistant', Jane Knight, who has spent countless days, weeks and months of her life to improve the quality of this work. Despite the thousands of pages of redrafting, all errors (regretfully) are mine.

Has it been possible to maintain objectivity in the face of constraints? I believe so. The Cabinet Office contracts for Official Historians make it explicit that the interpretation is the historian's alone, and that control is limited to matters of security. Furthermore, a frighteningly well-read advisory board has ensured that objectivity and analytical rigour are maintained throughout. The views of the JIC in 1947 when discussing ULTRA are equally as relevant today, and underline the rationale in allowing Official Historians unrestricted access to archives: 'It would be impracticable to expect Historians to complete their work realistically without giving them the necessary information to appreciate the implications of signal [or any] intelligence . . . the danger to security would occur where historians had insufficient information to enable them to recognise the dangers involved'.[20]

In 1962 President Kennedy, commenting on the Foreign Relations of the United States series, said that 'The effectiveness of democracy as a form of government depends on an informed and intelligent citizenry.'[21] The Official History series is part of this tradition. To conclude, Professor D.C. Watt, writing almost fifty years ago, noted that 'the [official] historian is among things the custodian of the national memory. It is his responsibility to see that memory is kept as free as possible from the distortions of distance in time from the events remembered, of imperfect biased recollection, and of prejudice or ignorance.'[22] I could not agree more and I hope that this book is testimony to that fact.

Notes

1   D Greenhill, Letter to the Editor, *The Times* (7 May 1977).
2   JIC(44)86(0), 'The British Intelligence Organisation', 3 March 1944. CAB 81/121.
3   A list, with dates, is in the Appendices.
4   'The Intelligence Machine', 10 January 1945. CAB 163/6. Emphasis added.
5   JIC(49)123rd Meeting, 25 November 1949. CAB 163/256.
6   JIC(48)14(0), 'General Directive to Chief Historians for Safeguarding Special Intelligence Sources in Compiling Official Histories', 11 February 1948. CAB 163/288.
7   HC Deb, 26 April 2007, c27WS.
8   Cited in O Chadwick, *Acton and History* (Cambridge: Cambridge University Press, 1998). p.29.
9   H Butterfield, 'Official History: Its Pitfalls and Criteria', *Studies: An Irish Quarterly Review* 38:150 (1949), pp.129–44.
10   H Trevor-Roper, 'Hitler: Does History Offer a Defence?', *Sunday Times* (12 June 1977).
11   P Cradock, *Know Your Enemy: How the Joint Intelligence Committee Saw the World* (London: John Murray, 2002).
12   F H Hinsley et al, *British Intelligence in the Second World War* (London: HMSO, 1979–94).
13   B Stewart, *Scrapbook of a Roving Highlander: 80 Years Round Asia and Back* (Newark: Acorn Publications, 2002). p.260.
14   Interview with Cecil Alldis, 21 September 2009.
15   'Joint Intelligence Committee', Note by J.H.Godfrey, n.d. ADM 223/465.
16   Hayter does, however, mention heading the Services Liaison Department, the forerunner to PUSD, which brought 'closer acquaintance with the Intelligence organizations'. W G Hayter, *A Double Life: The Memoirs of Sir William Hayter* (London: Hamish Hamilton, 1974). pp.82–3; B Burrows, *Diplomat in a Changing World* (County Durham: The Memoir Club, 2001).
17   Burrows, *Diplomat in a Changing World.* p.150.
18   D Greenhill, *More by Accident* (York: Wilton, 1992); P Cradock, *In Pursuit of British Interests: Reflections on Foreign Policy under Margaret Thatcher and John Major* (London: John Murray, 1997); E H Peck, *Recollections, 1915–2005* (New Delhi: Paul's Press, 2005). p.232.
19   *The UK Government's Official History Programme* (Cabinet Office booklet, 2010).
20   JIC/1345/47, 'Use of Special Intelligence by Official Histories', 21 November 1947. CAB 163/288.
21   Cited in D P Myers, 'Publication and Declassification of Records', *The American Journal of International Law* 56:1 (1962), p.158.
22   D C Watt, 'Foreign Affairs, the Public Interest and the Right to Know', *Political Quarterly* 34 (1963), p.123.

Part One

Origins, 1936–1939

1   Why Joint Intelligence?

The Need for Central Intelligence

On Tuesday 7 July 1936, a few weeks before the spectacular opening by Adolf Hitler of the Berlin Olympics, seven men sat around a large ornate table in a four storey building just opposite the entrance to Downing Street to discuss what was known of the growing military challenge that Germany posed for the British Empire. Six of the men were officers representing the intelligence staffs of the Royal Navy, Army and Royal Air Force. The seventh was a shadowy civilian whose background was in an organisation that had then no official existence, the Secret Intelligence Service (SIS) or MI6. The building in which the meeting was taking place, No. 2 Whitehall Gardens, had made history before when an earlier occupant, Benjamin Disraeli, had held meetings of his Cabinet there.[1] Outside the front entrance the trees were the last remaining remnant of the Privy Garden of the Old Palace of Westminster.[2] Now the large ornate rooms, modelled in the French style similar to the interior of the Palace at Versailles, housed the Committee of Imperial Defence (CID) and the Chiefs of Staff (COS) Committee and it was at their direction that the key figures in British intelligence were meeting formally in committee for the first time. Outside the storm clouds gathered overhead and as the clock chimed 11 o'clock in the Secretary's Room on the first floor the chairman, a Brigadier in the East Yorkshire Regiment, opened proceedings.[3] The Joint Intelligence Committee (JIC) had come into being.

No. 2 Whitehall Gardens has long been demolished and the present Ministry of Defence stands on its site; the CID disappeared with the end of Empire and decolonisation. While the military threat from Germany and the Axis was eventually defeated, followed by the demise of the Soviet Union after the long Cold War, threats to the UK and its interests remain but now come from diverse sources, including terrorists, proliferators and international criminal gangs. Throughout each of the last 78 years the JIC has, however, continued to meet in Whitehall, within a stone's throw of its original meeting place, to provide Ministers and other policymakers, diplomats, and military commanders with the best assessment of the intelligence available to the British authorities.

The machinery of British intelligence has one of the longest histories of any modern intelligence system. William Burghley and Francis Walsingham set up the first intelligence gathering machinery in Elizabethan times but it was not until 1909 that the modern British intelligence establishment was founded. In October of that year the Secret Service Bureau (SSB) was formed. This quickly developed into a home branch – what would become the Security Service (MI5) – and a foreign branch – the forerunner to SIS.

In 1936 a decision was made to create a central clearing house for intelligence: the Joint Intelligence Sub-Committee (JIC).[4] Its creation owed something to the origins of the modern British secret service. The rationale in creating the SSB in 1909 was driven by the emergence of an external threat. Though there had existed similar fears before, the perceived German menace was new in the sense that it directly threatened the British mainland itself. Spy fever, fuelled publicly by the novels of William Le Queux, was at its height. The belief that there were upwards of 80,000 German agents secretly working in the British Isles created the need for a two-pronged approach: an internal organisation to guard against such a threat, and an external organisation to watch for an indication of any war which might awaken the agents into action.[5] In the 1930s a new version of this threat was causing concern but in a different way, with fears over German re-armament confusing views about Hitler's intentions.

An appreciation of the international situation and the means of dealing with it helps explain why a centralised structure for intelligence was not initiated before 1936. Sir Harry Hinsley, author of the Official History of British Intelligence in the Second World War, suggests that the decision to create the JIC stemmed from the belief that while centralisation was not key, further collaboration between the various Service departments was. In this way, 'most of the pressures for change in the inter-war years resulted from the fact that increasing profession-alisation tended to separate these functions and to call for new, specialised inter-departmental bodies to undertake them.'[6] Yet the JIC was essentially ineffective in the build-up to the outbreak of war, and the reason for this lies in the nature of British intelligence in the mid-1930s.[7]

Within the British government there were several types of intelligence. Vice Admiral William James, the Deputy Chief of the Naval Staff, referred to them as 'service' and 'special' intelligence.[8] Of the 'service' variant there existed within the military three different intelligence organisations: one for the Admiralty, another for the War Office, and one for the Air Ministry. These organisations were affected by the perception of an increased German threat. Following Germany's occupation of the Rhineland in 1936, the post of a separate Director of Military Intelligence was re-established in the War Office. In the Air Ministry, concerns about the expanding German Air Force led to the creation of a Deputy Director of Intelligence.[9] Finally, in the Admiralty, an Operational Intelligence Centre was resurrected.[10] There was remarkably little discussion or collaboration between them. At a higher level, the CID provided a forum whereby military and civilian personnel met to discuss policy options, but it appears that such discussions only rarely involved intelligence matters. The product of these three Service intelligence organisations was, unsurprisingly, overwhelmingly military in content: it reflected analyses of enemy capabilities with little or no attempt to gauge intentions. Furthermore, each was concerned almost exclusively with the remit of its parent Service, be it the Royal Navy, the Army or the Royal Air Force.

Alongside the military organisations were the civilian or 'special' intelligence agencies. Following the investigations into the nature and scope of civilian intelligence in the early 1920s by the Secret Service Committee of the Cabinet, the various agencies had become central components – if undeclared – of government with more clearly defined roles.[11] SIS, under its Foreign Office (FO) supervision, was responsible for collecting information outside the British Empire. It was to remain separate from the FO itself, and as such some of its officers were stationed under the guise of 'Passport Control Officers', others under business cover.[12] The three Service intelligence branches seconded a number of staff to SIS yet, crucially, SIS was not solely concerned with military matters and could, if required, report on political topics. In addition to its overseas human intelligence operations, SIS had assumed responsibility for the Government Code & Cypher School (GC&CS), which itself had been formed in 1919 from the relevant single-Service Sigint organisations and been organised on an inter-departmental level. The Security Service retained a military intelligence designation – MI5 – though it too had a remit extending far beyond military concerns.[13]

The third strand of intelligence, though not explicitly recognised as such, was the political element residing within the FO. Through a mixture of diplomatic reporting and information gathering through private networks the FO had, since the late nineteenth century, collected what would today be described as political intelligence. Up to the end of the First World War this had been mainly ad hoc in nature, and the extent to which 'intelligence' was amassed largely reflected the current Permanent Under Secretary's (PUS) views towards its utility and value.[14] The system became more permanent but it was not until Sir Robert Vansittart's appointment as PUS in 1930 that it really developed into a sophisticated network. Vansittart was a consummate devourer and user of intelligence and his network was known within Whitehall as his 'private detective agency'.[15] It was out of this confusion – a disparate number of organisations dealing with intelligence and a resurgent German threat – that the JIC was created.

The First Tentative Steps to Joint Intelligence

The first steps towards an integrated governmental approach to intelligence assessment occurred in December 1923 with industrial and economic intelligence. Although in its early incarnation this was not a truly effective system it would, by 1929, become the model for the subsequent Joint Intelligence Committee. In 1931 the CID's 'Industrial Intelligence in Foreign Countries Sub-Committee' (FCI) had created within it a research body called the 'Industrial Intelligence Centre' (IIC). Although the IIC initially had no official terms of reference, its purposes were defined in 1934 as being twofold: firstly, to ensure the best economic intelligence was utilised by the FCI; and secondly, to ensure that all relevant information was amassed and effectively distributed to the consumers – thereby producing the first effective attempt at all-source analysis within the British intelligence machinery. Despite such an important role, the IIC system did not convince all the various departments that it should be the central clearing-house for economic intelligence: the main problem was that the IIC reports were still submitted to the various Service's intelligence departments before they went higher up the Whitehall hierarchy.[16] This should not, however, detract from its importance as a first step towards a centralised intelligence machinery.

The realisation that a wider-reaching interdepartmental intelligence assessment system was needed came from the military but was channelled through Sir Maurice Hankey. Hankey was born in 1877 and joined the Royal Marines, later serving in naval intelligence. He joined the Secretariat of the Committee of Imperial Defence in 1908, and from 1912 until 1938 served as its Secretary. He also assumed the position of Secretary of the Cabinet in 1916, the first in a long line of distinguished incumbents. Hankey is remembered for revolutionising the system of Cabinet government, but his importance to intelligence history lies in the creation of the Chiefs of Staff Committee: for bringing the disparate elements of the military into one common body. Described variously as 'brisk, businesslike and ultra conservative', Hankey was central to the development of the British government prior to the Second World War.[17] General Sir Henry Wilson, Chief of the Imperial General Staff (CIGS) at the conclusion of World War One, said of Hankey, 'If you once lose hold of Hanky-Panky, you are done, absolutely done'.[18]

While it might have been Hankey who converted the concept of centralised intelligence assessment into practice, the stimulus for change came from military quarters. On 22 July 1935 the Director of Military Operations and Intelligence (DMO&I) in the War Office, Major General John Dill, wrote to Hankey about the need for a better system of co-ordinating intelligence:

> . . . we find an increasing tendency for certain specific aspects of intelligence to develop, in which two or more separate Departments are equally interested, with the result that the danger of uneconomical duplication in the collection and recording of such intelligence is tending to increase. Again, the preparation of plans which depend on these forms of intelligence is unduly delayed by the necessity for a laborious process of co-ordination between Departments which are geographically widely separated.

As an example of how such an effective system might work, Dill extolled the virtues of the IIC. The issue, in Dill's mind, was that intelligence for the purpose of planning was missing. He continued, 'I feel very strongly that something is wanted', and put forward as a tentative suggestion that the scope of the FCI might be enlarged to 'embrace all the subjects of intelligence on which joint plans by different Departments might depend. The title would presumably be changed and might become the "Joint Intelligence Committee" or "Intelligence Co-ordination Committee".'[19]

Hankey's response on 29 July 1935 noted how he had 'felt myself, for some time, that the existing arrangements could be improved'. Although he did not want a 'super intelligence centre', Hankey did feel that better 'arrangements [could be made] for facilitating touch between all the departments who obtain information on any particular subject'.[20] Interestingly by referring to the 'obtaining' of information, neither Hankey nor Dill meant the 'civilian' collection agencies MI5 or SIS – instead, this was to be a purely military matter and designed solely to fulfil the needs of the military planners.

From their correspondence it is evident that the topic re-emerged just three months later and in various different fora. One aspect stemmed from an Air Ministry intelligence paper on 'bomb targets'. The problem was this: the First World War and the intervening years had revealed the importance of precise target selection for bombing. In 1935, and with discussions already underway as to the nature of British military strategy in any future European war, the Air Ministry had studied the subject. Its conclusion was that some sort of a 'Joint Co-ordinating Committee' be created to select targets. The issue lay not with obtaining information – it was felt that relevant expertise already existed – instead it was the problem of arranging contact with the experts and co-ordinating their information that was taxing the Air Ministry.[21] At this time the only central mechanism for co-ordinating intelligence effort was the Industrial Intelligence Centre (IIC). Its Director, a one time SIS officer called Desmond Morton, referred to the possible 'pending formation of a Joint Intelligence Committee', as being one available solution, though he felt that the IIC should be the natural home for it in the meantime. Clearly, Morton recognised that the answer to the problems of collating information was a central co-ordinating body.[22]

Morton's reference to a Joint Intelligence Committee suggests that concrete proposals had been made. The JIC was designed to serve various committees of which the most senior was the Committee of Imperial Defence (CID). This was chaired by the Prime Minister and included a large number of Secretaries of State, including those for the three Services. Its Secretary was Sir Maurice Hankey, the common link between the various committees. Below this was the CID's Chiefs of Staff Sub-Committee (COS), which was chaired by the Minister for Co-ordination of Defence (Sir Thomas Inskip) and included the three Chiefs of Staff, with Hankey as Secretary. Lowest in the hierarchy was the Sub-Committee of the Deputy Chiefs of Staff (DCOS) which, in addition to the three Deputy Chiefs, had Hankey as Chairman.

Following Dill's original letter Hankey, through his position as Secretary of the CID, discussed the idea with the COS. Their recommendation, in early October 1935, was that the matter should be debated by the DCOS Committee first, who should then send a proposal back to the Chiefs to discuss.[23] This decision caused much exasperation amongst Air Ministry officials, who felt it would take too long for a decision to be reached and any practical measures to be put in place.[24]

Despite strong support from the War Office, the Air Ministry, and the Industrial Intelligence Centre, not every department thought a central mechanism was such a good idea. Following initial discussions in late October, Vice-Admiral William James, the Deputy Chief of the Naval Staff, informed Hankey that although he 'approached the matter with an open mind', the problem was not just that the papers 'were not very illuminating', but that the discussion 'did not materially alter an earlier impression that we might be embarking on a large and perhaps expensive organisation as the result of finding weakness in our Intelligence system with regard to one specific point'.[25] In reply Hankey thanked James for his thoughts and reassured him that discussions were at a 'preliminary' stage, but ended by saying that 'personally I feel strongly that there is a good deal which could be done to put our intelligence on a better footing.'[26]

The 'specific point' raised by James was the Air Ministry's 'bomb target' report. There is some evidence of internal competition between the Royal Navy and the Royal Air Force. Although not immediately evident from the records pertaining to the JIC itself, there are hints from Admiralty and Air Ministry files. The debate between the Navy and the RAF over control of naval aviation has been well documented.[27] One of the central issues was the procurement of funds, over which the Admiralty and Air Ministry views were poles apart. Though this debate would continue up until the start of the Second World War, it is entirely possible that the effects were felt in the discussions about setting up the JIC; certainly it would have been present in the minds of senior naval figures.[28] One relevant clue comes from some notes produced by Admiral John Godfrey, wartime Director of Naval Intelligence who, referring to the origins of the JIC, commented that naval intelligence had been 'unhampered' by 'a desire to produce over-optimistic results (in terms of bomb success and enemy damage) which cramped the truth of air intelligence.'[29] These debates would resurface in the context of the Spanish civil war.[30]

Vice-Admiral James' concerns, first expressed at the end of October 1935, had, by the end of November, mellowed somewhat. He was now content that a change was necessary, but suggested that it be a revision to the procedures of the FCI rather than a whole new structure.[31] By late October 1935, the notion that something had to be done had reached a general consensus, despite the Admiralty's lukewarm response. As Hankey had foreseen, the topic was passed from the COS's hands to the DCOS Committee. The latter discussed Dill's original paper and, in true British committee style, instructed the Secretary to prepare a review. In addition it created an 'ad-hoc sub-committee' composed of the three Service intelligence directors to consider the question of a separate intelligence centre.[32] At the following meeting it was proposed that such a system was necessary, and that in the first place the FCI should be expanded. Such an enlarged FCI would include a provision to 'co-opt additional members' as and when needed in order to 'deal with specific problems'. Furthermore, the envisaged additional focus of the FCI was to be confined to the consideration of 'bombing targets intelligence'; it therefore had a somewhat limited scope.[33]

In structural terms nothing changed since representatives of the Services' intelligence departments had been attending the FCI since its first meeting in 1930.[34] Perhaps as recognition that these alterations did not go far enough, the 'ad-hoc sub-committee' of the DCOS, which had been tasked with preparing a report, went much further in its proposals. In defining the subject matter it concluded that 'service intelligence' referred to 'information which can be obtained through the Intelligence Staffs of the three Fighting Services; together with matters which are the principal concern of those Staffs'. The 'special' intelligence agencies of MI5 and SIS (including GC&CS) were never co-opted into the proposals as they lay outside the concerns of the military intelligence directorates.

The ad-hoc sub-committee also identified a list of topics of mutual interest to all three Services and on which co-ordination was vital. The final suggestion was that the new structure, to be called the 'Inter-Service Intelligence Committee', should solely include the intelligence representatives from the three Services.[35] This proposal was subsequently incorporated into a lengthier document – paper number DCOS 4. Much like the 1909 decision to create a Secret Service Bureau, the major cause for change was defined as the need to be 'properly prepared for the eventuality of war.' The three Services' intelligence directors concluded in the paper that 'our intelligence organisation requires some modification to cope with modern conditions.' The 'modern conditions' referred to the duplication that was becoming increasingly problematic and common. As such it was proposed that 'direct and permanent liaison between the many departments' was needed. The proposition to deal with these problems was two-fold: that the FCI be expanded further to include provision for bombing targets intelligence; and that a separate 'inter-service intelligence committee' be created to meet on an ad-hoc basis, at the 'request of one of the members', to achieve co-ordination across the three Services. [36]

The COS Committee met on 13 January 1936 and approved the report without reservation.[37] It was then passed upwards and the matter was considered at the meeting of the CID on 30 January 1936. The CID agreed with the recommendations as set out in DCOS 4, namely that the FCI be expanded and that a new Services' intelligence committee be established. This decision by the CID in January 1936 was a momentous one, something which would change the face of British intelligence and define its structure.[38]

Following the January 1936 decision, the FCI did not meet again until March. At its nineteenth meeting bomb targeting was discussed for the first time and, following a lengthy discussion, general consensus was reached: a new sub-committee of the FCI was to be created to concentrate specifically on this topic. Interestingly its composition was to be the same as the new JIC, to be created in the summer of 1936, and it was to consider topics which would subsequently preoccupy much of the JIC's time.[39] At the following meeting of the FCI in May, the new Sub-Committee reported back. Its Chairman, Wing Commander Charles Medhurst from the Air Ministry's intelligence directorate, stated that it should concentrate in the first instance on identifying targets in Germany, though subsequent ones should be identified by the CID itself. The precursor to the JIC – a committee of intelligence officials, tasked from above, and designed to assess information for the purposes of military planning – had been created.[40]

Far trickier to trace is the fate of the Inter-Service Intelligence Committee (ISIC). As it was, this proved to be a short-lived organisation. There do not seem to be any records of actual meetings. Although it did meet in its brief six-month lifespan, there is no evidence to indicate how often or what topics were discussed. The original proposal for the Committee reveals something of its remit:

(a)   Preparation of Intelligence Reports and provision of maps and plans for such publications.
(b)   Joint appreciations on possible enemy operations from the Intelligence point of view, e.g. Japanese operations against Hong Kong and Singapore.
(c)   Press liaison and security in combined exercises.
(d)   A.A. [anti-aircraft] defences of foreign countries.
(e)   Coastal defences of foreign countries.
(f)   Intelligence from Procedure Y. [signals intelligence]
(g)   Signal communications and developments.
(h)   Co-ordination of the work of the Intelligence Staffs of the three Services in special circumstances.
(i)   Questions involving the Defence Security Service where the three Defence Departments are concerned.[41]

The Committee could be convened only by one of the constituent members and only when they saw fit. Its range of functions was quite broad, but given the lack of records it is impossible to know what was discussed. What is clear is that one of the major problems the ISIC faced was that it had no established means of disseminating its product.

The Creation of the Joint Intelligence Sub-Committee

Less than five months after its creation, it had become clear that the ISIC was not capable of meeting the challenges it faced. As the military increasingly concerned themselves with a possible war with Germany, questions were raised about the role of intelligence in military planning. The DMO&I in the War Office, the newly promoted Lieutenant General John Dill, wrote to Hankey and the directors of intelligence in the Air Ministry and Admiralty in late May 1936, detailing the failings of the present system.

As with bombing targets, it was becoming increasingly clear that the work of civilian intelligence and military planning needed to be dovetailed together. Dill's suggestion was to expand the existing size of the ISIC to include Morton, and extend its remit to provide a specific responsibility for assisting the Joint Planning Committee (JPC), the military body designed to put policy into action.[42] Hankey concurred with Dill's suggestion: an expanded ISIC would provide the JPC with 'information necessary for the preparation of their papers direct from a co-ordinated source.'[43] All three Service intelligence chiefs approved of Hankey's suggestion. The reaction was so positive that it was felt that the DCOS did not need to approve the matter, not least because speed was of the essence in altering the present structure. The overall objective was no longer to find a way to co-ordinate intelligence as a means in itself, but rather as a way to increase the speed with which the JPC could produce its own reports.

The proposal went straight to the COS Committee on 16 June 1936. At that meeting, Hankey proposed to 'extend the functions of the Inter-Service Intelligence Committee in order to enable that body to assist the Joint Planning Committee when the latter required co-ordinated intelligence.' The COS whole-heartedly approved.[44] The title accorded this new body was the 'Joint Intelligence Sub-Committee', it being a sub-committee of the COS. In its first meeting, a few weeks later, the JIC re-iterated the conclusions of the COS.[45]

There were some similarities between the ISIC and the JIC. For example, the composition of both bodies was the same (though the JIC could ask the IIC for assistance as required). The major difference between the two, however, was structural. The JIC became a sub-committee of the COS, thereby increasing its importance and positioning it firmly at the centre of government, where it was drawn into the orbit of the COS planning machinery. The JIC thus had a wider scope, not only absorbing the roles and remit of the ISIC, but also acting in an advisory capacity to the JPC and the Joint Planning Staff (JPS).[46] Initially it had been decided that the best means of achieving cooperation was for both the JIC and the JPC to share a Secretary, but by its third meeting the JIC felt that this would jeopardise his JPC role (which was primary) and so a separate JIC Secretary had to be appointed. Furthermore, until this happened 'we cannot view with any confidence a successful inauguration of the new Joint Intelligence Committee'.[47] Be that as it may, the result was not quite as hoped, as both Committees continued to share a central secretariat.

There are two standard critiques of the pre-war JIC's organisation: that it did not use the expertise of MI5, SIS and GC&CS; and that it suffered because the FO did not want to be involved. But these misunderstand the role and nature of the JIC: the JIC was a military body, comprising a military membership, designed to assess military subjects, and pass recommendations to a military planning body. It was not established to consider the kind of subjects that the FO would have been involved with; the JIC was concerned solely with military capabilities and excluded the topic of intentions. This also explains why the 'civilian' intelligence agencies were not full members. At the same time, however, it is clear that the FO kept a keen eye on proceedings. Frank Ashton-Gwatkin, the FO representative on the FCI, sent a note at the outset, commenting on how the 'Foreign Office would be considerably interested', especially in the Committee's expanded remit, concluding that it 'will require watching'.[48]

It is surprising that the decision had not been taken earlier to create a joint intelligence body, given that there had been previous arguments for, and experience with, 'joint' intelligence. In 1925 the Secret Service Committee had been reconvened to consider the structure of British intelligence and evaluate its worth. In taking statements from leading figures, the Secret Service Committee heard the Chief of SIS, Admiral Hugh Sinclair, complain that the present organisation was 'fundamentally wrong'. Furthermore, he pointed out, there was 'no central control of policy, [and] a serious lack of coordination and cooperation which resulted in overlapping and waste of time'. While such words were prophetic, Sinclair's remedy was not a co-ordinating body, but instead a plea that all the various intelligence agencies be amalgamated into one big directorate – his.[49] Although the idea of working together was therefore not new, Sinclair's vision had been concerned primarily with intelligence collection and not assessment.

The idea of the military working together was also not new. A Joint Naval and Military Committee had been established in the 1890s to produce combined reports on topics of common interest, and it had been an unquestioned success.[50] Discussions in the early 1920s about the creation of a unified Ministry of Defence revealed that the Services could co-operate. Indeed, the 1922 Weir Committee, which had been created to look into such matters, had outlined recommendations on the 'amalgamation of Services', and several reviews had been conducted from that point on, outlining how this could and did work in practice.[51] Furthermore, following Weir's report, the JPC was created as a tri-Service gathering with representatives from naval and air intelligence as standing members.[52] In addition, the 1924 creation of the 'Cryptography and Interception' committee, comprising personnel from the three Services and civilian intelligence staff; and the 1928 formation of the committee on Industrial Intelligence in Foreign Countries, had shown that a joint, centralised approach to intelligence was extremely successful.[53]

The growing German threat ensured that British intelligence had to adapt: the intelligence community itself had to become more unified, and intelligence had to be brought closer to military planning. Both factors are evident in the JIC's role, as defined by the COS on its creation:

a. to extend its functions to include work in connection with papers under preparation by the Joint Planning Committee;
b. that the Joint Planning Committee would, as necessary, give terms of reference to the Joint Intelligence Committee asking for information required for the preparation of Joint Planning Reports;
c. that the Joint Intelligence Committee was empowered to co-opt the services of Major Morton in any enquiries which they undertook in this connection;
d. that the Secretary to the Joint Planning Committee would assist the Joint Intelligence Committee in an organising and liaison capacity only, his duties with the Joint Planning Committee not being interfered with.[54]

From Birth to War

Taking the chair at the very first meeting of the Joint Intelligence Committee on 7 July 1936 was Brigadier Desmond Anderson. Anderson was the Deputy Director of Military Intelligence in the War Office and would be promoted to Lieutenant General, having served as Assistant Chief of the Imperial General Staff and as Commander of various Corps during the war. He is the only JIC Chairman to have a school named after him.[55] He was joined by his counterparts from the Admiralty, Captain Claude Hermon-Hodge (later a Rear Admiral and the son of Conservative politician Baron Wyfold), and the Air Ministry, Wing Commander Charles Medhurst (later an Air Chief Marshal). All three were senior figures from their respective intelligence directorates, though they held different ranks. Also in attendance were Colonel Bernard Paget (War Office – later to become General Sir Bernard), Commander Eric Bush (Admiralty – later the author of many military books), and Major Desmond Morton (Industrial Intelligence Centre – later Churchill's adviser on intelligence matters). The Secretary, Major Leslie Hollis (Royal Marines – later General Sir Leslie and the senior Assistant Secretary of the War Cabinet), was also the Secretary of the JPC.[56]

At its first meeting the Committee wholeheartedly approved the COS recommendations on its role. However, four days prior to the meeting, on 3 July, Hollis questioned how the JIC would work vis-à-vis the ISIC. To most other observers, and indeed to secondary commentators, the JIC had subsumed the ISIC. The difference, Hollis felt, was that the ISIC should deal with problems common to all three Service intelligence directorates, whereas the JIC should address itself solely to problems identified by the JPC.[57] It was accepted that the Committee should help the JPC when it needed intelligence, but when no targets were identified by the JPC the role of the Committee was unclear. This never became a problem as the amount of work quickly grew. The consequence, though, was that the JIC did not adopt any formal terms of reference at this time.

By the time of its second meeting, almost three months later on 29 September 1936, this organisational debate had been partially resolved. The JIC would not only work on papers requested by the JPC, but would also take over the ISIC's responsibilities. Therefore almost from the outset the Committee had a remit to provide assistance to military planning, but also to act as the central forum for any tri-Service intelligence issues.[58] In order to make this process work efficiently, it was decided at the same time that the JIC Secretary should also be the JPC Secretary, a procedure already in place but one which had been called into question by the JIC's expanded workload.[59] And so the Committee set to work.[60]

The pace of the Committee's work increased, although there remained procedural doubts, in particular regarding the dissemination of its product. In an important letter in September 1936, Leslie Hollis, the JIC Secretary, wrote to Colonel Hastings Ismay, the Deputy Secretary of the COS, to emphasise that the JIC's work would only be useful if there existed a direct channel into the COS discussions. That channel, Hollis argued, should be through him, as he was already an Assistant Secretary to the COS committee in addition to his JIC role.[61] Two days later this request was forwarded to the chiefs of the three Services and was subsequently approved.[62]

At this time there were several tri-Service intelligence committees in addition to the JIC: the FCI and the FCI's Air Targets Bombing Committee. The IIC had been absorbed into the Department of Overseas Trade. The most important relationship was that between the JIC and FCI. In late 1937 the original and long-established Chairman of the FCI, Sir Edward Crowe, retired. His replacement as Chairman (and concurrently Comptroller-General, Department of Overseas Trade) was Thomas St. Quintin Hill. In assuming his post Hill questioned the rationale behind having separate JIC and FCI gatherings. Instead he proposed that they be amalgamated or, if that would result in too large a committee, have separate committees for military and civilian issues. Hill's proposal met with universal 'dislike', but perhaps his most important comment was on the value of the FCI's work, recognising the virtues of having a forum whereby 'officers of the Defence Services and the Civil Service have met round a table to discuss common problems'.[63]

One of Hill's other proposals was that any such committee should be chaired by someone from the Treasury. This idea, of having a civilian chairman of an essentially military committee, would re-appear several times in the build-up to the Second World War. In commenting on the proposals, Leslie Hollis, the JIC Secretary, noted the 'inappropriateness' of having a civilian chairman.[64] Upon receiving a critique of his plan from Hankey, Hill decided not to push for any changes.[65]

The two committees continued as before. By 1939 it had become clear, however, that the work of the FCI was no longer as crucial as it had been originally. A proposal was suggested through the new JIC Secretary, Captain Andrew N. Barnard, that the FCI should be subsumed within the JIC, particularly as Desmond Morton (the head of the IIC) attended JIC meetings on a regular basis.[66] The idea was supported by Ismay, now a Major General and Hankey's replacement as Secretary to the CID.[67] This was almost certainly a reflection of the increasing status of the JIC which, by 1939, especially with the involvement of the FO, had become a serious player within Whitehall.[68]

Foreign Office Involvement

The FO's inclusion was the catalyst for the JIC to start realising its potential. Once again it was external circumstances that prompted an internal change. It was generally recognised that during the Committee's first two years of existence it was producing 'good work'. The original Chairman, Brigadier Anderson, was briefly replaced in February 1938 by Brigadier Roger Evans, the Deputy Director of Military Intelligence (who would go on to command the 1st Armoured Division in France in 1940). His appointment was short lived though, and in September 1938 Brigadier Frederick Beaumont-Nesbitt, the new Deputy-Director of Military Intelligence, became the War Office representative on the JIC, FCI, and FCI (Air Targets Bombing) committees.

On the departure of Brigadier Evans the question arose as to who should now chair the JIC meetings. With the exception of one meeting when the Admiralty had taken charge, the War Office had consistently taken the chair from the outset. Hollis, the outgoing secretary, proposed that the War Office continue to lead. Almost certainly this was due to the ongoing disputes between the Admiralty and Air Ministry at this time.

Though initially reluctant, Beaumont-Nesbitt agreed to become the JIC's third Chairman. Beaumont-Nesbitt had been born in 1893 and after joining the Grenadier Guards in 1912 had a varied and fascinating career, including: the Military Attaché in Paris; Deputy, and then Director, of Military Intelligence; Military Attaché in Washington at the time that the Americans joined the war;

and, for over twenty years, various posts in the Royal Household.[69] In reminiscing about his early years in the army, Beaumont-Nesbitt recalled that as a 'callow youth' it was a 'miracle' that he survived. Indeed, his memoirs reveal a litany of pranks whilst a young officer, including memories of a champagne-infused stag party and how his appendix almost burst upon being told he was to be sent to fight in the First World War.[70] His son recalls him 'using a wooden door in the garden, as a target against which he could practise firing a handgun (Browning automatic)'. Beaumont-Nesbitt was certainly a colourful character, remaining known throughout his military career as 'Paddy', on account of his Irish ancestry.[71]

On taking the chair, Beaumont-Nesbitt conducted a review of the existing intelligence arrangements, resulting in a twelve-page report which he submitted to Hollis in December 1938. His proposal, considered 'interesting and, indeed, revolutionary' by the FO, was perhaps the first major step in making the JIC a truly inter-departmental committee.[72] Beaumont-Nesbitt began by distinguishing between 'military intelligence' and 'political intelligence'. Just this small step was, in itself, novel, though it revealed a growing recognition of the importance of political intelligence; it also marked something of an intellectual turning point in defining what 'intelligence' was.

The Services had traditionally seen intelligence as being a purely military matter, concerned almost entirely with capabilities and neglecting any mention of intent. This view had slowly begun to change as the possibility of a European War increased. In such an event it would be important to know not only the capabilities of the other side's forces, but also when or whether a decision might be taken to commence hostilities. As a result, in March 1938 Hankey had asked the FO to prepare an appreciation of the political situation in the event of war with Germany. On the occupation of the Sudetenland by Germany, the JIC had requested the FO to revise its paper, taking into account the JIC's comments and views.[73] It was at the JIC meeting on 16 November 1938 that the FO was in attendance for the first time and thereafter this became the norm. In informing the JIC of Beaumont-Nesbitt's chairmanship, Hollis stated that the Committee would be 'in for a rather busy time in the future', having to work with the FO to produce various political assessments.[74] This was a crucial suggestion, for as Edward Thomas, one of Hinsley's co-authors, has written, 'the really urgent problems of the late 30s called for weighing of both military and political factors.'[75] It was in this atmosphere that Beaumont-Nesbitt presented his report.

In essence the problem, as the JIC Chairman saw it, was that although FO reporting was sent to the Services, they did not know how best to assess it. Furthermore, the lack of integration between the Service departments in day-to-day affairs meant that the material was not being passed to those who needed it most. The situation was particularly acute because the Services needed to keep themselves abreast of the 'international political situation', but were not equipped to do so. The solution was to incorporate such work into the JIC's remit, which was still at this time 'somewhat ill-defined'. As Beaumont-Nesbitt concluded, 'here surely is a deficiency which could and should be made good'. He recommended the existing Committee be enlarged, with the 'inclusion of a senior FO representative, who would also be asked to act as Chairman'. This proposal was reinforced not only by the increasingly political content of deliberations, but also because it would stop any 'vested interests' from becoming 'too powerful'.[76]

Equally important was Beaumont-Nesbitt's proposal for dealing with the large amount of incoming information. Three different 'sections' should be created, dealing with 1) Europe, Africa and the Middle East; 2) India, Far East, North and South America; and 3) Economics and Propaganda. These sections would comprise representatives from the range of government departments involved in the collection of intelligence: the FO, Admiralty, War Office, Air Ministry, Colonial Office, India Office, Department of Overseas Trade, Home Office, and SIS. This, then, would signal the creation of a 'joint staff' to analyse and assess the incoming information.

Up to then SIS had not been involved with the JIC, attending a meeting for the first time in November 1938: the same meeting in which the FO came for the first time. The presence of both was a coincidence: SIS only attended for a specific item; the FO for the whole meeting. In commenting on the proposal, Colonel Stewart Menzies, the Head of the Military Section in SIS and a future Chief, emphasised the importance of the proposed structure: 'our own constantly recurring experience of being called upon for ad hoc notes on various aspects . . . is our strongest proof that such machinery is badly needed'. In addition, Menzies requested that SIS become a member of the JIC, but only at a point when 'inter-departmental discussions' were commonplace. Perhaps for this reason full SIS membership of the JIC would not happen until 1940.[77]

From the records alone there is no evidence as to whether Beaumont-Nesbitt's colleagues on the JIC approved of the idea of the FO taking the chair. The COS argued strongly that a committee that reported to them should not have an FO chairman.[78] The general reaction to Beaumont-Nesbitt's proposal was supportive. Hollis called it 'most attractive' and highlighted the extreme importance of creating a central intelligence authority within the government:

> I suggest that in an emergency, we shall find our existing intelligence arrangements would let us down. The government will be receiving disjointed reports from varying sources with no machinery for linking them up with other reports received from other sources on the same subject. Whereas on the Planning side we can, I think, adapt our planning organisation to meet emergency requirements, the weak link in the chain might be the lack of some authoritative body who could give us, at very short notice, co-ordinated intelligence.[79]

Before any decision was taken the paper was circulated to the FO. Sir Lancelot Oliphant, the Deputy Under-Secretary of State in the FO, commented on the necessity to do something about the duplication of effort. He mentioned that FO reporting had been insufficiently used by the Services in the past and approved of the FO being represented on the JIC.[80] Other parts of the FO, however, were not so keen; with one official writing that it would 'be a duplicate Foreign Office in miniature'.[81] The consensus was that a member of the FO should be made responsible for liaising with the Service departments and for ensuring that they 'accept the political appreciations of the FO'.[82] This idea, that the FO was still the only place in which political intelligence could be interpreted, meant that there had to be an FO involvement, and it seems to have persuaded any doubters.

Despite some initial reluctance the FO agreed to provide a representative. In replying to Oliphant, Beaumont-Nesbitt attempted to resolve the divergence of opinion on the role of the FO. Instead of either of the Services trying to assess political situations, or the FO doing it independently of Service requirements, Beaumont-Nesbitt suggested that 'what we want to do is to devise some organisation whereby all forms of intelligence can be fused into a properly co-ordinated picture. To do this, representatives of the Foreign Office and Service Departments . . . must work together.'[83]

This was not quite as novel as it sounded. In mid-1937 the FO discovered that the intelligence directorate in the War Office was preparing a report on the USSR. The problem was that the FO was also preparing one as was, it appears, the Admiralty.[84] The reaction in the FO was that not only should something be done to co-ordinate matters, but also that Service reports should include an FO summary on the political situation.[85] The Admiralty agreed.[86] Such moves were further crystallised in May 1938, when it was decided that FO political reporting should be incorporated into Service intelligence summaries.[87]

In practice the members of the FO, War Office, Admiralty and Air Ministry would represent the needs and requirements of their home departments. Once a topic had been passed to the JIC, each member would be responsible for liaising with his parent department in order to gather all relevant information. However, the problem of drafting the actual assessments remained and a joint staff was needed to prepare the reports, which would then be discussed at the JIC, and once approved, be passed up to the CID. These developments were recognition that the existing JIC structure could no longer cope with the demands placed upon it. 'Intelligence' now encompassed not only military information but political and economic appreciations too. Now that intelligence was recognised as being central to planning and to Britain's war effort, further change was needed.

The Situation Report Centre

While the discussions of Brigadier Beaumont-Nesbitt's proposals continued, outside events meant that plans had to be expedited. In March 1939 the German Army marched into Prague and Prime Minister Neville Chamberlain promised support to Poland in the event of German aggression. The following month, in April, the 'Situation Report Centre' (SRC) was created. It would prove to be a crucial body in improving the standing of the JIC in the run up to war.[88] One of the problems with the JIC's work up to this point was that it was long-term in focus. In March 1939 several events suggested that not only was war becoming imminent, but that short-term assessments were needed. In addition to the German invasion of Czechoslovakia, reports were received from the FO (through Vansittart's networks) that German submarines were purportedly on patrol near Plymouth, and a telex from the Minister in Berlin warning that German bombers would soon attack the Home Fleet. In essence, it was felt that an organisation was needed to look at these 'rumours' and assess their veracity.[89]

The SRC, though initiated by the Minister for Co-ordination of Defence, Lord Chatfield, was originally conceived in response to comments by the Prime Minister. Neville Chamberlain had two concerns: firstly, that before any 'action' should be taken it should be based on the best possible intelligence; and secondly, that something had to be done to further co-ordinate the Service departments.[90] In response, the SRC was tasked with collating intelligence and issuing 'daily situation reports in order that any emergency measures which might have to be taken should be based only on the most reliable and carefully co-ordinated intelligence.'[91] In May the remit was expanded to include, in addition to the daily reports, the production of weekly commentaries on general trends.[92] This crucially filled the void left by the JIC, which was concentrating on much longer term targets.

The SRC assessments were distributed to twenty four recipients, including the Prime Minister, Minister for the Co-ordination of Defence, the CID, Admiralty, Air Ministry, War Office, FO and SIS.[93] The SRC included the three Service members of the JIC as permanent members, together with Major General Ismay, the Secretary of the CID. Successive JIC Secretaries also serviced the SRC.[94] Despite being separate from the JIC, in circulating the reports the SRC/JIC Secretary, Barnard, informed recipients that the 'Reports should be referred to simply as "Joint Intelligence Committee Reports".'[95]

The SRC was chaired by a FO diplomat, Ralph Skrine Stevenson. Skrine Stevenson was born in India in 1895 and, following commissioned service in the First World War in the Rifle Brigade, joined the Diplomatic Service. Having served in Copenhagen, Berlin, Sofia, the Hague, Barcelona and Cairo, Skrine Stevenson returned to Whitehall in 1937 with the rank of an FO Counsellor, the equivalent grade to a Brigadier. In 1938 he was briefly appointed Minister [or Major General in military terms] in Madrid, the number two in the Embassy, and a key position given the civil war raging at the time. He subsequently returned to the United Kingdom, serving as Private Secretary to Foreign Secretaries Lord Halifax and Anthony Eden, and later as Ambassador in China and then Egypt.[96] Admiral John Godfrey, the wartime DNI, recalled that Skrine Stevenson was 'excellent, and he and his Foreign Office Assistant worked extremely hard to make the show a success'.[97]

At its first meeting on 25 April 1939, Skrine Stevenson outlined why the SRC had been created: 'for the purpose of sifting and disseminating day-to-day secret intelligence in a summarised form which would be available for a very restricted circulation'. It was agreed that there would be daily meetings at 4pm and that 'representatives should bring, in quadruplicate, summaries of the intelligence received in their respective departments up to 3pm on that day.'[98] Reports were divided into countries, and combined political, military, naval and air intelligence. All weekly reports began with a note that 'this commentary has been prepared jointly by the Foreign Office and the Directors of Intelligence of the Three Service Departments.'[99] It was, then, a truly inter-departmental product.

It is difficult to gauge the effectiveness of the SRC but it is possible to infer something from how its reports were received. Skrine Stevenson reported that 'the first report was circulated last night and a very useful one it was, on right lines'.[100] A few weeks later in mid-May, Skrine Stevenson wrote how the military information was not very reassuring, but that all available information was being utilised by the Service departments. 'C', the chief of SIS, was recorded as being 'entirely happy' with the process. However, another comment, referred to 'seemingly reliable information' having been ignored.[101]

In mid-May the War Office wrote to the Treasury to inform them that it was having staffing difficulties in filling its spot on the SRC.[102] The recipient of the letter, taking ten days to consider it, passed the request on to the FO because he could not 'recollect having heard of this [organisation]'.[103] The reply explained that 'the whole thing is kept as secret as possible', and that 'the extra work entailed by it is very considerable and is growing'.[104] At the same time, within the FO debates were underway about the future of its various intelligence and co-ordinating sections. Sir Alexander Cadogan, the PUS, commented on how the 'Dominions Intelligence' outfit should be combined with the SRC to provide a forum for 'liaison with the CID', and that a separate economic and co-ordinating section should be created.[105]

If the requests for copies of the daily Situation Reports are anything to go by, then the SRC was doing an extremely good job. Several prominent ambassadors asked to see copies of the daily reports, yet the SRC was reluctant to grant wider distribution because of the information contained within them. Indeed, from the outset a 'Note Regarding Secret Sources of Obtaining Information' was produced, detailing how important it was that the SRC reports were not circulated so that sources and methods would not be compromised. It was even felt that to send the reports outside London could pose a security breach.[106] Discussions at this time reveal the substantial SIS input to the reports. In fact, Admiral Sinclair, the Chief of SIS, requested that Ismay send him copies of the daily report 'so that I can be sure that our information has been correctly interpreted.'[107]

In mid-June Skrine Stevenson, through the auspices of the SRC, produced a paper on the co–ordination of intelligence in time of war. The report echoed Beaumont-Nesbitt's proposals of late 1938 in arguing that the present arrange-ments were not suitable for wartime. The difference between the two was that whereas Beaumont-Nesbitt's original proposal related to the JIC (at this time still concerned with long term threats), Skrine Stevenson's SRC report mentioned that short term threats were not being dealt with efficiently and in a co-ordinated manner. The two reports should be seen as complementary, essentially labouring the same point for the strategic JIC and the tactical SRC. In commenting on Skrine Stevenson's paper, Beaumont-Nesbitt, now Director of Military Intelligence, suggested that he look at his own proposal of six months earlier.[108]

Beaumont-Nesbitt's original proposal, despite the initial enthusiasm, had come to nothing. The primary reason seems to have been a desire to avoid changing the existing structure given the threat of war: any re-organisation would inevitably lead to upheaval and would take time – which might not be available – to settle down. The FO was, at this point, not attending the JIC regularly, though it was generally recognised that its attendance would be beneficial.[109]

The draft of the 'Co-ordination of Intelligence' memorandum, prepared by the SRC, includes a fascinating section on the 'need for the co-ordination of intelligence', which was omitted from the final version.[110] The draft outlined how the JIC was not able to adequately fulfil the central co-ordinating role between the FO and the Services because it lacked an FO representative. It is worth re-emphasising here that the original rationale for the JIC was as a military co-ordinating body, therefore an FO presence was almost a reversal of what it had been created to do. That FO attendance was now needed was a reflection of the changing times. The central issue, as Skrine Stevenson explained to Cadogan, was that to ensure effective co-ordination of intelligence, a permanent liaison relationship between the FO and the Services needed to be created. The solution was to 're-constitute the JIC' as the forum for this.[111] Although expressing some concern that the JIC was the 'handmaiden' of the COS, Cadogan supported the idea.[112]

The central obstacle to the proposition – which everyone agreed was, in theory, a good idea – was whether an FO representative should and could be allowed to chair a COS sub-committee. Skrine Stevenson noted that 'in principle it was doubtless quite wrong that an FO representative should serve on a Committee controlled by other Departments of State but, our aim being to increase efficiency in the coordination and presentation of intelligence, I would be in favour of accepting the situation and re-constituting the Joint Intelligence Committee, leaving it as an offshoot of the Chiefs of Staff Sub-Committee.'[113] The JIC met formally to discuss the matter on 29 June 1939 and approved it. In informing Ismay, Leslie Hollis called it a 'rather peculiar business', but at the same time said that it was 'quite unobjectionable'.[114]

The proposal then had to be ratified throughout the Whitehall chain before anything could actually be done. The DCOS Committee gave approval on 14 July 1939. Although the DCOS was happy for a FO member to attend the meeting, it initially rejected the proposal that the FO representative should take the chair, though the Deputy Chief of the Naval Staff then informed his counterparts that he wanted to give the matter 'further consideration'.[115] The DCOS re-considered the matter a fortnight later, with the Air Ministry and Admiralty representatives still expressing discomfort over having a non-military chairman. The Deputy Chief of the Imperial General Staff tried to reassure his colleagues by re-iterating the FO position that their representative had to be of a Counsellor rank, equating to what would now be known as a 1-star military officer, therefore on a par with the Service representatives, but if such a person was to be subordinate to the Services it would be difficult to find someone willing to fill the post.[116] Admiral John Godfrey, on the other hand, recalled that 'this seemed rather a good scheme as it would ensure that the Foreign Office took a lively interest in the proceedings of the JIC'.[117]

After some careful manoeuvring behind the scenes – Skrine Stevenson observed that this was 'privately' pointed out to the DCOS – the DCOS subsequently ruled that the JIC should make its own decision. The account that he provided for the FO file is the only surviving version of how it assumed the chairmanship, and clearly suggests that it was FO support for the idea that made it possible:

> [referring to JIC 130] . . . it will be observed that the Deputy Chiefs of Staff have omitted the recommendation dealing with the Chairmanship of the re-constituted JIC. I understand that at their first meeting to consider this matter the Deputy Chiefs of Staff desired to lay down the principle that as the handmaiden of the Chiefs of Staff the JIC could not have a Foreign Office Chairman. It was, however, pointed out to them privately that if they laid down any such rule the rank and responsibility of the Foreign Office representative would have to be re-considered. The Deputy Chiefs of Staff then had second thoughts and at a subsequent meeting decided to leave the question of Chairman to the JIC itself (as is the case with other Sub-Committees of the CID); and have contented themselves with deleting the relevant recommendations. As, however, the JIC have already decided the question, the Chairman will in fact be the FO representative except when questions of the internal organisation of the intelligence systems of the Fighting Services are under consideration. I think that we can leave the matter at that. The main point, i.e. the constitution of the JIC to include a FO representative, has been gained and it is well understood by the Directors of Intelligence that from every point of view it is more convenient that the FO representative should be Chairman.[118]

The matter was concluded on 3 August 1939 when the FO chair was formally accepted by the JIC. It was also on this date that, for the first time, the JIC was chaired by the FO, with Ralph Skrine Stevenson taking the role, something that it would do for the next forty-four years.[119] The JIC's composition and responsibilities were expanded and re-iterated:

(a) that this Committee should consist of a Counsellor from the Foreign Office and the Directors of Intelligence of the three Service Departments, or their Deputies, assisted or represented as might be necessary by the junior officers whose employment with the Situation Report Centre has already been sanctioned.

(b) That this Committee should continue to issue the Daily Reports and Weekly Commentaries at present produced by the Situation Report Centre and should also be charged with the following duties:

(i) The assessment and co-ordination of intelligence received from abroad with the object of ensuring that any Government action which might have to be taken should be based on the most reliable and carefully co-ordinated information obtainable.

(ii) The co-ordination of any intelligence data which might be required by the Chiefs of Staff or the Joint Planning Sub-Committee for them.

(iii) The consideration of any further measures which might be thought necessary in order to improve the efficient working of the intelligence organisation of the country as a whole.[120]

Through its amalgamation with the SRC, the JIC had assumed several new roles. It had taken on the responsibility for producing both short-term and long-term intelligence assessments, a radical departure from its previous incarnation. Furthermore, it was now accountable for overseeing all administrative arrangements relating to the intelligence machinery in its totality, and for taking the lead in highlighting any deficiencies in the existing system. This, then, was the shape that the JIC would take as events in Europe worsened.

The fact that intelligence had now taken on a political as well as the traditional, purely military, angle ensured that the various agencies had to begin to co-operate. Despite its involvement with SIS, one of the greatest factors that had prevented this occurring earlier was the reticence exhibited by the FO towards intelligence in general, and political intelligence in particular. Historically the FO had been averse to some of the personalities and methods involved in the acquisition of intelligence, considering it both un-gentlemanly and dishonest, and it especially did not want the activities of agents run from embassies abroad to ruin relations that had been developed with host nations. It also seems there was an element of jealousy at play, for the general FO attitude was that diplomats were the only people qualified to make appreciations of the international environment.[121] The growing severity of the German threat slowly eroded this view, but it would not be until the war was actually underway that it would fade.

Harry Hinsley, in writing on this period, hints at something of the environment in which the JIC had to operate:

> . . . collaboration between the Service departments and the Foreign Office, to ensure that military and political intelligence were considered together in appreciations for the Cabinet or its committees, went unrecognised, or was even resisted. To have thought on these lines would have been to affront Whitehall's deeply entrenched belief about the respective responsibilities of the Foreign Office and the Service departments for advising the government – the belief that they should tender independent advice, provided that the Service departments confined their advice to the military sphere.[122]

The idea of the JIC was, in itself, nothing new: Hankey had initially created the COS Committee as a forum in which defence matters could be discussed in a joined-up manner. What perhaps was new was the way in which intelligence began to take on a wider and more central role within government. This change was a reaction to the worsening international situation and a realisation that to cope effectively, all arms of the military and defence effort had to work as one. Although this was fine in theory, it would not quite work out in pracice.

The infant JIC had come into being without causing much of a ripple, yet its role was never effectively defined and there remained problems with its tasking and method of distributing its product. Despite a number of small reviews and proposals the Committee continued, gradually expanding its remit and influence as the 1930s wore on. In part this was due to the increasing weight given to intelligence; in part it was also due to the utility of the assessments being drawn up by the JIC and their use by the military planners. This changing perception of the value of intelligence by its customers was absolutely central. The nature of external events meant that a unified, central forum was needed, not only in ensuring that efforts were not duplicated, but also to enable effective transition from intelligence to policy. Thus, by 1939, it was clear that intelligence would underpin decision making over the inevitable conflict with Nazi Germany, and to this end the JIC would be crucial.

Notes

1 W F Moneypenny, *The Life of Benjamin Disraeli, Earl of Beaconsfield* (London: John Murray, 1920). p.285.
2 'Whitehall Gardens. The History of the Site', Churchill College Archives, University of Cambridge: Lord Hankey's Papers: HNKY 8/40.
3 The weather forecast is courtesy of the Meteorological Office archive. I am grateful to Glyn Hughes for this information.
4 For the remainder of the Official History the 'Joint Intelligence Sub-Committee' will be referred to as the 'Joint Intelligence Committee' or JIC. The original title, reflecting the fact that the JIC was a sub-committee of the Chiefs of Staff, officially remained until 1948, but it was referred to as 'JIC' throughout.
5 For more see D French, 'Spy Fever in Britain 1900–1915', *Historical Journal* 21 (1978), pp.355–70.
6 This is something hinted at by Hinsley but not really stated explicitly. See F H Hinsley et al, *British Intelligence in the Second World War: Volume 1* (London, 1979). pp.3–4.
7 For further details see C Andrew, *Her Majesty's Secret Service: The Making of the British Intelligence Community* (London: Heinemann, 1985).
8 W.M.James to M.Hankey, 22 November 1935. CAB 21/2651.
9 For an interesting account of pre-war air force intelligence see Air Marshal Sir V Goddard, *Epic Violet* (Unpublished). Liddell Hart Centre for Military Archives, King's College London (hereafter LHCMA): Goddard papers. This manuscript was later published as a book, *Skies to Dunkirk: A Personal Memoir* (London: William Kimber, 1982). Chapter 4, 'On False Deductions', which deals with intelligence was omitted from the published version. Goddard was Director of Intelligence in the Air Ministry, 1938–9.
10 Hinsley, *British Intelligence: Vol.1.* pp.11–12.
11 V Madeira, '"No Wishful Thinking Allowed": Secret Service Committee and Intelligence Reform in Great Britain, 1919–1923', *Intelligence and National Security* 18:1 (Spring 2003), pp.1–20.
12 For more information see K Jeffery, *MI6: The History of the Secret Intelligence Service, 1909–1949* (London: Bloomsbury, 2010).

13   On MI5 see C Andrew, *The Defence of the Realm: The Authorized History of MI5* (London: Allen Lane, 2009).

14   J Ferris, "Indulged in all Too Little"? Vansittart, Intelligence and Appeasement'. In his *Intelligence and Security* (London: Routledge, 2005). p.46.

15   Andrew, *Her Majesty's Secret Service*, pp.382–6.

16   Hinsley, *British Intelligence: Vol.1*, p.31. See also R Young, 'Spokesmen for Economic Warfare: The Industrial Intelligence Centre in the 1930s', *European Studies Review*. 6 (October 1976), pp.473–89. In addition, Desmond Morton, the Director of the IIC, ensured that reports also found their way to the Committee of Imperial Defence. See G Bennett, *Churchill's Man of Mystery: Desmond Morton and the World of Intelligence* (London: Routledge, 2006). pp.150–75.

17   As reported in *Time* magazine, 13 June 1938.

18   For more see S Roskill, *Hankey: Man of Secrets*, 3 Volumes (London: Collins, 1970–74).

19   J.G.Dill to M.Hankey, 22 July 1935. CAB 54/3.

20   M.P.A.Hankey to J.G.Dill, 29 July 1935. CAB 21/2651.

21   'Notes on ICF/52 dated 18.10.35 – Bomb Targets', Air Staff (Intelligence), 21 October 1935. CAB 21/2651.

22   'Bomb Targets', Note by D.Morton, 18 October 1935. CAB 21/2651.

23   'Central Machinery for Co-ordination of Intelligence – Note by the Secretary', 9 October 1935. CAB 54/3.

24   C.L.Courtney to M.P.A.Hankey, 18 October 1935. CAB 21/2651.

25   W.M.James to M.P.A.Hankey, 29 October 1935. CAB 21/2651.

26   M.P.A.Hankey to W.M.James, 31 October 1935. CAB 21/2651.

27   For instance, see G Till, *Air Power and the Royal Navy, 1914–1945: A Historical Survey* (London: Jane's, 1979).

28   For an account of this and the role of intelligence see J A Maiolo, *The Royal Navy and Nazi Germany, 1933–39: A Study in Appeasement and the Origins of the Second World War* (London: Palgrave, 1998).

29   'Joint Intelligence Committee (JIC) and Joint Intelligence Staff (JIS)', 2 May 1947. ADM 223/465.

30   See chapter 2 for more.

31   W.M.James to M.P.A.Hankey, 22 November 1935. CAB 21/2651.

32   DCOS 2nd Meeting, 29 October 1935. CAB 54/1.

33   DCOS 3rd Meeting, 29 November 1935. CAB 54/1.

34   For details see CAB 48/2.

35   DCOS 7, 17 December 1935. CAB 54/3.

36   DCOS 4, 'Central Machinery for Co-Ordination of Intelligence', 1 January 1936. CAB 4/24

37   COS/161st Meeting, 13 January 1936. CAB 53/5.

38   'Minutes of the 273rd Meeting of the Committee of Imperial Defence', 30 January 1936. CAB 2/6.

39   FCI 19th Meeting, 26 March 1936. CAB 48/2. The relevant papers that were discussed at this meeting, FCI 81 and FCI 84, can be found in CAB 48/4.

40   FCI 20th Meeting, 11 May 1936. CAB 48/2.

41   DCOS 7, 17 December 1935. CAB 54/3.

42   J.G.Dill to M.P.A.Hankey, 28 May 1936. CAB 21/2651.

43   M.P.A.Hankey to W.James, 28 May 1936. CAB 21/2651.

44   Minutes of the 178th Meeting of the Chiefs of Staff, 16 June 1936. CAB 53/6.

45   JIC 1, 30 June 1936. CAB 56/2.

46   For more see E Thomas, 'The Evolution of the JIC System Up to and During World War II', In C Andrew & J Noakes (eds), *Intelligence and International Relations, 1900–1945* (Exeter: University of Exeter, 1987), pp.223–4.

47   JIC 3, 14 July 1936. CAB 56/2.

48 W1382/80/50. Note by F.T.A.Ashton-Gwatkin, 17 February 1936. FO 371/20453.
49 'Prime Minister's Secret Service Committee – Minutes of 2nd Meeting, 2 March 1925', FO 1093/68.
50 'Memorandum on the Improvement of the Intellectual Equipment of the Services', 10 November 1902, St. J.B. [William St John Brodrick, Secretary of State for War]. CAB 37/63. The reports themselves can be found in CAB 18.
51 Viscount Weir was a Scottish industrialist who became a Privy Councillor and chaired various committees on behalf of the government in the 1920s. This particular committee focussed on co-ordination between the three Services. Its report is in ADM 1/8646/200. For subsequent discussions see Paper 695-B, Committee of Imperial Defence, 3 June 1926. CAB 4/14; Paper 772-B, Committee of Imperial Defence, 23 February 1927. CAB 4/16; Paper 870-B, Committee of Imperial Defence, 17 April 1928. CAB 4/17; Paper 933-B, Committee of Imperial Defence, 27 March 1929. CAB 4/18.
52 For details see ADM 1/8646/205.
53 On the former see HW 42/1. On the creation of the latter see Paper 906-B, Committee of Imperial Defence, 9 August 1928. CAB 4/18; Paper 909-B, Committee of Imperial Defence, 31 August 1928. CAB 4/18; Paper 932-B, Committee of Imperial Defence, 21 February 1929. CAB 4/18.
54 Minutes of the 178th Meeting of the Chiefs of Staff, 16 June 1936. CAB 53/6.
55 The Desmond Anderson Primary School in Crawley, West Sussex.
56 JIC 1st Meeting, 7 July 1936. CAB 56/1.
57 L.C.Hollis to H.Pownall [CID Assistant Secretary], 3 July 1936. CAB 21/2651.
58 JIC 3, 'Revised Functions and Working Arrangements Report', 14 July 1936. CAB 56/2. The adoption was at JIC 2nd Meeting, 29 September 1936. CAB 56/1.
59 JIC 12, "Revised Functions and Working Arrangements of the Joint Intelligence Sub-Committee', 26 September 1936. CAB 56/2.
60 The work of the Committee in the three years up to the outbreak of the Second World War will be addressed in chapter 2.
61 L.C.Hollis to H.L.Ismay, 22 September 1936. CAB 21/2651.
62 H.L.Ismay to CNS, CIGS, CAS, 24 September 1936. CAB 21/2651.
63 T.St.Q.Hill to M.P.A.Hankey, 11 October 1937. CAB 21/2465. See the responses by Colonel F.B.Webb, Hollis and Hankey in the same file for the rebuttal.
64 Note by L.C.Hollis, 14 October 1937. CAB 21/2465.
65 T.St.Q.Hill to M.P.A.Hankey, 26 October 1937. CAB 21/2465.
66 A.Barnard to Colonel Ives, 21 August 1939. CAB 21/2465.
67 H.L.Ismay to F.G.Beaumont-Nesbitt (JIC Chairman), 22 August 1939. CAB 21/2465.
68 Ultimately the FCI and the IIC would soon be subsumed into the newly-created Ministry of Economic Warfare. See D.Morton to H.L.Ismay, 6 September 1939. CAB 21/2553.
69 Information taken from the *Who's Who* entry for Beaumont-Nesbitt, Maj-Gen Frederick George.
70 F G Beaumont-Nesbitt, *Memoirs, 1893–1918*. (Unpublished). LHCMA: Beaumont-Nesbitt papers. See also his obituary in *The Times* (21 December 1971), p.12.
71 Brian Beaumont-Nesbitt, Email to author, 9 July 2009.
72 A copy of the report is in CAB 21/2651. The Foreign Office reaction is in W793/793/50. FO 371/23994.
73 JIC 78, 16 November 1938. CAB 56/4.
74 L.C.Hollis to K.C.Buss [Air Ministry representative on the JIC], 17 October 1938. CAB 21/2651.
75 Thomas, 'The Evolution of the JIC System', p.224.
76 See Beaumont-Nesbitt's report and cover note to Hollis, 21 December 1938. CAB 21/2651.

77 S.G.Menzies to F.G.Beaumont-Nesbitt, 14 December 1938. W793/793/50. FO 371/23994.

78 DCOS 41st Meeting, 14 July 1939. CAB 54/2.

79 L.C.Hollis to H.L.Ismay, 4 January 1939. CAB 21/2651.

80 W793/793/50. L.Oliphant to F.G.Beaumont-Nesbitt, 15 February 1939. FO 371/23994.

81 The author of this handwritten note is illegible. See the handwritten note in W793/793/50. FO 371/23994.

82 W793/793/50. Handwritten comment by R.W.A.Leeper [FO], 20 January 1939. FO 371/23994.

83 W5320/793/50. F.G.Beaumont-Nesbitt to L.Oliphant, 28 March 1939. FO 371/23994.

84 See various minutes in W2780/531/50. FO 371/21225.

85 W15468/531/50. Minute by F.Roberts, 30 July 1937. FO 371/21225.

86 W17211/531/50. H.Hodge to D.F.Howard, 9 September 1937. FO 371/21225.

87 E2768/2768/65. 'Arrangements for the Revision or Compilation of the Political Chapters of Service Department Intelligence Reports', 11 May 1938. FO 371/21839. For an example see N220/220/38. 'Intelligence Report on the Soviet Union', 15 January 1938. FO 371/22294.

88 D C Watt, 'British Intelligence and the Coming of the Second World War in Europe', In E R May (ed), *Knowing One's Enemies: Intelligence Assessment Before the Two World Wars* (Princeton: Princeton University Press, 1986), p.265. Andrew shares this view. *Her Majesty's Secret Service*. p.591.

89 W.E.van Cutsem [MoD] to E.E.G.L.Searight [JIC], 5 October 1954. Van Cutsem had been the Deputy Director for Military Intelligence at the time; Searight was the JIC Secretary. See also 'Joint Intelligence Committee and Offshoots', C.Morgan, c.1947. ADM 223/465. This is one of the Godfrey history volumes, and includes several different accounts on the origins of the JIC by wartime members.

90 Note by N.Chamberlain, 21 April 1939. CAB 21/2722.

91 JIC 114, 4 July 1939. 'Annex: Co-Ordination of Intelligence. Memorandum by the Situation Report Centre.' CAB 163/6. See also Hinsley, *British Intelligence: Vol.1.* p.43.

92 W7914/108/50. Note by R.C.Skrine Stevenson, 16 May 1939. FO 371/23984.

93 W7254/108/50. Lord Chatfield to Viscount Halifax [Foreign Secretary], 28 April 1939. FO 371/23984.

94 W8012/108/50. Situation Report Centre, meeting held on 16 May 1939. FO 371/23984.

95 'Daily Secret Situation Reports', Note by the Secretary, 6 September 1939. FO 1093/126.

96 These details are taken from the introduction to the Skrine Stevenson papers, held at the Manx National Heritage Library, Isle of Man. (Ms 10859). I am grateful to Roger Sims for his assistance with the collection. For some reason, Stevenson dropped the 'Skrine' part of his name in later life; documents from this period refer to him as 'R. Skrine Stevenson'.

97 'Joint Intelligence Committee', notes by J.H.Godfrey. ADM 223/465.

98 W6765/108/50. Situation Report Centre, 25 April 1939. FO 371/23983.

99 Situation Report Centre Volume, Foreign Office Archive. FO 1093/125.

100 Handwritten notes on the cover of W6765/108/50. FO 371/23983.

101 See the various minutes on file W7989/108/50. FO 371/23984.

102 X5572/G. H.J.B.Clough to Secretary, Treasury, 12 May 1939. FO 366/2382.

103 X5572/G. S.H.Wright to H.H.Quarmby, 22 May 1939. FO 366/2382.

104 X5572/G. C.Howard Smith to S.H.Wright, 25 May 1939. FO 366/2382.

105 X5572/G. Note by A.Cadogan, 25 May 1939. FO 366/2382.

106 H.L.Ismay to Minister [Lord Chatfield], 25 May 1939. CAB 21/2722.

107 'C' to Ismay, 25 April 1939. CAB 21/2722.

108 W9715/108/50. F.Beaumont-Nesbitt to R.C.Skrine Stevenson, 14 June 1939. FO 371/23986.

109 W9715/108/50. 'Co-ordination of Intelligence: Draft Memorandum by the Situation Report Centre', n.d. but probably late June 1939. FO 371/23986. The revised version of the report can also be found in this volume.

110 The draft is in W9715/108/50. FO 371/23986. The final circulated version is JIC 114, 4 July 1939. CAB 56/4.

111 W9715/108/50. R.C.Skrine Stevenson to A.Cadogan, 21 June 1939. FO 371/23986.

112 W9715/108/50. A.Cadogan to R.C.Skrine Stevenson, 27 June 1939. FO 371/23986.

113 W9715/108/50. Note by R.C.Skrine Stevenson, 27 June 1939. FO 371/23986.

114 L.C.Hollis to H.L.Ismay, 26 June 1939. CAB 21/2651. Although this pre-dates the formal acceptance, it appears that all members had discussed the issue beforehand and were in agreement.

115 DCOS 41st Meeting, 14 July 1939. CAB 54/2.

116 DCOS 44th Meeting, 28 July 1939. CAB 54/2.

117 'Joint Intelligence Committee', notes by J.H.Godfrey. ADM 223/465.

118 W9975/9805/49. Note by R.C.Skrine Stevenson, 1 August 1939. FO 371/23901.

119 JIC 32nd Meeting, 3 August 1939. CAB 56/1. In fact, Foreign Office incumbency of the chairmanship was longer than this: if those Chairmen, diplomats seconded to the Cabinet Office, are included, then the FO and its FCO successors only relinquished the role in 2001.

120 JIC 114 'Reconstitution of the Sub-Committee', 4 July 1939. CAB 163/6.

121 Hinsley, *British Intelligence: Vol.1.* pp.5–6.

122 Hinsley, *British Intelligence: Vol.1.* p.73.

2   Building a Foundation

In order to assess the Joint Intelligence Committee's pre-war performance it is essential to keep in mind what the pre-war JIC was set-up to do. The problem with most secondary accounts is that they assume that the JIC should have been tasked with exposing Nazi Germany's real intentions, yet this was not the Committee's role. The 1936 JIC never took the initiative in selecting topics; instead customers placed requirements upon it. On those occasions where it did produce papers on less than wholly military topics, such as Nazi espionage in the UK, its reports were not well received.

The period 1936–9 was characterised by several issues: arguments between the Admiralty and the Air Ministry over budgets and primacy in military strategy; the inability of politicians to agree on Hitler's true intentions; the failure to anticipate the Nazi-Soviet pact; and the lack of preparedness by the intelligence agencies for war in September 1939. While the JIC played a role in each, it was not always as directly or as forcefully engaged as it could, and arguably should, have been.

In the period from its creation in July 1936 to the outbreak of war in September 1939, the JIC held only 34 meetings, approving and disseminating 140 papers. In addition, an off-shoot sub-committee was created, dealing initially with aerial warfare in Spain, then with an expanded remit to include China. The papers produced reveal something of the diverse nature of the JIC's work. Generally speaking they are overwhelmingly military in content – unsurprising given the JIC's role in advising the JPC – but as war approached the JIC took on a wider responsibility. The key question is whether this was out of necessity or whether it was a reflection of the Committee's growing stature, or both.

Although never given explicit terms of reference, the pre-war JIC had several primary functions.[1] The original remit was to act upon requirements identified by the JPC by providing relevant information. Implicit in this was an assumption that the JIC would co-ordinate the work of the three Service intelligence directorates. By mid-1939 this area of activity had expanded greatly and was now threefold: to ensure that governmental action was based on co-ordinated intelligence; to produce data for the JPC; and finally, to consider any further measures to improve the intelligence machinery. While these roles were not formally adopted until relatively late, all three were apparent in the JIC's work going back as far as its first meeting in 1936. In the three year period to the outbreak of war, therefore, the Committee's work can be split into three primary tasks: examining the use of aerial warfare in the Spanish and Chinese civil wars; the management of the intelligence community, including the creation of liaison relations; and preparing for the imminent war.

The Spanish Civil War

The period of the Spanish civil war matches almost exactly that of the pre-war JIC. Starting in July 1936, Spain endured a devastating three year conflict, resulting in the deaths of over 200,000 people.[2] The war however, was not strictly civil in nature, being used also as a proxy conflict for several nations. A month after the outbreak of hostilities Britain signed a non-intervention agreement, and militarily played no overt part in the civil war, though there are hints of a more covert role having been employed at various times.[3]

The stimulus for the Committee's interest in Spain may have been a comment by Sir Thomas Inskip, the Minister for the Co-ordination of Defence, in early 1937 that 'I wish we had more red-hot information from Spain.'[4] As it was, in March 1937 the Admiralty sent a letter to the Home Office, FO, War Office, Air Ministry and CID suggesting that the civil war in Spain offered an unprecedented opportunity to observe the lessons of modern aerial warfare. In particular, the letter emphasised that up to this point any lessons from air warfare were limited to the experiences of the First World War, lessons which were 'not only very scanty but also in some degree misleading when applied to the improved material and technique of modern air war.' The letter called for an inter-departmental forum in which to discuss the implications of the Spanish experience and was passed to the JIC.[5]

At the meeting at the end of April 1937, the JIC discussed the matter and took a fairly ambivalent view towards the proposal. The Air Ministry could not understand why such a forum needed to be convened considering that it had already been conducting relevant work; a view similarly held, albeit to a lesser degree, by the Admiralty.[6] A month later the JIC met once more to consider the matter. In the interim a number of representatives from other government departments had visited the Air Ministry to discuss its work. The general feeling, subsequently recorded in a JIC memorandum, was that the recommended inter-departmental forum was indeed necessary.[7] The new 'Sub-Committee on Air Warfare in Spain' was subsequently approved, with the terms of reference to 'examine all available information on Air Warfare in Spain'.[8]

From the outset, the work of the new JIC sub-committee was flawed. The impression gained from the JIC minutes is that while everyone recognised that it was a sensible idea in theory, no-one really wanted the burden of a new sub-committee and those involved were sceptical from the outset as to what it could achieve. Wing Commander Victor Goddard, the Air Ministry representative, highlighted the problems in the reporting from Spain, specifically the reliance on 'unskilled or biased observers', and he added that the prospects of learning lessons were 'very limited'.[9] Most troublesome was the inherent view of the Spanish civil war and the use of aircraft. It was recognised from the outset that the use of aerial warfare in Spain 'may not be as intensive or as highly technical as that which may be visualised in a future war between first class European powers.'[10] Herein lay one of the central failings of the whole endeavour, but one which would not appear quite so explicitly until later.

Despite the limited scope of the new sub-committee, the JIC's remit on Spain was straightforward: it was not to assess the direction of the civil war per se, nor to comment on the involvement of foreign powers and the wider implications of the conflict; instead it was to examine the aerial conflict and to consider the lessons that could be identified. In reality the JIC's focus on the civil war had nothing to do with Spain itself, but rather more to do with what could be learnt from German and Italian involvement in the conflict.

Whilst the rationale behind the creation of the sub-committee was sound, it masked deeper stresses and tensions within the British military establishment. The importance of the military lessons from Spain lay as much in how foreign powers conducted tactical warfare as in how Britain might respond to and engage in similar operations. The JIC sub-committee, then, became the forum in which Admiralty and Air Ministry arguments over funding and military procurement could be played out. The sub-committee's first three papers were discussed by the JIC in September 1937. It seems to have been commonly agreed that sources of information were patchy. The War Office was particularly concerned about this, commenting that 'owing to the sudden outbreak of the civil war, MI1c [as SIS was designated then] have unavoidably been somewhat slow in developing their organisation in Spain.' Information from observers was not considered to be any better.[11] At the same time it was emphasised by Captain Claude Hermon-Hodge, the Admiralty representative, that the purpose of the sub-committee was to 'present conclusions based upon facts, and not to attempt to draw conclusions from those facts', and he was quick to point out that he was referring to future work.[12] Presumably this was an attempt to ensure that the JIC did not stray into policy recommendations. The comments are particularly apt given the large and very detailed wish-lists drawn up by the Service departments as to what lessons from Spain they wanted covered.

The first report, on anti-aircraft artillery defence, by way of example, began by referring to the difficulties in gathering information, the unreliability of observers, the untrained technical ability of observers, and the fact that only 'very general' appreciations could be made. Without reliable evidence from German sources, 'there is little prospect of our obtaining valuable A.A. [anti-aircraft] experience'.[13] Despite these caveats, the sub-committee produced a fairly detailed and lengthy report. One of its most telling conclusions was that it would be difficult to extract any substantial lessons because the findings 'fall far short of what should be expected from first class Powers'. The most interesting observations were those made on foreign involvement, principally that of German, Italian and Russian forces. The report made it clear that the foreign powers were far more effective than the native Spanish forces.

The first three reports were transmitted to the COS Committee for discussion in late 1937. In general the COS Committee was pleased with the results. It communicated that they had been 'admirably compiled', were 'extremely valuable', and perhaps most crucially, 'showed a commendable absence of Departmental bias'.[14] It was clear that foreign intervention, particularly German, was more efficient than Spanish efforts, the implication being that the JIC felt lessons from 'second' class powers could not easily be transposed on to 'first' class powers. While this conclusion has been criticised in the secondary literature as revealing an arrogant mind-set, the information available at the time did imply that there were different standards of military operations, so it was not a wholly unreasonable conclusion.[15] That said, the important 'so what' question arising from this was never addressed; if the whole purpose was to look at Spain with regard to what lessons could be learnt, the implications of facing Germany in a future conflict were never raised.

By late 1937 the numerous reports on aspects of the Spanish civil war were beginning to extend beyond mere observational reporting. Inskip informed the COS that MPs were beginning to ask why the government was not doing anything about the lessons from Spain.[16] This debate centred around more general discussions on Britain's rearmament policy, and reflected the earlier COS comments on 'departmental bias'.

Given the delay in procuring military technology it was essential for British planners to identify the future nature of warfare as soon as possible. Despite being restricted by the Treaty of Versailles, Germany had undertaken an ambitious rearmament programme. Discussions within the UK military in the early 1930s concerned not just the nature of Germany's efforts, but also the future of maritime and air strategies, and their relative primacies in any future conflict. One example of this was the debate over how vulnerable ships were to aerial attack. The Admiralty accepted that aerial attack was a risk, but concluded that ships could continue to survive alone; the Air Ministry, conversely, argued that this vulnerability made battlefleets relatively obsolete.[17] It was within this bitter debate that the JIC 'Sub-Committee on Air Warfare in Spain' came into existence. The issue, in strategic terms, was not so much who was right, but that the correct strategy should be enacted upon in sufficient time to meet any foreign threat.

In reporting on events in Spain, the various military attachés were not entirely objective in their coverage.[18] In addition, the different Services drew their own conclusions from the analyses produced. For example, there were a number of disagreements between the Admiralty and the Air Ministry over the value of anti-aircraft fire in defending ships from aerial attack.[19] In assessing the reports of the JIC sub-committee, the Admiralty was content as they supported its concern about the importance of safeguarding fuel reserves. Indeed, Hermon-Hodge, the Admiralty's JIC representative, commented on one of the sub-committee reports that it 'seemed that the very considerable expenditure which the Admiralty were now contemplating . . . was fully justified.'[20] On the question of the survivability of ships in the face of aerial attack, the Admiralty fared less well: the various reports on the matter declaring that no firm lessons could be learnt from Spain.[21]

Other disputes between the Air Ministry and the War Office surfaced, principally over the 'probable form of land operations' and the role of the RAF.[22]

Was the 'Sub-Committee on Air Warfare in Spain' a success? Despite the differences of opinion there was a recognition that it was essential to 'eliminate any possible sources of friction or disagreement in advance before war comes'.[23] But this never happened in any comprehensive fashion and, furthermore, such calls probably came too late. Those papers that did reach the COS were well received but generally speaking, it was left to the individual Services to heed the lessons from Spain.[24] The biggest failing was not the inherent biases, errors or lack of information, but rather that very little was done as a consequence of the sub-committee's report. This deficiency had been identified by Group Captain Kenneth C. Buss, the Director of Intelligence and Air Ministry representative in early 1939: 'it was not only a matter of collection and collation but also of deciding what use could be made of the information when it came to hand.'[25] The impact was obvious, for as one secondary commentator has observed, 'after three years of war in Spain from which the British had collected copious amounts of military intelligence, the Spanish civil war had still had no perceptible effect on British rearmament or strategy.'[26]

In a sense these problems were not the fault of the JIC. It was responsible for producing the analysis but not for acting upon it. But the JIC analysis itself was faulty – the lessons drawn from the Spanish civil war were applicable to other nations only they were ignored. In addition, rather than examining the specific detail, the JIC could have tackled the implications of its findings, yet the consistent argument was that lessons could not be learnt from the Spanish experience. The greatest illustration of this failing was that the German Air Force, having gained valuable experience in Spain, was able to take full advantage once the Second World War began.[27]

In October 1938 the remit of the sub-committee was expanded to include examination of the war raging between China and Japan, including what lessons could be learnt. While anti-aircraft operations were similar to those observed in the Spanish conflict, bombing methods were very different.[28] Subsequent reports included a comparison of the Spanish and Chinese experiences.[29] In total six such reports were produced.

On 1 April 1939 the sub-committee was wound up, its responsibilities passing to other bodies.[30] The reason behind this was that representatives were needed for more 'urgent' matters. Its dissolution was accepted as necessary by the DCOS Committee, which considered that the lessons from Spain were important and the sub-committee's reports had been of 'considerable interest and value'.[31] Thus a strange dichotomy emerged: on the one hand the sub-committee's reports were evidently considered useful, but on the other they seemingly had no discernible effect on policy. Nonetheless, the JIC's standing improved in the eyes of the COS Committee as a result. Furthermore, the sub-committee was able to extend links to other, related bodies – including the Home Office's Air Raid Precautions' department and the 'Sub-Committee on Bombing and Anti-Aircraft Gunfire Experiments' – thereby expanding its range of influence across Whitehall.[32]

There are frequent references to the great utility of the reports, and how any uncertain or disputed areas should be referred back to the JIC for clarification.[33] This was, in theory at least, the great value of having the forum hosted by the JIC. With its raison d'être as an inter-departmental committee, any inter-service rivalries were supposed to be minimised. The biggest differences were undoubtedly between the Air Ministry and the Admiralty, and this is explicitly why the War Office, certainly in the first instance, was often left to chair meetings before regular FO involvement became the norm.[34]

The JIC was criticised by Hollis, its Secretary (and also the Assistant Secretary to the CID), for not being able to comment on technical matters, therefore making its reports on Spain of only limited value, yet this was never its purpose.[35] In a sense this is the start of the JIC's ascendancy. If nothing else, through the existence of the sub-committee the COS and senior figures within the three Services became familiar with the work of the JIC on a regular basis, and this certainly helped the JIC establish itself within the governmental machinery for planning for war.

Management of the Intelligence Community

Of the various roles prescribed to the JIC in the pre-war period, the one which has received least attention was managing the intelligence community. This was a broadly defined responsibility, outlined in July 1939 as: 'The consideration of any further measures which might be thought necessary in order to improve the efficient working of the intelligence organisation of the country as a whole.'[36] This was not an original remit of the JIC, and certainly there are no efforts to tackle what might be described as community management until January 1939. The stimulus for the change was the JIC's sub-committee's work on aerial warfare in Spain and China. The War Office representative and Chairman of the JIC, Brigadier Frederick Beaumont-Nesbitt, commented that there was a general question mark over where responsibility lay for collecting and collating intelligence on foreign air defences. Furthermore, the problem involved not just the three Services but also SIS.[37] The result was a decision, taken at the JIC, as to which Service was responsible for which type of information.[38]

Despite involvement in other activities – which could be considered part of its management role, such as creating and running a role play 'war game' of an impending war with Germany – one of the JIC's main functions in this pre-war period was to create and manage relations with overseas intelligence organisations.[39] This was not at the tactical level, as it was understood this was dealt with on an agency-to-agency basis, but rather at the strategic level. Its involvement in such matters began in late 1937 following a request from the Commanding Officer in Malta that an 'Inter-Services Intelligence Bureau' be created in order to monitor and gauge Italian movements.[40] The JIC considered the matter and approved the supply of relevant intelligence to and from Malta.[41] This fell to the JIC to adjudicate because it represented the only relevant inter-service body. This brief experience would be useful because the JIC would develop two major liaisons, and one minor one, prior to the Second World War.

In October 1935, on orders from Benito Mussolini, the Italian army marched into Abyssinia (now Ethiopia) and seized control of the country. Britain, with an imperial stake in Eastern Africa, disapproved of the Italian aggression. Although the Italian invasion, as such, was never discussed by the JIC, the implications of the Italian action eventually would be. At the time the COS considered the Italian forces a distinctly second class military outfit. Admiral Sir Ernle Chatfield, the First Sea Lord, commented on how he felt the Italian navy would never 'prove really efficient at sea'; the army representative, Major General John Dill, stated that although 'highly developed', the Italian army was still 'Italian', and that therefore there was 'considerable doubt' over its efficiency; whereas Air Chief Marshal Sir Edward Ellington noted how 'a few knocks would reduce [the Italian air force's] enthusiasm'.[42]

The implication of the Italian invasion was obvious: to the War Office it had 'altered the whole strategic problem of the Middle East' and, for this reason, it was now seen as necessary to create a 'Combined Intelligence Bureau' for the Middle East. This reflected both the importance of the region to Britain and the necessity of integrating intelligence activities. There was a concern that British interests could be affected by events in neighbouring nations. Therefore with the increasing threat of 'foreign penetration' and propaganda efforts, it was essential to keep abreast of developments. For this, intelligence would be central, yet the existing system was too disjointed, with the result, in the JIC's words, that there were 'gaps in our Intelligence.'[43] The proposed Bureau would act as a clearing house for intelligence – it would produce assessed intelligence for distribution to London. The Air Ministry supported the proposal, especially its location in Egypt.[44]

The ensuing discussions about creating a Bureau are important as the JIC was attempting to replicate and export its own model abroad. The JIC was in 'complete agreement' that such a Bureau was needed; the problem was to precisely define its role and functions.[45] The JIC undertook a review of the 'attitude of the "Arab world" to Great Britain', which found generally favourable reports, concluding that it was unlikely that any of the nations would take action against Britain in the event of a European war (for more see below).[46]

The JIC's recommendations on the Bureau were transmitted to the COS Committee and thence to the CID for discussion.[47] The CID in approving the creation of the Bureau commented on how the 'problem of the co-ordination of intelligence is, of course, intimately connected with the co-ordination of command.' The new 'Combined Middle East Intelligence Centre' was therefore seen as an all-source intelligence organisation, responsible for collating information necessary for military planning, including monitoring foreign use of propaganda against the British Isles.[48] Importantly the new Centre was placed under the control of the JIC, becoming its first 'outpost'.[49] This body, albeit in a slightly different guise, would eventually play a valuable role in the Second World War. It was in discussions over the Middle East Intelligence Centre that Victor Cavendish-Bentinck first became involved with the JIC.[50] He would, in 1940, assume Chairmanship of the Committee for the duration of the Second World

War. Bentinck, a diplomat, acted as middle-man. His minutes on the matter make clear that he was impressed by the work of the JIC in relation to the Middle East Bureau.[51]

The JIC's other involvement with foreign intelligence was in a different context. In two separate instances it acted as the broker between British and French intelligence, and as the mediator between British and Turkish intelligence. Regarding the former, the role of intelligence in Anglo-French military and diplomatic relations in the years prior to the outbreak of war was just beginning to emerge.[52] In this context, in early 1939, the military staffs of both powers held a series of talks to discuss military strategy in the event of a war with Germany.[53] In the first round of these talks, the practicalities of exchanging military information were discussed, particularly the means by which it could be rapidly communicated in the event of war.[54] Such deliberations soon expanded to include a discussion on the exchange of all Service intelligence between Britain and France. These were initially discussed by the 'Strategical Appreciations Sub-Committee' of the COS Committee, but were soon passed to the JIC. Prior to this SIS had already begun to liaise on human intelligence (Humint, or agent running) and signals intelligence (Sigint, or the interception of communications) with the French.[55]

The JIC's remit was to turn the theory into practice; to establish how intelligence could be exchanged and whether it should take place in London or Paris, or locally in command centres.[56] The Committee consulted the individual Services.[57] Agreement was reached in April 1939 and consisted of approving existing liaison arrangements and establishing new ones. Essentially discussion was to take place at the Service-to-Service level. The intelligence components of both the Admiralty and the Air Ministry were already in touch with their French counterparts and the War Office was instructed to open channels. The fourth component, Economic Warfare Intelligence, was to continue establishing links which had only just begun. But no mention was made of the JIC product being transmitted to France.[58]

The new policy of bilateral exchange was implemented just a month later with discussions in Rabat, Morocco, about exchanging intelligence between British and French forces in North Africa.[59] The conference was followed by further discussions in Jerusalem and Aden.[60] Talks with the French about setting up intelligence exchange relations would prove to be fortuitous. In August 1939, and with war imminent, military missions were sent to several locations in Eastern Europe, comprising a sizeable intelligence detachment in addition to purely military officers. It was expected that the French would follow suit, and responsibility for intelligence liaison would be split evenly.[61]

At the same time the JIC was also responsible for establishing liaison links with the Turkish intelligence services. Although Turkey would not officially enter the war until early 1945, in October 1939 it concluded a mutual assistance pact with Britain and France.[62] As with a number of other countries, the British military had held 'Staff conversations' with the Turkish military. Amongst other things, the Turks exhibited a keen desire to learn about British intelligence assessments of the Italian forces; in return they would provide their own forecasts.

The matter was referred to the JIC, who concluded that such information should be exchanged.[63]

In these instances, although the actual discussions were conducted by military officers, the results were carefully transmitted back to the JIC in London, whose role was to make decisions on any aspects to do with intelligence. Everything was conducted under the auspices of the COS, and in this way the JIC was brought further into military planning, though it would still remain relatively peripheral in the run up to war.

Preparing for the Inevitable

In the pre-war period the JIC never had an official remit of watching for, or warning of, war. As the military planners became more involved with preparing for the outbreak of hostilities the JIC was inevitably drawn into the estimating process. Given that the focus of the Committee was overwhelmingly military and was designed to inform the JPC, then it is perhaps unsurprising that little attention was paid to gauging German intentions, with more effort placed on analysing their war-fighting capabilities. The advent of FO involvement in the year immediately preceding war marked something of a change, but ultimately the JIC was never asked to speculate, nor proffer a view, on when the Germans might provide the *casus belli* necessary for British involvement. It is not the remit of this history to provide an historical account of British intelligence on Germany in the lead-up to September 1939[64] but rather the JIC's role in what Churchill would later describe as the 'gathering storm'.[65]

Of the first topics the JIC would address in its initial months of existence, perhaps none would be as important as its studies of armaments, manpower and mobilisation of foreign forces. Its first paper set the scene for much of what was to follow, outlining the size of forces in various countries. It is revealing to see the countries on which it chose to concentrate and those which it did not.[66] The initial paper was prepared by the War Office but was subsequently approved as a JIC document with the request that the JPC provide a list of nations for the JIC to focus on in the future.

A country's war-fighting potential was based, according to the paper, on two limiting factors: manpower and armaments. Of these the JIC felt that the latter was more important, since 'very few countries possess an industry strong enough to manufacture sufficient armaments to maintain in the field the whole of the available trained man-power.' It was for this reason that Desmond Morton, the head of the IIC and subsequently Churchill's intelligence adviser, would become a regular attender at pre-war JIC meetings.[67] In this context, the JIC commented, a 'neutral' nation was of crucial significance if it was still prepared to offer industrial support, even if no overt military help was forthcoming. The tone of the document suggests that any coming conflict would be different from anything that had gone before, with frequent references to 'modern war'. The paper continued by remarking that it was only possible to understand force levels, given the emphasis on armaments and industrial supply, if nations were grouped together. In other words, it was not possible to simply study the German war machine in isolation because, in practice, Germany would not be fighting alone, and in the ensuing assessments Germany was rarely considered in this way.

The JPC discussed the report at the start of July 1936, subsequently issuing a large list of 23 countries of interest,[68] though the record of the relevant meeting of the JPC makes no mention of any such discussion.[69] The resulting paper was produced and approved by the JIC in November, subsequently becoming a Joint Planning paper.[70] The JPC studies fitted well with other work being authorised for the JIC: in particular there were two topics that had become constant by 1936. The first had its origins in a 1934 decision by the COS which had charged the JPC with 'contemplating in our defence preparations the possibility of a war with Germany'.[71] The assumption behind the paper was explicit: it should be supposed that war would occur between the UK and Germany in late 1939. This may have had more to do with the debates on Britain's own re-armament programme and which direction it should take than with consideration of external developments. The JPC was to consider not just military factors, such as troop levels, mobilisation speeds etc., but also political factors. At the same time though, these were to take secondary importance because it was recognised from the outset that 'we do not feel that a discussion of the detailed political factors likely to influence the attitude of the Powers in 1939 would have any great value.'[72]

The second task came from a higher authority and was set by the COS themselves, following a decision by the Cabinet. This followed a call by Foreign Secretary Anthony Eden in November 1936 that, given the 'anxiety as to the state of Europe', it would be useful to gauge Britain's strength vis-à-vis other nations. The COS passed the request downward in turn to the JPC and JIC. In assessing the situation certain assumptions were made, conforming to the previous premise that nations should not be considered solely in isolation: these were that Germany and Italy were hostile, France and Belgium were with the United Kingdom, and Russia was either neutral or with the UK.[73]

These two tasks – preparing for war with Germany and comparing British forces with foreign ones – would preoccupy the JIC in unequal measure throughout the period to September 1939; but they did not dominate the Committee's proceedings. At this time that the JIC had no secretariat: generally speaking, papers were produced by Service departments and then discussed at the JIC meetings, they were redrafted as necessary and then issued, usually to the Joint Planners. We know that the JIC drew upon several sources of intelligence, ranging from military attaché reporting to secret intelligence. Certainly the Service departments were heavily reliant on SIS reporting for their information.

A revealing vignette of the problems of collecting intelligence in the mid-1930s is provided by a document written by Admiral Sir Hugh Sinclair, the Chief of SIS. In it 'C' described the problems of financial cutbacks and how they had affected his organisation's intelligence gathering abilities. 'C' mentioned how SIS's main role was to procure information for the Services, but how the lack of funds meant that investigating secret foreign plans to re-arm had only been partially covered by the secret service. A bigger problem was that due to financial stringency it had been necessary to prioritise workloads, with the effect that since Italy had previously been considered friendly, there had been no SIS sources at the time of Mussolini's invasion of Abyssinia. Germany was and remained the number one priority, but there were weaknesses in SIS's operations against the other members of the Axis.[74] This was particularly acute as SIS was also responsible for providing the intelligence used to gauge foreign industrial mobilisation capability.[75]

Given SIS's centrality to the intelligence process, its own assessments of the worsening international situation and the likelihood of war with Germany are of interest. A November 1938 survey declared that Hitler's policy was one of 'atomisation', described as 'a process of creating small States on a racial and self-determination basis, which would be completely dependent on, and under the influence of, Germany. A start was to be made with Czechoslovakia.'[76] A further 'summary of information from secret sources' in January 1939 revealed the difficulties SIS encountered in trying to determine German actions: 'Germany is controlled by one man, Herr Hitler, whose will is supreme and who is a blend of fanatic, madman and clear-visioned realist'. Furthermore, 'his ambition and self-confidence are unbounded, and he regards Germany's supremacy in Europe as a step to world supremacy . . . Britain, meanwhile, is Enemy No.1.' The final conclusion was explicit: 'it is unfortunately no longer possible to assume that there is no likelihood of Germany "coming West" in 1939 . . . . all our sources are at one in declaring that he [Hitler] is barely sane, consumed by an intense hatred of this country, and capable both of ordering an immediate aerial attack on any European country and of having his command instantly obeyed.'[77]

In compiling its various reports the JIC amassed and published a vast array of statistics, yet although these reports were routinely accepted and approved by the JPC, it is difficult to judge their effectiveness. More often than not, JIC views were incorporated into JPC papers without comment or attribution, eventually being put before the COS Committee. In a sense this was how it should have been: the JIC was designed to provide information to the planners, but from the documentary record there is little by way of comment on the JIC's involvement and input. It can only be assumed that the work must have been considered important because it was widely used.

The very detailed comparison of manpower levels in Britain and other countries did not reach any conclusions, but the main message was that any impending war would be different from previous conflicts. For the first time, the JIC felt that all 'able-bodied citizens' would be called up in the 'shortest possible time'. The paper made some useful observations, including a warning of the danger of mobilising too quickly, thereby questioning the First World War timeframe of the lag between planning and actually putting men on the frontline ready to fight. Ultimately though, its conclusions were tentative given that it was especially difficult to make accurate predictions for large nations like the USA, Soviet Union, China and Japan.[78] Certainly the JIC was aware of the paper's shortcomings, as the Deputy Director of Military Intelligence made plain shortly afterwards, in particular the failure to relate troop numbers to mobilisation speeds.[79]

The JIC also provided information on rearmament. The Minister, Sir Thomas Inskip, asked in early 1937 for the JIC to provide him with details of foreign rearmament efforts, the rationale for which was their use as an argument for procuring support and funding for Britain's own programme. The resulting report was both detailed and authoritative, and a more useful document than the paper on manpower levels.[80] Despite this, the version that went to Inskip was watered down, for the JIC had decided that given that it was to be used publicly, all information derived from 'secret sources' should be removed.[81]

By this point international events had continued to deteriorate. In March 1936 Hitler had authorised the invasion of the Rhineland, an illegal act which caused consternation within His Majesty's Government.[82] The Rhineland was a defining point in the increased intelligence interest focussed on Germany. In early 1937 the COS Committee prepared a document entitled 'Planning for War with Germany'.[83] The report was passed upwards to the ministerial 'Defence Plans (Policy) Sub-Committee', chaired by the Prime Minister, who approved it and gave the various sub-committees of the COS, the JIC and JPC specific tasks.

The COS paper was, as its title suggested, a series of proposals for practical measures to be employed in preparation for a war with Germany. Its 24th recommendation was that the JIC should 'review the intelligence arrangements for the contingency of war', building upon the JIC's role as the managers of the intelligence community, and recognising its remit as going beyond merely providing assessments to the military planners.[84] The Committee instructed the Service departments to consider how war might affect them, but the topic does not appear to have been discussed any further within either the JIC or the JPC.[85]

In addition to assessments being produced on Germany, the JIC gave consideration to German and Italian espionage in the UK, and how foreign agents might be able to sabotage British plans for war. This was an example of a task allotted to the JIC which did not emerge from the military planners, a fact that would later cause some consternation. The subject had first been considered by MI5 and had been brought to the attention of the JIC to allow a more senior committee to look into the subject to see if anything further should be done.[86] Speed and haste were most certainly not characteristics of the pre-war JIC, with the report taking eight months to complete. The finished product was relatively substantial, detailing Nazi and Fascist organisations in Britain and the precautions necessary to deal with them. The JIC concluded that foreign agents posed a 'potential danger' which, if left unchecked, could 'produce very serious results'. The precautions outlined included not just ensuring that 'aliens' could not work in sensitive areas, especially the dockyards and munitions factories, but also that MI5 should continue to monitor such people.[87]

The JIC paper was transmitted to the COS for approval. The minutes of the discussion illustrate the various views held within the government at this time, particularly within the context of the appeasement debate. The Admiralty felt that foreign organisations should be 'liquidated' and that a request should be made to the Italian and German governments to remove their agents: this should be done at such a time when relations with Britain were 'reasonably satisfactory' so as to not 'precipitate a war'.[88] The following month MI5, through its Director General, Sir Vernon Kell, issued a further report to the JIC on Ireland, including an SIS intelligence report originating from someone close to the Nazi party that Germany would try and win over Ireland should war break out. The SIS report was distributed by the JIC as the optimum means of circulating its contents throughout the Service departments.[89]

The SIS report caused some resentment within the War Office because it was not a purely military topic, even though the matter was dealt with quietly and efficiently. The issue was not just that a paper had been requested without the COS authorisation, but also that, in the words of Major General Robert Haining, the Director of Military Operations and Intelligence (as the post had now become) in the War Office, 'with the amount of work there is at the moment I think it is a good thing to have some controlling authorities to see that time is not wasted as I think it has been in this case.'[90] Maurice Hankey's response was to do nothing. In his reply Hastings Ismay, the Deputy Secretary of the COS Committee, stated that Hankey had 'found from experience that it is as the general rule preferable to allow Committees to work out their own salvation rather than to tie them down too rigidly.' Furthermore, 'in the particular case of the JIC, he [Hankey] feels that they are doing such good work that it would be a pity to administer anything that might be interpreted as a snub at this stage.'[91]

Planning for War

1938 marked a watershed in the JIC's assessments of the changing international situation because, for the first time, it was asked to be far more forward looking in its estimates. The stimulus for this seems to have been Hitler's annexation of Czechoslovakia in March 1938. It was likely to affect the French, who had an obligation to protect the Czechs: by extension therefore, it was considered that an attack 'would clearly bring a French response that might force Great Britain to join in to bolster their ally'.[92]

In the months before the signing of the Munich Agreement in September 1938, the British intelligence and planning machinery turned its attention towards examining the implications of the annexation of Czechoslovakia. The JIC's work had already contributed to the JPC's 'Appreciation of the Situation in the Event of War Against Germany in 1939', a version of which had appeared in October 1938. Following a debate within the British Cabinet it was felt necessary to revise the paper, but its redrafting became influenced by the events in Czechoslovakia.[93] In examining the implications of the Nazi actions of March 1938, the JIC was asked by the JPC, acting on instructions passed down by the Prime Minister through the COS, to consider two 'hypothetical alternatives':

1)   that this country should concert with France, Czechoslovakia, Yugoslavia, Roumania, Hungary, Turkey, Greece, or any one of them, an undertaking to resist by force any attempt by Germany to impose a forcible solution of the Czechoslovak problem;

2) that this country should give an assurance to the French Government, that, in the event of the French Government being compelled to fulfil their obligations to Czechoslovakia, consequent upon an act of aggression by Germany, the United Kingdom would at once lend its support to the French Government.[94]

The JIC concluded that its earlier 1936 assessment was still substantially correct, though it also realised that events in Czechoslovakia, coupled with the annexation of Austria, had changed the industrial strength of those countries and therefore the consequent assessment of industrial, and by extension armament, pro-grammes would alter.[95] A revised intelligence appreciation was passed to the JPC, who in turn modified the document for the COS, which was approved by the CID in mid-April.

The JPC produced a further revised version of the document in July 1938, once more assessing the 'Situation in the Event of War Against Germany', though using the timeline of April 1939. Its conclusion, based in part on JIC assessments, was, in essence, that war with Germany would only occur if Germany militarily intervened in Czechoslovakia and, as a result, France became embroiled. If both these situations occurred, then 'we would be bound to come to her [France's] defence'.[96] The COS in July, though approving the report's contents, decided not to forward it to the CID because a study based on 'hypothetical political premises ... must inevitably suffer from a certain lack of reality.'[97] Despite this reservation, the COS Committee still agreed with the report's general conclusions. In discussion some illuminating views emerged as to Germany's intentions: Sir Maurice Hankey, the Secretary to the COS Committee and CID, considered that war would be a gamble for Germany as it could not know whether Britain and France would be prepared to go to war over Czechoslovakia; whereas Lord Chatfield, the First Sea Lord, thought that Germany would not dare risk it at this stage. What is clear is that all participants agreed and approved of the 'inter-dependence of political and military planning'.[98]

The international climate had altered drastically between mid and late 1938. At the start of 1938 Hitler had annexed Austria and made similar moves in Czechoslovakia. In the spirit of appeasement, in April 1938 the British signed an agreement with Italy, recognising its position in Abyssinia and ensuring that Italian troops would withdraw from Spain at the conclusion of the civil war. September saw a series of discussions between Prime Minister Neville Chamberlain and Hitler, culminating in the Munich Agreement and Chamberlain's declaration of 'peace for our time'. In these talks Chamberlain, amongst other things, acceded to the transfer of the Czechoslovakian Sudetenland to Germany. The Czechoslovak government was subsequently notified that it could either confront Nazi Germany alone or surrender: unsurprisingly it chose to capitulate. Chamberlain has been criticised for his naive view of the Germans. Throughout his dealings with the various dictators of the 1930s he was generally mistrustful of FO advice, which he claimed had 'no imagination'.[99]

As Chamberlain was meeting Hitler in September 1938 the COS Committee was urgently seeking assessments of what might happen if war broke out between Germany and the UK over Czechoslovakia.[100] Whilst there is no recorded response in respect of Munich in the JIC records, the JPC considered its previous assessments to be invalid and, therefore, instructed the JIC to work with the FO in preparing a new political assessment.[101] This was the first serious task undertaken by the JIC and FO jointly. The original assumption, outlined in the July 1938 JPC report, was that war would only occur if Germany attacked Czechoslovakia and the French intervened. Now the November report indicated that war might originate in any one of three ways:

1)   a German attack on the UK or France;
2)   an Italian attack on France;
3)   a German attack on one of her Eastern or South Eastern neighbours.

Of the three, it was felt that the final option was the 'least likely' to involve the UK; though as we now know this is precisely what happened approximately ten months later. Furthermore, it was confidently assumed that Germany would not dare risk a war without a guarantee of Italian support.[102] The assessment was passed to the JPC and circulated.[103]

It is never clear from the documents how such assumptions were reached, or what information they were based upon. The problem with all of the reports produced in this period, though never explicitly recognised as such at the time, is that no attempt was made to address the likelihood of such events happening. For example, would Hitler decide to use force to assume control in Czechoslovakia and, if so, what circumstances might prompt such a move or what measures might prevent it? The JIC never addressed these questions, presumably, because it was never asked to do so. To accuse the Committee of both short sightedness and an unwillingness to step beyond its remit would, therefore, be to misunderstand its role. It was designed to address questions posed by the planners and, on occasions when it did move beyond this, such as addressing MI5's request to examine Nazi espionage in the UK, it was challenged. To establish whose responsibility it was to monitor German intentions and warn of the possibility of war, if not the JIC, it is necessary to compare the assessments being produced by the JIC and by the individual intelligence agencies. The only one of relevance was SIS, for not only was it supplying military information to the Services, but was commenting actively on political developments.

An SIS memorandum to the FO in September 1938 entitled 'What Should We Do?' clearly sets out its thinking. In describing German aims, SIS concluded that Hitler sought 'supremacy' in Europe and a deal with Britain to allow him to achieve this. But absent from the paper is any indication that Hitler would either choose to invade Britain or provoke it into declaring war. Germany's primary method was stated as being the use of 'force', with the ultimate notion that 'strength begets allies'. The document then outlined what should be done, asserting that granting the Sudetenland land to Germany was a necessary move, not least because it would 'forestall the inevitable'. Amongst other recommendations were a covert move to disrupt German-Italian relations by signing an agreement with Rome; to build up British armaments; to ally Britain with France (though it was recognised that 'we cannot really trust any foreign country'); and finally, to increase friendly relations with a host of other countries, including Japan, Spain, Turkey and the USA. A final postscript on Russia added candidly: 'we can never bank on this country, but, to keep on the right side of this devil, we must sup with him to some extent, adapting the length of our spoon to circumstances at any given moment.'[104] The SIS assessment made no attempt to gauge the likelihood of war, nor what might trigger it, though it is clear that as 1939 wore on, an increasing number of SIS papers focussed on this.[105]

The FO had prime responsibility for monitoring German intentions. Much has been written on the actions of the British Ambassador in Germany, Sir Nevile Henderson, and his relationship with the Prime Minister, Neville Chamberlain, and Foreign Secretary, Lord Halifax.[106] One justification for signing the Munich Agreement, thereby deferring war, was based on the fact that Britain's own re-armament position was less advanced than Germany's.[107] Certainly this is something that Sir Alexander Cadogan, the PUS at the FO, recognised at the time.[108] In early 1939 a number of reports arrived at the FO suggesting that German and Italian attacks were imminent.[109] In disagreeing about what the reports meant, Cadogan and Henderson revealed their views on the secret intelligence flowing in. While Henderson was disparaging about SIS information, Cadogan was far more supportive, arguing that it was up to the FO to incorporate secret intelligence into normal diplomatic reporting and to decide upon its meaning.[110]

Despite his enthusiasm Cadogan did express 'some misgivings' about SIS reports in general, though he congratulated it on having predicted the 'September crisis'.[111] Something of the FO sentiments towards SIS can be inferred from Gladwyn Jebb, a diplomat who had been in Munich in September 1938 with Chamberlain, but as Cadogan's Private Secretary had been the 'link-man' between the FO and SIS.[112] Jebb informed a colleague that although Cadogan might have 'the impression that the reports of the SIS which are circulated in the office are obtained by "hired assassins" who are sent out from this country to spy out the land', this was 'not at all how the system works in practice'.[113]

By 1939 FO assessments were being incorporated into both Service estimates and JIC forecasts, though never, it would seem, in a wholly comprehensive fashion.[114] Some of the material may have come from secret sources or attaché reporting, but most came from diplomatic reporting, especially from the Embassy in Berlin.[115] There are, however, no JIC papers in 1939 specifically on the threat of war with Germany; indeed, it is not until the weeks immediately prior to the outbreak of war that it addressed the subject explicitly in discussing how the Committee would meet in the event of war. Perhaps crucially, despite 'great physical difficulties' in doing so, the JIC felt that it ought to continue meeting during war, primarily as it was felt necessary to maintain liaison between the various components of British intelligence.[116]

Were any branches of the intelligence community suggesting that war could be likely or possible? An SIS assessment from late 1938, based on '"inside" information in the proper sense of the word', referred to Hitler's 'incalculability', and listed amongst his characteristics 'ruthlessnsess, cunning' and 'fits of bitter and self-righteousness resentment, and what can only be termed a streak of madness'. Combined with these was 'an extraordinary clarity of vision'.[117] By March 1939 SIS could report that it had 'no serious indications of preparations being made'.[118] By July SIS, correctly, was confident that if war came it was likely to start with an offensive in Poland; at the same time it was concluded, also correctly, that there was evidence that many within Germany wanted a 'rapprochement' with Russia.[119]

Whilst such intelligence was not making its way directly to the JIC, other committees, in addition to the military JPC, were toiling away, preparing for the final act that might propel Britain into war. At the start of March a new 'Strategic Appreciation Sub-Committee' (SAC) was created. Operating under the CID, the SAC was chaired by the Minister for Co-Ordination of Defence, included both the military and parliamentary heads for the Services, and was supported by the pairing of Hastings Ismay and Leslie Hollis (together with Lieutenant Colonel Ian Jacob) as secretaries. The SAC was designed to assess incoming reports – the first was a COS Committee 'European Appreciation' – and to decide what should be done. By virtue of the fact that JIC reports were incorporated into JPC reports, which in turn were subsumed into COS reports, JIC work was being read at the highest levels, though the consumers probably did not know the source. The SAC was very short-lived, winding up after only six meetings, but it is a good example of how JIC assessments were being brought within the planning process, though by this time it could be argued that it was too little too late.[120]

The government continued to receive reports in the second half of 1939 on foreign preparations for war. Desmond Morton's IIC, for instance, was unrelenting in issuing economic forecasts of the threat posed by Germany's position.[121] Similarly, the FO was quick to assemble reports from its embassies on German preparations, including the movement of ships, transportation efforts on railway lines, and rumours about the construction of field hospitals.[122] By 20 August 1939 it was reported to the COS meeting that Nevile Henderson, the Ambassador in Berlin, had opined that 'the situation had deteriorated considerably'. Yet Henderson still felt that war could be averted with a 'personal letter' from Chamberlain to Hitler. It fell to the COS to consider what might happen if Hitler interpreted such a move as 'provocation'. By this time a variety of defensive measures had been put in place. For the JIC it was a question of when war came, not if.[123]

As the COS Committee was deliberating the extent of Britain's military preparations, the Germans were signing a Non-Aggression Pact with the Soviet Union. This event, in August 1939, was of great significance, for British military planners had constantly sought to ascertain what Stalin's position would be in the event of war. With the signing of the pact, this had become obvious. In Donald

Cameron Watt's words, the pact 'represents one of the biggest disasters ever to overtake British foreign policy'. Despite a number of warnings having been received by the FO, including SIS suggestions that such a move was possible and Military Intelligence producing a memorandum on the topic, the event itself was largely unforeseen within the policymaking circles of government.[124] It would appear that none of the intelligence ever reached the JIC.

Also of concern were events in the Far East. Since its creation the JIC had taken an interest in the region, unsurprising given the extent of Britain's colonial responsibilities. The major imponderable was Japan, especially its territorial aspirations.[125] The JIC first considered the matter at its second meeting in September 1936. Given the later fall of Singapore it is noteworthy to record its conclusions: 'it is possible that no knowledge of the preliminary preparations will reach us and that the Japanese will embark their troops and sail the convoy before any declaration of war or before information of their intentions could be received.'[126] The subject was never explicitly addressed again by the JIC prior to September 1939, though there were regular, weekly updates produced under the auspices of the SRC.

Throughout the summer of 1939 the SRC had disseminated a weekly series of reports, detailing German and Italian plans for war. By mid August, having now combined with the JIC and issuing reports under the JIC's name, it concluded that 'it is evident that Germany is taking all possible measures short of open mobilisation to bring her preparedness for war to the highest pitch.'[127] In the last few days of August 1939 Germany launched a series of covert measures designed, ostensibly, to show to the world that Poland was initiating hostilities towards her. A week earlier the SRC had reported that the 'atmosphere' was 'highly charged'. For the SRC the 'issue of peace or war will depend solely on Herr Hitler's decision on the question whether a war with Poland can in fact be localised or if not whether it can be successfully fought on two fronts'.[128]

On 30 August 1939, in the next of its weekly summaries, the SRC noted how 'the stage was being set for direct action against Poland'.[129] Two days later, on 1 September, Nazi intentions were revealed both in a speech by Hitler and by the German invasion of Poland. As the SRC had predicted, Hitler judged that given his earlier policy of appeasement, Chamberlain would merely prevaricate once more and allow him to continue; instead, the British Prime Minister demanded the immediate withdrawal of German troops. At 1100 on 3 September 1939, Britain declared war on Germany. One Cabinet minister later reminisced about how Chamberlain had 'said quietly: "Right Gentlemen, this means war". Hardly had he said it, when there was a most enormous clap of thunder and the whole Cabinet Room was lit up by a blinding flash of lightning. It was the most deafening thunderclap I've ever heard in my life.'[130] The SRC's immediate reaction was a perceptive one, yet in foretelling what lay ahead it underestimated the struggle that would await the country:

> The outbreak of war between Germany and the Allied powers signified the breakdown of Hitler's policy, so successful hitherto, of using the mere threat

of German strength to attain his ends. There is reason to believe that up to the last moment he still hoped that Great Britain and France would yield. The vast majority of Germans fully believed that Hitler would again bring off one of his bloodless victories and their surprise and disappointment is clearly one of the elements contributing towards the low morale and discontent which are reliably reported to be rife in Germany. The importance of this feeling can easily be exaggerated and although there may not be much enthusiasm for the fight against Great Britain and France the war against Poland is popular.[131]

The JIC may be held responsible for its inability to predict Hitler's true intentions, but this would be unfair for it was never created to fulfil such a role; its task was to ensure that intelligence arrangements were in place in case of war. The watch-dog for Hitler's aggressive plans should have been both the FO and SIS, and whilst both provided a number of reports on German actions, neither of them predicted the likely outcome with any certainty. A part explanation lies in SIS's assessment of Hitler's 'incalculable' personality. Although the Security Service did have information obtained through their agents in the UK, what is clear is that no-one on the JIC was sufficiently immersed in the German psyche to appreciate the evolving events of the late 1930s from the perspective of Berlin.

In assessing the JIC's performance it is worth remembering the conditions within which it worked. Its remit was to ensure that governmental policy was based on co-ordinated intelligence; to produce forecasts for incorporation into JPC assessments; and finally, to consider any necessary measures to improve the intelligence machinery. On these the JIC's performance was mixed. It is hard to conclude that its creation did much to alter the basis for governmental action in a wider sense, though it is fair to say that JPC products were based on information derived from the JIC. There are even examples of the JPC delaying production of its own work until it had received the JIC's input.[132]

On the intelligence machinery as a whole, certainly by the outbreak of war it was becoming widely accepted that assessments would not be complete without a mix of military and political reporting, and this was recognised in the FO's input to various Service forecasts, although political reporting regularly took second place to military matters. Regardless of whether the JIC was responsible for the FO's increased involvement or whether it was a reflection of a growing interdepartmental movement, certainly the JIC was instrumental in fostering further measures, especially foreign liaison and development.

It is less clear what the impact of JIC assessments may have been. Many of the JPC reports were not based on assessments that would be disseminated as full JIC papers, and of those issued under JIC auspices, it is not apparent how widespread they were circulated, whether they were read or what the reaction might have been. Despite meeting relatively infrequently – sessions were usually a month apart until late 1939 – the JIC did produce a large corpus of material. This is especially impressive in the pre-war period when there was no intelligence staff to draft reports, and the practice was for individual departments to create documents and then circulate them amongst the committee members.

Assessments of the Spanish civil war reveal that the JIC did become embroiled in inter-service debates, allowing some of the tension to be dissipated, though it unquestionably continued to simmer under the surface. The JIC's work on Germany prior to war was useful, particularly on the re-armament debate, and military planning might well have been less effective without the reports, though even the planners were too slow in realising the German threat. The Committee became an integral part of Britain's war machine, but it was certainly far from being in either the driving seat or central to planning. It was, however, becoming increasingly respected in various parts of the government and of value to the military planning machinery as a whole and was, as a result, in an ideal position to exert its influence as war intensified and the conflict became ever more global in nature. Perhaps this is the real test of the pre-war JIC: it thrived amidst the creation and dissolution of numerous other committees and when war arrived, it had become a truly inter-departmental intelligence organisation.

Notes

1 For more on these see chapter 1.
2 A Beevor, *The Battle for Spain: The Spanish Civil War 1936–1939* (London: Weidenfeld & Nicolson, 2006).
3 For instance see G D Macklin, 'Major Hugh Pollard, MI6, and the Spanish Civil War', *The Historical Journal* 49:1 (2006), pp.277–80. On the questions over Britain's involvement see G Stone, 'Britain, Non-Intervention and the Spanish Civil War', *European Studies Review* 9 (1979), pp.129–149.
4 Cited in M.P.A.Hankey to R.H.Haining [War Office], 8 March 1937. WO 106/1577.
5 JIC 32, 'Spain: Intelligence Regarding Air Warfare', 22 April 1937. CAB 56/2.
6 JIC 8th Meeting, 26 April 1937. CAB 56/1.
7 JIC 34, 'Spain: Intelligence Regarding Air Warfare', 7 May 1937. CAB 56/2.
8 JIC 9th Meeting, 26 May 1937. CAB 56/1. For an overview see B Armstrong, 'Through a Glass Darkly; The Royal Air Force and the Lessons of the Spanish Civil War, 1936–1939', *Air Power Review* 12:1 (Spring 2009), pp.32–55.
9 JIC 9th Meeting, 26 May 1937. CAB 56/1.
10 JIC 32, 'Spain: Intelligence Regarding Air Warfare', 22 April 1937. CAB 56/2.
11 Minute by G.S.Clark [MI3b, Directorate of Military Intelligence, War Office], 9 March 1937. WO 106/1577.
12 JIC 10th Meeting, 28 September 1937. CAB 56/1.
13 JIC 40, 'Report No.1: Anti-Aircraft (Artillery) Defence', 6 October 1937. CAB 56/3.
14 JIC 45, 'Spain: Intelligence Regarding Air Warfare', 22 October 1937. CAB 56/3. For the COS discussions see CAB 53/33.
15 For example see N Cerda, 'The Road to Dunkirk: British Intelligence and the Spanish Civil War', *War in History* 13 (2006), pp.42–64.
16 Chiefs of Staff 219th Meeting, 19 October 1937. CAB 53/8.
17 For more details see G Kennedy, 'The Royal Navy, Intelligence and the Spanish Civil War: Lessons in Air Power, 1936–39', *Intelligence and National Security* 20:2 (June 2005), pp.239–40.
18 This problem was not just confined to Spain, see A Best, 'Constructing an Image: British Intelligence and Whitehall's Perception of Japan, 1931–1939', *Intelligence and National Security* 11:2 (July 1996), pp.403–23.

19 See Kennedy, 'Lessons in Air Power', pp.249–50.

20 JIC 13th Meeting, 9 February 1938. CAB 56/1.

21 JIC 48, 'Report No.3 Air Attack on Ships', 17 February 1938. CAB 56/3. For further details see Kennedy, 'Lessons in Air Power', pp.253–5.

22 See, for instance, 'Deputy Director Plans to Deputy Chief of the Air Staff', 1 December 1937. AIR 2/2190.

23 'C.Newell [Chief of the Air Staff] to Viscount Gort [Chief of the Imperial General Staff]', 8 February 1938. AIR 2/2190. It is not entirely clear whether such advice was reciprocated at lower levels within the Services, though there are other examples of calls for collaboration and discussion within this file.

24 The COS recorded in its minutes that the secretary should 'convey [to the JIC] an expression of the Meeting's appreciation of their work'. COS 219th Meeting, 19 October 1937. CAB 53/8.

25 JIC 21st Meeting, 11 January 1939. CAB 56/1.

26 Cerda, 'The Road to Dunkirk', p.50. Similar observations are made by Frederick Winterbotham, a Royal Air Force officer seconded to SIS at this time. F W Winterbotham, *The Nazi Connection* (New York: Dell, 1978). p.149.

27 W Murray, 'The Luftwaffe before the Second World War: A Mission, A Strategy?', *The Journal of Strategic Studies* 4:3 (September 1981), pp.261–70.

28 JIC 62, 'Proposal to Set Up a Sub-Committee on Air Warfare', 9 May 1938. CAB 56/3.

29 For example, JIC 89, 'Spain and China: Intelligence Regarding Air Warfare: Report No. 1. Air Attack on Sea Communications', 10 June 1939. CAB 56/4.

30 See CAB 56/6. Also, JIC 93, 'Dissolution of Sub-Committee on Air Warfare', 13 March 1939. CAB 56/4.

31 DCOS 40th Meeting, 10 July 1939. CAB 54/2.

32 JIC 18th Meeting, 8 July 1938. CAB 56/1.

33 For an example see the handwritten comments on the jacket of HO 144/20884.

34 This was the rationale used to persuade Brigadier Evans to chair the JIC. 'Hollis to Evans', 11 January 1938. CAB 21/2651.

35 'Note by L.C.Hollis', 14 October 1937. CAB 21/2465.

36 JIC 114 'Reconstitution of the Sub-Committee', 4 July 1939. CAB 163/6.

37 JIC 82, 'The Responsibility for Collecting and Collating Foreign Air Defence Intelligence', 10 January 1939. CAB 56/4. On SIS' role in such matters, see below. In fact a similar question had been raised as far back as February 1937, but no decision seems to have been taken. JIC 6th Meeting, 9 February 1937. CAB 56/2.

38 JIC 84, 'The Responsibility for Collecting and Collating Foreign Air Defence Intelligence', 10 January 1939. CAB 56/4. See also JIC 21st Meeting, 11 January 1939. CAB 56/1.

39 The war game, including detailed background narrative, is in JIC 86, 'Exercise to Test the War Rooms', 27 January 1939. CAB 56/4.

40 JIC 37, 'Inter-Services Intelligence Bureau, Malta', 15 September 1937. CAB 56/3.

41 JIC 10th Meeting, 28 September 1937. CAB 56/1.

42 These quotes are cited in W K Wark, 'British Intelligence and Small Wars in the 1930s', *Intelligence and National Security* 2:4 (1987), p.69. The original material is in COS 150th Meeting, 13 September 1935. CAB 53/4. See Wark's article for the general lessons of Abyssinia for the British military.

43 JIC 77, 'A Combined Intelligence Bureau for the Middle East', 26 October 1938. CAB 56/4.

44 JIC 79, 'A Combined Intelligence Bureau for the Middle East', 14 November 1938. CAB 56/4.

45 JIC 20th Meeting, 16 November 1938. CAB 56/1.

46 JIC 83, 'Attitude of the "Arab World" to Great Britain, with Particular Reference to the Palestine Conference', 20 February 1939. CAB 56/4.

47 1548-B, 'Establishment of a Combined Intelligence Centre in the Middle East', 20 April 1939. CAB 4/29.

48 1556-B, 'Establishment of a Combined Intelligence Centre in the Middle East', 27 June 1939. CAB 4/30.

49 JIC 28th Meeting, 13 June 1939. CAB 56/1. See also DCOS 106(JIC), 'Establishment of a Combined Intelligence Centre in the Middle East', 21 June 1939. CAB 54/7.

50 JIC 28th Meeting, 13 June 1939. CAB 56/1. Coincidentally this was also the first meeting attended by both MI5 and SIS, the latter in the person of Stewart Menzies, the future chief but at that time War Office liaison officer.

51 For example see the minute, dated 16 May 1939, in J1993/126/66. FO 371/23391. There are numerous other examples in the same file.

52 For instance, see M Thomas, *Britain, France and Appeasement: Anglo-French Relations in the Popular Front Era* (New York: Berg, 1996); also P Jackson & J Maiolo, 'Strategic Intelligence, Counterintelligence and Alliance Diplomacy in Anglo-French Relations before the Second World War', *Militärgeschichtliche Zeitschrift*, 65, 2, (2006), pp. 417–461.

53 R A Doughty, 'The Illusion of Security: France, 1919–1940', In W Murray et al (eds) *The Making of Strategy: Rulers, States and War* (Cambridge: Cambridge University Press, 1994). p.487.

54 For further details see successive meetings of the Joint Planning Committee from March 1939 onwards. CAB 55/3.

55 For more see Jeffery, *MI6*. pp.289–94.

56 SAC 6th Meeting, 17 April 1939. AIR 9/113. On the JIC see JIC 96, 'Exchange of Intelligence Between French and British Staffs', 18 April 1939. CAB 56/4.

57 JIC 25th Meeting, 20 April 1939. CAB 56/1.

58 AFC(J)35, 'Anglo-French Staff Conversations, 1939', 21 April 1939. CAB 56/4.

59 JP 258th Meeting, 21 June 1939. CAB 55/3. Further details of the discussions are in JIC 111, 'Franco-British Staff Meetings at Rabat, May 1939', 23 June 1939. CAB 56/4.

60 JIC 112, 'Franco-British Conference at Jerusalem on 2nd June 1939', 23 June 1939. CAB 56/4; JIC 113, 'Franco-British Conference at Aden from 30th May to 2nd June 1939', 23 June 1939. CAB 56/4.

61 COS 967(JIC), 'Military Missions in Eastern and South Eastern European Theatres of War', August 1939. CAB 53/54.

62 B Millman, *The Ill-Made Alliance: Anglo-Turkish Relations, 1934–40* (Montreal: McGill-Queens University Press, 1999).

63 DCOS 105(JIC), 'Staff Conversations with Turkey', 20 June 1939. CAB 54/6.

64 Despite its age the best is still W K Wark, *The Ultimate Enemy: British Intelligence and Nazi Germany, 1933–1939* (Oxford: Oxford University Press, 1986).

65 W S Churchill, *The Second World War, Volume I: The Gathering Storm* (London: Cassell, 1948).

66 These included: France, Belgium, USSR, Italy, Czechoslovakia, Germany and Japan.

67 JIC 2, 'Notes on the Armament Supply to Certain Countries in the Event of War in 1936/7', July 1936. CAB 56/2.

68 JIC 5, 'Note by the Secretary, Joint Planning Committee', 13 July 1936. CAB 56/2.

69 JP 107th Meeting, 9 July 1936. CAB 55/2.

70 JP 180, 'The Principles Governing and Factors Affecting the Size and Composition of Forces which can be Mobilised and Maintained in the Field by Certain Foreign Countries in Time of War', November 1936. CAB 55/8.

71 JP 155, 'Appreciation of the Situation in the Event of a War against Germany in 1939', 26 October 1936. CAB 55/8. The original decision can be found in COS 354, 2 November 1934. CAB 53/24.

72 JP 155, 'Appreciation of the Situation in the Event of a War against Germany in 1939', 26 October 1936. CAB 55/8. The original decision can be found in COS 354, 2 November 1934. CAB 53/24.

73 The various documents are grouped together in JIC 19, 'The Estimated Preparedness for War of Great Britain and Certain Other Powers on 1st May 1937', 5 December 1936. CAB 56/2. The document was passed to the Committee of Imperial Defence and approved in February 1937. 1311-B, 'Preparedness for War of Great Britain in Relation to Certain Other Powers by May 1937', 25 February 1937. CAB 4/26.

74 C/39. 'Memorandum on Secret Service Funds', 'C', 9 October 1935. CAB 127/371.

75 C/7244, Sinclair to E.Crowe [Department of Overseas Trade], 17 May 1932. CAB 127/371.

76 'Germany: The Crisis and Aftermath: Tendencies and Reactions', 14 November 1938. CAB 104/43.

77 FP(36)74, 'Possible German Intentions', 19 January 1939. CAB 27/627. The Foreign Secretary gave a summary of this report to Cabinet shortly afterwards. See Hinsley, *British Intelligence: Vol.1*. p.83; also, Jeffery, *MI6*. p.300.

78 JIC 20, 'Man Power in Certain Foreign Countries', 11 February 1937. CAB 56/2.

79 JIC 22, 'Man Power in Certain Foreign Countries: Note by the Deputy Director of Military Intelligence, War Office', 24 December 1936. CAB 56/2.

80 JIC 26, 'Foreign Armaments', 16 February 1937. CAB 56/2.

81 JIC 6th Meeting, 9 February 1937. CAB 56/1.

82 R Miller, 'Britain and the Rhineland Crisis, 7 March 1936: Retreat from Responsibility or Accepting the Inevitable?', *Australian Journal of Politics and History*, 33: 1 (1987), pp.60–77.

83 COS 549, 'Planning for War with Germany', January 1937. CAB 53/30.

84 JIC 35, 'Planning for War with Germany', 19 May 1937. CAB 56/2.

85 JIC 9th Meeting, 26 May 1937. CAB 56/1.

86 JIC 2nd Meeting, 29 September 1936. CAB 56/1. Unfortunately the original MI5 document has not been preserved in this series. For more detail see Andrew, *Defence of the Realm*. pp.186–216.

87 JIC 23, 'Nazi and Fascist Party Organisations and Activities in British Territory', 5 May 1937. CAB 56/2.

88 COS 606(JIC), 29 July 1937. CAB 53/32.

89 JIC 36, 'German Activities in the Irish Free State', 21 June 1937. CAB 56/3.

90 R.H.Haining to H.L.Ismay, 7 June 1937. CAB 21/2651.

91 H.L.Ismay to R.H.Haining, 10 June 1937. CAB 21/2651.

92 Murray, 'Appeasement and Intelligence', p.54. On the French see P Jackson, 'French Military Intelligence and Czechoslovakia, 1938', *Diplomacy and Statecraft* 5:1 (March 1994), pp.81–106.

93 COS 678(JP), 'Appreciation of the Situation in the Event of War Against Germany', 3 February 1938. CAB 53/36. Also, JP 188th Meeting, 18 January 1938. CAB 55/2.

94 JIC 58, 'Situation in the Event of War Against Germany', 16 March 1938. CAB 56/3.

95 JIC 14th Meeting, 16 March 1938. CAB 56/1.

96 COS 747(JP), 'Appreciation of the Situation in the Event of War Against Germany in April 1939', 15 July 1938. CAB 53/40.

97 COS 754, 'Planning For War With Germany', 2 September 1938. CAB 53/40.

98 COS 245th Meeting, 25 July 1938. CAB 53/9.

99 Cited in E Goldstein, 'Neville Chamberlain, The British Official Mind and the Munich Crisis', In I Lukes & E Goldstein (eds), *The Munich Crisis, 1938: Prelude to World War II* (London: Frank Cass, 1999). p.284.

100 COS 769, 'The Czechoslovak Crisis', 23 September 1938. CAB 53/41. The reaction in the Joint Planning Committee is in CAB 55/13.

101 JP 319, 'Revision of Appreciations', 25 October 1938. CAB 55/13.

102 JIC 78, 'Appreciation for a European War: Political Setting', 16 November 1938. CAB 56/4.

103 JP 334, 'Appreciation for a European War: Political Setting', November 1938. CAB 55/14.
104 C14471/42/18. 'What Should We Do?', 18 September 1938. FO 371/21659.
105 Jeffery, *MI6*. pp.303–12.
106 For a good overview see P Neville, 'Rival Foreign Office Perceptions of Germany, 1936–9', *Diplomacy and Statecraft* 13:3 (September 2002), pp.137–52. Also, B J C McKercher, 'The Foreign Office, 1930–39: Strategy, Permanent Interests and National Security', *Contemporary British History* 18:3 (Autumn 2004), pp.87–109.
107 K Neilson, 'The Defence Requirements Sub-Committee, British Strategic Foreign Policy, Neville Chamberlain and the Path to Appeasement', *English Historical Review* 477 (June 2003), pp.651–84.
108 C14471/42/18. Note by A.Cadogan, 8 November 1938. FO 371/21659.
109 Some examples of these can be found in FO 1093/86.
110 A.Cadogan to N.Henderson, 26 February 1939. FO 800/294.
111 Handwritten comments on the bottom of G.Jebb to G.M. 31 March 1939. FO 1093/86.
112 Jeffery, *MI6*. p.303.
113 G.Jebb to G.M. 31 March 1939. FO 1093/86.
114 C10651/9878/18. Covering minute, 12 July 1939. FO 371/23091.
115 C10651/9878/18. Covering minute, 27 July 1939. FO 371/23091.
116 JIC 33rd Meeting, 24 August 1939. CAB 56/1.
117 'Germany: Factors, Aims, Methods, Etc', 20 December 1938. FO 1093/86.
118 SIS memorandum, 9 March 1939. FO 1093/86.
119 Minute covering comments by 'C', 27 July 1939. FO 1093/88.
120 The minutes and memoranda are in CAB 16/209.
121 See CAB 21/2553.
122 For example, see file 11764 in FO 371/23091.
123 COS 960, 'Minutes of an Informal Meeting', 20 August 1939. CAB 53/53.
124 D C Watt, 'An Intelligence Surprise: The Failure of the Foreign Office to Anticipate the Nazi-Soviet Pact', *Intelligence and National Security* 4:3 (1989), p.512. See also correspondence in N4146/243/38. FO 371/23686.
125 A Best. *British Intelligence and the Japanese Challenge in Asia, 1914–1941* (London: Palgrave, 2002).
126 JIC 2nd Meeting, 29 September 1936. CAB 56/1. Also, WO 106/5399.
127 SWR 13, Weekly Commentary, Week Ending 17th August 1939. FO 1093/125.
128 SWR 14, Weekly Commentary, Week Ending 23rd August 1939. FO 1093/125.
129 SWR 15, Weekly Commentary, Week Ending 30th August 1939. FO 1093/125.
130 Cited in M Gilbert, *Winston S. Churchill, Vol. V, Companion Part 3, Documents: The Coming of War, 1936–1939* (London: Heinemann, 1982). pp.1608–9.
131 SWR 16, Weekly Commentary, Week Ending 6th September 1939. FO 1093/125.
132 For instance, they stalled answering a COS request for information in preparation for the 1937 Imperial Defence Conference. JP 124th Meeting, 13 November 1936. CAB 55/2.

Part Two
War, 1939–1945

3   The Onset of War: 1939–1940

By September 1939 the Joint Intelligence Committee had become a relatively well established entity within Whitehall, yet its true value would not be tested until the war was well underway. With the outbreak of hostilities, though the JIC remained subordinate to the COS Committee, it was reconstituted as a Sub-Committee of the War Cabinet, the latter having replaced the Committee of Imperial Defence (CID). In this way the most important development was simply that the JIC survived; this would remain so until its potential would be realised: 'on the eve of the war Whitehall had thus at last acquired a vision of the intelligence community as a whole which was to be of enormous importance for the conduct of the war. But neither the SRC [Situation Report Centre] nor the reorganised JIC which absorbed it achieved any overnight pre-war miracles.'[1]

Sir Harry Hinsley's Official History of intelligence in the war provides a vast amount of detail on how British intelligence, in particular signals intelligence, was organised, what role it played and how effective it was. In the context of the JIC, however, the volumes do not provide an answer to an important question of this period: how and why did the JIC's position improve from its weak standing in 1939, to its central role in 1945? Many of the developments that were to gradually improve its status arose during the initial stages of the war. This can, in part, be attributed to the improving performance of the JIC; but also to the increasingly desperate need to have good, co-ordinated intelligence. Whatever the reason, the JIC, operating at the centre of government, was to assume greater importance.

The outbreak of war

The galvanising effect of the war in unifying against a common enemy was not felt immediately across the intelligence community. This was evident in that the Services' intelligence directors were never all present at the same meeting of the JIC until 1940, instead usually sending deputies in their place. At a strategic level the whole corpus of British intelligence, including the Services' intelligence directorates, was slow to respond. Aside from the JIC structure, other bodies existed which were tasked with information collection and with intelligence analysis. The objective to incorporate everything into a single, joint and centrally directed structure, geared towards winning the war, was no easy feat.

With the FO now coming on board, the biggest stumbling block, ironically, became the COS. On the day war was declared the Chiefs had moved the JPS, the cadre of military officers who wrote the planner's papers, to an office physically next door to them so that they could 'always be at hand.' However, no similar arrangement was made for the JIC (not least because it had no staff at this time), and although the JIC and JPS were theoretically supposed to be working together, in practice this did not always happen. So, for example, until March 1940 the JIC was not shown any papers prepared by the JPS for COS meetings, and by the fall of France the JIC as a whole had only attended one COS meeting (in April 1940).[2]

At the same time though, there was a definite recognition by them that intelligence would be of central importance in directing the war. At the COS meeting on 3 September 1939 the JIC Chairman, Ralph Skrine Stevenson, promised the Chiefs that he 'undertook to do my best to keep them informed of all political developments at their daily meetings at 10 a.m.'[3] He was, however, quick to highlight the time needed for the 'collection, collation, sifting and assessment of the value of intelligence', thus underlining the difficulties involved. Ultimately, and significantly, it was agreed that very urgent matters would be put before the Chiefs, even if they had not been assessed or commented upon by the relevant intelligence department.[4]

From the outset of the Second World War, therefore, the JIC had a specific responsibility for providing assessments for the military planning aspect of the war effort. Every morning the COS, before the start of their meeting at 1000, had to be appraised of the latest developments by the JIC, including both political and military intelligence. The Daily Situation Report, which had become a JIC responsibility once it had absorbed the SRC in July 1939, also had to be issued daily, at 1730.[5] In addition, relevant FO telegrams had to be sent to the JPC twice-daily, at 0930 and 2015. If this service was not enough, Skrine Stevenson had also volunteered to attend any COS meeting to provide a personal briefing.[6] To assist an increasingly over-worked JIC, the Chiefs offered that 'some use' might be made of the Map Room organisation at the Central War Room (see the appendices for a map).[7] Whilst therefore not residing physically near to the COS, the JIC was not completely divorced from the planning machinery (contrary to the conclusion that Hinsley reached on the point); whether the JPC took notice of JIC assessments is another matter.

Producing these three sets of daily summaries was not the full extent of the JIC's work. Its members were not seconded full-time to the JIC; rather they attended meetings as and when necessary. Within their own departments they were also responsible for submitting a weekly résumé of developments, be they naval, military or air. These were to be submitted to the JPC, who would collate them and issue them to the COS directly.[8] Such papers were also to be sent to the JIC which, in turn, produced its own weekly summary of intelligence. The obvious point was not raised until late September 1939 by the Deputy Director of Military Intelligence, Colonel W. C. van Cutsem, who asked whether any checks were being made to compare and contrast the information being sent to the planners, not least to avoid duplication. The implications of this, notably the sheer quantity of material being received by the JPC and the COS, would become a serious issue a few months later.

Only fragments of the various daily and weekly summaries have been preserved. We can find clues as to their worth from the disparate views of those who received the material. One important piece of information is contained in a short note by Victor Cavendish-Bentinck, who replaced Skrine Stevenson as Chairman of the JIC in December 1939. In it, he states that SIS wanted to receive copies of the JIC daily and weekly summaries, as well as any memoranda prepared for the COS. The reply by Gladwyn Jebb, the Private Secretary to the PUS was 'all to the good'.[9] This was a significant move. SIS had rarely been involved in the early work of the JIC and was not, at this stage, a full member of the Committee, though it had continually expressed an interest in the JIC product.

Not all this work was being conducted by the main JIC. At some point, and it is by no means clear when, a delineation was made between the 'senior' and 'junior' members of the JIC.[10] The 'senior' members comprised the committee chaired by Skrine Stevenson, and included the heads of the Services' intelligence directorates. With the outbreak of war this group met as the JIC every Friday at noon at Richmond Terrace, a building on Whitehall opposite Downing Street. The 'junior' members were, in effect, the drafters. The vast majority of the pre-war JIC papers had been produced by a single Service department and, where there was discussion, it took place at the JIC itself to decide whether a paper should be issued or not. The increasingly widespread and comprehensive nature of papers meant that this had to change.

The 'junior' members were never formally convened in a committee as such; rather they were officers chosen by the individual Service departments whose task it was to write the papers on their own area of expertise. This process involved two separate tasks: the first was the production of the daily JIC summaries; the second was the writing of the assessments for consideration at the 'senior' JIC meetings. It is not clear whether the same people were involved in both jobs, but the likelihood is that they were different.[11] In practice therefore, the 'junior' members of the JIC did not comprise an official committee at all, but instead came together in an ad hoc arrangement for the sole purpose of producing papers. Consequently, results were mixed. A 1957 internal history of the JIC explains why this was so: 'major Intelligence papers . . . were written by a team of officers already overworked in their own offices, who met spasmodically as occasion arose and who had little or no experience of working in committee. Moreover, the team changed according to the subject.' The implications of this were clear: 'few papers were initiated, they took long to write, and the standard was not always high.'[12]

A key development was the appointment, in December 1939, of a new chairman. Ralph Skrine Stevenson's appointment in June of 1939 had only ever been seen as a temporary one. His dual position as Chairman of the JIC and head of the Dominions Intelligence Section of the FO was felt sufficient for a promotion to Counsellor level. It had always been intended that as soon as a 'permanent post' became vacant he would move on. Indeed, when chairing his first meeting in August, Skrine Stevenson had already been given his next posting – as Private Secretary to the Secretary of State Lord Halifax – to start in December 1939. His involvement with the JIC therefore, was only ever to be transitory from the outset.[13] Views of Skrine Stevenson's tenure are contradictory. Contemporaries described his chairing as 'excellent'[14], that he did 'extremely well'[15], and that the government 'owe . . . a great debt of gratitude'.[16] Yet at the same time it is generally accepted that the Committee's performance only improved once his successor assumed chairmanship.

Victor Cavendish-Bentinck was no stranger to the JIC; he had previously attended a number of meetings and had been working alongside it in his normal guise as a FO official. One of the problems in choosing Cavendish-Bentinck was whether he too should be appointed at the level of Counsellor. The issue was whether the Treasury would support another Counsellor on the FO payroll. After much wrangling it was agreed that Cavendish-Bentinck could be appointed at that rank.[17]

Heir to the Duke of Portland and a relative of the Duke of Devonshire, Cavendish-Bentinck had a privileged Victorian upbringing, enjoying a brief military career before joining the FO in 1918. He was posted to a number of European capitals, and was involved in some of the most important discussions of the inter-war period, including attending both the Lausanne and Locarno Conferences, and working with the League of Nations. Always dressed immaculately in striped trousers and black jacket, Cavendish-Bentinck could often be found walking across St. James' Park accompanied by his pet dog, who would sit with him in the FO each day. Unsurprisingly, it was not long before Angus, a Kerry Blue Terrier who had earlier served with his master in Chile, became known as the 'Intelligence Dog'.[18] Unfortunately Angus would become one of the war's casualties. Kennedy Walker-Sloan, one of Cavendish-Bentinck's FO colleagues who worked with him on the JIC later in the war, recalled how one day he was taking Angus for a walk when 'crossing Hyde Park Corner he [Angus] spied another dog coming up Constitution Hill, he shot out and ran straight under a taxi. I had the awful business of explaining to Bill [as Cavendish-Bentinck was known to friends] that his little poodle was no longer with us.'[19]

In the mid-1920s Cavendish-Bentinck had met Clothilde Quigley, an American heiress. They had married and she had accompanied him to his posting in Paris and then to Greece. Whilst in Athens Clothilde began to exhibit characteristics that would later embarrass Cavendish-Bentinck: she was rude and antagonistic and, partly as a result, he was sent to the Embassy in Chile, a diplomatic backwater. Here she continued in her 'extravagance' and 'tempestuousness' and Cavendish-Bentinck 'began to have doubts about her sanity'. Upon his assuming chairmanship of the JIC, she upped sticks and left for the United States, together with their two children. This would, however, not be the last Cavendish-Bentinck heard from her (see chapter 5).[20]

Cavendish-Bentinck continued Skrine Stevenson's practice of being both head of the FO's Dominions Intelligence Section and Chairman of the JIC.

On leaving office Skrine Stevenson wrote a memorandum on what the work of JIC chairman involved. He described how the workload was 'heavy' and how, as both de facto chairman and the FO representative on the Committee, his job was to act as FO liaison, including involvement in the preparation of JIC summaries and the separate FO summaries.[21] The implications of this – the sheer volume of paper produced – would become important once Winston Churchill assumed the premiership.

Assessments during the Phoney War

During the 'phoney war', the period from the German invasion of Poland in September 1939 to the fall of Norway in April 1940 when little happened in the way of open conflict in Europe, the JIC produced a huge number of papers on a wide array of topics. Once more its pre-war role as manager of the intelligence community tended to overshadow the other work being done; certainly it occupied a large amount of the Committee's time. Yet again the JIC was reluctant to consider anything unless under direct instruction, though by this time the added pressure of a heavy workload meant that even had it wanted to initiate extra assessments, it would have been extremely difficult to do so.

Structurally the JIC was similar to its pre-war incarnation. Perhaps the only significant difference was the increased workload. Meetings had become more regular and, as a result, the Committee could immerse itself in a greater number of papers. In the first four months of the war the JIC produced a total of 37 assessments and held 18 meetings; in addition it continued to produce various daily and weekly summaries. Of the topics covered the majority were of a general administrative nature, looking at, for instance, the weekly Service summaries; the Middle East Intelligence Centre; the management of Anglo-French cyphers; whether the Germans had broken international law in their conduct of the war; the despatch of secret documents by air; and the security organisation in Aden.[22]

The first proper assessment came at the instruction of the COS following a suggestion by Lord Hankey, in his new position as Minister without Portfolio, that attention should be focussed on what resources Germany could gain by invading Holland and Belgium.[23] The dense 28 page report was finished promptly in early October 1939 and approved just a week later. It concluded that there were a number of economic and industrial targets that would benefit Germany and which should be kept out of their hands at all costs. A more important study was the investigation as to what Hitler meant when he referred to a 'secret weapon' that would soon be targeted on England. Once more the assessment followed a COS request. In considering this the JIC examined a range of different weapons, including such unconventional options as chemical, bacteriological or entomological warfare. The conclusion was that the 'most probable' delivery system was the German Air Force, though they did not agree on what novel weapon an aircraft might deploy.[24] In all likelihood Hitler was referring to what would become the V-Weapons.

The final task allotted by the COS to the JIC in 1939 was to 'draw up an appreciation of possible enemy intentions in the spring of 1940'.[25] The subsequent report, completed just over a week later, was the first proper assessment by the JIC as to the war's future conduct. The lengthy study (27 pages) considered a variety of factors, including the German economy and military, its relations with Russia, Italy and Japan, and examined the different options open to Germany. Though a useful assessment, none of the report's conclusions were strong; indeed, the analysis began with the caveat that 'it is difficult at present to predict which course or combination of courses Germany is likely to adopt'.[26]

Of the conclusions offered, the JIC stated that it was against Germany's interests to attack Russia in the spring of 1940, that economically a decisive German victory was needed somewhere, and that militarily attention would be focussed on crushing allied forces. In commenting on the report Sir Alexander Cadogan, the PUS in the FO, recognised that it was 'difficult to choose between Germany's various alternatives'. The implications were that 'we can merely do our best to be prepared, as well as we can be, to counter any one (or more) of them.'[27] Of perhaps more importance were the comparative tables produced, which showed that British aircraft production was behind German levels. Though in a general sense these were all sensible conclusions, the problem remained, and it was a critical one, that nothing specific could be offered.[28] A subsequent report, equally imprecise, was produced by the Allied Military Committee in January 1940. In commenting on it (the paper was circulated to the JIC for examination), Cavendish-Bentinck observed that they 'had not produced any more definite prophesy [sic]' than the JIC.[29]

The first half of 1940 saw a vast proliferation in the nature, depth and breadth of topics covered by the JIC. This expansion can be explained by the increasingly active German war effort and, consequently, the heightened number of demands for assessments and reports. Despite the enlargement in scope, there was no corresponding increase in the number of papers requested by the COS themselves: requests, instead, were coming from a variety of government departments.

Once more the JIC became embroiled in an ever expanding number of administrative and managerial roles, both within the British intelligence community and in liaison with foreign establishments. In between these few assessments were produced. One of its first substantial assessments in 1940 was approved in mid-March. The paper updated the previous assessment on Germany's armed forces by looking at its 'productive capacity'. In doing so, it operated on an assumption that the pre-war JIC had made, namely that a country's war fighting potential was intrinsically linked to its industrial prowess and the speed by which it could re-arm.[30]

The final report was the JIC's longest to date – a total of 44 pages – with each section being prepared either by the relevant Service department or the Ministry of Economic Warfare.[31] The report itself, though rich in detail, was once more of limited value – it revealed statistics and numbers that could be used as a comparison with British capabilities, but it did not reveal anything about the future nature or direction of Germany's war effort. Despite these shortcomings, the JIC was able to provide more meaningful information in other ways. Following the signing of the Russo-Finnish Treaty in March 1940 it was tasked with evaluating the Treaty's significance for the future conduct of the war. The report, relatively succinct and precise in nature was, with the benefit of hindsight, accurate.[32]

Whether it was due to a shortage of information, a lack of interest by the COS and the planners in requesting topics, or an already over-burdened workload, the JIC's main role was not in the production of assessments, but rather in the organisation and management of the intelligence war effort. Early 1940, for instance, saw the JIC concentrate on the security of plans, the organisation of scientific intelligence, and the security of Anglo-French communications. A key discussion started in March 1940 on the creation of an 'Inter-Services Project Board'. This rather innocuous sounding body was, in fact, concerned with planning and co-ordinating sabotage and other 'irregular' operations – it helped form part of what would become the Special Operations Executive (SOE). Such work was organised under the auspices of the JIC, the first of many instances over the coming decades where the JIC would be concerned with both the assessment and planning of intelligence operations.[33]

The discussion of the Inter-Services Project Board at the COS meeting on 1 April 1940 was the first in which all members of the JIC, attending as a single body, were present. In defending the Board's creation against charges by the First Sea Lord, Admiral of the Fleet Sir Dudley Pound, 'as to whether such machinery was really necessary', Cavendish-Bentinck put forward a convincing rationale for why it needed to be inter-departmental in nature. He argued that it was important to weigh 'irregular' operations against ongoing 'regular' operations. In doing so he was ably supported by Colonel Stewart Menzies, the recently appointed SIS chief, and Major General Frederick Beaumont-Nesbitt, the former JIC Chairman and current Director of Military Intelligence (DMI).[34]

Cometh the hour . . .

The JIC's relatively calm introduction to the demands of war would change dramatically from April 1940 onwards. Whereas the Committee that met up until this point had been similar to its pre-war incarnation, the post-April 1940 JIC would be a very different beast, not only in its expanded remit, but more importantly in how it was received and perceived across Whitehall. Several factors contributed to this: the JIC taking a more forthcoming approach certainly helped, but it would be external events – the occupation of Norway and Winston's Churchill's ascent to the premiership – that would confirm this change in fortunes.

The first move came in March 1940, with Cavendish-Bentinck expressing his surprise that the JPC were producing papers for the COS and the War Cabinet which 'had not at any stage' been considered by the JIC.[35] Hinsley makes great play of the fact that the JPC and the JIC were not in contact during this early period of the war, yet other papers suggest that this was not quite so straightforward. In commenting on the situation, Beaumont-Nesbitt, the DMI, outlined the JIC/JPC relationship:

(a) Where time is not very limited, the JIC is asked to prepare a report on particular terms of reference.

(b) Where time is very limited:

  (i) Members of the JPC, before commencing planning, consult their own Service Intelligence Directorates and obtain data.

  (ii) The draft JP paper is circulated to the Intelligence Directorates for comment.[36]

In discussion the Committee members felt that it was impractical for the JIC itself to prepare the intelligence component of JPC papers given their urgent nature, but that all JPC drafts should be submitted to the JIC before they passed to the COS.[37] After further consideration it was decided that once a Service director of intelligence was made aware of the inception of a JPC paper, it was incumbent upon them to consider whether the full JIC need discuss the intelligence background material.[38] The JPC's reaction was mixed: it was happy for the Service directors of intelligence to receive the papers, but did not want Cavendish-Bentinck, as the FO representative, to be sent them.[39] No explanation was given as to why.

On 9 April 1940 an event took place that was to have profound consequences for the JIC. In the early hours of the morning the German war machine attacked Norway, overrunning the capital, Oslo, by midday. The subsequent fall of Norway, and in particular the failure of British intelligence to effectively forewarn or forestall it, had direct implications for the JIC, which was partially held accountable. Was this an accurate or fair critique?

The general consensus across the intelligence community, quite reasonably, seems to have been that any hostile move by the Germans would be directed against Belgium or Holland.[40] Despite this confidence, assessments were produced on German intentions toward Scandinavia. A paper concentrating on Sweden had been completed in February 1940. Though detailed, it addressed the wrong question. Instead of asking whether the Germans might invade Sweden, it looked at how such an attack might take place. The JIC did this because it had been given a specific request issued by the COS and so it did not question the parameters for the paper.[41] From the mainstream JIC records alone it would appear that a possible German invasion of Norway was never discussed, though British intelligence certainly had information that the Germans were interested in the region.[42] Although the JIC's Daily Summaries have not survived, there is a brief synopsis of the kind of detail they contained in a submission from Cavendish-Bentinck to Chamberlain. This revealed that it was well known that troops were being massed, and that German aircraft had been spotted building up on Germany's north-west coast. Despite these details, Cadogan concluded that 'none of this was a very exact pointer to what was actually afoot.'[43]

Following the German attack on Norway, the JIC met on 11 April to assess the situation, producing a paper that depicted the imminence of an attack on the Low Countries. Indeed, in commenting on this the Committee concluded that 'we should consider ourselves fortunate to have even this measure of warning'. The attacks in Scandinavia were, according to the JIC, part of a larger plan to bring about the downfall of the United Kingdom. An attack on Holland would be next, 'to be followed, simultaneously or shortly afterwards, by a large scale air offensive against England.'[44] This assessment, though never formally distributed as a JIC report, was eventually put before the War Cabinet in mid-April 1940.[45]

This marked the start of a new phase in the JIC's war. On 12 April the Committee was instructed to prepare a daily 'Scandinavian Intelligence Summary' for the Military Co-ordination Committee, the body created at the outbreak of war to advise the War Cabinet.[46] Meanwhile there was another important development. On 3 April Prime Minister Neville Chamberlain accepted the resignation of Lord Chatfield, the Minister for the Co-ordination of Defence. The following day Chamberlain made a statement to the effect that the post would remain vacant and that the First Lord of the Admiralty would take over responsibility for chairing the Military Co-ordination Committee. The man filling that position was Winston Churchill.[47] Churchill had been a long-term admirer of Britain's intelligence services, but the true effects of this for the JIC would not be felt until he became Prime Minister.[48]

Despite the JPC's earlier reluctance to involve the FO (in the form of Cavendish-Bentinck) in intelligence discussions, in April Cavendish-Bentinck was invited to a JPC meeting. The subject for discussion was Operation 'RUPERT', the plan for the capture of Narvik from the Germans, who had occupied it the previous day. The JIC's involvement was not so much with the planning of the operation, but with the safeguarding of communications and the plans themselves.[49]

However, moves were afoot to raise the Committee's profile. Just a week or so later a request was raised by the JPC and put to the JIC to offer its 'considered views' on how the present situation might develop, 'in order to assist the Joint Planning Sub-Committee in the preparation of certain reports'. In summary the JIC repeated its views that the invasions of Denmark and Norway were part of a bigger plan, and that the next German attack would take place further to the west, probably involving a 'knock out' blow against Britain or France. Of the two, it was felt more likely that Britain would be the next target.[50] In submitting the report to the FO, Cavendish-Bentinck commented on the great haste in which it had been written, and how a better job could have been done with more time.[51]

The instant reaction to this was a request, initiated by the Director of Intelligence at the Air Ministry, for the JIC to review the imminence and likelihood of a German attack on the UK.[52] Although the COS Committee had considered the subject in late 1939, it was felt necessary not only to review the situation, but also to submit the paper to the COS once completed. This was an important, albeit unrecognised, milestone for the JIC – the Committee was suggesting a paper that had not first been commissioned by the JPC or COS. This initiative was not the only forward-thinking move taking place.

At the same time the JIC suggested that given its workload was now so over-burdened, it was impossible to continue without additional staff.[53] One of the precursors to this plea was a decision by the COS to ask for a weekly summary of the war from the enemy's perspective. Concurrently, it was requested that the JIC reduce the number of figures in their daily intelligence summary.[54] Informally, the COS's Secretary, Lieutenant Colonel Leslie Hollis, told the JIC that the Military Co-ordination Committee did not have enough time each day to wade through a lengthy paper that included 'a mass of detailed information'.[55]

What can be made of these two moves, one an attempt to reduce the JIC's detailed output, the other a request to produce a new summary? Perhaps they should be read as an attempt to streamline the sheer volume of material being produced and distributed by the JIC; certainly several earlier discussions had taken place at COS meetings about receiving too much information, to the detriment of the speed with which they received other summaries.[56] Indeed, the FO had also attempted to curtail the JIC's weekly intelligence summary.[57] Ultimately both initiatives would become more important as the war effort gathered pace in 1940.

To assist matters the JIC decided to incorporate a forecast of German intentions into its Daily Situation Report summary for the COS.[58] Additionally, if a matter was too urgent to wait for the daily summary, for which all information had to have been received by 1500 in order to reach the COS for 1700, it was to be dispatched immediately via the relevant Service director of intelligence, provided that the other two directors approved. This meant that papers could be distributed in the JIC's name without the FO having first approved it. These were important developments for not only did they symbolise the increased fusion of military intelligence in the JIC, but they also brought the JIC further into the military planning sphere. Whilst it is difficult to assess the immediate significance of the moves, because almost none of the daily summaries have survived, Major General Hastings Ismay, who had just been appointed as Churchill's staff officer and the liaison between the War Cabinet and the COS Committee, produced an invaluable paper on the nature of the intelligence product (see below).[59]

The suddenness with which Germany had invaded and occupied Norway had left an indelible mark on several senior members of the government, including Chamberlain. Even within the intelligence community it was felt that this exemplified a classic case of intelligence failure.[60] Several informal post-mortems were held to see what had gone wrong and why. Cavendish-Bentinck informed Cadogan that although the Air Ministry had received some information through its reconnaissance flights, this had not been communicated to the JIC.[61] Menzies, now 'C', was instructed to provide a report on what knowledge SIS had had of the invasion, and he confirmed that although there had been numerous hints, there had been nothing specific.[62] Sir Samuel Hoare, the Secretary of State for Air and a former SIS officer, confirmed that SIS had passed information to both the Admiralty and War Office.[63] Lord Hankey, who had commissioned Menzies' report, exonerated SIS, given that most of the information had been given to the Admiralty.[64] Hoare went further, complimenting SIS on having presented a 'cast iron case. They [SIS] have given warnings which, in the aggregate, are as definite as you could expect to receive'.[65]

The obvious problem, identified by Hankey, was that these SIS reports were not incorporated into the JIC Daily Summaries, with the result that 'we were caught napping.'[66] Menzies' report was passed to Sir Horace Wilson, the head of the Civil Service, for distribution to Neville Chamberlain. Arthur Rucker, Chamberlain's Principal Private Secretary, reported to the Prime Minister in the simplest terms the problem: 'the position is that we were fully warned of the preparation by the Germans of an Expeditionary Force on a big scale . . . we could not, of course, foretell where that Force would be sent.'[67] The implications were clear, that in order to avoid such a surprise attack in the future, intelligence would be key. The difficulty, in the collective minds of Hankey, Wilson and Chamberlain, was not so much the collection of intelligence, but rather its assessment and assimilation. It was therefore decided that the JIC be charged with maintaining 'a running and connected story based upon such intelligence material as seems to point to the need for action.'[68]

The importance of Norway was in sounding a warning that there were lessons to be learned. As Hankey wrote: 'it is no use crying over spilt milk . . . nevertheless, it is a good thing to look back on our mistakes – and this is by no means the only one – in order to try and rectify them in the future.'[69] There were, however, three problems standing in the way, as Ismay identified in his report:

(i) To ensure that the machinery of the Joint Intelligence organisation is set in motion with the least possible delay after the receipt in the Intelligence Departments or the Foreign Office of a piece of information which may be of vital importance.

(ii) The machinery of the Joint Intelligence organisation must be speeded up so that the considered and co-ordinated views of our Intelligence Service may be produced very quickly.

(iii) Means must be found of ensuring that these views are immediately brought to the notice of those responsible for taking executive action at any hour of the day or night.[70]

Speed was therefore of the essence in getting intelligence to the right people at the right time, yet the current process was too slow and unwieldy to be effective. By this time in spring 1940, the JIC was meeting every day, primarily to discuss the regular 'Daily Situation Report', with formal meetings taking place (and being recorded) variously as required. The request for extra staff at the end of April was a reflection of the sheer effort needed to produce the steady stream of papers. Matters were not helped when, on the evening of 22 April 1940 Major Barnard, the JIC's Secretary, was killed in a motor accident.[71]

On 10 May 1940, in the wake of severe criticism from all sides of the House of Commons over his running of the war, particularly during the so-called 'Norway Debate' of 7 and 8 May, Neville Chamberlain resigned. The premiership passed to Winston Churchill as head of a new wartime coalition government.[72] Churchill shared Chamberlain's concerns about the need for intelligence to reach the planners in a faster and more efficient manner.[73] His sentiments echoed points raised by Ismay in his seminal report: (1) The JIC and individual Service intelligence directors should be given responsibility for initiating reports. (2) Measures should be taken to strengthen the JIC's secretariat in an attempt to 'oil the wheels'. With a recognition that 'the burden of work . . . is continually increasing', the appointment of two further military secretaries was approved, one with the rank of a General Staff Officer 1st Grade (GSO(1)), and another at GSO(3). (3) Finally, it was felt that the JIC should produce reports on specially coloured paper – for the eyes of the Prime Minister, War Cabinet and COS only – on anything that was sufficiently urgent that it could not wait for the normal daily summary.[74] Ismay's proposals were subsequently endorsed by the COS, with the result that the JIC was made 'responsible for taking the initiative in preparing, at any hour of the day or night, as a matter of urgency, papers on any particular development in the international situation.'[75]

As a consequence, for the first time the JIC had been given a formal role to play in defining what was felt to be a threat, rather than waiting for the military departments to identify a topic of interest. This stemmed from the belief that, as the purveyors of all matters secret, the Committee was best placed to decide.[76] In practice it meant a re-think about the numerous summaries being produced. Most importantly it reflected recognition that intelligence was central to military planning and the war effort. In discussion the JIC now approved the production of the following reports:

(i)   the daily 1030 summary for the War Cabinet
(ii) the daily 1600 Situation Report
(iii) the daily 1630 JIC Intelligence Report
(iv) the daily 0700 and 1800 War Cabinet Map Room summaries [the former being a summary of information on force dispositions; the latter a more domestic operational summary].[77]

In addition, the JIC was still producing longer, more strategic assessments. The sudden fall of Norway had resulted in a May 1940 paper focussed on the likelihood of a German invasion of the United Kingdom. The first version, a revision of the previous assessment of November 1939, contained few alterations. It concluded that provided that British control of the North Sea remained intact, there was little to fear from a potential German airborne or seaborne attack. The discussion of the paper was perhaps the most heated of all JIC papers to date. In particular, the presence of two Home Office officials served to annoy the permanent members of the Committee. In reporting back to the FO, Cavendish-Bentinck noted how 'at today's meeting we had a first-class fight with the Home Office, whose representatives were full of unjustified self confidence and supercilious arrogance. They seemed to base their attitude not on the necessity for complete security but on "political [i.e. departmental] considerations".'[78]

Suffice it to say they were overruled, and the report was approved by the COS two days later.[79]

A complicating factor in the assessment however, was the judgment of the mood of 'aliens and disaffected elements' within the UK itself, and accordingly a separate report was commissioned on Fifth Column activities. It was generally pessimistic in tone, arguing that Germany had developed effective networks elsewhere and so it should be assumed that some such system was in deployment in the UK.[80] Furthermore, Cavendish-Bentinck felt that British preparations for a German attack were not advanced enough – he based this on the testimony of Brigadier Hawes, Chief Staff Officer of the Eastern Command at a JIC meeting – and that this was a worrying situation, so much so that he confided it 'would keep a lighter sleeper than myself awake at night'.[81]

The effects of the JIC's new-found position within the military planning structures were felt immediately. No sooner had its report been accepted by the COS than word came down that the JPC, which was also interested in the question of a German invasion of the UK, was working on a similar paper, albeit from a different perspective. The JPC therefore requested the JIC to consider the matter on the basis that the Germans had managed to neutralise Britain's control of the sea and that as a consequence, an attack might take place from continental Europe.[82] In addition, following on from the discussion on Fifth Column activities, the JIC prepared a paper on the use of German airborne troops for an invasion.

The JIC continued to focus throughout May on the likely nature of a German attack on the UK. On 6 May it was noted that any invasion of the UK would be preceded by an invasion of Holland which, on 10 May, was precisely what happened with concurrent assaults on Belgium and France.[83] The attack was devastating. The Dutch government capitulated just six days later. Taken together, the suddenness, abruptness and efficiency of the German invasions of Poland, Norway, Denmark, France and the Low Countries offered an important lesson, and the JIC was quick to grasp it. In addition to assessing the nature of a German attack on the UK, the JIC also concentrated on how best to prepare for one. It is clear that it was convinced that an attack would take place. Accordingly, a list of twenty security recommendations was prepared for the COS, including the internment of all 'enemy aliens' between the ages of 16 and 70, both male and female.[84] This list, essentially a set of policy prescriptions, went beyond the traditional role of intelligence assessment and took the JIC into new territory.

The result was spectacular. In discussing the implications of the JIC's various reports, the COS introduced the Committee as 'our advisers on intelligence matters'. Furthermore, the JIC's recommendations were enthusiastically adopted, and emphasis was placed on the fact that they were based on the lessons learnt from previous German moves. In particular, the nature of German attacks was 'stressed': 'the completeness of the German plans for such an invasion, their effectiveness in sabotaging all attempts at resistance, and the secrecy with which the German preparations had been carried out'.[85] One implication discussed by the COS on the basis of the JIC reports, was whether Britain's military effort in Narvik, Norway, should be withdrawn in order to concentrate on preventing an attack on the UK. The outcome, though such a move was rejected at that time, was also significant: to instruct the JIC to assess when an invasion of the UK might begin.[86]

This was an important step. The JIC had now been used for the first time to consider the nature of a German attack and what preparations could be made, but up to this point it had not speculated on when such an attack might take place. The significance the JIC attached to this instruction was clear. The same day as the COS instruction – 24 May – the JIC decided to call an immediate meeting for 1700, following the end of their normal meeting which was to begin at 1500, with a view to producing a report to be approved by 2100 by the Service intelligence directors, for immediate dispatch to the COS Committee in time for its morning meeting on 25 May.[87] The conclusions of the JIC report were unequivocal: 'Germany is in a position now to undertake an invasion of Great Britain by sea or air'. However, it was also noted that without full air support, the Germans were unlikely to launch such an offensive, and that the British military should certainly not withdraw from Norway, because such a move might signal to the Germans that their chances of success were high enough to warrant an immediate attack.[88]

The Director of Naval Intelligence (DNI), Rear Admiral John Godfrey, requested that the JIC strengthen the intelligence system 'by all possible means with a view to obtaining the earliest possible warning of an enemy attack'.[89] This was an important suggestion. To have full forewarning, information would have to be obtained from the various occupied countries, as they were the likely bases for any invading forces. The problem, however, was that the present intelligence organisation 'was not designed to cover so wide a subject; it was inadequate for the purpose, and steps must be taken urgently to organise an adequate system.'[90] The implications of this were vast, entailing not only an increase in aerial reconnaissance, but also serving to underline just how important it would be to penetrate German ranks in occupied countries. More specifically, the JIC proposed to create a special 'inter-service intelligence staff' to focus specifically on the collection, collation and assessment of intelligence on the German question.[91] This was given a special endorsement by the COS Committee, and in discussion it reiterated the fact that the JIC should take the initiative in warning them of any hostile action.[92]

Whilst such discussions were continuing, the composition of the JIC was once more changing. In late May the JIC decided that SIS and the Ministry of Economic Warfare should become full members of the Committee and, after discussion, it was agreed that MI5 should also join. In addition, not only would all three organisations become full members of the senior committee, they should also send representatives to the daily meeting of the junior team, to discuss and approve the various daily summaries. Here then, for the first time, was a unified JIC, comprising the major civilian and military intelligence agencies.[93]

The JIC continued to concentrate on other topics too, both of a procedural and intelligence nature including, on the one hand, reporting on the situation in Italy, the general progress of the war and the importance of Ireland; and on the other, questions over the employment of aliens, leakages of information, and overseas intelligence commands. In June steps were taken to further increase and improve the JIC's links with the military planners. It was recorded that 'the importance of all planning being based on the most accurate information available cannot be over emphasised', and that accordingly JIC and JPC relations had been improved, but that it was now vital to strengthen links with the Allied Military Committee, the Anglo-French planning body.[94] It appears that the JIC was now thinking that its information should go beyond the COS Committee in helping to inform policy.

The question of whether a German invasion of the UK was likely continued to be the main priority for the JIC. By the end of May the Germans had reached the English Channel and with the British Expeditionary Force in full-scale retreat, the evacuation of Dunkirk was effected. In spite of this, views oscillated throughout the early summer months of 1940 yet at no point did it look, with any degree of certainty, as if the Germans might launch an offensive against Britain. In early June the JIC concluded that the 'invasion of this country will be for Germany her culminating effort of the war. She may be expected therefore to press it with the utmost intensity regardless of loss, and to throw into the balance all her available resources.'[95]

The Inter-Service Intelligence Section had been created in the Admiralty following the JIC's earlier discussions, and had been tasked with a responsibility for the intelligence effort on the invasion question. From the outset it, too, had passed a daily summary to the COS.[96] In mid-June the JIC discussed and approved the formation of a staff, working for the Commander-in-Chief, Home Forces, to keep him informed about relevant intelligence information. Furthermore, it also suggested an Inter-Service Intelligence Section be convened daily within the War Rooms once an invasion was actually underway.[97] Pressure on producing assessments of German intentions regarding an invasion now came from General Sir Edmund Ironside. Much like his namesake who had lived 900 years earlier and who had fought to fend off the threat of Danish invasion, Ironside, who had been Chief of the Imperial General Staff, had been appointed on 27 May by Churchill as the Commander-in-Chief Home Forces. Ironside was to co-ordinate activities in the UK to guard against a German invasion and his 'army' was to be the last line of defence. Accurate intelligence would be central to his mission.

The impasse continued. By mid-June the JIC could only conclude that 'we do not consider that any forecast can be made as to the probable German timetable for operations against this country'.[98] No doubt a central difficulty in assessing this was the crucial question of how long France could survive and, by extension, how quickly the Germans could re-equip themselves for an attack on the UK. Assessments were made as to whether the Germans might employ special measures in their invasion plans, including the use of gliders, smoke, mustard gas, and rhesus monkeys to spread yellow fever. More important was a survey of the impact of the war effort on Germany itself, its population and its resources.[99] By late June it was noted that Germany would not want to endure another winter of war, and that a start date for any possible invasion must be fast approaching. It was therefore considered that 'from the 1st July they [German invasion plans] must be regarded as imminent', especially given that as each day passed, Britain's own defensive plans improved and supplies from America enhanced Britain's strength.[100]

Complicating matters was the question mark over Italy's potential role in the war. A JIC paper in late May 1940 saw Italian intervention as a certainty, remarking that Italian forces had been 'engaged busily in preparing for war'. Furthermore, if evidence of Italy's capabilities was not enough, its intentions were equally transparent: 'Signor Mussolini, on whose decision all depends, has publicly placed himself on Germany's side'. Il Duce, it was felt, was not only 'afraid of Germany', but was also 'dominated' by it, to the extent that Mussolini was 'no longer a free agent' and that Hitler was 'in real control'. Strategically, therefore, Italian participation in the war was not in doubt. Tactically, though, what was missing was an idea as to when: 'all the indications point to the fact that Signor Mussolini has made up his mind to enter the war on the side of Germany, but there is no evidence available from which the date of such entry may be deduced'.[101] The JIC was on the right lines – just two weeks later the Italians declared war on Britain and France.

While the finishing touches were being put to the JIC report on 'Germany's Next Move' the French will to resist German aggression collapsed. Although never discussed explicitly in the papers, such a move may well have been expected because it did not alter JIC views on Germany's plans. But it was still not possible to assess whether an attack would be airborne, seaborne or both, or when it would begin.[102] In early July Churchill requested a further review by the JIC. In its reply, though 'little further conclusive evidence' had come to light, the JIC asserted that 'Germany is making preparation' for the invasion of the United Kingdom, though this would not take place before mid-July.[103]

The Battle of Britain began on 10 July 1940, when the German Air Force began a series of aerial raids, both by day and by night. The start of the air war triggered no new JIC papers, nor did it bring about any immediate change to the assumptions about invasion. The JIC had had no advance warning of the German aerial bombardment, though fortunately signals intelligence had managed to provide notice.[104] The JIC's first assessment, on 16 July, did not concentrate explicitly on the aerial attack. It concluded that the re-arming of the German Air Force had been slower than originally perceived, but did not expand on the implications of this.[105]

One attempt to counter the German threat was to propagate a myth about a British 'secret weapon'. Several JIC reports were issued on the value of deception, and perhaps something of the desperation of the time is evident in the attempt to persuade the Germans that Britain had a new, powerful weapon – a 'special ray' – that could set fire to approaching aircraft and ships. To support this, it was suggested that wooden towers be erected at various points around the coast, with a 'brightly polished ball on top of them'. There is no evidence that the scheme was ever adopted.[106]

As a voracious reader and absorber of information, Churchill had been a keen recipient of the JIC's various papers, yet even he struggled with the volume of material. In late July 1940 he complained and asked not to be shown the 'palmolive' any more – the name given to the JIC's 'Daily Situation Report Summary' because of the green paper used.[107] Eric Seal, Churchill's Private Secretary, wrote to Ismay to inform him that scrapping the palmolive would 'certainly relieve us of the unpleasant duty of reading through all the reports in the hope (generally unrealised) of finding a speck or two of grain amongst bag-loads of chaff.'[108] In fact the Prime Minister was not alone in his views, as earlier critiques had made plain. The JIC, though not acknowledging Ismay's input, decided that the Daily Situation Report need no longer be daily.[109]

The JIC was not short of work. Although Nazi Germany was the pre-eminent threat, it was not the only one. To give an idea of the extent of its workload, for the short period 25–30 July 1940, the Committee produced, approved and issued twenty different reports, including, once more, a mixture of administrative and intelligence topics. Amongst these were a number of assessments for the JPC, including one on the future conduct of the war, and another on whether British military effort should be re-directed towards the defeat of Fascist Italy.[110]

In late July 1940 the JIC discussed the means by which information could and should be obtained, concluding that every military effort should be extended to helping SIS garner information and that, simultaneously, steps should be taken to destroy German means of communication.[111] The majority of the papers in August were concerned with propaganda, both checking the veracity of German efforts and deciding on a deception strategy. No substantive JIC papers on the German invasion were issued, though there was discussion following a suggestion by the Director of Combined Operations that 'agents' be sent to Ireland, Iceland, the Faroes, Shetlands and Orkneys, to report back information once the Germans did mobilise their forces.[112]

The increasingly successful fight in the skies over Britain led to a request by the COS for the JIC to re-assess the threat of a German sea-borne invasion. The JIC concluded that such an invasion could not be ruled out, but that any attack depended on air supremacy and this could not be obtained by the Germans. The implication was that the Germans would probably intensify their aerial attacks for the remainder of September.[113] Though the report itself is not explicit, the minutes of the discussion make it clear: 'it was generally agreed between the Services that invasion or raids were at least as likely to occur now as at any time during the last three months'.[114]

The COS Committee, however, was not happy with the report, complaining that it 'was not what was required'. The assessment should, instead, be based upon German intentions, not their capabilities.[115] The JIC produced a further paper, stating unequivocally that 'it is considered that these [German invasion] preparations are so advanced that invasion could be attempted at any time.'[116] Because of the German Air Force's tactical switch to the bombing of London, it is clear that the JIC thought that the initiative was being lost by the Germans. Perhaps as a consequence, attention began to be focussed elsewhere. In mid-September the

JPC produced an enormous wish list for regions of the world where it required information, including specific targets for each.[117]

German plans for invasion were dissected in a series of reports starting in early October 1940. The first, approved on 10 October, considered Germany's next move. It concluded that whilst an invasion of Britain could not be ruled out, given Germany's failure to secure either sea or air supremacy and Britain's increased strength, invasion was now regarded as 'hazardous'. Instead, the Germans would be likely to utilise their invading forces through the Balkans, the Italians would intensify attacks in North Africa, and pressure would be put upon Spain to join forces.[118] The battle had also, by now, spread to the Middle East and the Mediterranean. In other words, German failure to secure British surrender had resulted in the spread of the war into a global conflict.

Hinsley has argued that the German failure in the Battle of Britain was less to do with the successes of British intelligence than with the limitations of German military capabilities.[119] Certainly the JIC's contribution to the conflict was minimal, and without any real indication of how its assessments were perceived, it is difficult to know whether its product affected decision makers, particularly as the JIC's daily summaries have all been lost. At the same time though, the military planners and the COS in particular, were hungry for any nuggets of information the JIC could provide. The assessments themselves were strategic in nature, and while this would have been useful for gauging trends, they were perhaps never designed to convey immediate enemy movements to the planners, particularly once attention was focussed on the threat.

A German Perspective

With his assumption of power, Prime Minister Winston Churchill instigated a number of changes. The JPC, in a sense the guardian of the JIC's product, was split into three new bodies: a Strategic Planning Section; a Future Operational Planning Section; and an Executive Planning Section. Of more relevance here was a set of questions that a rather concerned Churchill put to the COS in November 1940:

(i) ... We were deficient in intelligence as to Norway. Was any change of personnel made?
(ii) We are now found very late in obtaining information about Crete (aerodromes).
(iii) Have we adequate knowledge of other possible theatres of war?
(iv) I should like to know who is responsible and how long he has been in charge.[120]

The Lord Privy Seal, Clement Attlee, suggested the failure to predict the invasion of Norway 'seems to me to have demanded a thorough overhaul of the Intelligence Services.'[121] The matter was, almost inevitably, referred to the JIC for comment and expansion. The junior committee met at 1730 on Sunday 10 November to draft a response, so that the full JIC could discuss it the following day, for the COS to receive it on 12 November.[122]

The JIC report absolved itself and the wider intelligence community of any real blame. Indeed, it suggested, and was supported by the Air Ministry, that intelligence on Cretan aerodromes was very good, and that therefore Churchill must have been misinformed by the Defence Committee, who had originally raised the point. Furthermore, the fact that pre-war intelligence activities had been curtailed by budgetary cuts was emphasised throughout.[123] The COS Committee endorsed the report's contents, but before passing it up to the Prime Minister it decided to embellish a number of the points raised. Its conclusion offered a resounding note of support for the intelligence community:

> So far as the past is concerned, we do not for one moment claim that intelligence has been altogether satisfactory. We are satisfied, however, that the blame for such shortcomings that there have been cannot be attributed to any particular individual; indeed the respective heads of the Intelligence Services are constantly taking steps to improve matters . . . it seems to us very undesirable that a drastic reorganisation of this magnitude should be attempted at the moment when we are fighting for our lives.[124]

At the same time a number of other changes were being introduced, including a further revision to the number and nature of daily reports being issued, with the previous list being bolstered by a daily 'Greek Situation Report', instigated following Italy's invasion of Greece in late October 1940.[125] Unrelated to this, Churchill's succinct suggestion was to 'try now and simplify, shorten and reduce' the intelligence summaries.[126] In addition it was decided to discontinue the JIC's 'daily summary' (which was no longer actually daily) as a stand alone product, but incorporate the information into the daily 'Cabinet War Room Record' instead. The daily 'situation report' continued unabated, though circulation was tightened up.[127] More important was an idea to resurrect a First World War practice of looking at the war from the opponent's perspective: the so-called 'enemy's syndicate', a practice that broadly equates today with the idea of 'red teaming'.

1940 had been an important year for melding the intelligence and planning communities together, and there had been a series of meetings, looking at different topics, where both Committees met as one. This had even led Godfrey, the DNI, to suggest that they be amalgamated, though ultimately nothing came of it.[128] The most important bilateral discussion took place in late November, following an initial suggestion by the War Office's Director of Plans, Brigadier Ian Playfair.[129]

The first meeting to discuss the creation of an enemy planning section was convened by the JPS, and although the Services' directors of intelligence were present, the remaining members of the JIC did not attend. Despite this, the record of the meeting was subsequently issued as a JIC paper.[130] The rationale behind the suggestion was simple: to 'watch continually . . . the course of the war as a whole from the enemy point of view, and in particular of working out possible enemy plans'.[131] The JIC and JPS were unanimous in supporting the creation of the 'Future Operations (Enemy) Section' (FO(E)S, or FOES, as it became known). At the end of November a combined JIC and JPS team presented FOES at a COS meeting, where it received a thorough endorsement.[132]

FOES was to comprise officers from the Services, together with representatives from the FO and the Ministry of Economic Warfare. All, with the exception of the War Office representative, had had recent experience of Germany, having served in various positions in the British Embassy.[133] They were to be based in the War Cabinet Offices and although it was suggested that they owe allegiance to the JIC, in fact FOES would have little to do with the JIC (though they were in fact welcomed by the JIC Secretary on their first day).[134] Instead it reported directly to the COS Committee, which would also issue it with their requirements. FOES was to have unrestricted access to intelligence material, but would have no access whatsoever to allied planning – therefore they were supposed to know all that they could about the Germans, but nothing about what the allies were up to.[135] The members themselves were chosen on the basis that members could 'absorb the enemy's mentality and develop an enemy point of view'.[136] Having received its first set of instructions, the chairman, Major General Piers Mackesy, informed the COS that it would take a further period of a few weeks before they could 'get into the "skin of the Germans".'[137]

The first FOES paper, signed by the 'German' General Keitel, was a broad strategic survey from the German perspective.[138] The response, however, was not good. Admiral of the Fleet Sir Dudley Pound commented that it 'gave the impression of having been written by a Neutral and that, in consequence, it failed to lead up to any definite recommendations.'[139] The revised version[140], though better, was still not felt to go far enough, with the COS Committee agreeing that 'if regarded as a captured enemy document, [it] told us little that we did not know already.'[141]

Part of the problem was that the initial COS decision that FOES should have no access to allied plans, did not allow for German penetration of the planning machinery. It was therefore suggested that FOES have some access to planning material, because it had to be assumed that German military intelligence might have procured some of the allied plans through espionage operations.[142] As General Mackesy highlighted, 'British intelligence is our O&P [operations and plans]! British O&P is our intelligence!'[143] The other new measure was for the COS, now 'acting' as Hitler, to issue FOES with a directive for more precise information, with result that many assessments were signed off with 'Heil Hitler'.

These had not been the first assessments to be written from the German perspective.[144] In the midst of the German invasion fears Admiral Sir Reginald Aylmer Ranfurly Plunkett-Ernle-Erle-Drax, Commander-in-Chief, The Nore, produced a report on the 'Battle for Britain'. Pretending to be a German General Staff Officer, Admiral Drax, using his new nom de guerre, wrote about what strategy he would adopt in invading Britain, ending with 'Heil Hitler'.[145]

The Foreign Operations (Enemy) Section produced approximately thirty reports in its brief existence, though not all have been preserved.[146] Following initial teething problems the COS warmed to the appreciations, and they even began to instruct the JIC to examine them as pieces of intelligence.[147] In March 1941 FOES was disbanded, to be replaced by an Axis Planning Section which, itself, would be transformed into the Joint Intelligence Staff in late 1941 (see chapter 4). This move would, once more, see an upsurge in the nature of the JIC product and in the performance of the Committee itself. Although not strictly a JIC venture, FOES would play an important role in the JIC's development.

In examining the performance of the JIC in the first months of the war we are hindered by gaps in documentation. The JIC assessments exist in their entirety, as do the minutes, and these reveal a Committee concerned with managerial issues, whose only assessments were long-term in scope and nature. They were all as a result of a direct request by the military and were relatively infrequent in nature. These paint a one-dimensional picture of the JIC as an organisation that spent far more time on co-ordination than on intelligence provision.

It is hard to offer a comprehensive evaluation of the JIC given the lack of papers. The JIC's daily and weekly summaries have almost all been destroyed. The few examples which remain show the operational and tactical side of the JIC's work. For instance, both the JIC's 'Intelligence Summary' and the 'Daily Secret Situation Report', reveal that the Committee was at the centre of incoming information, that this was specific, timely in nature, and distributed on a daily basis. These summaries are exceptionally interesting, and it is obvious what a benefit they would have been to military planners, attempting to keep abreast of the latest developments.[148] But in solely considering the assessments that survive, there is be a danger of being unduly critical of the JIC's performance because of the inability to assess its main workload: the provision of daily information to the military planners.

At the outbreak of war in September 1939 the JIC was an integral component of the war planning machinery, yet it remained relatively aloof from the main set-up. This was confirmed by the decision to move the Planners closer to the COS, but to leave behind the intelligence apparatus. Events of 1940 were decisive for the JIC, in particular the reception of its reports within Whitehall. The failure to foresee the Nazi attacks in Scandinavia led to the first moves to integrate the JIC into the war fighting effort. Its fortunes were improved by the COS Committee's recognition that intelligence was vital to the war effort, and its direc- tive for the JIC to take the initiative in preparing assessments, whenever the need arose. It was perhaps this move, more than any other, that allowed the JIC to escape from the creative vacuum that had characterised the pre-war period.

Yet despite these positive moves, the JIC was still inhibited. Hinsley identifies three characteristics which, he argues, explain why the JIC was slow to develop following the outbreak of war: 1) it was too pre-occupied with administration; 2) without a staff of its own the JIC had to adopt individual Service department assessments; 3) the planners used the JIC's daily and weekly summaries but did not pay much attention to the normal assessments – they were provided with intelligence directly by the Services so it was not clear why they needed the JIC product as well.[149]

Are these fair criticisms? It is immensely difficult to provide a judgement of the JIC in the first eighteen months of the war. Although it became far more involved in the work of the Planners and the COS, there are very few contemporary comments to tell us what was really thought of the JIC. Certainly, an amount of assurance can be given from the increased presence the JIC had, both as a Committee and in terms of its product, but is this the whole picture? It is impossible, for example, to provide a definitive answer to the question to what extent the JIC influenced the policies of the war effort. What the JIC did attempt to offer, with some success, was timely, strategic warning of German intentions and an appreciation of their vulnerabilities in order to aid the formulation of British military planning.

In 1940 alone, the senior JIC held seventy-five meetings and produced four hundred and thirty-six papers. In addition, the various daily and weekly summaries would have run into the thousands. From the detailed assessments it is possible to gain an impression of the vast array of topics that the JIC considered, from administration, through assessment, to intelligence planning. However, given that only a handful of immediate assessments remain, it is impossible to gauge whether the JIC reports strengthened Britain's strategy to respond to German plans.

Of Hinsley's critiques we can disregard the first. The JIC did spend a large amount of time on administration, but given that it was charged with co-ordinating the country's intelligence efforts, this was inevitable; it certainly did not stop the Committee from producing a wealth of reports. Hinsley is correct in his second assertion about drafting, but only as it pertains to the six-month period following the outbreak of war. With the creation of a 'junior' JIC, people sec-onded from Service departments to compose individual reports, the Committee did have something resembling a drafting team, though it would not become effective until late 1941. The difference between this and later periods is that the junior JIC members were not seconded full-time for a dedicated period to work explicitly on JIC papers. The final point, that the JPC only read the immediate JIC assessments, was probably true. To planners, tactical assessments would have had more real world relevance than long-term strategic papers.

By 1940 the JIC had also become a broader body. It had a full-time FO chair-man, and this was representative of the changing views of the FO which, by the outbreak of war, had started to show a clear interest in the work of the JIC. JIC reports were regularly distributed throughout various parts of the FO, with handwritten annotations often commenting on the usefulness of the assess-ments.[150] Furthermore, the introduction of MI5, SIS and the Ministry of Economic Warfare as permanent members, also strengthened the Committee's position as the central co-ordinator for intelligence. Therefore whilst it might be difficult to label the 1939–1940 period as an outright success for the JIC, it certainly laid the foundations for the full-blown intelligence organisation that would emerge as the war progressed, a structure that would become absolutely integral to the war effort.

Notes

1 Andrew, *Her Majesty's Secret Service*. p.592.
2 Hinsley, *British Intelligence: Vol.1*. p.93.
3 W13193/12800/49. Cover note by Stevenson, 6 September 1939. FO 371/23912. At this time the COS met twice daily, once in the morning and once in the late afternoon.
4 COS(39) 2nd Meeting, 3 September 1939. CAB 79/1.
5 COS(39) 2nd Meeting, 3 September 1939. CAB 79/1.
6 W13193/12800/49. Cover note by Stevenson, 6 September 1939. FO 371/23912.
7 W13193/12800/49. A.N.Barnard to R.C.Skrine Stevenson, 3 September 1939. FO 371/23912.
8 JIC(39)1, 'Weekly Resume of the Naval, Military and Air Situation', 6 September 1939. CAB 81/95; JIC(39)1st Meeting, 7 September 1939. CAB 81/87; W13319/13319/49. Note by R.C.Skrine Stevenson, 8 September 1939. FO 371/23914.
9 W18366/15616/49. Notes by V.Cavendish-Bentinck and G.Jebb, 11 December 1939. FO 371/23949. See also JIC(39)15th Meeting, 8 December 1939. CAB 81/87.
10 The earliest reference found is a note by Colonel van Cutsem, 10 September 1939. CAB 81/95.
11 'The Development of I.S.(O)', note for the attention of J.H.Godfrey [wartime Director of Naval Intelligence], 2 November 1943. ADM 223/465.
12 JIC(57)40, 'Joint Organisation for Intelligence', 5 April 1957. CAB 163/50.
13 X7763/G. Letter from C.Howard Smith [Foreign Office] to E.Hale [Treasury], 8 August 1939. FO 366/2382.
14 'Joint Intelligence Committee', note by J.H.Godfrey, n.d. but probably late 1940s. ADM 223/465.
15 F.Beaumont-Nesbitt to H.L.Ismay, 18 December 1939. CAB 21/2722.
16 H.L.Ismay to R.C.Skrine Stevenson, 7 December 1939. CAB 21/2651.
17 See various correspondence in X7763/G and X11961/G. FO 366/2382.
18 P Howarth, *Intelligence Chief Extraordinary: The Life of the Ninth Duke of Portlan.* (London: Bodley Head, 1986). p.130.
19 Interview with K.Walker-Sloan. 24 March 2010.
20 Details can be found in J Colville, *Strange Inheritance* (London: Michael Russell, 1983). pp.152–66. Colville was Churchill's Assistant Private Secretary during the war years.
21 X11961/G. 'The Co-ordination of Secret Intelligence', November 1939. FO 366/2382.
22 Discussion of these papers is in CAB 81/87.
23 JIC(39)13, 'Measures to be Taken in the Event of Germany Overrunning Holland or Belgium or Both', 28 September 1939. CAB 81/95.
24 JIC(39)18, 'German Secret Weapon', 9 October 1939. CAB 81/95.
25 COS(39)101st Meeting, 9 December 1939. CAB 79/2.
26 JIC(39)37, 'Possible German Action in the Spring of 1940', 18 December 1939. CAB 81/95.
27 C6470/5/18. Handwritten note by Cadogan, 20 December 1939. FO 371/24379. In the same file Cavendish-Bentinck effectively apologises for the length of the report. He also describes how some of the statistics used in the assessment were reached, including some details on how the numbers changed between various drafts.
28 JIC(39)37, 'Possible German Action in the Spring of 1940', 18 December 1939. CAB 81/95.
29 C1199/5/18. Minute by Cavendish-Bentinck, 24 January 1940. FO 371/24379. A copy of the report itself is in JIC(40)4, 'Possible German Action in the Spring of 1940', 22 January 1940. CAB 81/96.
30 JIC(40)13, 'Assessment of German Productive Capacity', 4 March 1940. CAB 81/96.
31 JIC(40)14, 'Assessment of German Productive Capacity', 4 March 1940. CAB 81/96.

32 JIC(40)18, 'Strategic Implications of the Russo-Finnish Treaty', 21 March 1940. CAB 81/96.

33 JIC(40)15, 'Inter-Services Project Board', 16 March 1940. CAB 81/96.

34 COS 62nd Meeting, 1 April 1940. CAB 79/3.

35 JIC(40)14th Meeting, 15 March 1940. CAB 81/87.

36 'Memorandum by Director of Military Intelligence', n.d. but early April 1940. CAB 21/2651.

37 JIC(40)14th Meeting, 15 March 1940. CAB 81/87.

38 JIC(40)22, 'Preparation of Papers for the Chiefs of Staff', 23 March 1940. CAB 81/96.

39 JP(40)17th Meeting, 16 March 1940. CAB 84/2.

40 Hinsley, *British Intelligence: Vol.1.* p.129.

41 JIC(40)10(S), 'Possible German Action', 19 February 1940. CAB 81/135.

42 O Riste, 'Intelligence and the 'Mindset': The German Invasion of Norway in 1940', *Intelligence and National Security* 22:4 (August 2007), pp.521–536.

43 Memorandum by V.Cavendish-Bentinck, 6 May 1940, and handwritten note by Cadogan at the bottom. Neville Chamberlain Papers, University of Birmingham: NC 8/35/59.

44 JIC(40)18(S), 'Possibility of an Imminent German Invasion of the Low Countries', 11 April 1940. CAB 81/135.

45 In addition to normal memoranda, at some point in late 1939/early 1940, a second series of JIC memoranda was initiated, with the suffix (S). Though it is never stated explicitly what the (S) stood for, it is possible to surmise that given that the majority of the papers are 'notes by the Secretary', it is likely that these were the secretary's files, a practice that was certainly in existence from the middle of the war onwards. Where there are reports in this series, it seems that they were either early drafts, or were JIC papers which were never issued as such, often instead being appended to JPC papers.

46 JIC(40)21st Meeting, 13 April 1940. CAB 81/87.

47 Churchill, *Second World War: Vol.I.* p.528.

48 D Stafford, *Churchill and Secret Service* (London: Abacus, 1997). Also, Bennett, *Churchill's Man of Mystery*.

49 JP(40)26th Meeting, 10 April 1940. CAB 84/2.

50 JIC(40)23(S), 19 April 1940. CAB 81/135.

51 C5848/5/18. Minute by Cavendish-Bentinck, 20 April 1940. FO 371/24381.

52 JIC(40)34, 'German Invasion of the United Kingdom', 19 April 1940. CAB 81/96.

53 JIC(40)24th Meeting, 23 April 1940. CAB 81/87.

54 COS(40)86th Meeting, 19 April 1940. CAB 79/3.

55 JIC(40)24th Meeting, 23 April 1940. CAB 81/87.

56 For instance, see COS(39)31st Meeting, 28 September 1939. CAB 79/1.

57 W156/56/49. Minute by Cavendish-Bentinck. 6 January 1940. FO 371/25156.

58 JIC(40)24th Meeting, 23 April 1940. CAB 81/87.

59 COS(40)352, 'Urgent Intelligence Reports', 13 May 1940. CAB 80/11.

60 Director of Military Intelligence Major General Francis Davidson later examined Norway as a case-study of intelligence failure to heed the lessons for future work. LHCMA: Davidson 4/3.

61 V.Cavendish-Bentinck to A.Cadogan, 6 May 1940. Chamberlain Papers: NC 8/35/58.

62 'The Scandinavian Invasion', 14 April 1940. PREM 1/435.

63 S.Hoare to M.Hankey, 23 April 1940. CAB 127/375.

64 M.Hankey to H.Wilson [Permanent Secretary of the Treasury], 29 April 1940. PREM 1/435.

65 Hoare to Hankey, 23 April 1940. CAB 127/375. For more on SIS see Jeffery, *MI6.* pp.344–6.

66 Hankey to S.Hoare [Secretary of State for Air], 24 April 1940. CAB 127/375.

67 A.N.Rucker to Prime Minister, 6 May 1940. Chamberlain Papers: NC 8/35/61.

68 Wilson to Ismay, 1 May 1940. CAB 127/375.

69 Hankey to Hoare, 24 April 1940. CAB 127/375.

70 COS(40)352, 'Urgent Intelligence Reports', 13 May 1940. CAB 80/11.

71 L.C.Hollis to Major General A.N.Floyer-Acland [Military Secretary to the Secretary of State for War], 23 April 1940. CAB 21/2651.

72 For more see N Smart, 'Four Days in May: The Norway Debate and the Downfall of Neville Chamberlain', *Parliamentary History* 17:2 (1998), pp.215–43.

73 The message from Churchill was communicated by Sir Edward Bridges, the Cabinet Secretary. See JIC(40)60, 'The Production of Intelligence Summaries by the Joint Intelligence Sub-Committee and Service Departments', 15 May 1940. CAB 81/96.

74 COS(40)352, 'Urgent Intelligence Reports', 13 May 1940. CAB 80/11.

75 COS(40)360, 'Urgent Intelligence Reports', 17 May 1940. CAB 80/11.

76 JIC(40)71, 'Urgent Intelligence Reports', 17 May 1940. CAB 81/97.

77 JIC(40)29th Meeting, 15 May 1940. CAB 81/87. Details of the additional yet separate Services' intelligence summaries are given JIC(40)60, 'The Production of Intelligence Summaries by the Joint Intelligence Sub-Committee and Service Departments', 15 May 1940. CAB 81/96.

78 C6846/5/18. Minute by Cavendish-Bentinck, 1 May 1940. FO 371/24382.

79 COS(40)314(JIC), 'German Invasion of the United Kingdom', 3 May 1940. CAB 80/10.

80 JIC(40)47, '"Fifth Column" Activities in the United Kingdom', 2 May 1940. CAB 81/96.

81 C6846/5/18. Minute by Cavendish-Bentinck, 1 May 1940. FO 371/24382.

82 JIC(40)50, 'German Invasion of the United Kingdom', 3 May 1940. CAB 81/96.

83 JIC(40)56, 'German Invasion of the United Kingdom', 6 May 1940. CAB 81/96.

84 JIC(40)68, 'Security Measures Against Air Invasion', 16 May 1940. CAB 81/96.

85 COS(40)366, 'Security Measures Against an Invasion of the United Kingdom', 18 May 1940. CAB 80/11.

86 COS(40)146th Meeting, 24 May 1940. CAB 79/11.

87 JIC(40)82, 'German Invasion of the United Kingdom', 24 May 1940. CAB 81/97.

88 JIC(40)83(Revise), 'German Invasion of the United Kingdom', 25 May 1940. CAB 81/97.

89 JC(40)84, 'Early Warning of Invasion', 25 May 1940. CAB 81/97.

90 JIC(40)35th Meeting, 26 May 1940. CAB 81/87.

91 JIC(40)88, 'Early Warning of Invasion', 30 May 1940. CAB 81/97.

92 COS(40)161st Meeting, 1 June 1940. CAB 79/4.

93 JIC(40)34th Meeting, 24 May 1940. CAB 81/87.

94 JIC(40)103, 'Co-Operation with the Allied Military Committee', 5 June 1940. CAB 81/97.

95 JIC(40)101, 'Summary of the Likely Forms and Scales of Attack that Germany Could Bring to Bear on the British Isles in the Near Future', 6 June 1940. CAB 81/97.

96 For more information see Hinsley, *British Intelligence. Vol.1.* p.169.

97 JIC(40)109, 'Home Defence Inter-Services Intelligence Section', 12 June 1940. CAB 81/97; Also, JIC(40)44th Meeting, 14 June 1940. CAB 81/87. The daily records produced are in AIR 40/1637.

98 JIC(40)121(Revise), 'Seaborne and Airborne Attack on the United Kingdom', 15 June 1940. CAB 81/97.

99 These are all contained within CAB 81/97.

100 JIC(40)143, 'Germany's Next Move', 27 June 1940. CAB 81/97.

101 JIC(40)81, 'Italian Situation', 24 May 1940. CAB 81/97.

102 JIC(40)144, 'Germany's Next Move', 2 July 1940. CAB 81/97.

103 JIC(40)152, 'Imminence of a German Invasion of Great Britain', 4 July 1940. CAB 81/97. Interestingly, this report includes an appendix that lists the evidence used to reach this conclusion, including something about its provenance and reliability.

104 Hinsley, *British Intelligence: Vol.1*. p.176. Quite why the Sigint intercepts were not brought to the JIC's attention is not obvious.

105 JIC(40)163, 'Sea-Borne and Air-Borne Attack on the British Isles, Scales of Attack', 16 July 1940. CAB 81/97.

106 JIC(40)177, 'Secret Weapon', 18 July 1940. CAB 81/97.

107 An example of this colour paper and of the JIC's 'Daily Secret Situation Report' can be found in CAB 163/10.

108 E.A.Seal to H.L.Ismay, 22 July 1940. PREM 3/254/3.

109 JIC(40)215, 'Daily Secret Situation Reports', 29 July 1940. CAB 81/98.

110 These can be found in CAB 81/98.

111 JIC(40)184, 'Supply of Intelligence from Enemy and Enemy Occupied Territories', 20 July 1940. CAB 81/97. See also the Confidential Annex to this report in CAB 81/89.

112 JIC(40)257, 'Supply of Information in Certain Areas', 29 August 1940. CAB 81/98.

113 JIC(40)268, 'Sea-Borne Invasion of the United Kingdom', 5 September 1940. CAB 81/98.

114 JIC(40)57th Meeting, 5 September 1940. CAB 81/87.

115 COS(40)296th Meeting, 6 September 1940. CAB 79/6.

116 JIC(40)273, 'Possible German Action Against United Kingdom', 7 September 1940. CAB 81/98. This account does not quite tally with the version given in Howarth, *Intelligence Chief Extraordinary*. p.134. Howarth did not have access to the JIC papers in preparing his account.

117 JP(40)459(O), 'Provision of Intelligence for Planning', 19 September 1940. CAB 84/19.

118 JIC(40)306, 'Possible Axis Intentions', 10 October 1940. CAB 81/98.

119 Hinsley. *British Intelligence: Vol.1*. p.164. For a recent review see S Puri, 'The Role of Intelligence in Deciding the Battle of Britain', *Intelligence and National Security* 21:3 (June 2006), pp.416–39.

120 COS(40)376th Meeting, 6 November 1940. CAB 79/7.

121 Minute by C.R.Attlee to the Prime Minister, 28 November 1940. PREM 4/97/11.

122 JIC(40)362, 'Intelligence', 9 November 1940. CAB 81/98.

123 JIC(40)367, 'Intelligence', 11 November 1940. CAB 81/98.

124 COS(40)932(FINAL), 'Provision of Intelligence', 14 November 1940. CAB 80/22.

125 These can be found in WO 106/3122–3124.

126 JIC(40)376, 'Daily Summaries: Avoidance of Duplication of Information', 13 November 1940. CAB 81/98.

127 See the various correspondence in CAB 120/744.

128 JIC(40)381, 'Proposed Formation of Joint Planning and Intelligence Committee', 18 November 1940. CAB 81/98.

129 JP(40)122nd Meeting, 3 November 1940. CAB 84/2. Playfair subsequently wrote several of the Official Histories of World War Two.

130 JP(40)126th Meeting, 6 November 1940. CAB 84/2. Also issued as JIC(40)68th Meeting, 8 November 1940. CAB 81/87.

131 JIC(40)387, 'Formation of Future Operations (Enemy) Planning Section', 26 November 1940. CAB 81/98.

132 COS(40)401st Meeting, 25 November 1940. CAB 79/8.

133 'The FOES', Vice Admiral Sir T.Troubridge. Churchill College, University of Cambridge Archives: MLBE 2/39. Troubridge was the naval representative on FOES.

134 Handwritten note by C.Edwards, 7 December 1940. CAB 121/241.

135 COS(40)407th Meeting, 28 November 1940. CAB 79/8.

136 JIC(40)387, 'Formation of Future Operations (Enemy) Planning Section', 26 November 1940. CAB 81/98.

137 COS(40)422nd Meeting, 10 December 1940. CAB 79/8. Mackesy had been the land commander for the Narvik area of Norway following the invasion. He had then retired from the War Office, to be brought back into service with the creation of FOES.

138 FOES(40)1, 'Appreciation of the Situation', 31 December 1940. WO 193/792.

139 COS(41)11th Meeting, 7 January 1941. CAB 79/8.

140 FOES(40)1, 'Appreciation of the Situation', 8 January 1941, CAB 81/64.

141 COS(41)17th Meeting, 14 January 1941. CAB 79/8.

142 Minute by Major General John Kennedy [Director of Military Operations and Plans, War Office], 15 January 1941. WO 193/792.

143 P.Mackesy to J.Kennedy, 15 January 1941. WO 193/792.

144 For various initiatives see D McLachlan, *Room 39, Wherein Took Place the Exciting Story of British Naval Intelligence During World War II* (New York: Atheneum, 1969). pp.252–6.

145 JIC(40)181, 'The Battle for Britain', 18 July 1940. CAB 81/97.

146 Details can be found in CAB 81/64, which includes copies of the first six.

147 COS(41)107th Meeting, 24 March 1941. CAB 79/10.

148 An example of both summaries can be found in PREM 3/254/3. An example 'Intelligence Summary' from November 1940 can be found in CAB 120/744.

149 Hinsley, *British Intelligence: Vol.1*. pp.94–6.

150 For example see File 15616/49. FO 371/23949.

4 Stabilisation: 1941–1942

On 19 December 1940 the Joint Intelligence Committee moved from its home in Richmond Terrace, where it had resided since July 1936, to the new Cabinet Offices in Great George Street. The offices, which had originally housed the Board of Trade, were newer than those in Richmond Terrace, but more importantly, they brought the JIC into closer proximity to the War Cabinet and the military planners.[1] The main Committee met two or three times a week, though there were no set times. In addition, the junior members of the Committee, those responsible for drafting the papers, met twice weekly in the 'Operations Intelligence Centre' in the sub-basement of the Admiralty building.[2]

Despite the existence of minutes of the JIC meetings, in which the decisions taken are recorded, nothing is conveyed of their tone and nature. The precise composition of the JIC in 1941 is an interesting example of how people, from different backgrounds, with different ranks and stature, worked together. Within the Committee the three Services' Directors of Intelligence – a Major General, a Rear Admiral, and an Air Vice Marshal – were all the same rank. The newly-introduced 'civilian' intelligence agencies, MI5 and SIS, were also represented by senior military officers, albeit junior in rank to their Service colleagues. SIS's normal envoy was its chief, Colonel Stewart Menzies[3]; whilst MI5 sent its Assistant Director, Brigadier Henry Allen. The other permanent member, from the Ministry of Economic Warfare (MEW), was an academic seconded to the government, in the shape of Professor Noel Hall.[4] The Secretary was drawn from the War Office, and usually of Lieutenant Colonel rank. That left the Chairman, the FO representative, Victor Cavendish-Bentinck who, by 1941, had attained the position of Acting Counsellor.

Approximately speaking, an FO Counsellor was equivalent to a 1-star military officer (for example, a Brigadier), whereas the Services' Directors of Intelligence were 2-star officers (for example, a Major General); this therefore made Cavendish-Bentinck junior to his colleagues and this was emphasised by the fact that he was also younger than them. This was not the only difficulty to overcome. Cavendish-Bentinck has recalled how he 'found the situation a little difficult, as I was lower in rank than the Directors of Intelligence, who all thought that a war was no matter for a civilian.'[5] At one stage in 1941 Cavendish-Bentinck did suggest to his superiors that he be replaced by someone more senior, but the reply from Major

General Hastings Ismay, the Secretary to the COS Committee, was to 'soldier on.'[6] Perhaps as a sign of the JIC's and his own increasing prestige, Cavendish-Bentinck continued to be promoted on the FO scale throughout the war and was awarded a CMG for his efforts in the 1941 New Year's Honours list.[7]

Throughout the period 1941–2 the JIC represented the high point in the intelligence hierarchy, with reports moving upwards to the planners. Until the middle stages of the war there seems to have been little of the top-down system that would later characterise the JIC; there was only infrequent instruction passed down through the JIC to the agencies themselves vis-à-vis intelligence requirements. In this period the JIC was brought much closer to the planners, culminating in its active involvement in planning Operation TORCH – the invasion of North Africa in November 1942.

Creation of a Secretariat

In December 1940 Major General Frederick 'Paddy' Beaumont-Nesbitt, the Director of Military Intelligence (DMI) in the War Office (and former JIC Chairman), was replaced as DMI by Major General Francis Davidson. Davidson, described by a contemporary as a 'trim, compact figure with twinkling eyes – a genial uncle' would make an immediate impact on the JIC.[8] Like his predecessor, Davidson produced a flurry of papers for the JIC, commenting on current practice, where the deficiencies were and what might be done to rectify them. One of his first, produced in January 1941, was an examination of the JIC system, reflecting on whether it was meeting the requirements placed upon it. Davidson's biggest complaint was that the JIC was still not effectively co-ordinating the machinery of intelligence. To this end, he argued, the COS were still receiving 'parallel and simultaneous information'. For Davidson, the solution was to strengthen the junior committee by 'assisting in the production of appreciations'.[9] Furthermore, he felt that the drafters should be a more professional cadre with experience in writing reports for senior readers.[10]

In response to this the JIC approved a memorandum in February 1941, dictating how its papers should be written in the future so that they would be more useful and more agreeable to the COS:

(a) To present the conclusions to the Chiefs of Staff in as concise a form as possible.
(b) To include in the paper the essential arguments on which the conclusions are based.
(c) To keep the paper as short as possible.[11]

In a persuasive minute, Davidson outlined how FOES needed to be part of the intelligence setup: given its location outside this machinery, there was an inevitable amount of duplication because the JIC did not know what FOES was producing, and vice versa. Commenting on the drafting process in general, Davidson argued that the current system, whereby papers were prepared by individual departments, could never be representative of a combined intelligence viewpoint, even with the discussions in the junior JIC. His suggestion was for a full-time drafting team, comprising representatives from the military intelligence departments, the FO and the Ministry of Economic Warfare (note the absence of MI5 or SIS here): 'this section should be to the JIC what the planners are to the COS'.[12] In discussion, the JIC's response was somewhat tepid: it agreed with Davidson's views but decided to 'defer consideration' of the paper. As a temporary remedy, the Committee decided that FOES should send representatives to the junior committee.[13]

Despite the JIC's decision to 'defer consideration', its discontent with FOES was communicated to the COS Committee which, in turn, called representatives of the JIC and the JPS to attend a meeting in early March 1941.[14] Davidson himself was present at the COS meeting. Once again, he argued forcefully that the JIC needed a permanent staff responsible for drafting assessments, his main rationale being that this would speed up the process. Common sense prevailed: the COS agreed that such a body should be placed within the JIC structure, that it should answer to the JIC itself, and that a permanent staff be forged from the Service departments, the FO, and the MEW.[15]

The new organisation was to be called the 'Axis Planning Section' (APS). APS was scheduled to take over from FOES at the end of March 1941 and work on similar topics. According to its official remit, APS was to continue the role of FOES, though now report to the JIC.[16] In practice however, APS was to have two primary functions:

(a) Prepare appreciations from the enemy point of view.
(b) Draft papers for the Joint Intelligence Sub-Committee covering normal JIC activities.

The difficulty was that whilst those topics under (a) had to be written from the enemy's perspective, those under (b) had to be written with full access to all intelligence material. The two jobs, therefore, were mutually exclusive. To further confound matters, the general view prevalent amongst the JIC members was that the APS was the 'JIC in permanent session'. To the JIC's Secretary, Lieutenant Colonel Stephen N. Shoosmith, the role of the APS was clear: 'they are in fact the JIC Drafting Committee'.[17]

The APS, therefore, was in an unenviable position from the outset: it could not hope to perform an effective or efficient job in writing as the enemy because it had access to too much information, therefore blighting any objective assessments it tried to produce. This was clearly in evidence in the reaction of the COS to APS papers. Furthermore, it was felt that as APS's work was increasingly becoming concerned with drafting JIC assessments, it was stepping on the toes of the junior JIC, to the detriment of both organisations. An additional complicating factor was the delay in APS papers reaching the COS, having to pass through the JIC first. As a result its chairman, Captain Thomas Troubridge, suggested that it would be better to speed up the system.[18] Troubridge also had another valuable contribution to make, advising his team that it was best to 'never tackle the difficult matter on the agenda first. Bring it up about an hour before lunch and it will be settled quickly.'[19] At a meeting in early May 1941, the JIC unanimously decided that the APS would, forthwith, 'function as the drafting Sub-Committee of the JIC'.[20] This change was recognised by the COS who, anxious that the APS was becoming overburdened with drafting, instructed the JIC to ensure that both tasks could be fulfilled adequately. Assurances were, of course, given.[21]

It is this organisational alteration which, above all else, signalled the start of the JIC's growth into maturity. In practice it now meant that the APS would draft all JIC papers. Once a first draft was prepared it would be distributed to the various Services' intelligence departments for discussion and perusal by the Directors who would then, once a week, convene to discuss, amend and ultimately approve and disseminate the papers.[22] Comparing this to the modern Assessments Staff and Current Intelligence Groups shows how little processes have changed and thus how significant this decision was.

Even at the time it was recognised that this was an important change. Earlier in June 1940 the decision had been taken for the JIC's junior secretariat to draft reports, which would only be discussed by the senior JIC if there were wide divergences of opinion – this may explain why there are so many assessments which are never referred to in the minutes of the full committee.[23] The introduction of APS as the drafters meant that the junior JIC was no longer needed and so the APS now became, as Hinsley has observed, 'the inner committee of the JIC.'[24] This was significant for it ensured that the JIC could occupy itself with other matters while the APS could spend its time preparing reports, which would then be discussed at JIC meetings if and when necessary.[25]

At the end of May the JIC and the JPS met and discussed future collaboration. Here, for the first time officially, the APS was referred to as the 'Joint Intelligence Staff' (JIS), a title that was to stick until a re-organisation took place in 1968.[26] The close relationship between intelligence and planning meant, according to a memorandum by Air Vice Marshal Charles Medhurst, the Assistant Chief of the Air Staff (Intelligence), that it was now increasingly obvious that an 'appreciation of the situation from our own point of view and that of the enemy' was needed, and that this could only be possible if certain changes were made. On a practical level it was suggested that both organisations should be moved into the same building. It was further proposed that both the JIC and the JPS share a common secretariat, though this was sensibly rejected.[27]

The central tenet of the JIS's work was based on the principles of Cabinet government – which also underpinned the JIC's work – namely that the COS should be given assessments based on consensus, with one unanimous view. In essence the JIS had two main duties, defined as: '(a) to think out and produce drafts on subjects submitted by Directors of Intelligence, COS; (b) to assist the Directors of Plans and Joint Planning Staffs by providing the information required by them for the problems they have under consideration.'[28] The JIS practice of producing drafts was as follows: a topic would be chosen; each representative would research the matter; and it would be 'exhaustively discussed' by the relevant experts when required. During the discussion one of the assistants, usually Donald McLachlan (Royal Naval Volunteer Reserve and subsequent author of *Room 39*), would take notes and in doing so produce the first draft of the assessment. Once polished it would be forwarded to the Service Directors of Intelligence.[29] In practice, as one JIS member has recollected, drafting of papers would typically be started at 9pm and finished at 5am in time for JIC meetings.[30] The JIS was to liaise daily with the JIC Secretariat to keep the main Committee informed of progress.

The creation of the JIS was a success. As the DMI, Davidson subsequently testified, 'having got a highly trained body of professionally competent officers, who can produce high grade inter-service papers . . . [they] have strung together the fruits of the labour of the Intelligence sections into an admirable paper.'[31] It was not without its problems though. Captain Stuart Paton was the first naval representative on the JIS. He has recalled the difficulties from the outset in persuading the Directors of Intelligence of the urgent need to read some of the JIS papers; a greater problem still was getting all the Directors' together to resolve differences in opinion. These difficulties, according to Paton, were soon ironed out and the system proved to be invaluable.[32]

At the same time the COS, in a move designed to further integrate the intelligence and planning machineries, decided in April 1941 that the JIC itself, or a representative of the Committee, should now attend COS meetings every Tuesday. The idea was that the JIC should 'give a brief summary of the general situation and to report any dangerous developments', and their presence meant they could answer questions put to them by the Chiefs.[33] This stemmed from the decision taken after the fall of Norway that the JIC should track developments, not just provide intelligence snapshots of events. It was decided that the JIC would hold a weekly meeting, immediately prior to attending the COS meeting, to ensure that any 'outstanding business' was cleared up.[34] As it transpired, meetings with the COS would not always be as frequent as once a week, but certainly this was a significant move by the Chiefs. The overall result of these changes was that the JIC was now brought wholly into the planning aspects of the war effort. At the JIS level, too, close relations with the planners were forged. Major Gordon Waterfield, a member of the JIS, has written that much of its work 'consisted in [providing] quick answers for the Planners'.[35]

Did these various organisational changes, both in terms of the JIC structure and its relationship to the planners, actually make any difference? In early June Major General Davidson circulated a minute amongst the JIC representatives that sheds some light on this. He commented that 'the fact is that many JIC papers do not go to the COS at all, or if they do they are merely noted, as the COS are very busy with problems of immediate urgency.'[36] The question then, is that if the COS were paying very little attention to the JIC, why had its stature risen? Some of the answers were provided by Cavendish-Bentinck, who responded to Davidson by saying that each Service Director passed relevant papers directly to his respective Chief of Staff, thereby meaning that many of the JIC papers reached the individual Chiefs, even though they circumvented the COS committee itself.[37]

Furthermore, many of the JIC papers found their way to the COS through the JPS. In short, by the summer of 1941 the intelligence and planning components of Britain's war fighting capability had become unified, in what DMI Major General Davidson described as a 'balanced machinery'.[38] This would be fortuitous timing, for the war would suddenly turn eastwards.

Germany Turns Eastward

One of the major pre-war quandaries had been to determine to which side the Soviet Union would ally itself. The Nazi-Soviet pact of August 1939 had revealed a partial but not necessarily definitive answer. Since the outbreak of war the JIC had debated whether the Soviet Union would enter the conflict and, if so, in what circumstances. Many of the initial assessments had concentrated on the security of Soviet oil supplies,[39] but subsequent papers examined its policies towards various regions along the periphery.[40] Following the cessation of the Russo-Finnish war in March 1940, the JIC considered its strategic implications by providing answers to a series of specific questions set by the JPS. Victory over Finland implied that significant Soviet forces would be available for use elsewhere, either on its Western Front or to oppose German expansion into South-East Europe. The conflict had provided two immediate advantages for the Soviet Union:

(1) The strengthening of her position against Germany which is one of the immediate, as well as long-term objectives of Soviet policy.
(2) The territorial gains on the Finnish mainland will facilitate Bolshevik cultural revolution into Sweden and Norway as well as Finland itself in pursuit of the world revolution which is another long-term objective of Soviet policy.[41]

Despite acknowledging that the Russians feared a German attack at some stage, the majority of assessments produced by the JIC in the summer of 1940 suggested that Germany's next major offensive would be against the United Kingdom, and in a series of papers addressing Germany's 'next move' produced in late 1940, the suggestion that Hitler might move eastwards was seemingly never envisaged.[42]

By spring 1941 the JIC concluded that Germany's next move would take place in the Eastern Mediterranean, possibly followed by attacks in the Western Mediterranean.[43] This was followed by a more detailed paper in April, focussing on the Mediterranean island of Crete. The conclusion, highly accurate as subsequent events would reveal, was not only that an attack was 'certain', but that Germany would utilise airborne troops as an invading force.[44] On 20 May 1941 the Germans launched Operation MERCURY, the invasion of Crete.

One of the first papers on German attitudes towards the Soviet Union was produced by FOES in January 1941. This argued that the only circumstance in which Germany would attack the Soviet Union would be in time of 'dire necessity'.[45] A further FOES paper in March repeated this belief. It was written as if by the German High Command and stated that 'there is no reason to change our long standing decision to postpone the settlement of accounts with Russia until England has been crushed'.[46] Such a categorical viewpoint was overturned just a fortnight later by FOES' successor body, the APS. The APS wrote that two events had irrevocably altered its assessment of Germany's eastward policy: 1) the German invasion of Yugoslavia on 6 April, which had not been anticipated; and 2) the existence of a number of intelligence reports that suggested that the Germans were readying themselves to attack the Soviet Union. Despite recognising this German aspiration, it was still concluded that a 'direct attack on Russia is unlikely at present'; yet it was also accepted that Germany's military preparations in the east would continue, as this could provide the basis for an invading army or, at the very least, would 'provide a threat'.[47]

The first clues as to the JIC's thinking reveal a sharp divergence of opinion on the matter. Briefing the COS Committee personally, DMI Davidson suggested that there would be no advantage to Germany in attacking Russia, though if it did, this would not happen until early autumn. Cavendish-Bentinck, conversely, reflected the FO line that the threat to Russia was a serious one and would develop much sooner than the autumn.[48] Although considering where else Germany might strike next, including several assessments on Hitler's policies towards Spain and Portugal, the JIC finally turned its attention towards producing an assessment on the Soviet Union in mid-May 1941.

To make its paper more accessible for the COS, the JIC adopted its earlier principle of producing a detailed report, together with a cover note that highlighted the main conclusions. These revealed that assessments had, once more, vacillated. It was now concluded that 'indications' suggested that 'a new agreement between the two countries may be nearly complete', thereby reversing the APS' earlier assessment. This was supported by a line of reasoning that Germany's major focus was on procuring economic resources and therefore a war with Russia would be detrimental to the overall war effort; instead, Germany would try to exert pressure on Russia to sign a new agreement, granting it various economic concessions. In conclusion the JIC added a warning: 'if in the course of negotiations she [Germany] sees no prospect of reaching agreement she will implement her threat of force'. The assessment was based on detailed sound reasoning, and although not specifying the intelligence basis, Hinsley shows that both human and signals intelligence played a role. Certainly there would have been adequate intelligence coverage, for the JIC confidently ended by commenting that 'from present intelligence, agreement is the more likely event.'[49]

As we now know, information provided through the breaking of German cyphers revealed that Hitler's plans were of a military nature. This raises the question over the access that members of the JIS, and indeed the JIC, had to intelligence material. During the war ULTRA – the reading of the German Enigma codes – was one of the most closely guarded secrets. Certainly the three Services' Directors of Intelligence were on the list of those cleared to see material from the outset, as was Menzies, given SIS's control of GC&CS. According to a distribution list produced in April 1940, which may be illustrative of access, then neither Cavendish-Bentinck, the MEW or MI5 representatives, or the Secretary were privy.[50] If anything, the list of those cleared to use Sigint was tightened as the war went on, a decision on which the Directors of Intelligence were directly involved.[51] At some point though, Cavendish-Bentinck was indoctrinated and allowed access,[52] as was the JIC Secretary, Denis Capel-Dunn. Indeed, Capel-Dunn was involved with a complaint in late 1942 about how widely known was the existence of ULTRA.[53]

Years later Cavendish-Bentinck recalled that all the JIC members had become ULTRA-cleared with the exception of Vickers, the new MEW representative.[54] Churchill, who was a keen devourer of single source intelligence, was also particularly susceptible to believing ULTRA material. The difficulty was the COS did not like him receiving intelligence which had not been properly assessed. Consequently, as Cavendish-Bentinck recalled, 'it was arranged that this material should be evaluated by the JIC'.[55] In addition, it is clear that the JIS members, who would go back to their parent departments in the search for all relevant information, would also have had access.[56] One of the great difficulties was, as the DNI later recalled, in 'preserving the security of the source'. This was especially tricky as the Services' personnel had greater access to the breadth of ULTRA material than their FO colleagues.[57] The Battle of the Atlantic, for instance, was an Admiralty matter and one in which the JIC played only a peripheral part. Being operational in nature, Admiralty reports bypassed the JIC on the way to the COS Committee. Where the JIC was involved, through the ad hoc meetings of one of its sub-committees, the Inter-Services Security Board, was in the security of information and protection of convoys.

Kennedy Walker-Sloan, one of the FO members of the JIS, has said that without ULTRA they would have been 'fumbling all over the place'.[58] Rear Admiral John Godfrey, the DNI, was even more forthright:

> If, therefore, there had been a turning off of the top of S.I. [Special Intelligence, or ULTRA material], before the end of the war, and before the result was beyond any reasonable doubt, the intelligence directorates would have been hard put to find those capable, by a keen analytical examination of the lesser grades of intelligence, of producing an accurate forecast or estimate of the enemy's intentions and dispositions.[59]

Ronald Lewin has described how, as the war went on, Cavendish-Bentinck became increasingly convinced of the importance of ULTRA in JIC assessments.[60] Indeed, in discussions Cavendish-Bentinck confirmed to Lewin that 'ULTRA was central to its [the JIC's] operations'.[61]

A week after the May 1941 assessment the JIC had, once more, revised its viewpoint. It was now concluded, with confidence, that Germany would make good its threat of force, with a probable date for action being the end of June.[62] Noel Annan, a member of military intelligence and who would later join the JIC structure, has commented on the difficulties Cavendish-Bentinck faced in persuading his JIC colleagues that Germany's intentions against the Soviet Union were hostile. According to Annan, it was the accumulation of information provided by ULTRA that persuaded the Committee that Cavendish-Bentinck was right.[63] The following day the COS were briefed on the large German military build-up.[64] Hinsley criticises the apparatus for being slow to react to Germany's eastward moves. He identifies the fact that other considerations distorted the picture, including an early example of the 'cry wolf' syndrome – that there had been rumours about German plans to invade the USSR that predated Hitler's decision, so that when more concrete information was obtained, it was dismissed. A further complicating factor was the British government's attempts to entice the Soviet Union away from Germany.[65]

Hinsley generally exonerates the JIC from blame; instead pointing the finger at the FO and the fact that diplomatic information was allowed to override military and political intelligence.[66] Meanwhile, ULTRA information increasingly suggested that German moves were hostile. In assessing that war was likely, the JIC took it upon themselves to produce a detailed report on what the effects of a German-Soviet war would be. The report was overwhelmingly focussed on military and economic factors, without predicting who might win or what the greater impact on the war in general would be.[67] To be ready for all eventualities, the JIC also prepared a paper on the effects of a German-Soviet rapprochement.[68] Neither document assessed the likely course of events, and so a third paper was penned at the same time, which was unequivocal in its conclusion: 'fresh evidence is now at hand that Hitler has made up his mind to have done with Soviet obstruction to Germany and intends to attack her . . . matters are likely to come to a head during the second half of June.'[69] Intelligence was able to reveal something of Hitler's intentions and could postulate a timeframe.

On 22 June 1941, the event that Churchill had described as 'too good to be true' happened, with over three million German troops crossing the border into the Soviet Union, along a 1500 mile long front.[70] Major General John Kennedy, the Director of Military Operations and Plans in the War Office, recalled that 22 June was a 'hot stuffy' day in London. He had been alerted to the attack at 0700, commenting in his diary that 'the thieves have fallen out'.[71] The immediate summaries that presumably would have been produced by the JIC are lost, along with the rest of the daily reports. From COS records it is clear that the JIC was charged with 'keeping a day to day watch on the position'.[72] Almost immediately the JIC met, and although any discussion of the invasion itself was not recorded, it did deliberate about how intelligence could be transmitted to the British liaison mission in Moscow.[73]

The first detailed assessments following the onslaught of Operation BARBAROSSA considered the impact of the attack on Germany's plans to invade Britain, something that the intelligence community had always thought would precede any invasion of the Soviet Union.[74] The first assessments of the progress of the war itself were hugely pessimistic about the Soviet Union's chances of survival, and focussed on the implications of an impending surrender. The possibility was also aired that Germany might make a peace offer to the United Kingdom, though it was assumed that such a move would be vehemently rejected by the government.[75] A subsequent report stressed that it was unlikely the Soviet Union would surrender and that they would fight to the bitter end, something which it was thought Hitler would try to neutralise as quickly as possible so that the German forces could then extricate themselves.[76]

As it was, the initial pace of progress of the German army was not maintained. Despite only having 'not very exact' information as to the rate of advance, by August the JIC noted the reduction in pace, and the tone of the assessment is almost one of surprise at the resilience of the Soviet Union.[77] In September the JIC re-assessed the nature of the German advance. It was noted that the German High Command must have been surprised at the levels of resistance faced, and that there was evidence that plans were being put in place for 'a winter in Russia'. On a broader level the JIC also considered morale both within the German armed forces and at home, discounting the suggestion that Hitler had become unpopular and concluding that 'Germany is far from breaking point'.[78] As the weather on the Eastern Front worsened the JIC produced a further update on the situation, concluding that the 'length and wastage of the Russian campaign' had utilised Germany's best troops, and that a period of rest would be needed before any further fronts or large-scale invasions could be planned.[79] The following month, in December, the JIC produced an assessment based on the first six months of the Soviet campaign. Its conclusion was that the German military was 'stretched to its utmost'.[80] With the German army floundering in the snow, attention would be sharply refocused by events in the Pacific, which would, decisively, bring the United States into the war.

Relations with the United States

The United Kingdom and the United States had first discussed military equipment and plans in 1937.[81] There had been relatively little discussion of intelligence; what there had been was confined to dialogue between the two navies. In the first months of 1940 intelligence relations were extended with the creation of British Security Co-ordination – the SIS office in New York responsible for liaison with the Americans; and by the visit of several FBI officers to London.[82] In June 1940 General Raymond Lee was sent to London as military attaché and head of intelligence. Lee had previously been the military attaché in London from 1935–9, but had been recalled to Washington upon the outbreak of war to 'whip American peacetime soldiers into shape'. As the early months of the war proceeded and the German army advanced, 'his superiors decided that once again he was the man America needed in London'.[83]

In July 1940, on the insistence of the President, an American representative, Colonel William Donovan, was despatched to London as the President's Special Envoy. A veteran of the First World War, Donovan had earned the nickname 'Wild Bill' in recognition of his fearless nature. He spent most of the interwar period as an attorney in New York, before becoming one of President's Roosevelt's trusted aides.[84] Colonel Donovan's primary role was to assess Britain's chances – both in terms of its ability and its will – to withstand a German invasion, and whilst in London in July 1940 he met Churchill and the various intelligence chiefs.[85] Perhaps as a response, the JIC was instructed in August by the Director of Plans to prepare a memorandum on how Washington, in organisational terms, was approaching the war.[86] The same month it was decided that the Dominion Wire, a regular product based on the JIC's daily summary, should be forwarded to the US Ambassador in London, with Lord Lothian, the British Ambassador in Washington, also instructed to show it to President Roosevelt.[87]

In late August 1940 a meeting was held in London between the British COS and Brigadier General George Strong, the Assistant Chief of Staff for the US Army. At the meeting Strong disclosed the fact that the Americans were reading Japanese codes and that 'considerable progress' had been made in reading Italian ones. In fact, knowledge of the US breaking Japanese codes had first been communicated to the then CIGS, Field Marshal Lord Gort, two years previously, but the 1940 meeting was far more significant as it was proposed by Strong that the time was now ripe for the free exchange of intelligence.[88] This was agreed by the COS, and a few weeks later President Roosevelt approved the dissemination of all relevant information to the British. In early 1941 a succession of further meetings strengthened this new alliance at a time when, it should be borne in mind, the United States had not yet entered the war.[89]

On a further fact-finding mission in March 1941, Colonel Donovan attended a joint JIC/JPS meeting, informing them of his visits to Spain, the Middle East and the Balkans.[90] The JIC was also involved in discussions about the means by which American information would be transmitted back to the UK.[91] The timing was opportune: in March 1941 the US had approved the Lend-Lease Act, thereby allowing defence and other supplies to be passed across the Atlantic. Donovan's appointment in June 1941 as 'Coordinator of Intelligence' was welcomed by the British, including one FO official, who noted that he 'should prove a very good man from our point of view'.[92] Yet despite all this, the British remained sceptical of the intelligence benefits the Americans could offer. Cavendish-Bentinck, for instance, wrote in a fascinating minute how 'we must bear in mind that Washington is far worse informed than ourselves (odd as this may seem to those who complain of our intelligence) . . . I believe that their intelligence departments are primitive and rather inexperienced . . . there is little contact or collaboration between American Government Departments.'[93]

Cavendish-Bentinck's last point, about the lack of co-ordination in the American machinery, was increasingly vexing the British. In June 1941, Rear Admiral Godfrey, the DNI, visited the United States.[94] In reporting back to the JIC he also referred to the problems and about the need to create 'a joint intelligence machinery at Washington'.[95] At the same time General Lee, the US representative in London, wrote to Washington emphasising the 'necessity for a Joint Intelligence Committee in Washington.' The justification was a strong endorsement of what Lee had encountered in London: 'we cannot get along much longer without something like this. The Joint Committees here are so numerous and so effective that nothing that comes to the attention of any department fails to reach all the others in a very short time'.[96]

In the meantime, as Godfrey informed the London JIC, two British bodies had been created: a 'senior' and a 'junior' JIC (Washington). Both were set up along the lines of the London JIC, with representatives from the same organisations as permanent members. The Chairman of the 'senior' Committee was Major General Frederick Beaumont-Nesbitt, former DMI and chair of JIC (London). The 'senior' JIC was only to meet on matters of major policy. By contrast, the 'junior' JIC(W) met every day and was tasked with collating all information from the US government and producing reports that were dispatched daily to London. It was also tasked with liaising with relevant American authorities and distributing London JIC assessments as necessary. Finally, it was at the beck and call of the American Joint Chiefs of Staff, 'for such purposes as they see fit'.[97] In practice, the 'senior' British committee had never met by the time Beaumont-Nesbitt stood down as Chairman in October 1941, and it was decided that the 'junior' JIC should drop its prefix as it was unlikely the 'senior' committee would actually ever meet.[98]

Although the JIC had been involved in the creation of overseas intelligence structures before, JIC(W) was a novel move.[99] Here, for the first time, was the creation of a body designed specifically to manage the intelligence relations of two countries.[100] Cavendish-Bentinck's initial reaction was one of unease. He informed Sir Alexander Cadogan, the PUS at the FO, that it 'somewhat disquiets me, as I have always tried to prevent the JIC spreading out.'[101] Although there were bilateral links between the various components of British intelligence and their American counterparts, there was no unified attempt to ensure that material was not duplicated. The creation of JIC(W) therefore, was driven by similar reasons to those which prompted the creation of the JIC itself in 1936. Intelligence exchange between the London and Washington JICs was not always straightforward and there were occasions where JIC(W) complained about the lack of information it was receiving from London. Yet this should not overshadow its main contribution at this time: a direct line of communication between London and Washington.[102] This would prove to be invaluable as the United States was propelled into war.

In creating JIC(W) it was hoped that it might 'induce' the Americans to set up their own co-ordinating body.[103] Initially, at least, such developments were not regarded favourably by the Americans. Despite these British moves and Lee's impassioned pleas from London, it would be some time before an American equivalent to the JIC was created. According to a note received by Lee from Colonel Hayes Kroner, who would soon become the head of the War Department's Military Intelligence Service, the War Department had serious reservations:

(1) We are not going to copy British organisation and procedure.
(2) We are not convinced that such a central clearing house and assimilating centre are needed here.
(3) It is far more difficult to put into effect than Lee imagines.
(4) The 'high ups' still don't feel the danger of incompleteness in their information.
(5) The fact that Beaumont-Nesbitt, Godfrey and Noel Hall are here and that they serve in the Joint Intelligence Committee and recommend it, is having an unfavourable effect.

(6) The British have not been successful, so far, in the war; why should they advise us?

(7) Many other alarmingly ignorant and prejudiced reactions.[104]

Eventually the Americans began to change their mind, assisted largely by Donovan's appointment and the fact that he had gained Roosevelt's confidence.[105] So, in early 1942, an American JIC was finally created, comprising representatives from the directors of intelligence from the army and navy (there was no separate air force at this time), State Department, Board of Economic Warfare, and Donovan, the Co-ordinator of Information.[106] Both the American JIC, and the JIC(Washington), would work closely with the main JIC in London. Following its creation in 1942 they would also work closely with the Anglo-American 'Combined Intelligence Committee', which reported to the Combined Staff Planners, in turn responsible to the Combined Chiefs of Staff.[107]

War in the Far East

Although the war raging in Europe occupied the majority of the JIC's time, increasingly the threat of war in the Far East became an important consideration. Part of the reason for this was that so much less was known about the region, with collection priorities having been reduced in the inter-war period, seriously hampering SIS' capabilities.[108] The Far East was crucial to Britain, not least for the security of the Empire. Yet the general consensus from a number of detailed studies of British intelligence and the Japanese threat in the build-up to Pearl Harbor is that the Japanese military were misunderstood by Britain; and the idea that they might pose a threat was never seriously entertained.[109]

British intelligence first turned its attention to the Far East in 1929, following the rise of the Nationalist Guomindang and the threat posed to British commercial interests, when it was realised that very little was known about China. Thereafter, both SIS and GC&CS began to collect information, though problems – primarily the unreliability of reporting – continued to plague their efforts.[110] In the 1930s the JIC had spent some time examining the lessons of the Sino-Japanese war, as part of its larger study on the Spanish civil war and the use of aerial bombardment. No attention had been focussed on Japan itself; indeed, the first JIC paper was not produced until May 1940. Other papers had been produced on the threat to British interests in the Middle East and various parts of Africa; it was, however, the first paper to question Japanese intentions in the region. The planners emphasised its importance by stressing that although the COS had not asked for it, 'it is an issue which will very shortly have to be faced'.[111] The overwhelming tone of the JIC assessment was that Japanese intentions were indeed hostile, although they might not act against Britain because of their commitments elsewhere in the region. It was emphasised that 'from a strategical point of view the danger of a clash with the United States appears to outweigh all other considerations'.[112]

Following a request by the Colonial Office, the JIC turned its attention to the region again the following month, in June 1940, concluding that a maximum of three days warning should be expected before any Japanese attack.[113] Across Whitehall, the consensus amongst senior planners was that while Japan was inherently cautious, it was recognised that it was also ambitious.[114] This dichotomy was certainly in evidence in the JIC's assessment in September regarding Japanese intentions vis-à-vis Indochina.[115] A further report, completed at the same time, concentrated on Malaya and included very detailed forecasts as to how long it would take Japan to stage an attack. It concluded with a sombre note of caution: 'it is unlikely that warning of these preparations would be available to us'.[116]

These various reports stemmed, it seems, from no fresh intelligence (there was a general lack of evidence on Japanese intentions), but rather a desire by the COS to cater for all eventualities. Hence, further JIC reports were prepared, including on Japanese chemical warfare capabilities, and a further assessment of Japanese policy towards Indochina and Malaya. Throughout, the fate of Singapore was of primary concern. An integral component of the Empire, Singapore was important to Britain, not least as a naval staging post in the Pacific and the largest overseas base east of Suez. From August 1939 the Far Eastern Combined Bureau had been based in Singapore – a Services' intelligence centre that was in daily contact with London. Problems remained, however, with collecting information. In October 1940 the JPS had commented on how 'SIS is not functioning in Japan', with the result that 'we cannot rely upon receiving from Japan any information of the assembly and despatch of an expedition' towards Singapore.[117] The complaint was reiterated in January 1941, when it was emphasised that 'little or no reliance is placed upon SIS information'.[118] As a result an SIS representative was sent from London to improve matters.[119]

Sigint, too, was lacking and it was perhaps the paucity of accurate intelligence that led to a war scare in February 1941. Reports were received in late January, suggesting that the Japanese were mobilising a large expeditionary force in the region around Formosa. The JIC was immediately tasked with investigating whether this was a hostile move that could lead to war. Its report began with a warning caveat that the final move for war was never likely to be 'affirmed', hence an assessment had to be based on a balance of probabilities. These suggested that Japan was 'ready to run the risk' of launching hostilities, and that the most likely target for an attack would be the Dutch East Indies.[120] However, the threat failed to materialise. Almost simultaneously, the Americans presented GC&CS with its own machine for reading Japanese cypher traffic.[121]

In April 1941 the JIC approved its most detailed report to date on Japan. The APS prepared a lengthy assessment on Japanese strategy, concluding that economic pressures meant that Japan would become progressively weaker whilst at the same time the defences in Singapore would strengthen: therefore 'the incentive will be to attack sooner rather than later'. It was thought that Japanese strategy would be directed towards expanding southwards. Despite such a confident assurance, no detailed forecast was given as to whether this was actually likely to happen, or indeed when such an attack might take place.[122] The war scare of February may have affected JIC thinking, because when similar reports emerged of Japanese troop movements in April, they were readily discounted.[123]

There is certainly evidence that thinking with regard to the Japanese threat was changing at this time. In an absorbing minute, the ever-astute DMI, Major General Davidson, wrote how 'recent experience has shown that we cannot guarantee any definite warning of Japanese military operations'. The requirement was clear, 'the time has come to adopt a more aggressive intelligence policy in the Far East'.[124]

The general idea was to use Consuls in the Far East as the channels through which intelligence could be passed to London. Furthermore, 'C' suggested that SIS send an officer into Japan itself.[125] All intelligence in the Far East was to be centralised through the Far Eastern Combined Bureau, with further steps taken to completely integrate British and American intelligence on the Far East.[126] This would be the first time that the JIC effectively undertook management of the intelligence community, identifying gaps in intelligence coverage and deciding, as a Committee, how they should be plugged.

The picture by the summer of 1941 was changing. Up to this point intelligence collection had clearly been deficient, but steps were being taken to remedy this through an increased SIS presence in the region and by codebreaking, together with the opportunities presented through the formalising of links with US intelligence. The assumptions underlying the assessments had also changed. It was no longer thought probable that any forewarning would be given of a Japanese attack. Such a conclusion was borne out by the Japanese occupation of southern Indochina in July, the northern part of the country having been overrun in September 1940. By August 1941 it was felt that the next Japanese move would be against Thailand, which would be 'swift and sudden, and we shall receive only very short notice.'[127]

A Russo-Japanese neutrality pact had been signed in April 1941, but attention was also focussed on whether Japan would attempt to attack Siberia, now that the Soviet Union was engaged in a war with Germany, and whether various fronts could be attacked simultaneously. In mid-November the JIC revisited its previous assessments on Japanese intentions. In July the Americans had imposed a trade embargo on Japan, which had had a disastrous impact on the Japanese economy. Although it was unlikely Japan had reached a decision on a course of action, its increasingly dire economic situation meant that it would imminently be faced with having to make the decision one way or another. The main options were economic capitulation, launching an offensive against the UK and the US, or getting further involved in the war in China. Of these, it was thought that the primary course of action would be to try and resolve matters diplomatically with the US; if this failed (and it was not stated whether this was likely or not), then there would be war, probably starting against Thailand as this posed the least risk of bringing in the major powers.[128]

By this time American intelligence, and by extension British intelligence and thence the JIC, had reasonably good access to Japanese cyphers, providing a degree of confidence in their assertions. Perhaps as a result, in late November the JIC produced its most detailed forecast to date on the subject. It considered, once more, where an attack might take place. The underlying rationale behind the assessment was still the belief that, at heart, the Japanese were cautious; hence, it was thought unlikely that the Japanese navy would split its main fleet. Furthermore, the presence of the main American Pacific Fleet at the Pearl Harbor naval base, Honolulu, together with Dutch and British ships elsewhere, would act as a possible deterrent.[129]

By the end of November the Japanese-American discussions had effectively broken down.[130] At this time the sense conveyed by JIC papers was of the inevitability of war: the difficulty lay in determining precisely where, when and how it would come. On 2 December the JIC was instructed to prepare a daily telegram on the situation in the Far East for Air Chief Marshal Sir Robert Brooke-Popham, the Commander in Chief, Far East.[131] Through its reading of Japanese traffic, GC&CS received some warning of Japan's true intentions, but these are more easily understood with hindsight than they would have been at the time.[132] When war did come, with devastating efficiency, it was not unexpected strategically but the location and scope of Japan's attack was a tactical surprise.[133]

The simultaneous declaration of war by Japan on the United Kingdom and the United States propelled America into the war. Churchill, with his usual clarity, informed the COS that 'this removes all political difficulty from initiating naval or air action' [against Japan].[134] The JIC's immediate task was not to investigate why it had been unable to predict the attacks, but to estimate what Japan's next move might be. It was concluded that Japanese intentions were to remove all Allied power from East Asia: therefore Malaya and Singapore were primary targets.[135]

By this time the war was truly global in nature. One of the first consequences for the new allies was to further increase Anglo-American exchange of intelligence through strengthening liaison channels.[136] Domestically, plans were made to give the JIC an increased role in operational affairs (see below). The JIC was producing a stream of papers, ranging from analyses of Axis offensives in North Africa, through the status of the German front in the Soviet Union and German threats to Turkey, the Caucasus and Malta, to internal morale within Italy and Germany. In addition it was still involved with administrative tasks, including the aliens, refugee and war registers, the creation of various interrogation centres abroad, deception plans, propaganda efforts, and liaison relations. Amidst this effort, concerns over the Far East and Britain's Empire continued unabated. This was, therefore, a Committee heavily burdened but also vital to the continuing and increasing war effort.

Following the Japanese incursion into Malaya, the Philippines, Hong Kong and Borneo, a number of papers produced in late December 1941 looked at where Japan might strike next, focussing principally on the Dutch East Indies (latter day Indonesia) and South Africa.[137] The most likely course, so the JIC concluded, was for the Japanese to move south against Sumatra, thereby cutting off British access to Malayan aerodromes.[138] Surprisingly, although it neighboured Sumatra, a Japanese attack on Singapore was never seriously considered. The reasoning behind this was similar to American preconceptions on Pearl Harbor – given the size and strength of forces there, it was felt that any Japanese attack would be suicidal and therefore inconceivable. What is more surprising is that the lessons of Pearl Harbor were not heeded: previous assumptions that the Japanese were cautious were never seriously re-evaluated by the JIC.

Following the Japanese invasion of Malaya on 8 December 1941, there had been a series of bloody battles which the Japanese had dominated. In retreat, at the end of January 1942 the final British troops left Malaya, blowing up the causeway between Johore and Singapore in the process. Dressed as Singaporean civilians, a number of Japanese crossed in rubber dinghies. At the same time the JIC received several reports from military commanders that Japanese forces were amassing nearby. In replying to regional field commanders, the JIC informed them that although 'we have here [in London] no repeat no evidence other than is available to you', it was concluded that an attack 'might . . . start at any time'.[139] From 3 February British forces were bombarded by Japanese aerial attack, and on 8 February Japanese forces invaded the island. On 15 February Lieutenant General Arthur Percival, the General Officer Commanding Malaya, surrendered, signalling the largest military capitulation in British history. Percival would later be a spectator in Tokyo Bay to Japan's surrender in 1945.

Had British intelligence failed in the Far East? A distinction needs to be drawn here between intelligence and policy. On reflection the JIC's performance was mixed: it was rarely wide of the mark, and strategically its assessments were accurate; yet there was one notable strategic failure, and it would prove to be significant: the inability to realise that Japan would attack both the UK and the US simultaneously. In the aftermath Major General Davidson had his own study produced, looking back at a vast number of JIC predictions and gauging their accuracy. His conclusion was that the 'JIC estimate of sequence of events and scales of attack were on the whole good.'[140] This was supported by a post-war retrospective report by the then DNI Rear Admiral Godfrey. In considering the importance of JIC reports of 1941, Godfrey concluded that 'the War Cabinet and COS Committee was fully and accurately advised as to Japanese intentions and preparations'.[141]

At a strategic level the JIC forecasts were sound, though they failed to heed the lesson of 7 December where Japan threw caution to the wind. More problematic was tactical intelligence, which was repeatedly lacking. Intelligence collection efforts in the Far East had made a slow start, and it was not until 1941 that SIS and GC&CS began to really penetrate Japanese intentions. Also, the JIC focussed on the quantity of Japanese forces and failed to look at their quality. As with intelligence during the Spanish civil war, it was assumed that there was a difference between 'first' order powers like Germany, and 'second' order powers like Spain. So it was with Japan. Views of the Japanese, starting with Churchill and working downwards, were stereotypical.[142] The Japanese were seen as technically and militarily inferior, and even if this had been the case, the implications for strategy were never entertained. When backed into a corner, facing a militarily superior enemy, an asymmetric attack is an attractive proposition. Japan in 1941 was neither the first nor the last country to employ such a tactic. Thus, while strategic assessments were made as to Japanese intentions, little was done to portray the threat that Japan posed, with devastating effect on policy.

Intelligence for Planning; Planning for Intelligence

The 1942 JIC was still housed in the Cabinet War Offices on Great George Street. The introduction of the JIS as the drafters for the Committee had revolutionised how it operated. Captain Thomas Haddon (Army), the Deputy JIC Secretary appointed in November 1941, explained how the system worked:

> . . . usually what happened was that they [JIS] had a meeting at which they put over their parent office's view, then the Secretary produced a working draft. At the next meeting the team corrected that draft, a revised draft was then prepared by the Secretary and so on until they were all satisfied, and the final paper was produced by the Secretary and circulated in the main Committee. Usually this was approved be it either by telephone, or if there was time, at a meeting, before being sent to the Chiefs of Staff Committee, or whoever had asked for it in the first place.[143]

Although most commentators ascribe the Committee's wartime successes to the quality of its chairman, mention also needs to be made of the Secretary's role. Denis Capel-Dunn had become Assistant Secretary in 1941, though it was not until November 1942 that he became the main secretary. Born in Leipzig in 1903, Capel-Dunn studied Modern Languages with History at Trinity College, Cambridge, though it appears that he never graduated.[144] Following a brief spell in the Diplomatic Service, including a stint at the British Embassy in Havana, Capel-Dunn read for the Bar and in 1938 started practise as a Barrister. He was involved with the enquiry into the sinking of HMS Thetis, a submarine disaster in which ninety-nine people had lost their lives.[145]

Capel-Dunn was also a member of the Essex Regiment Territorial Army, had attended the Junior War Staff Course at Camberley in 1940 and held a military rank of Lieutenant Colonel.[146] He seems to have divided opinion, with John Colvin, who knew Capel-Dunn through their membership of the St James' Club, recalling him as 'very fat, extremely boring . . . his conversations were hideously detailed and humourless. We all disliked him very much indeed'.[147] Yet this was a minority view. Noel Annan called Capel-Dunn 'secretive' and 'elusive'; while Major General Davidson, called him 'extremely capable'.[148] The wife of Thomas Haddon, who knew Capel-Dunn as their husbands worked together, recalled that 'despite his rather bizarre personality', he had great 'ability and character'.[149] The Directing Office of his Staff Course commented on his attributes: 'quick brain, level-headed, wide outlook, calm demeanour, recommended for work in the higher formation'.[150]

The record certainly seems to have been in Capel-Dunn's favour, and his achievements within the JIC and his plans for post-war British intelligence were numerous and significant. It was felt by many members of the Committee that

Capel-Dunn brought an objectivity to proceedings that had been lacking in the past. As Admiral Godfrey subsequently recalled: 'Capel Dunn, a barrister, relieved a regular soldier as Secretary – an improvement as the particular soldier could never forget that he was a soldier.'[151] As Secretary, Capel-Dunn was responsible not just for minute taking, but for ensuring the smooth operation of the Committee. The majority of JIC liaison with other government departments was conducted by him, and he was instrumental in relocating the JIS into the same building as the planners. As the Air Ministry informed its representative in Washington, '. . . Capel Dunn has been very successful in revitalising Intelligence Committee here'.[152] In 1944 he was awarded the OBE in the King's Birthday Honours List. In its recommendation letter the Office of the War Cabinet had written that Capel-Dunn's work on the JIC 'has been an outstanding success. He has organised the work well and he has a clear mind and a flair for the presentation of a case. Moreover, he has the gift of inducing those with whom he works to pull together as a team'.[153]

What of the JIS? Did the various military and civilian members work harmoniously together? There are a few surviving testimonies of JIS veterans, and these reveal the role that departmental affiliations played in the assessment process. As one naval representative, Charles Fletcher-Cooke (who would become MP for Darwen, Lancashire after the war), has recalled, most of the problems being dealt with were not of a naval dimension, so he spent the majority of his time as 'cross-examiner', getting the army, air force and FO representatives to prove their arguments, a very useful challenge function.[154] Furthermore, Noel Annan, a War Office representative (and later Vice-Chancellor of London University), has recalled how the Air Ministry were 'consistent optimists', whereas the War Office were 'consistent pessimists', with the Admiralty being generally ambivalent about most things.[155] Kennedy Walker-Sloan, an FO representative, has described how consensus, generally speaking, was easily reached.[156]

By 1942 the original JIS had a second 'team' created underneath it, responsible for examining more mundane topics, often statistical and less controversial.[157] At this point there were ten members, five in each team, a number that was maintained, more or less, throughout the war. Another important change was initiated in 1942, which served to grant the JIS members more independence:

> Before January 1942, the members of the Joint Intelligence Staff received instructions from their Directors on the general line to be followed before they started to discuss a paper ... it was realised, however, that this arrangement did not give enough flexibility and it was finally agreed not without considerable discussion, that the Joint Intelligence Staff should be left free to work out their own arguments and conclusions. From that time it became very much more important as a body and began to have an entity of its own.[158]

Despite initially expressing a desire that the JIS be moved into the same building as the JPS, this did not immediately take place, yet the JIC, and indeed the COS, were increasingly of the opinion that intelligence had to be brought further into the planning sphere. Indeed, Desmond Morton, Churchill's adviser on intelligence, had earlier written to the Prime Minister to state that 'intelligence' and 'plans' were too 'rigidly' separated.[159]

The JIC had had some experience with planning. Following the failure to foresee the Nazi attack on Norway, a sub-section of the JIC had been created, focussed on the requirements, priorities, and provision of topographical intelligence. Though not strictly a planning role, the rationale behind this was that topographical intelligence would be used for operational purposes.[160] This sub-section of the JIC ensured that a direct channel of communication was maintained with the planners.[161]

In November 1941 the JPS produced a memorandum on the situation. 'It has become apparent', the report began, 'that the existing system . . . is not entirely satisfactory.' Through the JIS, information was gathered for planning purposes – this much was fine – the problem was that the intelligence machinery was becoming overloaded with demands for intelligence, to the detriment of the work and speed of delivery.[162] The response was the creation of a new body, the Intelligence Section (Operations), or IS(O). The instigation of this was organised through a combined meeting of the JIC and JPS, where it was decided that IS(O)'s role would be to 'collate intelligence for operational planning'. It would work under the aegis of the Services' intelligence directors and would be guided and supplied with information by the JIS, but would be administratively linked to the JIC.[163] This was an important move, not only for further cementing the JIC into the planning machinery, but also as it signified a realisation by the JPS that they needed the intelligence community for operational purposes.[164] The duties of the IS(O) were confirmed at the end of December 1941.[165]

A further move was the introduction of a weekly report, produced by the JIS and distributed to the COS by the JIC, on enemy appreciations of Allied plans.[166] These two moves – the creation of an intelligence-derived body for planning purposes; and the decision to focus attention on what the enemy knew about British plans – would become intertwined immediately with planning for Operation TORCH – the Allied invasion of French North Africa in November 1942. For this the intelligence community would have a new role to play: providing assessments of enemy reactions to Allied plans as their armies descended into North Africa.[167]

Unsurprisingly, one of the biggest questions facing the military planners at the start of 1942 was over the future direction of the war. The German army had become bogged down in the Soviet Union, yet Stalin was adamant that a new Allied western front be opened up in order to divert German resources and effort. Many of the American planners were keen to support this in the form of a new cross-Channel offensive, yet British planners favoured, and eventually had approved, a move into French North Africa. The JIC itself had previously produced a number of assessments on North Africa, looking not only at regions where there were British interests, but also French and other colonial powers.[168]

Although complaining about the previous deficiencies in intelligence for planning purposes, the planners did accept some responsibility for not having provided enough direction in the past. They now felt more confident in predicting where information would be needed, and almost immediately produced a large list of regions and topics for which they required intelligence.[169] One commission was for the JIC to produce a paper on North Africa. The request had originated with Churchill and the COS, and may well have stemmed from the Anglo-American military discussions at the time. The JIC's conclusion would be an important one: 'we believe that anything in the nature of an overwhelming force which attempted invasion would meet with a mere token resistance.'[170]

The original British plans for an invasion of French North Africa were code-named Operation GYMNAST. The first discussion of this by the JIC was in December 1941. Here it was merely noted that plans for North Africa were being made and that relevant 'cover' would be adopted in due course.[171] By early 1942 arguments were raging between the British and American JCS as to the best location for invasion, and over the first few months conclusions vacillated wildly.[172] For the first half of 1942 GYMNAST was a constant topic within the intelligence and planning machineries, with the JIS producing a series of papers on aspects of the plan and what resistance might be expected.[173]

An assessment of 'German Intentions' in January 1942 suggested that increased forces were being sent to the Russian front, while in North Africa, attempts would be made to reinforce Rommel's forces in order to seize and exploit oil reserves.[174] Following the fall of Singapore in February, the JIC produced a further series of studies of Axis intentions. It was stated in March that Germany's primary objective was the defeat of the Soviet Union, whereas Japan's was to secure control of East Asia. Importantly, it was concluded that Japan did not want to get involved in the war in Europe, and that she would only fall in line with German objectives where they 'further[ed] her own intentions'.[175]

At this time, in recognition of the increased workload and diverse responsibilities of the Committee, it was decided that the JIC should meet twice a week: on Tuesdays with all the directors present to discuss papers, and on Fridays, with only Cavendish-Bentinck as chair and the Services' deputy-directors present, to discuss administrative matters of a purely military nature.[176] To emphasise how encompassing the JIC's product now was, and the central role it occupied within planning circles, a new survey was instigated, focussing on 'the probable strength, efficiency, equipment, training, and morale of the Axis forces in 1942, economic factors, morale on the home front, and the bearing which these may have on the Axis plans of campaign for this year.'[177]

One of the main American proposals for offensive action in 1942 was Operation SLEDGEHAMMER, a plan for the invasion of North West Europe. As a means of testing its worthiness, the JIC considered a brief paper on the possible reaction in North Africa.[178] There is no record of any discussion of the plan having taken place. In early July, SLEDGEHAMMER was finally rejected by the British COS. Part of the issue was over the priority of focus: the US Joint Chiefs of Staff (JCS) wanted to devote far more American strength to the

Pacific, whereas the British were concerned that this would dilute the war effort against Germany. To settle matters, President Roosevelt dispatched the JCS, together with his personal envoy Harry Hopkins, to London. In sending them, Roosevelt had stated that while the defeat of Japan did not imply the defeat of Germany; the defeat of Germany did imply the defeat of Japan. Therefore, focussing on the European dimension of the Axis threat was central to winning the war.[179]

Meanwhile, the JIC in mid-July was working on a paper about German intentions, which concluded that if the Germans could be driven out of North Africa in 1942, then it would leave them 'faced with a difficult campaign in the spring of 1943.' The assessment satisfied two concerns of the military planners: firstly, the notion the British favoured, that the new front needed to be opened in 1942 rather than the following year; and secondly, provided that Mediterranean operations were expanded, then attacking North Africa would open and keep clear important shipping routes.[180] To what extent this influenced military planning is not clear; what is evident is that at the bilateral discussions in late July, the decision was made to focus on North Africa.

By early August, the JIC was hard at work on an assessment of the effect of an Allied invasion of North Africa – now codenamed Operation TORCH. The initial conclusion was that regardless of the conduct of the war against the Soviet Union, Germany would have to withdraw troops and equipment for maintenance and recuperation at some point in the autumn of 1942. Therefore an attack on North Africa, particularly one that used the element of surprise, would be an effective way of diverting German attention and securing a relatively quick victory.[181] One of the naval members of the JIS, Donald McLachlan, has recalled how useful it was to have the JIS draft the assessments because they were uniquely positioned to perceive the invasion through enemy eyes.[182]

The planners were, at the same time, working towards an early October date for the invasion.[183] A further series of JIC papers produced throughout August supported this timescale, focussing on whether Spain might get involved in any conflict, the status of Vichy France's forces, and what German strategy might be upon the commencement of Operation TORCH.[184] By late August the JIC was producing a number of reports – by and large accurate – for Force Commanders on the nature and type of opposition to be faced, thereby suggesting suitable locations for invasion.[185]

Planning continued throughout September 1942, including lengthy discussions between British and American military officials as to the precise places to attack first. By October an examination of the JIC papers shows just how all-encompassing planning for Operation TORCH was to their workload. A paper in late October concluded that the 'timing and destination of TORCH have not yet been correctly appreciated by the enemy', though it was recognised that the general intention to attack North Africa was 'clearly suspected'.[186] This assessment was now produced weekly for the COS Committee and based on ULTRA decrypts, and focussed on how well known Allied plans might be to the enemy and what enemy troop dispositions were.[187]

Continuing the weekly discourse on Operation TORCH, the JIC reported again on 3 November that the Axis powers had 'not yet appreciated the exact destination, timing or scale of the attack'.[188] Just five days later, on 8 November 1942, Operation TORCH was put into action. In the early hours British and American forces launched a multi-pronged attack on the coast of North Africa, invading parts of Morocco and Algeria. Although no formal JIC assessments had been produced in the few days leading up to the attack, detailed information was provided through ULTRA about the locations of German U-boats. Active deception measures employed by the Allies and accurately reported on by the JIC in the build-up were successful.[189]

As a sign of the important role that the intelligence community had played in the preparations for Operation TORCH, General Dwight Eisenhower, the Supreme Commander Allied Expeditionary Force in North Africa, personally asked for his gratitude to be conveyed to Cavendish-Bentinck with congratulations on the 'invaluable help given', particularly 'the regular flow of information [which] has enabled planning to be kept up to date.'[190] Operation TORCH was the first military plan that involved the JIC in any detailed and central way. Information provided through the JIC umbrella, including the IS(O) and direct reporting by the JIS to the planners, ensured that those making strategy were kept abreast of the most detailed intelligence available. The system worked as it had originally been set up to do, albeit several years into the war. Almost immediately a request was made to increase the size of the Intelligence Section (Operations).[191]

At approximately the same time – late 1942 – space was found in the Cabinet War Rooms for members of the JIS, thereby ensuring that for the first time they were physically located in the same building as the planners and within easy reach of Churchill. Indeed, in the rooms in Great George Street officers of the JIS and JPS formed a mess, where they often ate meals together (see figure 6.14).[192]

The remainder of 1942 was concerned with the usual array of topics, ranging from the purely administrative, through controlling and ensuring the security of intelligence, to the production of assessments. Of the notable fresh developments were two decisions in August 1942. The first was to authorise production of a regular survey of enemy morale; the second was to assume responsibility for assessing enemy oil supplies.[193] As a further sign of its integration into the planning machinery, in October 1942 the JIC agreed to provide all relevant intelligence to the newly created 'Post-War Planning Section'.[194] Other decisions in late 1942 were to reproduce the JIC model abroad, with the creation of a JIC West Africa in October. This followed from the first expansion of the model to the United States, and a further offspring – the JIC(Middle East Front) – in early 1942.[195] The JIC was finally fighting on all fronts.

The middle years of the war saw a great expansion in the JIC's role, remit and responsibilities. In commenting on these in mid-1942, the Secretary, Denis Capel-Dunn, informed General Ismay that the JIC has a

> ... dual responsibility. In the first place, they fulfil the role of charter proph-
> ets and are responsible for trying to forecast what the enemy is going to do.

In the second place, they are responsible for creating and administering the machinery through which Intelligence is gathered and upon which Intelligence their prophecies are, or should be, based.[196]

Throughout the period the permanent representatives on the JIC struggled to keep pace with their workload. The creation of the JIS – a full-time cadre of drafters – substantially eased matters, as did the subsequent formation of a second team of JIS writers. A further help was the instigation of a second weekly meeting of the JIC composed of deputies and designed to discuss more routine matters. This released the JIC to concentrate on other things. It was these changes, as DMI Davidson has recalled, that signalled a reversal in fortunes: 'thus the quantity and quality of JIC performance increased as the war went on, and played an increasing part of the COS machinery on the Intelligence side.'[197]

The most well known function of the JIC was the production of assessments; yet by just considering this aspect the wide role that the JIC played during the war is overlooked. In addition, the JIC looked after security, formalised and conducted strategic foreign liaison, considered propaganda, and produced a flood of daily, weekly and long-term assessments. It was far more than a Committee designed to provide intelligence for planning, and its helpful role in forming good relations with the United States intelligence authorities attests to this.

To be useful intelligence has to meet four criteria: it has to be relevant; correct; timely; and useable. The JIC radically improved its performance in all of these areas during this period. The introduction of Sigint material revolutionised the ability of the JIC to make predictions and afforded it greater confidence in its assessments. A criticism of the pre-war JIC, and indeed the wartime JIC up to the fall of Norway, was that despite producing good intelligence, rarely if ever was it influential. The key improvement at this time was the merging of relations with the planning elements of the war effort and the closer working relationship between the JIC and the JPS. Furthermore, the JIC briefed the COS Committee regularly and produced a daily stream of tactical assessments. Not only did the JIC product thereby become more relevant (and therefore more read by its customers), but it also began to contribute to the planning and conduct of military operations. Here was a JIC that, for the first time, was properly and effectively integrated with those it was designed to inform.

Notes

1 Note by the Secretary, Joint Intelligence Committee, 17 December 1940. CAB 21/3622.
2 C.T.Edwards [JIC Secretary] to P.Mackesy [Chairman, FOES], 8 February 1941. CAB 21/3622.
3 In January 1944 Menzies was promoted to Major General, having been given the local rank of a Brigadier earlier in the war. For background details see FO 1093/132.
4 Hall was a distinguished figure: he taught at UCL pre-war, becoming the first Director of the National Institute of Economic and Social Research and founded what would become the Henley Business School.

5   Cited in Howarth, *Intelligence Chief Extraordinary.* pp.112–3.
6   Howarth, *Intelligence Chief Extraordinary.* p.149.
7   K Strong, *Men of Intelligence: A Study of the Roles and Decisions of Chiefs of Intelligence from World War I to the Present Day* (London: Cassell, 1970). p.123.
8   N Annan, *Changing Enemies: The Defeat and Regeneration of Germany* (New York: Cornell University Press, 1995). p.64. Cavendish-Bentinck was scathing in his memory of Davidson: 'a very mediocre officer . . . with a permanent desire to make our reports fit in with the views of the CIGS [Chief of the Imperial General Staff].' Howarth, *Intelligence Chief Extraordinary.* p.165.
9   JIC(41)10, 'Development of the Junior Joint Intelligence Sub-Committee as a Means of Assisting in the Production of Appreciations', 5 January 1941. CAB 81/99.
10 'High Level Intelligence', F.Davidson, n.d. Major General F.H.N.Davidson Papers, LHCMA: Davidson 4/3.
11 JIC(41)48(Revise), 'Form of JIC Papers', 8 February 1941. CAB 81/100.
12 JIC(41)58, 'Study of Enemy Intentions', 6 February 1941. CAB 81/100.
13 JIC(41)5th Meeting, 7 February 1941. CAB 81/88.
14 COS(41)90th Meeting, 8 March 1941. CAB 79/9.
15 COS(41)93rd Meeting, 11 March 1941. CAB 79/9.
16 JIC(41)112, 'Axis Planning Section', 22 March 1941. CAB 81/101.
17 Shoosmith to Cavendish-Bentinck, 29 March 1941. CAB 163/6. Shoosmith would become the Principal Staff Officer to the Deputy Supreme Commander, Allied Powers in Europe.
18 'The FOES', Vice Admiral Sir T.Troubridge. British Naval Intelligence Papers, Churchill College, University of Cambridge Archives: MLBE 2/39.
19 Cited in McLachlan, *Room 39.* p.409.
20 JIC(41)12th Meeting, 8 May 1941. CAB 81/88.
21 COS(41)251st Meeting, 18 July 1941. CAB 79/13.
22 JIC(41)12th Meeting, 8 May 1941. CAB 81/88.
23 JIC(40)126, 'Procedure for Drafting Joint Intelligence Sub-Committee Report, Etc.', 16 June 1940. CAB 81/97.
24 Hinsley, *British Intelligence: Vol.1.* p.298.
25 JIC(41)13th Meeting, 15 May 1941. CAB 81/88.
26 JIC(41)14th Meeting, 30 May 1941. CAB 81/88.
27 JIC(41)222, 'A Combined Inter-Service Intelligence and Planning Committee', 24 May 1941. CAB 81/102. The two staffs were not moved until late 1942.
28 'Joint Intelligence Staff', Paper by DMI Major General Davidson, 6 October 1941. CAB 163/5.
29 'The FOES', Troubridge. Churchill College, Cambridge: MLBE 2/39.
30 Interview with K.Walker-Sloan, 24 March 2010.
31 'Duties of the Joint Intelligence Staff', Paper by DMI Major General Davidson, 7 December 1941. CAB 163/5.
32 'The Joint Intelligence Staff', S.Paton, 19 February 1949. Churchill College, Cambridge: MLBE 2/39.
33 COS(41)143rd Meeting, 22 April 1941. CAB 79/11.
34 JIC(41)11th Meeting, 24 April 1941. CAB 81/88.
35 JIC/856/46, 'The Joint Staff and Cabinet Secretariat', 25 June 1946. CAB 176/11. Waterfield produced a book immediately after the war entitled 'The Joint Staff and Cabinet Secretariat – Developments in Fifty Years'. This included his reminiscences of the war, including detail on the JIS and the offices and working environment. The book was passed to the JIC to review but was refused publication. This file includes the chapter on the 'Co-ordination of Intelligence', but unfortunately the rest has not been located.
36 Minute by F.H.N.Davidson, 3 June 1941. CAB 21/3622.
37 Minute by V.Cavendish-Bentinck, 4 June 1941. CAB 21/3622.

38 JIC(41)297, 'Report on the Joint Intelligence Staff', 25 July 1941. CAB 81/103.

39 For instance, see JIC(39)29(Revise) 'Russia: Vulnerability of Oil Supplies', 21 November 1939. CAB 81/95.

40 For instance, see JIC(40)179, 'Soviet Foreign Policy', 27 July 1940. CAB 81/97.

41 JIC(40)18, 'Strategic Implications of the Russo-Finnish Treaty', 21 March 1940. CAB 81/96.

42 For instance, see JIC(40)306, 'Possible Axis Intentions;, 10 October 1940. CAB 81/98.

43 JIC(41)90, 'German Action in the Mediterranean Area', 5 March 1941. CAB 81/100.

44 JIC(41)181, 'Scale of Attack on Crete', 27 April 1941. CAB 81/102.

45 COS(41)23, 'Strategical Appreciation', 9 January 1941. CAB 80/25.

46 JIC(41)119, 'German Operations Following the Balkan Campaigns', 25 March 1941. CAB 81/101.

47 JIC(41)138, 'German Strategy in 1941', 7 April 1941. CAB 81/101. For details of these 'rumours', see WO 190/893.

48 COS(41)143rd Meeting, 22 April 1941. CAB 79/11.

49 JIC(41)218(Final), 'German Intentions Against the USSR', 23 May 1941. CAB 81/102.

50 'CXFJ Work', 8 April 1940. HW 14/4.

51 See various correspondence in Cabinet Office papers.

52 B F Smith, *The ULTRA-Magic Deals and the Most Secret Special Relationship, 1940–1946* (Shrewsbury: Airlife, 1993). p.102. Smith states that Cavendish-Bentinck was one of the two FO officials indoctrinated, he does not state who the other one was, but presumably it was the PUS, Cadogan.

53 D.Capel-Dunn to J.Buckley [GC&CS], 1 October 1942. Cabinet Office papers.

54 'Victor Cavendish-Bentinck'. Ronald Lewin Papers, Churchill College Archives, University of Cambridge: RLEW 5/2.

55 V.Cavendish-Bentinck to R.Lewin, 25 May 1977. Lewin Papers, Churchill College Archives: RLEW 5/2.

56 Further details can be found in a questionnaire completed by the JIS, on the value and use of ULTRA during the war. HW 3/172.

57 'The Value and Use of Special Intelligence in JIC Work', Paper in the Godfrey Archive. ADM 223/107.

58 Interview with K.Walker-Sloan, 24 March 2010.

59 'The Value and Use of Special Intelligence in JIC Work', Paper in the Godfrey Archive. ADM 223/107.

60 R Lewin, *ULTRA Goes to War* (London: Grafton Books, 1978). pp.108–9.

61 Victor Cavendish-Bentinck'. Lewin Papers, Churchill College Archives: RLEW 5/2.

62 JIC(41)229(Final), 'Germany's Next Move After Crete', 30 May 1941. CAB 81/103.

63 Annan, *Changing Enemies*. p.61.

64 COS(41)197th Meeting, 31 May 1941. CAB 79/11.

65 Hinsley, *British Intelligence: Vol.1*. pp.429–30. Similar claims have been made as to why Stalin did not heed all the warnings that he was given. See B Whaley, *Codeword Barbarossa* (Cambridge, MA: MIT Press, 1973). These false claims may have had something to do with the fact that the original German plans were drawn up in December 1940.

66 Hinsley, *British Intelligence: Vol.1*. p.462.

67 JIC(41)234(Revise), 'The Possible Effect of a German-soviet War', 14 June 1941. CAB 81/102. In one of the few surviving examples, there are comments on the first draft of this paper by MI14, the section of the War Office responsible for intelligence on Germany. See WO 208/1761.

68 JIC(41)251(Final), 'Some Effects of German-Soviet Collaboration', 13 June 1941. CAB 81/103.

69 JIC(41)252, 'German Soviet Relations', 12 June 1941. CAB 81/103.

70 W S Churchill, *The Second World War: Volume III, The Grand Alliance* (London: Cassell, 1964). p.317.

71 Diary entry for 22 June 1941. Major General Sir John Kennedy Papers, LHCMA: Kennedy 4/2/3. See also J Kennedy, *The Business of War* (London: Hutchinson, 1957).

72 COS(41)272nd Meeting, 2 August 1941. CAB 79/13.

73 JIC(41)19th Meeting, 26 June 1941. CAB 81/88.

74 JIC(41)272, 'German Invasion of the British Isles', 8 July 1941. CAB 81/103.

75 JIC(41)288(Final), 'A Possible German Peace Move', 28 July 1941. CAB 81/103.

76 JIC(41)290(Final), 'The Effects of a Russian Collapse', 31 July 1941. CAB 81/103.

77 JIC(41)307(0), 'The Effect of the Russian Campaign on the Prospects of Invasion', 1 August 1941. CAB 81/103.

78 JIC(41)355(Final), 'Alleged Views of the German General Staff on the Present Situation', 7 September 1941. CAB 81/104.

79 JIC(41)433(Final), 'Germany's Future Intentions', 8 November 1941. CAB 81/105.

80 JIC(41)452(Final), 'The Russian Campaign', 2 December 1941. CAB 81/105.

81 For more see D Reynolds, *The Creation of the Anglo-American Alliance, 1937–41: A Study in Competitive Cooperation* (London: Europa Publications, 1981).

82 N West (ed.), *British Security Coordination: The Secret History of British Intelligence in the Americas, 1940–1945* (London: Fromm International, 1999); D M Charles, '"Before the Colonel Arrived": Hoover, Donovan, Roosevelt and the Origins of American Central Intelligence, 1940–41', *Intelligence and National Security* 20:2 (June 2005), pp.225–37.

83 James Leutze's introduction to R E Lee, *The London Observer: The Journal of General Raymond E. Lee, 1940–1941* (London: Hutchinson, 1971). p.xv.

84 T F Troy, *Donovan and the CIA: A History of the Establishment of the Central Intelligence Agency* (Washington, DC: CIA Center for the Study of Intelligence, 1981).

85 Lee, who discussed Donovan's findings with him before his return to brief Roosevelt, noted that Donovan felt Britain's chances of 'beating off' the Germans were 60–40, whereas Lee was more confident, arguing 2 to 1, 'barring some magical secret weapon'. Lee, *The London Observer.* pp.27–8. For an interesting earlier American discussion on Britain's survival chances see M S Alexander, 'Perceptions by US Officials in Washington DC and London of Britain's Readiness for War in 1939', *Contemporary British History* 25:1 (March 2011), pp.101–24.

86 JIC(40)233, 'American War Organisation', 10 August 1940. CAB 81/98.

87 JIC(40)56th Meeting, 27 August 1940. CAB 81/87.

88 COS(40)289th Meeting, 31 August 1940. CAB 79/6. The JIC reaction is in JIC(40)263, 'Exchange of Information with the United States Authorities', 1 September 1940. CAB 81/98. The JIC version contains the full text of what Strong said; the version in the COS Committee minutes omits most of the detail.

89 R L Benson, 'The Origin of US-British Communications Intelligence Cooperation (1940–41)'. Available on the National Security Agency's website: www.nsa.gov

90 JP(41)33rd Meeting, 7 March 1941. CAB 84/3.

91 JIC(41)12th Meeting, 8 May 1941. CAB 81/88.

92 A4904/769/45. Handwritten note, 26 June 1941. FO 371/26231. Unfortunately it is not possible to work out who the person was from his signature. The date and name cited above are taken from the FO document. American sources, by contrast, state that Donovan was appointed in July 1941 and that his job title was 'Coordinator of Information'. See, for instance, M Warner, *The Office of Strategic Services: America's First Intelligence Agency* (CIA, 2000). Available at www.cia.gov

93 A3295/101/45. V.Cavendish-Bentinck, 2 May 1941. FO 371/26179.

94 For Godfrey's own account see his unpublished memoir in Churchill College Archives, University of Cambridge: John Godfrey papers: GDFY 1/6.

95 JIC(41)17th Meeting, 17 June 1941. CAB 81/88.

96 Lee, *The London Observer.* p.277.

97 JIC(41)253, 'A Telegram from Rear Admiral Godfrey', 14 June 1941. CAB 81/103.

98 MM(41)191, 'British Joint Staff Mission in Washington: Joint Intelligence Committee', 21 October 1941. CAB 122/1584.

99 For the minutes of the first few of the JIC(W) meetings, see CAB 122/1584.

100 'Notes on the Organisation and Responsibilities of the British JIC Washington', 8 December 1941. CAB 122/1584.

101 V.Cavendish-Bentinck to A.Cadogan, 13 June 1941. FO 371/29030.

102 For instance, F.W.Vogel [British Army Staff, Washington] to War Office, 13 October 1941. CAB 122/1584.

103 F.Hoyer-Millar [British Embassy, Washington] to V.Cavendish-Bentinck, 4 June 1941. CAB 122/1584.

104 Lee, *The London Observer.* p.319.

105 L A Valero, 'The American Joint Intelligence Committee and Estimates of the Soviet Union, 1945–1947', *CIA Studies in Intelligence* (Summer 2000).

106 'Directive by the Combined Chiefs of Staff for Combined Intelligence', 11 February 1942. CAB 122/1584. See also L L Montague, 'The Origins of National Intelligence Estimating', *CIA Studies in Intelligence* 16:2 (Spring 1972), pp.63–70. Montague had been a former Secretary of the US JIC.

107 F H Hinsley et al, *British Intelligence in the Second World War, Volume 2: Its Influence on Strategy and Operations* (London: HMSO, 1981). pp.42–44.

108 C/39. 'Memorandum on Secret Service Funds', 'C', 9 October 1935. CAB 127/371. See also Jeffrey, *MI6.* pp.262–6.

109 For instance, see the most recent account on this: D Ford, *Britain's Secret War Against Japan, 1937–1945* (London: Routledge, 2006).

110 Best, 'Constructing an Image', pp.403–23.

111 JP(40)168, 'Implications of the Capture by the Japanese of the Dutch East Indies', 13 May 1940. CAB 84/13.

112 JIC(40)65, 'Possible Japanese Action Against the Dutch East Indies', 17 May 1940. CAB 81/96.

113 JIC(40)135, 'Straits Settlement: Warning of a Japanese Attack', 21 June 1940. CAB 81/97. See also JIC(40)335, 'Period of Warning of an Attack on Singapore', 23 October 1940. CAB 81/98.

114 A Best, '"This Probably Over Valued Military Power": British Intelligence and Whitehall's Perception of Japan, 1939–41', *Intelligence and National Security* 12:3 (1997), p.77.

115 JIC(40)267, 'The Probable Effect on Japan of an Extension of the Far Eastern Hostilities to Indochina', 6 September 1940. CAB 81/98.

116 JIC(40)272, 'Time Required for the Japanese to Stage an Attack Against Malaya', 7 September 1940. CAB 81/98.

117 JP(40)621, 'Period of Warning of an attack on Singapore', 4 November 1940. CAB 84/22.

118 JIC(41)21, 'Intelligence Organisation in the Far East', 14 January 1941. CAB 81/99.

119 JIC(41)26, 'Intelligence Organisation in the Far East', 17 January 1941. CAB 81/100.

120 JIC(41)55, 'Japanese Intentions', 5 February 1941. CAB 81/100.

121 Details are in ADM 199/1477.

122 JIC(41)155, 'Future Strategy of Japan', 17 April 1941. CAB 81/101.

123 JIC(41)160(Final), 'Reported Japanese Intention to Attack Malaya', 20 April 1941. CAB 81/101.

124 JIC(41)221, 'Action to Counter Pro-Axis Activities in the Far East', 24 May 1941. CAB 81/102. Unfortunately the annex to this paper, where Davidson described what this meant in practice, has been lost. The War Office prepared a report on this, which was circulated amongst the JIC, the original of which has also been lost. JIC(41)243, 'Action to Counter Pro-Axis Activities in the Far East', 3 June 1941. CAB 81/102. Some clues can be extracted from the minutes of the JIC meeting where this was discussed. See below.

125 JIC(41)14th Meeting, 30 May 1941. CAB 81/88.

126 JIC(41)15th Meeting, 6 June 1941. CAB 81/88.

127 JIC(41)309, 'Japan's Next Move', 2 August 1941. CAB 81/103.

128 JIC(41)439(Final), 'Japanese Intentions', 18 November 1941. CAB 81/105.

129 JIC(41)449(Final), 'Possible Japanese Action', 28 November 1941. CAB 81/105.

130 For more detail see D Borg & S Okamoto (eds), *Pearl Harbor as History: Japanese-American Relations, 1931–1941* (Columbia: Columbia University Press, 1973).

131 COS(41)405th Meeting, 2 December 1941. CAB 79/16.

132 Details are in HW 1/288.

133 There is nothing to substantiate the claims made by various revisionist historians that the JIC had foreknowledge of the Japanese intent to sail towards Pearl Harbor. In particular, Constantine Fitzgibbon, who claims the information came from Cavendish-Bentinck, has written that the JIC met on 5 December to discuss the impending attack. There are no records of the JIC, as a full committee or as individual members, meeting that day. Furthermore, what autobiographical information does exist (for instance, Admiral Godfrey) makes no mention. An internal account of the JIC's assessments of Japanese intentions in 1941 also makes no reference. A memoir by the JIS member responsible for the Far East states that radio monitoring lost track of the Japanese fleet in mid-November. See 'JIC Appreciations in 1941 of Japanese Intentions'. ADM 223/494. On Godfrey, see National Maritime Museum: GOD/104. For the JIS see Sir Julian Ridsdale's unpublished memoir in Churchill College Cambridge: RIDS 1. On the revisionist accounts see C Fitzgibbon, *Secret Intelligence in the Twentieth Century* (London: Hart-Davis, 1976); R J Aldrich, 'Never-Never Land and Wonderland? British and American Policy on Intelligence Archives' *Contemporary Record*, 8:1 (1994), pp.133–52; and D C S Sissons, 'More on Pearl Harbor' *Intelligence and National Security*, 9:2 (1994), pp.373–79.

134 Minute from the PM to the COS, 7 Dec 1941. CAB 79/16.

135 JIC(41)471, 'Japanese Intentions', 11 December 1941. CAB 81/105.

136 'Minutes of JIC(W) meetings, held on 8, 9, 11 December', 13 December 1941. CAB 122/1584. Also, JIC(41)38th Meeting, 16 December 1941. CAB 81/88.

137 These can be found in CAB 81/105.

138 JIC(42)1, 'Possible Japanese Actions Against the Netherlands East Indies', 1 January 1942. CAB 81/106.

139 The various messages are contained within JIC(42)37, 'Timing and Scale of a Sea-Borne Attack on Singapore', 1 February 1942. CAB 81/106.

140 Minute, 3 January 1942. WO 208/871.

141 'JIC Appreciations in 1941 of Japanese Intentions', J.Godfrey. ADM 223/494. This is part of the Godfrey histories – a large number of files he produced documenting the history of Naval Intelligence.

142 Aldrich states that this was so extensive that political bias neutralised the value of the intelligence. R J Aldrich, *Intelligence and the War Against Japan: Britain, America and the Politics of Secret Service* (Cambridge: Cambridge University Press, 2000). p.50.

143 Brigadier T.Haddon Papers, Imperial War Museum (94/8/1): *Looking Back* (unpublished memoir). p.21. Haddon would return to the JIC at the end of the war as Secretary, with the rank of Lieutenant Colonel.

144 I am grateful to Jonathan Smith, the Trinity College archivist, for this information.

145 I am indebted to Barnaby Capel-Dunn, his son, for this biographical information.

146 I am grateful to Aaron Cripps, archivist at the Defence Academy, for this information.

147 'Obituary: John Colvin', *The Daily Telegraph* (17 October 2003). It is also mentioned in 'Awful Widmerpool is Unmasked At Last', *The Daily Telegraph* (30 December 1991). Rather cruelly Anthony Powell had based the character of Widmerpool in *A Dance to the Music of Time* on Capel-Dunn; the dramatisation needs to be read in the context that Capel-Dunn refused to keep Powell on his staff.

148 Annan, *Changing Enemies*. p.17; F.N.H.Davidson to J.G.Dill [Chairman of the British Joint Services Mission, Washington], n.d. but 1943. CAB 163/6.

149 'Letter to the Editor', *The Daily Telegraph* (3 January 1992).

150 Detail taken from Cabinet Office papers.
151 Note by J.H.Godfrey, 2 May 1947. ADM 223/465. This is another of Godfrey's wartime 'memoirs' – the volumes he produced to commemorate the role of Naval Intelligence in the war. This particular volume focuses on the JIC and central intelligence. Emphasis in original.
152 'Air Ministry to Britman, Washington', 15 December 1942. CAB 121/230.
153 A copy is in WO 373/156.
154 C.Fletcher-Cooke to J.H.Godfrey, 18 March 1949. Churchill College, Cambridge: MLBE 2/39.
155 Annan, *Changing Enemies*. pp.67–8.
156 Interview with K.Walker-Sloan, 24 March 2010.
157 See the various correspondence in CAB 163/5.
158 JIC/856/46, 'The Joint Staff and Cabinet Secretariat', 25 June 1946. CAB 176/11. The writer of the comments was one of the War Office representatives.
159 D.Morton to W.S.Churchill, 20 January 1941. PREM 4/97/11. For more on Morton see Bennett, *Churchill's Man of Mystery*.
160 JIC(41)56, 'Report on the Joint Intelligence Committee Topographical Section', 8 February 1941. CAB 81/100.
161 Details can be found in CAB 119/74.
162 JP(41)988, 'Intelligence for Planning', 20 November 1941. CAB 84/37.
163 JIC(41)470, 'Intelligence Section (Operations)', 24 December 1941. CAB 81/105.
164 JP(41)171st Meeting, 18 December 1941. CAB 84/3.
165 JIC(41)499, 'Intelligence Section (Operations)', 30 December 1941. CAB 81/105.
166 See various correspondence in CAB 120/744.
167 Hinsley, *British Intelligence: Vol.2*. p.463.
168 For instance, see JIC(41)443(0), 'The Position in French North Africa', 21 November 1941. CAB 81/105.
169 JP(42)63, 'Intelligence for Planning', 20 January 1942. CAB 119/74.
170 JIC(41)458(Final)(0), 'Situation in French North Africa', 6 December 1941. CAB 81/105.
171 JIC(41)462(0), 'Operation Gymnast – Cover', 8 December 1941. CAB 81/105.
172 M Howard, *Grand Strategy: History of the Second World War: Volume IV, August 1942-September 1943* (London: HMSO, 1972). pp.xvii-xviii.
173 'Operation Gymnast – Scale of Air Attack', 10 March 1942. CAB 119/74. This was drafted by the Air Ministry representatives on the JIS.
174 JIC(42)34(Final), 'Germany's Intentions', 25 January 1942. CAB 81/106.
175 JIC(42)75(Final), 'Enemy Intentions', 14 March 1942. CAB 81/106.
176 JIC942)11th Meeting, 31 March 1942. CAB 81/90.
177 JIC(42)113(Final), 'Axis Strength and Policy, 1942', 10 April 1942. CAB 81/107. This was the second of these papers, the first had been produced in February 1942.
178 JIC(42)164(0), 'Reactions in French North Africa to "Sledgehammer"', 1 May 1942. CAB 81/108.
179 Howard, *Grand Strategy*. p.xxi.
180 JIC(42)265(Final), 'German strategy in 1942/3', 16 July 1942. CAB 81/109.
181 JIC(42)299(0)(Final), 'Operations in a Certain Country', 3 August 1942. CAB 81/109. See also JIC(42)304(0)(Final), 'Operation "TORCH" – Intelligence Appreciation', 7 August 1942. CAB 81/109.
182 McLachlan, *Room 39*. p.251.
183 Details are in CAB 121/490.
184 These can be found in CAB 81/109.
185 JIC(42)320(0), 'A Certain Operation – Information for the Force-Commander', 20 August 1942. CAB 81/109.
186 JIC(42)415(0), 'Recent Intelligence Affecting Operation TORCH', 20 October 1942. CAB 81/111.

187 For an interesting Bletchley Park perspective on this see R Erskine, 'From the Archives: A Bletchley Park Assessment of German Intelligence on TORCH', *Cryptologia* 13:2 (1989), pp.135–42.

188 JIC(42)432(0), 'Recent Intelligence Affecting Operation "TORCH"', 3 November 1942. CAB 81/111.

189 Hinsley. *British Intelligence: Vol. 2.* pp.478–83.

190 JIC(42)431(0), 'Letter by Brigadier Mockler-Ferryman on a Certain Operation', 30 October 1942. CAB 81/111. Mockler-Ferryman was Head of Intelligence Section, Allied Forces in North Africa.

191 JIC(42)444, 'Intelligence Section (Operations) – Increase of Establishment', 12 November 1942. CAB 81/111.

192 C.Fletcher-Cooke to J.H.Godfrey, 18 March 1949. Churchill College, Cambridge: MLBE 2/39.

193 Details can be found in CAB 81/90.

194 JIC(42)52nd Meeting, 16 October 1942. CAB 81/90. The Post-War Planning Section looked at what reconstruction efforts would be needed in the future. For more see CAB 119/64.

195 Some of the Middle East JIC papers can be found in WO 201/2712.

196 D.Capel-Dunn to Ismay, 2 July 1942. CAB 163/6.

197 'High Level Intelligence', F.Davidson, n.d. Major General F.H.N.Davidson Papers, LHCMA: Davidson 4/3.

5 Preparing for the End, 1943–1945

In 1942 the British government published a White Paper, designed to inform the public about the way in which the war effort was being planned and fought. Detailed within this was a description of the 'Joint Intelligence Sub-Committee', a body with responsibility 'to collate and assess all information about the enemy and, in particular, to prepare appreciations of the most likely course of enemy action from time to time.' The role of the JIC within the war effort was also spelt out: 'the Joint Planning Staff and the Joint Intelligence Sub-Committee work hand in hand, and both of them are regularly summoned to discuss problems with the Chiefs of Staff'.[1]

By 1943 the JIC had become a valuable part of the establishment. It had fulfilled the role it had been created to play, becoming an essential cog within the planning and wider military machinery. By this time the JIC had demonstrated its value with the planning for Operation TORCH, the invasion of North Africa, where intelligence assessments had played a crucial role in helping the Allied planners decide which course of action to adopt. The JIC had also developed regional variations in places as far afield as the United States, Africa and the Middle East. In London, too, the JIC now had a number of subordinate bodies. Principal amongst these was the JIS, the permanent cadre of specialists seconded from the Services and other government departments, whose job it was to research, prepare and write the assessments that would subsequently be issued as JIC papers. In addition, the Intelligence Section (Operations) (IS(O)) had been created to monitor military operations throughout their duration, on behalf of the intelligence community, ensuring that all relevant information was made available to planners. The Inter-Services Security Board (ISSB) looked after the security of all plans and other intelligence duties, while the Inter-Service Topographical Department (ISTD) had responsibility for collating and disseminating topographical intelligence. Presiding over these sub-committees, and ensuring that all relevant information was passed to the planners and the COS, were the full members of the JIC – the Directors of Intelligence in the War Office, Admiralty and Air Ministry, the Chief of SIS, and senior representatives from MI5 and the Ministry of Economic Warfare. The Committee was chaired by Victor Cavendish-Bentinck, the FO representative, and assisted by its Secretary, Lieutenant Colonel Denis Capel-Dunn.

One important body that fell outside the JIC's purview, albeit sharing many of the same members, was the XX Committee. Also known as the Double Cross Committee, it focussed on the work of double agents in supporting, influencing and monitoring the reports they sent back to Germany. To ensure that this work was effectively co-ordinated across Whitehall another organisation, the 'W Board', was created. It comprised the three Services' Directors of Intelligence, the Chief of SIS, the Deputy Director-General of MI5, and was chaired by Sir Findlater Stewart, the Director-General of the Ministry of Information. Importantly the W Board, in Sir Michael Howard's words, 'reported to no one and was responsible to no one'. Given the sensitivities of double agents and their activities, the JIC was excluded from knowing what went on on the grounds that it 'was felt to be too large and too public a forum for the discussion of so sensitive a subject', though quite how much information was shared informally given the common membership is unknown.[2] Certainly through the activities of ISSB in the first half of war, where papers entitled 'rumours of a military nature intended to mystify or mislead the enemy' were routinely discussed, the Committee must have had some awareness of what was going on.[3]

From January 1943 to the end of the war in mid-1945, the JIC continued to meet at least once a week in its own right, but also attended COS meetings and held combined sessions with the JPS. The JIS worked from its underground offices in the Cabinet War Rooms.[4] Elizabeth Norman, a member of IS(O), recalled what this was like: '[we were] situated in the bowels of the earth beneath the Treasury . . . we had two sets of steel doors, each guarded by armed Marines to descend to these darker regions. Once there, we were out of touch with the outside world, sun, cold, rain, air-raids, rockets and finally buzz bombs'.[5] The rooms themselves were 'bright with artificial lighting'.[6] Norman recalled one particularly hair raising moment:

> One evening I had been dancing with my current young man . . . he dropped me off at the Treasury, not knowing where I worked . . .
> . . . he was with the 8th Army in Southern Italy, had unexpected leave and wanted to find me. Being a tall, good looking Marine and smartly uniformed young Officer with plenty of battle Ribbons, and knowing I worked at the Treasury Offices officially, he came along, strode in, saluted sharply and they let him through the steel doors without a pass and the same again with the next lot of doors. He then meandered down one of the most secret and protected corridors in war-time London, opened our door, my desk was nearest and he was about to greet me lovingly when he saw the look of horror on everyone's face, including mine and beat a hasty retreat . . .
> . . . When I got back from escorting him [off the premises] there was a terrible atmosphere, I was questioned, and was finally let off . . . he could have been shot.[7]

The second half of the war was characterised by the JIC's newfound status and integral role in military planning, beginning with the strategy in the Mediterranean and culminating with the landings on D-Day. Yet the JIC's role, and that of all of its subordinate bodies, was far wider; it continued to play a crucial part in the production of both strategic and tactical assessments, and increasingly turned its attention to the shape and nature of the post-war world. Central to many of these deliberations was the burgeoning relationship with the United States.

Allies at last

British intelligence had played a crucial role in the creation and establishment of an American intelligence community, with the JIC instigating a representative body in Washington (JIC(W)) to work alongside an American JIC.[8] This 'special' relationship would prove to be of critical importance. By late 1942 there was a feeling in London that relations were not as close as they should be and that JIC(W) needed 'improvement'. This was despite the fact that steps had recently been taken to ensure that the 'special intelligence', the sobriquet given to ULTRA intelligence, was transmitted to Washington.[9] Many of the British intelligence officers saw themselves as the elder statesmen in the partnership, and were keen to offer their thoughts and advice whenever possible. In considering an American JIC paper on Japanese capabilities, for instance, the Deputy Director of Military Intelligence commented that although the paper

> is headed capabilities, the conclusions in paragraph 5 refer to intentions. We have previously noticed this tendency on the part of American intelligence papers. They confuse capabilities and intentions, and are apt to assume that, because Japan is capable of a certain course of action, she intends to take that course. We feel that this paper provides a good opportunity to tactfully raise this point with America.[10]

The response was to send Denis Capel-Dunn, the JIC's Secretary, over to Washington to gauge progress, offer advice, and report back to the JIC upon his return to London.[11] One of Capel-Dunn's main tasks, as he saw it, was to ensure that the intelligence set-up was optimised given that 'the Americans are right into the war in the West' and that 'a good deal may depend on the 'I' party in Washington'.[12] Capel-Dunn submitted the report on his visit at the end of January 1943. His impression was not one of an overly developed system. There were two American JICs: a 'senior' committee, comparable to the JIC in London, and a 'working committee', analogous to the JIS. The American JIC had never, as far as he could tell, met either the US JCS or the planners. Furthermore, the British JIC in Washington had no direct contact with the US JIC. Whilst in the United States Capel-Dunn had been 'embarrassed' to be asked to address a combined meeting of the JIC(W) and US 'working committee', where he had commented on the closeness of intelligence and planning in the UK, and how 'we lived together and worked together'.[13]

Capel-Dunn's solution, to suggest an interchange of British and American officers, was greeted with muted enthusiasm by the JIC, with the Air Ministry and

Admiralty wanting more time to consider how this might work in practice.[14] Relations between both nations' intelligence communities in London had not been quite so inhibited, with weekly meetings being held between the US intelligence representative and the 'junior' JIC – the Deputy-Director's level of the committee. These discussions must have been useful because by April some improvements were being noted. The DMI, Major General Francis Davidson, noted how JIC(W) had been 'regularly' called upon by the senior American JIC to discuss and comment on papers. Furthermore, US JIC papers were increasingly taken more seriously by the US Joint Chiefs.[15]

This improvement in both internal and external relations continued through-out 1943. In late April it was recorded by the JIC that the different American factions were now in regular communication, both with one another and with their British counterparts, and that where there were differences in opinion they were reasonably and sensibly debated.[16] May was a very important month for the subsequent planning of the Allied war effort, with the British COS travelling to the US for the second Washington conference, codenamed TRIDENT. Although the JIC did not attend, an intelligence representative was present who reported back to the Committee. Brigadier John Kirkman, the Deputy Director of Military Intelligence, and a regular attender at the JIC's Deputy Director meetings, informed the JIC that discussions had gone well and that he had formed a positive impression of the closeness between intelligence and planning. He finished by saying that a JIC representative should attend the next bilateral meeting. Echoing Capel-Dunn's earlier conclusion, he also emphasised the importance of having a frequent interchange of officers between UK and US intelligence.[17]

At the same time, discussions between British and American military planners were continuing on the future conduct of the war. The following month Edward Mason of the newly created Office of Strategic Services (OSS), the American counterpart to SIS and SOE, visited London and was invited to attend a JIC meeting. Discussions appear to have been cordial, with topics including the improved intelligence relationship, and a comparison of some UK and US assessments. This was followed by a visit in October of Stanley Hornbeck, of the American senior JIC.[18] A further Anglo-American conference in August – QUADRANT – had, this time, been attended by two members of the JIS, as Brigadier Kirkman had suggested earlier in the year,[19] followed by the fourth meeting – SEXTANT – in December, where UK-US intelligence relations were described as 'very good'.[20] The Anglo-American intelligence communities were therefore beginning to operate much more closely together, yet the question remained: could the military planners operate with such unanimity?

Japan or Germany?

Operation TORCH signalled, in some respects, a watershed in the intelligence/planning relationship. The numerous discussions that would follow in 1943 revealed two facts: that the war required that British and American planners work in tandem; and that intelligence was now central to any and all military operations. Working together was not a new idea – there had been frequent collaboration before the United States' entry into the war and, immediately following the attacks on Pearl Harbor, the British COS had discussed 'Strategy' with their opposite numbers.[21] Thereafter a series of COS papers were issued on 'Anglo-American Grand Strategy', continuing throughout 1942. Yet despite these positive aspects, as Sir Michael Howard has described, long-term strategic plans for winning the war were often fraught with disagreement between the British and American planners.[22]

Even before the invasion of North Africa, the big issue for Anglo-American military planners, given that it was felt that both countries could not be defeated simultaneously, was whether it was best to concentrate effort on the downfall of Germany or Japan. Intelligence made an important contribution to this decision (an area that Howard could not divulge when writing his own account). In Britain the COS commissioned the JIC to provide the necessary intelligence for the planners to produce a 'worldwide strategic review'.[23] Against this backdrop, the British Joint Staff Mission (JSM) in Washington, the military body designed to liaise between both countries, wrote to the COS in London querying whether it would be Germany or Japan next, and concluded that 'it would be better to show quite clearly that we are approaching the problem with a completely open mind'.[24] The reply, unequivocal in nature, stated that 'you should know at once that we have anything but an open mind on this subject'. The directive issued to the planners was therefore not an objective one: 'the JPS will examine how best we can implement our agreed strategy of defeating Germany first.' The difficulty was that the US Strategical Committee (which had been created to draft war plans), as the JSM informed London, was leaning towards concentrating all efforts on defeating Japan, a policy that the COS felt was 'madness'.[25] It was subsequently decided by the Chiefs that the paper should not, at that time, be passed to the Americans.[26]

With an offensive aimed at defeating Germany first on the British agenda, attention was focussed on planning the possible strategies needed to achieve this, beginning with operations in the Mediterranean.[27] Underpinning these was a conclusion drawn by the JIC in late September that Germany should not be allowed any respite.[28] Within a few days of the invasion of North Africa, the JIC was instructed to prepare papers on the implications of TORCH for Germany and Italy. The resulting assessment declared that, as a consequence, Germany would seek to reinforce the Mediterranean, as would Italy in Sicily and Sardinia.[29] Quite how widely distributed this paper was is not clear, but just a few days later Churchill, writing as Minister of Defence, issued a lengthy memorandum to the COS on how the successes in Africa should be used to set up bases on the African Mediterranean coast to 'strike at the under-belly of the Axis'.[30] It was emphasised that the memorandum reflected COS thinking; in receiving it the JSM in Washington commented on its 'great value' for use in combined discussions with the Americans.[31] Churchill's report was subsequently passed to President Roosevelt as an expression of the British desire for the direction of the war effort.[32] Roosevelt replied to Churchill, saying that the report had been passed to his military planners who were 'studying the possibilities'.[33] Churchill considered this a 'poor response'.[34]

In London, Brigadier General Walter Bedell Smith, the American Chief of Staff for the European Theatre at the Allied Forces Headquarters and a future director of the CIA, was briefed by the British on the latest intelligence reports, which he was to take back to Washington.[35] Meanwhile, the JIC was busy preparing and approving a paper on German strategy, which began by stating that 'evidence is accumulating of weaknesses which limit German strategy as a whole', including manpower, transport, raw materials and food. The implications, and indeed the opportunities, were clear: 'the present is a critical moment when the duration if not the final outcome of the war may be dependent on the vigour of Allied action during the winter.'[36] The COS approved the report as it stood, though they also asked for a statistical table comparing the number of Axis divisions in different scenarios.[37] It was also dispatched to Washington for use in planning discussions, as were later JIC papers on the Mediterranean region.[38] Further papers similarly were produced on factors that might lead to a German collapse, and an examination of German morale.[39] Assessments were also made of Italian morale, concluding that Mussolini's popularity continued to decline and, if military defeats were suffered, a 'general collapse' was a realistic expectation.[40]

The combination of these assessments provided the military planners with a basis for strategy. Major General Leslie Hollis, the Secretary of the COS Committee, commenting on the JIC paper on German strategy, said: 'it is a very good paper ... it gives a very good lead as to what we hope our future strategy will be.'[41] Similarly, in discussing whether Italy might collapse and the potential impact on Germany, it is clear that military commanders valued the JIC's opinion.[42] Papers were now, as a matter of routine, being passed up to the COS for approval, the majority of which were then transmitted to Churchill in his dual roles as Prime Minister and Minister of Defence.

Within the UK, preparation of strategic options papers often used JIC assessments as a basis for planning. The JIC papers on the German effort had maintained that while its economy was finding it increasingly difficult to sustain the war, a victory over Russia without any other Allied operations having started would enable the economy to recover quickly.[43] It was decided that a united British front had to be presented to American military planners. Despite all the deliberations no joint Anglo-American decisions had been made. The response was Casablanca (codenamed SYMBOL) – an Allied military and political conference held on the shores of Morocco and designed to foster unity on winning the war. The conference, held in the second half of January 1943, began with good news from the Russian front. The Soviet counter-offensive at Stalingrad had been a success and the German forces had suffered a significant defeat. Agreement was reached at Casablanca that the overall defeat of the Axis powers had to begin in Europe, and only then could the Far East could tackled. The American preference was for a cross-channel invasion of north-west Europe in the summer of 1943, something they had been requesting for some time. There was also a concession by the American contingent to agree further operations in the Mediterranean, as they would divert German attention away from the war in Russia. Disagreements arose over the way to achieve the collapse of Italy, which was of primary importance.[44]

To prepare for the conference the British had examined a range of military operations, compiling detailed plans and weighing the pros and cons of involvement. These included the invasion of Sicily (Operation HUSKY) and Sardinia (Operation BRIMSTONE). The implications of opening a Sicilian offensive, according to the JIC, would be to cause 'devastating results' in Russia as Germany would have to divert substantial effort to the Mediterranean.[45] As a result the COS were fully equipped to argue the British position with their American counterparts. This proved to be particularly significant because the American contingent was divided as to what to do.[46] After much deliberation, it was decided to proceed with the invasion of Sicily, a move which Churchill had wanted from the start. It has been argued that the American concession 'went the British way', simply because 'the British were still the dominant of the two powers in the Anglo-American partnership'.[47] Though overly simplistic, it does nonetheless reveal the nature of the relationship at this time, especially in the Mediterranean context. The decision was a momentous one, for as Matthew Jones has argued, 'the Casablanca Conference of January 1943 had a decisive impact on the development of the war in the Mediterranean, and more generally on the whole evolution of Allied grand strategy.'[48]

The JIC now had to revisit a number of its papers that dealt with German strategy and Axis manpower.[49] A request was issued by the War Cabinet, subsequently passed on by the COS, for the JIC to consider the 'German military situation', especially in light of the turning of the tide in Russia, and its effect upon German strategy on the Eastern Front and North Africa.[50] At the same time plans for Operation HUSKY were continuing to develop. In early March 1943 the COS once more asked the JIC to revise its assessments of German strategy and force dispositions.[51] Two days later General Sir Alan Brooke, the Chief of Imperial General Staff (CIGS) and Chairman of the COS Committee, emphasised the 'importance of obtaining the best possible intelligence' for planning purposes.[52] The JIC continued its survey of worldwide events, discussing and producing assessments on 'Possible Developments in the Balkans', 'Supplies for the Swiss Army', 'Japanese Armament production', 'Scale of Attack on the Falkland Islands', 'French resistance in National Territories', and operations in Burma, Sumatra and Malaya.[53] Yet its most important role remained the provision of intelligence for planning purposes. Throughout March and April the JIC continued to issue reports on the war in the Soviet Union and its effect on the German war effort. Cavendish-Bentinck ensured that JIC discussions were relevant to the work of the JPS and that all information was passed on to them – a far cry from the poor JIC/JPS relationship of the early years of the war.[54]

Ralph Bennett has argued that with regard to the war in the Mediterranean 'intelligence is less necessary to offence than to the defence.'[55] In the case of the progress of the war from 1943 onwards this could not be further from the truth.

With Operation HUSKY confirmed, the JIC was asked to produce assessments on the speed by which German forces might be brought into Italy to counter an Allied invasion,[56] and what means might induce an Italian surrender.[57] With the Battle of Stalingrad now concluded, Churchill asked the JIC to prepare a fresh assessment on German strategy on the Eastern Front, pleading that 'we ought to get the report before it is all over'.[58] If this is a criticism of the speed with which the JIC prepared papers then it is an unfair one, as time and again the JIC responded to the request for information with the timely production of a report. Indeed, in submitting the request to Capel-Dunn, Hollis almost apologised for the comment, adding 'I am not certain to what the Prime Minister is referring'.[59] Within a week the JIC assessment was disseminated and the COS discussed it at their meeting two days later.[60] Although Brooke was impressed by the report's appendices, he was less sure about its main conclusions, for as Hollis subsequently informed Capel-Dunn: 'the conclusions drawn from them [appendices] in the covering paper were not definite enough, and almost appeared as if designed to cover the JIC for every eventuality (an ignoble thought, I know!)'.[61] To the approval of Brooke, the report was subsequently revised and finally distributed just over a week later.[62]

By early May the JIC had produced a variety of reports on strategy, considering a whole raft of possible eventualities. Included amongst these were plans for further operations in the Mediterranean, starting fresh avenues in the Pacific, and a cross-English Channel invasion.[63] Concurrently the JIC issued revised assessments on the nature of German manpower and strength, considering whether it signalled the 'disintegration' of its military power. The JIC Chairman, Victor Cavendish-Bentinck outlined the problem: 'during the past 3½ years the Joint Intelligence Sub-Committee have prepared a number of appreciations on enemy strategy and strength which have proved correct. All this good work will, however, be forgotten if we fail to appreciate the impending disintegration and thus enable our forces to take advantage thereof with the minimum of delay.'[64] The result was the instigation of a monthly process to review signs of German collapse, based on a list of conditions developed by the JIC in December 1942 on the basis of criteria evident in the collapse of the German army in 1918.[65] A revised version of this, produced in October 1943, was considered so valuable by Churchill that he decreed 'this paper is so important that it should be printed, and I will then give directions as to the circulation'.[66]

Planning continued throughout the early summer months of 1943, with the JIC producing a flurry of regular papers on what opposition might be expected to Allied plans. From May 1943 a weekly series began considering what the enemy knew about Allied intentions to invade, a practice that had been used to great effect earlier in the war.[67] To further smooth the lines of communication between the intelligence and planning realms, in mid-June it was decided to merge the JIC and JPS secretariats. Capel-Dunn, the JIC Secretary, became Deputy Secretary of the new 'Joint Planning and Joint Intelligence Staffs', with Lieutenant Colonel Edward King-Salter taking over full-time responsibility for the JIC.[68] King-Salter had previously been the military attaché in Norway at the time of the German invasion and British evacuation, and held the distinction of having been seconded to the German army in 1935 for training purposes.[69]

On 7 July 1943 – the seventh anniversary of its first meeting – the JIC reported that the enemy now knew that Sicily was to be the target for a new offensive, as significant naval and air activity had been spotted the previous evening. The result was that a 'high state of readiness' was being maintained.[70] Two days later, on 9 July, one of the largest amphibious operations in history was launched. Operation HUSKY was a strategic success, paving the way for the Italian Campaign. The war effort now took on a greater momentum, with an increased urgency in the preparation of intelligence assessments. In early August the JIC was asked to prepare a wide-ranging review of German intentions in the latter half of 1943. For the first time the JIC outlined its concerns over the task, for while 'there has probably never been a time since the war with Germany started when it was more difficult to make this appreciation . . . the initiative has now passed to the Allies in every theatre of war and Germany can have no planned strategy in the broad sense other than to counter the strategy of the Allies'.[71]

Was this the turning of the tide in the Allies' favour? The JIC certainly thought so: it was now a case of focussing on German reactions to Allied plans, rather than finding ways to counter and roll back the German menace. By the time the JIC reported the COS had embarked for QUADRANT – a further Anglo-American planning conference, this time to be held in Quebec. On their behalf the report was received by the Vice Chief of the Imperial General Staff, Lieutenant General Sir Archibald Nye, who declared: 'I consider that this paper gives a very good review of German plans . . . the paper is so important that I would like to raise a number of points . . . for discussion with the Chiefs of Staff. I have in mind the possibility of sending these points to the Chiefs of Staff in Quebec.'[72] The paper was indeed sent to the COS, who, in turn, suggested passing it to the Americans and using it as a basis for discussion at QUADRANT.[73]

Crossing the Channel

By the time of the QUADRANT conference in August 1943 Benito Mussolini, the Italian Fascist leader, had been deposed. Within the JIC there was little consensus about whether this might lead to Italy's surrender and collapse of its forces. The Anglo-American discussions concentrated on further tightening the screw against Nazi Germany. Once more, Churchill urged that the British should be 'masters of the topic', to ensure that we 'have a view to contribute to any the Americans may have'.[74] Principal amongst these was Operation OVERLORD, the cross channel invasion of Europe.

Plans for such an invasion had been under discussion for some time. For planning purposes it had been agreed that the new Chief of Staff to the Supreme Allied Commander (COSSAC), Lieutenant General Sir Frederick Morgan, needed an intelligence body answerable to him. The JIC was involved in the initial discussions over this.[75] One of COSSAC's primary functions was planning for the invasion of Europe. The JIC concluded that the newly created intelligence section of COSSAC had to be dependent on existing structures for the provision of intelligence – this implied working not only alongside the JIC, but also British and American Service intelligence directorates.[76]

It was decided at the QUADRANT conference that OVERLORD was to proceed. According to the Combined COS, it was to be the 'primary United States-British ground and air effort against the Axis in Europe', with a target date of 1 May 1944. Before that point it was essential to plan several, smaller operations, designed to ensure that when the cross channel invasion did take place, Germany would be in no position to retaliate effectively.[77] For OVERLORD to work certain pre-conditions had to be met: the German Air Force fighter strength had to be reduced; tactical surprise had to be assured; and, finally, German defences in north-west France, specifically around Caen, needed to be contained.[78]

Upon their return to London in September 1943, the COS instructed the JIC to provide warning for 'when the situation was suitable' for OVERLORD to be carried out.[79] Included in these discussions were plans for Operation RANKIN, the occupation of Europe in the event of a German collapse or even defeat. Throughout the late summer and autumn of 1943 the JIC continued to produce reports on the war in Europe, focusing on specific areas, troop dispositions and strengths, morale, and intentions. Similar reports were produced on the war in Asia, not to mention the more mundane aspects of the JIC's work, including security reviews, organisational and administrative matters. By December the JIC was, once more, asked for a fresh appraisal of the conditions in Europe, and whether RANKIN was still possible. The Committee decided to instigate a monthly series of reports on signs of German collapse, especially tailored with Operation RANKIN in mind.[80] The first of these, produced in late December, concluded that if RANKIN was carried out it would face serious opposition from the populations of occupied Europe, therefore implying that it was untenable at that time, particularly given the 'war weariness' of Germany's allies.[81]

By the start of 1944 the Allied armies had landed in southern Italy, marched into southern Europe, and were readying themselves for the battle of Monte Cassino and the subsequent taking of Rome. The JIC thought that the Germans would pose little threat in this march through central Italy.[82] A variant of this assessment had been derided, correctly, by Brooke, as 'too optimistic a basis on which to plan'.[83] Furthermore, the JIC had earlier (and correctly) estimated that the war in Russia had reached a point whereby the Germans were 'incapable of regaining the initiative'.[84] One of the first papers produced in 1944 was a detailed consideration of the opposition to be expected for OVERLORD if it was carried out in mid-May 1944. Overshadowing these discussions was a new German threat – that of the ballistic missile (see below).[85]

Further updates were issued to the monthly progress reports on German troop levels and planning for RANKIN. Of the more substantial papers that had been regularly issued, the JIC's assessment of 'German intentions' was perhaps the most significant. In preparing for the next revision of this, Hollis asked that it be drafted in such a way as to be useful for the planning of OVERLORD, demonstrating how integrated the intelligence and planning sides of the war effort had become: 'before long we shall have to review the position . . . and ultimately take a decision whether the conditions are such that we can go ahead or not'.[86] In general terms the report was accepted by the COS, though Brooke did suggest that the impact of the war in Russia on plans for OVERLORD needed strengthening. Following minor revisions it was transmitted to Eisenhower and other senior Allied military commanders, evidence of the central JIC role in allied planning.[87]

Planning continued unabated, with the military receiving and updating their ideas on an almost daily basis.[88] Although the JIC continued to provide a stream of assessments on OVERLORD, from March 1944 it also began to consider post-OVERLORD operations.[89] In March alone, more than ten papers dealt with different aspects of OVERLORD, in addition to a steady supply of daily assessments. One of the most important assessments was to gauge German awareness of Allied plans – knowledge of which, it was felt, would underpin Germany strategy. In early March 1944 the JIC wrote that 'Germany is aware that Allied forces are rapidly being built up in the United Kingdom and there is some evidence that at present she expects that the main attack will be made against the coastline facing the English Channel.'[90] The report was received with approval by the COS who authorised its despatch to Churchill and the Supreme Headquarters Allied Expeditionary Force (SHAEF).[91]

Of the various sources of intelligence for the planning of OVERLORD, signals intelligence, above all else, was crucial. Intercepts throughout April and May had a decisive impact on the conduct of operations, with the result that D-Day, the date for the invasion, was pushed backwards.[92] To increase the likelihood of concealing the true landing location, active deception measures were undertaken to mislead the German command.[93] Cavendish-Bentinck recalled how Operation FORTITUDE, the codename given to the OVERLORD deception plan was one of the 'most important and fruitful pieces of deception in the war . . . we made the Germans believe that there was going to be a second landing in the Pas de Calais under General Patton, which led them to keep five divisions in that area.'[94] However, in the run up to the invasion, the JIC was less clear about the disposition of German forces. From late May, the JIC undertook a weekly review of German knowledge of OVERLORD. The first of these, disseminated on 22 May, stated that:

> The main assault is expected against the northern coast of France from Boulogne to Cherbourg inclusive. Although the German High Command will, until our assault takes place, reckon with the possibility that it will come across the narrow Straits of Dover to the Pas de Calais area, there is some evidence that the Le Havre-Cherbourg area, including as it does those two first class ports, is regarded as a likely, and perhaps even the main, point of assault.[95]

Such assessments were essential, for knowledge of the level of the opposing German forces had always been one of the deciding factors in choosing when to launch the invasion. The difficulty in May was that the lull in the war with the Soviet Union meant that the Germans had not needed to transfer any more units eastwards. This led to further revisions in JIC assessments over what Allied forces might expect to face in France,[96] a report that was approved by the COS and immediately sent to the JSM, SHAEF and Supreme Allied Commander for the Mediterranean.[97]

A revised report was issued again at the start of June 1944. It was accepted that 'there has been no intelligence ... to suggest that the enemy has accurately assessed the area in which our main assault is to be made', it was concluded that 'he appears to expect several landings between the Pas de Calais and Cherbourg'.[98] Assisting the JIC in the production of its forecasts was accurate Sigint on the nature, disposition and location of German formations.[99] The Allies could be confident, therefore, that their deception endeavours had been successful. Three days later, on 6 June 1944, 160,000 troops crossed the channel, accompanied by just under 7,000 vessels and almost 12,000 aircraft. To the Germans it was a tactical surprise.[100] To the British it was an intelligence and military success, for as the JIC was subsequently to note: 'all the evidence suggests that the Germans did not accurately assess in advance the timing, scale or location ... in particular they do not appear to have appreciated that the weather was sufficiently favourable for large scale amphibious operations'.[101]

The successful landing in north-west France was not, of course, the end of the campaign. The deception operation to convince the Germans of a landing in the Pas de Calais region continued to cause confusion. Even by early July, the JIC could report that intelligence suggested the Germans still suspected an invasion there and so were maintaining a sizable military presence in the region.[102] By the end of July some of these units had begun to move on, some being diverted to the battles in Normandy, others to protect the sites where Hitler would unleash his weapon of vengeance.

Hitler's Secret Weapon

Upon the declaration of war Hitler, in a speech on 19 September 1939, proclaimed that Germany had an unassailable 'weapon'. Hitler's terminology was fairly ambiguous. The actual word used – 'waffe' – could be interpreted to mean a specific weapon, for instance a gun, or a much larger entity, like the air force. To investigate the basis for Hitler's claim the JIC was introduced to the world of scientific intelligence.[103] Although not central to the JIC's role, intelligence on scientific and technical targets would become increasingly important.

Detailed assessments of the German technical capacity, as opposed to basic estimates of numbers of tanks or aircraft, would not be studied until 1943. This first enquiry was at the instigation of the Ministry of Supply, who had asked the JIC to comment on various reports, all of which seem to have been procured by SIS.[104] The conclusion, described only as 'tentative', was that the Germans were experimenting with long-range rockets at a site at Peenemunde, near the Baltic coast. The more difficult question was the purpose of the rockets: anti-aircraft (considered likely) or for carrying 'very heavy quantities of high explosive' (considered less likely). The final conclusion was that they 'must still be some way from the operational stage.'[105] What is interesting here is how the JIC was only brought into the picture tangentially. It expressed disquiet that it had no technical or scientific basis of analytical expertise on which to provide assessments, but still managed to manoeuvre itself to take the lead for intelligence on German rocketry.

From the first days of the conflict, the Air Ministry's intelligence branch had brought on board a scientist to help interpret enemy developments, and in this capacity he had become attached to SIS. Born in 1911, Dr Reginald Victor Jones, or R.V. as he preferred it, held a doctorate from Oxford, where he had worked at the Clarendon Laboratory on infra-red detection.[106] Jones had first become aware of the importance of Peenemunde in 1939 with the 'Oslo Report' – a mysterious package delivered to the British Embassy in Oslo, detailing German scientific developments – even though this had not been in connection with flying rockets. It was not until the end of 1942, however, that detailed information appeared suggesting that rocketry experiments were being conducted at the site. A number of additional reports were received in early 1943 – hence the date of the JIC assessment – by which point it had been concluded by Jones' team that 'it looks as though we'll have to take those rockets seriously!'[107] By April 1943 the COS had concluded that this was, indeed, a serious threat, and accordingly the Prime Minister was informed. The COS suggested that a special section be convened to investigate the various claims about a long-range German rocket. Furthermore, it was declared that it would be best if one individual was put in charge, thereby ensuring that 'a considerable amount of his time' could be devoted to the matter.[108]

The onus was put on the Prime Minister to appoint someone, and Churchill chose Duncan Sandys for the job. Sandys was Churchill's son in law and Joint Parliamentary Secretary to the Ministry of Supply. Sandys' terms of reference were to investigate whether the intelligence was reliable, what it indicated, and what counter-measures should be employed.[109] One of Sandys' first steps was to ask the JIC for its opinion, hence the report in April.[110] Subsequently, further information was obtained through aerial reconnaissance, which began working more closely with Jones, who often directed the RAF towards various targets.[111] Intelligence was passed to Sandys by the JIC, through the office of Denis Capel-Dunn.[112] By mid-1943 the new photographic evidence, together with testimonies from Polish resistance and several prisoners of war, suggested that a long-range military rocket was being developed. Here, however, the intelligence forecasts came up against hard science.

Earlier in the war Churchill had appointed Professor Frederick Lindemann (Lord Cherwell) to be his scientific adviser. Cherwell was an Oxford physicist who, when confronted with the intelligence assessments, concluded that they could not be correct for several reasons. Firstly, and most significantly, he was innately sceptical of German scientific achievements. Furthermore, he could not accept that a rocket weighing seventy tonnes, as identified by aerial reconnaissance, could actually get off the ground; and argued that such a rocket could not be fired without arousing the suspicion of locals, who had so far not reported anything strange. His conclusion was unambiguous: he did 'not favour directing any considerable effort to cope with what seems to be a remote contingency.'[113] Jones, however, did not agree, powerfully arguing his case and destroying Cherwell's faulty and unimaginative reasoning.[114] Cherwell would, for some time, remain unconvinced and continued to argue that intelligence was being inaccurately assessed, though he did admit that 'no doubt I am biased by the fact that I do not believe in the rocket's existence.'[115] Jones subsequently retorted that while 'there are obvious technical objections which, based on our own experience, can be raised against the prospect of successful rockets, it is not without precedent for the Germans to have succeeded while we doubted.'[116] By June Sandys, sensibly, opted to believe the worst-case scenario, agreeing with Jones that offensive counter measures – an aerial attack – would be necessary to deal with the threat.

From mid-June to mid-July 1943 further reports emerged from SIS and photographic reconnaissance that indicated increased German efforts and suggested that Sandys had been right in calling for an airstrike on Peenemunde. To help collate all the incoming information, the JIC decided that an ad-hoc sub-committee should be convened by Sandys' staff.[117] This group would meet weekly and would include representatives from the Service departments. It was chaired by Colonel Kenneth Post, the Military Assistant to Duncan Sandys in the Ministry of Supply. Although the JIC did not regularly discuss the group's activities, it did express some consternation about its lack of minute taking.[118] In mid-August 1943 pre-selected targets at Peenemunde were bombed, destroying many of the industrial installations and killing several of the leading scientists and technicians.[119] Despite this tactical success, Sandys and the special sub-committee continued to investigate the German long-range rocket, as did Jones. Evidence at Peenemunde suggested that the Germans were also developing a pilotless aircraft – which would become known as the V1. By the end of September 1943 a sizable quantity of material had been amassed: 159 reports from SIS, 35 from prisoners of war, 37 from diplomatic postings, plus a wealth of photographic evidence.[120] Despite the targeted bombing, work had continued to progress to such an extent that Sandys concluded at the end of October that: 'we must . . . reckon with the possibility that the equivalent of some 2,500 to 10,000 tons might be delivered on London during the course of a single week in November or December.'[121]

At the same time the JIC was beginning to question the unusual arrangement of Sandys' sub-committee. In early October it had been asked by Brigadier Ian Jacob, the Assistant Military Secretary to the War Cabinet, to inform the COS when an attack was imminent.[122] The JIC's problem, as it correctly recognised, was that it lacked sufficient information to be able to offer an informed opinion.[123] To Hollis it appeared as if the JIC was dragging its feet and he stated 'do not let us make heavy weather of this.'[124] In the end the COS dictated that the JIC should be responsible for commenting on Sandys' reports to them, apart from on purely scientific subjects.[125]

Problems persisted however. In late October Cavendish-Bentinck informed the JIC of his concerns that Sandys' sub-committee was not doing an effective job of 'sifting all the evidence', and that he had doubts that it was the best organisation to do so. In its place he recommended convening a proper JIC Sub-Committee, as opposed to the less regularised arrangement that existed under Sandys, to take over responsibility.[126] The JIC discussed the proposal again at its next meeting, where it was approved, and the COS informed of the decision at the next joint session at the start of November. As a result, the JIC created the 'BODYLINE' Sub-Committee, under the chairmanship of Commander Ian Fleming, whose job it was to 'sift and appreciate the intelligence on "BODYLINE" contained in CX [SIS] reports'.[127] 'BODYLINE', referred to all German developments of rockets, pilotless aircraft, and glider bombs. Sandys though, was not content. He complained to the COS about the confusion in responsibility for warning about rockets and the inevitable duplication in effort between his sub-committee under Colonel Post, and the new JIC Sub-Committee. The COS retort was unequivocal: the JIC should assume the lead.[128]

The new JIC Sub-Committee on 'CROSSBOW' was created in late November 1943. The codename had replaced its earlier incarnation 'BODYLINE'. The JIC CROSSBOW Sub-Committee was to meet daily in the Air Ministry and produce a weekly report for the JIC. Importantly R.V.Jones was a member, presumably as the de facto SIS representative, a useful position in that one of the Sub-Committee's specific roles was to sift through SIS reporting for relevant information.[129] Its work was considered so important to the war effort that when the COSSAC representative complained about his workload and that he would only be able to attend CROSSBOW meetings once a week, the full JIC concluded that this should take priority over any theatre intelligence responsibilities.[130]

The first report by the CROSSBOW Sub-Committee highlighted the 'imminence of a threat against this country'. Recent reports had revealed the existence of 'ski sites', the sloping ranges needed for launching the V1, although it was not referred to as such at this stage. These sites were all targeted towards London, so there was no disagreement on their objective. There was a significant amount of detailed information on the rockets themselves, the nature of the ski slopes, and the operational readiness of the sites.[131] There was also some information on the A4 – the German rocket that would subsequently become known as the V2. Taken as a whole, it is clear that the JIC had a good picture of the threat posed by both weapons, and it was concluded that the pilotless aircraft (the V1) – codenamed BIGBEN – posed the more immediate threat.[132] In its second report the Sub-Committee concluded that 'a minimum theoretical scale of attack equivalent to a 2,000 ton bomb raid could be launched from 100 ski sites in under 24 hours. It might be 4 or 5 times as great.' The only consolation, of sorts, was that it was considered that the pilotless aircraft would not be operational in great numbers until February 1944. In many respects this was considered a graver threat to the United Kingdom than it had faced in 1940 with the possibility of German invasion.[133]

From mid-December 1943 onwards the RAF and US Army Air Force conducted a series of bombing raids directed against the ski slopes and suspected
production sites. At the same time the Air Staff began to prepare a series of papers
on further sites to attack.[134] In early January, the JIC met the COS Committee and
informed it that the CROSSBOW Sub-Committee could be wound up, barely
two months after its creation. It argued that the Sub-Committee had fulfilled
its remit in bringing together the disparate elements of government working on
rocketry intelligence, and that future work would be best located within the Air
Ministry itself, which would also assume responsibility for the weekly surveys. This
was accepted by the COS and so, from January 1944 onwards, the JIC had little
more to do with CROSSBOW or rocketry intelligence.[135]

The JIC also focussed on the other elements of what would become referred to,
in due course, as weapons of mass destruction. Starting in the latter half of the
war, periodic assessments had been made of German chemical and biological
weapons (CBW), both of which had been utilised effectively in the First World
War. Assisting the JIC was the Inter-Services Committee on Chemical Warfare.[136]
Scant details were known about biological weapons, though better information
was available about German advances in the chemical weapons field. The more
important question was one of intent: would Hitler actually deploy and use
chemical weapons?[137] By the summer of 1944, following the successful Normandy
landings, the Allied forces began to advance through Europe. The question
considered by the JIC was how Hitler would react if faced with 'imminent military
disaster'. Would he resort to the use of chemical warfare? The JIC's assessment
was that even if such an order was given, the German General Staff would
disregard it as not a sound military suggestion.[138] Further assessments as the war
progressed did not change this view, though by early 1945 it was still recognised
that 'the possibility always remains of Hitler resorting to gas warfare if he felt that
it was Germany's last resort.'[139] Another assessment considered the effect on Axis
morale – both amongst troops and at home – if the Allied forces used CBW.[140]
Somewhat surprisingly, the papers almost exclusively cover German developments
of CBW. The JIC assessment that the Japanese were of a 'very great technical
inferiority' in this sphere would turn out to be a serious underestimation.[141]

By August 1944 it had become apparent to the JIC that the Germans had made
advances in a whole raft of scientific areas, including U-boat technology, types
of mine, torpedoes, infra-red devices, rockets and tanks. It was felt that the
Germans 'may be ahead of the Allies' in approximately two-thirds of these areas;
of more concern was that at least half 'have presented or may present counter-
measure problems'.[142] Despite this dire warning, it was not considered that such
developments would drastically alter the future pattern of the war.

Notoriously absent from the list of enemy developments was the most potent
and symbolic advance of all, the atomic bomb. British intelligence had focussed
on German plans to build a nuclear device from the earliest days of the war,
with SIS, in particular, taking a keen interest.[143] Subsequently, intelligence on
German advances was considered by a body named the Tube Alloys Technical
Committee.[144] For much of the war, Britain had refrained from liaising with the

US on the German atomic programme, the Americans finally getting involved in 1943. In January 1945 the 'Tube Alloys Intelligence Committee' was created to concentrate on such matters, assuming the role previously filled by the Tube Alloys Technical Committee. It comprised British and American officials, was restricted to SIS of the intelligence agencies, and excluded Jones and other members of scientific intelligence.

Throughout the war neither SIS (who took the lead), the Tube Alloys Technical Committee, or the Tube Alloys Intelligence Committee reported to the JIC on nuclear matters, nor interacted with it in any way whatsoever; furthermore, this exclusion was deliberate. During the war, knowledge of the atomic bomb was a secret on a par with ULTRA and yet the members of the JIC were cleared to that level, so why were they not privy to atomic intelligence? The answer is two-fold: for reasons of security, access to information was extraordinarily closely guarded; the other reason, related to the first, was that the Americans had kept atomic intelligence separate from scientific intelligence, and they decreed that the British do likewise.[145] Given SIS's lead on atomic matters, 'C' would have known, and it is possible that Cavendish-Bentinck was given a partial briefing on atomic developments so that other members of the Committee could be steered away if discussion arose, though there is no evidence to confirm this. Writing in the immediate aftermath of the war in October 1945, Air Vice Marshal Thomas Elmhirst, the interim JIC Chairman, did concede that there had been 'reasons why they [the JIC] were excluded from contributing to the study of the intelligence aspect of the subject', but urged that 'now that the existence of the atomic bomb is public knowledge', then the JIC should be kept informed – this is precisely what happened (see chapter 10).[146]

In preparing for Operation OVERLORD, the COS Committee did consider some reports – not through the JIC – that the Germans might deploy some sort of radiological weapon. It was suggested by Ismay, Churchill's chief of staff, that 'the Joint Intelligence Staff must be brought into the picture', yet the reply was a resounding 'no'.[147] Even when it became clear that the Germans did not have a viable atomic programme, the JIC was not privy to the fact that the Allies did have one. This became slightly absurd when, in early August 1945, it produced a paper on the 'Japanese Attitude to Unconditional Surrender', in which it had dutifully to report, upon finishing it on 10 August, that its conclusions were no longer entirely valid given the atomic bombing of Hiroshima and Nagasaki a few days earlier.[148] Regardless of what the members of the JIC thought of their exclusion from atomic matters the Committee would try to play an active part in ensuring that all the information on 'secret weapons and scientific war effort' were gathered at the end of the war.[149]

The Defeat of Germany

The successful D-Day landings forced the German lines to pull back across Europe. The Allied armies continued to push eastwards with a series of offensives. The JIC, too, continued to work on all fronts. It produced, as was now its custom, papers ranging from the war in Europe and the abilities of the Germans to withstand bombing offensives, through to Japanese strategy and the co-ordination of intelligence and planning in the Far East with the Americans. In addition it still maintained a focus on procedural matters; issues relating to security; and increasing links with overseas intelligence authorities.

From the summer of 1944 a series of papers looked towards the end of the war, the outcome of which no longer seemed to have been in doubt. Given the variety of military outfits that would accompany and follow the Allied Expeditionary Force, the question arose as to who would co-ordinate the intelligence effort. The JIC, which first discussed this in January 1944, was interested in learning the lessons of the war for future use: 'we were ignorant of many of the factors that caused the last war to end, and we must not repeat our mistake and fail to obtain the information this time.'[150] The result was the JIC's 'Intelligence Priorities Committee', created following D-Day in June 1944. Its remit was slightly wider than originally envisaged, and included receiving, co-ordinating and submitting requests to SHAEF for intelligence.[151] The new Committee met under Cavendish-Bentinck's chairmanship and, at its first meeting, produced a list of priorities for collection.[152] This Committee would subsequently be absorbed by the Combined Intelligence Objectives Sub-Committee, usually abbreviated to CIOS and pronounced as chaos.[153] SHAEF itself would subsequently have its own JIC, with a special sub-committee on counter-intelligence.[154]

The JIC had become central to British and Allied military planning through such endeavours as Operation HUSKY and Operation OVERLORD. It had excelled in producing timely, accurate and reliable intelligence assessments. Yet its performance would not remain untarnished, particularly concerning the Ardennes offensive. The Supreme Commander Allied Expeditionary Force, General Eisenhower, set his sights on advancing into Germany itself through a series of offensives in the autumn of 1944. Using its experience with the flying bombs, the JIC produced a number of papers on German strategy, looking at it in isolation as well as with special reference to 'new weapons'. It was in this latter area that the JIC felt Germany would reveal its hand. The JIC anticipated that Germany would aim to thwart Allied advances in the west through the development of novel weapons, particularly the pilotless aircraft and the rocket.[155]

In his Official History of British Grand Strategy, John Ehrman has stated that the three weeks from mid-August to early September 1944, were 'among the most dramatic of the European war'.[156] At the start of the period the JIC produced its latest assessment of 'German strategy and capacity to resist'. This series had, by now, become a monthly feature of the Committee's work. The assessment in mid-August was noticeably more upbeat than previous versions. The successes of D-Day and subsequent advances had resulted in 'new and major disasters' for the Germans which had brought 'her to the verge of defeat'. Furthermore, 'German strategy can only continue to be one of improvisation in a desperate effort to hold the advancing Allies.' To the JIC, the implications were clear: 'such a defeat will come about before the end of this year.'[157] A month later the JIC was even more certain of its conclusions. Germany had suffered 'catastrophic disasters' and now 'the process of final military defeat leading to the cessation of organised resistance has begun in the West'. In fact, the Committee felt that there was nothing the German High Command could do to halt this deterioration; the only question was the speed with which the collapse would occur.[158]

Such a forecast was fundamentally inaccurate. At the time Brooke called the report 'somewhat optimistic', though he also stated that 'he had no reason to disagree with it'.[159] Churchill, too, felt it 'errs on the side of optimism', and that, while he did not reject the JIC's findings, 'no one can tell what the future may bring forth'. For Churchill, any German collapse would be 'political rather than military'.[160] Without any record of the original JIS material it is impossible to tell what specific intelligence contributed to the JIC's assessment. From the document itself though, it is clear that there were certain criteria on which its forecast was based: morale levels; production levels of stocks and supplies, particularly oil; and the reducing size of the armed forces. Active Allied efforts had been undertaken to disrupt supplies and it was noted that troop numbers were now 'at a low'. Were these the correct criteria to use? Pre-war the JIC had often fallen back on a similar system – a nation's armed forces could only be as good as its supply lines and research and development programme – and this had served it well. What it did not take into account, and arguably should have done, was the effect of Allied advances on increasing German military efforts. Similarly, a weakness in the reasoning was to underestimate the German High Command's capacity to inflict a counter-blow, a mistake that would cost the Allied war effort dearly.

From September the JIC produced a constant flurry of reports, detailing German movements in Europe. Despite suffering further setbacks, German resistance proved to be far stronger than predicted. In its next monthly update, in mid-October, the JIC recognised these mixed fortunes. Yet overshadowing all else, in the Committee's opinion, was the fact that German supplies were in a dire situation, her economy and manpower levels were weak, such that 'she cannot for long resist sustained Allied attack'. It was hard to disagree with these conclusions; however, the implications drawn by the JIC revealed a clear case of mirror-imaging – projecting onto the enemy one's own thoughts and feelings. Germany's weaknesses, according to the JIC, 'must be clear to many, if not all, of Germany's leaders'. Perhaps they were, but this did not mean that they would have perceived them in the same way as the Allies would have done. By October the predicted pace of German collapse, although still considered inevitable, had become slower than at first thought.[161]

Throughout the autumn of 1944 the Allied armies continued to advance. Discussions at the OCTAGON military conference in Quebec in September 1944 had set the agenda for winning the war. Amongst General Eisenhower's plans was the directive to focus effort on northern Europe, defeat the German forces west of the Rhine, seize control of the numerous bridgeheads, and then advance into Germany for the final confrontation. One of the initial moves was to be the ill-fated Operation MARKET GARDEN, the plan to capture several bridges in Holland. The tactical failures here, in particular the inability to gauge German opposition levels and to factor these into the very ambitious

Allied plans, were not the fault of the JIC, nor indeed the result of faulty intelligence – high level intercepts had provided a wealth of evidence.[162] Indeed, the setback at Arnhem contributed to the JIC's revised assessment of the pace of German decline.

Sigint continued to provide a stream of high-level military information on German intentions and contributed to a JIC assessment on the subject in mid-November. In trying to explain why the Germans were moving air force and army contingents from Germany to the Western Front, the JIC outlined the alternatives before providing its own viewpoint: 'we do not think that the evidence . . . warrants the conclusion that the Germans are planning a spoiling offensive [implying that Germany would attack the Allies while plans were underway to launch an offensive].'[163] There is a fascinating glimpse here into the changes made between drafts. An earlier version had been more definite: 'we conclude that the enemy are planning to spring a surprise which would almost certainly include attacks on Allied airfields'.[164] In fact, this earlier view would be closer to what would happen, so why did it not appear in the final version? Upon receiving the paper, the COS asked to meet the JIC to discuss the judgment and it was subsequently agreed that it should be removed.[165] From the records it is not clear why the COS were so adamant about this. Hinsley states that it was because the original paragraph took attention away from the main conclusion, which supported the COS position, and so it was best not to divert the reader's focus.[166] This raises an interesting point about the operational interference in intelligence assessment. Today this practice might be frowned upon but, for the JIC at this point, it was simply part of the intelligence process: assessments were prepared principally for use by the COS and military planners and therefore they had to satisfy the customer.

On the Eastern Front the Red Army had begun to hinder German progress, and it was clear that a major Soviet winter offensive was being planned. To the Germans therefore it made tactical sense to strike a blow against the western flank, as it was far less well defended and had poorer supply lines. The operation was planned in utmost secrecy, with troops being moved at night and very little radio traffic. By early December Air Ministry intelligence could report that 'the original plan for "lightning blow" and sudden attack in the west may with some certainty be said to have lapsed.'[167] The JIC itself did not prepare an assessment, and while it is tempting to conclude that information was lacking on which to base one, Sigint was available which suggested the Germans were certainly planning something.[168]

In the early hours of 16 December 1944 the German army launched a major counter offensive against the Allied forces in the Ardennes, an attack that would ultimately claim over 80,000 Allied lives. Focussing on the move a few days later, the JIC provided a reasoned analysis of Hitler's motives: it had not been the last throes of a madman intent on holding onto power, but rather was a sensible move, both militarily and strategically. The report does not convey any feelings of panic or desperation, instead portraying the offensive as what it was – an attack by the German military to secure concessions from the Allies and interrupt their progress.[169] At no point did the JIC question why the attack came as a surprise – an event which one JIS member later described as a 'most spectacular blunder'.[170] It is clear from a fascinating post-war document on the use made by the JIS of ULTRA material why this was so. ULTRA decrypts suggested that it was likely to be an air offensive, and without any other good sources of information, it was decided 'to avoid giving the tactical picture'.[171] On the other side of the Atlantic several post-mortems were conducted, though none seem to have been entertained in London. The difficulty, of course, was that a combination of long-held views of German intentions, and a tendency to see the German military through Allied eyes, ensured that intelligence reflected biased perceptions.[172]

Within a few days the JIC had revised its view of German objectives, now stating that the long term planning that must have gone into the operation suggested 'more ambitious ultimate objectives'.[173] As it was, the German advances petered out in the New Year following an Allied counter offensive. Revising its paper on 'German strategy and capacity to resist' in January, the JIC, in stark contrast to previous versions, was less clear on when Germany might collapse. It now depended on a variety of factors, largely military, but it was judged Germany would survive until at least April 1945.[174] The COS Committee approved the report, noting that it tallied with its estimated dates for the end of the war.[175] Churchill's response, in typically abrupt prose, was to ask Ismay to compare recent JIC forecasts with previous predictions, noting that he should 'not let the officers concerned know that what they said a few months ago is being compared with what they say now. It would only dishearten them.'[176] Having received the report Churchill cut straight to the point: 'they [JIC] manage to get it exactly wrong in their report of September 5 [JIC(44)395 – see above]. It would be impossible to state the opposite of what has happened more exactly. I know the difficulty of prophecy, but this is a pretty bad one.'[177]

Throughout the early months of 1945 the JIC continued to produce a variety of reports on the developing European war. On the continent, following the German setback after the Ardennes attack, Allied forces spread throughout Europe. In terms of supporting military planning in Europe, the JIC's role was almost over. Attention therefore turned towards other subjects. The JIC was not entirely convinced of the possibility of a German national redoubt, some sort of inner fortress in the Alpine provinces, though it recognised that 'some reports' suggested the existence of such a plan. Overall, it was not felt that 'large scale resistance' would prove possible.[178] By March the situation was clear: the German High Command was now facing 'a disaster more complete than any that has yet befallen the German Nation'. Despite this, it was accepted that Hitler had 'probably not yet abandoned all hope of turning the tide'. Given the previous difficulty in assessing German attitudes independently from the Allied position, this was a reasonable verdict. The final defeat now rested more on Allied capabilities – how quickly and effectively operations could be conducted – than on German strategy or capacity to resist.[179]

In the spring of 1945 the Allied forces made a series of spectacular advances through Europe. By March, the largely British and American contingent from the west, and the Soviet army from the east, sped towards Berlin in a final dash to the finish. On 20 April the Red Army, having arrived first, encountered bloody resistance in the Battle of Berlin, which lasted until 2 May when the German forces in the city finally surrendered. News of the capitulation arrived a few days after another momentous event had occurred: in a bunker underneath the city, Hitler and some of his entourage, in a final act of defiance, committed suicide. Just a few days later the Germans, under Grand Admiral Karl Doenitz, signed surrender terms. After six long years the war in Europe was finally over.

Victory in the East

Whilst defeat of the Axis powers in Europe was the JIC's top reporting priority for the second half of the war, it was not its only area of concern. The entry of the Japanese into the Second World War had helped crystallise the developing Anglo-American intelligence relationship. On the planning side the decision was taken to concentrate first on the defeat of Europe. On the intelligence side, a series of seminal Sigint agreements ensured that Britain retained responsibility for European codes, whereas the Americans took primacy in relation to Japan, where the US was heavily committed.[180] This delineation of the tasks was reflected, to an extent, in the production of assessments. The American JIC spent far more time on Japan than the JIC in London, though its assessments were routinely shared with its British counterpart. It appears that British intelligence, and in particular SIS, had no great sources of information in the region.[181] Despite this, the JIC was by no means ignorant of developments in Asia, and still produced its own forecasts, but at a slower pace and less frequently. What is clear is that both London and Washington felt that the Axis powers were disunited, with no common aims or objectives, for as the American JIC made clear: 'Japan's policy is dictated throughout by self interest. She is not prepared to make any effort involving serious risk in order to give relief to her Axis partners, even should they appear to be in danger of defeat.' This divergence was also evident in what Japan might hope to achieve, with the US concluding that its only policy was to 'defend her sphere against the Allies and to rely on their exhaustion and war weariness to bring about a negotiated peace.'[182] The JIC in London expressed its 'satisfaction' with the US report.[183]

Assessments of Japan only began to gather pace once it became clear that Germany was on the ropes and facing imminent defeat. The successes of the D-Day landings led the JIC to widen its remit and from the autumn of 1944 it disseminated regular updates on Japanese intentions. The majority of these were not, however, JIC papers; rather they were produced by such groups as the American JIC, the FO, or South East Asia Command. In September 1944 the Services' Directors of Intelligence paid a visit to Washington. One of the main items for discussion with the Americans was co-ordinating the intelligence effort in the Far East, and they were joined by the Australian Director of Military Intelligence, the Chief of the Intelligence Section for the Eastern Fleet, and a representative of the FO. The talks went favourably and everyone seems to have returned to London content.[184] This series of meetings followed on from another successful venture that had taken place at the start of September, where the JIC had organised a conference on the 'co-ordination of Far East intelligence', which had aimed to formalise relations within and amongst the countries of the British Commonwealth.[185] By the end of 1944, therefore, much of the intelligence effort necessary to support operations against Japan had been put in place.

JIC assessments of Japanese intentions were continually based on a key assumption: the date by which Germany would be defeated. This was considered important because following such a capitulation, Soviet forces would be diverted to the Far East and this would change the strategic balance. The forecast in August 1944 was predicated on a 1944 German defeat, and concluded that Japanese intentions were primarily defensive, aiming to delay Allies advances in the Pacific for as long as possible.[186] The revised paper, produced in December 1944, now judging that Germany would be defeated by June 1945, stated that Japan had not yet begun to withdraw its forces to prepare for the final Allied assault on the mainland.[187] By spring 1945, both the American and British JICs agreed that on the assumption that Germany would be defeated by July 1945, then fighting against the Japanese would continue into early 1946, with an assault on Japan's outer zone – including Indochina, Sumatra, Borneo and Java – to begin in the spring of 1946.[188]

What is interesting here is that no connection was drawn between the status of the Allied forces, Japan's defences, and what might be expected to trigger a Japanese surrender; one of the difficulties faced in gauging this was an understanding of where the real power lay in Japan. In early April the Koiso Cabinet fell. Although a significant event, the FO informed the JIC that within the Japanese system there was a 'visible Administration (the Cabinet of the moment) and an "invisible" one'; this latter group comprised military chiefs, former Prime Ministers and figures within the Imperial Household.[189] Complicating the situation further, from an Allied perspective, was the FO belief that the Japanese population had 'reached the conclusion that the war is lost'.[190] The implications of this were difficult to estimate. Assuming that Germany would be defeated by July and that Russia would not declare war on Japan until October, then it was concluded that Japan would not try to conclude a peace deal with the UK and US. On the other hand, the JIC could not 'exclude the possibility' that faced with a battle against the UK, US and Russia, the Japanese might choose to surrender instead. In other words, the JIC assessment included both scenarios – which were mutually exclusive – and suggested that both were possible.[191]

Throughout May the number of assessments on Japan grew steadily, including American JIC views on the likely troop disposition and strength to be faced in an invasion, a FO view of the current political climate, and a JIC report on whether the release of photographs of Japanese PoWs would induce surrender (it was considered worthy of an attempt).[192] As a basis the military planners used the assumption that war with Japan would continue well into 1946, and so the JIC was asked to provide its views accordingly. To this end, the JIC was tasked by the JPS in late June with considering whether a 'modification' of the unconditional surrender terms might be sufficient to end the war. These terms, which many historians have since considered to be too harsh, were subsequently agreed by the Allied leaders at the Potsdam conference in July 1945. The JIC's report, an example of the Committee's skilful and considered experience by this point, concluded that acceptance of 'unconditional surrender' would be extremely unlikely because it implied the overthrow of the Imperial House. For the military, furthermore, surrender would only be possible if it did not discredit their warrior ethos. A better option would be to stop using that term and to refrain from suggesting that a Japanese capitulation implied an overthrow of their institutional structures. The final assessment, taking these points into account, was that 'they would probably surrender more readily before invasion than immediately after it'.[193]

The JIC were unaware that at the same time high-level discussions were underway in Washington and London about the deployment of a new weapon, the atomic bomb. On 1 July, Churchill, in perhaps his most important final decision as wartime Prime Minister, signed a minute confirming his acquiescence to the use of the bomb. Importantly this decision was taken without consulting the COS.[194] The JIC, too, was equally in the dark. From July onwards the majority of the JIC's work focussed on trying to assess how Japan might react to various military moves, and what factors would induce surrender.[195] Immediately prior to the dropping of the first atomic bomb on Hiroshima, the JIC had observed that 'there is evidence that the Japanese Cabinet, and indeed the Emperor himself, desire to bring hostilities to an early close. They are prepared to accept peace on the Allied terms provided these avoid the form of unconditional surrender and ensure the preservation of the Japanese "National Structure".' Thereafter, a further bomb had been dropped, this time on Nagasaki, and Russia had declared war. The impact of both was such that 'we do not feel able to confidently predict the effect on the Japanese of these tremendous events.'[196] On 15 August 1945 Emperor Hirohito broadcast a radio message, declaring that Japan had accepted the peace terms proffered at Potsdam – the war in the Pacific was over.

End of an Era

The day before VJ-Day the JIC met, as normal, in the Secretary's room on Great George Street in Whitehall. Atypically the meeting was chaired by Rear Admiral Rushbrooke, the DNI. There were two important items on the agenda. The first was to report the death of Colonel Denis Capel-Dunn, who had become the JIC's Assistant Secretary in November 1940 and its Secretary from December 1941. Although he had become Secretary of the Joint Staff upon the amalgamation of the JIC/JPS secretariats in June 1943, he had continued to be involved with the JIC. Capel-Dunn had been in San Francisco, taking part in the creation of the United Nations Charter and, together with several British officials, including Sir William Malkin, the senior legal adviser in the FO, had been aboard a plane leaving Montreal for London that had gone missing on 3 July 1945.[197] Although no body was found, the search for Capel-Dunn was abandoned in mid-July and he was presumed dead.[198] Cavendish-Bentinck and Ian Jacob (one of Ismay's deputies who had worked alongside the JIC and who had worked with Capel-Dunn in San Francisco) published a glowing tribute to Capel-Dunn in *The Times*. 'Equipped with a clear logical mind', they wrote, 'a sound judgment, and a marked ability for organisation, Capel-Dunn was able to profit to the full from his wide experience and varied activities . . . he was particularly concerned with the development of the Joint Planning and Intelligence Staff, the inter-service organisation which grew in scope and importance with the progress of the war.'[199]

The second significant item on the agenda was the departure as Chairman of Victor Cavendish-Bentinck, who had been appointed in December 1939, and served almost the entire duration of the war. His appointment had been lengthy and he had successfully managed to avoid a posting as Field Marshal Montgomery's Political Adviser in 1944. As a result, when he was asked to become His Majesty's Representative in Poland, he felt he 'could not get out of it'.[200] Speaking on behalf of the JIC, Rear Admiral Rushbrooke stated that they 'very much regretted' his departure, and 'wished to record a sincere vote of thanks for the invaluable work done by Mr Cavendish-Bentinck on behalf of the Services and of Intelligence.'[201] That same morning Cavendish-Bentinck appeared before the COS Committee for the last time. Commenting on his departure, Field Marshal Alan Brooke, the CIGS, stated 'that he would like to take this opportunity of expressing on behalf of the Committee, the deep gratitude for the excellent work done by Mr Cavendish-Bentinck during the past six years. The Chiefs of Staff Committee and the Joint Intelligence Sub-Committee were greatly indebted to him for all the help and assistance he had given them throughout this long period'.[202] Despite such warm sentiments on the invaluable role he had played, Cavendish-Bentinck would end up leaving public office under a cloud within just a few short years.

In the mid-1920s Cavendish-Bentinck had met and subsequently married Clothilde Quigley, an American heiress. She had accompanied him on several of his pre-war diplomatic postings, causing quite a commotion wherever she appeared. At the start of the war, with Cavendish-Bentinck poised to assume the JIC's chair, she had taken their children and departed for the United States. His biographer has stated that this was, in many respects, a blessing in disguise: 'relieved of a marriage which now offered little but emotional stresses, he was able to devote all his mind and energies to the task facing him'.[203] Wishing to re-marry, Cavendish-Bentinck instituted divorce proceedings whilst he took up his position in Warsaw.

While his divorce progressed in private, Cavendish-Bentinck relocated to Poland. His posting would only last two years, ending somewhat ignominiously. In November 1946 the Polish government arrested Count Ksawery Grocholski on espionage charges, alleging that he had passed secret information to the British Ambassador, Cavendish-Bentinck, who was accused of being a spy.[204] Grocholski initially denied such matters, but after 'interrogation' by the Polish authorities, subsequently admitted guilt and was executed. To the detriment of Anglo-Polish relations, Cavendish-Bentinck then proceeded to publicly state that the national elections in January 1947 were neither free nor fair. To the Poles he promptly became persona non grata and was recalled to London.[205] It was rapidly decided to post Cavendish-Bentinck to Rio de Janeiro as Ambassador to Brazil.

At the same time, in early spring 1947, Cavendish-Bentinck's divorce proceedings were coming to a conclusion. They were messy and *The Times* carried large extracts, as did other broadsheets. The decision went against Cavendish-Bentinck after he admitted to having had a number of affairs whilst he was separated during the war.[206] He appealed, attracting more attention, but this time was successful and was granted a decree nisi.[207] A counter-appeal to the House of Lords was launched, but subsequently withdrawn.[208]

There the matter should have lain, but unfortunately for Cavendish-Bentinck it did not. Under FO rules of the time, no one in the diplomatic service was permitted to re-marry without the permission of the Secretary of State.[209] There were precedents: Ralph Skrine Stevenson for instance, Cavendish-Bentinck's predecessor as JIC Chairman, had been allowed to re-marry; the difference here was the way that Cavendish-Bentinck's divorce had been widely covered in the press. According to Sir John Colville, Churchill's wartime Assistant Private Secretary and someone who had known Cavendish-Bentinck, this publicity, together with the Polish spy allegations, and the intervention of the media baron Lord Beaverbrook on Cavendish-Bentinck's behalf, doomed any future career. According to Colville, the Secretary of State, Ernest Bevin, could not 'abide' Beaverbrook, and he sought to take this out on Cavendish-Bentinck.[210] His FO career was terminated, as were his pension rights.[211] It was an extraordinary change of fortune for someone who had spent twenty-eight years in the diplomatic service, including six years at the helm of the JIC. To add insult to injury, it was later revealed by Sir Pierson Dixon, the Foreign Secretary's Principal Private Secretary, that Bevin had retorted at the time: 'I could have saved him if his name had been Smith'.[212] There is nothing to confirm or refute this; in writing to Dixon, Cavendish-Bentinck did say that 'the Secretary of State was very nice to me when I saw him last Monday; I am one of his strong admirers'.[213] In July 1948, the matter now finally resolved, Cavendish-Bentinck married Kathleen Tillotson. He would go on to pursue a successful second career in business and finance.

A Joint Intelligence War?

With the end of the war came a proposal for the JIC to produce a study on why Germany had collapsed.[214] The final report was not issued until October 1946 and was a lengthy 196 pages. It was written by the JIS and relied upon the testimony of numerous witnesses and the archives of various branches of the German military and the Ministry of Foreign Affairs. In discussing German weaknesses, it made no mention of Allied successes. For the JIC there were 'factors which first and fundamentally interfered with the basic Germany strategy:

(a) Germany's failure to appreciate the long-term consequences of Great Britain entering the war when she did, and her failure to eliminate Great Britain before becoming engaged with Russia.

(b) Germany's misappreciation that Russia could be disposed of very quickly, which resulted in the fatal war on two fronts.

The report continued, 'Among the weaknesses which came to light as a result of these fundamental errors, we consider it of interest to examine the following:

(a) Characteristics inherent in Hitler's personality as leader of the State and Supreme Commander of the German Armed Forces.
(b) The deficiencies of the working of the machinery of joint command, as shown in practice.
(c) The inadequacies of German intelligence.
(d) The organisation of German war production.[215]

The report was warmly endorsed by the COS Committee, even though it was recognised that subsequent Official Histories might record that it contained 'errors and omissions'.[216] What, therefore, of the role of intelligence and the part played by the JIC?

At an organisational level the JIC had a good war, moving from a relatively obscure and distrusted position to one of influence and respect. The changing status of the JIC can be attributed to various factors. Christopher Andrew attaches importance to what he calls 'the powerful influence of the Prime Minister himself.'[217] By contrast, both Patrick Howarth and Kenneth Strong (both of whom worked with him) place considerable weight on the character and personal abilities of the JIC Chairman, Victor Cavendish-Bentinck.[218] Hinsley does not attach great significance to any one factor, and overall tends to downplay or ignore the role of personalities. Edward Thomas, one of Hinsley's co-authors, gives credit entirely to the JIS.[219]

What is certainly clear is that the JIC's stature, in the eyes of the military, rose immeasurably. By mid-1944 the JIC could state in a review that its present duties were to 'advise the Chiefs of Staff and through them the Minister of Defence and the Cabinet upon the immediate and long term intentions of the enemy and the probable course of events.'[220] At a tactical level, too, the JIC had much to offer. Throughout the war it produced a series of daily and weekly papers, the vast majority of which no longer survive, but where they do exist it is clear that their value would have been immense. One example was the transmission by Cavendish-Bentinck of a weekly report to senior figures in the FO, summarising discussions between the JIC and the COS together with comments and views.[221] In addition, with the creation of the JIS the military planners had a body that they could task to answer specific queries. The vast majority of the JIS papers have not been preserved either, but surviving examples reveal their value: the JIS, for instance, was often called upon to provide assessments of very precise information or questions put to it and to do so in a very short time. In this way the planners had a body, albeit with a short institutional memory, that could evaluate incoming information against what was already known. These were never issued as formal JIC papers and exist sporadically in the archive: just how often the JIS was asked to complete such tasks we cannot know. What this does reveal is the less well recognised aspect of the JIC's work as an umbrella organisation.[222]

From 1942 onwards JIC assessments were routinely disseminated onwards and upwards. In passing JIC assessments to Churchill, Hollis would almost always add, as the final line, 'the Chiefs of Staff concur'. The CIGS, Brooke, was perhaps the most vocal of the COS, and he often expressed his views in comments on a first draft, but these were often ironed out in the revised version. In this way the JIC worked hand in hand with the COS and military planners. In general the JIC lived to serve the COS and so papers were re-drafted to address their concerns. Does this undermine the Committee's objectivity? Possibly to a small extent, but it seems clear that no papers would have been issued with which the JIC did not entirely agree. Furthermore, in the build up to OVERLORD for instance, a variety of notes were passed from Hollis to Churchill, keeping him updated on the intelligence situation, and often these JIC assessments were passed to Churchill before the COS had either seen or approved them.[223]

The role of personalities was fundamental to the JIC's increasingly important place within the war effort. Churchill himself was an admirer of intelligence. It is a well known fact that he had delivered to him every morning, personally by the Chief of SIS, the 'golden eggs' – the daily ULTRA decrypts. Less well known is the fact that his daily intake also included JIC papers, a box to which he alone had the key.[224] Churchill was a strong advocate for wanting to see the original single source intelligence itself which, from the perspective of the intelligence community, carried dangers. David Stafford suggests that several failures, citing the JIC's inability to predict the Ardennes offensive as an example, led Churchill to increase his calls for this un-digested information.[225] Whatever his reasoning, it is certainly clear that Churchill took a keen interest in the work of the JIC, and evidently saw it as an integral and valuable part of Britain's war effort.

Undoubtedly the most influential figure in the JIC's success was its Chairman, Victor Cavendish-Bentinck. He played an increasingly hands-on role in steering the JIC, and while he was not solely responsible for the system's improvement, as its helmsman he was pivotal. Chairing the JIC was not Cavendish-Bentinck's only duty: he became the FO representative on the JPS and attended COS Committee meetings, usually in his FO guise. Both of these were weekly occurrences in the second half of the war, and both would have been important and time-consuming. In addition, he also chaired the JIC's sub-committee on Intelligence Priorities. Furthermore, he appears to have become the FO's man for all matters secret: he was heavily involved in re-structuring SIS to equip it for the post-war world; in evaluating SOE and calling for its demise[226]; in SIS discussions about assassination plots and preparations for OVERLORD[227]; and was involved with a deception ploy in the Cicero espionage affair.[228]

The official minutes reveal little of Cavendish-Bentinck's deft handling of matters as Chairman, but details have been provided by Noel Annan, a wartime member of the JIS. He wrote how,

> Bill Bentinck sometimes dropped into our mess before dinner to pick our brains ... he held informal meetings to discuss enemy intentions, and

encouraged junior as well as senior officers to speak their minds. No one was better informed about every intrigue in the War Cabinet Offices, and he never disclosed his sources . . . he was both astute and prescient . . . he had the gift of producing harmony among the service intelligence chiefs. He would listen, his long fingers touching his chin, looking relaxed and cunning, defusing disagreement with banter.[229]

Cavendish-Bentinck was both the Chairman of the JIC and its FO representative. In theory therefore, his participation in the Committee was to represent and promote the FO line. However, as Laurence Kirwan, a member of the JIS, has recalled, 'he was supposed to represent Foreign Office policy, but I sometimes wondered whether if it was Bentinck policy'.[230] Major General Sir Kenneth Strong, later head of the Defence Intelligence Staff (DIS) but during the war Eisenhower's chief of intelligence, also testified to Cavendish-Bentinck's abilities as Chairman:

> when Bill Cavendish-Bentinck came upon the scene in October 1939 the British Intelligence community was confused and seeking leadership. This leadership was to be Cavendish-Bentinck's greatest contribution . . . in retrospect, the most unlikely feature of the structure was the fact that the three service Intelligence chiefs were prepared to subject themselves to the chairmanship of a non-service diplomat with no previous experience in intelligence . . . his new colleagues found that he was an excellent chairman, tactful, relaxed and good-tempered; he would lean back in his chair with his hands pressed together and listen, looking very wise and cunning, and keeping the discussion to the point. Eventually he would intervene in a slightly bantering manner which would remove the heat from really contentious issues.[231]

Cavendish-Bentinck also acted as FO representative at various junctures, for instance, travelling to SHAEF and through Germany in April 1945 and assisting the War Crimes Commission on the advisability of using intercepted messages as evidence.[232] Yet Cavendish-Bentinck's primary function was to serve the JIC. Unlike some of his successors as Chairman, who saw their role as essentially facilitators, he was keen to get involved and regarded himself as an equal contributor alongside his more senior military colleagues.

On the subject of consensus and agreement, upon which the JIC was predicated, the minutes of meetings reveal little in the way of conflict or major disagreement, though it is clear that there were several heated discussions; certainly by the middle part of the war the JIC was operating as an effective inter-service committee. David Stafford suggests that a powerful motivating factor here was the need to appear as a united front to 'protect themselves against Churchill'. The COS unquestionably needed insulating, so it would be no surprise that the JIC felt a similar urge.[233] Indeed, John Ehrman has argued that for the COS 'their power derived from that fact that they formed a close team'.[234]

The JIC model was not unique to Britain, though this is where it originated. By the end of the war it had been successfully replicated in a variety of countries and organisations. Perhaps the most important was the American JIC and its relationship with the British JIC (Washington). In addition the Canadians had their own version – the Canadian Joint Intelligence Committee – instigated in 1943 and specifically designed so as to foster liaison with the British.[235] A JIC had been created in Algiers in 1943 and another version in Cairo in 1944. Towards the end of the war a JIC (Control Commission Germany) had been initiated to organise and co-ordinate the British intelligence effort in support of the occupation, as had a similar body in Austria – the JIC (Allied Commission for Austria).[236] The JIC model was truly exportable, or so it was felt at the time.

The JIC, although created before the Second World War, matured during the six year conflict. Statistics are impressive: from September 1939 to VJ-day in August 1945 it held a total of 391 meetings; produced 729 assessments, most over 5 pages in length; amassed a staggering 5,295 secretariat minutes; and compiled an unknown number of daily and weekly summaries:

Table 5.1 Frequency of wartime JIC meetings, memoranda and secretariat paperwork

	Meetings	*Memoranda*	*Secretariat Minutes*[237]
September to December 1939	18	7	N/A
January to December 1940	75	65	N/A
January to December 1941	40	92	N/A
January to December 1942	63	51	383
January to December 1943	65	188	2,084
January to December 1944	75	233	1,675
January to 15 August 1945	55	93	1,153

Overall, then, this was a hard working committee. In addition to its written record, the Services' members of the JIC, together with Cavendish-Bentinck, met the COS weekly from the middle part of the war onwards. The meeting was designed to resolve any issues, but also for the COS Committee to be presented with recent tactical intelligence, often provided by ULTRA.[238] A fascinating glimpse of the experience can be taken from a note by Cavendish-Bentinck, who declared the three COS to be 'stubborn and short-sighted'.[239] At these meetings oral briefings would be given on current military activities affecting the German and Japanese Naval, Army and Air Forces.[240] These must have been valued by the COS, because even after the conclusion of the War in Europe, it was decided to continue them.[241] In addition the JIS produced a steady supply of answers to Churchill's incessant questioning.[242] Throughout the war the JIC was involved with a large cast list of characters, some of whom would attain fame for one reason or another, including Ian Fleming, Lord Rothschild, Anthony Blunt and Kim Philby.[243] Perhaps a final reflection can be left to Denis Capel-Dunn, who in replying to yet another missive from Churchill, informed Ismay that:

> The Prime Minister asks if there is no arrangement by which all Intelligence of the Departments is brought together. The answer is that it is for this precise

purpose that the Joint Intelligence Sub-Committee and its permanent Staffs [exist] . . . It is round my table that the ultimate distillate of all this mass of material is turned into an agreed Joint Staff view for submission to the Chiefs of Staff and the Minister of Defence. The process is continuous.[244]

The Joint Intelligence Committee had finally come of age.

Notes

1 Cmd.6351, *The Organisation for Joint Planning* (London: HMSO, 1942). p.3.
2 M Howard, *British Intelligence in the Second World War: Volume 5 – Strategic Deception* (London: HMSO, 1990), p.7.
3 A number of these are in CAB 81/100.
4 A list of staff and a map of their location can be found in CAB 21/1995.
5 Elizabeth Fitzgerald papers, Imperial War Museum. Norman was her wartime maiden name.
6 Interview with E.Norman, 8 June 2009.
7 This is a mixture of information from an account in the Fitzgerald papers, and from the interview on 8 June 2009.
8 For an American perspective see L L Montague, 'The Origins of National Intelligence Estimating', *CIA Studies in Intelligence* 16:2 (Spring 1972), pp.63–70. For a good overview see 'History of the Joint Staff Mission', C.P.Warren. CAB 102/388.
9 Correspondence about this is in CAB 163/6.
10 'MI2 Comments on US(JIC68) JIC(42)510', 22 December 1942. WO 208/2059A. This file is full of comments by MI2 (the War Office's intelligence section on the Middle and Far East) on various JIC papers.
11 V.Cavendish-Bentinck to D.Capel-Dunn, 7 November 1942. CAB 121/230.
12 D.Capel-Dunn to L.Hollis [Secretary, COS], 8 November 1942. CAB 121/230.
13 'Visit to Washington January 1943', 25 January 1943. CAB 163/6.
14 JIC(43)6th Meeting, 2 February 1943. CAB 81/91.
15 F.H.N.Davidson to D.Capel-Dunn, 12 April 1943. CAB 163/6.
16 JIC(43)21st Meeting, 20 April 1943. CAB 81/91. For an example see the comparison of British and US JIC papers on German Strategy in 1943. US National Archives and Records Administration II Archive (hereafter NARA II), College Park, MD: RG 319, Box 2143.
17 JIC(43)28th Meeting, 1 June 1943. CAB 81/91.
18 JIC(43)50th Meeting, 12 October 1943. CAB 81/91.
19 JIC(43)44th Meeting, 31 August 1943. CAB 81/91.
20 JIC(43)63rd Meeting, 14 December 1943. CAB 81/91.
21 COS(42)7(0), 'American-British Strategy', 5 January 1942. CAB 80/61.
22 Howard, *Grand Strategy*.
23 COS(42)256th Meeting, 5 September 1942. CAB 79/23.
24 JSM376, JSM Washington to Chiefs of Staff London, 3 September 1942. CAB 121/145.
25 OZ1206, COS to JSM, 8 September 1942. CAB 121/145.
26 COS(42)315th Meeting, 12 November 1942. CAB 79/24.
27 For details see CAB 121/127.
28 The file that this should be in: CAB 81/110, has been mislaid by The National Archives – clues can be obtained in JPS papers in CAB 84/49.
29 JIC(42)447(0), 'Operations Consequent on "TORCH"', 14 November 1942. CAB 81/111.
30 COS(42)397(0), 'Future Strategy and Planning', 17 November 1942. CAB 80/65.

31 JSM487, JSM to COS, 19 November 1942. CAB 121/127.

32 OZ1923, COS to JSM, 18 November 1942. CAB 121/127.

33 Roosevelt to Churchill, 19 November 1942. CAB 121/127.

34 Handwritten note, 20 November 1942. CAB 121/127.

35 COS(42)(O)189th Meeting, 25 November 1942. CAB 79/58.

36 JIC(42)462(Final), 'German Strategy in 1943', 3 December 1942. CAB 81/112.

37 This was subsequently produced as JIC(42)477, 'German Strategy in 1943', 7 December 1942. CAB 81/112.

38 OZ2150, COS to Commanders-in-Chief, 7 December 1942. CAB 121/412.

39 Both of these can be found in CAB 81/112.

40 JIC(42)474, 'Italian Morale', 4 December 1942. CAB 81/112.

41 L.C.Hollis to Haddon [COS secretariat], 26 December 1942. CAB 121/412.

42 CC/149, Commanders-in-Chief to COS, 5 December 1942. CAB 121/127. In fact this would be one reason why the JIC wrote the paper on German strategy.

43 Hinsley, *British Intelligence: Vol.2*. pp.111–2.

44 Air Ministry officer (whose name is illegible) to J.Taylor [Air Ministry], 24 July 1943. AIR 40/2448. This refers to some of the drafting problems and disagreements that arose.

45 JIC(42)447(0)(Final), 'Operations Consequent on "TORCH"', 14 November 1942. CAB 81/111.

46 Details can be found in *Foreign Relations of the United States: The Conference at Washington, 1941–2 and Casablanca, 1943* (Washington, US Department of State, 1968).

47 D E Delaney, 'Churchill and the Mediterranean Strategy: December 1941 to January 1943', *Defence Studies* 2:3 (2002), p.17.

48 M Jones, *Britain, the United States and the Mediterranean War, 1942–44* (London: Macmillan, 1996). p.40.

49 JIC(43)6th Meeting, 2 February 1943. CAB 81/91.

50 JIC(43)60, 'The German Military Situation', 9 February 1943. Also, JIC(43)65, 'The German Military Situation', 12 February 1943. CAB 81/113.

51 COS(43)93(0), 'Future Strategy', 1 March 1943. CAB 80/67.

52 COS(43)33rd Meeting(0), 3 March 1943. CAB 79/59.

53 These can all be found in CAB 81/114.

54 See, for instance, JP(43)13th Meeting, 2 March 1943 and JP(43)14th Meeting, 3 March 1943. CAB 84/6.

55 R Bennett, 'Intelligence and Strategy: Some Observations on the War in the Mediterranean 1941–45', *Intelligence and National Security* 5:2 (1990), p.456.

56 JIC(43)160(0)(Final), 'Operations Subsequent to "HUSKY"', 11 April 1943. CAB 81/114.

57 JIC(43)163(0), 'Defeat of Italy by Air Attack Alone', 13 April 1943. CAB 81/114.

58 Churchill to CIGS [Brooke], 14 April 1943. CAB 121/412.

59 Hollis to Capel-Dunn, 15 April 1943. CAB 121/412.

60 COS(43)(0)83rd Meeting, 22 April 1943. CAB 79/60.

61 Hollis to Capel-Dunn, 23 April 1943. CAB 121/412. The original conclusions stated that Germany's main problem was the 'balancing of risk' on the various Fronts being fought; that Russia would remain Germany's 'main preoccupation'; that Germany would retain the Tunisian bridgehead, 'even at great cost'; that Germany's strategy on the Western Front would be defensive; and that attacks on shipping would be intensified. JIC(43)171(O), 'German Plans and Intentions During the Summer and Autumn of 1943', 20 April 1943. CAB 121/412.

62 JIC(43)171(Revise), 'German Plans and Intentions During the Summer and Autumn of 1943', 28 April 1943. CAB 81/114. The revised conclusions were more definite in their wording and repeated the view that attacks on shipping would intensify and that Russia would present Germany's 'overriding preoccupation', whilst also judging that: Germany and Russia would not agree on a separate peace; and that on all other Fronts, Germany's strategy would be 'strictly defensive'.

63 Details can be found in CAB 121/128.

64 JIC(43)211(0), 'Disintegration of German Military Strength in the West', 13 May 1943. CAB 81/115.

65 JIC(42)473(Final), 'Indications of a German Collapse', 8 December 1942. CAB 81/112.

66 Note by WSC, 5 October 1943. CAB 120/744. The revised version was paper JIC(43)367. It is not recorded who Churchill chose to place on the distribution list.

67 Examples can be found in CAB 81/115. See chapter 4 for more.

68 JIC(43)256, 'Joint Planning and Joint Intelligence Staffs', 18 June 1943. CAB 81/115. Some further details on the impact of this on the ISTD see CAB 119/74.

69 Sir Basil Liddell Hart papers, LHCMA: Liddell: 11/1935/108.

70 JIC(43)277(0)Final, 'Recent Intelligence Affecting Operations in the Mediterranean', 7 July 1943. CAB 81/115.

71 JIC(43)324(Final), 'German Plans and Intentions During Second Half of 1943', 3 August 1943. CAB 81/116.

72 COS(43)463(0), 'German Plans and Intentions During Second Half of 1943', 11 August 1943. CAB 80/73.

73 COS(43)471(0), 'QUADRANT: Part I', 17 August 1943. CAB 121/154.

74 Minute by Churchill for the COS, 19 July 1943. CAB 121/154.

75 F H Hinsley et al, *British Intelligence in the Second World War: Vol.3, Part 2 – Its Influence on Strategy and Operations* (London: HMSO, 1988). pp.749–52.

76 JIC(43)195(0), 'Sphere of Responsibility and Function of the Intelligence Branch of Chief of Staff to Supreme Allied Commander (COSSAC)', 29 April 1943. CAB 81/114.

77 CCS303/3, 'Strategic Concept for the Defeat of the Axis in Europe', 17 August 1943. CAB 121/154.

78 Hinsley, *British Intelligence: Vol.3, Part 2*. pp.6–8.

79 This was discussed in JIC(43)47th Meeting (0), 21 September 1943. CAB 81/91. The Chiefs of Staff directive is in COS(43)217th Meeting (0), 16 September 1943. CAB 79/64. The military dimensions of preparations for OVERLORD, and its precursor operations, have been dealt with in John Ehrman's Official History: *Grand Strategy: Vol.V, August 1943-September 1944* (London, HMSO: 1956).

80 JIC(43)63rd Meeting (0), 14 December 1943. CAB 81/91.

81 JIC(43)511(0), 'Situation in Europe in Relation to "RANKIN"', 20 December 1943. CAB 81/119.

82 JIC(43)444(0)(Final), 'German Capabilities in Italy', 1 November 1943. CAB 81/118.

83 COS(43)267th Meeting (0), 29 October 1943. CAB 79/67. Brooke was referring to paper JIC(43)377, 'The Situation in Italy'.

84 JIC(43)430(0)(Final), 'German Intentions in Russia', 19 October 1943. CAB 81/118.

85 JIC(43)524(0)(Final), 'Operations "OVERLORD" and "Anvil"', 2 January 1944. CAB 81/119.

86 L.C.Hollis to D.Capel-Dunn, 14 February 1944. CAB 121/413.

87 For another good example of the JP use of JIC assessments, see JP(44)4(Final), 12 January 1944. CAB 121/390. A further sign of this was the creation in March 1944 of the Joint Intelligence Committee (Allied Force), JIC(AF), as an 'inter-Allied' sub-committee of the JIC, reporting to and responsible to the main Committee in London. (Examples of some of the minutes can be found in WO 204/12582) It dealt with purely Service issues, providing reports to the Supreme Allied Commander, Mediterranean Theatre, but crucially was not responsible for either operational or 'day-to-day intelligence'. (For the composition and functions of JIC(AF) see JIC(44)118, 'Joint Intelligence Committee, Allied Force', 23 March 1944. CAB 81/121) Each week JIC(AF) disseminated a paper on the 'major points of intelligence interest affecting political, naval, military and air matters', which became known as the 'Commander's

Bulletin'. (Minute by G.R.Thomson [Security Intelligence Middle East], 21 February 1944. WO 204/12968. This file also includes some examples of this weekly series.)

88 For details see CAB 121/128.

89 For instance, JIC(44)82(0)(Final), 'Operations Subsequent to "OVERLORD"', 3 March 1944. CAB 81/121.

90 JIC(44)66(0)(Final)(Revised), 'German Plans and Intentions During the First Half of 1944, with Particular Reference to "OVERLORD"', 1 March 1944. CAB 81/120.

91 L.C.Hollis to W.S.Churchill, 2 March 1944. CAB 121/413.

92 See Hinsley, *British Intelligence: Vol.3, Part 2*. pp.41–102.

93 There are a large number of studies of this. A good introduction is T L Cubbage, 'The Success of Operation FORTITUDE: Hesketh's History of Strategic Deception', *Intelligence and National Security* 2:3 (July 1987), pp.327–46.

94 Cited in Howarth, *Intelligence Chief Extraordinary*. p.186.

95 JIC(44)214(0)Final, 'German Appreciation of Allied Intentions Regarding "OVERLORD"', 22 May 1944. CAB 154/64.

96 JIC(44)215(0), 'Periodic Review of Conditions in Europe and Scale of Opposition to "OVERLORD"', 25 May 1944. CAB 81/122.

97 COS(44)175th Meeting (0), 30 May 1944. CAB 79/75.

98 JIC(44)232(0)(Final), 3 June 1944. CAB 154/64.

99 Hinsley, *British Intelligence: Vol.3, Part 2*. pp.81–2.

100 T L Cubbage, 'The German Misapprehensions Regarding OVERLORD', *Intelligence and National Security* 2:3 (July 1987), pp.114–74.

101 JIC(44)250(0)(Final), 'German Appreciation of Allied Intentions in the West', 12 June 1944. CAB 154/64.

102 JIC(44)299(0)(Final), 'German Appreciation of Allied Intentions in the West', 10 July 1944. CAB 154/64.

103 See chapter 3 for the analysis.

104 F H Hinsley et al, *British Intelligence in the Second World War: Vol.3, Part 1 - Its Influence on Strategy and Operations* (London: HMSO, 1984). p.360.

105 JIC(43)188(0)(Final), 'German Long-Range Rockets', 25 April 1943. CAB 81/114.

106 R V Jones, *Most Secret War: British Scientific Intelligence, 1939–1945* (London: Hamish Hamilton, 1978).

107 Jones, *Most Secret War*. p.332.

108 COS(43)189(0), 'German Long Range Rocket Development', 14 April 1943. CAB 121/211.

109 Details can be found in CAB 121/211.

110 JIC/492/43, 'German Long Range Rocket', 21 April 1943. CAB 176/1. This document includes the JIC's analysis of SIS reporting on the threat.

111 Jones, *Most Secret War* .pp.336–7.

112 Note by L.C.Hollis, 26 May 1943. CAB 121/211.

113 Details are in PREM 3/110.

114 Jones, *Most Secret War*. pp.342–5. For a transcript see DO(43)5th Meeting, 29 June 1943. CAB 121/211.

115 Cherwell to Ismay, 29 July 1943. CAB 121/211.

116 COS(43)592(0), 'German Long Range Rockets: Report on Reliability of Evidence Collected', 29 September 1943. CAB 80/75.

117 JIC(43)36th Meeting (0), 13 July 1943. CAB 81/91.

118 JIC(43)49th Meeting, 5 October 1943. CAB 81/91. The Chairman declared that this was a result of its 'unconstitutional' character. See JIC/1549/43, 'BODYLINE', 5 October 1943. CAB 176/2.

119 For more see M Middlebrook, *The Peenemunde Raid: The Night of 17–18 August 1943* (London: Cassell, 2000).

120 Hinsley, *British Intelligence: Vol.3, Part 1*. p.394.

121 COS(43)652(0), 'German Long Range Rocket: 13th Interim Report by the Joint Parliamentary Secretary, Ministry of Supply', 24 October 1943. CAB 80/76.
122 E.J.King-Salter [JIC Secretary] to Hollis, 12 October 1943. CAB 121/211.
123 JIC(43)50th Meeting, 12 October 1943. CAB 81/91.
124 Hollis to King-Salter, 14 October 1943. CAB 81/91.
125 COS(43)253rd Meeting (0), 19 October 1943. CAB 79/66.
126 JIC(43)53rd Meeting, 26 October 1943. CAB 81/91.
127 JIC/1733/43, 'JIC BODYLINE Sub-Committee', 1 November 1943. CAB 176/2.
128 COS(43)276th Meeting (0), 11 November 1943. CAB 79/67.
129 JIC(43)468(0)(Revise), 'Composition and Terms of Reference of JIC CROSSBOW Sub-Committee', 23 November 1943. CAB 81/118.
130 JIC(43)63rd Meeting, 14 December 1943. CAB 81/91.
131 See for instance JIC(43)516(0)(Final), 'CROSSBOW', 18 December 1943. CAB 81/119.
132 JIC(43)483(0)(Final), 'CROSSBOW', 24 November 1943. CAB 81/119.
133 JIC(43)501(0)(Final), 'CROSSBOW', 4 December 1943. CAB 81/119.
134 These were issued as COS papers. Some examples can be found in CAB 121/211.
135 COS(44)2nd Meeting (0), 4 January 1944. CAB 79/69. For details of the intelligence effort against the V1 and V2 for the remainder of the war, see Hinsley, *British Intelligence: Vol.3, Part 1*. pp.415–58 and Hinsley, *British Intelligence: Vol.3, Part 2*. pp.533–72.
136 On its origins see CAB 21/3912.
137 For more information see Hinsley, *British Intelligence: Vol.3 Part 2*. pp.573–83.
138 JIC(44)311(0)(Final)(Limited Circulation), 'Use of Chemical and Biological Warfare by the Germans', 18 July 1944. CAB 81/124.
139 JIC(45)18(0), 'Use of Chemical Warfare by the Germans', 17 January 1945. CAB 81/127.
140 JIC(44)328(0)(Final)(Limited Circulation), 'Axis Reactions in Relation to C and B Warfare', 26 July 1944. CAB 81/124.
141 JIC(44)328(0)(Final)(Limited Circulation), 'Axis Reactions in Relation to C and B Warfare', 26 July 1944. CAB 81/124. On the technical advances of the Japanese programme see D Barenblatt, A *Plague Upon Humanity: The Secret Genocide of Axis Japan's Secret Germ Warfare Operation* (London: HarperCollins, 2004).
142 JIC(44)359(0)(Final), 'German Armament Developments', 24 August 1944. CAB 81/124.
143 Jones, *Most Secret War*. pp.306–9.
144 Hinsley, *British Intelligence: Vol.2*. pp.122–9. 'Tube Alloys' was the British codename for atomic matters.
145 For more see M S Goodman, *Spying on the Nuclear Bear: Anglo-American Intelligence and the Soviet Bomb* (Stanford: Stanford University Press, 2007).
146 JIC/1468/45, 'Intelligence on Atomic Energy', 11 October 1945. CAB 176/8.
147 Ismay to W.L.Gorell Barnes [Personal Assistant to Attlee], 13 May 1944. CAB 126/177.
148 JIC(45)242(0)(Revised Final)(Limited Circulation), 'Japanese Attitude to Surrender', 10 August 1945. CAB 81/130.
149 Details are in FO 1093/189.
150 JIC(44)2nd Meeting (0), 11 January 1944. CAB 81/92.
151 JIC(44)238(Final), 'Intelligence Priorities Committee', 7 June 1944. CAB 81/123.
152 Details can be found in CAB 81/144.
153 JIC(45)65, 'Combined Intelligence Objectives Sub-Committee', 22 February 1945. CAB 81/127.
154 Details can be found in WO 219/1659; WO 219/1680; WO 219/1699.
155 JIC(44)316(0)(Final)(Limited Circulation), 'New Weapons in Relation to German Strategy', 22 July 1944. CAB 81/124. This report was approved by the COS and

disseminated to the Prime Minister, Supreme Commander Allied Expeditionary Force, and the Supreme Allied Commander, Mediterranean Theatre. Details are in CAB 121/413.

156 Ehrman, *Grand Strategy: Vol.V.* p.377.

157 JIC(44)354(0)(Final), 'German Strategy and Capacity to Resist', 14 August 1944. CAB 81/124.

158 JIC(44)395(0)(Final), 'German Strategy and Capacity to Resist', 5 September 1944. CAB 81/125.

159 COS(OCTAGON)3rd Meeting, 8 September 1944. CAB 121/413.

160 Minute by the Prime Minister, 8 September 1944. CAB 121/413.

161 JIC(44)437(0)(Revised Final), 'German Strategy and Capacity to Resist', 16 October 1944. CAB 81/125.

162 Hinsley, *British Intelligence: Vol.3, Part 2.* pp.382–9.

163 JIC(44)463(0)(Final), 'Recent Intelligence on German Intentions in the West', 11 November 1944. CAB 121/413.

164 JIC(44)463(0)(Final), 'Recent Intelligence on German Intentions in the West', 11 November 1944. CAB 81/126. Although this appears to be the final version, it is clear from the COS papers that it was further revised.

165 COS(44)368th Meeting (0), 14 November 1944. CAB 79/82.

166 Hinsley, *British Intelligence: Vol.3, Part 2.* p.415.

167 Cited in Hinsley, *British Intelligence: Vol.3, Part 2.* p.428.

168 Hinsley, *British Intelligence: Vol.3, Part 2.* pp.431–4.

169 JIC(44)509(0)(Final), 'The German Counter Offensive', 22 December 1944. CAB 81/126.

170 Annan, *Changing Enemies.* p.117.

171 'Use of ULTRA by the Military Secretariat of the JIS', n.d. HW 3/172. The DMI, Major General John Sinclair, produced his own critique of what had gone wrong, though his views were rebuffed by Edward Travis, later head of GC&CS. See HW 14/119.

172 For more see Annan, *Changing Enemies.* pp.122–3.

173 JIC(44)512(0)(Revised Final), 'German Ability to Sustain the Present Counter-Offensive', 27 December 1944. CAB 81/126.

174 JIC(45)22(0)(Final), 'German Strategy and Capacity to Resist', 21 January 1945. CAB 81/127.

175 Ismay to Churchill, 23 January 1945. CAB 121/413.

176 Churchill to Ismay, 25 January 1945. CAB 121/413.

177 Churchill to Ismay, 28 January 1945. CAB 121/413. Three years earlier, in relation to an assessment of the German Air Force, Churchill had written that 'though all prophecy is dangerous the Joint Intelligence Sub-Committee have been right to make the attempt'. W.S.Churchill to Chiefs of Staff Committee, 7 June 1942. CAB 121/412.

178 JIC(45)55(Final), 'German Situation After Capture of Berlin and Loss of the Ruhr', 18 February 1945. CAB 81/127.

179 JIC(45)90(0)(Final), 'German Strategy and Capacity to Resist', 19 March 1945. CAB 81/128.

180 For more see R Erskine, 'The Holden Agreement on Naval Sigint: The First BRUSA?', *Intelligence and National Security* 14:2 (1999), pp.187–97. Also, J C Sims, 'The BRUSA Agreement of May 17, 1943', *Cryptologia* 21:1 (1997), pp.30–8.

181 JIC/1449/43, 'Report by the DDMI India', 22 September 1943. CAB 176/2.

182 JIC(43)281(0), 'Japanese Intentions', 11 July 1943. CAB 81/115.

183 JIC(43)36th Meeting, 13 July 1943. CAB 81/91.

184 Some brief details are in CAB 122/1417.

185 JIC(44)404(0), 'Conference on Co-Ordination of Intelligence in the Far East', 16 September 1944. CAB 81/125.

186 JIC(44)337(0)(Final), 'Japanese Strategy', 12 August 1944. CAB 81/124.

187 JIC(44)491(0)(Final), 'Possibility of Japanese Withdrawal from the Outer Zone', 8 December 1944. CAB 81/126.
188 The US view is in JIC(45)112(0), 'Japanese Reaction to Assault on Tokyo (Kwanto) Plain of Honshu', 3 April 1945. The British view is JIC(45)114(0), 'Japanese Strategy', 4 April 1945. CAB 81/128.
189 JIC(45)120, 'The Japanese Cabinet Crisis', 10 April 1945. CAB 81/128.
190 JIC(45)131(0), 'Conditions in Japan – Summary for March, 1945', 14 April 1945. CAB 81/128.
191 JIC(45)136(0)(Final), 'Japanese Strategy and Capacity to Resist', 28 April 1945. CAB 81/128.
192 These are all in CAB 81/129.
193 JIC(45)204(0)(Final), 'The Japanese Attitude to Unconditional Surrender', 27 June 1945. CAB 81/129.
194 Ehrman, *Grand Strategy, Vol VI*. p.298.
195 The various papers can be found in CAB 81/130.
196 JIC(45)242(0)(Revised Final), 'Japanese Attitude to Surrender', 10 August 1945. CAB 81/130.
197 'A Liberator Missing, British Officials on Board, San Francisco Staff', *The Times* (7 July 1945).
198 'Obituary: Col. D.C.Capel-Dunn', *The Times* (19 July 1945).
199 'Col. D.C.Capel-Dunn: An Appreciation', *The Times* (25 July 1945). Both authors appear in initials only.
200 V.Cavendish-Bentinck to N.Annan [Annan had served in the JIS during the war], 20 April 1983. Noel Annan Papers, King's College, University of Cambridge: NGA/5/1/813.
201 JIC(45)55th Meeting (0), 14 August 1945. CAB 81/93.
202 COS(45)198th Meeting, 14 August 1945. CAB 79/37.
203 Howarth, *Intelligence Chief*. p.113.
204 FO 371/66097 contains despatches from Warsaw detailing the allegations against Cavendish-Bentinck.
205 'Smear Technique', *Time Magazine* (10 February 1947). Also, J Colville, *Strange Inheritance* (Wiltshire: Michael Russell, 1983). p.187.
206 'Law Report, March 27', *The Times* (28 March 1947).
207 'Law Report, November 6', *The Times* (7 November 1947).
208 'Mrs V.F.W.Cavendish-Bentinck, Appeal to House of Lords Withdrawn', *The Times* (6 July 1948).
209 Colville, *Strange Inheritance*. p.191.
210 Colville, *Strange Inheritance*. p.192. Cavendish-Bentinck also seems to have disliked Beaverbrook, describing him to his biographer as 'dreadful'. Cited in Howarth, *Intelligence Chief*. p.195.
211 V.Cavendish-Bentinck to P.Dixon, 17 May 1947. Sir Pierson Dixon private papers. I am grateful to Dixon's son and daughter for allowing me access to his papers.
212 Cited in Howarth. *Intelligence Chief Extraordinary*. p.223.
213 V.Cavendish-Bentinck to P.Dixon, 17 May 1947. Sir Pierson Dixon private papers.
214 JIC(45)29th Meeting (0), 1 May 1945. CAB 81/93.
215 JIC(46)33(Final), 'Some Weaknesses in German Strategy and Organisation, 1933–1945', 20 October 1946. CAB 121/413.
216 COS(46)169th Meeting, 20 November 1946. CAB 79/63.
217 Andrew, *Secret Service*. p.677 & p.678.
218 Strong, *Men of Intelligence*. pp.115–23. Also, Howarth, *Intelligence Chief*. pp.111–204.
219 Thomas, 'Evolution of the JIC System', pp.231–2.
220 'Charter for the JIC', 13 July 1944. CAB 163/6.
221 These are contained within FO 1093/192.
222 An example can be found in CAB 121/464.

223 Details are in CAB 120/745.
224 M Gilbert, *Continue to Pester, Nag and Bite: Churchill's War Leadership* (London: Pimlico, 2004). p.13.
225 Stafford, *Churchill and Secret Service*. p.363.
226 On both of these see chapter 6.
227 This idea had originated with SHAEF but was rebutted by SIS. See Jeffery, *MI6*. pp.538–40. Also, FO 1093/292.
228 C Baxter, 'Forgeries and Spies: The Foreign Office and the "Cicero" Case', *Intelligence and National Security* 23:6 (December 2008), p.816. 'Cicero' was the name given to Elyesa Bazna, the Albanian valet to the British Ambassador in Turkey, who photographed and sold classified documents to the Germans. See Jeffery, *MI6*. pp.503–4.
229 Annan, *Changing Enemies*. pp.61–2.
230 Cited in Howarth, *Intelligence Chief*. p.170.
231 Strong, *Men of Intelligence*. pp.115–118.
232 On the former see V.Cavendish-Bentinck to A.Cadogan [FO PUS], 8 April 1945. FO 1093/190. On the latter see a note by V.Cavendish-Bentinck, 25 May 1945. FO 1093/192. This was actually a valuable role, for as Cavendish-Bentinck informed the FO, intercepted material would be absolutely crucial to proving that German military leaders were guilty of atrocities. For correspondence see FO 1093/191.
233 Stafford, *Churchill and Secret Service*. pp.222–3.
234 Ehrman, *Grand Strategy*. p.326.
235 Details are in RG24-E-1-b (JIC memoranda) and RG24-C-1-a (JIC minutes), Canadian National Archives, Ottawa. On the first visit to Britain of the Canadian JIC Chairman and attempts to improve relations, see also JIC(43)61st Meeting, 30 November 1943. CAB 81/91.
236 For JIC(CCG) see FO 1038/100. For JIC(ACA) see FO 1020/1258. For details of the JIS role in Austria see FO 1020/1259.
237 These only begin in 1942.
238 An example of this tactical information can be found in HW 1/3522. No other examples have been found.
239 V.Cavendish-Bentinck to A.Cadogan, 31 May 1944. FO 1093/188. This note also includes detail on how the three Chiefs of Staff disliked General de Gaulle and did not want to meet with him prior to D-Day, despite the JIC's recommendation that they do.
240 An example on German Air Force training, February 1945, is in CAB 121/230.
241 COS(45)127th Meeting, 15 May 1945. CAB 79/33.
242 Examples can be found in CAB 163/3.
243 In a BBC radio show years later, Cavendish-Bentinck recalled that when Philby appeared before the JIC he was 'rather a dark, sallow faced fellow. I had a hunch there was something rather odd about him.' BBC Radio 4 Series 'The Profession of Intelligence', broadcast 16 August 1981.
244 D.Capel-Dunn to Ismay, 6 November 1942. CAB 163/3.

Part Three

New Threats, 1945–1957

6   A New Identity, 1945–1957

Perhaps the greatest success of the JIC was that it was destined to survive the war. Sir Kenneth Strong, the future head of the JIB, has recalled that 'at the end of the war, the British Government was forced to make economies, the Chiefs of Staff believed that whatever reductions might be made in the armed forces budgets, the Intelligence structure should remain intact.'[1] As a Committee, the JIC began to look towards the post-war world as early as 1943, some time prior to the beginning of higher level discussions on its post-war survival. Separately each member had, under the guise of his parent department, been involved in such deliberations. Why was there a belief that the committee structure, with the JIC at the heart of British intelligence, was the system for facing an uncertain world? Part of the answer lies in the growing success of the JIC during the war, not only as an organisation controlling and disseminating information but also as an inter-departmental forum. Indeed, it is this latter aspect which would become an increasingly important factor in the JIC's evolution.

The first discussions and reviews were conducted by the JIC itself. The JIC continued to be a sub-committee of the COS Committee and so, above all else, it was a military forum. Although it did discuss non-military matters, frequently straying into political or economic assessments, the underlying rationale was that this was a COS sub-committee. What is clear, however, is that the structure of British intelligence in the decade immediately following the end of the conflict was never entirely resolved. The successive reviews, which after the war were conducted by outsiders, were testament to this. The constant tinkering is not necessarily a sign that the intelligence machine was not working, rather that it needed constant refinement to deal with an evolving threat.

This chapter focuses on the organisational development of the JIC from 1943, when it started thinking about the post-war world, to 1957, a crucial year in its evolution when it moved from the Ministry of Defence (MoD) to the Cabinet Office. During this time the JIC also went through a series of reviews and revisions, as did its sub-committees and regional off-shoots. Further, often under the guidance of its FO Chairman, the JIC was involved in a number of reviews of national intelligence structures as a whole, reviews that have hitherto been inaccessible to the public. The underlying message of this chapter is to show how the JIC's role in the British intelligence community went beyond providing assessments and that, by 1957, its work had become integrated with the Whitehall foreign, defence and security policy machinery.

Crystal Gazing

The first discussions about the post-war organisation surfaced in August 1943. The impetus came from the JIC's Chairman, Victor Cavendish-Bentinck, whose 'principal concern [was] to ensure that upon hostilities with Germany coming to an end the present Joint Intelligence organisation should be kept alive'. Cavendish-Bentinck had several ideas on how the system ought to change:

– the JIC should cease to be a Chiefs of Staff Committee but should report to the Secretary of the Cabinet;
– the reports of the Committee should be circulated to the Departments concerned and in important cases to the Cabinet;
– the Committee should have a whole [full] time Chairman from the Foreign Office and its membership (and that of the JIS) should be slightly enlarged so as to deal with the political and economic problems which are likely to predominate after the war with Germany has ended.[2]

The JIC Secretary, Denis Capel-Dunn, warned Cavendish-Bentinck that moving the JIC away from the COS would not be 'wise'. His reasoning was simple: there would be no question that the COS 'machine' would continue into the post-war world and it was therefore essential that the JIC remain part of it, even if the JIC took an increased interest in non-military matters.[3] Cavendish-Bentinck's ideas were too novel for most of his colleagues and they would not be taken up until 1957, when the JIC moved away from the COS and into the Cabinet Office (see Volume II).

After some revision, including the deletion of the suggestion that responsibility for the JIC should move away from the COS, Cavendish-Bentinck presented his paper to the JIC for discussion in October 1943.[4] Briefing the Committee he stated that: 'as post-war considerations were being discussed in other departments . . . the time had now come for the Sub-Committee to formulate their views.'[5] The JIC, and Cavendish-Bentinck in particular, would be central to many of the debates about the post-war intelligence machinery. Indeed, reminiscing many years later Cavendish-Bentinck acknowledged that he had 'taken a real part in shaping the post-war planning organisation'.[6] One point of discussion was whether the JIC should focus on a broad array of subjects or restrict itself to purely military matters. The members of the JIC were united in their views: the Committee should continue to function after the end of the war but 'the time had not yet come for crystallising points of detail.'[7] Despite the reluctance to think more deeply about their future, to Cavendish-Bentinck the situation in late 1943 was clear:

Our Committee has changed considerably since the war began, both in organisation and in function. We were set up originally as an advisory body.

Now, in addition to our principal task of advising the Chiefs of Staff on enemy intentions, we have become in some respects an executive body, and take many decisions on our responsibility without referring to the Chiefs of Staff. We lay down the policy affecting a large number of Inter-Service organisations. The question arises whether it is desirable that the JIC after the war should revert to their previous shadowy form or whether something approaching the present organisation should be maintained.[8]

What, then, did the JIC actually do at this point? Two documents from 1944 give some indication of this. The first is a definition of the JIC's work, endorsed by the Committee itself:

The Joint Intelligence Committee in addition to its responsibility for co-ordinating the product of the various collectors of intelligence into the form of agreed advice on enemy intentions, has the additional responsibility of watching, directing and to some extent controlling the British Intelligence organisation throughout the world, so as to ensure that intelligence is received at the most economical cost in time, effort and manpower, and so as to prevent overlapping.[9]

Critical
Claim

This understated yet ambitious set of responsibilities was formalised in the summer of 1944 when a revised charter was issued. Rather than introducing anything new, it confirmed the need for the existing disparate set of functions and subordinate committees. Thus: 'as a body the JIC have a dual responsibility: (i) compiling all day to day combined intelligence Situation Reports and making long-term and short-term appreciations of enemy intentions. (ii) Co-ordinating administrative arrangements relating to the Intelligence machine as a whole.'[10] From the outset, then, it was highlighted that the JIC's functions went far beyond the production of intelligence assessments.

These internal deliberations were complemented by a resounding vote of support from a high level conference in late 1944 on the 'Co-ordination of Intelligence in the Far East.' Ostensibly this was concerned with wartime developments, but on the final day discussion turned toward post-war machinery. There was unanimous agreement that the London JIC should be the hub of all intelligence efforts, with additional JICs created in various locations within the Far East, all subordinate and reporting back to Whitehall.[11] These discussions were useful in highlighting the support for the continued existence of the JIC, but they did little to address the specific points about the structure of the post-war Committee, what its remit should be, and who should be represented. The first attempt to address these came from members of the JIC itself.

In a remarkably prescient document, Cavendish-Bentinck and Capel-Dunn set out their plans for the future. Their task had been set by the JIC and approved by the Cabinet Secretary, Sir Edward Bridges and, initially, they aimed solely to consider the future of the JIC itself.[12] However, it was decided that the remit should be broadened 'so as to ensure that so far as possible, the benefit of the lessons learned during the war in inter-service and inter-departmental co-operation in intelligence matters should not be lost.'[13] For the first time in an official document 'intelligence' was defined, both its composition and its utility: 'intelligence is, however, of high importance as a servant of those conducting military operations. It is no more. It cannot win battles, but if it is absent or faulty, battles may easily be lost'. Herein lay the crux of the argument: intelligence was as vital in the post-war period as it had been during the war. In particular the drafters were keen to highlight the deficiencies of the intelligence apparatus prior to the Second World War, and to ensure that in future the intelligence machinery of His Majesty's Government was ready to meet the next challenge, whatever that might be. At the same time, as the pace of peacetime intelligence would differ from that of wartime, it was acknowledged that changes and reductions had to be made. Thus, a review of the present, wartime, system was offered, with a depiction of a possible post-war model.

To the authors, one of the great successes of the war had been the 'considerable degree of inter-departmental co-operation through the machinery of the Chiefs of Staff organisation' and, as such, 'we recommend its extension, involving the surrender of some departmental sovereignties, we do so in the firm belief that it is essential'. Cavendish-Bentinck and Capel-Dunn also drew a distinction between the different members of the Committee, and how their role at the JIC affected their other responsibilities. In so doing they highlighted, for the first time, the dangers of the politicisation of intelligence, and how the JIC model attempted to get around such hazards:

> Whereas in the Service Departments intelligence is the sole responsibility of certain officers specially selected for dealing with it, in the Political Departments, e.g. the Foreign Office and Colonial Office, the officials who receive, collate and assess information are also responsible for formulating policy. This is not necessarily a bad thing, but the system does possess a serious weakness. One who is concerned in devising and recommending policy, and in assisting in its execution is likely, however objective he may try to be, to interpret the intelligence he receives in the light of the policy he is pursuing. To correct this possible weakness, it is clearly desirable that some quite objective check be placed on all intelligence received. So far as intelligence affecting the conduct of the war is concerned, the problem has been to some extent solved in the Foreign Office by the establishment of the Services Liaison Department, whose function it is to take part at all levels in the deliberations of the JIC in the preparation of intelligence appreciations, and to interpret to the Planning Staffs the foreign policy of His Majesty's Government. This departure has justified itself in war, and we hope that it will be decided to continue it in peace. We believe that no Department, however experienced and well staffed, has anything to lose by bringing the intelligence directly available to it to the *anvil of discussion* and appreciation among other workers in the same field.[14]

Here, then, was an insight into how the JIC system could not only cross inter-departmental boundaries, but also ensure that individual departmental concerns could not dominate. The key was to ensure that the JIC would be 'controlled at the top by a strong inter-service and inter-departmental body, representing the needs of producers and consumers of intelligence.'[15]

The JIC continued to revise the paper and a new version, approved in early September 1945, was based on the successes of the wartime experience, and how this could be applied to its post-war incarnation. The JIC was forthright in admitting that its pre-war failings had 'led to the need for rapid and largely improvised expansion under the imminent threat.' Furthermore, having now 'set our house in order', the JIC made five recommendations as to the future of British intelligence:

(a) An intelligence organisation must be centrally directed and fitted to the system of command;
(b) Its collecting agencies must cover the world;
(c) Its collating staffs must work as far as possible on an inter-service basis;
(d) All commanders must be provided with intelligence staffs able to give them the intelligence picture which they require for their tasks;
(e) London has been the focal point of British intelligence during the war and should remain the hub of the intelligence organisation.[16]

The COS agreed to endorse the report as a 'defence requirement', stipulating that it be sent to the Prime Minister for authorisation. In approving the paper the COS stated that the objective was to 'lay the foundations for an efficient and economical intelligence machine, taking into account the lessons of past experience.'[17] The proposal was not discussed again by either the JIC or the COS; in fact, any formal change would take a further three years to accomplish.

Committees Beget Committees

From the outset, to assist the JIC in managing the transition of intelligence machinery into the post-war world there were to be a number of sub-committees, dealing with various aspects of intelligence. Intelligence collection agencies were to continue to exist, but as part of Cavendish-Bentinck's and Capel-Dunn's original 1945 proposal, to assist them a new 'Central Intelligence Bureau' was suggested: essentially a new organisation to process, collate and assess incoming information. The Bureau would also be the conduit for intelligence to pass between different governmental departments. It was suggested that the Bureau should come under SIS' purview, given that 'C' was also responsible for signals intelligence as the head of the Government Code and Cypher School (GC&CS), although 'C' himself could not head it as he was not 'a public figure'. The report concluded by stating that 'we think it essential that all the intelligence authorities should be brought under the JIC umbrella.'[18]

The initial reaction of Edward Bridges, the Cabinet Secretary, to Cavendish-Bentinck and Capel-Dunn's report was that it was a 'lucid and important paper'.[19] The JIC called a special meeting of the Committee on Sunday 11 March 1945 to discuss the report, some two months later. There was general agreement on the concept of a Central Intelligence Bureau, but it was decided that a special sub-committee should be convened to look into it in more depth. Two interesting conclusions were drawn: that there needed to be a better mechanism for gathering 'overt' intelligence, which should be co-ordinated through SIS to complement covert sources; and that while it was considered necessary to continue the practice of having a FO Chairman, it largely depended on the 'personal qualities' of the person chosen, and so there needed to be a mechanism for removing the Chairman if the required standard was not met.[20] Quite why it was decided the FO should continue to occupy the chair is not explicit as the minutes of the special JIC meeting to discuss it have not been preserved; certainly Cavendish-Bentinck was convinced of the necessity to do so, and had been for some time.[21]

The 'Ad Hoc' committee to discuss plans for the 'Joint Intelligence Bureau' (JIB), as it had now become known, met in mid-April 1945 under Cavendish-Bentinck's Chairmanship. It concluded that the JIB should adopt the procedures outlined in the original report but should be confined to 'static intelligence', possibly meaning non-time sensitive intelligence. Furthermore, the JIB should also assume responsibility for overt intelligence. However, it was quite a different beast from the original proposal for a Central Intelligence Bureau as it would no longer act as the central assessment organisation for intelligence and would be one step removed from the current intelligence picture.[22]

As the meetings of the special ad-hoc committee proceeded, the JIB concept continued to evolve. Its central rationale was to be an inter-service organisation, with the explicit purpose of ensuring information was shared across the Services, whilst also avoiding any duplication of effort, similar to the JIC's original remit almost a decade earlier. By the summer of 1945 the JIB was seen as an intelligence organisation designed largely to focus on 'economic intelligence for defence purposes'. As a military intelligence agency this would encompass consideration of defence economics, including trade, raw material, fuel, power, ship building, and military production. The JIB would also be responsible for logistical and topographical intelligence, including airfields, static defence systems, and tele-communications systems.[23] The reason for this change of emphasis is not clear.[24] Nonetheless, the JIB model was approved by the JIC and was included in a wider paper on the British intelligence machine to be submitted to the COS.[25]

The JIC submitted its proposal for the creation of the JIB which, in turn, were approved by the COS Committee.[26] Even the Treasury supported the proposals, though not 'in writing'.[27] Thereafter a further committee, chaired by Ian Fleming, was convened to turn the concept into reality.[28] The JIB was eventually born in August 1945, with the JIC taking a hands-on role in the appointment of its first Director-General, Major General Sir Kenneth Strong (Eisenhower's former intelligence chief and a relatively frequent attender at JIC meetings).[29] In 1946 with the passing of the Ministry of Defence Act, the JIB would operate within the Ministry of Defence organisation.

The creation of the JIB was not the only substantial restructuring to take place in the summer of 1945. In 1943 Victor Cavendish-Bentinck had been heavily involved in the review and restructuring of SIS: the first amongst the constituents of the intelligence community to anticipate the post-war world.[30] The SOE, so famously popularised by Churchill's instruction to 'set Europe ablaze', had fulfilled a valuable and important wartime role. It had been created initially out of part of SIS, and this was remembered with some dismay by many SIS officers.[31] In early 1945 Cavendish-Bentinck, now seen as the FO's man on all matters secret, was asked to chair a special committee, entirely separate from the JIC, to look at the future of SOE.

From the start Anthony Eden, the Foreign Secretary, was convinced that SOE and SIS should be amalgamated.[32] Cavendish-Bentinck worked on the matter throughout the first half of 1945.[33] In May, Lord Selborne, the outgoing Minister of Economic Warfare (and therefore the Minister in charge of SOE) wrote a long report to the COS on SOE's wartime achievements, including how it should be re-organised for the future.[34] On receipt of a statement from the FO, Cavendish-Bentinck suggested, and the COS subsequently approved, that the JIC discuss 'what SOE organisation would be required in the near future'. In response yet another 'Ad Hoc Committee' was established, again chaired by Cavendish-Bentinck. The underlying rationale was for an organisation to conduct 'clandestine operations'[35], yet almost no mention was made of the future threat and, apart from Germany and Austria, no European target was thought necessary.[36] In discussing the initial report, 'C' made reference to the Soviet Union, though admitting he was 'quite unaware of what additions will be required'.[37] That no post-war enemy was identified was unsurprising given the continuing arguments between the military and the FO (see chapter 8).

The debate on the post-war role of sabotage provides an insight into bureaucratic politics, and the difficult line between establishing requirements and the post-war realities. As Cavendish-Bentinck confided to Harry Sporborg, the vice-chief of SOE:

> I entirely agree with you as regards the value to this country of the weapon of clandestine and subversive activity, but we must cut our coat according to the cloth, and if we produce too large an establishment it will be turned down, and there will be no S.O. [special operations] organisation whatsoever in peacetime. I remember that after the last war various schemes were put forward which would have been of the greatest use, but they were turned down, and the promoters were not given a second hearing, just because they put forward what was considered to be too large an establishment.[38]

Sporborg's reply was also telling: 'I differ fundamentally from you on this issue as I am convinced that if we adopt the old "coat and cloth" formula we shall merely be condemning this country to participation in further wars. We do not know what our cloth is and our duty, as I see it, is to design the right sort of coat and put our design forward to HMG.'[39] Such discussions were symptomatic of problems in formulating the future direction of British policy and, more particularly, defining the nature of the future threat.

The next session of the JIC's Ad Hoc Committee on SOE was taken up by a lengthy discussion about the virtues of amalgamating SOE and SIS, which some members had thought obvious, whereas others had not even begun to contemplate.[40] The discussions reveal something of Cavendish-Bentinck's abilities as chairman. Judging from the minutes he quietly imposed his authority, gently trying to swing the discussion back on topic. From a private note he wrote afterwards to the PUS in the FO, Sir Alexander Cadogan, he confided that Gubbins, the head of SOE, had taken him aside following the meeting to castigate him for the position he adopted. Furthermore, Cavendish-Bentinck opined that while he was on leave, Cadogan should expect to hear 'some vigorous lobbying' from Gubbins and 'some complaints' from Lord Lovat, the Parliamentary Under-Secretary for Foreign Affairs and a former army Brigadier. Cavendish-Bentinck also made his position clear with regard to SOE, stating he held 'a deep prejudice' against it, though he did not explain why.[41]

The final report, sent to the COS in late July 1945, concluded that a 'special operations' organisation was needed, and quoted Eden's 1944 minute that it should come under the control of SIS, which the Ad Hoc Committee stipulated should only take place after the defeat of Japan.[42] The COS endorsed the report and subsequently forwarded it to the Prime Minister.[43] In private correspondence with Cadogan, Cavendish-Bentinck admitted that the final report was a 'compromise' between the various positions. In a handwritten annotation at the end Cadogan confided: 'Maybe. But this doesn't appear from the report'.[44]

Partially excluded from the JIC's deliberations, from the outset, was signals intelligence. Initial responsibility for this lay with SIS, usually represented at the JIC by 'C', who chaired the London Signal Intelligence Board (LSIB) – another cross departmental body but which only discussed matters relating to signals intelligence. Quite how the two inter-agency bodies collaborated and co-ordinated matters is not clear. Certainly from the JIC records alone there is no substantial evidence that they communicated; perhaps this is no surprise given that the terms of reference and minutes of the LSIB reveal a completely different set of responsibilities.[45] Whenever there was some debate on Sigint within the JIC, special permission seems to have been sought from 'C'.[46] By 1948 however, the JIC was assuming more responsibility for signals intelligence, producing a set of requirements for Sigint which, it was stated, should 'guide the Sigint Board in allocating its resources'.[47] Its presence at the apex of British intelligence was growing.

External Examination: The 1947 Evill Report

In the immediate post-war years, the JIC continued to produce a regular series of papers and held frequent discussions on how British intelligence could be improved, as part of its management function, totally separate from its assessment capacity. Despite efforts to forge a new post-war organisation, little had actually changed. In some quarters a demand arose for an external review of the entire intelligence structure, rather than one conducted by the JIC itself. For instance, in the words of Lieutenant General Sir Leslie Hollis, the Chief Staff Officer to the Minister of Defence, 'there seems to be a definite need for a general stock-taking of our Intelligence machine'.[48] Responsibility lay with the COS Committee, to whom the majority of the intelligence structures were technically subservient, which in turn appointed Air Chief Marshal Sir Douglas Evill as the man to lead the review.

Evill had had a long and distinguished military career, culminating as Vice Chief of the Air Staff. Earlier, in one of the first post-war reviews, he had conducted a study into the organisation of signals intelligence.[49] His initial remit was to consider the resources available, whether effort was being duplicated, and where insufficient attention was being given. In addition, he would look at the agencies subordinate to the FO – SIS and GCHQ (which had changed its name from GC&CS in 1946) – but only so far as the degree of overlap between the military and political intelligence spheres were concerned.[50] Evill started work in June 1947 and his terms of reference included a concern recurrent in various letters between the COS, the Defence and Foreign Secretaries, and which encapsulated Britain's post-war position: 'we must ensure that the acquisition and use of intelligence in peace is brought to its highest pitch of efficiency, since good intelligence can, to some extent, make up for exiguous forces.' Evill's task was to undertake a general review of the intelligence structure of HMG,[51] assisted throughout by the JIC who, from the outset, appear to have been very helpful.[52]

The JIC provided Evill with information on the various aspects of intelligence, including 'military, economic, industrial, technical, scientific and political' and, in particular, where efforts were concentrated and where there was inadequate intelligence coverage.[53] Perhaps the most interesting of these was SIS's requirements and its relative successes in managing to meet them (for more see chapter 8). Evill found the information useful but also asked for further advice on whether increased money or personnel would improve intelligence coverage.[54] Evill circulated his preliminary findings to the JIC in draft form for comment and approval in July 1947 and the Committee met with him at the beginning of August to discuss them. Generally speaking Evill approved of the existing intelligence structures. Commenting on the JIC's function at the heart of British intelligence Evill stated 'that he had been impressed with the importance of the central direction of intelligence requirements'. However, he also stated that he felt the JIC itself should spend more time on collating reports and on 'pure intelligence', in other words, that they should also produce assessments, not just rely on the JIS to draft them. In response William Hayter, the FO Chairman of the JIC, explained that it was 'not practicable to write intelligence appreciations in Committee'. Evill promised to take the advice and information 'into account'.[55]

Of far more significance was a further report produced by Evill in late September, on the 'Higher Direction and Coordination of Intelligence', aimed squarely at the JIC itself. Evill's underlying belief was that a 'profitable' system was a 'highly centralised one'. He had examined the newly created Central Intelligence Agency (CIA) in the US, though he admitted that information was 'hard to come by'. Nevertheless, he had some clear and confident statements to make. The British system was 'loose' in comparison, albeit better suited to the traditions of Ministerial responsibility. As a whole, Evill found the JIC product to be 'indispensable' to the COS for 'sound advice on defence matters'. But the requirements for the various members of the JIC, to be accountable for their parent department's wishes and concerns, was too much, however 'able' they were. Evill felt that the JIC, with its total complement of seven permanent members[56], was too large and unwieldy a body to properly supervise the collation and direction of British intelligence. Furthermore, looking at its role and remit, the JIC was too 'preoccupied' with 'organisational and security issues'. To remedy these Evill suggested two separate committees: one for requirements and assessments, and the other to focus on security, organisational and administrative matters. He also suggested the issuing of a new charter to take into account the broad range of activities undertaken. Finally, Evill turned his attention to the position of Chairman, arguing that this needed to be both enhanced and increased in stature, so that it could carry full weight and authority.[57] The JIC met Evill once more to discuss this latest report. It is difficult from the minutes of the meeting to get a real feel for how the dialogue went, but it seems clear that the Committee members were not overly impressed with Evill's findings, not least because they felt much of what he proposed was already being done.[58]

Evill finally submitted his report to the COS in November 1947, who described it as being 'important and far reaching'.[59] Evill's conclusions were both wide-ranging and varied. On the performance of British intelligence as a whole he declared himself to be 'very disturbed', largely because so little was known about the Soviet Union, though he also accepted the difficulties in penetrating such a difficult target and the relatively short time for which it had been a priority (see chapter 8 for more). The JIC readily accepted this criticism. Organisationally however, he saw other weaknesses. Although he approved of the JIC model, he felt it needed greater power, specifically an 'increase of responsibility and a strengthening of authority'. Thus, 'it is in and from that body that both efficiency and economy in our intelligence operations as a whole must be sought and the Committee must be correspondingly empowered for that purpose'. Central to this was the role of the JIC's Chairman who, Evill concluded, needed to be a 'more powerful appointment . . . so as to afford to that body the added authority that is needed to give more forcefulness and influence to our intelligence organisation as a whole'.[60]

The difficulty lay in implementing his findings. Even with hindsight, Evill's report sounds as sensible today as it did then. His comments on the chairmanship, in particular, were prophetic. The JIC, upon receipt of the report, decided to wait for some direction from the COS before doing anything.[61] In turn, the COS threw the initiative back to the JIC to make suggestions on its own functions. To William Hayter, the JIC Chairman, a new charter would formalise what the Committee already did. The members of the Committee were unanimous in agreeing that the Chairman's powers should be increased, commenting impishly that had that been the case then there would have been no need for Evill's review in the first place. In addition, responsibility for the more detailed recommendations by Evill on Service and other departments was passed directly to those concerned for comment.[62]

The JIC's functions had been laid out in the 'Cabinet Committee Book'. This stipulated two primary functions:

(a) To collate Intelligence and make reports to the Chiefs of Staff.
(b) To consider measures to improve the Intelligence organisation of the country as a whole.[63]

It was accepted that these terms were very broad and that it was up to the JIC to interpret them as it saw fit.[64] Furthermore, the importance of the JIC was emphasised by the COS which observed that, at a time when the military capabilities of Britain had been and were continuing to be reduced, 'It is of the greatest importance that our Intelligence Organisation should be able to provide us with adequate and timely warning. The smaller the armed forces, the greater is the need for developing Intelligence Services in peace, to enable them to fulfil this responsibility.'[65] The JIC endorsed Evill's suggestion for a revised charter, amending it to more accurately reflect its work, and agreeing that it would be best for the FO to continue to supply the Chairman.[66]

The JIC submitted its conclusions to the COS in January 1948, arguing not only for a revised charter but for a name change from 'Joint Intelligence Sub-Committee' to just 'Joint Intelligence Committee'.[67] A special working party was created to advise on translating Evill's recommendations into practice, which reported back to the JIC in February.[68] Most noteworthy was the need for a clearer delineation between the work of the Directors of Intelligence in the three Services, and what could be left to their deputies; and an expansion of the JIS.[69] In broad terms the report was accepted by the JIC, who sent a revised version to the COS a few weeks later. At the heart of the report was a recognition that: 'this situation is due, to a great extent, to increased requirement for intelligence, a requirement which may be expected to increase still further'. In addition, although problems lay ahead, the time and effort spent on extending links to the United States (see chapter 7) had begun to pay dividends: 'the flow of reports from the American Central Intelligence Agency has now started and it is most desirable that these reports should be fully examined and commented upon in order to ensure the most profitable results for our own purposes and to encourage the Americans to continue their supply.'[70]

The JIC's proposals were endorsed by the COS[71] and were accompanied by the approval of a new Charter:

The Joint Intelligence Committee is given the following responsibilities:

(i) Under the Chiefs of Staff to plan, and to give higher direction to, operations of defence intelligence and security, to keep them under review in all fields and to report progress.

(ii) To assemble and appreciate available intelligence for presentation as required to the Chiefs of Staff and to initiate other reports as the Committee may deem necessary.

(iii) To keep under review the organisation of intelligence as a whole and in particular the relations of its component parts so as to ensure efficiency, economy and a rapid adaptation to changing requirements, and to advise the Chiefs of Staff of what changes are deemed necessary.

(iv) To co-ordinate the general policy of Joint Intelligence Committees under United Kingdom Commands overseas and to maintain an exchange of intelligence with them, and to maintain liaison with appropriate Commonwealth intelligence agencies.[72]

The JIC therefore, for the first time, now had a formal Charter, a detailed remit, and a wide ranging responsibility for intelligence. The final outcome of the review in 1947/8 was to elevate the JIC to full committee status – no longer merely a sub-committee of the COS. As a reflection of this the FO Chairman was promoted to a rank of Assistant Under-Secretary, equivalent to the military intelligence Directors at Rear Admiral, Major General or Air Vice Marshal level.[73] Hence, by early 1948, the JIC was becoming better equipped to operate in the post-war world.

Life on the Committee

One of Victor Cavendish-Bentinck's greatest legacies was to instil in the FO a recognition that it should provide top class candidates for JIC Chairman. Indeed, it is illuminating to consider the notable careers of the early Cold War FO post holders once they moved on from chairing the Committee; certainly a spell as the JIC Chairman was good for future progression.[74] Consider this note sent by one former Chairman to the outgoing one: 'you do not say to what higher sphere you have been called, if indeed one ex-Chairman of the JIC can admit to another Chairman that there is any higher sphere.'[75]

In the period up to 1957 the JIC had four Chairmen, all FO, and all destined for great things. Cavendish-Bentinck's successor was Harold Caccia. An old Etonian and a rugby player, he was cited on one occasion in *The Times* as having 'run well and opened up the game by means of a number of accurate and well-timed passes to the wings'.[76] Caccia had joined the FO in 1929, subsequently serving in China, and as Assistant Private Secretary to Foreign Secretaries Anthony Eden and Lord Halifax, followed by stints in Greece and Algiers. Caccia returned to the FO and in November 1945 assumed Chairmanship of the JIC, though he remained in post only until August 1946. Unfortunately there are no records that tell us anything of Caccia's style as Chairman. Lord Sherfield (Sir Roger Makins), his predecessor as Ambassador in Washington, has written that Caccia was 'short, stocky, and bald with a fair complexion. He was forthright in speech and energetic in action, and he retained throughout his life a cheerful and light-hearted, almost boyish, manner, which concealed a serious and thoughtful disposition'.[77] Upon his departure the COS 'expressed their great regret at losing the valued services and advice of Mr Caccia'.[78] Caccia is particularly remembered as being the man who repaired the Anglo-American special relationship in the wake of the Suez debacle, when he became Ambassador to the US in 1956. He returned to London in 1962 to become the PUS in the FO and shortly thereafter head of the Diplomatic Service.

Caccia's successor as Chairman was another high flyer. William Hayter entered the FO in 1930, subsequently serving in Vienna, Moscow, China and Washington. He returned to London in 1944, and in October 1946 became the JIC's seventh Chairman. Sir John Ure, a contemporary in the FO, has written that during his time in Washington, Hayter was the man who passed on the message to London that Pearl Harbor had been attacked. Remembered as 'able, polished, and with an academic turn of mind . . . only his closest friends broke through the canopy of charm to discover real warmth in his personality'. Hayter's FO career culminated as Ambassador to the Soviet Union; he resigned in 1958 over his 'disillusionment over Suez'.[79] Although he produced an autobiography and left papers in Oxford, Hayter did not mention his chairmanship of the JIC.[80]

Patrick Reilly took over as Chairman in January 1950, remaining in post until April 1953. Reilly had joined the FO in 1933, serving in Tehran, Algiers, Paris, and Athens. Unlike his predecessors, Reilly had already had a varied and in-depth involvement with the intelligence world, having spent approximately a year in the middle of the war as the personal assistant to the Chief of SIS.[81] Following his spell on the JIC Reilly became Ambassador, firstly to the Soviet Union and then to France, and was also for a time a Deputy Under-Secretary in the FO. Reilly's papers, held in Oxford, are more revealing about his time on the JIC.

One episode, in particular, reveals something of the pressures imposed on the FO Chair. In 1951 two British diplomats, Donald Maclean and Guy Burgess, defected to the Soviet Union. Reilly recalled the impact of this event in his memoir:

> Being still exceedingly busy I had reverted to my wartime habit of returning to my office after dinner and working there for several hours. One evening I found myself reading a minute by Carey Foster [head of security in the FO] in which he pressed me quite properly to take action on some recommendation of his on which I had been sitting. This entirely justified reproach touched off a violent nerve storm. Within seconds I had demolished the solid wooden armchair in which I had been sitting. I stood for a long time looking aghast at its ruins. Then I collected the debris together, put my papers away in my safe, and went off to bed, deeply shaken and ashamed of myself. Next morning the debris had been removed and another chair provided . . . no one ever said a word to me again about this distressing incident: and I have demolished no more chairs!'[82]

Although it is not possible to gain an appreciation of his style of chairmanship, Reilly's term had been well received. Sir Kenneth Strong, the head of JIB, commented on the 'sorrow of the JIC at your departure and their deep gratitude for all you had done during your term of office'.[83] Similarly, Sir John Sinclair, the chief of SIS, recalled that 'I have no feelings other than admiration and gratitude for all you have done as Chairman of the JIC'.[84]

The final Chairman in this period was Patrick Dean. His FO career started unusually. Graduating in law he was called to the bar in 1934, and then worked as a barrister until the outbreak of war, when he accepted a position as one of the FO's legal advisers. In this capacity he was involved with the Nuremburg war crimes trials, following which he was offered, and accepted, a position in the Diplomatic Service. He was subsequently made head of the German Political Department and also served in the Embassy in Rome, before returning to London where, in April 1953, he became Chairman of the JIC. He served in this position for seven years, eventually leaving in July 1960 to become the United Kingdom Permanent Representative to the UN, followed by a stint as Ambassador in Washington. Dean did not write a memoir or leave any private papers. He has been described as 'utterly straightforward and loyal both to his superiors and to his subordinates ... although clear-sighted and sometimes harsh in his judgments of people he was invariably courteous and tolerant of colleagues who fell short of his standards.'[85] The US State Department was similarly effusive: 'Dean has a strong, dominating personality and is an extremely hard worker. He has an analytical mind and an easy mastery of detail. A frank and friendly man, he has always been cooperative with American officials'.[86]

Involvement with the JIC, however, was not the only task of the FO Chairman. Caccia, Hayter, Reilly and Dean were all Assistant Under-Secretaries (AUS – comparable to a Major General), though Dean was promoted to Deputy Under-Secretary (DUS – comparable to a Lieutenant General) partway through his tenure. As such they were responsible for intelligence within the FO, thereby having titular responsibility for the Permanent Under-Secretary's Department (PUSD), though the day to day attention of PUSD was controlled by someone of Counsellor rank. PUSD had been created after the war, subsuming the old Services Liaison Department. In practice it was responsible for FO liaison with SIS (including GCHQ) and MI5, for looking after the FO's security department (hence Reilly's tantrum over the defections of Burgess and Maclean), and for providing FO representation at the COS meetings, the JIC meetings (including chairing), and the Joint Planners meetings.[87] Furthermore 'representation' was a two-way street, involving a constant dialogue back and forth between the FO and relevant departments. In Hayter's time PUSD was a small team with no administrative or secretarial support.[88] Chairing the JIC therefore, was not a full-time or sole position; rather it was one task among many.[89] The Chairman was not the only busy member, Lieutenant Colonel Thomas Haddon, one of the Committee's post-war Secretaries, recalled that he rarely got home before 9.30pm each night.[90]

What was it like working on and with the JIC? A fascinating glimpse into this is provided by Chester Cooper, an American, one of whose tasks was to act as liaison with the JIS. Occasionally Cooper would be asked to attend a JIS meeting, and in his memoir he recalls the first time he did so:

> I was ushered into a gloomy, crowded, and cluttered conference room dominated by a table covered with a green, tea-stained baize cloth. A dozen or so men were slumped in chairs at the table or haphazardly seated around the room ... the owlish-looking man next to me (who mumbled "economist, JIB" when we were introduced) was thoughtfully absorbed in a Greek pentameter he was composing. The navy commander on my other side was dozing ... the door flew open and someone shouted, "240 for 60!" I heard cheers and groans. The intruder slammed the door behind him. I barely had a chance to make my profound contribution ... when there was a gentle knock on the door. The navy officer stirred himself, opened the door, and happily announced, "Elevenses!" Tea and biscuits were passed around. And then, once again, the door swung open and the mysterious interloper yelled, "310 for 80!" ... I quickly learned that my first impression of this group was completely wrong. Yes, they were laconic. Yes, cricket, elevenses, afternoon tea, and Greek pentameters were nontrivial considerations ... But, as I was soon to discover, they were bright ... they were also serious and hardworking.[91]

Clearly Cooper did not get the hang of cricket scores whilst in London! In fact the frequent discussion of cricket scores was a deliberate move, according to one Assistant Secretary of the time, to demonstrate the 'Englishness of the meetings'.[92]

Of life on the JIC itself there is scant evidence. The only real detail comes from Cecil Alldis, an RAF Officer who was seconded to the JIC in the early 1950s as Assistant Secretary and was responsible for taking the minutes in the JIC meetings. Alldis has recalled something of his experiences of minute taking:

> I was told to just to turn up and get on with the job. After a week in the job I got called into Searight's [Colonel Eric Searight, JIC Secretary] office who said [discussing Alldis' draft minutes of a JIC meeting] "you can't make so and so say that". I said "but he did say it" and Searight said "but it's absolute tripe. You can't send that around Whitehall over his name". I said "well, what can I do about it?" "Oh no", he said, "your job is to make the minutes readable and correct and not to send out absolute nonsense". We didn't alter them factually, we just made them sound like they were uttered by intelligent and gifted and knowledgeable people. Sometimes you had to change them if they said something against the policies of their Department. Very rarely did Committee members want them [the resulting minutes] changing.

Of the meetings themselves, Alldis has reminisced that the 'atmosphere was good', and 'even if two departments were arguing on different sides of the coins; it was done in a very civilised fashion. I didn't see any fights break out.' Of the members the Chairman was 'always dominant'. The 'standard of debate' was good and this was all thanks to the FO Chairman, whose quality was 'always high'.[93] The only other comment, albeit brief, comes from Major General Arthur Shortt, the DMI, who described one 1950 meeting in his diary as 'v. interesting'. In contrast, he was far less impressed with meetings that he attended of the Hong Kong Local Intelligence Committee ((LIC), see chapter 7), which he thought were 'not very impressive'.[94]

The Committee in Action (i) – Meetings and Membership

Following the end of the war the JIC continued to meet frequently, always once a week but quite often two or three times if the need arose. During the latter stages of the war the JIC had met in two different groupings: at Director-level and at Deputy Director-level. This practice continued into the post-war period. This differentiation was not always immediately obvious, because frequently one of the Directors would send a deputy in their place. In practice therefore, the personnel of the two Committees tended to overlap. The senior Committee was expected to concentrate on assessments; whereas the junior Committee was to focus on administration, including security, codeword allocation and so on. In reality, the practical necessity of co-ordinating the COS Committee requirements meant that both Committees covered similar grounds.

Evill had recommended that the senior JIC members should spend more time on intelligence matters and less on administrative concerns. The JIC fully endorsed this and decided to use one JIS team to produce drafts of assessments, and the other to work on organisational issues.[95] From February 1948, the two committees became known as the JIC (Directors) and JIC (Deputy Directors).[96] This latter also convened as the JIC (O[rganisation] & S[ecurity]) meeting.[97] By the mid-1950s the various groups lined up as follows:

- Directors – to deal with important matters regardless of their category
- Deputy Directors (Intelligence) – to deal with less important "intelligence" matters
- Deputy Directors (Organisation) – to deal with less important "organisation" matters
- Deputy Directors (Security) – to deal with less important "security" matters[98]

One of the more pressing problems to be tackled by the Deputy Directors was how to improve intelligence procurement (see chapter 8). Other organisational developments saw the creation in late 1948 of a new Security Sub-Committee;[99] and in 1952 the Bridges Committee of Permanent Secretaries on Intelligence, designed to oversee budgets, which shortly became known as the PSIS (Committee of Permanent Secretaries on Intelligence Services).[100]

The nature of the changing threat and its impact on the Committee's work and practice meant that, by the 1950s, procedures had to alter once more.

The previous structure remained the same but the substance of the meetings changed. There were now to be weekly meetings of the full, Directors' JIC, weekly meetings of the Deputy Directors' Committee on Security; and a weekly meeting of either the Deputy Directors' Committee on Intelligence or the Deputy Directors' Committee on Organisation. This system was continued into the late 1950s.[101]

The main Committee's minutes reveal a certain hierarchy within the JIC. The FO Chairman and the three Services' Directors of Intelligence – after all, the JIC was still a military forum – were the most important members: they were concerned on a daily basis with intelligence for planning purposes and support to policymaking. As a result this inner group was involved in a constant dialogue with the COS, the joint planners, and other relevant bodies from which the other JIC members, essentially the heads of the agencies, were excluded. Records of these discussions, particularly with the COS, were usually noted at the JIC, but it does not appear that the other members were consulted beforehand. While this might be expected to have had a detrimental effect or cause resentment amongst the Committee's members, it almost certainly did not. The JIC at that time was a subordinate body to the COS, therefore to brief them personally was an intrinsic part of the job, and as the main liaison between the intelligence world and the military, these four individuals were the best placed to act on the JIC's behalf.

As Cold War requirements changed so did the membership. During 1948 the Chairman of the Joint Scientific and Technical Intelligence Committee (JSTIC), Dr D. Brunt, had become a full-time member of the JIC, though the position did not last long.[102] He was joined in October 1948 by a representative from the Colonial Office, George Seel, then Assistant Under-Secretary. The Committee's ranks were further swelled in 1951 by a GCHQ representative in the shape of its Director, Sir Edward Travis, a decision welcomed by the JIC Chairman for ensuring that 'even more direct contact' could be established between them.[103]

By 1955 the Committee had nine permanent members, comprising: the FO, the three Service Directors of Intelligence, the Director of the JIB, the Chief of SIS, the Director-General of the Security Service, the Director of GCHQ, and a Colonial Office representative. Occupying a slightly vague position was the newly created post of 'Scientific Adviser, Intelligence' to the Ministry of Defence (MoD), which had replaced the Director of Scientific Intelligence as the MoD intelligence representative. The incumbent was invited to meetings but was seemingly not a full member.[104]

The most important issue to consider about this organisational evolution is how well the Committee structure and system worked in practice. Certainly the JIC thought it did. In opposing the suggestion that the Commonwealth Relations Office (CRO) become a full member – as suggested in General Sir Gerald Templer's review into intelligence in the colonies[105] – Patrick Dean wrote a compelling summary of the arguments both for and against. He spoke about the 'present close and satisfactory arrangements which exist among the various organisations responsible for security/intelligence in the United Kingdom and the Commonwealth countries. Intelligence people undoubtedly speak much more frankly to each other than they will to outsiders, however friendly.'[106] Dean and his colleagues eventually won the argument, though they did concede that the CRO could attend meetings as and when necessary, but only as observers. However, just a year later this decision was reversed and the CRO became a full member of the JIC.[107]

The Committee in Action (ii) – Product

Although the JIC had several functions, its raison d'être was the production of intelligence forecasts. During the Second World War these were of two main types: strategic and tactical. The production of daily, immediate assessments had ceased with the end of the war. By July 1950 however, with the temperature of the Cold War rising and the invasion, just a few weeks earlier, of South Korea by the communist North, it was decided to review the process by which assessments were produced on the Soviet Union. This review concluded that the JIC should produce a weekly review of Soviet activities to identify where the next 'hot' spot might arise, which should become a weekly item at the Directors' JIC to be appended to the records of the meeting. At the same time, the JIC was quick to highlight that any particularly time-sensitive piece of intelligence should be brought directly to the attention of the COS, bypassing the main Committee entirely.[108]

Shortly after this introduction of a weekly review of the Soviet threat, it was agreed that, in addition, the heads of the 'Russia Sections' of the FO, JIB and three Services should meet weekly to discuss the 'threat'.[109] At the same time, at the Deputy Directors' meeting, weekly discussions were held on the communist threat to the Far East and South-East Asia, an indication that these areas were seen as a lesser priority. In November, with the Korean War intensifying, these became topics for the Directors' meeting and were considered in the context of the Soviet threat.[110] This move resulted in the introduction in December 1950 of the weekly 'Review of the Situation Round the Soviet and Satellite Perimeter'.[111]

Over the next few years the nature of this weekly review of current intelligence changed slightly, with the introduction in 1951 of a section on the Middle East. As time moved on and the intelligence coverage improved, these assessments became increasingly highly classified often with two versions appearing, one including Sigint-derived material and the other without, in order to facilitate a wider distribution. As an indication of the importance of this latter document, it was decided in early 1951 that a suitably redacted version should be shared with the Supreme Headquarters Allied Powers Europe (SHAPE). Similarly, in January 1953, General Sir Nevil Brownjohn, the Chief Staff Officer in the Ministry of Defence, requested that a copy be passed directly to the Minister of Defence, and then to the Prime Minister, thereby bypassing the COS for the first time.[112]

By 1953 the weekly summary had become the 'Perimeter Review', characterised by its opening statement that 'there are no indications of Soviet military aggression'.[113] From 1955 a similar phrase was repeated in respect of China. These documents covered the globe but excluded the colonies – any communist inspired activity in these regions was covered by the 'Colonial Office Review of Current Intelligence', which included material from the regional LICs (see chapter 7) that had already been passed to the JIC.[114] The JIC evidently saw the Perimeter Review as a key product, and was keen to ensure that it was as authoritative and accurate as possible, with a conscious effort to ensure 'collective memory', by frequently revisiting earlier Reviews.[115]

In early 1954 the JIC discussed how the Perimeter Review might be disseminated more widely, largely because 'more publicity might need to be given to the Committee's views on current intelligence'.[116] By this time it had grown from its initial 1–2 page summary to 10 or more pages. The JIC saw the purpose of the Review as twofold: to provide a 'mind-clearing exercise' and to 'draw the attention of a fairly wide circle of non-intelligence authorities to important likely developments'. This second factor raised obvious classification issues, and so it was decided that two versions should be produced, a highly classified 'Weekly Review of Current Intelligence', and a less sensitive, more widely disseminated 'Weekly Summary of Current Intelligence.'[117]

By 1955 the Weekly Review had become a staple ingredient of the JIC's workload; if anything, it was probably the single JIC report which was most widely read and known about across Whitehall and beyond. By this time three separate 'heads of sections' meetings were held each week, concentrating on the Western Sector, the Far East and South East Asia, and the Middle East. Every Tuesday representatives from other departments would attend meetings to discuss any relevant items that had occurred since the last JIC meeting. They would then produce a 'brief' for the Directors' JIC meeting, which took place on Thursday mornings. In between the preparation of the brief on Tuesday, and its discussion by the JIC on Thursday, it was shared with the US so that American views could be incorporated. At the same time, a summary of the brief was prepared for wider circulation. To the Secretary of the JIC, there were four main purposes of the Weekly Review:

(a) To identify and evaluate immediately any indicators of Soviet preparedness for war.
(b) To identify and evaluate immediately any indicators of other disturbances that may lead to a requirement for the use of UK defence forces.
(c) To identify and evaluate intelligence that may indicate the future policy of other nations.
(d) To provide a forum in which Directors can discuss with other Directors events with which their own Departments may not be immediately concerned, and so ensure that all Directors are equally well briefed on world-wide events.[118]

This, therefore, was a far broader and more varied interpretation of the assessment function contained within the JIC's Charter. It is noteworthy that this included a warning function, something which the JIC would be repeatedly accused of failing to perform effectively. It also provides a clear statement of the benefits of having senior intelligence officials meet around the table once a week just to discuss matters of common interest. This is a crucial point which became of increasing importance.

Some attention was paid to whether the summaries should continue to be appended to the JIC minutes. The Weekly Summary, in particular, was noted as having a wide circulation, and that it therefore might be beneficial to 'print and bind it specially' as this would be a 'good advertisement', yet at the same time it was recognised that 'it is not a particularly stirring production'.[119] A list produced in December 1955 reveals just how widely distributed the various versions were. In addition to the parent departments of the JIC members, the most highly classified version, together with the 'special supplement' (in essence a Sigint-heavy annex), was sent to the Prime Minister; the normal 'Weekly Review' went to regional JICs, military liaison offices within the Commonwealth, senior figures in the Ministry of Defence, the Cabinet Secretary, and the CIA. The 'Weekly Summary', the least classified version, went to all of the above, as well as the Secretaries of State for the Colonies and Commonwealth, and also the military liaison staff of Commonwealth nations. Sporadically a further, even more diluted version, was sent to NATO headquarters. While the JIC product was widely disseminated, it is more difficult to know how useful it was, but the benefits of having a single, co-ordinated view of current intelligence is apparent from its continued production.[120]

In early 1956 these various products were reviewed and reformed into two series, the names of which would become synonymous with JIC assessments. The constant tinkering with the weekly assessment since 1950 had still not resulted in a product which satisfied the Committee. It began by re-iterating the purpose of the weekly reports:

(a)   To ensure that the Committee has the opportunity of reviewing all the developments of the past week, and of assessing the significance of trends.
(b)   To produce a document for the information of Ministers and senior officials giving an intelligence evaluation of important information received and of trends revealed.
(c)   To keep other interested parties abreast of current intelligence.

It concluded that 'in its present form the Review did not meet this requirement and was therefore of limited value'. There was a need for a new review, one that would identify trends without being constrained by classification. This new weekly product, different in name from the previous versions so as to emphasise the discontinuity, would be a specially published document.[121] At a practical level, as good an idea as this was it was held up by a lack of properly indoctrinated personnel to produce the paperwork.[122] The new documents were now given the names 'Weekly Survey of Intelligence' for the highly classified document; and the 'Weekly Review of Current Intelligence' for the less sensitive and widely disseminated study. The former of these would soon become characterised by its distinctive red cover, forever more becoming known simply as the 'Red Book'.[123]

This digression on the origins of the Red Book is important, not only for how the Committee saw itself and its assessment role, but also for a methodological point. Although many of the 'Grey Books' (named after the cover colour of the Weekly Review of Current Intelligence) have now been released, all of the Red Books remain classified. This poses a problem because the JIC has traditionally been seen as a longer term, strategic-looking assessment body, and while this is true to an extent, the unavailability of all Red Books from 1956 onwards is misleading about its current, pro-active and tactical commentary. Certainly it could, and did, react speedily when called upon to do so, particularly at times of tension and crisis.

The pre-war and early wartime JIC had produced very few assessments which might be described as non-military in nature – papers were predominantly concerned with capabilities rather than gauging intentions. As the threat from the Soviet Union grew, it continued to be vital to have good in-depth knowledge of the Soviet war machine, but understanding the motivations, rationale, fears and psyche of the Soviet leadership became equally important. As a COS Committee, the JIC retained an underlying military responsibility but gradually the topics for assessments changed as the definition of 'intelligence', in terms of what was required, also altered. This cannot be defined explicitly, but rather it was a piecemeal shift in trends. What is important here is to note the changing emphasis in the reports issued in the twelve year period from the end of the war to 1957, and how 'intelligence' had less of a military focus.

The first recognition of the change was noted by JIC members in 1950. In a discussion about the scale of the JIS' workload, Major General Arthur Shortt, the DMI, suggested that less time be spent on political appreciations and more on solely military ones. Patrick Reilly, the Chairman, dismissed the idea out of hand, commenting that 'he considered that the Committee's responsibility to the Chiefs of Staff were such that this suggestion could not be accepted. Moreover, political considerations were tending to become more and more closely related to military affairs and, from the planning point of view, the political aspect was an important factor in dealing with a large number of current problems'. Reilly was supported in his stance by the Air Ministry representative.[124] A justification of Reilly's position came in 1955, with a discussion on the leadership of the Soviet Union. Briefing the COS Committee, Patrick Dean outlined how the JIC had concluded that Khrushchev was now the real power in the Kremlin, and identified what he, and the other leading Soviet figures, saw as their foreign policy aspirations.[125]

The Committee in Action (iii) – Process

The lifeblood of the Committee was the JIS. Originally reduced to one 'team' of five people at the end of the war, it quickly became apparent that this was insufficient for the task ahead. The practice had been for the JIS – all seconded members from the Services and policy departments represented at the JIC, though not from the intelligence agencies – to write assessments, which would then be circulated for comment. Once approved by all, the JIS would 'affix Directors' signatures' and the paper would be disseminated as a JIC report. The JIS role was therefore vital, for not only did it produce the paper, but was also responsible for ensuring that 'Departmental comments and amendments had been adequately co-ordinated before a paper was thus finalised'.[126]

A paper in 1948, on Soviet intentions, had, for the first time, been supervised by Brigadier Valentine Boucher, who normally represented the DMI at the Deputy Directors' meetings. The DNI, Rear Admiral Eric Longley-Cook, commented in the Directors' JIC on the 'value' of having someone supervise and guide the work of the JIS. On further discussion it was decided that thereafter the most relevant Deputy Director would take responsibility for a paper, with the exception of particularly important topics, for which the JIC's Chairman would take the lead.[127] In subsequent discussion with the JIC, the JIS highlighted the importance of 'free discussion' and how the presence of a 'senior member' might inhibit this. Importantly, the JIS re-emphasised the fact that it was 'not an independent body but a staff of representatives'.[128] It proposed that a Chairman should be drawn from the ranks of the JIS itself, and that whenever possible the relevant JIS member should attend the JIC meeting when their paper was discussed. The JIC agreed to all these suggestions.[129]

The DNI, however, remained unconvinced about the setup of the JIS. He raised the matter again in December 1948, only to be confronted by universal support for the system by the other members of the JIC. To reinforce this the Chairman, William Hayter, offered his view that 'our intelligence is not wonderful, but is probably better than that of any other country except the Soviet Union . . . the Americans may end up better than us – they are richer in manpower, money and resources.' Although warning against complacency, 'C' added 'that the Americans will not reach anything like our standard in our lifetime in spite of their vast expenditure.'[130] It would appear, therefore, that the DNI's concerns were overruled. These rather bureaucratic wranglings were actually very significant. Having two JIS teams fundamentally increased the ability to produce assessments, and the recognition of the role of the JIS, to represent departmental views, was a further sign of the inter-departmental and communal-focus of proceedings.

Following the 1948 reforms three different weekly meetings of the JIC took place. Every Monday afternoon the FO Chairman of the senior JIC would agree with his counterparts chairing the Deputy Directors' meetings on the allocation of agenda items between the three meetings. The idea was to ensure, above all else, a balance in the workload.[131] The rationale behind this was to create as much time as possible for the main Committee to discuss 'general problems and in exchanging ideas'. In broad terms, topics for papers were approved beforehand though time was set aside, 'limited to a maximum of half an hour', for discussing 'unforeseen matters'.[132] By 1950 it was recognised that the time taken to produce papers was 'steadily increasing'. It was decided that the scope of assessments could only be decided by the Services' Directors' of Intelligence.[133] Once more, the reasoning behind this was straightforward, as Patrick Reilly informed the Committee, 'before any report was put in hand by the Committee, proper thought should be given as to whether it was required and that the lines on which a report should be written were clearly laid down.' This was obviously seen as an important point and it was now decided that terms of reference for papers could only by issued by the main JIC itself, something the COS had previously done.[134]

Once the topic for a paper had been approved and terms of reference established, members of the JIS consulted their parent departments to collect and collate all relevant information, then in committee they would produce a first draft of the report. At this stage the JIS consisted of two teams, one more senior than the other. The senior team comprised three General Staff Officers, 1st Grade ((GSO1 or Lieutenant Colonel level); one from each Service), and representatives from the FO and JIB; a similar composition for the second team, albeit with more junior appointments, was at General Staff Officer, 2nd Grade ((GSO2 or Major level) level and FO and JIB equivalent).[135] The first draft of a paper would be shown to the Services' Directors' for approval, with the FO Chairman usually seeing a second or third revision of the draft. The intention, therefore, was that by the time the 'revised draft' had been issued, it represented 'the co-ordinated views of the Directors, and should not normally require any subsequent amendments of consequence'. For the remaining JIC members, they would only see the 'revised draft' once it got to the JIC, and they were told to confine their comments to 'major points of principle'.[136] It is for this reason that so few JIC memoranda are recorded as having been discussed in the full Committee and why there are almost no recorded instances of disagreements over assessments. The JIS did not include anyone from the intelligence agencies so, generally speaking, it would not be until a relatively late draft that SIS, MI5, and GCHQ would see a JIC paper. Sometimes the JIS member who wrote the paper would be asked to attend the JIC to answer any questions that might arise or to defend their judgements. Pending discussion of their paper they were, in the words of one Assistant JIC Secretary, 'kept in the kennels outside until required'.[137]

Servicing both the JIS and the JIC was the Secretariat (see below). Its role was vital, for as the Secretary in the early 1950s confided, 'the Secretariat is to the Joint Intelligence Committee very much what the engine and steering gear are to a ship'.[138] Though largely administrative, the role of the JIC Secretariat was crucial to the successful working and organisation of the Committee: one former Assistant JIC Secretary from the early 1950s has described it as looking after the 'drudgery', in other words, 'keeping the JIC machinery ticking over'.[139] Included amongst its roles was responsibility for: circulating papers to the JIC; organising the business of the sub-committees; setting up meetings and recording the discussions of all meetings of the JIC and its sub-committees; acting as conduits for information between the JIC and outside bodies; passing instructions from the COS to the JIC; and, finally, acting as an intermediary between the JIC and the planners. Heading this team was the Committee's Secretary, usually holding the rank of Colonel, and who, in all but name, also became a de facto member of the Committee.[140] Assisting the Colonel was a small team, composed in the mid-1950s of a GSO 1, a GSO 2, three civil service officials, and four clerical staff (usually female). Thus, there were two teams of five people staffing the JIS, and a total of ten people in the Secretariat, providing a grand total of twenty people 'manning' the entire system.

Once finished and approved, all the JIC papers were then transmitted to the COS for further endorsement which, generally speaking, in the overwhelming majority of cases they received. It was then up to the COS to distribute the papers further as they saw fit. Receipt of papers from the JIC was important, for it was recognised that they represented 'the official opinion of the UK intelligence organisation'.[141] In some instances papers were referred back to the JIC to either re-word or, where the COS wanted to see different conclusions, re-draft.

At this juncture it is necessary to make several observations on the purpose and role of JIC assessments at this time. As an outgrowth of Churchill's wartime directive that the JIC take the initiative in producing drafts, assessments could be produced that had not been commissioned by the COS nor reflected its thoughts. In a sense, therefore, the JIC was producing papers for which there was no obvious readership. Did this negate the value of them? Until the late 1960s, there is no recorded instance of the JIC trying to discover, or even being concerned about whether its reports were read by its consumers.

In trying to gauge the importance and impact of JIC papers it is important to note that although relatively rare, at times the COS did reject a JIC paper, almost always because they disagreed with its contents. Two notable examples of this were papers produced in the late 1940s that dealt with the Soviet Union's strategic intentions, and both were a reflection of wider COS/FO disagreements. In these instances the COS did not agree with the JIC's position, and decreed that the papers should not be circulated further. In one sense these are examples of politicisation: when policymakers found the intelligence they were receiving unpalatable and papers were suppressed. In a slightly underhand tactic, and using terms of reference whereby papers were allowed to be shared with regional JICs and allies, the two papers in question were disseminated. In informing the Chairman of the regional JIC(FE) (see chapter 7) about this, Lieutenant Colonel John K. Gardiner, the JIC Secretary in London, confided 'please treat it as personal to your Committee, under the counter with JIC(48)26 and JIC(47)42!'.[142]

An Umbrella Organisation

By the late 1940s, then, the JIC was firing on all cylinders. Its composition was settled, it had the support of its members, was liked and listened to by those it was designed to serve, and had a good team of drafters preparing assessments. Subordinate to the Committee were a series of sub-committees. By late 1948 these included: Security; Service Attachés; Inter-Services Language; Carrier Pigeons; Aerial Reconnaissance; and Mobilisation Plans. These six sub-committees, as different as they were, reveal much about the Committee's main functions aside from producing intelligence assessments.[143] Broadly speaking the intelligence machine was perceived favourably across Whitehall, having been validated by the 1949 Harwood Report into the armed forces, which called for increased funding for intelligence work. Evill's proposals, widely discussed in the Committee at the time and for some years afterwards, had had a significant impact. Writing in mid-1949, the Committee's Secretary, Gardiner, wrote that Evill's recommendations had resulted in an atmosphere of increased vigour, keenness and efficiency that had not been experienced 'ever before. I believe that we have a healthy and effective organisation for higher direction'.[144]

Within a matter of months the number of subordinate committees had doubled in size, now comprising: the Joint Scientific Intelligence Committee; the Joint Technical Intelligence Committee; the Exchange of Military Information Sub-Committee; the Security Sub-Committee; the British Metric Security Sub-Committee; the Inter-Service Languages Sub-Committee; the Intelligence Mobilisation Plans Sub-Committee; the Monitoring Requirements Sub-Committee; the Services Attachés Sub-Committee; the Joint Air Photographic Intelligence Board; the Carrier Pigeons Sub-Committee; and the Evasion & Escape Sub-Committee.[145] This diverse and disparate array of bodies reveals the sheer scale, breadth and depth of the JIC's work, far beyond just the production of intelligence assessments. Yet despite these responsibilities, producing finished intelligence for the COS and military planners remained the Committee's central raison d'être.

By the early 1950s the standing of the JIC as the central body for British intelligence had certainly been confirmed, and its relationship to other intelligence entities was frequently raised. The Sigint Board had been traditionally chaired by 'C', who was, of course, ultimately responsible for it in his position as Director General of Signals Intelligence. With discussions underway in the early 1950s to find a successor to Menzies as 'C', it was queried whether the new 'C' should continue to chair the Sigint Board. Sir William Strang, the PUS in the FO, thought it odd that this should not pass to the Chairman of the JIC because 'it was wrong to have two bodies of equal standing in the Intelligence Organisation with overlapping functions but different Chairmen'.[146] The COS agreed to this in late 1951. However, the 'C' designate, together with the outgoing Chief, successfully argued the SIS corner and so whilst 'C' remained Chairman of the Sigint Board, a special provision was written into the Charter to ensure that any 'differences of opinion' between GCHQ and other government departments would be passed to the JIC for resolution. The Sigint Board itself included the members of the JIC and therefore the problem experienced in wartime when some of the JIC members did not have direct access to relevant signals intelligence was no longer an issue.[147] By the mid-1950s it had been decided that whenever 'C' could not chair the Board, the JIC Chairman would assume responsibilities as his deputy.[148] From the late 1940s onwards the JIC, as a Committee, not just its constituent members, would have far more to do with signals intelligence, not only because Sigint made up an increasingly large proportion of the intelligence that went into JIC assessments, but also as the JIC spent more and more time on considering how to improve Britain's intelligence coverage.

In addition to creating the JIB and dismantling SOE, the JIC spent a considerable effort reviewing the existing organisation for scientific and technical intelligence. Wartime efforts against German technological advances had been a resounding success, and the lessons of the war were not lost on the JIC. Alongside the Ad Hoc committee on the JIB, the JIC also created a committee to consider how scientific and technical intelligence should be approached in the post-war world. This was justified in a note by Capel-Dunn to the Cabinet Secretary, Sir Edward Bridges, which divulged that 'many of us have felt the need during the war years for some closely-knit and more logical machinery.'[149] Meeting under the Chairmanship of Professor Patrick Blackett the group focussed on the 'collection, collation, assessment and appreciation' aspects of scientific and technical intelligence. Included amongst its members was the respected scientist R.V. Jones, who had achieved widespread success with his intelligence forecasts during the war (see chapter 5). One of the group's first conclusions, and perhaps its most prescient, was that 'by far the most important intelligence requirement for a country such as ours will be accurate information rapidly acquired of scientific and technical development in other countries'. The group's proposal was for the creation of a 'Joint Technical Intelligence Committee' to assess weapon capabilities, which would complement the JIC's work, given that its expertise lay in less technical areas.[150]

Recognising its lack of any substantial technical know-how, the JIC endorsed the conclusions and issued the Ad Hoc group's final report as a JIC paper. It stated that there needed to be dedicated scientific intelligence personnel in each Service intelligence directorate; that SIS should maintain a special section; that an overt scientific section be established within the JIB; and that these disparate groups should convene regularly as a Joint Technical Intelligence Committee, which would subsequently report to the JIC itself.[151] The recommendations were approved; the only negative voice being that of the Security Service, which had deliberately been left out of the proceedings because it was not felt that it could offer much or benefit. Its Director-General, Sir David Petrie, complained about its exclusion whilst also pleading to be allowed to be involved.[152] 'C' attempted to delay a decision, but ultimately the JIC agreed to include Petrie in the discussions.[153]

The one omission in the scientific discussions, as indeed it had been during the war, was atomic intelligence. Following the attacks on Hiroshima and Nagasaki the JIC was now patently aware of the potential of atomic warfare, though it was not apprised of the most recent developments. In intelligence terms the JIC's initial view was that 'we consider that all intelligence on this important subject should be handled within the established intelligence organisation and not by independent agencies.'[154] There was, however, a problem with this concept. The preservation of the wartime Anglo-American partnership was paramount. There had been some discussion in the summer of 1945 about the post-war atomic intelligence system, and 'C' had expressed his desire to bring atomic matters within the scope of the rest of the intelligence machinery. The difficulty, as indeed he recognised, was that for security reasons the Americans were very keen that atomic intelligence should remain separate from the rest of scientific intelligence, 'as it was necessary to maintain the closest collaboration possible with them, we should do well to fall in with the American views in this matters.'[155] Thus, the JIC's bid was rejected, and despite several attempts by R.V.Jones to amalgamate scientific and atomic intelligence, they remained separate. From this point onwards the subsequent atomic intelligence organisation, created within the Directorate of Tube Alloys in the Ministry of Supply, reported its findings to the JIC, many of which were subsequently incorporated into broader JIC papers on the Soviet military threat.[156] It is evident that the JIC was not entirely happy for, in the early 1950s, the Chairman, Patrick Reilly, informed the Cabinet Secretary, Sir Norman Brook, that 'the JIC had always regarded the present arrangements, which excluded atomic energy intelligence from its field of authority, as unsatisfactory'.[157]

In 1954 Admiral Sir Charles Daniel, who had had sporadic involvement with the JIC, was called upon to write a report on the organisational aspects of atomic intelligence. Daniel agreed that this separation was warranted and should continue, but suggested that an oversight body should be created. The Atomic Energy Intelligence Committee (AEIC) was therefore constituted and whilst being separate from the JIC it would report to it. Importantly the JIC, through its Chairman Patrick Dean, would be represented on the AEIC. Although agreeing to this, it is clear that Dean was slightly perturbed at the creation of a parallel intelligence body to the JIC, which he suggested should eventually subsume it; a view shared by the COS.[158] The launch of the Soviet satellite 'Sputnik' in October 1957 proved to be a catalyst for resolving this debate. It was now clear that nuclear and missile intelligence could no longer be treated separately, and so 'atomic' and 'scientific' intelligence were finally merged. In parallel the AEIC became a specialised sub-committee of the JIC, and was re-named the 'Sub-Committee on Intelligence on Nuclear Weapons'.[159]

An Augmented Committee

By the mid-1950s the JIC model was working well and it is evident from the records that both the JIC and COS thought so. To strengthen its position further, in 1955 the JIC was issued a revised Charter:

(i) To give higher direction to, and to keep under review, intelligence operations and defence security matters.
(ii) To assemble, appreciate and present intelligence as required by the Chiefs of Staff and to initiate such other reports as may be required or as the Committee may deem necessary.
(iii) To keep under review the organisation and working of intelligence and defence security as a whole at home and overseas so as to ensure efficiency, economy, and a rapid adaptation to changing requirements, and to advise what changes are deemed necessary.

(iv) To co-ordinate the activities of Joint Intelligence Committees under United Kingdom commands overseas and to maintain an exchange of intelligence with them.

(v)   To maintain liaison with appropriate intelligence and defence security agencies in the self-governing Commonwealth countries and the United States and other foreign countries, and with the intelligence authorities of international defence organisations of which the United Kingdom is a member.[160]

This is a useful summary of the activities of the JIC in the mid-1950s. It is immediately clear how varied its tasks were, and how the production of intelligence assessments – frequently seen as its primary role – was but one of many. The JIC itself does not appear to have made any explicit distinction between the relative importance of its functions. It is clear from the division of labour that the full Committee, which spent most of its time on assessments, was far less concerned with administrative issues (i.e. principally anything that did not involve assessment) and more involved with the organisational aspects of the Charter (i.e. the work of regional and sub-committees). Foreign liaison was considered important, as was ensuring that the COS and the planners were fully briefed on all relevant items. Indeed, an internal 1955 history of the Joint Intelligence Organisation emphasised that the Services' Directors and the FO Chairman would frequently attend COS Committee meetings, and the JIC Secretary would always be present if any item 'with a possible intelligence implication' was discussed. Similarly with the planners: the senior figures met at irregular intervals to discuss papers, but at a more junior level the Committee's Secretaries were in daily contact. This, therefore, was a JIC immersed in the operations of the state.[161]

By 1957 the JIC had ten permanent members: the FO, the DNI, the DMI, the Assistant Chief of the Air Staff (Intelligence), the Director of the JIB, the Chief of SIS, the Director-General of the Security Service, separate representatives from the Commonwealth Relations Office and the Colonial Office, and the Director of GCHQ. Below this were two JIS teams, a small secretariat servicing it, and a plethora of sub-committees, regional committees, and liaison relationships to maintain. This was certainly a busy Committee, composed of senior men all of whom, including the chairman, had other responsibilities to fulfil aside from JIC work. A revealing picture of how they viewed themselves can be found in the report of a short-lived working party set up by the JIC to consider whether the British intelligence system was prepared for the eventuality of war:

> The British Intelligence machine in the UK is required to deal with a welter of miscellaneous subjects at top speed. It might, in fact, be said without exaggeration that the machine is propelled by a succession of panics, due to insufficient time being available to deal with questions of the highest importance . . . one cause is undoubtedly the difficulty of sorting out the mass of detailed intelligence available into the form of reasoned appreciations.[162]

From the final stages of the war, when the JIC began to anticipate the post-war world, until 1957, at no stage did the JIC question whether its model was the best or whether it was the optimal system to deal with what transpired to be the threat from communism. The underlying problem in the pre-war period, a lack of any inter-departmental structure to supervise the intelligence effort, had been solved through the JIC. Created by, and working to, the Committee was a network of subordinate bodies, yet it is not apparent from the records how closely the JIC really supervised them. In practice most were self-sufficient, often only reporting at times of crisis or need, yet the support network served as a two-way street between Whitehall and overseas. Indeed, it is quite astounding to consider the number of committees, sub-committees, and ad hoc committees that the JIC created – certainly this was a Committee that liked and saw the value of other committees! To this extent the JIC, rightly, saw itself as an umbrella organisation.

The JIC was central to the entire British intelligence machine. From setting requirements and priorities, through matters of security and administration, to producing assessments, the main functions of intelligence flowed through the JIC. Its role was much broader than the production of assessments, yet even here its function was two-fold: to produce both long-term and short-term forecasts for a wide variety of customers. Central to these was the role of the Chairman, and in this twelve year period the JIC had four very able, very successful, FO men, all of whom carried the mantle created by Cavendish-Bentinck during the war. The British system, unlike its American counterpart, was small enough for personal contacts to count for much.

Since the JIC was a subordinate body to the COS Committee the reaction of its consumers to its product can be gauged, and the COS were content with the majority of reports disseminated in their name. What is less obvious is whether those reports that the COS did not comment upon or distribute had a wider impact outside the JIC structure. The creation of the Red and Grey Books ensured that the shorter, more current intelligence assessments were disseminated more widely than just the military community, and this helps explain the longevity and stature of the JIC as more than a military sub-committee. The main Committee was able to focus its efforts on assessment by passing matters to do with security and organisation to the Deputy Directors' JIC. But the Committee also became increasingly exercised by liaison matters. Indeed, it was through liaison that the JIC really began to exert ever greater influence and play a role in the affairs of state. It would be through the creation of a world-wide network of intelligence that the JIC became not just a window on the world, but a vital element of British policymaking.

Notes

1 Strong, *Men of Intelligence*. p.123.
2 D.Capel-Dunn to V.Cavendish-Bentinck, 18 September 1943. FO 1093/194.
3 D.Capel-Dunn to V.Cavendish-Bentinck, 18 September 1943. FO 1093/194.

4 JIC/1605/43, 'Future Organisation of Intelligence', 13 October 1943. FO 1093/194. This file also contains the views of the different members of the JIC on the paper.

5 JIC(43)53rd Meeting, 26 October 1943. CAB 81/91.

6 W.Bentinck to J.Lewis, 9 October 1980. I am extremely grateful to Dr Julian Lewis, MP, for providing me with some of his research correspondence relating to wartime planning for the post-war period. Cavendish-Bentinck in later life called himself Bill (William) Bentinck.

7 JIC(43)53rd Meeting, 26 October 1943. CAB 81/91. The minutes refer to various papers on this subject by Committee members, these can all be found in FO 1093/194.

8 JIC/1801/43, 'Future Organisation of Intelligence', 9 November 1943. Cabinet Office papers.

9 JIC(44)86(O), 'The British Intelligence Organisation', 3 March 1944. CAB 81/121

10 'Charter for the JIC', 13 July 1944. CAB 163/6.

11 JIC(44)404(O), 'Conference on Co-ordination of Intelligence in the Far East', 16 September 1944. CAB 81/125.

12 D.Capel-Dunn to E.E.Bridges [Cabinet Secretary], 7 July 1944. Cabinet Office papers. See also JIC/1735/43, 'Draft Letter from Chairman, JIC, to Sir Edward Bridges', 2 November 1943. FO 1093/194.

13 JIC/1424/44, Cavendish-Bentinck to D.Petrie [D-G, Security Service], 27 October 1944. Cabinet Office papers.

14 'The Intelligence Machine', 10 January 1945. CAB 163/6. Emphasis added. For a more detailed examination of this paper see M Herman, 'The Post-War Organization of Intelligence: The January 1945 Report to the Joint Intelligence Committee on "The Intelligence Machine"', In R Dover & M S Goodman (eds), *Learning from the Secret Past: Cases in British Intelligence History* (Washington: Georgetown University Press, 2011). This includes a copy of 'The Intelligence Machine' document.

15 'The Intelligence Machine', 10 January 1945. CAB 163/6.

16 JIC(45)265(O)(Final), 'Post-War Organisation of Intelligence', 7 September 1945. CAB 81/130.

17 COS(45)220th Meeting, 11 September 1945. CAB 79/39.

18 'The Intelligence Machine', 10 January 1945. CAB 163/6.

19 Bridges to Robbins [Ministry of Economic Warfare], 23 January 1945. Cabinet Office papers.

20 JS/108/45, Note by D.Capel-Dunn, 'The Intelligence Machine', 21 March 1945. CAB 163/6. The minutes do not exist apart from the general conclusions.

21 U3498/2231/G70. Note by V.Cavendish-Bentinck, 3 July 1943. FO 371/35449.

22 JIC/512/45, 'Minutes of 1st Meeting of the Ad Hoc Committee on the Joint Intelligence Bureau', 18 April 1945. CAB 176/5.

23 JIC/687/45, 'Minutes of 6th Meeting of the Ad Hoc Committee on the Joint Intelligence Bureau', 24 May 1945. CAB 176/6.

24 JIC/836/45, 'Minutes of a Special Meeting of the Joint Intelligence Bureau', 20 June 1945. CAB 176/6. The preceding minutes are also in this volume.

25 JIC(45)36th Meeting (O), 29 May 1945. CAB 81/93.

26 COS(45)198th Meeting, 14 August 1945. CAB 79/37.

27 JIC/1162/45, 'Joint Intelligence Bureau', 17 August 1945. CAB 176/7.

28 Examples of some of the minutes can be found in CAB 176/7.

29 Strong had also been a lead candidate for the Director-General of MI5 at the same time. Note by L.C.Hollis, 11 October 1945. CAB 121/230. The matter was only resolved when Cabinet Secretary Sir Edward Bridges decided in the JIB's favour.

30 For more details see FO 1093/252. For more on this review see chapter 8.

31 M Seaman, '"A New Instrument of War" The Origins of the Special Operations Executive', In M Seaman (ed.) *Special Operations Executive: A New Instrument of War* (London: Routledge, 2005). pp.7–21.

32 PM/44/735, A.Eden to Prime Minister, 30 November 1944. FO 1093/198.
33 He had had some earlier involvement with SOE. See CAB 102/648.
34 COS(45)360(O), 'Future of SOE', 27 May 1945. CAB 80/94.
35 JIC/821/45, 'Minutes of the 1st Meeting of the Ad Hoc Committee on the Future of SOE', 18 June 1945. CAB 176/6.
36 JIC/859/45, 'Future of SOE', 23 June 1945. CAB 176/6.
37 JIC/861/45, 'Future of SOE', 24 June 1945. CAB 176/6.
38 V.Cavendish-Bentinck to H.N.Sporborg, 22 June 1945. FO 1093/198. Emphasis in original.
39 Sporborg to Cavendish-Bentinck, 23 June 1945. FO 1093/198.
40 JIC/867/45, 'Minutes of the 3rd Meeting of the Ad Hoc Committee on the Future of SOE', 25 June 1945. CAB 176/6.
41 Cavendish-Bentinck to A.Cadogan, 25 June 1945. FO 1093/198.
42 COS(45)504(O), 'Future of SOE', 31 July 1945. CAB 80/96.
43 COS(45)198th Meeting, 14 August 1945. CAB 79/37.
44 Cavendish-Bentinck to Cadogan, 14 August 1945. FO 1093/198.
45 As envisaged in 1945 its role was: 'The Signal Intelligence Board is responsible to the Chiefs of Staff for instituting and carrying out within the British Empire, and in collaboration with other nations when authorised, the Chiefs of Staff policy in respect of the interception of all communications and radio transmissions of other nations; the cryptography and traffic analysis required for their interpretation; the resulting Intelligence and the manner and extent of its distribution'. I am grateful to the GCHQ Departmental Historian for this information.
46 JIC(46)28th Meeting (O), 22 May 1946. CAB 81/94. A similar point can be made in regard to the earlier 'Y Board', which included the three Services' intelligence Directors, plus the Director of GC&CS, but did not seem to include anyone from the FO. Some details are in HW 42/31.
47 JIC(48)19(O), 'Sigint Intelligence Requirements – 1948', 11 May 1948. CAB 158/3. A copy is reproduced verbatim in R Aldrich & M Coleman, 'The Cold War, the JIC and British Signals Intelligence, 1948', *Intelligence and National Security* 4:3 (1989), pp.546–9.
48 L.C.Hollis to Lord Tedder [Chief of the Air Staff]. 22 April 1947. CAB 121/231.
49 'Sigint Enquiry – Report by Sir D Evill', 11 September 1946. CAB 158/73.
50 Draft Letter to the Foreign Secretary, n.d. but either April or May 1947. DEFE 7/1953. An abridged version was sent by the Minister for Defence, A.V.Alexander, to the Foreign Secretary, E.Bevin, 17 May 1947. DEFE 7/1953.
51 Evill interpreted the instructions given to him as including: 'i) the extent to which available intelligence, regardless of sources, seemed to meet defence requirements; ii) the organisations which exist to receive and collect this intelligence and their relation to one another, including the avoidance of waste and outlay; iii) the existing methods of co-ordinating and direction of intelligence operations with a view to making the best use of resources; iv) the internal organisation of the Service Intelligence Directorates and Joint Intelligence Bureau'. JIC/1159,49, 'Recommendations Made by Sir Douglas Evill in his Review of Intelligence Organisations, 1947, and their Implementation', 4 July 1949. CAB 163/7.
52 Various discussions by the JIC can be found in CAB 159/1.
53 JIC(47)38th Meeting (O), 20 June 1947. CAB 159/1.
54 Evill to Secretary, JIC, 15 July 1947. CAB 163/7.
55 JIC(47)50th Meeting, 6 August 1947. CAB 159/1.
56 Comprising a Foreign Office Chairman, the three Service departments, MI5, SIS, and the JIB.
57 JIC/1017/47, 'Review of Intelligence Organisation', 26 September 1947. CAB 163/7.
58 JIC(47)65th Meeting (O), 1 October 1947. CAB 159/2.
59 COS(47)140th Meeting, 12 November 1947. CAB 121/231.

60 Misc/P(47)31, 'Review of Intelligence Organisations, 1947', 6 November 1947. CAB 163/7. Note the similarities here with Lord Butler's view of the role of the JIC Chairman: '. . . someone with experience of dealing with Ministers in a very senior role, and who is demonstrably beyond influence'. HC 898. *Review of Intelligence on Weapons of Mass Destruction: Report of a Committee of Privy Counsellors.* (London: The Stationary Office, 2004). p.158.

61 JIC(47)77th Meeting, 12 November 1947. CAB 159/2.

62 JIC(47)85th Meeting, 3 December 1947. CAB 159/2.

63 JIC/761/47, 'Review of Intelligence Organisation', 2 August 1947. CAB 163/7.

64 JIC/761/47, 'Review of Intelligence Organisation', 2 August 1947. CAB 163/7.

65 COS(47)102. DEFE 5/2.

66 JIC(47)90th Meeting, 18 December 1947. CAB 159/2.

67 JIC(47)84(O)(Final), 'Review of Intelligence Organisations – 1947', 3 January 1948. CAB 158/2.

68 JIC/54/48, 'Review of Intelligence Organisations 1947', 9 January 1948. CAB 163/7.

69 JIC/278/48, 'Review of JIC Organisation and Procedure', 11 February 1948. CAB 163/7.

70 JIC(48)20(O), 'Review of JIC Organisation and Procedure', 27 February 1948. CAB 158/3.

71 COS(48)33rd Meeting, 8 March 1948. CAB 121/231.

72 DO(48)21, 'Charter for the Joint Intelligence Committee', 24 February 1948. CAB 131/6.

73 Bevin to Alexander, 4 February 1948. DEFE 7/1953.

74 This remains the case. Sir Peter Ricketts, JIC Chairman 2000–2001 and subsequently the PUS, Foreign and Commonwealth Office, and the first National Security Adviser, Cabinet Office, confirmed this. Interview with P.Ricketts, 18 May 2009.

75 H.Caccia to D.P.Reilly, 15 April 1953. P.Reilly Papers. Bodleian Library, University of Oxford: c.6866, folio 3.

76 'Eton v. Old Etonians', *The Times* (19 March 1923).

77 'Caccia, Harold Anthony', *Oxford Dictionary of National Biography*.

78 COS(46)129th Meeting, 23 August 1946. CAB 79/51.

79 'Hayter, Sir William Goodenough', *Oxford Dictionary of National Biography*.

80 Hayter, *A Double Life*. His papers are in New College, Oxford.

81 Reilly produced a fascinating mini-memoir on this: 'The Secret Service, 1942–3'. Reilly Papers: c.6918, folios 200–250.

82 Reilly papers: c.6920, folios 245–6.

83 K.W.D.Strong to D.P.Reilly, 21 April 1953. Reilly papers: c.6866, folio 6.

84 Sinclair to Reilly, 24 April 1953. Reilly papers: c.6866, folio 11.

85 'Dean, Sir Patrick Henry', *Oxford Dictionary of National Biography*.

86 'Dean, Sir Patrick Henry', May 1958. NARA II: RG 59, Lot 58D 776, Box 22.

87 Fuller details can be found in 'Permanent Under-Secretary's Department', Note by G.L.McDermott [head of PUSD] 18 November 1953. PUSD Files, FCO.

88 PUSD comprised a 1st Secretary who worked with the JPS; a 2nd Secretary who was a member of the JIS; and a 1st Secretary on permanent secondment to SIS.

89 This description is provided by Reilly. Reilly papers: c.6920, folio 222. Further details can be found in JIC/1017/47, 'Review of Intelligence Organisation', 26 September 1947. CAB 163/7.

90 Brigadier T.Haddon Papers, Imperial War Museum (94/8/1): *Looking Back* (unpublished memoir). p.32.

91 C L Cooper, *In the Shadows of History: 50 Years Behind the Scenes of Cold War Diplomacy* (New York: Prometheus Books, 2005). pp.137–8.

92 Interview with Cecil Alldis, 21 September 2009. The post of Assistant Secretary was, in essence, a clerical one; it should not be confused with the FO grading of Assistant Under Secretary.

93 Interview with Cecil Alldis, 21 September 2009.
94 The JIC reference comes from his diary entry for 17 August 1950, the LIC reference from 13 May 1952. Shortt's diary for his tenure as DMI are very brief, though there is a nice mixture of work references and pleasure: 16 August 1950: 'JIC met COS at 1030 – 1/2hr earlier than expected . . . briefed for tomorrow's JIC at 1630 . . . test match collapse . . . ordered new hat'. 19 August 1950: 'Got up late. Had a haircut . . . v.early bed'. 20 August 1950: 'Spent morning doing housework!' Major General A.C.Shortt Diaries, Defence Intelligence and Security Centre, Chicksands.
95 JIC(48)14th Meeting, 18 February 1948. CAB 159/3.
96 JIC(48)16th Meeting, 25 February 1948. CAB 159/3.
97 JIC(48)20th Meeting, 10 March 1948. CAB 159/3.
98 JIC/2899/54, 'Outline of the UK Joint Intelligence Organisation', 9 November 1954. PUSD Files, FCO.
99 JIC(48)104th Meeting, 23 September 1948. CAB 159/4.
100 On the origins of this see PSIS(74)1, 'The Role and Responsibilities of PSIS. Note by the Chairman', 17 January 1974. CAB 163/228.
101 JIC/2781/52, 'Organisation of JIC Meetings', 4 December 1952. CAB 163/8.
102 JSTIC was one of the JIC's sub-committees. See chapter 10.
103 JIC(51)95th Meeting, 13 September 1951. CAB 159/10.
104 COS(54)114, 'Scientific Intelligence Organisation', 6 April 1954. DEFE 32/4. The post of Scientific Adviser Intelligence to the MoD lasted from 1955–60. Its only incumbent was Eric Williams, who went on to become the Chief Scientist at the Department for Trade and Industry.
105 For more see R Cormac, 'Organising Intelligence: An Introduction to the 1955 Report on Colonial Security', *Intelligence and National Security* 25:6 (2010), pp.800–22.
106 COS(55)229, 'Membership of the Joint Intelligence Committee', 12 September 1955. CAB 163/8. See also various correspondence in CAB 21/3622.
107 P.H.Dean to N.Brook [Cabinet Secretary], 2 June 1956. Also, Brook to the Prime Minister, 6 June 1956. CAB 21/3622. For further background detail see 'Revision of Charter', 1955. PUSD Files, FCO.
108 JIC(50)72nd Meeting, 13 July 1950. CAB 159/8.
109 JIC(50)75th Meeting, 20 July 1950. CAB 159/8.
110 JIC(50)130th Meeting, 30 November 1950. CAB 159/8.
111 JIC(50)133rd Meeting, 7 December 1950. CAB 159/8.
112 These facts are drawn from a history of the weekly summary. JIC/2326/53, 'Perimeter Review', 29 September 1953. CAB 176/44.
113 Peter Hennessy makes great fun of this in his book *Secret State: Whitehall and the Cold War* (London: Penguin, 2003).
114 JIC(55)28, 'Colonial Intelligence and Security', 23 March 1955. CAB 158/20.
115 JIC/2477/52, 'World Wide Intelligence Organisation in Peace and War', 28 October 1952. CAB 176/39.
116 JIC(54)4th Meeting, 14 January 1954. CAB 159/15.
117 JIC/1512/54, 'Form of the Perimeter Review', 28 June 1954. CAB 176/49. Despite the change of name, the opening paragraph began the same way. See the first 'Review of Current Intelligence', JIC(54)60th Meeting, 8 July 1954. CAB 159/16.
118 JIC/2652/55, 'Form of the Weekly Review of Current Intelligence', 4 October 1955. CAB 176/55.
119 JIC/3146/55, 'Form of the Weekly Review of Current Intelligence', 30 November 1955. CAB 176/55.
120 JIC/3287/55, 'Form of the Weekly Review of Current Intelligence', 16 December 1955. CAB 176/55.
121 JIC(56)19th Meeting, Confidential Annex, 'Form of the Weekly Review of Current Intelligence', 23 February 1956. CAB 159/22.

122 JIC/598/56, 'Form of the Weekly Review of Current Intelligence', 2 March 1956. CAB 176/56.
123 JIC/1353/56, 'Form of the Weekly Survey of Intelligence', 23 May 1956. CAB 176/57. The Red Book would survive until January 2008.
124 JIC(50)13th Meeting, 3 February 1950. CAB 159/7.
125 COS(55)8th Meeting, Confidential Annex, 'Meeting with Directors of Intelligence', 9 February 1955. CAB 158/79.
126 'Procedure for Finalising JIC Papers', 17 July 1946. PUSD Files, FCO.
127 JIC(48)135th Meeting, 3 September 1948. CAB 159/4.
128 Compare this to the 1968 creation of the Assessments Staff – see Volume II.
129 JIC(48)138th Meeting, 10 December 1948. CAB 159/4.
130 'Organisation of JIC and JIS', 3 December 1948. CAB 163/5.
131 JIC/423/50, 'Conduct of the Work of the Committee', 4 March 1950. CAB 163/8.
132 JIC(50)11th Meeting, 27 January 1950. CAB 159/7.
133 JIC(50)13th Meeting, 3 February 1950. CAB 159/7.
134 JIC(50)19th Meeting, 17 February 1950. CAB 159/7.
135 JIC/272/51, 'A "Child's Guide" to Certain Intelligence Organisations', 2 February 1951. CAB 163/8.
136 JIC/423/50, 'Conduct of the Work of the Committee', 4 March 1950. CAB 163/8.
137 Interview with Cecil Alldis, 21 September 2009.
138 JIC/2430/53, E.E.G.L.Searight (JIC SEC) to H.Parker (PUS, Ministry of Defence), 9 October 1953. CAB 163/8.
139 Interview with Cecil Alldis, 21 September 2009.
140 JIC/2430/53, .Searight to .Parker, 9 October 1953. CAB 163/8.
141 JIC/2450/48, 'Circulation of JIC Reports', 22 December 1948. CAB 176/20.
142 JIC/2450/48, 'Circulation of JIC Reports', 22 December 1948. CAB 176/20. The two reports themselves can be found in CAB 158/1 and 158/3.
143 JIC/2340/48, 'Joint Intelligence Committee Organisation and Procedure', 7 December 1948. CAB 163/6. The terms of reference for the Carrier Pigeons Sub-Committee can be found in the Appendices to this volume.
144 JIC/1185/49, Note from Gardiner to Elliot [Air Marshal, Chief Staff Officer to Minister of Defence], 4 July 1949. CAB 163/7.
145 JIC/1416/49, 'Intelligence Organisation', 10 August 1949. CAB 176/23. For further details see the appendices to this volume.
146 'Chairmanship of the Sigint Board', 16 May 1952. CAB 158/75.
147 LSIB(52)1(Final), 'The Signal Intelligence Organisation', 26 June 1952. CAB 158/75.
148 'Signal Intelligence (SIGINT) and the Sigint Organisation', 3 May 1955. CAB 158/79.
149 D.Capel-Dunn to E.E.Bridges, 2- April 1945. CAB 21/3622.
150 JIC/551/45, 'Minutes of the First Ad Hoc Committee on the Organisation of Scientific and Technical Intelligence', 26 April 1945. CAB 176/6.
151 JIC(45)229, 'Organisation of Scientific and Technical Intelligence', 26 July 1945. CAB 81/129.
152 JIC/1231/45, 'Organisation of Scientific and Technical Intelligence', 29 August 1945. CAB 176/7.
153 JIC(45)60th Meeting (O), 4 September 1945. CAB 81/93.
154 JIC(45)311(O), 'Intelligence on Tube Alloys', 6 November 1945. CAB 81/131.
155 JIC/1275/45, 'Intelligence on Tube Alloys', 5 September 1945. CAB 176/7.
156 For more details see Goodman, *Spying on the Nuclear Bear*.
157 'Record of Meeting to discuss Atomic Energy Intelligence', 3 April 1951. CAB 126/246. Also in attendance were Lord Portal (Controller of Atomic Energy, Ministry of Supply), Sir Roger Makins (Deputy Under-Secretary, FO), and 'C'.

158 Confidential Annex to COS(54)30th Meeting, 17 March 1954. DEFE 32/4. See also Amplification to Confidential Annex to COS(53)135th Meeting, 27 November 1953. DEFE 32/3.
159 Goodman, *Spying on the Nuclear Bear*. pp.168–73, 186–9.
160 JIC(55)74, 'Charter for the Joint Intelligence Committee', 7 November 1955. CAB 158/22.
161 JIC/1/56, 'History of the Joint Intelligence Organisation', 31 December 1955. CAB 163/8.
162 JIC/2221/52, 'World-Wide Intelligence Organisation', 30 September 1952. CAB 176/38.

Figure 6.1 Desmond Anderson,
Chairman of the JIC
(July 1936 – December 1937)

Figure 6.2 Roger Evans, Chairman of the JIC (February 1938 – July 1938)
Front row, second from left.

Visit of General Gamelin (Chief of General Staff and of National and War Defences, and C.-in-C. Armies of France)

Government House, Aldershot, June 7th, 1939

Figure 6.3 Frederick Beaumont-Nesbitt, Chairman of the JIC (November 1938 – July 1939)
Back row, fifth from right.

Figure 6.4 Ralph Skrine Stevenson, Chairman of the JIC (August 1939 – December 1939)

Figure 6.5 Victor Cavendish-Bentinck, Chairman of the JIC (December 1939 – August 1945)

Figure 6.6 Harold Caccia, Chairman of the JIC (November 1945 – August 1946)

Figure 6.7 William Hayter, Chairman of
the JIC (October 1946 –
November 1950)

Figure 6.8 Patrick Reilly, Chairman of the JIC (November 1950 – April 1953)

Figure 6.9 Patrick Dean, Chairman of the JIC (May 1953 – July 1960)

Figure 6.10 Denis Capel-Dunn, Secretary of the JIC (March 1941 – June 1943)

Figure 6.11 Joint Intelligence Staff, 1943
L-R: Henry Haslam [Ministry of Economic Warfare], Francis Ogilvie [Air Ministry], Kennedy Walker-Sloan [Foreign Office], Charles Fletcher-Cooke [Admiralty], Noel Annan [War Office]

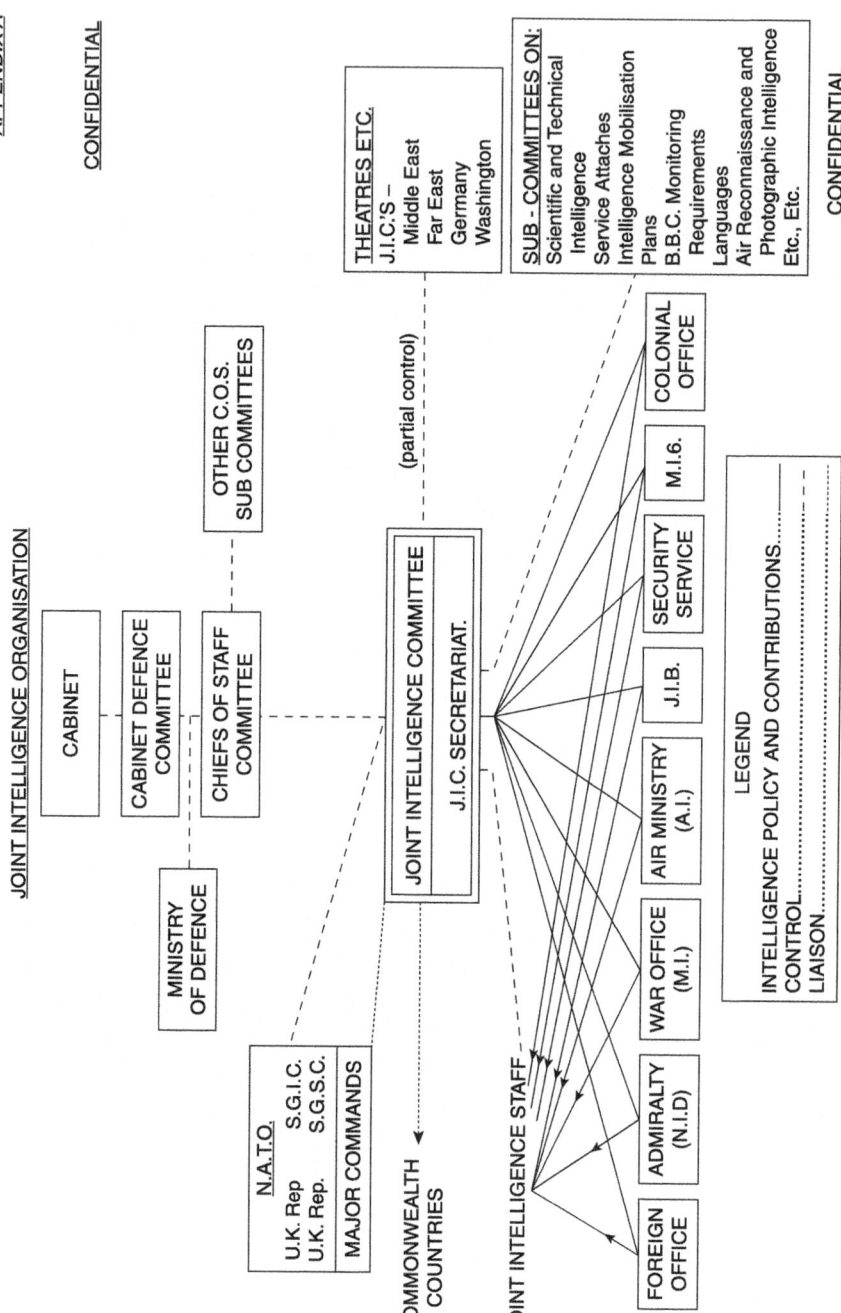

Figure 6.12 JIC Organisational Chart, 1955

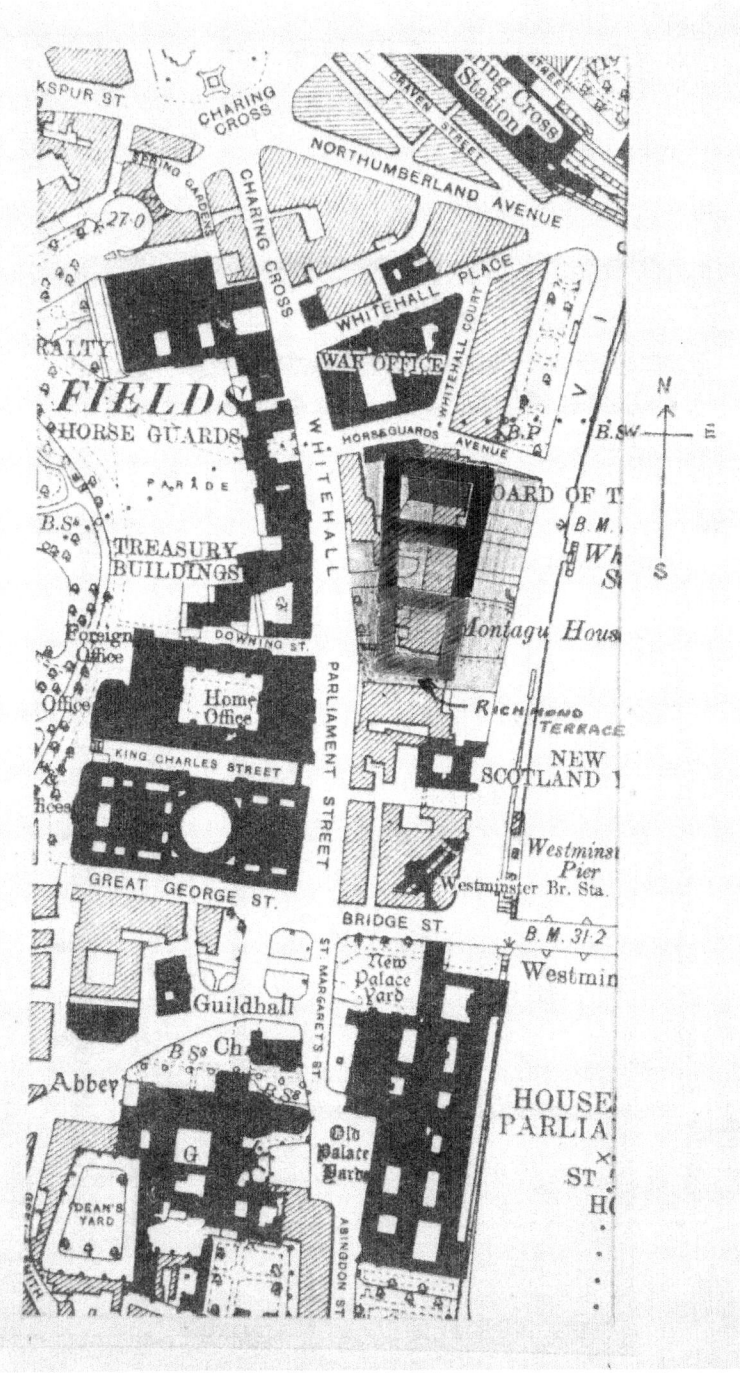

Figure 6.13 Map of Whitehall, c.1940

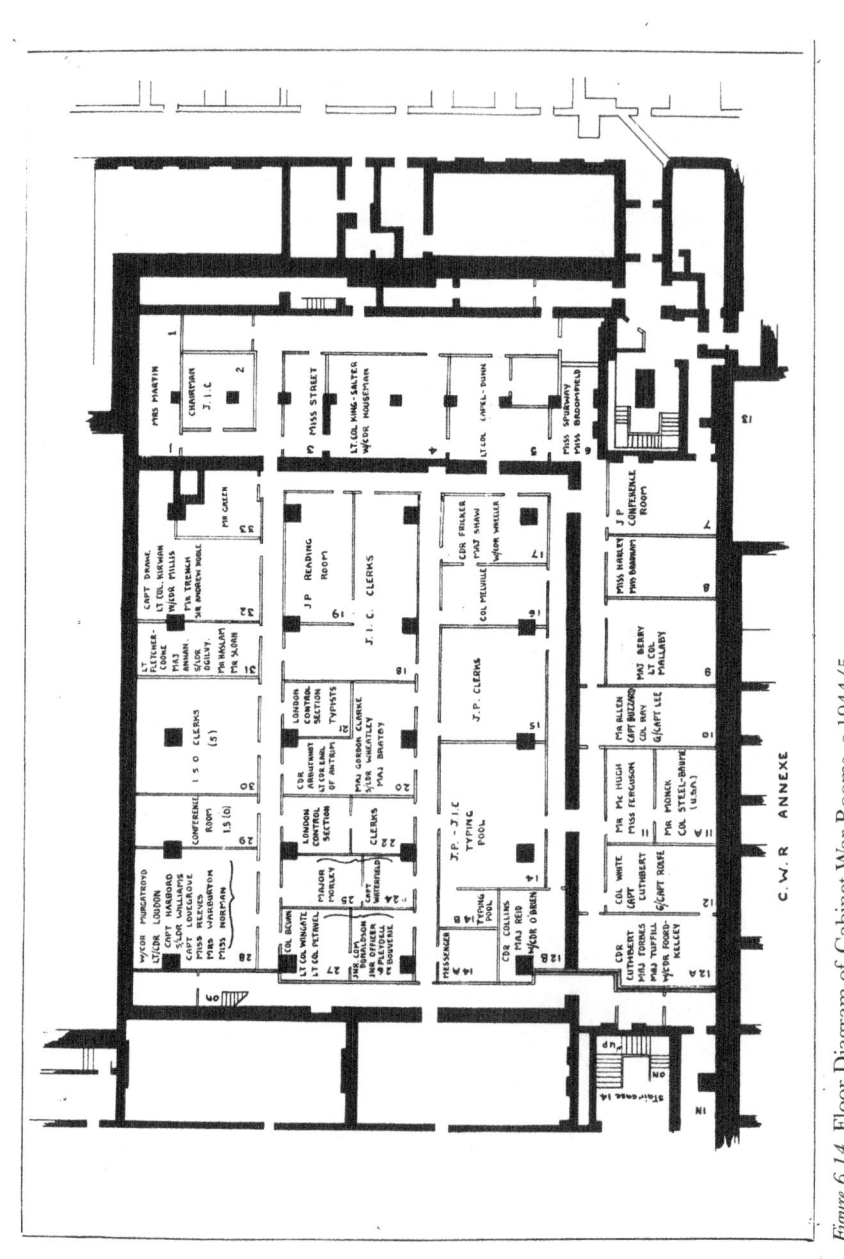

Figure 6.14 Floor Diagram of Cabinet War Rooms, c.1944/5

7 Creating a World-Wide Intelligence Network

By the mid-1950s the JIC was producing a stream of assessments, with a large series of long-term papers complementing the various short-term, weekly reviews. Intelligence now covered a variety of topics, not just purely military matters. Yet, aside from the production of assessments, the JIC had a number of other functions. Perhaps primary amongst these, particularly in the immediate post-war period, was establishing and maintaining allied and foreign liaison. This took several forms: monitoring regional outposts of British intelligence; maintaining liaison with Commonwealth and other allied countries; but perhaps above all, it was concerned with cementing the foundations developed during the war with the United States.

Liaison was a crucial aspect of the JIC's role. It included: sharing intelligence assessments; contributing to and commenting upon other countries' papers; allowing other nations to participate in the British JIC system; helping establish allied intelligence organisations, often based on tried and tested British models; maintaining a window on distant parts of the world; and, finally, ensuring that British intelligence forecasts could have a greater impact on Cold War policymaking beyond the confines of Whitehall. It is difficult to measure the importance of the relationships that were created at this formative stage of the Cold War although certainly the longevity of many of them shows how valuable they must have been, both in London and elsewhere.

What is clear is that the members of the JIC, by the end of war, saw themselves as the elder statesmen of the intelligence world. Whilst this might seem a blasé, even arrogant stance now, it is important to remember that Britain had one of the longest traditions of intelligence and, in the form of the JIC, had a unique, central system for the production of assessments and the management of the intelligence community. It is no surprise, then, that the JIC model was copied and exported to many other countries. What is perhaps more unexpected though, is how frequently this system would flounder. Indeed, it was destined to survive only in Britain, British colonial possessions or other Commonwealth members: in other words, in systems modelled on the Whitehall Cabinet system of government where officials maintained a strict political neutrality.

Dining with the Americans

The most important relationship was the Atlantic alliance, formed during the war and strengthened through a succession of treaties and agreements. In early 1946 JIC(Washington) (JIC(W)), the British JIC based in Washington, wrote a detailed report to its counterpart in London, outlining how Anglo-American intelligence collaboration had progressed since the end of the war. The report covered military and economic intelligence, deliberately excluding political topics. Of these, naval and military intelligence relations were strong, though air force collaboration had suffered because of the changing personnel involved and the lack of any constant RAF presence in the US. Economic intelligence, a much newer field for collaboration, was less established but good foundations had been laid.[1] As to civilian agencies, the war had left something of a void in the United States. President Truman had disbanded the OSS in September 1945, despite having no clear proposals for what should follow. Following the short-lived Strategic Services Unit (SSU), the creation of the Central Intelligence Group (CIG) in January 1946 was merely an interim step, designed to accommodate the remaining fragments of OSS. It was, however, through the Central Intelligence Group that it became increasingly clear that 'central' co-ordination was of paramount importance.[2]

In late 1945 a review of the British intelligence system was completed by William H. Jackson on behalf of General Donovan, who had been head of OSS. Jackson, a future Deputy-Director of Central Intelligence and a noted Anglophile, produced a report that focussed specifically on whether elements of the British system could be used to create an American centralised system. In turn this led, via several other studies, to the creation of the American estimate process.[3]

In April 1946 Lieutenant Commander W. M. Scott, the Chief of Mission for the SSU/CIG at the American Embassy in London, wrote to its head in Washington on the difficulties faced by the uncertainty over US intelligence. 'For months', he wrote,

> we have been "hanging on" with an indefinite status, changing our organiza-tion's name and generally lacking a fixed place in the intelligence picture . . . our friends here have been exceedingly patient and we, by dodging issues and slightly "coloring" our status, have been able to hold our own in practi-cally all phases of liaison with the British . . . in all conversations with British intelligence personnel they have repeatedly stressed the need for more co-ordination of our intelligence services . . . for the good of the American government the question of the status of our organisation must soon be settled one way or the other; relations which are of extreme importance to American intelligence are not going to be possible to maintain unless we have a definite status soon.[4]

In August 1946 Colonel William Quinn, the head of SSU, visited London. Reporting on his trip, Quinn had emphasised to British counterparts his desire for the SSU to stand on its two feet and for liaison on 'secret' and 'special operations' to be limited; nonetheless, he continued, 'I personally feel that if at all possible, such liaison as is effected with the British should be maintained in London'.[5]

Back in London the JIC took a keen interest in developments on the other side of the Atlantic. It requested and was given regular updates from its British counterparts in the US, who described and analysed progress.[6] Despite their wartime closeness, there were still some in the UK who questioned how much information should be shared with the Americans. At the Service level intelligence exchange was extensive, yet at the higher level – the realm at which the JIC operated – collaboration had largely dropped off after the war, with reports generally only being passed between the British COS and American JCS. In April 1946 the question was raised within the JIC, whether a series of reports on Russia should be released to the Americans, not because of their sensitivity (and some were Sigint codeword documents), but because they would 'reveal to the Americans the extent of our concentration in that particular field'.[7] In turn, Brigadier Arthur Cornwall-Jones (the Secretary of the British Joint Staff Mission (BJSM) in Washington and of the Combined COS, and who had been a pre-war Secretary of the JIC), gave his opinion: 'we have a feeling that it would pay us to try to develop our association with the Americans ... the present time, when Russian activities are causing us much concern in the world, would appear to be an appropriate moment to start off.'[8]

The JIC was evidently persuaded by this. It was nevertheless decreed that papers should be 'topped and tailed' so that anyone reading them in the US would not know that they were British JIC reports. The rationale behind the decision was clear: 'the Sub-Committee [i.e. JIC] fervently hope that an exchange of appreciations on such matters will result'.[9] To the British, the great originator and purveyor of modern intelligence, this was not a purely altruistic move, for it was felt by the Services' Directors of Intelligence that 'it was desirable to educate United States departments in our views'.[10]

An ongoing concern in passing information to the Americans, in particular, was security in the State Department. Many within the JIC system, particularly those in the committee in Washington, had grave doubts about circulating assessments to them. Fortunately, it was reported that within the new Central Intelligence Group structure in the US, there were only two State Department officials, both junior, and neither privy to JIC papers. Thus satisfied, the JIC approved and the matter was passed to the COS, who also agreed, and it was decided to start transmitting JIC papers on the Soviet Union to the Americans.[11] This was not, however, the full extent of the JIC's dealings with the US. In considering how collaboration might be increased, the JIC produced a brief report on what it considered to be an optimum system, whereby British officers would be in 'direct working contact' with US intelligence officers.[12]

By the end of 1946 then, the backbone of the Anglo-American intelligence partnership had been forged. Bilateral links that had been created during the war between the Services' intelligence departments were extended, and also through a special Sigint agreement – known subsequently as the UKUSA agreement – which had been formalised by the LSIB in March 1946.[13] Individually, the members of the JIC would have been privy to these details, and some may have been involved with its negotiation. At the Committee level, British assessments were making their way across the Atlantic, and in return US views on them and separate American appreciations were being received. In addition, on the rare occasions that they visited London, senior US intelligence officers attended the JIC, though only for specific items on the agenda.

The creation of the Central Intelligence Agency (CIA) in the late summer of 1947 presented a new opportunity for the British, one that they were keen to grasp, for as the JIC(W) recorded, 'CIA under the new Act has very wide powers and it is felt here that we should do all we can to meet their wishes'.[14] It was decided at a special meeting of the Services' Directors of Intelligence that from the outset, JIC papers could be passed to the CIA directly, though the preference was that they go through the British JIC(W) and the US JIC when possible.[15]

Anglo-American dealings were not always straightforward and cordial. Relations, albeit strong at the departmental level, were often undermined by differing views at the political level. One difficulty was gauging the reactions of American politicians, who were exhibiting an increasingly introspective view of the world, and this was, in the JIC's eyes, having an impact on how much information the Americans might be prepared to share.[16] A further complicating factor was the American reluctance for their information to be communicated to Commonwealth countries, or indeed to Commonwealth officers working with their British counterparts. This was no trivial matter. An FO paper on the subject concluded that

> if we fail to move the Americans from the position they have taken up, we shall be faced with a choice, on vital defence questions, and as a consequence possibly in wider spheres, between co-operation with the United States and co-operation with the Commonwealth, both of which may be indispensable to our survival as a Great Power.[17]

The JIC's view was more subtle, stating that 'there is no need to inform the Americans officially' when this might happen. Although this sounds under-handed, it reflected the British belief that relations with US intelligence agencies at the working level were cordial and considered to be important, whereas at a more senior, political level doubts persisted and so there was no reason to discuss the technicalities of the relationship.[18] American politics were integral to these thoughts. In early discussions about US-UK relations, the Americans had informed the JIC that one of the arguments used to persuade Congress to pass the 1947 National Security Act, had been the necessity pre-war to rely on the British for intelligence. Congress had, consequently, wanted an assurance that the CIA would be able to rely on its own sources of intelligence and not depend too much on foreign assistance. Therefore, although collaboration was desirable, certain information had to be withheld from Congress.[19]

It was occasionally necessary to muddy the waters. For instance, in discussions over the decision to partition Palestine in early 1948, it was agreed not to circulate relevant JIC papers to the CIA because of perceived Jewish sympathies in Washington.[20] Despite the occasional hiccup, on the whole the system worked well and the level of trust and collaboration exhibited by the British increased. The 'topping and tailing' procedure for JIC papers, for instance, was scrapped in 1948.[21] Similarly, with the restructuring of US intelligence in 1946/7, came a significant move to increase the working relationship at the JIC level. In a meeting in 1946, and at a time when the US was just creating the Central Intelligence Group, two US representatives (one of whom was Jackson) visited the UK and attended a JIC session. Anglo-American collaboration was discussed, and the British were frank in their concerns about security. An interesting point to emerge was the suggestion that a US representative be appointed, part of whose job it would be to liaise with the JIC.[22]

Against the backdrop to these and ensuing discussions, was the rapidly developing Cold War and a succession of US actions. The August 1946 Atomic Energy Act, better known as the McMahon Act after the Senator who sponsored it, ended the technical exchange of atomic information between the US and UK, and this had an immediate effect on intelligence sharing. The 1947 Truman Doctrine and Marshall Plan ensured an American commitment to Europe, much to the relief of the British, and were followed by the military guarantees established by the creation of NATO in 1949. The January 1950 Burns-Templer Agreement, designed to ensure the complete exchange of military information between the UK and US, was useful in reinforcing relations, and would later be used by the JIC as part justification for its collaboration with the CIA.[23] By early 1950 it was calculated that 90% of JIC reports were being passed to the Americans; however, problems remained in getting reciprocation, with no US JIC papers being sent to London, and with only very few US comments received on British JIC papers.[24] The Americans cited several factors for this: that the US JIC produced very few papers; that manpower commitments meant that there was very little time to offer comments; and that once US JIC assessments were approved, they became US JCS papers, and so were prohibited from being exchanged. In the spirit of cooperation it was decided that papers could be forwarded 'on an informal basis and on the understanding that the source would not later be quoted.'[25] Within a few months the situation had improved, with London receiving American papers 'from time to time'.[26]

As we now know, even by the late 1940s the US JIC had become a largely redundant body: the work of the US JIC, a military committee, was meant to be complemented by the non-military assessments produced by the CIA but who, in practice, had subsumed much of its work. This was not immediately obvious to the British JIC, though it would rapidly become so. On the US side, the major catalyst for collaboration was the CIA. The JIC was informed that the Director of Central Intelligence (DCI), General Walter Bedell-Smith (who had worked with the British on intelligence matters in SHAEF), was 'most anxious, as part of his reforms, to ensure closer co-operation between our respective

Intelligence Organisations'.[27] For JIC Chairman Patrick Reilly this was a crucial development because there could now be liaison at the formative phase of the assessment process, not just at the finished product stage. For the JIC, this was seen as the start of a merging of relations which was to be reciprocated on the other side of the Atlantic,[28] and was considered particularly crucial, for while relations at the agency-to-agency level were good, a recent UK-US assessment conference had revealed the differences between the two nation's strategic positions.[29]

In mid-1951, Colonel Dante Edward Pemberton Hodgson, late Welsh Guards, was chosen to represent the JIC in Washington. His duties, broadly defined, were to 'act in a liaison capacity and represent JIC (London) with any US intelligence agency which may request your services.'[30] His role including attending meetings discussing early drafts of papers by the newly established Office of National Estimates (ONE).[31] A month after starting Hodgson wrote back to give London his impressions of attending ONE meetings in the CIA. If Cooper had been startled by his first experiences of London, then it is fair to say that Hodgson had a similar baptism:

> I was very impressed by the very great care which was taken by this Committee in drafting, every word was considered and the exact shade of meaning was eventually arrived at . . . I was introduced to each individual member by [the Chairman of ONE] . . . Thereafter the members sat down removing what clothing they thought fit. The gentleman on my right removed his shirt and vest and remained clad in a pair of bright red braces depicting a pair of very undressed ladies. The chair on my left was empty. The late arrival sat down and apparently did not feel the heat as he retained his hat and coat throughout the proceedings. More than half the members sat through-out with their feet on the table. You can imagine my feelings when I thought back on the meetings in the JIC in London![32]

The ONE gradually assumed the responsibilities, originally allocated to the US JIC, for preparing assessments. ONE differed from the British JIC in that its members were not representatives of parent departments; indeed, of the eight full-time members in 1951, three were university professors, two were retired military men, and a further two were classed as 'professional' intelligence officers. Perhaps as a result of this disparate composition, Hodgson reported a far greater level of debate and argument. Of the members, it is worth mentioning the presence of Sherman Kent, a university history professor, who would write about the theory and practice of strategic intelligence production in the United States.[33] Sitting above the ONE was a small 'Board', chaired by Ray Cline, who would eventually become a Deputy Director of the CIA.[34]

Hodgson produced a further report to mark his first three months in Washington. Relations with the CIA were considered to be 'firmly established'; by contrast, the US JIC had shown almost no interest in his presence, and he certainly had not been able to make any inroads into regularly attending its meetings.[35] Perhaps, in hindsight, these were the first signs of the post-war shifting of intelligence power. The American community, and the CIA in particular, were now much more self-sufficient and the previous London bias had swung firmly in Washington's favour. As evidence of this, Ray Cline was despatched to London to act as a second US representative, while shortly thereafter in the US, Hodgson suddenly found his access to ONE curtailed. The reason given by the CIA was that Hodgson's presence was inhibiting discussion, but this bemused Sir Christopher Steel, the Minister in Washington, who reported that 'there can be no earthly reason why the Americans should benefit from our infinitely better geared machine while we get nothing from them.'[36] Subsequently, and following much diplomatic wrangling, Hodgson was given permission to see drafts of ONE papers, but was no longer allowed to attend meetings.[37] In London it does not appear that any reciprocal restriction was even considered.

From an American perspective, then, the relationship was functioning well. Cline has written about how his new position provided

> the benefits of seeing how the evidence on common strategic problems looked from the viewpoint of another nation, a close ally with similar but separate interests . . . my real awakening in London was the discovery of how much we still benefitted from formal liaison exchanges.[38]

It is interesting to note here how Cline's attitude altered once in London, from the typical US view on liaison. The more senior representative attended relevant JIC meetings, whereas Cline, as the junior member, was involved with the JIS. The JIC noted that Cline's presence was positive, and that he provided 'much useful information', the collaboration was, therefore, a two-way street as far as relations in London were concerned. In Washington, however, Hodgson was still being given only restricted access to papers and personnel, and to the JIC back in London, this was a result of the 'rigidity of the American system and to inter-service and inter-departmental jealousies in Washington'. The decidedly lopsided balance of exchange was not lost on the JIC: 'the position thus is that for five months [the senior US representative] has been attending at least part of nearly every JIC meeting and Mr Cline has had something like a free run of our JIS, without our enjoying any comparable treatment in Washington: and that we have been maintaining in Washington a full Colonel's post which is almost valueless.' Despite this imbalance, the JIC was not as concerned as might be imagined, largely because of the value of the London-based liaison:

> even if we remain unable to obtain reciprocal treatment in Washington, the balance of advantage lies in allowing the [US] representatives in London access to the JIC and JIS as at present. In this way they are able to give us a good deal of useful information about American thinking in Washington and we in turn are able through them to feed our views into the American intelligence machine.[39]

The spate of British spy cases, including the identification of Guy Burgess, Donald Maclean, and Klaus Fuchs as Soviet agents, certainly reinforced US reluctance to engage in a full exchange of intelligence. This was the view of the Pentagon who, in the summer of 1952, had argued that with the tightening of their security the British should no longer be involved in the early stages of the preparation of intelligence estimates.[40]

Part of the problem, as Cline had earlier informed the JIC, was that with elections looming in 1952 in the US, nobody was prepared to take any risks politically.[41] The JIC recognised that the system of governance in the US meant that regardless of his position as CIA director, Bedell-Smith could not simply decide to increase British access to US intelligence. Yet maintaining the Anglo-American intelligence relationship was absolutely vital, not least as it provided an underpinning to political relations.[42] Shortly after President Eisenhower's inauguration, he installed the Deputy Director, Allen Dulles, as the new Director of Central Intelligence. Dulles wasted no time, and within a month of his appointment had invited Hodgson to call on him. In a frank discussion Dulles promised that he was to take the question of access to a 'very high level', which Hodgson took to mean the National Security Council or the President himself.[43]

One noticeable contrast between the US and UK approaches was the sheer scale of effort. In reporting on a discussion with a representative of the Office of Current Intelligence in the CIA, Colonel Eric Searight, the JIC Secretary, informed the Committee that the comparable body in the States responsible for the equivalent of the 'Perimeter Review', numbered three hundred people, compared to less than ten in the UK. It was suggested that another US representative be sent to London, to work exclusively with the British team producing the Perimeter Review, and that a similar arrangement be formalised in the States.[44] To inform its discussions with the Americans, the JIC consulted various members, to see how well individual departments were faring. On the whole, those who dealt with the CIA were content; those who had to deal with the Pentagon were less so.

By June 1953 it is clear that Committee members felt that while the quality of the shared CIA product was now beginning to match the material the US was receiving, the quantity of exchanged material was still heavily in America's favour.[45] Briefing Prime Minister Winston Churchill in June 1953 before his talks with President Eisenhower in Bermuda, the JIC wrote that 'for some time now we have been concerned at the one-sidedness of our intelligence co-operation with the United States ... the best way to improve co-operation is to convince the Americans that they stand to gain by it. Many Americans already appreciate this and are aware that we are not getting our fair share of the bargain. We believe that Mr Allen Dulles ... is among them.'[46] As prophesised, the forces for change were now beginning to spread across the Atlantic. In a forthright letter to the JIC Chairman, Patrick Dean, Dulles himself admitted that relations had been strained, but that 'the need has become substantially greater, or at least more evident, for close working-level contact.'[47] Following a discussion at the JIC, Dean wrote a remarkably candid reply, emphasising in private that the aim was to 'squeeze Dulles a little on his offer'. In contacting Dulles, Dean was keen to highlight, in very plain language, the contrast between the relative access granted in London and Washington. Dean ended by confirming why the British were so intent on pursuing American collaboration: 'it is our [the JIC's] belief that our joint effort in all matters of intelligence is the firmest foundation [on which to base policy] . . . which is of such value to both our countries particularly in times of emergency.'[48]

Within the Committee itself there was a feeling that, despite the promises, if matters did not improve then the US representative in London would have to have his access withdrawn. However, the JIC was able to detect small glimmers of improvement: 'we fear, however, that there is little hope of an early general improvement in UK/US Intelligence Cooperation, and we feel that probably the only real sympathy in America . . . comes from the CIA, especially its Director, Mr Dulles, who certainly appreciates the value of our contribution'.[49] The necessary change of views in Washington lay, as the JIC had already realised, with the politicians and not the CIA. In late 1953 the Committee was informed that the increased threat posed by the Soviet Union had led to a step change on Capitol Hill, where it was now felt necessary to improve any warning that might be given of a Soviet nuclear attack. In practical terms this meant a warmer approach to liaison relations, especially with the British.

These shifts in the political landscape were conveyed to the JIC by the London-based US representative.[50] Their impact is recorded in a memorandum by the JIC, produced for the COS in preparation for a visit from the Chairman of the US JCS. In this, the JIC noted several 'talking points' for discussion, including highlighting 'the shortcomings of the defences of the West', and how they 'can to some extent be compensated by good intelligence . . . it would clearly be uneconomical and inefficient for the US and the UK intelligence organisations to work in semi-isolation . . . a full and frank interchange of intelligence between our two countries on all levels would go far towards the improvement of our warning system.'[51]

The reverberations of the US decision can be inferred from later moves. Foremost amongst these was the approval of a new JIC liaison officer in Washington, who was to achieve greater access than his predecessor. Upon the completion of his two year tour in the States, Colonel Hodgson was recalled to the UK. His replacement was Dr Alan Crick, who was to be attached to the Deputy Director for Intelligence in the CIA. This was a novel but calculated move as Hodgson had been attached to ONE, and over lunch one day Sherman Kent had informally told the then JIC Chairman that the 'Hodgson approach would never get us anywhere'.[52] Hodgson had been privy to the debates and discussions within ONE between the different military factions regarding the content of assessments, and was aware that the Americans did not want to air their 'disputes in the presence of a British representative'; Crick's attachment to the CIA was considered beneficial as it would avoid these concerns.[53]

Crick was no newcomer to the secret world. He had served in the army during the Second World War, including a spell as intelligence officer to SHAEF.

After the war he had joined the JIB, becoming its first representative on the JIS in 1946. Following his two year spell with the JIC, he returned to the JIB. In the summer of 1953 he was sent to Washington, where he remained for three years. Following a further period back at the JIB, he returned to Washington as JIC representative for the years 1963–5, before becoming the Chairman of the JIS (1965–8) prior to its conversion into the Assessments Staff. Shortly before his departure for the US, Crick was briefed by the JIC as to his future role. Broadly speaking this included: liaison with the CIA generally, participation in the work of the US Watch Committee (the comparable body to the Perimeter Review producers) and the Office of National Estimates.[54] Crick was instructed to 'work tactfully'.[55]

In May 1954 Patrick Dean visited the United States and Canada. The 'really big item', as he put it, was meeting Allen Dulles and securing closer co-operation with the United States. Discussions went well, helped, no doubt, by Crick's successful appointment. As Dean subsequently informed the JIC, 'Crick seemed to me to have done amazingly well. He is very popular and well known throughout the CIA . . . the doors are opening for him all round and he has settled down very quickly and expanded his influence just as we hoped.' Dulles re-iterated his desire to strengthen relations and, as an incentive, Dean suggested that the Americans participate in the deliberations of the JIC (Far East).[56] Thus, it would seem that by late 1953 the JIC had finally secured a substantial line of access into the CIA and the American assessment procedure.

Writing in mid-1955, the JIC Secretary, Colonel Searight, neatly summed up the state of the JIC-CIA relationship:

> the exchange of intelligence is of course by no means perfect, nor will it ever be. It has had, and will continue to have, its "ups and downs", as personalities and politics change, but the JIC is firmly of the opinion that in both the general and the particular Service spheres it is as good as can be expected and has undoubtedly improved over the past two years.[57]

On leaving Washington in late 1956, Crick provided a valedictory note for the JIC, which revealed something of the closeness between the intelligence communities yet, in other respects, the differences in policy: 'in recent years there has been a growing exchange of National Estimates and JIC reports and each country now takes fuller and more critical cognizance of the other's appreciations. This has done much to reduce the gaps in Intelligence thinking even if it has not led very appreciably to the reduction of major differences in policy.' The earlier imbalance was still, to an extent, present, for Crick was never allowed the same kind of access as his opposite numbers were granted in London. To Crick the reason behind this was simple, 'the sensitiveness of the Americans about revealing to other nationals, even their most trusted collaborators, anything they consider likely to look foolish when received, or any product they consider slipshod or unworthy.'[58]

The details of the rise and fall in relations are less important than what they tell us about the changing balance of power at this time. The earliest documents clearly show that the JIC saw itself as the senior partner in the relationship. Gradually, and perhaps unnoticed at the time, this began to change. The reversal of the relationship is never explicitly recorded, but it is clear from the JIC's unrelenting desire to maintain and improve the liaison that it must have realised that the US intelligence effort had much to offer, and that it was no longer simply a case of educating them in the finer arts of intelligence analysis. Indeed, even in the face of the decisions by the US – whereby they retained full access whilst withdrawing a reciprocal arrangement – the JIC never once complained, perhaps a reflection that it understood the relative balance of power involved. Relations would only improve with a new President, a new Director of Central Intelligence and, perhaps most importantly, a new (and pervading) sense of threat. With this came a new emphasis on acting in concert, which called for common intelligence analysis.

A final word can be left to an unidentified British speaker in an undated speech delivered to the Intelligence Advisory Committee, the closest thing in the American intelligence community to the JIC at that time:

> We realise in London that our effort can in many respects not compare with yours. You devote a much larger amount of manpower, money and other resources to the whole field of intelligence and you have developed facilities and resources for collation and research which we admire and envy but cannot expect to emulate . . . but to set against this we have certain special facilities and advantages, which are of great value in present conditions. The main advantage is that we are so widely dispersed and can maintain a world-wide intelligence organisation . . . I should make it plain that we intend to remain deployed in this fashion and the facilities and advantages which it gives us compensate to a great degree for our comparatively smaller organisation in London.[59]

The speech acknowledged the balance in the developing Anglo-American intelligence partnership. The US had the money, the resources, and the technology; Britain had the people, the organisation and, perhaps above all else, the global real estate for intelligence access.

Regional Outposts

If the JIC's relationships with the CIA developed in the latter's favour, then relations with Commonwealth and other friendly nations remained firmly to London's benefit. During the war the JIC had exported its model to a variety of countries, which continued in the post-war period, as did the creation of regional JICs. The result was a global support network of subsidiary bodies that would be used to great effect as the Cold War diversified and, from the late 1940s, became much more than just a European concern. What is also startling for this period is not just the sheer number of Commonwealth, colonial and foreign agencies with whom the JIC liaised, but the nature of these relations, particularly amongst those nations which would not immediately be perceived as friendly allies. What emerged was a hierarchical system with the main JIC in London at the top.

In its review and proposals for the post-war intelligence organisation (see chapter 6), the JIC was quick to ensure that the pre-war mistakes of insufficient intelligence coverage should not be repeated. Intelligence had to serve British policy worldwide – in practice this required an international network of executive bodies controlled, directed and led by the JIC from London. Assisting the London organisation was to be a network of regional JICs, that would be staffed by Commonwealth nationals. These outposts were to be created in Commonwealth nations, to provide a global intelligence structure, working at both the operational agency-to-agency level, and at a more strategic JIC-to-JIC level.[60] This was not a British intelligence orchestra but a Commonwealth one, albeit conducted in London; certainly this was the impression that the JIC was keen to promote, often referring to the 'Empire's commitment' in messages to Commonwealth allies.[61]

Alongside the Commonwealth intelligence system were a number of other organisations. Of the JIC model itself, comparable bodies had been created in the Second World War in such diverse places as Washington, Algiers, Ottawa and Cairo. Some of these did not survive the end of conflict, while others were gradually wound up as their usefulness declined. Far more important were the regional JICs and sub-committees, staffed by Britons serving abroad. JIC(W), referred to above, became less critical as the JIC liaison with the CIA grew in importance. Perhaps of the greatest significance were those outposts that were at the forefront of the Cold War.

It is important to realise, from the outset, that the JIC remained a military body, despite its FO Chairman and other civilian representatives. This model was continued with the regional committees, some of which were more military-focussed than others, largely depending on their location and role.[62] Towards the end of the war a JIC(Control Commission Germany) had been created to organise and co-ordinate intelligence. In January 1947 it was re-designated JIC(Germany).[63] JIC(G), as it was usually referred to, survived until the dissolution of the Commanders-in-Chief Committee (Germany) in 1990, and although its importance diminished as the Cold War wore on, it played a central and important role in the formative years of the post-war intelligence world.[64] Subordinate to JIC(G) was the Berlin Joint Intelligence Sub-Committee[65], which dealt largely with Brixmis, the British military mission in the Soviet zone of Germany; the Public Order Sub-Committee[66]; and something known simply as the 'Sub-Committee'.[67] As a broad structure, JIC(G) provided a range of military information for the JIC; by the 1950s it also became increasingly concerned with defectors, including consideration of the means to induce people to defect.[68] As one internal JIC history put it, JIC(G) 'act[ed] as a "Window" for JIC(London) on the Soviet Union'.[69]

In Austria there also existed a JIC, though this was more peripheral than its sibling in Germany. More important were the JIC(FE) and the JIC(ME). These two committees would become increasingly significant following the communist party's victory in the Chinese civil war in 1949 and increased tension in the Middle East from the early 1950s onwards. JIC(FE) grew out of the intelligence structure in Singapore, and was designed to co-ordinate intelligence matters in the Far East. Working under JIC(FE) was a specialist JIS team, operating under much the same rules and conditions as the JIS in London. One of JIC(FE)'s other tasks was to maintain liaison with Australia's and New Zealand's intelligence services.[70] JIC(ME), similarly, had its own JIS team, and covered the Middle East region and the Balkans.[71] Both these organisations were referred to as 'theatre JICs'. In other words, they were replicas of the main JIC in London, complete with JIS teams, and had much broader functions than the other regional outposts. The JIC in London exercised 'partial control' over them, in that it issued their Charters and was 'free to call on them for such appreciations as may be required'.[72]

As well as these there were other, smaller, regional bodies. In 1947 a JIC(Jamaica) was created: it was solely a military body and focussed on central and Latin America. Additionally, a string of Local Intelligence Committees (LIC) were established – colonial organisations concentrated on their specific locale, reporting to the local Governor and technically subordinate to either the JIC(FE) or JIC(ME). In 1948 LICs were created in Borneo, Sarawak, Brunei, Malaya, Singapore and Hong Kong. These LICs had several specific responsibilities: to advise the local military on intelligence matters; to co-ordinate intelligence and security activities; and to provide JIC(FE) with reports.[73] A similar function was carried out by the 'Central African Intelligence Co-Ordinating Sub-Committee', which operated under JIC(ME).[74] By the early 1950s an enormous structure of LICs had been built-up, all reflecting British foreign policy interests and all reporting to either JIC(ME) or JIC(FE), and then to the JIC in London. It comprised: Aden, North Borneo, British Guiana, Cyprus, Fiji, Gambia, Gibraltar, Gold Coast, Hong Kong, Northern Rhodesia, Nyasaland, Sarawak & Brunei, and Singapore.[75] To this list an LIC for Berlin was added a few months later, to be complemented by further LICs for the Persian Gulf and Somaliland.

With only a few exceptions, none of the papers for the LICs in this period have been preserved.[76] Relations between the LICs and JIC(ME) and JIC(FE) seem, on the whole, to be have been conducted satisfactorily; indeed, no serious problems are recorded. There are examples of some debates, more constructive than destructive in nature. For instance, in 1955 the Chairman of JIC(FE), the diplomat Andrew Gilchrist, wrote to the JIC in London to comment on complaints that not enough information was being provided. Denying this, Gilchrist noted that he had 'never heard such nonsense in my life', yet at the same time he did have two criticisms, namely that the JIC was not taking seriously enough the threat of atomic warfare in south-east Asia and, perhaps more importantly, telling London that 'you have written a really rotten paper on Indo-China'. It is not clear what the JIC made of this critique; certainly it would not have been something it was used to hearing from its regional outpost.[77] Less clear is the value of the LICs to the JIC back in London; given their charter it is likely that they served an operational role in the relevant territories, providing a supervisory and organisational function, but they probably contributed little in the way of assessments.

The two main regional outposts, JIC(ME) and JIC(FE) were far more crucial, and their specific operational performance will be examined in relation to events later. At a general level they provided a regional window on the world that simply would have been inaccessible from a committee room in Whitehall. It is perhaps no surprise, given this, that a number of individuals worked in a regional JIC before becoming a full-time London JIC member, and at least three of the Cold War Chairmen had first served in either JIC(ME) or JIC(FE). In contrast, JIC(W) and JIC(G) had more specific roles to fulfil. JIC(G) was arguably less important, and largely, it would seem, this was a reflection of the changing emphasis of the Cold War. Even when there were 'hot' points in Germany, the Berlin Blockade being a prime example, JIC(G)'s role was limited.

Spreading the Gospel

The JIC, in its management and liaison role, not only had to concern itself with agencies and directorates within Whitehall, but also other organisations across the entire world. In addition to the Americans, this also included the other members of the community that would form the backbone of an intelligence alliance that spanned the globe: UK, US, Canada, Australia, and New Zealand. The JIC also maintained liaisons with a range of other nations, extending far beyond the typical allies or the Commonwealth.

In 1942 Canada had created its own JIC, an entirely military committee designed on the British model explicitly to foster collaboration with London and Washington.[78] In the post-war period the Canadian JIC remained extremely keen to share assessments with London and to move beyond purely military matters.[79] This was an important move, for as one retired Canadian intelligence officer has noted, 'a generally decentralized intelligence community emerged after World War II, mainly as a result of the Cold War. Up to that point Canadian intelligence activities were so small, ad hoc or subordinate as to be irrelevant here. The first "real" system of independent intelligence analysis was a copy of the British system'.[80]

Australia too, expressed an interest in learning from the UK. Its strategic location and close proximity to Asia made it a valuable ally for Britain, and accordingly every effort was made to produce a community shaped upon the model employed in London. In this way, 'dependency certainly marked the origins of the Australian intelligence community, established in the first two years after the Second World War under British tutelage and to serve largely British aims'.[81] The initial Australian JIC was more concerned with organisational issues than assessment, but this began to change by the late 1940s with the creation of a JIS.[82]

Links were also established with other countries of the Commonwealth, including New Zealand, South Africa, and India. At this point in the immediate post-war period most attention was focussed on Services' intelligence, on security matters, and on JIB-type systems.[83] Of these New Zealand must have been considered the most important, for it worked hand in glove with Australia and, as a result, was allowed access to British JIC assessments.[84]

By 1947 there existed, therefore, a complex set of relationships between elements of the Commonwealth, all operating at varying levels, with different objectives and degrees of liaison. In London much of the interaction was conducted with the Commonwealth Service Liaison Staffs, including the representatives from Australia, New Zealand, Canada and South Africa. On the JIC side it was handled by Colonel Parry. In an interesting submission to the JIC, he outlined the different procedures and relationships with these Commonwealth allies. In general Parry felt that the background knowledge of military liaison officers was inadequate. He offered several reasons for this: there were not enough of them; they did not fully understand the joint system, either not having their own system at home or having very little experience of it; their JIC responsibilities were secondary to their Services' liaison roles, and so therefore were relegated as of lesser importance. To the JIC the impact of this was evident: 'the New Zealand and South African representatives would appreciate meetings of whatever nature, but make little use of them; the Australian representative would support them energetically and the Canadian representative would appreciate them only so long as they deal with subject matter of value and of direct bearing on their own country.'[85] This, then, was a tacit acceptance that the power and experience lay in British hands and, unlike the relationship with the United States, this remained firmly in London's favour.

In 1949 New Zealand took the plunge and created its own JIC. The impetus had come from the New Zealand COS, and it was to be constructed along British lines, albeit with a smaller membership. A corresponding JIS was also to be formed.[86] The jewel in the Commonwealth intelligence crown remained Australia however. Its importance lay, primarily, in its location: with the ability to maintain a watchful eye on the Far East, JIC(Melbourne), working closely with JIC(FE), kept London abreast of key developments. The two organisations also shared assessments, often passing them to one another before being despatched to Whitehall. Similarly, British representatives often attended JIC(Melbourne) meetings.[87] Furthermore, there existed close links between intelligence agencies, with Sigint in particular being useful to London. By the mid-1950s the worldwide community was firmly established, bolstered unquestionably by the decision in 1954 to allow representatives of Canadian, Australian and New Zealand intelligence to attend JIC meetings in London.[88]

It was not just friendly allies or Commonwealth members that the JIC liaised with in the immediate post-war period. Indeed, if anything it is surprising quite how widely the JIC network spread in this period, and perhaps the maxim 'my enemy's enemy is my friend' had something to do with this. For example, a plea by the French in 1946 for the British to pass more, higher classified intelligence was discussed by the JIC but fell on deaf ears.[89] Yet within a few years the Cold War environment had led the JIC to be much more willing to grant assistance. This culminated in the JIC's 129th meeting of 1952, when the French Director of Military Intelligence was allowed to attend. The reason was clear: he had come across from Paris to learn about how the British approached 'joint intelligence'.[90] Thereafter relations seemed cordial, at least for a while.

The JIC was regularly involved in discussions with, and about, passing information to other countries, evidence that the JIC's role within the intelligence machinery went beyond the production of assessments. Discussions within the Deputy Directors' meetings on security were held on liaison and intelligence exchange with the Swedes, the Turks, the Yugoslavs and the Spanish.[91] Decisions varied according to the nation, the type of information sought, and the nature of the Cold War at that precise time; further evidence of the JIC's pragmatic approach to intelligence liaison amongst the non-aligned states. Furthermore, the JIC supplied a number of papers for NATO dissemination, often diluted versions of existing JIC reports.

Within a decade the JIC had created across the globe a series of assorted relationships with regional and local committees, friendly allies, and Commonwealth nations. The most important was undoubtedly the United States, who provided assistance at a variety of levels. JIC relations with the CIA had their share of peaks and troughs before being put on a firm basis in 1953. These reflected the shifting intelligence tectonic plates between the two nations, with the British initially seeing themselves as the dominant partner, but this quickly changed to equal partner, before then moving equally as speedily to junior partner. Despite this, the relationship would prove to be invaluable to the long-term health of British intelligence.

By contrast, relations within the Commonwealth and beyond firmly remained in Britain's favour, with a number of countries eager to come and learn from the British experience. Regional relations fell into three categories: local British committees (be they JICs or LICs) operating abroad; provincial Commonwealth JICs that liaised with JIC(FE) or JIC(ME); and non-Commonwealth nations, whose liaison arrangements varied on a case by case basis. Certainly in this period Australia, due to its resources, eagerness to embrace liaison, and crucially its location, was the most valuable. At a broad level these relations were crucial: not only did they increase access to relevant material but they also provided a common intelligence assessment to underpin policy discussion and decision making, thereby ensuring a united front against a potential common enemy.

The seeds sown at this time would eventually mature and blossom. The majority of these liaisons, conducted in the years immediately following the end of the war, were established at a time when the UK had no clearly defined enemy: the Cold War was in its formative stage, when a general wariness of the Soviet Union had yet to develop into outright hostility. Efforts by the JIC in the late 1940s to bolster Britain's offensive intelligence capability often encountered the same starting problem: that it would take a number of years before any intelligence efforts bore fruit. But the farsighted efforts in the immediate post-war years to create a world-wide intelligence network stood Britain in great stead for the conflict that was to follow.

Notes

1 JIC(46)18(O), 'British Joint Intelligence Committee in Washington: State of Collaboration with the United States', 26 February 1946. CAB 81/132.
2 M Warner (ed), *Central Intelligence: Origin and Evolution* (CIA History Staff, 2001). Available at www.cia.gov
3 Details of the Jackson's review and of its original location can be found in Valero, 'The American Joint Intelligence Committee', footnote 11. On the impact I am grateful to information provided by Dr Michael Warner, formerly an historian in the Office of the Director of National Intelligence.
4 W.M.Scott to W.W.Quinn, 30 April 1946. NARA II: RG 263, HS/HC 804, Item 14.
5 W.W.Quinn to Colonel D.Galloway [the representative of the Director of Central Intelligence], 16 August 1946. NARA II: RG 263, HS/HC 804, Item 14.
6 For an example of this see JIC/152/46, 'New US Intelligence Organisation', 3 February 1946. CAB 176/9.
7 JIC/434/46, 'Inter-Change of Intelligence with the USA', 6 April 1946. CAB 176/10.
8 JIC/434/46, 'Inter-Change of Intelligence with the USA', 6 April 1946. CAB 176/10.
9 JIC/458/46, 'Interchange of Intelligence with the USA', 11 April 1946. CAB 176/10.
10 JIC/822/46, 'Exchange of Intelligence with the Americans', R.M.Munro [Secretary, JIC(W)] to Secretary, JIC (London), 12 June 1946. CAB 176/11.
11 JIC/972/46, 'Exchange of Intelligence with the Americans', 22 July 1946. CAB 176/12.
12 JIC/1413/46, 'Exchange of Intelligence with the Americans', 16 October 1946. CAB 176/13.
13 See HW 80/4 for further information.
14 JIC/953/47, 15 September 1947. CAB 176/15.
15 JIC/867/47, 28 August 1947. CAB 176/15. On the British JIC(W) and the US JIC see chapters 4 and 5.
16 For instance, see JIC(46)62nd Meeting (O), Confidential Annex, JIC/1546/46, 'Exchange of Intelligence with the Americans', 13 November 1946. CAB 81/94.
17 'Brief for Defence Committee Meeting January 9th', 6 January 1950. PUSD Files, FCO.
18 This can be inferred from various discussions on the subject. The quote comes from JIC/241/48, 'United States Policy for Passing Information to the UK', J.R.Canham [Secretary JIC(W)] to Secretary, JIC London, 29 January 1948. CAB 176/17.
19 JIC/830/47, 'Visit of Brigadier General Wright, US Army', 21 August 1947. CAB 176/15. This had also been the view of the 'Dulles Survey', a lengthy report on US intelligence which had used Jackson's earlier findings. It can be viewed at www.foia.cia.gov/helms/pdf/dulles_correa.pdf
20 JIC/264/48, 'Circulation of JIC Papers to CIA', 7 February 1948. CAB 176/17.
21 See various papers in CAB 121/231.
22 JIC(46)46th Meeting, 2 August 1946. CAB 81/94.
23 For details see CAB 163/14.
24 For some examples of the type and range of JIC papers sent to the US see NARA II: RG 59, Lot 58D 776, Box 2.
25 JIC/258/50, 'Exchange and Disclosure of Intelligence', 7 February 1950. CAB 176/25.
26 JIC/616/50, 'Action by JIC(Washington) on Certain Reports', 12 April 1950. CAB 176/25.
27 W.Elliot [BJSM, Washington] to D.P.Reilly, 14 November 1950. DEFE 11/349.

28 D.P.Reilly to W.Bedell-Smith, 3 November 1950. DEFE 11/349.
29 JIC(50)106, 'Liaison Between UK and US Intelligence Organisations', 5 December 1950. CAB 158/11.
30 'Charter for Colonel Hodgson', 17 May 1951. DEFE 11/350.
31 JIC/1255/51, 'Liaison Between United States and United Kingdom Intelligence Organisations', 5 June 1951. CAB 176/30.
32 JIC/1494/51, 5 July 1951. CAB 176/31.
33 See, for instance, 'The Law and Custom of the National Intelligence Estimate'. Available on the CIA's Center for the Study of Intelligence website.
34 JIC/1784/51, 'Organisation and Function of ONE', 13 August 1951. CAB 176/31.
35 JIC/2124/51, 29 September 1951. CAB 176/32.
36 JIC/1951/52, 28 August 1952. CAB 176/37.
37 JIC/1982/52, 1 September 1952. CAB 176/37.
38 R S Cline, *Secrets, Spies and Scholars: The Essential CIA* (Washington, DC: Acropolis, 1976). pp.123–5.
39 JIC/99/53, 12 January 1953. CAB 176/40.
40 BJSM Washington to MoD London, 20 June 1953. PUSD Files, FCO.
41 JIC/2113/52, 15 September 1952. CAB 176/38.
42 JIC/99/53, 12 January 1953. CAB 176/40.
43 JIC/736/53, 24 March 1953. CAB 176/41.
44 JIC/1134/53, 'UK/US Intelligence Cooperation', 11 May 1953. CAB 176/42.
45 JIC/1307/53, 'UK/US Intelligence Cooperation', 8 June 1953. CAB 176/42.
46 JIC(53)63, 'United Kingdom/United States Intelligence Co-operation', 19 June 1953. CAB 158/1. In fact the JIC held a special meeting on 16 June to discuss this very topic. See JIC/1447/53, 'UK/US Intelligence Co-operation', 15 June 1953. PUSD Files, FCO.
47 JIC/1549/53, 'UK/US Intelligence Cooperation', Dulles to Dean, 17 June 1953. CAB 176/42.
48 JIC/1787/53, 'UK/US Intelligence Co-operation: Liaison with the Central Intelligence Agency', 27 July 1953. CAB 176/43.
49 JIC(53)72, 'UK/US Intelligence Co-operation, Liaison with the Central Intelligence Agency', 9 July 1953. CAB 158/16.
50 JIC/2557/53, 23 October 1953. CAB 176/44. In a quasi-memoir Williard Matthias recounts the background to this change of atmosphere in Washington. W C Matthias, *America's Strategic Blunders: Intelligence Analysis and National Security Policy, 1936–1991* (Pennsylvania: Penn State Press, 2003).
51 JIC(53)107, 'Meeting with the Chairman, United States Joint Chiefs of Staff: Brief on United Kingdom/United States Intelligence Co-operation', 29 October 1953. CAB 158/16.
52 D.P.Reilly to R.Makins, 11 April 1953. PUSD Files, FCO.
53 R.Makins to D.P.Reilly, 17 April 1953. PUSD Files, FCO.
54 JIC/2841/53, 'Directive to the Joint Intelligence Committee's Representative with the Central Intelligence Agency', 20 November 1953. CAB 176/45. For further details on the exchange of information on the Watch Committee and Perimeter Review, see H.Caccia to R.Makins, 5 February 1955. PUSD Files, FCO.
55 G.L.McDermott [Head of PUSD, FO] to H.Beeley [British Embassy, Washington], 20 November 1953. PUSD Files, FCO. This file also includes the Directive for Crick's appointment.
56 JIC/1263/54, 'Chairman's Visit to Canada and the USA', 26 May 1954. PUSD Files, FCO.
57 JIC/1332/55, 'Exchange of Information with the United States', 12 May 1955. CAB 176/53.
58 JIC/240/57, 28 January 1957. CAB 176/60. The timing of this suggests that the events of Suez might have figured in his sentiments.

59 'Talk to IAC', A.J.P.Crick Papers, LHCMA, King's College London. There is no date for the speech, but given its contents it would probably have been 1955. It would seem likely that the speaker was Major General Kenneth Strong, the Director of the JIB.

60 JIC(45)265(O)(Final), 'Post-War Organisation of Intelligence', 7 September 1945. CAB 81/129. See also S Anderson, 'The Evolution of the Canadian Intelligence Establishment, 1945–1950', *Intelligence and National Security*, 9: 3 (1994), p.459.

61 JIC/1635/45, 'Arrangements for Post-War Intelligence Collaboration with Australia', 9 November 1945. CAB 176/8.

62 I am indebted to Nick Weekes for his tireless efforts in tracking down details of these regional JICs.

63 There is no complete set of JIC(G) paperwork, it is scattered across CAB, FO and DEFE papers. For some of the post-war papers from the late 1940s see FO 1005 series.

64 For more information see S Case, *The Joint Intelligence Committee and the German Question, 1947–61* (PhD Thesis, Queen Mary, University of London, 2009).

65 For instance FO 1032/190.

66 The Public Order Sub-Committee met weekly and produced reports on the level of morale and public opinion within the British zone in Germany. It also looked at public safety and wrote assessments on subversive activity. For details see FO 1050/367.

67 The mysteriously named 'Sub-Committee' of JIC(Germany) was designed to inform the Commanders-in-Chief Committee, British Forces Germany and the Principal Staff Officers Committee about any intelligence-related issues they sought information on. Papers included, for instance, a report on the creation of Brixmis, and another on 'Intelligence Information in a Period of Tension Amounting to Emergency Prior to Anticipated Invasion of Western Germany'. Details can be found in FO 1032/901.

68 On this latter point see M S Goodman, 'British Intelligence and the British Broadcasting Corporation: A Snapshot of a Happy Marriage', In R Dover & M S Goodman (eds), *Spinning Intelligence: Why Intelligence Needs the Media, Why the Media Needs Intelligence* (London: Hurst, 2009). pp.127–30.

69 JIC/1009/55, 'History of the Joint Intelligence Organisation', 22 April 1955. CAB 163/8.

70 For more details see JIC(54)33, 'Intelligence Organisation in the Far East', 17 March 1954. CAB 158/17.

71 For more details see JIC(54)32, 'Intelligence Organisation in the Middle East', 17 March 1954. CAB 158/17.

72 JIC/2899/54, 'Outline of the UK Joint Intelligence Organisation', 9 November 1954. PUSD Files, FCO.

73 JIC/1567/48, 'Draft Charter for Local Intelligence Committees – Far East', 18 August 1948. CAB 176/19.

74 JIC/1199/50, 'Charter for Central African Intelligence Co-Ordinating Sub-Committee', 10 July 1950. CAB 176/26.

75 JIC/1280/1953, 'Relations Between Local Intelligence Committees and Joint Intelligence Committees', 27 May 1953. CAB 176/42.

76 Examples of where they do exist include: LIC (Singapore) – CO 1022/206 & CO 1022/207; and LIC (Hong Kong) – CO 1030/251. Some others can be found amongst the India Office papers in the British Library.

77 JIC/1794/55, 'Relations between JIC and JIC(Far East)', 1 July 1955. CAB 176/53. It is not clear why Gilchrist thought the paper was 'rotten' – he sent a longer and more detailed critique but it has not been preserved in the JIC archive.

78 W K Wark, 'The Evolution of Military Intelligence in Canada', *Armed Forces and Society* 16:1 (Fall 1989), pp.77–98. For greater detail see RG24, Volume 5190 (Canadian JIC Correspondence, 1942–5); RG24, Volume 2468 (Canadian JIC Minutes, 1942–6); and RG24, Volume 8088 (Canadian JIC Reports). Canadian National Archives, Ottawa.

79 JIC/583/46, 'Exchange of Intelligence of Appreciations with the Canadian Joint Intelligence Committee', 4 May 1946. CAB 176/10.

80 C O Spencer, 'Intelligence Analysis Under Pressure of Rapid Change: The Canadian Challenge', *The Journal of Conflict Studies* XVI: 1 (Spring 1996).
81 G Woodward, 'Enigmatic Variations: The Development of National Intelligence Assessment in Australia', *Intelligence and National Security* 16: 1 (2001), p.2.
82 JIC/437/47, 'Organisation of the Australian Joint Intelligence Committee', 8 May 1947. CAB 176/14.
83 Details can be found in various papers in CAB 176/9.
84 JIC(46)72nd Meeting, 4 December 1946. CAB 81/94.
85 JIC/693/47, 'Commonwealth Liaison Staffs', 17 July 1947. CAB 176/15.
86 JIC/523/49, 'New Zealand – Joint Intelligence Organisation', 17 March 1949. CAB 176/22.
87 JIC/663/50, 'Visit by the Chairman, Joint Intelligence Committee Far East, to Melbourne', 17 April 1950. CAB 176/25.
88 Confidential Annex to JIC(54)48th Meeting, 27 May 1954. PUSD Files, FCO.
89 JIC/222/46, 'Exchange of Technical Information with the French', 18 February 1946. CAB 176/9. Also, JIC(46)9th Meeting, 20 February 1946. CAB 81/94.
90 JIC(52)129th Meeting, 20 November 1952. CAB 159/12.
91 Details are spread across a range of CAB 176 and CAB 159 files.

8 Changing Enemies

The Rise of the Soviet Union, 1945–1947

Some time before the end of the Second World War the JIC had begun to look towards the future, attempting to gauge how to structure the intelligence apparatus of the United Kingdom so as to be ready to meet any potential threat. The JIC was not the only part of the Whitehall machinery to do so: in 1942 the military, too, began to look towards the post-war world, as did the FO shortly afterwards. This crystal gazing was hugely important for, as the JIC admitted, the pre-war deficiencies in intelligence coverage had been detrimental to the war effort and it was crucial to know where to focus energy and attention in the future (see chapter 6). This proved to be a contentious debate, with the FO and the COS at loggerheads. The JIC, so often a harmonious forum, became the battleground in which the future course of British policy would be played out.

By early 1946, with the aid of a stream of invaluable reporting from the front line in Moscow, the FO slowly began to reappraise Stalin's Russia. Yet despite this shift the debate across Whitehall continued. Was the primary motivation for Soviet policy one of aggressive expansion of her borders or a rather a defensive ploy to increase her security and assuage Stalin's paranoia? The growing crisis in Persia in the spring of 1946 helped define issues in a situation where Soviet forces had been reluctant to withdraw as had previously been agreed. This gave rise to the question of the extent to which the intelligence community was reactive or proactive with regard to the Soviet threat. Were conclusions only drawn as the consequence of events, or was there an attempt to forecast them?

This chapter focuses on the discussions within Whitehall about the future aspirations of Soviet foreign policy, and how the battles between the FO and COS were reflected in the JIC, with Cavendish-Bentinck playing a central role. It will then examine how the British intelligence community, once the Soviet threat had been identified, became central to post-war planning. Several key questions dominated the period from 1943 to the declaration of the Truman Doctrine in early 1947: To what extent would the US get involved in Europe? What were the Soviet intentions? Were they fuelled by expansionist aggression or by defensive security concerns? Central to all these issues were the forecasts provided by the JIC.

Whither the Soviet Union?

It has become something of an historical convention that the members of the wartime Grand Alliance – the United Kingdom, United States and Soviet Union – were united only in hatred of, and desire to defeat, Nazism. It was a "marriage of convenience". Pre-war there had been major issues centred on the political stances of the US and Soviet Union if war were to come. By 1941, with the British forewarned through ULTRA of the German army's deployment eastwards, veiled messages were sent to try and alert Stalin. That these warnings were vague and had a minimal impact on Soviet strategy and policy should not detract from the fact that the British were prepared to work with the Soviet Union. With Hitler's decision to attack the Soviet Union in June 1941, the British offered assistance, including military technology, discussion of operational planning and, to a lesser extent, the exchange of intelligence. Even without the assistance of the Cambridge spy ring, the Russians were well aware of the existence of the JIC by the end of the war.

Despite such collaboration, the wartime alliance did little to dispel fear and distrust of communist Russia. Thus, from 1943 as post-war planning and discussion got underway, the future of Britain's relations with the Soviet Union became an increasing concern. One of the first serious efforts to plan for the future was the creation, in 1942, of the Military Sub-Committee (MSC) of the Ministerial Committee on Reconstruction Problems. The initial plan was for the MSC to become a sub-committee of the COS Committee, operating along similar lines to the JIC and the JPS. However, with frequent opposition from the higher echelons of the FO, this aspiration was never to mature.[1] What was needed, all sides agreed, was a more senior body, one that would be answerable to the COS themselves but with a senior FO input, whose views and reports would be respected. The Post-Hostilities Planning (PHP) sub-committee was the answer. To understand the findings of the PHP, its composition and its sources of information, it is first necessary to consider why the Soviet Union became such a major focus.

By 1943 the deeply entrenched views of the FO and the three military Services, which had essentially been overridden because of the importance of maintaining co-operation with the Soviet Union after the German invasion in June 1941, once again, rose to the surface. An underlying difficulty was the fact that the military and political planners would have to work together: the post-war world would, in the words of one historian, be an 'awkward bureaucratic interface' between the two.[2] This 'awkwardness' is not immediately obvious from the records from this time; indeed, the FO appeared content for the COS to take primacy in tackling such questions. In beginning to consider post-war problems, the FO was initially keen to incorporate military thinking into its projections.[3] Another practical reason for the two to work together was the responsibility of the COS for advising the War Cabinet, and each had to accommodate the other's thinking. The difficulties appeared to focus on the practicalities of reaching a consensus.

Initial discussions focussed on the respective attitudes of the United States and the Soviet Union. Would the US stay in Europe or would it retreat into isolationism as it had following the previous war? Was the Soviet Union likely to continue to be an ally of the West and would co-existence be possible? As was and remains the Whitehall custom, the solution was sought in the creation of a committee. In this context the PHP sub-committee was restricted to a consideration of Russia, which was inevitable: in 1943 it was inconceivable that the United States would ever become a future foe, and whilst its commitment to Europe was uncertain, a more urgent question was to ascertain the future course of Soviet policy.

The intention was for the PHP to examine the fate of post-war enemy territories about to fall into Allied control and, more broadly, a consideration of how future military issues might affect policy requirements.[4] The PHP, furthermore, was to be the forum in which the Services and the FO could exchange views.[5] As a result, it was imperative that the new PHP had a senior membership, access to information and the means to produce reports. The PHP was to be chaired by Gladwyn Jebb, a high-flyer in the FO, with representatives from the Service departments. It had no intelligence component in its membership as such: as a more senior committee it was to rely, in theory at least, on JIC reporting for its information.

The JIC itself was not officially involved in the discussions surrounding the creation of the PHP. Commenting on the original proposals in the spring of 1943, Denis Capel-Dunn, the JIC Secretary, wrote that the aims of the PHP tackled the wrong kind of questions.[6] Although not a member of PHP, Victor Cavendish-Bentinck, the JIC Chairman, was one of the few FO recipients of its reports.[7] By mid-1943 the JIC's role, and that of the PHP, was to use intelligence information to produce forward-looking strategic assessments with the PHP and then draw on these products to prepare diplomatic and defence policy papers. The JIC, therefore, became the engine-room of the PHP's work. It was in this forum that the FO and COS clashed.

The first PHP paper stemmed from a request by the COS Committee to undertake a study of Britain's position vis-à-vis the Soviet position in the post-war world. HMG's underlying policy was 'to remain on terms of close friendship with the USSR'.[8] The study had the approval of the FO and by October 1943 its terms of reference had been produced.[9] The PHP drafters worked throughout late 1943 and early 1944. In the meantime the JIC, too, had been tasked with a similar issue, this time focused on the nature of post-war Soviet foreign policy. As some commentators have noted, the JIC had virtually no intelligence on which to draw its conclusions, and so relied on input from the FO.[10] As a result the first JIC paper to address policy towards the post-war Soviet Union was, more accurately, a FO paper, sent to the JIC for comment and eventual transmission to the PHP drafters.

The Soviet Union's major tasks were seen as reconstruction, and underlying its foreign policy, a 'search for security'. On the assumption that the US and UK would pose no threat to the Soviet Union, it was assessed that 'Russia will welcome a prolonged period of peaceful relations'. If the Soviet Union anticipated a more hostile Western policy then 'her attitude to this country will be suspicious and potentially antagonistic'. The FO thought that over the next five years, post-war reconstruction would be more likely to preoccupy Russian leaders and the Soviet Union would, therefore, 'constitute no menace to British strategic interests.'[11]

The only record of a reaction to the paper is from SIS, which found it hard to disagree with its general tone, but cited evidence that undermined the conclusion that the Soviet Union would be isolationist. Some information suggested that the Comintern – the organisation created in 1919 to export communism and the ideals of a worldwide revolution, and which was thought to have been dissolved in 1943 – had remained in place, and in a position to 'give direction to the national Communist parties of other countries'. The implications of this led SIS to question the conclusions of the FO's paper, suggesting that the Soviet Union might 'adopt a more forward policy essentially as a defensive measure by using the instruments which lie ready to her hand and seek to aid the establishment in power of the Communist parties in several countries'.[12] The question of when the decision to create the successor to the Comintern – the Cominform – was taken is still open to some debate, though the most recent evidence suggests it was not until 1946.[13] As a committee, and after some reflection, the JIC took a slightly more optimistic position than the FO, and was certainly more positive than the SIS paper. It did, however, warn that the Soviet Union might not take as long to recover as the FO had predicted, and that to 'overestimate the need for rehabilitation may lead to an underestimate of the Soviet Union's defensive potential.'[14]

At the same time a PHP paper was in preparation. Based largely on FO reporting, its conclusions were unsurprising. It argued that 'a real endeavour to secure the full and friendly participation of the USSR in any system of world security appears to be the best means of avoiding friction between us'. In highlighting its conclusion, the paper acknowledged that no attempt had been made to 'deal with the possibility that Soviet Russia might attempt to extend her influence over Western Europe and thus dominate the whole continent'.[15] In discussion the COS Committee was not as resistant to the paper as might have been expected – certainly by this point in mid-1944 both the Services and the FO were still on polite terms – its only criticism being that the paper did not sufficiently take into account Russian developments in air power.[16]

The PHP paper was duly amended and re-issued, but the divergence in opinion between the Services and the FO more generally had become apparent.[17] In writing to the Vice-COS Leslie Hollis, the Senior Assistant Secretary to the War Cabinet, outlined the problem:

> The Service Directors in PHP feel strongly that our future long term planning must take account of the possibility, however remote, of Russia as a potential or even an actual enemy. On the other hand Mr Jebb as Chairman of PHP and a member of the FO points out that the FO would probably be most reluctant to accept such a hypothesis on the grounds that it was politically highly dangerous [that is, if the fact emerged] and, indeed, does not represent the facts of the situation.[18]

While Anglo-Soviet relations remained good – this debate occurred at a pivotal moment in the war – attempts at collaboration were made which achieved differing levels of success. At the military level the British tried to secure information necessary for the planning of Operation OVERLORD (see chapter 5), yet continually found their approaches rebuffed. The result, as Christopher Warner of the FO told his colleagues, was that 'the War Office from the CIGS downwards feel resentment [toward the Soviet Union], I understand, at the mere withholding by the Russians of information'.[19] Cavendish-Bentinck adopted the role of mediator whilst also maintaining his FO allegiance:

> I have tried without success to impress on my colleagues that the trouble lies mainly in the personalities of the Service representatives we have sent to Russia. This is one of the few cases in which I feel some sympathy with the Russian attitude. If I had had to deal with most of the Services representatives we have sent to Russia I should have difficulty in resisting an inclination to be obstructive and tiresome.[20]

Shortly afterwards, Cavendish-Bentinck noted that military relations had improved slightly: 'I believe that the Russians are now playing up a bit better about this, but they have in the past been exceedingly tiresome.'[21] In a clear demonstration of his finesse in handling inter-departmental matters, Cavendish-Bentinck would record in discussion with his biographer that at a subsequent meeting of the JIC he asked the DMI to raise an issue 'in order that it should not be thought that I used the JIC for pushing ideas that receive no support from elsewhere'.[22]

Information on the attitudes of individual members of the JIC towards the Russians can be gleaned from a note written in March 1944. Commenting on the unwillingness of the Russians to share information with the British, Cavendish-Bentinck noted that 'their refusal . . . might be attributed to spite if one did not remember that the Russians are Asiatics and cannot be judged by European standards.'[23] Views like this were not uncommon in the 1940s. If anything, the statement is mild by comparison to some.[24]

The review in 1943/4 on the future of SIS is also revealing. In October 1943, Sir Alexander Cadogan, the PUS in the FO, created a small committee of diplomats chaired by Sir Nevile Bland and comprising Cavendish-Bentinck and Peter Loxley (of the Services Liaison Department, the interface between the FO and SIS). Their initial task was to consider post-war relations between SIS and the FO. This was not as straightforward as it seemed, for as Cavendish-Bentinck noted, 'one point that has continually emerged in our discussions is the great desirability of our giving 'C' before the war is over an indication of the tasks on which we think that the SIS should concentrate after the war.'[25] To this end Cavendish-Bentinck sought views from the Services' intelligence Directors on their priorities for intelligence collection in the post-war world.

Each Service replied individually, and each, without exception, placed Russia at the top of its priority list. The reasoning was succinctly summed up by Commodore Edmund Rushbrooke, the DNI, who explained that Russia 'is clearly indicated as the most unpredictable quantity in the post-war world. Information about Russia is exceedingly hard to come by'.[26] Major General John Sinclair, the DMI and future 'C', was also explicit in his calculation: 'whatever our relations with the Russians in the post-war period they are unlikely to tell us more than they do now. Though the question is one of high policy and SIS work in Russia is at present forbidden [see below], the organisation of an efficient SIS in Russia is essential and should have high priority.'[27]

The FO was also heavily involved in the review and, like the military, provided responses to Cavendish-Bentinck. Each of the different political departments replied, but the most relevant in this context was the Northern Department, responsible for Russia. Its head, Christopher Warner, was a diplomat who had spent the majority of his time based at the FO in London. Warner was more anti-Soviet than many of his colleagues and he made this clear in his report: 'I feel quite certain that we shall want to collect as much information as possible about Russian activities'.[28] By contrast, Sir Orme Sargent, the Deputy Under-Secretary in the FO, in commenting on the Services' submissions exclaimed that 'I must frankly say that I am shocked to see that both the Admiralty and the Air Ministry place Russia alone in the first category [i.e. top priority], instead of Germany. I am afraid I do not understand the mentality of people who reason in this fashion. I am certain the FO should do all they can to prevent this reasoning from being accepted as the basis of British foreign policy.'[29] As these two stances indicated, not only did the FO oppose the military view, but there were also internal divisions.[30]

The Bland Report on the 'Future Organisation of the SIS' was completed in October 1944. Its conclusions are not of concern here save for the general fact that it stated that SIS had a crucial part to play in the post-war period.[31] Meanwhile, the Post-Hostilities Planning Staff (PHPS), as it was by then known, continued to produce a number of reports, the majority of which were unrelated to the issue of post-war Russian relations. As the FO representative (and chairman) on the PHP, Gladwyn Jebb regularly informed his superiors of progress. Increasingly these missives complained about the anti-Soviet stance of the military whereas Jebb, echoing the FO line, opposed them. The FO was not pro-Soviet as such, and many were suspicious of the Russians. Rather they advocated that it would be politically risky to start to target the Soviet Union actively as an intelligence priority because if this became known, as they doubtless thought it would, then Anglo-Soviet relations would break down. Rapprochement was, therefore, the order of the day, and to plan on the basis of a hostile Russia was both foolhardy and premature.

By the summer of 1944 the split between the military's position and that of the FO was starkly clear and it was beginning to play a divisive role in the production of planning papers. To some, including the former JIC Secretary Denis Capel-Dunn, the arguments were 'spurious' and 'built up in an area where very little real division of opinion exists'. Capel-Dunn summarised what he saw to be the reality of the situation:

> Nobody, I am sure, in the FO or anywhere else would attempt to sustain the argument that the Chiefs of Staff should entirely exclude from their minds, when advising the Government as to our future strategic needs, the possibility that at some time and in some circumstances, Russian policy might be a danger to the interests of the British Empire. Similarly, I hope that no responsible person on the military side of the house would deny that it would be criminally foolish for HMG to embark on a foreign policy which could give the Russians the impression that it was directed against them.[32]

Such sensible views were not universally shared. In June 1944, Jebb informed the FO that he had told his military colleagues on the PHP that the FO did not support their view that the Soviet Union was the 'sole potential enemy'. The Air Ministry and Admiralty representatives had declared their disagreement, stating that 'it was "unrealistic" not to contemplate what measures should be taken to secure our interests against attempts to undermine them on the part of the Soviet Union in the event of things going wrong.'[33] Once more Cavendish-Bentinck, with his greater experience of inter-departmental committees and working with the military, tried to smooth matters. Responding to Jebb's minute, he wrote that 'my experience during the past $4\frac{1}{2}$ years has led me to believe that you get more out of them [the military] by humouring them regarding the form of papers and letting them take the assumptions that they like provided that the conclusions and recommendations are what we want.'[34] He offered a further thought on dealing with the military several months later: 'it is far easier to secure satisfactory papers if the FO view is inculcated when the paper is first being drafted. If the papers begin on the wrong lines, it is difficult to get them right.'[35]

From the internal FO discussions of PHP papers on the arguments with the military about the vexed question of Russia, it becomes increasingly clear that Cavendish-Bentinck was a skilled Whitehall warrior. In commenting on yet more FO disagreement of the military's views, he observed that:

> I do feel that if we give the impression of persistently refusing to allow any mention that Russia may later on be non-co-operative and even hostile, we shall have in the Service Departments this same reputation vis-à-vis Russia as Sir Horace Wilson had as regards Germany from 1937 to the outbreak of the present war, with the result that they may tend to discount our opinions and regard us as being ostrich like so far as Russia is concerned.[36]

In circulating the latest PHP paper to the COS, Hollis reported back to Jebb that it had, in general, been received favourably. However, the COS Committee felt that the PHP had not sufficiently taken into account that 'in the long run the most important factor will be our relationship with Russia' and that accordingly, some planning should be undertaken in the event that relations broke down.[37] Jebb, by contrast, had believed that the original paper was already too direct in 'contemplating a hostile Russia', and thought the COS position was too extreme. Once more it fell to Cavendish-Bentinck to try and smooth matters, by carefully explaining that the military's concerns were based on a genuine and proper fear at the surprise of Russian military advances, and that it was 'natural that they should therefore regard Russia as a potential danger'.[38]

A question that emerged from all of this was whether the military concern about an unfriendly Russia was merely a worse case scenario, or whether there were genuine concerns that the Soviet Union posed a threat to future British interests. The PHP, in August 1944, asked the JIC to provide some clarity.[39] It was implicit from the preceding discussions that the JIC would need to strike at the heart of the debate. Were the Russians hostile? What were their post-war intentions? Did they pose a threat to British interests?

The response, produced a few weeks later, was the first JIC paper on the matter since March 1944. The result was disappointing – it re-iterated those conclusions, stating that no further information had come to light, and declaring that a re-review of Russia's intentions would therefore not be attempted. Instead, the paper concentrated predominantly on Russian capabilities and military advances, outlining in detail how these were progressing faster than had been expected.[40] If it had been anticipated that the JIC would resolve the dispute one way or another then some were disappointed. Admittedly it adhered to the FO line, but not conclusively enough to end military doubts; by maintaining that the Soviet military capability was greater than first thought, it incorporated COS thinking. In the FO there was quiet pleasure on receipt of the report. Jebb's deputy called it a 'most interesting and valuable paper', and declared that it 'endors[ed] the FO view – ought to (but probably won't) cool the heads of the PHPS.'[41] A useful, though not necessarily representative, view was provided by Patrick Davison (Lord Broughshane), the Assistant Secretary (Military) to the War Cabinet and PHP Secretary: 'no particularly new thought comes out of this, and it represents rather a set back for the would be drinkers of Russian blood'.[42]

Unsurprisingly, the matter remained unresolved, though some progress had been made. A PHP revision of an earlier paper that had never been formally approved had been based on the assumption that Russia was Britain's 'potential enemy No.1', but was also predicated on the assumption that 'there was little likelihood of a threat from the USSR for a period of ten years'.[43] In many ways this paper appeared designed to please everybody, yet it was not taken seriously and it, too, was never formally approved as it stood.[44] In fact PHP papers were being read less and less and losing much of their credibility, probably owing to the fact that the authors themselves could never agree and, as a consequence, papers were generally inconclusive in tone and content.

By September 1944 relations had reached crisis point. Gladwyn Jebb, the chairman of PHP, resigned, and with his departure the FO became 'associate members'. The cause was simple: 'a result of a fundamental difference of opinion in the approach towards our post-war relationship with the USSR'. As Jebb's deputy, Ward, was told by Sir Orme Sargent, he should 'hold aloof from these anti-Russian studies, and not attempt to correct their extravagances, on the principle of giving the PHPS all the rope they want to hang themselves.'[45] The impact was instant. The first draft of a PHP paper in September 1944 began with the premise that 'a hostile Russia is one of our basic assumptions', and suggested that the JIC consider the statement's accuracy.[46] Cavendish-Bentinck informed the FO that, at that day's JIC meeting, a copy had 'suddenly' been produced and advised his colleagues 'to have nothing to do with it. They agreed.'[47] Following Jebb's resignation as chairman of PHP, the paper had not been seen by the FO in advance. The result, as Ward wrote, was 'the usual story, but this time even more foolishly worded'.[48]

During the early stages of the Second World War a short-lived attempt had been made to produce assessments from the enemy's perspective. A team of drafters, adopting fictitious German names and military ranks, produced a series of papers on German strategy (see chapter 3). This endeavour to get into the mind of the enemy ultimately had little impact. The concept, however, lingered, and with the dearth of intelligence on which to base assessments of post-war Russian intentions it was once more suggested that the best approach would be for a group of people to 'situate' themselves in Moscow to see how the world looked. The initiative came from the PHP in its draft paper which was passed to the JIC, with the hope that it might be able to produce 'an independent strategic appreciation made from the point of view of a Russia intending to embark on an expansionist policy.'[49] This proposition prompted Cavendish-Bentinck's exclamation of 'having nothing to do with it'.

Although the JIC was not keen, the idea itself was sensible. Intelligence was seriously lacking and an objective and non-departmental view was needed, so it would have made sense for the JIC – or more accurately its drafters, the JIS – to write the study. The problem, as Patrick Davison explained, was that the previous attempt by the FOES (see chapter 3) had been so disastrous that 'the JIC are against it, and the best opinion that I can obtain is that the precedents are <u>not</u> arguments in favour'.[50] The JIC's reluctance might also have stemmed from a desire not to intervene in the debate; however, in a change of heart – which cannot be explained by the surviving files – the JIC did undertake to produce an assessment on how it felt Russia viewed the world.

The first draft of the paper was produced for circulation to the JIC members in mid-October 1944. Two interesting facts emerged. Firstly, the paper was not entirely written by the JIS but was, in Cavendish-Bentinck's words, 'largely the handiwork of Sir A.Noble'. Andrew Noble, a FO colleague of Cavendish-Bentinck's, had taken over much of the responsibility for the Services Liaison Department in communicating with SIS. In assisting with the preparation of the report, Noble 'kept in close touch' with the FO and the Northern Department in particular.[51] This raises the question, for which there is no good answer, of how frequently in its early years the JIC made use of drafts written by departments rather than the JIS.

The paper, 'Russia's Strategic Interests from the Point of View of Her Security', when discussed by the JIC, was evidently referred back for revision.[52]

The revised version, some two months later, was quite different and opened with several caveats. In contrast to the original draft it did try to predict future Soviet actions. The tone, detail and sophistication of argument became far more advanced in the revised paper, which was a longer 13 page assessment.[53] It is perhaps the best and most prescient of all JIC papers produced up to this point and so it is unfortunate that it was never appreciated as such.

'Any study of Russia's strategic interests', it began, 'must be speculative as we have little evidence to show what view Russia herself takes of her strategic interests or what policy she intends to pursue. Moreover, Russian policy at present depends very largely on the decisions of Marshal Stalin'. The assessment then examined the Soviet Union's capabilities and intentions, before concluding with a judgment on the threat. Russia's size, natural resources, and military prowess (which, it was expected, would continue to advance) meant that she was a considerable force to be reckoned with – the COS must have been pleased with this outcome. Soviet intentions, however, were predicated not on potency, as might have been expected, but on a sense of vulnerability – here the FO readers may have been satisfied.

The Soviet Union's primary concern, it was assessed, was to achieve 'absolute security', the fear being that a resurgent Germany might invade, for a third time in less than fifty years. Germany therefore had to be physically crushed, and any perceived attempt by the West to expand or ally with Germany would be seen as a hostile move. To ensure this, Russia would 'build up a system of security outside her frontiers in order to make sure, so far as is humanly possible, that she is left in peace and that her development is never again imperilled by the appalling devastation and misery of wars such as she has twice experienced within a generation.' Here was the first recognition that the Soviet Union envisaged a series of buffer states outside her own borders.

Given these views of its capabilities and intentions (taken together perceived as constituting a 'threat'), what was the likely course of future Soviet policy? Firstly, it was felt that she might 'experiment' with a 'policy of collaboration' with the UK and US; secondly, that she would create a system of allied territories, a so-called 'sphere of interest', that would protect her; and thirdly, that everything would be done to ensure that Germany was incapable of future aggression. In summary, Soviet actions would be 'directed primarily towards achieving the greatest possible measure of security'. And so the question remained, did the Soviet Union constitute a post-war threat to British interests or not? The JIC's response was clear, throwing responsibility back to the policymakers:

> . . . Russia will not, in our opinion, follow an aggressive policy of territorial expansion, her suspicion of British and American policy will nevertheless continue to cause difficulty as will also her tactlessness in the handling of international affairs. Accordingly Russia's relations with the British Empire and the United States will depend very largely on the ability of each side to convince the other of the sincerity of its desire for collaboration.[54]

In late December the COS met Cavendish-Bentinck, the three Services' intelligence chiefs and the JIC's representative from the MEW. The COS Committee found the report to be a 'valuable study of the problem', and 'the conclusions reached by the JIC seemed sound'.[55] They approved its circulation but in doing so gave it a very restrictive marking, with the result that it was not widely disseminated. This had two unrelated consequences: the distribution was limited in the hope that the Russians would not discover that this type of study was taking place (though unknown to anyone in Whitehall, the Soviet spy Donald Maclean was passing all such papers to Moscow[56]); and secondly, the report was passed to the Foreign Secretary but the COS refused permission for it to go to the whole of the War Cabinet, for fear that they would object to 'their [the COS] undertaking studies of this kind'.[57] Even when the Foreign Secretary, who thought the study was 'well done', requested that it should go to the War Cabinet, the COS once more refused.[58]

The COS Committee clearly did not want the paper to be too widely disseminated but, by contrast, the FO was extremely eager for it to do so. It had originally been sent to the Foreign Secretary, in Cavendish-Bentinck's words, so that 'we should have at our disposal a report with which the Chiefs of Staff agreed.'[59] The turn of the year in 1944/5 marked the high point of the FO's antipathy towards the COS view of the Soviet Union. From this point, and inexorably in the light of events, the FO had to alter its opinion of post-war Russian policy until it was forced to accept the reality of Russian hostility.

Consensus on the Soviet Union

According to historian Martin Folly, in the most comprehensive account of FO views of the Soviet Union, it was Stalin's actions against liberated countries as the Red Army swept towards Germany that began to alter opinions in London.[60] In a despatch from Moscow in January 1945 the Minister, John Balfour, informed the FO that 'In all this there is a well-defined long-term policy which, so far as can at present be foreseen is summed up in the word "security".' This was a reiteration of the JIC's conclusions of December 1944 but, as Balfour continued, 'I say "at present" because the self-confidence of the Soviet Union, which victory has immeasurably increased, combined with a love of power for its own sake . . . might cause this policy as it unfolds itself to assume dangerous forms.'[61] The feeling that the Russians were becoming more confident, less trustworthy and generally colder in their relations with the British is clearly evident in other FO papers of the time.

Yet old habits died hard. Despite the gradually changing perception, some sections of the FO remained much less hostile than the military. In commenting on a PHP paper in May 1945, Geoffrey Wilson, a diplomat who had spent most of the war years in the Embassy in Moscow, observed that it 'painted the most terrifying picture of what the Russians might do'. Davison, the PHP secretary, had explained to him that 'one of his objects was to get some political ammunition to support the military conclusions which had already been drawn!'[62] This PHP paper, on the 'Security of the British Empire' was, after numerous redrafts sent in June 1945 to the JIC for comment on the political section. Although there is reference to a joint JIC-PHPS meeting, no record exists of the discussion.[63]

The JIC itself had continued its work, the majority of which was concerned with the end of hostilities in Europe and the expectation of the termination of the war in the Pacific. In April 1945 reports of Soviet activities in Bulgaria had been greeted with disconcerted pessimism. Sir Stewart Menzies, 'C', informed the Committee that he too had received reports from Bulgaria, and that the Russian troops were 'of the worst type'.[64] In an assessment in May, the JIC judged that, by July 1945, Soviet military strength would be considerable.[65] This report, issued on VE Day, was followed shortly thereafter by a new study, aimed at considering 'Relations with the Russians' now that the war in Europe had ended.

This first post-war study, completed shortly after VE Day, adopted the middle ground. In commenting on whether the British government should continue to share information with the Soviet Union, the JIC set the initial context: 'we assume that the policy of His Majesty's Government is to achieve the maximum collaboration with the Soviet Union, compatible with our own vital interests'. Furthermore, 'our relations with Russia during the last four years have been governed by the necessity for maintaining Russia's war effort', and so, with the end of the war, 'there is no longer any reason for giving Russia military assistance'. Consequently, 'the only effective means of using reciprocity is by driving as hard a bargain as possible when requests are first received.' It was carefully worded but ultimately hesitant in approach: the UK should aim to collaborate with the Soviet Union but this should be limited and based on what could be obtained in exchange. It was cautious advice and probably would have done nothing to assuage the concerns of those who were suspicious of Soviet motives.[66] In another paper produced at the same time, the JIC identified the Soviet Union as the primary concern for British intelligence as a whole. Accordingly, in its report on SIS requirements, the JIC noted that 'the USSR is likely to be the greatest potential danger to the strategic interests of the British Empire during the immediate post-war years, and should be a first charge on our intelligence resources.'[67] Yet even here, in the use of verbal qualifiers such as 'likely to be', 'potential', and 'should be', the JIC's equivocal position is reflected.

In the months following the end of the war in Europe it became more than just of passing interest to the JIC to monitor Soviet activities in her 'sphere of influence'. Some countries would remain under the control of Moscow, including Hungary, Romania and Bulgaria. More debateable was the slightly amorphous 'sphere' of southern Europe, where the Cold War intensified as the 1940s progressed. As early as August 1945 the JIC considered possible Soviet moves into Italy. There is, in these JIC documents, an unmistakeable acceptance that Europe had been divided into two: the Soviet sphere and the Anglo-American one. In the East the Soviet Union would attempt to control nations. Further West it would try to impose harsh peace terms on the defeated nations, whilst trying to limit their regeneration. The JIC appeared implicitly to accept this division as the way of the new world.[68]

Another country lying outside the Soviet sphere but clearly at risk was Turkey. For most of the war Turkey had been neutral, only becoming more closely involved in the last few months but never actively participating. Turkey was important for several reasons: geographically it was of interest to the Soviet Union; the Soviet leadership resented the Turks for their wartime position[69]; and, furthermore, the Soviet government saw Turkey as 'a very dangerous and unfriendly power'.[70] In June 1945 the Turkish Ambassador in Moscow had been informed that the Soviet Union wanted to create a base in the Straits so as to safeguard the transit of shipping between the Black Sea and the Mediterranean. The Turks rejected this and informed the British. At the Potsdam peace conference the following month the Soviet Union stated, in no uncertain terms, that it was a private matter between itself and Turkey, and that it should be dealt with bilaterally. In September 1945 reports began to reach London that the Soviet Union was moving troops towards the Caucasus. The JIC was concerned that, depending on the lines of advance, the West might not receive any prior warning of what might happen. In a subsequent discussion the Chief of the Air Staff, Marshal of the RAF Sir Charles Portal, posed an interesting question, and one that would continue to vex the JIC throughout the Cold War: 'whether it was possible accurately to distinguish between reported movements in connection with the war of nerves and reported movements which might be part of a build up prior to the use of force'.[71] It was never satisfactorily answered. Despite this, the JIC concluded that the Soviet Union was not preparing to attack Turkey, though the anti-Soviet press and radio campaign would continue.[72]

The JIC's major work on the Soviet Union in this period was its paper 'Russia's Strategic Interests and Intentions'. The first to be disseminated had been produced in December 1944, which concluded that the Soviet Union posed no strategic threat to the UK. It is surprising that this was not updated until January 1946, when the JIC was asked to revise it by the COS. The JIC was allowed to produce papers on its own initiative if it felt a topic worth pursuing; it did not need to wait for a directive to be issued. The JIC had not done so until that point, possibly because it was concentrating on the final throes of the war, or perhaps because its members, as individuals, were too concerned about straying from their departmental line, or simply that they were unable to take on more than they were already doing. Whatever the reason this hiatus created a gap at the centre of British intelligence about the Soviet Union and its intentions.

The updated JIC paper was finished in March 1946, a crucial time as post-war attitudes towards the Soviet Union matured. The difficulties in collecting intelligence on the Soviet Union were emphasised from the outset, notably the constant problem of penetrating the leadership of an authoritarian state. The tone and general conclusions of the revised report were not starkly different from those in 1944. The Soviet fear of attack was highlighted, as was the related need to create a 'belt of satellite States with governments subservient to their policy'. Thus, the Soviet Union would still try to avoid any hostile acts that might propel the West towards conflict. The security 'belt', no longer referred to as a 'sphere of influence', would be expanded if it was at all threatened, or at least perceived itself to be, and therefore Turkey and Persia were clearly of concern. Crucially, it was assessed that 'Russian policy will be aggressive by all means short of war', and that consequently, 'attention should be drawn to the dangers inherent in Russian policy as we see it'.[73]

The JIC's report was a careful consideration of the Soviet mentality and policies. The Soviet desire to expand was not seen as deliberate aggressive expansion but born out of necessity, a sense of vulnerability and a need to shore up her defences. Yet within this need lay a ruthless determination, a drive to achieve her 'security belt' regardless of any opposition. In commenting on a draft of the paper, the COS displayed a similarly nuanced understanding of the drivers behind Soviet policy.[74] The COS Committee approved the revised version and it was sent to the Prime Minister and Foreign Secretary, though their views were not recorded.[75]

The JIC report also concluded that the Soviet Union would wish to avoid war for at least five years. This stemmed from a belief that the Soviet Union would pursue its five year plan – a key tool for industrial planning – and would not be in a position to launch a 'major' war until that point. The point here was that the military planners needed as much detail as possible to back-up the assessment on which to base their post-war efforts for maintaining old equipment and introducing new technology. To confuse matters the Defence Committee, whose membership comprised leading politicians and was chaired by the Prime Minister, had stated that the UK would not be called upon to wage major war for two or three years, thus creating a dilemma over which estimate to use for planning purposes. The FO was duly called upon to adjudicate and the response, from PUS Sir Orme Sargent, reveals the assumptions on which the Defence Committee and the JIC's forecasts were based:

> It does not appear from the minutes of that meeting [the Defence Committee's] that this conclusion was based upon any agreed appreciation of the international situation, but was rather accepted as a reasonable estimate bearing in mind the crisis in manpower and the consequent necessity for the reduction in the strength of the armed forces . . . since this meeting of the Defence Committee an appreciation has . . . been written by the JIC on Russia's strategic intentions . . . the FO accepted this conclusion. In doing so we would draw attention to the fact that the JIC did not say that in their estimation there would be no war for five years, and we are most anxious that their paper shall not be misread on this point. All they did say was that the Russians would wish to avoid a major conflict before January 1951 and this led to an important caution that the danger would always exist that Russian leaders may misjudge how far they can go. On this basis . . . we cannot suggest a better course than to accept the line suggested in the JIC paper.[76]

The FO's approval of the JIC paper may have been based largely on despatches from the British Embassy in Moscow back to London. Such telegrams from

Moscow would prove invaluable in trying to understand the psyche of the Soviet leadership.

Crisis in Persia

In its March 1946 report, the JIC had highlighted that the Soviet Union's 'southern frontier' was unprotected, and that Turkey and Greece were therefore of strategic concern. Having discounted reports of Soviet troop movements in Turkey the previous October, the JIC conceded in March 1946 that there was evidence of military activity in the region.[77] For Turkey the judgment remained that there was still no military threat; for Greece, however, recent political activity and the decision by the communist-influenced Greek EAM party to withdraw from elections was seen as significant. This was really the first post-war sign, albeit never explicitly identified as such, that the Soviet threat to the West might not be solely military in nature.[78]

More worrying were reports, at the same time, of Soviet troop movements in Persia. Under the conditions of the 1942 Tripartite Treaty, the Soviet Union was to withdraw all of its forces by 2 March 1946. Although some Russian troops had been withdrawn, a great number remained and reports, 'particularly from American sources', suggested that they were being readied for 'major military operations'. The JIC reviewed this information, together with reports from the British Consul at Tabriz (in north west Persia, close to the Soviet border). Although details were scant, it was concluded that 'while we have no definite evidence to contradict these American reports, we are inclined to think they are exaggerated'. Despite this, there were clearly signs of Russian troop movements, and coupled with the fact that all Soviet forces should have been withdrawn by this time, something seemed to be afoot.[79]

What motive could the Soviet Union have in maintaining a military presence in the region? The possibilities were two-fold: firstly, to ensure, as the JIC had forecast, that Soviet forces would be available to exploit any situation to their advantage; secondly, it was believed that the Soviet Union needed external oil supplies to maintain her industrial growth, and the South Persian oilfields were a preferred source.[80] The FO asked the Embassy in Moscow, 'Given that Russia's policy will be aggressive by all means short of war, just how far will she push that policy before she sees the red light and holds back? In other words, how far does the Soviet Government think that they can with impunity disregard the interests and challenge the policy of His Majesty's Government and the United States Government?'[81] The JIC undertook to review the intelligence every two weeks,[82] and the first study, completed at the start of April, reported that although Soviet troops appeared to be returning to the Soviet Union, as yet there had been 'no confirmation' that any had actually departed.[83]

Information provided by Frank Roberts, a diplomat and, at that time, Minister (i.e. the deputy to the Ambassador) in Moscow, was invaluable.[84] Much as the American George Kennan would be later remembered for his clear analysis of the situation in Moscow, Frank Roberts provided a steady stream of reports and answers to questions posed by the FO.[85] For him, the only means of stopping the Soviet Union was to convince it that the Americans would support the British in any military response. Furthermore, he felt that although Soviet activities in Persia and Turkey could be seen as part of the move to secure a security belt, at the same time he did not feel that 'Soviet expansion' would stop with these two countries.[86] Roberts agreed with the JIC's report of March 1946, but added that it did not sufficiently take into account 'the importance of Marxist-Leninist ideology in the formation of Soviet foreign policy'.[87] The implications of this were that 'it may be misleading in dealing with the Soviet Union to distinguish between offensive and defensive moves and between long-term and short-term aims'. Thus, 'her long-term ambitions are dangerous to vital British interests'.[88] From the vantage point of Cairo, JIC(ME) supported Roberts' views, though it was less convinced that Soviet planning was fundamentally bellicose, seeing the Soviet Union instead as opportunist.[89]

Others in the FO supported Roberts' analysis. Robert Hankey, son of JIC founder Lord Hankey and himself a diplomat respected for his insight, recorded that 'Soviet policy is extremely dynamic, ambitious and opportunist and is fundamentally hostile to British liberal and democratic ideas'. He added 'I hope that when the JIC and/or the Chiefs of Staff finally reconsider this question, they will look at the whole matter on really broad lines. In my opinion it is not a matter any longer whether divisions stationed here can cover such and such a territory, it is a matter whether we can afford to allow a Power with so much ambition and such lack of scruple to control such colossal manpower and industrial potential.'[90] This represented a more hard-line FO attitude towards the Soviet Union. No longer could co-operation be seen as the key, but rather the aggressive expansionism needed a strong response. In May the change in policy was confirmed in its most powerful form in a memorandum by Christopher Warner, the head of the new Russia Section in the FO, entitled 'The Soviet Campaign Against This Country and Our Response to It'.[91]

What was the impact of these views on the JIC? The fortnightly update on events suggested, by late April, that the Soviet Union was withdrawing its forces from Persia, albeit at a leisurely pace, and that there had been no variations in numbers in Turkey.[92] By early June the JIC could report that all Soviet troops had now left Persia.[93] Despite this positive news, however, the outlook was overshadowed by the overriding problem of oil. In the mid-1940s forty percent of worldwide British-controlled oil was produced in Persia; the potential threat from the Soviet Union towards these oilfields was therefore considerable.[94] The threat to oil resources, coupled with Roberts' rather pessimistic reporting from Moscow, must surely have struck a nerve. Such was the gravity of the situation that the fortnightly papers reporting on Soviet actions in Persia were immediately despatched, with COS approval, to the Prime Minister and Foreign Secretary.[95] In the FO, JIC papers on Soviet intentions were warmly received. Thomas Brimelow, a diplomat who had served in Moscow in the latter half of the war and who would eventually become the PUS, recorded that 'there is rarely any hard thinking on what the Russians are up to and what we ought to do about it except when a JIC paper is on the stocks'. Similarly, Warner added that the only correct body to consider such questions was the JIC – praise indeed.[96]

A report on Soviet intentions in the wider Middle East, approved in June 1946, suggested that Russian activity in Persia was geared towards using the forthcoming elections to install a pro-Soviet regime. More generally, and in Persia particularly, it was concluded that 'the Soviet Union will take every opportunity to foment anti-British feeling and to reduce British influence throughout the Arab world, and will ultimately hope to supplant it.'[97] This may have been explained by the changing status quo; of Russia's need to strengthen its security belt or of the UK's inability to prevent Soviet moves of this kind. The impression conveyed by the report is that of no serious threat to the UK. The COS Committee enthusiastically endorsed its contents, instructing that it be sent to the Prime Minister, Foreign Secretary, the various Ministers responsible for the Colonies and Dominions, and numerous British Embassies abroad.[98]

What is clear throughout the reporting on Soviet actions in this period is that the JIC had no good sources of intelligence at its disposal (see chapter 9 for further details). This was to have an impact on the nature and type of assessments that were produced, for as Harold Caccia, then JIC Chairman, informed the COS Committee:

> . . . the means whereby the Joint Intelligence Sub-Committee proposed to keep the Chiefs of Staff fully informed on military activities in Europe and the Middle East had been based on the scope of information which was likely to be obtained and upon the capabilities of the Committee in time of peace. It was not proposed to issue detailed reports at regular intervals, but rather to base the reports on such information as came to light from time to time, so as to indicate major changes as they occurred.[99]

Within the FO, Caccia was more explicit on the problems. Referring to a 1946 JIC paper on Soviet strategic interests, he confided that:

> The approach is <u>strategic</u> and it has been compiled on the information available. We admit that that is insufficient for a proper intelligence appreciation, since we do not even know such fundamental things for any military study as the proposed rate of demobilization in Russia in 1946 . . . we have therefore been compelled, as in 1944, to crystal gaze rather than to marshal facts and figures in such a way that deductions are inescapable.[100]

The JIC's decision to produce papers only when new intelligence became available would be a policy that would last for some time. As the JIC was to inform the COS, this was part of a wider review 'examining the question of the availability of information concerning the Soviet Union, the sources of such information, and what our requirements will be in order to assess Soviet intentions'.[101] This problem had been identified before the end of the war and had been the reason that the JIC had tried to assess what, and who, the future enemy would be. With the focus now directed towards the Soviet Union, this lack of intelligence would have far-reaching implications.

Shifting Sands

The events in Persia between the spring and summer of 1946, taken in isolation, were hardly serious: initial reports of troop increases and movements were quickly proven to be inaccurate, and although the Soviet Union did retain a military presence beyond the terms of the 1942 agreement, this did not last for long. What was of significance is how Soviet actions were interpreted by the British Embassy in Moscow and in London. No longer was there a dispute within Whitehall as to the real motivation and intentions of Soviet foreign policy, although the gaps in intelligence coverage continued to hamper detailed forecasts. A re-review in August of an earlier paper on Soviet intentions in the Middle East clearly showed how JIC thinking had changed by this point. In suggesting that oil remained a high priority for the Soviet leadership – as did extending its influence beyond the already-defined East European security belt – the JIC concluded that 'the Soviet Government have, in fact, resumed the traditional policy of southern expansion . . . the Soviet Government will implement this historic policy by every means short of war. Their ultimate goal is clear; but the intermediate moves will be opportunist and their order of priority flexible.'[102]

The implications of such a forecast were clear: Britain could either accept or challenge the Soviet policy. At the political level Britain continued to meet the Soviet leadership to discuss plans for Europe, as they did other European leaders and the Americans too.[103] Below this level, conversations continued between the military and intelligence establishments. In discussion of the revised JIC paper, the COS emphasised how crucial the oil factor would be in determining Soviet actions. Given this, and the related moves to undermine British influence in the region, doing nothing was not an option. The response was to suggest that, as Lieutenant General Frank Simpson, the Vice Chief of the Imperial General Staff, put it: 'we should initiate strong counter propaganda to these Russian activities.' The JIC Chairman Harold Caccia, in attendance, is recorded as having agreed, as did General Hastings Ismay, who commented that 'we were at present adopting a somewhat negative attitude in the face of continued Russian provocation'. The result was that the JIC was asked to suggest a course of action to the COS, who in turn would recommend it to the politicians.[104] Thus, the COS instructed the JIC, assisted by the Joint Planning Staff, to hold a joint meeting to 'examine the possibility of taking some positive action to counter Russian subversive propaganda'.[105]

The JIC and JPS met in late August and agreed that it needed to be discussed further with Ivone Kirkpatrick, a future PUS but then head of the FO's Information Section, before any concrete plans could be laid. In the meantime, members of both the JIC and JPS complained about the difficulty of formulating a response without knowledge of the British government's policies in the Middle East. Furthermore, Sir Stewart Menzies, 'C', argued that even when a plan had been devised and approved, it would still take a year before any measures would become effective.[106] Kirkpatrick's subsequent report was approved by both the FO and the COS Committee and was used as a basis for planning.[107]

The JIC advocated both overt and covert propaganda campaigns. The former would present the 'positive advantages of the British way of life' whilst also dealing 'factually with Russia's campaign of misrepresentation'. The covert effort would be directed by the FO and SIS.[108] In addition, SIS was instructed to give priority to the preparation of plans for 'special operations' (i.e. SOE-style activities) in the event that the Middle East was overrun by the Russians.[109] Responsibility for organising this was split: on the 'special operations' front it was to be organised through the JIC,[110] whereas on the propaganda side responsibility for co-ordinating action rested with the 'existing machinery' in the FO.[111] This may have referred to the Cultural Relations Department, an approximate forerunner of the 1948 Information Research Department. Working alongside this was the FO's 'Russia Committee'; a group, to which Kirkpatrick belonged, charged with political warfare activities that would ensure that JIC intelligence assessments were factored into policy advice.[112] Integral to all was the role of the FO JIC Chairman.

In London the anti-Soviet faction was clearly in the ascendant. Even the most sceptical of FO advisers had become convinced of the need to co-ordinate policy against the Russians. One complicating issue was the American perspective. At a strategic level uncertainty continued over their future commitments to Europe, but in the intelligence and military realm, the JIC and the COS were keen to stress the seriousness of the situation with their transatlantic counterparts. However, the Americans had been, in Cavendish-Bentinck's opinion, 'too late' in seeing 'what the Russian game was', by late 1946 there can have been no doubt as to their general views.[113] The problem was one of scale – would the US see the Soviet threat to the European mainland as serious and severe enough to warrant some sort of military commitment? At various junctures, and particularly as the assessments grew more sombre, the military had been eager to circulate JIC papers to the Americans. In the Middle East particularly, where Soviet intentions had become clear, possibly for the first time, the COS were especially keen to impress upon the Americans the 'seriousness of the situation', which they did by forwarding various JIC assessments.[114] Likewise, the FO requested that JIC papers were sent to the US Joint Chiefs of Staff and to the President.[115] Any American response was not recorded.

At the same time the JIC was busy working on other papers, designed to gauge the extent of Moscow's reach. Concern continued unabated about the influence of Soviet-inspired agitation in Greece and the communists' political campaign.[116] By December the JIC members decided that periodic reports on Soviet troop activities in South East Europe and Persia should be expanded to include all regions outside the USSR with the exception of the Far East. In Eastern Europe, although it was reported that troop numbers were falling in all satellite states, Soviet forces still numbered in excess of 1,500,000 troops.[117] In addition, as a further report made clear, fifth column activities were on the increase, and thus 'communism is a serious menace to the interest of the British Commonwealth both outside British territory, and to a lesser extent inside it and we are of the opinion that it is essential that some immediate counter-action be taken against this danger'.[118]

The Cold War was truly underway and the situation in Greece was of particular concern to the British. A civil war had begun in 1946 between the army, backed by the UK, and the communist party, a proxy of Moscow. The JIC had reported on the situation throughout 1946. At a more senior level British policymakers had spoken to their American counterparts about the need to strengthen the Greek flank. In February 1947 the British were forced to concede to the Americans that they had to withdraw support. Historical analysis of this has centred on two theses: either that the decision was motivated by economic considerations – Britain had to plough what resources it had into the reconstruction of the UK; or that the British withdrawal was a deliberate attempt to draw the US into European affairs.[119] Whichever is the more accurate, the result was that on 12 March 1947 President Harry Truman stood up before the US Congress and announced that it was the policy of the United States to 'support free peoples who are resisting attempted subjugation by armed minorities or by outside pressures.' The immediate result was a programme of military and economic aid to Turkey and Greece, the two nations most at threat from communism. Subsequently this was followed by the Marshall Plan – a massive aid programme geared towards economic reconstruction in Europe. The Soviet Union and its satellite states rejected the terms of the Marshall Plan; in doing so the political divisions of the world were reinforced by its economic partition. The transformation was completed by the late 1940s with the creation of NATO, thereby also institutionalising the military separation between East and West.

Within the United Kingdom two further momentous decisions were taken: to maintain a military presence east of the Suez Canal and to proceed with the indigenous development of an atomic bomb. Within Whitehall, and indeed the military and intelligence establishments, a consensus had been reached that the Soviet Union posed a threat to British security. The precise dimension and scale of the threat was not quite so clear, and here the JIC would have a central role to play in the ensuing decades of the Cold War. In trying to interpret and predict the actions of those occupying the senior positions in the Kremlin, the JIC continually strove to assess the balance of forces as seen from London and Moscow.

In the evolution of British policy towards the Soviet Union the JIC had played an integral role. Often sitting uneasily between the hawkish military and the dovish diplomats, the JIC, and in particular its FO Chairman, was in an unenviable position. As it was, events themselves resolved the internal disagreements, but without the tactful and nimble footwork of Victor Cavendish-Bentinck Britain could have entered the Cold War in a far more divided state. In the face of this, JIC assessments are noteworthy for their caution. Even after the Soviet Union was declared to be the number one priority, the JIC remained relatively objective about its foe, often providing a more balanced assessment than the more strident voices emanating from some quarters of the FO. Initial assessments which interpreted Russian foreign policy from a Russian perspective were extremely sound and should have stood the test of time, but these proved to be short-lived.

JIC forecasts, taken as a whole, were good. Generally speaking they were balanced, well-written and, crucially, well-received. Hindering matters throughout, however, were the difficulties in procuring intelligence on the Soviet Union. Soviet intentions were difficult for the JIC to comprehend from London. The JIC made an effort to offer an objective account and to give the Russians the benefit of the doubt. Within just over a year Britain would face her first serious Cold War challenge in Berlin, and for this intelligence would prove to be paramount.

Notes

1 J Lewis, *Changing Direction: British Military Planning for Post-War Strategic Defence, 1952–1947* (London: Frank Cass, 2003). pp.17–54.
2 M Folly, *Churchill, Whitehall and the Soviet Union, 1940–45* (London: Macmillan, 2000). p.104.
3 A.Cadogan [PUS, FO] to H.Ismay [Churchill's Chief of Staff], 19 February 1942. CAB 119/64. For some general work on FO thinking see G Ross, 'FO Attitudes to the Soviet Union 1941–45', *Journal of Contemporary History* 16 (1981), pp.521–40; R Smith, 'A Climate of Opinion: British Officials and the Development of British Soviet Policy, 1945–7', *International Affairs* 64:4 (Autumn 1988), pp.631–47; and A Adamthwaite, 'Britain and the World, 1945–9: The View from the FO', *International Affairs* 61:2 (Spring 1985), pp.223–35.
4 'Note, 5 June 1943'. CAB 119/64. It is unclear who wrote this note, but its purpose was to outline the future requirements for 'post-hostilities'.
5 COS(43)199, 'Military Problems Arising on the Cessation of Hostilities', 25 July 1943. CAB 80/40.
6 JIC/485/43, D.Capel-Dunn to Howkins. CAB 119/64. Instead Capel-Dunn thought the focus should be more squarely aimed at 'the disintegration of the war'.
7 U3556/2231/70, 'Minute by S.Hood [FO]', 11 August 1943. FO 371/35449.
8 COS(43)224th Meeting (0), 23 September 1943. CAB 79/64.
9 PHP(43)1(0)(TofR), 'Effect of Russian Policy on British Strategic Interests', 5 October 1943. CAB 121/64.
10 R J Aldrich, *The Hidden Hand; Britain, America and Cold War Secret Intelligence* (London: John Murray, 2002). p.50; also, Lewis, *Changing Direction*. p.60.
11 JIC(44)60(0), 'Soviet Foreign Policy After the War', 11 February 1944. CAB 81/120.
12 JIC/334/44, 'Soviet Foreign Policy After the War', 27 February 1944. CAB 176/3.
13 C Bekes, 'Soviet Plans to Establish the COMINFORM in Early 1946: New Evidence from the Hungarian Archives', *Cold War International History Project* Bulletin 10 (1998), pp.135–6.
14 JIC(44)105(0)(FINAL), 'Soviet Foreign Policy After the War', 20 March 1944. CAB 81/121.
15 PHP(43)1(0)(Final), 'Effect of Soviet Policy on British Strategic Interests', 1 May 1944. CAB 81/45.
16 COS(44)172nd Meeting (0), 25 May 1944. CAB 79/75.
17 PHP(43)13(0)(Final), 'Effect of Soviet Policy on British Strategic Interests', 6 June 1944. CAB 81/45.
18 Note by L.Hollis, 13 June 1944. CAB 121/64.
19 N1829/26/G38, Note by C.F.A.Warner, 22 February 1944. FO 371/43284.
20 N1829/26/G38, Note by V.Cavendish-Bentinck, 23 February 1944. FO 371/43284.

21 N1437/26/G38, Note by V.Cavendish-Bentinck, 10 March 1944. FO 371/43284.
22 Howarth, *Intelligence Chief.* p.193.
23 N1437/26/G38, Note by V.Cavendish-Bentinck, 10 March 1944. FO 371/43284.
24 For instance see Folly, *Churchill, Whitehall and the Soviet Union.* pp.44–47.
25 Note by V.Cavendish-Bentinck, 17 April 1944. FO 1093/252.
26 E.G.N.Rushbrooke to V.Cavendish-Bentinck, 27 April 1944. FO 1093/252.
27 J.A.Sinclair to V.Cavendish-Bentinck, 16 May 1944. FO 1093/252.
28 C.F.A.Warner to P.N.Loxley, 3 May 1944. FO 1093/252.
29 Note by O.Sargent, 14 July 1944. FO 1093/252.
30 Folly, *Churchill, Whitehall and the Soviet Union.* pp.127–8.
31 A copy of the final report is in FO 1093/252. See Jeffery, *MI6.* pp.599–623 for more information.
32 D.Capel-Dunn to V.Cavendish-Bentinck, 8 October 1944. FO 1093/188.
33 U6254/748/G70. Note by G.Jebb, 15 June 1944. FO 371/40741A.
34 U6254/748/G70. Note by V.Cavendish-Bentinck, 16 June 1944. FO 371/40741A.
35 V.Cavendish-Bentinck to O.Sargent, 9 October 1944. FO 1093/188.
36 U6791/748/G70. Note by V.Cavendish-Bentinck, 18 July 1944. FO 371/40741A.
37 U6793/748/G70. L.Hollis to G.Jebb, 27 July 1944. FO 371/40741A.
38 U6793/748/G70. Note by V.Cavendish-Bentinck, 31 July 1944. FO 371/40741A.
39 PHP(44)20(0)Final, 'USSR – Questionnaire to JIC', 11 August 1944. CAB 81/45. This includes a detailed set of questions put to the JIC by the PHP.
40 JIC(44)366(0)FINAL(Limited Circulation), 'Russian Capabilities in Relation to the Strategic Interests of the British Commonwealth', 22 August 1944. CAB 81/124.
41 U6875/748/G70. Note by J.G.Ward, 16 August 1944. FO 371/40741A.
42 P.Davison to A.T.Cornwall-Jones [BJSM Washington], 30 August 1944. CAB 122/1566.
43 U7618/748/G70. Note by J.G.Ward, 19 September 1944. FO 371/40741A.
44 The relevant paper, PHP(44)17(0)Revise(Revised Draft) was revised again and eventually distributed as PHP(44)27.
45 U7841/748/G70. Note by J.G.Ward, 15 September 1944. FO 371/40741A.
46 The paper in question is PHP(44)23(0)(Final), 'Procedure for Assessing the Size of Post-War Forces Report', 3 October 1944. CAB 81/54.
47 U7619/748/G70. V.Cavendish-Bentinck to J.G.Ward, 18 September 1944. FO 371/40741A.
48 U7619/748/G70. Note by J.G.Ward, 25 September 1944. FO 371/40741A.
49 PHP(44)23(0)(Final), 'Procedure for Assessing the Size of Post-War Forces Report', 3 October 1944. CAB 81/54.
50 P.Davison to A.T.Cornwall-Jones, 21 September 1944. CAB 122/1566. Emphasis in original.
51 This comes from Lewis, *Changing Direction.* p.136.
52 JIC(44)56th Meeting (0), 24 October 1944. CAB 81/92. There are two versions of the paper, some two months apart. The JIC met to discuss it at an extraordinary meeting on 26 October, but there are no further details. No minutes of the meeting have been preserved, and the relevant secretariat paperwork has since been destroyed.
53 The original version was JIC(44)442(0)(Draft), 'Russia's Strategic Interests from the Point of View of Her Security', 18 October 1944. CAB 81/125.
54 JIC(44)467(0)(Final), 'Russia's Strategic Interests and Intentions from the Point of View of Her Security', 18 December 1944. CAB 81/126.
55 COS(44)411th Meeting(0), 27 December 1944. CAB 79/84.
56 Aldrich, *Hidden Hand.* p.57.
57 O.G.Sargent to L.C.Hollis, 22 January 1945. CAB 121/64.
58 COS(45)29th Meeting, 26 January 1945. CAB 79/29.
59 N678/20/G38. Note by V.Cavendish-Bentinck, 4 January 1945. FO 371/47860.
60 Folly, *Churchill, Whitehall and the Soviet Union.* p.142.

61 WP(45)156, 'Soviet Foreign Policy', 12 March 1945. CAB 121/64.

62 U3390/36/G70. Note by G.Wilson, 12 May 1945. FO 371/50775. The paper in question was PHP(45)29(0), 'Security of the British Empire'.

63 U4024/36/G70. Various notes on file. FO 371/50775.

64 JIC(45)25th Meeting(0), 10 April 1945. CAB 81/93.

65 JIC(45)148(0)(Final)(Limited Circulation), 'Russian Strength on 1st July, 1945', 8 May 1945. CAB 81/128.

66 JIC(45)163(0)(Revised Final), 'Relations with the Russians', 23 May 1945. CAB 81/129.

67 JIC(45)268(0)(Final), 'Requirements from SIS', 5 October 1945. CAB 81/130.

68 JIC(45)261(0)(Revised Final), 'Russian Policy Towards Finland, Hungary, Romania, Bulgaria and Italy', 28 August 1945. CAB 81/130.

69 E Athanassopoulou, *Turkey: Anglo-American Security Interests, 1945–1952* (London: Frank Cass, 1999).

70 A A Ulunian, 'Soviet Cold War Perceptions of Turkey and Greece, 1945–58', *Cold War History* 3:2 (2003), p.39.

71 COS(45)244th Meeting, 9 October 1945. CAB 79/40.

72 JIC(45)289(0)(Final), 'The Russian Threat to Turkey', 6 October 1945. CAB 81/131.

73 JIC(46)1(0)(Final)(Revise), 'Russia's Strategic Interests and Intentions', 1 March 1946. CAB 81/132.

74 COS(46)32nd Meeting, 27 February 1946. CAB 121/64.

75 L.C.Hollis to Prime Minister, 7 March 1946. PREM 8/342.

76 COS(46)83(0), 'Strategic Intentions – Assumptions for Planning Purposes', 14 March 1946. CAB 121/64. It is interesting to note that Sargent sent a draft of his letter to Harold Caccia before submitting it to the COS. Details in FO 1093/357.

77 Secondary sources appear vague on whether Soviet troops were actually inside Turkey at this time.

78 JIC(46)21(0)(Final), 'Implications of Recent Russian Movements in South East Europe', 16 March 1946. CAB 81/132.

79 JIC(46)24(0)(Final), 'Implications of Recent Russian Movements in Persia', 16 March 1946. CAB 81/132.

80 On this latter point see No.761, FO to Moscow, 12 March 1946. PREM 8/342.

81 No.759, FO to Moscow, 12 March 1946. PREM 8/342.

82 It is reported in the first of these reviews that the decision was taken at the meeting on 27 March 1946, though it adds that it was 'not recorded in the minutes'. See JIC(46)35(0) (T. of R.), 'Russian Troop Movements in South East Europe and Persia', 27 March 1946. CAB 81/132.

83 JIC(46)35(0)(Final), 'Russian Troop Movements in South East Europe and Persia', 6 April 1946. CAB 81/132.

84 Following his series of telegrams from Moscow he returned to London to brief the JIC in May and again in August 1946.

85 S Greenwood, 'Frank Roberts and the 'Other' Long Telegram: The View from the British Embassy in Moscow, March 1946', *The Journal of Contemporary History*, 25 (1990), pp.103–22.

86 N3812/605/G38. No.1092, Moscow to FO, 21 March 1946. FO 371/56831.

87 N3742/605/G38. Note by T. Brimelow [FO, later the PUS], 23 March 1946. FO 371/56831.

88 N3742/605/G38. No.1090, Moscow to FO, 21 March 1946. FO 371/56831.

89 N4544/605/G38. JIC Middle East to JIC London, 29 March 1946. FO 371/56831. For a subsequent view see JIC/1243/46, 'Russian Anti-British Activities in the Middle East', 10 September 1946. CAB 176/12.

90 N3756/605/G38. Note by R.M.A.Hankey, 25 March 1946. FO 371/56831.

91 Copies of this abound in the archives. One version can be found in N6344/605/G38. FO 371/56832.

92 JIC(46)44(0)(Final), 'Russian Troop Movements in South-East Europe and Persia', 27 April 1946. CAB 81/133.

93 JIC(46)56(0)(Final), 'Russian Troop Movements in South-East Europe and Persia', 17 June 1946. CAB 81/133.

94 JIC(46)55(0)(Final), 'Situation in South Persia', 7 June 1946. CAB 81/33.

95 For instance see COS(46)82nd Meeting, 24 May 1946. CAB 79/48.

96 N4157/97/38. Notes by T.Brimelow, 29 March 1946 and C.F.A.Warner, 5 April 1946. FO 371/56763.

97 JIC(46)38(0)(Final)(Revise), 'Russia's Strategic Interests and Intentions in the Middle East', 14 June 1946. CAB 81/132.

98 COS(46)90th Meeting, 7 June 1946. CAB 79/49.

99 COS(46)77th Meeting, 15 May 1946. CAB 79/48.

100 H.A.Caccia to O.Sargent, 22 February 1946. FO 1093/357. (Emphasis in original)

101 'General Review of Intelligence Concerning Russian Military Activities in Europe and the Middle East', 14 May 1946. CAB 121/64.

102 JIC(46)76(0)(FINAL), 'Russia's Strategic Interests and Intentions in the Middle East', 22 August 1946. CAB 81/134.

103 For a slightly outdated but excellent examination see J W Young, *Britain, France and the Unity of Europe, 1945–51* (Leicester: Leicester University Press, 1984).

104 COS(46)129th Meeting, 23 August 1946. CAB 121/64.

105 G.Mallaby [Ministry of Defence] to L.Hollis, 28 August 1946. CAB 121/64.

106 JIC/1181/46, 'Russian Strategic Interests and Intentions – Middle East', 28 August 1946. CAB 81/94.

107 A copy is in COS(46)242(0), 'Middle East – Propaganda Activities', 9 October 1946. CAB 80/102.

108 JIC/1440/46, 'Anti-British Subversive Activities', 22 October 1946. CAB 81/94.

109 C/172, 'C' to L.Hollis, 28 March 1946. FO 1093/347.

110 JIC/406/46, 'SOE Operational Planning', 1 April 1946. FO 1093/347.

111 JIC(46)100(0), 'Anti-British Subversive Activities – Middle East', 18 November 1946. CAB 81/134.

112 Aldrich. *Hidden Hand*. pp.122–32. See also the Terms of Reference in FO 371/56885 and R Merrick, 'The Russia Committee of the British FO and the Cold War, 1946–47', *Journal of Contemporary History* 20 (1985), pp.453–68.

113 Howarth, *Intelligence Chief.* p.198.

114 For instance, COS to JSM Washington, 16 September 1946. CAB 121/64.

115 JIC/1218/46, 'Russian Strategic Interests and Intentions – Middle East', 5 August 1946. CAB 176/12.

116 JIC(46)104(0)(Final), 'Foreign Assistance to the Greek Communists', 9 December 1946. CAB 81/134.

117 JIC(46)107(0)(Final), 'Movements of Russian Troops Outside the USSR Except in the Far East', 31 December 1946. CAB 81/134.

118 JIC(46)70, 'The Spread of Communism Throughout the World and the Extent of its Direction from Moscow', 23 September 1946. CAB 81/133.

119 For an interesting account see R Frazier, 'Did Britain Start the Cold War? Bevin and the Truman Doctrine', *The Historical Journal* 27:3 (1984), pp.715–27.

9 The Emergence and Stabilisation of the Cold War, 1947–1957

By the start of 1947 there was no doubt that the Soviet Union represented the primary threat to the United Kingdom. The cementing of the Iron Curtain and the Cold War fronts would have surprised few. For the JIC there was a serious and practical issue: prior to the outbreak of war in 1939 intelligence on Nazi Germany had been seriously lacking and the JIC was adamant that a similar situation should not occur again. But it faced a major hurdle in the shape of the Soviet Union. The problem was penetration – how could accurate, timely and reliable intelligence be procured against such an inaccessible target? As Churchill famously had stated in 1939, Russia was a 'riddle, wrapped in a mystery, inside an enigma'.

As the Cold War intensified a series of hot points arose. So, too, did the value and importance of intelligence. What might trigger a Soviet assault? Would the threat be an external military attack or a political assault from the inside? How could the defence of UK mainland be balanced against securing the interests of the territories overseas? Such questions continued to preoccupy a succession of JIC members, particularly the concern over when and where the Soviet Union might attack and whether intelligence would be able to provide any warning. Underpinning everything was the sticky question of resources. The JIC took it upon itself to lobby the COS Committee regularly with requests for more men, more money, and more operations.

By 1947 the Soviet Union had become priority number one but the belated Whitehall recognition of this was to be reflected, in a practical manner, in the means by which intelligence could, or rather could not, be collected. A succession of events served to highlight just how crucial good intelligence coverage was: from the Berlin Blockade, through the Korean War, the death of Stalin and Khrushchev's denunciation speech, to the Hungarian revolution in 1956. The JIC, as the hub of the intelligence and planning machinery, was central to post-war deliberations, yet a major problem remained throughout: how could forecasts be produced in the face of a compartmentalised, security-conscious and difficult to penetrate target? This was the problem facing both Humint and Sigint operations.

By the mid-1950s these efforts had achieved some success, and the level of intelligence coverage of the Soviet Union had significantly improved. At the same time, with relations having reached something of a plateau, the Cold War stabilised with the geo-strategic battle lines now drawn. Increasingly the JIC became more concerned with questions of a political nature, less so of a military kind, and accordingly the JIC underwent something of a transformation, leaving its COS home behind and eventually moving to the Cabinet Office.

Improving Intelligence

A theme highlighted continually in post-war JIC assessments of the Soviet Union, was the deficiency in intelligence coverage. This must have been felt particularly acutely given the contrast with the overwhelming successes of penetrating Nazi Germany. In fact, operations against Germany were a high point in intelligence collection, and the differences between the gathering of information in times of peace and times of war were not lost on senior civil servants, including the Cabinet Secretary, Sir Norman Brook.[1] In a 1950 review, at the height of the concerns over collecting intelligence, the JIC made a point of stressing the 'wartime advantages now lacking':

(a)   Adequate numbers of suitably trained agents ready to face the risk involved.
(b)   Widespread dissident elements within the target countries, prepared to facilitate the work of SIS agents.
(c)   Increased staff and funds.
(d)   Acceptance of diplomatic incidents.
(e)   The infiltration of agents, mainly by air, but to some extent by submarine.
(f)   A wider use of wireless communications by agents.[2]

Compounding matters was the nature of the Soviet state, with its characteristics of totalitarian leadership, strict compartmentalisation, and obsession with security. Recognising the difficulties in gathering information generally, the JIC therefore paid great attention to efforts on how to improve intelligence coverage.

In 1944 Victor Cavendish-Bentinck had played a central role in reconfiguring SIS for the post-war world, culminating in the Bland Report (see chapter 8). Crucial to these deliberations had been an attempt to gauge the contours of the post-war international environment, specifically where SIS's effort would have to be focussed. The result had been an almost total shift in priority and resources eastwards towards the Soviet Union. Despite this there were strict FO regulations on how SIS should tackle its priorities. According to the Bland Report, there was an FO edict that whilst Britain and Russia were wartime allies, SIS should not collect intelligence inside Russia. Importantly, the report continued that 'this restriction need not, however, preclude SIS from endeavouring to obtain intelligence data about Russia from outside that country'.[3]

The feasibility of this was discussed at the end of the war in the summer of 1945 by 'C' and several leading FO officials, including the new JIC Chairman Harold Caccia. The issue was clear, for as 'C' complained to the FO, 'to be told that intelligence in regard to what is happening inside Russia is of supreme importance and to be denied leave to act inside the Russian frontier is to invalidate the directive from the outset'.[4] The decision on whether this practice should continue ultimately lay with the PUS in the FO, Sir Alexander Cadogan. The difficulty was that in late 1945 the policy of the FO remained one of conciliation and collaboration (see chapter 8). Thus, 'C' was informed he could continue to collect intelligence from outside the Soviet Union, but could not have a permanent base inside. To help temper the impact of this self-imposed restriction it was decided that SIS should be allowed to set up 'representation' in Bulgaria, Romania and Hungary, in addition to those already in existence elsewhere.[5] This ruling was re-affirmed in March 1946, which is perhaps surprising given that by this time FO views towards the Soviet Union had hardened.[6]

The effect of these decisions would be long lasting. One of the JIC's most important tasks was the setting, and regular review of, requirements and priorities for the collection agencies. Consequently the JIC played a central role in the affairs of SIS and GCHQ at a strategic level. This process, about which virtually nothing has hitherto been declassified, has been a serious gap in public understanding of the JIC and its activities. In early 1946 the JIC undertook a 'statistical assessment' of SIS reporting. This task, which would become common practice in ensuing years, involved a comparison of the SIS product with the 'effort and cost' involved, both to see where gaps existed and also to highlight where effort should be re-directed.[7] A similar exercise was undertaken for Sigint. A COS ruling instructed that a significant proportion of GCHQ's effort should be directed towards 'Russian and satellite traffic'. In his 1946 review of the Sigint organisation, Air Chief Marshal Sir Douglas Evill noted that to improve penetration, increased means were needed, and he concluded: 'the overall objectives of Sigint are always likely to exceed the reach of the resources that can be made available'.[8]

The impact of the Evill review did not become apparent until the following year. In assisting Evill in 1947 with his post-war review of the intelligence machinery (see chapter 6) the JIC prepared a summary of the British intelligence organisation, together with a note on 'areas inadequately covered'. Of these the largest missing dimension was the Soviet Union. In its submission to Evill the JIC carefully outlined the problem:

> the study of Russia was only started seriously within the last two years. The virtual absence of the most elementary and basic forms of intelligence on that country meant that there was, and still is, a very great leeway to be made up concerning Russia as compared with the rest of the world. Furthermore, we find the greatest difficulty in remedying this situation . . . the problem of Russia [is] so difficult as to differ in kind from the problems with which we are faced in any other country where we are attempting to procure intelligence . . . in general, over the whole field, the principal limitations to procuring intelligence are the lack of cover, the lack of money and shortages in trained personnel at home and in the field.

Furthermore, the JIC continued, not only was the covert gathering of intelligence difficult, but it was extremely hard to find any open source information.[9] Additionally, SIS reported that although they were receiving 'copious' amounts of political and military reporting, the 'quality is not all that we could hope for'.[10]

By the spring of 1948 the situation had not improved. At the instigation of the naval intelligence representative, it was decided that from that stage onwards, the Deputy Directors' meeting of the JIC should regularly include an agenda item 'devoted to the consideration of long term problems and of how to improve the procurement of intelligence'.[11] Despite this, little was done to address any specific issues and in mid-1949 the subject was once more raised by the senior JIC.

By this time the Cold War had deepened. The 1947 declaration of the Truman Doctrine and Marshall Plan had resulted in something of a split. Western European nations were quick to grasp the finances on offer as were, at least initially, several Eastern European states but these, under the watchful eye of Moscow, rapidly rescinded their requests. In practice this meant that the division of Europe was now determined. Economically dependent to either American or Soviet masters, the battle lines of Europe were drawn. Yet for Britain, the issue of military alliances continued to be unresolved. With uncertainty over the US position, Britain sided initially with the French, signing a treaty of alliance at Dunkirk in March 1947. This was followed a year later by the Treaty of Brussels, a mutual defence agreement signed by the UK, France, Belgium, Luxemburg and Holland. Its intention was to present a common bulwark in Western Europe against possible Soviet expansion.

The signature of the Treaty of Brussels in March 1948 was opportune. A month before the Communist Party of Czechoslovakia, with Soviet support, had come to power following a coup, and in April the communists lost the general election in Italy following significant involvement by the Americans. Just a few months later, in June, Soviet forces cut off transportation links between West Berlin and the outside world. A reflection of this deterioration in East-West relations was the creation of the Western Union Defence Organisation in September 1948, a dedicated military entity headed by Field Marshal Viscount Montgomery. Significantly this did not include any US representation or involvement, something considered integral to the defence of Western Europe by its signatories. Thus, in Washington in April 1949, the North Atlantic Treaty was signed, effectively creating NATO. Several months later, in October 1949, the communists triumphed in the Chinese Civil War and proclaimed the birth of the People's Republic of China (PRC). These events ensured that the Churchillian 'Iron Curtain' had extended across the globe.

Against this backdrop the JIC once more addressed the intelligence coverage of the agencies, and whether it was good enough to be able to uncover any Russian plans for war. The JIC's findings did not make for pleasant reading. SIS material, it was concluded, was 'often unreliable and lacking in factual information', and Sigint coverage was hardly any better, though there was a realisation that this was primarily hampered by a lack of resources. Menzies, as 'C', was upset that a paper describing SIS's performance as 'disappointing' would be passed to the COS.

After a debate it was decided to delete the word but let the criticism stand. Throughout the report and the discussion, it was constantly emphasised just how hard a target the Soviet Union presented. Major General Kenneth Strong, the Director of the JIB, suggested that 'it was most undesirable that the confidence of the Chiefs of Staff should be undermined in this respect.' As such, the final report was 'tempered'.[12]

The report itself, as well as identifying the inadequacies in coverage, concluded that unless improvements were made, then 'little or no physical' indication could be expected before hostilities were launched.[13] Six months later the JIC once more reviewed the situation, to see whether its report had had any discernible impact. Some of the earlier identified shortcomings were highlighted – particularly the failings of SIS and the 'decline' in Sigint coverage – but the ban on 'clandestine air reconnaissance' (in other words, overflights of the Soviet Union) was given greater prominence than previously. What could be done? To the JIC the way ahead lay clearly with improving Sigint coverage: 'it must be constantly borne in mind that Sigint is, with certain exceptions, our most important means of penetrating the Soviet Union.'[14]

Despite dire warnings, within a year the quantity and quality of intelligence coverage afforded by the agencies had deteriorated still further. Without further resources, the JIC reported, the situation would continue to worsen.[15] The result was, in the JIC's words, that 'we are seriously concerned about the inadequacy of intelligence.'[16] In response, a new sub-committee of the JIC was created to examine methods to increase the flow of defectors. In addition, the LSIB, the oversight committee for Sigint, produced a report on how the Sigint effort might be improved: the central issue, as would so often be the case, was resources.[17]

At the end of November 1950 Patrick Reilly, the JIC Chairman, met the COS. He summarised the JIC's work over the previous eighteen months, the various surveys that had been produced and the recommendations that had emerged. One point he was keen to highlight was the challenge faced in penetrating Soviet communications. A recent JIC survey had made this explicitly clear:

> We and the Americans are not able to read currently any Soviet high grade cypher material. A considerable research effort is being made but the outcome is unpredictable and Sigint is unlikely to read in the foreseeable future secret messages dealing directly with Soviet intentions, war plans, war preparations . . . [our efforts are] limited by lack of manpower and accommodation and by the difficulties of hearing the more distant and low powered transmissions from existing interception sites.[18]

The COS accepted the difficulty of the task being faced, but told Reilly that the intelligence obtained was 'insufficient'. They therefore approved the numerous recommendations suggested by the LSIB, principally aimed at increasing the capabilities of GCHQ.[19]

Yet problems persisted and herein lay the nub of the issue: there was relatively good information on the nations other than the Soviet Union in the Eastern bloc, and adequate material on the Order of Battle, capabilities and methods of the Soviet armed forces; the problem lay with maintaining continued access to intelligence to allow regular assessment of senior figures, both military and political.[20] Furthermore, even where there had been high-level successes, such as the Sigint operation Venona, the result was very limited.[21] Thus, the collection agencies could fulfil some of the requirements placed upon them, but they could not answer the most critical questions that constantly plagued the JIC: would any warning be given if the Russians prepared for hostilities, and would this be picked up and transmitted in time?

Further pleas were issued in early 1952 by GCHQ, which were raised through the LSIB and passed via the JIC to the COS and the PUS in the FO, for another increase in the size and scale of its efforts. Once more the argument was made that Sigint alone offered the means by which 'we should thus improve our ability to fight the "Cold War"'.[22] Interestingly, the basis for this was not that GCHQ could necessarily penetrate the most secret cyphers, but rather, as its Director later stated, 'the cumulative intelligence value of collating a large quantity of individually innocuous messages'.[23] This was to lead to a system of traffic analysis by which it could be determined which communications were active but not what they were saying.

The JIC and COS endorsed the LSIB paper, which was subsequently transmitted to the Minister of Defence and the Prime Minister for approval. In tandem a new committee approved its suggestions. Created in early 1952 the 'Bridges Committee of Permanent Secretaries on Intelligence' had been convened to look, primarily, at the financing of the intelligence services. The group, chaired by the Cabinet Secretary, Sir Edward Bridges, and including the Permanent Secretaries of the Ministry of Defence, Home Office and FO, would subsequently become known as the 'Committee of Permanent Secretaries on Intelligence Services' (PSIS), meeting relatively frequently from this point onwards.[24]

At the same time the JIC presented a sombre and very depressing picture to the COS Committee of how well Britain's intelligence services were faring vis-à-vis the Soviet target:

> Soviet security maintains a high level of efficiency and we obtain little information directly revealing the policy and intentions of the Soviet leaders . . . to sum up, although our basic knowledge of the political and economic life of these countries is sound, we are less and less able to keep pace with developments in their armed forces and in science. Thus, in spite of undiminished efforts on the part of agencies, it is becoming increasingly difficult to forecast intentions and to estimate capabilities . . . the standard of our intelligence, upon which we must largely rely for guidance in both the "cold" war and a possible "hot" war, is much too low . . . the general position continues to deteriorate. The acceptance of greater risks and the provision of greater resources are clearly necessary if we are to be in a position to assess more adequately for the Chiefs of Staff the intentions and capabilities of the Communist bloc.[25]

Such a downbeat assessment of Britain's intelligence abilities cannot have made for welcome reading; perhaps as a result, the JIC's recommendation for further, more invasive operations was approved.[26] A subsequent letter from the JIC Chairman, outlining a radical expansion of GCHQ's capabilities beyond those approved by PSIS, was also endorsed by the COS.[27] Underpinning this was a belief, shared by the JIC members, that Sigint continued to be 'its most valuable source of intelligence, both actual and potential.'[28]

To assist matters the JIC created the new 'Sub-Committee on Measures to Improve Intelligence'. It was to meet monthly with the same departments represented as on the JIC itself; the sub-committee was tasked to keep under review efforts to improve intelligence collection.[29] The sub-committee's first report was issued as a JIC paper in October 1952. Like earlier studies it began by outlining the difficulties in penetrating a system such as that of the Soviet Union. Furthermore, it drew a useful distinction about the conditions in which intelligence was sought: 'we are operating under what are virtually war conditions, but against a backdrop of peacetime restrictions and economics'. It argued the need for more money, more men, more research, greater flexibility and the acceptance of 'risks' in collecting intelligence. To the JIC these recommendations were vital, not just for increasing knowledge about the Soviet Union, but also for the acquisition of enough material with which the UK could hold its own with the United States' intelligence community.[30] To these the COS agreed.[31]

The Sub-Committee on Measures to Improve Intelligence was abolished in late 1953 after holding eleven meetings. According to its Chairman, its main purpose had been to produce 'new ideas for improving the quality and amount of our intelligence', but it was reported that there had been 'little or no achievement'.[32] For Patrick Dean, the JIC Chairman, there were other, equally valid, reasons for its dissolution. The proposals in the annual JIC papers had, generally, been approved by the COS Committee and so, as Dean confided to Colonel Eric Searight, the JIC Secretary, 'I do not think we need feel dissatisfied.' The issue, for Dean, was that 'we have done so largely by painting gloomy pictures of the state of our intelligence. I doubt whether it would be wise to keep harping on this in reports to the Chiefs.'[33] This was clear evidence of how finely attuned the JIC FO Chairman was to wider Whitehall concerns and perceptions, in much the same way as had been his predecessors.

In late 1953 the JIC accepted that there were three major failings with its coverage of the Soviet Union:

(a) inadequacy of the sources on which we must rely to give early warning of Soviet aggression;
(b) our lack of information on Soviet intentions and plans;
(c) the inadequacy of our coverage in the USSR.[34]

Assessments such as these were used by the COS to urge Ministers to approve increasingly daring collection operations.[35] For the JIC, if nothing else, they were seen as 'mind clearing exercises'.[36] Within six months, however, the JIC could report to the COS that efforts to improve intelligence coverage had actually paid off. Information on the strength of Soviet armed forces was known with 'reasonable accuracy'; more was known about the economy; and although it was accepted that there was no reliable information on strategic planning, the JIC did 'believe that we should be able to report on preparations for war'.[37]

By 1955 the gathering of intelligence had been bolstered by the fruits of photographic reconnaissance and FERRET flights.[38] Yet despite the increased coverage of the Soviet Union and its satellites, doubts remained, particularly in the mind of Patrick Dean. For the JIC the main requirement was to report when and where a Soviet attack might take place and to ensure that there was adequate intelligence to provide advance warning. As the Cold War progressed it had become increasingly clear that specific events could not be treated in isolation but rather as part of a larger, integrated conflict. Thus, Dean queried, 'are our intelligence priorities, targets and methods properly directed and conducted to meet this attack?' Dean, a conscientious and particularly insightful Chairman, thought not and that therefore 'this suggests to my mind serious questions', including:

(a) Are we devoting far too much effort proportionately to gathering and collating intelligence which would solely or primarily be of use for global war?

(b) Is not too much effort being devoted to the collection of too wide a variety of intelligence, much of which, especially in the case of Sigint, is unlikely to be usable?

(c) Are we not losing sight of the essentials, i.e., Sino-Soviet major intentions, for the sake of a mass of detailed information, much of it of short range and relatively low quality?

(d) Are we not looking too much to Sigint and MI6 for information, much of which could be more simply obtained by overt methods, e.g. travellers, Attachés, press readings and so on?

(e) Are we being unrealistic or dishonest in assessing our chances of obtaining first class direct intelligence on the highest priority targets?

(f) Are our methods of procuring and collating overt intelligence given insufficient centralised organisation and direction to enable us to foresee and present <u>as a whole</u> the essentials both for possible global war and for Cold War purposes?

To Dean the answer to all of these questions was 'yes'. Therefore a change of emphasis was required and, more broadly, a change in expectations of what the intelligence community could hope to deliver. Efforts should be 'concentrated on those targets which are:

(i) most likely to give us reliable evidence about these [Sino-Soviet] intentions, and

(ii) reasonably within our compass.[39]

Dean's paper was circulated to the rest of the JIC for discussion in preparation for a meeting with the COS. The reaction of the rest of the JIC is not known. The relevant minute, given its acute sensitivity, was stored separately and has not survived. The only reference in the JIC minutes was to the postponement of any discussion with the COS. This reveals much about the JIC and the direction of British intelligence. For Dean, too much effort and responsibility was being placed on the intelligence community to be the watchdogs, to warn of the first sign of preparations for war, and this was simply unrealistic given the practical difficulties of obtaining high-grade, decisive, intelligence. Clearly Dean felt that insufficient emphasis was being placed on overt means of gathering information. These enquiries would prove to be timely.

Estimating the Inestimable

With intelligence on the Soviet Union seriously lacking, how could the drafters in the JIS produce informed assessments of Soviet policies and intentions? Wing Commander Cecil Alldis, the JIC Assistant Secretary in the early 1950s, recalled something of the difficulties faced: 'it was recognised that what we had to do was get into the Soviet mind ... we tried very hard to do so ... the problem was how.' The practical effect of this was that JIS papers on Soviet intentions were often subjected to far more critical analysis than other papers, simply because there was less information on which to base conclusions. Frequently, as a result, JIS drafters would be called into the JIC meetings themselves to defend their judgments.[40]

Despite a lack of high-grade reliable intelligence, a substantial number of papers on Soviet intentions were produced from 1947 onwards. JIC papers now reflected the sombre environment in which they were produced: the Soviet Union was no longer an ally, co-operation (of any form) might not be possible, and the existence of a hostile and aggressive Stalin had to be recognised. Rarely did the JIC record on paper its concerns about forecasts of Soviet intentions. A report produced by the JIC in 1951 was the exception: an innovative and extremely interesting review, re-examining its past assessments of Communist intentions since 1947. Aside from constant references to gaps in intelligence coverage, this one paper is the only attempt to address the quality of intelligence analysis, and even then it stops far short of an examination of methodological issues. The rationale behind the study was made clear in its introduction: 'in order to determine to what extent they have been proved correct by subsequent events and, in cases where their conclusions have been proved wrong, to discover why false conclusions were drawn.'[41] In the period 1947–51, the study concluded that thirty-three different assessments had either proved to be correct, or at least had not yet proven to be incorrect. In comparison only three had conclusively been wrong and the JIC examined these to identify what had caused the mis-judgment.

Despite the favourable statistics, it was conceded that 'our assessment of Communist intentions has not however, been as good as the small number of our miscalculations suggests. In the first place we failed altogether to forecast the

Blockade of Berlin in 1948 and the attack on South Korea in 1950.' Furthermore, a comment was made on the nature and tone of the assessments themselves: 'We have also, in many cases, drafted our conclusions somewhat equivocally and so allowed ourselves a fairly wide margin of error. The present tendency is to make the conclusions more definite'.[42]

On the Korean War (see chapter 11) the JIC had concluded that the Chinese would not 'embark on operations'.[43] The reasoning behind this, not based on intelligence but rather on a reading of the communist leadership, was that the Chinese would not dare risk war with the UN. However, just a few weeks after the assessment was approved, the Chinese army had swept into Korea and attacked the UN forces based there. How had the JIC managed to get its assessment completely wrong? Once more the 1951 review was very honest in its examination of the intelligence community's failings, and identified two factors as prevalent:

(a)   That our intelligence about Communist intentions in the Far East is even less adequate than our intelligence about the Soviet Union . . .; and
(b)   That we do not yet understand the mind of the Chinese Communist leaders.[44]

The report was approved by the JIC in December 1951, and the Secretary was tasked with circulating it 'for examination in Departments, in order that study should be made of the lessons to be learnt from previous intelligence appreciations and of measures to improve future estimates'.[45] Unfortunately such optimistic aspirations were never fully realised: despite efforts to improve the quality and quantity of collected intelligence, and with variations in the analytical process adopted, no in-depth study was commissioned to follow up on such recommendations.

Watching the Bear

How did the gaps in coverage translate into solid assessments? Throughout this period the JIC produced a mixture of papers which can roughly be divided into two types: the first concerned specific issues, areas where the Soviets posed an immediate or likely threat, and what might be expected to transpire; the second, and arguably more important, were the longer-term more strategic-looking forecasts of Soviet intentions and likelihood of launching hostilities. The latter was closely allied to assessments of Soviet military capabilities, discussed in the following chapter, yet underlying it was an examination of the rationale behind the Kremlin's actions. When would the Soviet Union launch a war? What actions might propel them? How would war come? And, did the Soviet calculation of what necessitated war match calculations in the West?

The conclusion reached in late 1946 had been that the Soviet Union would not risk war for five years; this was based on an examination of the Soviet economy and the overriding necessity for recovery and reconstruction (see chapter 8). In mid-1947 the JIC set itself the task of re-assessing the basis for this, predicated on two crucial questions: what was Russia trying to do and how far was she capable of doing it? The answer to the first question was clear: 'the Soviet leaders are inspired by the conviction that it is their long-term task to hasten the elimination of capitalism in all parts of the world'. This was not based on any hard intelligence, but rather on a reading of the 'published maxims of Lenin and Stalin'. The issue then, as the JIC posed implicitly in its second question, was how was this to be achieved? In a 66 page report the JIC set out its findings. With a pressing need to reconstruct the Russian economy, it was felt that policy would strive towards dependence on its own natural resources, and that until this was achieved Stalin would attempt to avoid war whilst continuing to establish a 'protective belt' around his borders and through the 'continued aggressive promotion of communism'. Thus, taking everything into account, it was unlikely that war would occur before 1955–60.[46]

The impact of this paper was not quite as the JIC had predicted. The conclusion that took hold was the projected date for war. In fact this date, some ten years hence, fitted neatly with those elements of post-war British planning that assumed the post-First World War 'ten year rule' still applied – that there would be no war for ten years, with the resultant impact on the development of domestic strategy and technology. By December 1947 discussion in the JIC focussed on what aspects might propel the Soviet Union into war before 1955–60, including miscalculation by or on behalf of the Soviet leadership, or if it thought conditions were so positive that war was perceived to be winnable.[47] These ideas were elaborated in a slightly longer paper which recommended that the COS Committee should approve the paper and authorise a wide circulation to clear up any misunderstanding.[48]

This judgement continued well into the 1950s. In a memorandum to the COS in 1955, the JIC Chairman Patrick Dean laid out his thoughts on 'The State of Our Intelligence'. The underlying rationale was that war was unlikely for five years – this was the JIC's view and it was shared by the COS and Ministers alike. By implication, then, the priorities for the intelligence community, as set by the JIC, were slightly outdated. It was now felt necessary to monitor long-term trends, not just to expect the sudden bolt out of the blue. Furthermore, with the broadening out of the Cold War and the increased use of proxies in Soviet policies, intelligence coverage had to extend further than the Soviet Union and China, and resources consequently needed to be spread to encompass the Middle East, Africa and beyond. The main threat, therefore, was 'a Cold War vigorously and flexibly conducted by the Communists'.[49] No longer was this a simple battle between West and East. How had this situation come about? To find an answer it is necessary to return to the late 1940s and consider the evolution of the Cold War following the Marshall Plan.

In January 1948 the JIC had its status elevated, received a new Charter and began to enjoy an enhanced standing across government (see chapter 6). In addition, the recommendations made by the Evill report had meant that a second JIS team was now in place. Nevertheless, the first major confrontation of the Cold War – the Soviet Blockade of Berlin – went completely undetected by the JIC until after it had actually begun. Coincidentally, just as the Soviets were making their final preparations, the JIC issued a paper, two months in the making, on 'Indications of Russian Preparedness for War'. An earlier American report on the same subject had produced a list of 112 different indicators that might suggest that the Soviet Union was ready to move. The JIC had revised this list to a mere 81 indicators, with the conclusion, on 18 June, that 'we believe the Russian armed forces to be in a high state of mobilisation and therefore able to undertake a limited offensive with little warning'.[50] Just a few days later the Soviet Union cut transport links (road, rail, and river) between the western sectors of Berlin and western Germany. Thus the classic situation existed: evidence that something was about to happen but no information on timing or location. Consequently, the JIC produced no advance warning of the Blockade.

The Blockade itself lasted for eleven months: from June 1948 to May 1949. The first reference to it by the JIC, albeit indirectly, was at the meeting of 2 July 1948. William Hayter, the Chairman, introduced the topic by stating that the 'general situation demanded constant vigilance', and therefore proposed the introduction of a short periodical report on 'Russian preparations for war'. This was a style of publication that had served the JIC well during the Second World War. The Committee agreed to the production of a quarterly series.[51] Within a fortnight, and despite deteriorating relations in Berlin, the JIC concluded that there was no evidence that the Soviet Union was preparing to launch hostilities. At the same time it was decided that the Committee should revisit this question every week.[52]

The Blockade of Berlin and the failure of the JIC to give any warning seems to have been something of a wake-up call, just as the fall of Norway had been in 1940. The COS demanded that the JIC produce a report on what might be done to anticipate any Soviet attack. This paralleled the concurrent debates on measures to improve intelligence and, more precisely, on the gaps in coverage. The subsequent report did little to allay fears, not least because it assessed 'the Russian armed forces to be in a high state of mobilisation and therefore able to undertake a limited offensive with little warning. Preparations for war on a larger scale might, however, become apparent, despite all attempts at concealment.'[53]

The first substantial attempt to place the Berlin Blockade within wider Soviet intentions was completed in early 1949. Despite Soviet sabre-rattling, events in Berlin revealed much to the JIC about the Soviet psyche. It was still judged that the Soviet leaders would wish to avoid war before 1956, and that if anything, the Berlin airlift had revealed the limits of Soviet policy, for despite their 'protests and threats' over the Western response, 'there has been no serious attempt to prevent it'. Germany was seen as a critical arena because it 'stands out as the most important single prize in the political and ideological struggle now in progress between the Soviet Union and the West'.[54]

One analysis of the JIC records during this crisis argues that its assessments were 'reassuring rather than alarmist'.[55] For the JIC there were two issues in respect of the Blockade: the failure to predict it, and the ability, once underway, to provide a series of useful assessments. This pattern would be repeated often. What does this reveal about the JIC system? Firstly, it shows that it was able to adapt, relatively quickly, to developing situations. It also exposes something of the problems in identifying and reading Soviet intentions: a feeling that something was about to happen but no detailed information as to the specifics. Finally, it also underlines the steadying tone of balanced JIC forecasts. It is clear that the Foreign Secretary, Ernest Bevin, appreciated the JIC's views as Hayter, the Chairman, was tasked with personally briefing him on a weekly basis.[56] This was important, and the significance of Berlin should not be underestimated: at its meeting on 9 July 1948, for instance, the COS Committee even considered whether it was worth a war.[57]

Surprise Surprise

1948 was an important year in the course of the Cold War. Early that year, in Czechoslovakia, the Soviet-backed communist party seized power, while in Berlin the Soviet Union surprised the West with its Blockade. These two events were followed in 1949 and 1950 with more unexpected developments: the first test of a Soviet atomic device; the success of the communists in the Chinese civil war; and the outbreak of hostilities in Korea.[58] These momentous events influenced the JIC's survey of the world, of Soviet intentions, and the likelihood of war.

The first test of a Soviet nuclear device in August 1949, was between two and three years earlier than predicted, though the intelligence services were in a position to detect accurately and define the scale and nature of the detonation after the event.[59] The impact of the test, though important, was mitigated by the JIC's assessment that the Soviet Union would choose to avoid nuclear war whilst it built up an atomic arsenal. On the other hand, if war were to occur it would now be nuclear in character and the issue was one of whether any warning would be possible. The JIC was pessimistic: 'we would, however, emphasise that the decision as to whether or not the Soviet Union will initiate the use of atomic bombs in a war against the Western Powers will be taken by one man, or a small group of men . . . the decision is, therefore, unpredictable.'[60] This forecast would become particularly relevant with the death of Stalin.

The impact of Soviet atomic progress, the communist victory in China, and the outbreak of the Korean War hastened a fresh review of Soviet intentions, produced in November 1950. The lengthy report (over seventy single-spaced pages) began with an interesting description of the enemy: 'The Soviet Union can only be understood if it is realised that it is not merely, like Nazi Germany, a totalitarian dictatorship engaged in power politics, but a unique and abnormal member of international society, inspired by a dynamic ideology with strong international appeal'. The Soviet aim was again assessed to be the collapse of the capitalist world, but now the JIC predicted that 'the Soviet leaders are also convinced that the capitalist world, aware of the growing strength of Communism, is likely eventually to resort to force in an attempt to avert its own collapse.' Soviet policy would focus on security.[61] The COS Committee approved the paper, which was circulated across the senior echelons of the government.[62]

A further report at this time developed some of these themes further. Whilst recognising that the overthrow of the capitalist system was the ultimate Soviet goal, the question was how this might be pursued in the interim, and whether the Soviet Union thought that capitalism would collapse without the need for a major war. In the meantime it was assumed that more covert methods of warfare would be used, including ideological attack, subversion and fomenting civil war. Furthermore, given the Marxist-Leninist orthodoxy, the JIC assessment was that Moscow would assume that to avoid disaster, war would come at the instigation of the West in a final effort to defer defeat. Taken together, although an imminent war could not be ruled out, it was still thought that there would be no conflict before 1955.[63]

The invasion of South Korea by its northern neighbour had not been expected by the JIC (or the US). From the outset it was suspected that the North Korean regime was a 'puppet' of the Soviet Union, and taken together with recent developments in Berlin and Czechoslovakia, it suggested a shift in Soviet thinking. Thus, 'these developments indicated that the Soviet leaders had grown less sensitive to Western susceptibilities and to the danger of heightening the existing tension'.[64] Despite this rather sombre warning, the JIC assessments gave no indication that an attack was considered to be imminent nor that there were gaps in the intelligence coverage.

In September 1950 an innovative meeting took place between analysts from the British and American intelligence communities. Working from the same source material, both addressed the question of when the Soviet Union might choose to initiate a major war and both came up with different dates: the British thought a mid-1950s date most likely; the Americans concluded that an earlier date was more probable.[65] From the documentary record it is impossible to know what frameworks or analytical techniques were used, but the British were not overly impressed with the American conclusion. It was suggested that the COS digest the combined 107 page report and use it as a basis for discussions with the American JCS.[66] The COS did so and professed themselves pleased with the combined report (including the divergent UK/US views), but stated that it was 'not entirely a satisfactory document on which to base detailed plans'.[67]

The JIC reports were generally strong in their conclusions, but the firm nature of these assessments belies the serious gaps in intelligence coverage. Reading Soviet intentions was not, it would seem, based on any hard intelligence but rather on an analysis of how the situation might be perceived by the Politburo, from the ideology underpinning its goals, and an assumption of a growing Soviet determination to undermine the West through all measures short of outright conflict.[68] Most often, the changing nature and tone of the JIC assessments reflected a combination of an interpretation of Marxist-Leninist ideology on the one hand, and observed Soviet actions on the other. Therefore predictions based on past and existing practice were used to forecast the future, without any allowance for a sudden change in policy. Whilst in other contexts this might have been considered poor analytical tradecraft, in the case of the Soviet

Union – with the intelligence gaps and difficulties in penetrating effectively a one-person one-party state – there was simply no alternative.

Against this backdrop a fresh assessment was produced in early 1951. By now the initial shock of the Soviet testing of an atomic bomb, the victory of the Chinese communists and the surprise of the Korean War had receded. The JIC once more tried to assess developments from the Kremlin's perspective: the 'immense scale' of American and West German rearmament might be seen as threatening. This, together with the possession of a stockpile of atomic weapons (albeit small), might propel the Soviet Union into an early war, in order to strike before Western rearmament plans were complete. The JIC concluded that 'the period of greatest danger appears to be about the end of 1952.'[69] The COS approved the report and it was forwarded to the Minister of Defence and thence to the Defence Committee.[70]

The ramifications of the Korean War were to be felt far beyond the Korean peninsula, contributing to the belief in the JIC that the Cold War could not be seen in isolation. Events in the Middle East, Far East, Europe and Africa were all inter-connected. This was not an early precursor of the US domino theory, but rather a belief that disparate events had a common thread, that the hand of Moscow was everywhere, and that proxy conflicts were just as significant as major war.

Alexander Craig has written how it was 'largely the Korean War that alerted the Committee to the danger of other potential conflicts.'[71] In its examination of Soviet Cold War strategy, completed in early 1952, the JIC made clear that separate, isolated events, should be seen as parts of a bigger picture. At the instigation of the Directors of Plans, the JIC undertook to produce brief and regular assessments of 'sore spots' around the globe; what would subsequently become the 'Perimeter Review'.[72] The first set of these considered a varied and, on the face of it, rather bizarre mixture of regions: Germany, Finland, British Honduras, the Falkland Islands and Dependencies, Formosa, Spitsbergen and Austria.[73]

In late 1952 the JIC undertook a fresh review of Soviet actions. The earlier papers had used 1954 as a possible date for war but this had now slipped, for planning purposes, to 1955. Taking the world as a whole the results from a Western perspective were disheartening, for as the JIC detailed: continuing Western military efforts in Malaya, Korea, and Indochina were not encouraging, the communists had been successful in elections in India, and the signs indicated growing communist support in Persia. In addition there were indications of a growing communist presence in Egypt, and continued unrest in French North Africa, Kenya and South Africa. Yet despite these bleak observations, the JIC was relatively upbeat: 'it is also significant that, despite their subversive and aggressive activities in many spheres, whenever the Soviet leaders have been faced with a situation carrying a serious threat of conflict with the United States, eg in Korea and in Berlin, they have acted with great caution'. Taken as a whole, the JIC concluded, as in previous assessments, that the Soviet Union would avoid war itself whilst doing everything in its power to undermine the West.[74]

In this particular paper there is a footnote to the effect that the Admiralty was at odds with the rest of the Committee. One of the key factors behind the creation of the JIC, and indeed a central tenet of its and the Cabinet system of governance, was consensus: all intelligence appreciations should be produced on the basis of complete agreement, so that policymakers should only receive a unanimous view. The issue was one of whether 'the psychological effect of the growing preparations for war' would increase the likelihood of conflict. The Committee members felt that this was not significant in the period up to 1955, whereas the Admiralty thought it was. Whether or not the COS were aware of the divergence of opinion is not clear because in the file copy the footnote has been crossed out by hand.

The Demise of Uncle Joe

Underlying all forecasts and assessments was the continual problem of a dearth of reliable, high-level intelligence. The significance of this was clear. In an update to its November 1951 paper on the likelihood of war, the JIC stated that there had been no 'new aggressive action' by the Soviets, equally 'nor is there, or has there been, any intelligence which would suggest that action of an unambiguously aggressive character is imminent'.[75] Earlier JIC papers had concluded that no such warning might be received.

The JIC foresaw three types of attack and addressed what kind of warning might be expected:

(a)   Should the Kremlin decide to launch a surprise attack with existing resources, even though this would sacrifice all the advantages of complete partial mobilisation.

(b)   Should the Kremlin decide not to launch their attack until their full strength had been mobilised.

(c)   Should the Kremlin choose, or be compelled to strike a balance, between the advantages of surprise and full mobilisation.

Of these, case (a) – surprise attack – was clearly the most dangerous. At best it was felt that only a few hours advance warning would be received. Full mobilisation would inevitably affect other areas of Soviet economic and public life, so warning signs were thought to be identifiable. The Soviet Union would need forty-two days to completely mobilise its resources. For case (c) it was impossible to address warning times, given the varying timescale involved.[76] In a 'strictly limited circulation' supplement, the JIC also considered what different types of intelligence might reveal. The report identified thirty-four different factors that might indicate preparations, and commented on whether overt or different types of covert reporting might detect them. In the JIC's opinion, the chances of any advance positive indication being provided by intelligence was low.[77]

The JIC's paper was based on an earlier report by its 'Sub-Committee on Measures to Improve Intelligence'. Its conclusion had been explicit, albeit rather depressing, that 'with the resources at our [i.e. British intelligence] disposal, there were no special intelligence operations which could be mounted which would ensure that the intelligence required . . . would be provided in time to be of use, if indeed it could be obtained at all.'[78] The implications for both Patrick Dean and Geoffrey McDermott, the two FO officials most involved in intelligence matters, was clear. Approval for intelligence operations within and targeted at the Soviet Union had to be 'considered from the angle of the amount of irritation which they might cumulatively be causing the Russians . . . are they likely . . . to cause Soviet policy to harden appreciably against the West? . . . this angle is, if anything, more important than ever at present'.[79] Given that little or no warning might be expected of an attack, it had to be carefully calculated whether ever more daring and risky intelligence operations might provoke the Soviet Union to take action.

The JIC seemingly did not address the process of decision-making in the Kremlin, a crucial and often overlooked factor. Since the death of Lenin in 1924, Stalin had manoeuvred himself into a position of absolute and unassailable power. At its meeting on 4 March 1953, the JIC took note of reports of Stalin's illness – he had suffered a stroke – and inquired what procedures ought to be followed to obtain further information from the Soviet Embassy about his condition. Within a few days the behemoth of the Soviet system had died.[80] The death of Stalin is often seen as one of the defining events of the 1950s, yet its significance was certainly lost on the JIC, at least to start with. In the 'Perimeter Review' of 10 March – the weekly current assessment looking at critical events in the world – the succession to Stalin was discussed, and the leading three contenders were all judged likely to continue his policies.[81]

The central question was how would the new leadership address Soviet policy and actions vis-à-vis the West? The first and possibly most important conclusion was that the new Soviet leadership had decided to govern by committee. This was seen as a novel move, though not one, in the JIC's mind, that would last.[82] Within a short period Georgi Malenkov emerged as *primus inter pares*, though it was noted that he was not treated with the same level of respect that Stalin had enjoyed. To determine his future policy, his speeches and movements were monitored and interpreted.[83] Second in line to Malenkov in the reshuffle was Lavrenti Beria, the feared and powerful head of the Soviet secret police and intelligence apparatus. In machinations behind the scenes, Beria was subsequently the victim of a coup that removed him from power. Commenting on his fall in mid-July 1953, some two weeks after it had taken place, the JIC concluded that it was the 'first crack . . . in the apparent solidarity of the post-Stalin leadership' and had come 'sooner than expected'. It was not felt that there would be 'any material change' in the conduct or course of Soviet foreign policy.[84]

In mid-August 1953 the JIC reported in its 'Perimeter Review' that the Soviet leadership's 'new look' policy was continuing, and that in various speeches Malenkov had stressed that 'there are no outstanding issues which could not be settled in a peaceful way on the basis of mutual agreement'. From this, the JIC concluded that Soviet policy 'aims at a further relaxation of tension', although no further concessions should be expected; indeed, Malenkov's more peaceful overtures coincided with his announcement of a Soviet test of a hydrogen bomb, even though his claims were not entirely believed.[85]

At the same time the Soviet leadership had to suppress an uprising in East Germany that looked as if it would quickly spread out of control: to restore calm the Kremlin authorised the use of tanks and troops. This evidence of unrest and of Soviet willingness to contain it using force was not lost on the JIC. Both were significant: the riots themselves were perceived to have been as much of a shock to the Soviet Union as they had been to the British; once underway, the Soviet leadership had 'acted prompted and firmly' but crucially 'with restraint', though it would 'be most unwise to assume that the Soviet Government will act with similar restraint if further rebellions occur'.[86]

What conclusions could be drawn from these events? Writing in a September 1953 update of its regular assessment on the likelihood of war, the JIC concluded that 'we see no reason to alter any of the conclusions of our last report, except that we believe the Soviet Government, temporarily at least, will be more cautious in the conduct of their cold-war struggle against the West'.[87] Read as a whole, however, the report is more perceptive than this statement suggests. Several recent events were seen as significant:

(a)   The re-organisation of the Soviet Government and the emphasis on collective leadership.
(b)   The measures taken by the new Soviet Government to make their regime more acceptable to the ordinary Soviet citizens . . .
(c)   The riots and unrest in Eastern Germany.
(d)   A change of economic policy in E. Germany and Hungary . . .
(e)   Political and economic concessions in E. Germany and Austria and to a certain extent in some of the Satellites.
(f)   The downfall of Beria . . .
(g)   The conclusion of an armistice in Korea.
(h)   Malenkov's speech at the closing session of the Supreme Soviet, in which he announced plans for improving the supply of consumer goods, a change in agricultural policy, and an apparent levelling of defence expenditure.
(i)   The first experimental Soviet thermo-nuclear explosion.[88]

Whilst the JIC accepted that 'there is nothing in these events to show that the basic aims of Soviet policy have changed', there were 'nevertheless certain broad inferences to be drawn from the events'. The Soviet leadership would be 'more careful than before not to run the risk of precipitating the unintentional war', and consequently would be 'more cautious'. In addition, the growing nuclear arsenals of the US and the USSR, both in terms of sophistication and sheer numbers, meant that 'as we near and reach the point when either side could destroy the other and when war might well result in the annihilation of both, neither will risk a deliberate war'.[89]

This assessment was approved by the COS in October 1953 and paved the way for a far more optimistic report in April 1954, the JIC's 'most hopeful assessment since 1945'.[90] The death of Stalin was labelled by the JIC as a 'major crisis' for the Soviet Union. The result was, in the JIC's view, a relaxation of 'tension in international affairs'. Stalin's death had 'aroused hope' that the 'Cold War might have died', but after the fall of Beria 'Soviet foreign policy assumed a more intransigent air'. Furthermore, a careful analysis revealed that the Soviet Union tried to 'constantly dangle the carrot of peace by negotiation within sight but out of reach'.[91]

Was this all a façade? In a separate assessment in April 1954 the JIC, perceiving a significant change, gave a far more upbeat view of the world and of Soviet actions. War, it was thought, would only result from either a deliberate decision or as the result of unintended consequences. Of these, the first could effectively be discounted: 'it is hard to believe that Russia would deliberately embark on war until all other means had failed . . . Russia desires to prosecute her policy by means other than war'. Of the second possibility, this too was deemed to be unrealistic, for 'the Russians have on the whole shown themselves careful in the last resort'. This was a tacit acceptance that whilst the Soviet leadership still desired an over-throw of the capitalist system, the principal means by which it should be achieved had altered.[92]

It is difficult to establish how these assessments were received within the military or whether they altered the basis of British defence planning. Conclusive evidence is hard to come by, but the likelihood is that it made little difference. The COS approved the paper[93], and although the JIC assessment reduced some of the urgency in terms of defence planning, in its conclusion it provided a clear justification for such preparations:

> the aim of the two sides remain in conflict and there is no apparent probability of change. The present state of "Cold War" is therefore likely to last for a long time, though there will be periods of greater or less tensions.[94]

The thaw in relations with the Kremlin, however, was not destined to last long. At the start of February 1955 the JIC reported that 'since December there has been a definite hardening in the Soviet Government's attitude on international affairs'.[95] More worrying was the news, also in early February, that Malenkov, the Soviet Premier, had been forced to resign, though it was not clear why. This was a matter of concern for two reasons: 1) there had been no advance warning; and 2) Malenkov's leadership and foreign policy had, on the whole, eased tensions. The JIC recorded in the minutes that 'this further emphasized the unfortunate truth that the majority of our intelligence on Russia was quite marginal.'[96]

What of the effect on policy? In briefing the COS on Malenkov's removal, the JIC Chairman, Patrick Dean, informed them that 'although the façade of collective leadership in the USSR was being maintained, Khrushchev was now the real power in the Government and Russia was, in fact, tending to go back to Dictatorship. Khrushchev's attitude vis-à-vis the Western Powers was likely to be more tough than that of Malenkov.'[97] This view was supported by an SIS assessment of the character of Nikolai Bulganin, Malenkov's successor as Premier of the Soviet Union: 'he is too old, and reached an important position too late, to exert any considerable influence in his own right. He should therefore be considered as an homme de paille [i.e. stooge] for Khrushchev.'[98] The view that Khrushchev was now the main player in Soviet politics was reiterated in a JIS paper, which concluded that he had been playing an increasingly large role behind the scenes before Malenkov's resignation.[99]

Despite these views the trend in optimistic JIC assessments continued. A report written in September 1955, specifically as preparation for those attending the Conference of Foreign Ministers in Geneva, argued that the Soviet policy was one of a 'relaxation' of international tension. However, a warning note was issued: if the Conference did not produce results then there was a distinct 'possibility' that the Soviet Union might resort to more hard-line tactics.[100] No firm conclusions were reached at the Conference in October, but the JIC saw no reason to change its earlier view. What was apparent, however, was that the Soviet Union was now focussing more attention on the Middle East and Asia.[101]

In February 1956 the Communist Part of the Soviet Union held its 20th Party Congress. These conference gatherings were routinely monitored for signs of promotion and demotion within the Soviet hierarchy, and for a general reading of Soviet intentions. The overarching theme of the conference, as the JIC reported, was unremarkable, though it was noted that Stalin was barely mentioned.[102] As we know now, the real event of significance was a four hour diatribe by Khrushchev on 25 February, the so-called 'secret speech', to a closed session. This speech was far more vitriolic in its denunciation of Stalin and Stalinism than anything ever heard before, asserting that Stalin's cult of personality had damaged the communist cause.

Within weeks the US intelligence community had got wind of the speech, eventually receiving a copy of the text via the Israeli security agency Shin Bet.[103] The JIC reported the effects of the denunciation of Stalin in late March 1956.[104] Khrushchev's speech was seen as important and its effects were immediately noticeable, with rioting reported in Georgia and Azerbaijan.[105] The bigger question concerned the impact Khrushchev would have as leader, particularly in terms of foreign policy and intentions towards the West. Although the JIC concluded that Khrushchev was more bellicose than his predecessor Malenkov, it did not change its forecast on the likelihood of war.[106] Qualifying this relative optimism was the realisation that, should the Soviet Union decide to initiate hostilities, there would be little or no warning. In the case of ballistic missile attack the time between the decision to strike and the actual assault would be very short. One aspect of the warning was to focus on 'alert procedures' – what measures might indicate an attack, and what should be done. To fulfil this task the JIC and its membership worked extremely closely with the United States and Canada.[107]

Much of the middle part of 1956 was taken up with assessments of the Egyptian leader Gamal Abdel Nasser and of an impending Arab-Israeli conflict. This overshadowed whatever else was going on in the world (see chapter 14). Following

Khrushchev's secret speech in February, a process of 'de-Stalinisation' had begun across the Soviet bloc. One immediate effect was to give implicit encouragement to those elements hostile to communist rule, particularly in the satellite states in Eastern Europe. Thus, starting in June there were a series of strikes in Poland by workers demanding better conditions. The JIC, in its new publication the 'Weekly Survey of Intelligence' (WSI), or the 'Red Book' as it quickly became known (due to the colour of its cover), by producing a short and accurate note on the protests: clear evidence that the JIC could still produce assessments at both a strategic and tactical level. In the WSI the JIC provided clear and concise assessments of developing situations worldwide.[108]

The revolt in Poland in late June 1956 was short-lived and was quickly suppressed by the secret police and armed forces. Subsequent reports suggested that the Soviet Union was reducing the size of its armed forces in Eastern Europe.[109] In late October the JIC reported further signs of unrest in Poland, noting that the Soviet Union was moving troops towards the Polish border, and concluded that these showed a 'Soviet readiness to impose their will if necessary'.[110] That 'will' was ultimately exercised in Hungary, not Poland. In the same Red Book the JIC reported that there had been a 'spontaneous outbreak of popular anti-Soviet feeling'. This was intimately linked to the fall of Stalin, his denunciation, and changes within the Soviet bloc.

Revolution in Hungary

In May 1955 the Warsaw Pact had been created. It tied the smaller, satellite states into a formal politico-military alliance with the Soviet Union, though its principal features included a specific reference to respect for the independence of sovereign states and a commitment that the Soviet Union would not interfere in their internal affairs. That was the theory. The practice was different. On 23 October 1956 in Hungary, a large group of protesters began to publicly and volubly express discontent, seemingly buoyed by the aftermath of the Polish uprising in which the government had agreed to open discussions with workers. Very quickly the scale of the demonstrations swelled, and feeling unable to control the situation, the Hungarian leadership requested assistance from the Soviet Union. These events were reported by the JIC in brief terms.[111]

The JIC summary of the situation emphasised the inherent chaos: 'the Hungarian uprising is a spontaneous nation-wide revolt against Soviet domination and the Police State, with no unifying political principle and no integrating leadership.' The situation could not be resolved favourably, and to the JIC it:

> appear[ed] inconceivable that the Hungarian people will be reconciled to the continued overlordship of Moscow. The Soviet leaders are consequently in a dilemma: either they must re-impose complete military control over Hungary in the face of awakened world criticism, or they must accept the Hungarian demand for complete withdrawal . . . it is not yet clear which way the Soviet leaders intend to resolve their dilemma.[112]

In Hungary events quickly spiralled out of control. The number of protesters grew, as did their volatility, and accordingly the number of Soviet troops and tanks increased. An immediate and significant outcome was that the Hungarian government fell, with its leaders retreating to Moscow. A week later the JIC reported that 'the position in Hungary is not at all clear', though it was known that Soviet forces were under the control of Moscow and not Budapest.[113] The JIC was especially interested to see whether the discontent would spread into neighbouring countries and in particular Poland, not least because of the implications for Soviet lines of communication to East Germany. It was concluded that 'the Russians are placing themselves in a state of complete readiness to strike at once if any trouble should develop'[114] Shortly afterwards, the JIC assessed that 'all the East European States are in a state of tension'.[115]

As events unfolded the JIC took a close interest, seeing developments in Hungary as a discrete event and considering its impact on other Eastern bloc countries. Throughout its discussions the Americans were actively involved, attending the weekly JIC meetings and conveying the US view on developments.[116] To the JIC, the increased readiness of the Soviet armed forces and the tension within the leadership was ominous, but there is no evidence that the JIC thought the conflict would spread outside the communist bloc. The JIC noted on 4 November that 'operations to crush Hungarians' had begun, and that Khrushchev had 'stated that the Soviet Union will apply whatever force is needed to extinguish it [the Hungarian resistance]'.[117] The actions of the Hungarian Legation in London were closely monitored by the Security Service: with the events of 4 November it was observed that the majority of the senior officials were against the Soviet actions (indeed, one junior member of the Legation sought asylum in Britain).[118]

On 1 November the Lord Privy Seal, RAB Butler, had responded to a question in the House of Commons to the effect that 'Her Majesty's Government have in no way the intention of exploiting events in Eastern Europe to undermine the security of the Union of Soviet Socialist Republics'.[119] Despite international condemnation of the Soviet military action and pleas from the Hungarian leadership for foreign assistance, good knowledge and coverage of the evolving situation led the JIC to its assessment of 8 November, that 'there is no sign of any Soviet intention to use its forces in Eastern Europe for action outside the boundaries of the Bloc in Europe'.

The Hungarian Revolution ended on 10 November in failure. For Patrick Dean it had been a sobering experience. Writing to the Foreign Secretary in early December 1956 he conceded that:

> personally I believe that we were nearer to global war about a fortnight or three weeks ago than is commonly believed. I think the Russians, with their present divided leadership, are more than ever prone to suspicions and fears and that they might feel compelled to take some action, say, in the Satellites or Eastern Germany, which would make it very difficult for the Americans not to intervene and which might lead rapidly to a very serious situation.[120]

As a Committee the JIC as a whole was less alarmed, there were vital lessons to be learnt from the Soviet leadership's response. The first observation it made was perhaps the most important, that: 'there is no evidence of Soviet preparations to launch a global war'.[121] More broadly, it was concluded that the Soviet Union would try to regain control over its satellites, but would do so in a pragmatic fashion: 'they will be prepared to make limited concessions to remedy popular discontent, but will not hesitate to use force to crush any radical undermining of their position'. In general terms, however, the Soviets would continue with the 'façade' of 'peaceful co-existence', whereas in reality they would do all they could to 'drive wedges' between the UK and the US.[122] Taking these factors into account, together with the recent experiences of Hungary and the Middle East, the JIC concluded that whilst the Soviet leadership 'do not want war', the chances that war might occur by accident 'have somewhat increased'.[123]

Pondering the Imponderable

Between the emergence of the Truman Doctrine in 1947 and the collapse of the Hungarian Revolution in 1956, the Soviet Union was the primary British intelligence target. In this ten-year period the assessments made by the JIC provided a foundation for judging the remainder of the Cold War. The initial problem, which had been only slightly ameliorated by the mid-1950s, was inadequate intelligence coverage. With the relatively late consensus over where the main threat lay, and after the FO prevaricated over the approval of covert collection efforts in the Soviet Union itself, the intelligence community found itself precisely where the JIC had predicted and feared it would be. The inability to wage the intelligence Cold War was revealed, in stark clarity, by the failure to warn of the Berlin Blockade in 1948, and provided the JIC with a valuable lesson in the continued importance of current intelligence support for informing decision makers as both military and political confrontations developed.

That intelligence coverage did begin to improve from the 1950s onwards was due, largely, to the efforts of the JIC. Through its reporting channels to the COS Committee and beyond, it was able to press continually for greater resources, including increased personnel, and promote the need to take more risks to procure intelligence. Sigint was recognised as the primary means of gathering information, and slowly the JIC's demands began to pay dividends. Intelligence coverage was, as always, far from comprehensive, and the JIC failed to receive any clear indications of several key events. There were significant failings, but as with the Hungarian Revolution, the JIC demonstrated that even when it could not predict an event, it was quick to grasp its significance and to monitor developments once underway.

Amongst the vast array of papers and topics covered in this period, assessments can be grouped into two principal types: examination of current events and identification of long-term trends. Of these it can be argued that the latter was the more important. For these the JIC was quick to identify the lessons of proxy conflicts and to argue that, while the Soviet Union was prepared to use force, it would wish to avoid escalating a local conflict to an international level. Running alongside these assessments was the regular forecast of the date when general war might be expected as a serious possibility. In retrospect these dates seem almost arbitrary, not quite plucked out of thin air, but certainly based on little in the way of concrete information. The JIC itself appears to have been aware of this deficiency. Despite the understandable defence need for a date to underpin its strategy and plans, the JIC ran the risk of implying that war was ruled out before that point. Clearly this was never the intention, and the JIC continued to be reluctant to point to a specific year.[124]

Another characteristic that emerges in this period is the changing nature, and arguably definition, of intelligence. Pre-war intelligence was focussed primarily on military targets; there was little emphasis on questions of policy or intent. This had begun to change during the war, though the emphasis remained overwhelmingly military. The developing Cold War changed this approach. Monitoring Soviet military capabilities was still a major priority, but the calculation had altered. Whereas during the war it might be assumed that once the Germans had a weapon they would use it, now the key intelligence problem became one of intent. To JIC members the implications were clear. Whilst being a military committee responsible to the COS, they should also broaden their focus to include political, economic and scientific issues.[125]

Notes

1   N.Brook to Prime Minister, 25 October 1950. PREM 8/1527.
2   JIC(50)81(Final), 'Present State of Intelligence and Measures to Improve It', 3 November 1950. CAB 158/22.
3   'Future Organisation of the SIS', N.Bland. FO 1093/195. See also Jeffery, *MI6*. pp.567–9; 610–11; and 705–6.
4   C/9541, 'C' to M.J.Creswell [Services Liaison Department], 5 September 1945. FO 1093/196.
5   H.A.Caccia to 'C', 6 November 1945. FO 1093/196.
6   F.Roberts to H.A.Caccia, 2 April 1946 & Caccia to Roberts, 5 April 1946. FO 1093/347.
7   JIC(46)4th Meeting (0), 23 January 1946. CAB 81/94.
8   'Sigint Enquiry – Report by Sir D Evill', 11 September 1946. CAB 158/73.
9   JIC(47)34(0)(Final), 'Review of Intelligence Organisation', 10 July 1947. CAB 158/1.
10 SIS Officer to JIC Secretary, 25 June 1947. CAB 163/7.
11 JIC(48)38th Meeting (0), 28 April 1948. CAB 159/3.
12 JIC/1223/49, 'Review of the State of Intelligence Available on Russian Intentions and Preparations for War', 8 July 1949. CAB 158/72.
13 JIC(49)12(Final), 'Review of the State of Intelligence Available on Russian Intentions and Preparations for War', 26 July 1949. CAB 158/72.
14 JIC(49)61(Final), 'Measures to Improve the State of Intelligence Available on Russian Intentions and Preparations for War', 5 December 1949. CAB 158/72.
15 JIC(50)50(Final), 'Measures to Improve the State of Intelligence Available on Russian Intentions and Preparations for War', 3 November 1950. CAB 158/72.
16 JIC(50)81(Final), 'Present State of Intelligence and Measures to Improve It', 3 November 1950. CAB 158/72.

17 DGC/1213(Final), 'Present State of Intelligence and Measures to Improve It', 3 November 1950. CAB 158/72.

18 JIC(50)81(Final), 'Present State of Intelligence and Measures to Improve It', 3 November 1950. CAB 158/72.

19 COS(50)186th Meeting, 24 November 1950. CAB 158/72.

20 JIC(51)45(Preliminary Draft), ' Review of Our Present State of Intelligence', 22 June 1951. CAB 158/73.

21 Venona was an Anglo-American programme to decypher the communications of Soviet diplomatic and intelligence agencies.

22 LSIB(51)10(Final), 'Measures to Improve Signal Intelligence', 7 January 1952. CAB 158/74.

23 Cited in COS(55)72, 'Services Transmission Security', 6 April 1955. DEFE 32/4.

24 Details of PSIS discussions and subsequent financial considerations can be found in T 220/1383. The records of PSIS are somewhat patchy, with the majority still retained given their financial data. Details on the origins can be found in CAB 163/228.

25 JIC(51)126(Final), 'Present State of Our Intelligence on the Soviet Union, The European Satellites and China, and Measures to Improve It', 7 January 1952. CAB 158/74.

26 COS(52)11th Meeting, 22 January 1952. CAB 158/74.

27 COS(52)387, 'Measures to Improve Signal Intelligence', 23 July 1952. CAB 158/74. Also, COS(52)105th Meeting, 22 July 1952. CAB 158/74.

28 LSIB(53)6(Final), 'Measures to Improve Intelligence', 22 December 1953. CAB 158/78. Although this is dated later, it nicely encompasses similar views held at the time.

29 JIC(52)8(Revise), 'Charter for the Sub-Committee on Measures to Improve Intelligence', 5 February 1952. CAB 158/14. Examples of some of the Sub-Committee's minutes can be found in 'Sub-Committee on Measures to Improve Intelligence'. PUSD Files, FCO.

30 JIC(52)56(Final), 'Measures to Improve Intelligence', 6 October 1952. CAB 158/75.

31 COS(52)152nd Meeting, 4 November 1952. CAB 158/75.

32 JIC/2656/53, 'Sub-Committee on Measures to Improve Intelligence', 2 November 1953. PUSD Files, FCO.

33 P.Dean to E.E.G.L.Searight, 5 October 1953. PUSD Files, FCO.

34 JIC(53)101(Preliminary Draft), 'State of Our Intelligence and Measures to Improve It', 31 December 1953. PUSD Files, FCO.

35 Further detail is in 'Report on the Present State of Our Intelligence and Measures to Improve It'. PUSD Files, FCO.

36 JIC/2412/53, 'State of Our Intelligence and Measures to Improve It', 7 October 1953. PUSD Files, FCO.

37 JIC(54)31(Final), 'State of Our Intelligence on the Communist Bloc and Measures to Improve It', 8 June 1954. CAB 158/76.

38 JIC(55)29(Final), 'State of Our Intelligence on the Sino Soviet Bloc and Measures to Improve It', 13 July 1955. CAB 158/79. An early draft of this paper is in 'Report on the Present State of Our Intelligence and Measures to Improve It'. PUSD Files, FCO. 'Ferret' flights were special aircraft equipped with electronic gadgetry to detect when Soviet radar 'lit up'.

39 JIC/3240/55, 'Meeting: Chiefs of Staff/Directors of Intelligence 20th December, 1955', 12 December 1955. CAB 158/79. Emphasis in original.

40 Interview with Air Commodore C.A.Alldis, 21 September 2009. This practice has since become standard.

41 JIC(51)87(Terms of Reference), 'Review of Assessments Made Since January 1947 by the Joint Intelligence Committee on Communist Intentions', 20 September 1951. CAB 158/13.

42 JIC(51)87(Final), 'Review of Assessments Made of Communist Intentions Since January, 1947 by the Joint Intelligence Committee', 12 December 1951. CAB 158/13.

43 JIC(50)88, 'Chinese Communist Military Intentions and Capabilities in the Non-Communist States Bordering China', 11 October 1950. CAB 158/11.

44 JIC(51)87(Final), 'Review of Assessments Made of Communist Intentions Since January, 1947 by the Joint Intelligence Committee', 12 December 1951. CAB 158/13.

45 JIC(51)87(Final), 'Review of Assessments Made of Communist Intentions Since January, 1947 by the Joint Intelligence Committee', 12 December 1951. CAB 158/13.

46 JIC(47)7(Final), 'Soviet Interests, Intentions and Capabilities', 6 August 1947. CAB 158/1.

47 JIC(47)85th Meeting, 3 December 1947. CAB 159/2.

48 JIC(47)76(0)Final, 'Possibility of War Before the End of 1956', 23 January 1948. CAB 158/2.

49 JIC/3240/55, 'The State of Our Intelligence', 12 December 1955. CAB 158/79. For more detail see 'Report on the Present State of Our Intelligence and Measures to Improve It'. PUSD Files, FCO.

50 The American and British papers are both in JIC(48)42(0)Final, 'Indications of Russian Preparedness for War', 18 June 1948. CAB 158/3.

51 JIC(48)67th Meeting (0), 2 July 1948. CAB 159/4. The first such report is JIC(48)70(0) Final, 'Short Term Indications of Soviet Preparedness for War', 1 October 1948. CAB 158/4.

52 JIC(48)73rd Meeting (0), 16 July 1948. CAB 159/4.

53 JIC(48)78(0), 'Measures to Prevent the Russians Obtaining Strategic Surprise', 16 July 1948. CAB 158/4.

54 JIC(48)121(Revised Final), 'Possibility of War Before the End of 1956', 27 January 1949. CAB 158/5.

55 A J Craig, *The Joint Intelligence Committee and British Intelligence Assessment, 1945–1956* (PhD: University of Cambridge, 1999). p.96.

56 JIC(48)80th Meeting(0), 30 July 1948. CAB 159/4.

57 COS(48)96th Meeting, 9 July 1948. DEFE 4/14.

58 These are dealt with in later chapters.

59 For more see Goodman, *Spying on the Nuclear Bear*.

60 JIC(49)111(Final), 'Soviet Use of Atomic Bombs', 14 March 1950. CAB 158/8.

61 JIC(50)6(Final), 'Basic Review of the Foreign Policy and Strategy of the Soviet Union', 9 October 1950. CAB 158/9.

62 COS(50)179th Meeting, 13 November 1950. DEFE 4/37.

63 JIC(50)77(Revise), 'The Likelihood of War with the Soviet Union and the Date by Which the Soviet Leaders Might be Prepared to Risk It', 18 August 1950. CAB 158/11.

64 JIC(50)75, 'Probable Soviet Short Term Developments', 23 August 1950. CAB 158/11.

65 See, for instance, the US document NSC-68. For more, see S F Wells, Jnr, 'Sounding the Tocsin: NSC 68 and the Soviet Threat', *International Security* 4:2 (1979), pp.116–58.

66 JIC(50)92, 'Soviet Intentions and Capabilities, 1950–1954', 28 September 1950. CAB 158/11.

67 JIC(50)100(Final), 'Soviet Intentions and Capabilities and the Date When the Soviet Union Might be Prepared to Engage in a General War', 21 December 1950. CAB 158/11. This is a copy of the UK/US combined report.

68 The FO's Information Research Department, in addition to the propaganda work, also spent time trying to understand communism. It even commissioned an internal manual, later published as R N Carew Hunt, *The Theory and Practice of Communism* (London: Pelican, 1969).

69 JIC(50)111(Final), 'Likelihood of Total War with the Soviet Union up to the End of 1954', 15 February 1951. CAB 158/11.

70 COS(51)34th Meeting, 21 February 1951. DEFE 4/40.

71 Craig, *The Joint Intelligence Committee and British Intelligence Assessment.* p.149.

72 JIC(52)15(Terms of Reference), 'Possible Soviet Cold War Strategy During 1952–1954', 14 February 1952. CAB 158/14.

73 JIC(52)15(Final), 'Examination in the Light of Soviet Cold War Strategy of Potential Trouble Spots Throughout the World', March-August 1952. CAB 158/14.

74 JIC(52)67(Final), 'Likelihood of General War with the Soviet Union up to the End of 1955', 22 December 1952. CAB 158/14.

75 JIC(52)32(Final), 'Likelihood of Total War with the Soviet Union up to the End of 1954', 21 May 1952. CAB 158/14.

76 JIC(52)51(Final), 'Warning of Soviet Attack 1952–1954', 18 December 1952. CAB 158/14.

77 JIC(52)51(Final)(Supplement), 'Warning of Soviet Attack', 18 December 1952. CAB 158/77.

78 JIC/1234/53, Ninth Meeting of the Sub-Committee on Measures to Improve Intelligence, 18 May 1953. PUSD Files, FCO. For further information see 'Russia: Warning of Attack'. PUSD Files, FCO.

79 G.L.McDermott to C.D.Wiggin [FO], 26 August 1953. PUSD Files, FCO.

80 The most detailed account is J Brent & V Naumov, *Stalin's Last Crime: The Plot Against the Jewish Doctors, 1948–1953* (London: HarperCollins, 2004).

81 JIC(53)28th Meeting, 12 March 1953. 'Perimeter Review as at 10th March, 1953'. CAB 159/13.

82 JIC(53)28th Meeting, 12 March 1953. 'Perimeter Review as at 10th March, 1953'. CAB 159/13.

83 For instance, JIC(53)31st Meeting, 19 March 1953. 'Perimeter Review as at 17th March, 1953'. CAB 159/13.

84 JIC(53)75th Meeting, 16 July 1953, 'Perimeter Review as at 14 July 1953'. CAB 159/14.

85 JIC(53)87th Meeting, 13 August 1953, 'Perimeter Review as at 11 August 1953'. CAB 159/14.

86 JIC(53)68(Final), 'Disturbances in East Germany, June 1953'. CAB 158/16.

87 JIC(53)79(Final), 'Likelihood of General War with the Soviet Union Up to the End of 1955', 10 September 1953. CAB 158/16.

88 By this point Malenkov's earlier claim about an H-bomb had been substantiated through intelligence. See chapter 10.

89 JIC(53)79(Final), 'Likelihood of General War with the Soviet Union Up to the End of 1955', 10 September 1953. CAB 158/16.

90 Craig, *The Joint Intelligence Committee and British Intelligence Assessment.* p.198.

91 JIC(54)10(Final), 'Survey of World Communism in 1953', 1 March 1954. CAB 158/17.

92 JIC(54)37(Revise), 'The Likelihood of War', 14 April 1954. CAB 158/17.

93 COS(54)45th Meeting, 22 April 1954. DEFE 4/70.

94 JIC(54)37(Revise), 'The Likelihood of War', 14 April 1954. CAB 158/17.

95 JIC(55)12th Meeting, 3 February 1955, 'Review of Current Intelligence as at 3rd February 1955'. CAB 159/18.

96 JIC(55)13th Meeting, 9 February 1955. CAB 159/18.

97 COS(55)8th Meeting, Minute 2 (Confidential Annex), 9 February 1955. CAB 158/79.

98 JIC(55)13th Meeting, 9 February 1955. CAB 159/18.

99 JIC/469/55, 'Review of Recent Changes in the Soviet Government', 15 February 1955. CAB 176/52.

100 JIC(55)58(Final)(Revise), 'Likely Soviet Courses of Action up to 1st January 1957', 30 September 1955. CAB 158/21.

101 JIC(55)76(Final), 'Probable Soviet Policy in the Light of the Geneva Conference of Foreign Ministers', 13 December 1955. CAB 158/22.

102 JIC/523/56, 'Proceeding of the XXth Party Congress of the Soviet Union', 23 February 1956. CAB 176/56.

103   Y Melman & D Raviv, 'The Journalist's Connections: How Israel Got Russia's Biggest Pre-Glasnost Secret', *International Journal of Intelligence and Counterintelligence* 4:2 (1990), pp.219–225.

104   JIC(56)30th Meeting, 22 March 1956. CAB 159/22. It was subsequently published a few months later.

105   JIC(56)32nd Meeting, 28 March 1956, 'Review of Current Intelligence as at 28 March 1956'. CAB 159/23.

106   JIC(56)21(Final), 'Likelihood of Global War and Warning of Attack', 1 May 1956. CAB 158/24. An earlier draft and discussion can be found in 'Likelihood of War and Warning of Attack'. PUSD Files, FCO.

107   JIC(56)39, 'UK Intelligence Alert Procedure', 12 March 1956. CAB 158/24.

108   'Weekly Survey of Intelligence', No.9, 28 June-5 July 1956. CAB 179/13.

109   'Weekly Survey of Intelligence', No.16, 16 August-23 August 1956. CAB 179/13.

110   'Weekly Survey of Intelligence', No.25, 19 October-25 October 1956. CAB 179/13.

111   'Weekly Review of Current Intelligence for Period Ending 25 October 1956'. CAB 179/1.

112   'Weekly Survey of Intelligence', No.26, 28 October-1 November 1956. CAB 179/13. Similar reports, albeit less detailed, are in 'Weekly Review of Current Intelligence for Period Ending 1 November 1956'. CAB 179/1.

113   'Weekly Survey of Intelligence', No.28, 9 November-15 November 1956. CAB 179/13.

114   JIC(56)119, 'Soviet Military Activity in Poland and Adjacent Areas', 9 November 1956. CAB 158/81.

115   JIC/2784/56, 'Threat to Austria', 14 November 1956. CAB 158/81.

116   This is clear from the records of the JIC meetings at this time. See CAB 159/25.

117   'Weekly Review of Current Intelligence for Period Ending 8 November 1956'. CAB 179/1.

118   JIC(56)131, 'Reactions in the Hungarian Legation in London to Recent Events in Hungary', 26 November 1956. CAB 158/81.

119   HC Deb [Hansard], 1 November 1956. Vol 558, cc1616–7. See also C Bekes, 'The 1956 Hungarian Revolution and World Politics', *Cold War International History Project*, Working Paper No.16 (September 1996), p.18.

120   P.H.Dean to Private Secretary, 7 December 1956. PUSD Files, FCO. It was the custom at the time to address all formal communications intended for Ministers to their Private Secretaries.

121   'Weekly Survey of Intelligence', No.31, 30 November-6 December 1956. CAB 179/13.

122   JIC(56)123(Final)(Revise), 'Soviet Policy in the Light of the Situation in the Middle East and the Satellites', 6 December 1956. CAB 158/26.

123   JIC(56)136(Final), 'The Extent to Which the Present State of Tensions Has Increased the Chances of Miscalculation Which Might Lead to Global War', 13 December 1956. CAB 158/26.

124   See, for instance, JIC(48)4th Meeting (O), 14 January 1948. CAB 159/3.

125   JIC(50)13th Meeting, 3 February 1950. CAB 159/7.

10 Studying the Soviet War Machine

One of the crucial lessons of the Second World War was the way in which science had altered warfare. Subsequent wars might involve yet another conventional conflict employing the massing of troops on a battlefield, improved weapons, chemical and biological armaments, and long range guided missiles, or even nuclear weapons. To plan for all eventualities the JIC had to focus on a broad array of military capabilities and technologies.

For all its problems with strategic leadership, the German High Command and the defence, research and industrial establishment that it had available, had proved adept at making scientific and technological advances. With the exception of nuclear weapons, much military innovation in the post-war period owed its origins to wartime German projects; in anticipation of this, as the war was drawing to its close, the race between the UK, US and USSR for Axis scientists and technicians increased. This move was particularly evident in Germany, though it was not confined to central Europe alone and German experts were not the only targets.[1] These German scientists and technicians would eventually make an invaluable contribution, not only in utilising their scientific expertise but also in providing insights into Soviet developments.

Assessments of post-war Soviet military capabilities depended upon a varied evidential base. For example, the JIC had to produce assessments ranging from the opaque atomic, and later nuclear weapons programme, to the relatively transparent bomber force. Underpinning these was the need to acquire accurate information. Measures to improve intelligence collection on Soviet intentions were particularly important, though Soviet military capabilities would continue to be a very high priority. But the nature of these two requirements was markedly different. The elements of defence capability were easier to identify, and quantitative estimates could be prepared and compared. Overall there was far less infighting and debate over interpretation of such material than over intentions. The JIC therefore faced an unenviable task: to achieve a balance between improving its understanding of the scale, location and capabilities of the Soviet war machine, including insight into Soviet thinking about the way in which it was being constructed, and producing forecasts of how and the circumstances in which it might be used. In the absence of access to intelligence on what the Soviet leadership was planning, intelligence gaps could only be filled by analytical judgments and so, as would often be the case, high-quality intelligence analysis and assessment would be just as crucial a part of the process as intelligence collection.

Capturing Germans

As the Allied forces swept through Europe heading towards the final prize of Berlin, a small army of scientists and technically-trained intelligence officers followed. Often only a few hours behind the liberating forces, the Alsos Mission – named after General Leslie Groves ('alsos' being Greek for 'groves'), the head of the Manhattan Project (codename for the wartime atomic bomb programme) – proved to be a success: a large number of technicians were secured, together with documents and other technical equipment. In parallel efforts were made by the Combined Intelligence Objectives Sub-Committee (CIOS), and the later British Intelligence Objectives Sub-Committee (BIOS), both of which aimed to capture material and produce surveys on German progress in a wide variety of scientific fields.

First prize was the German atomic bomb programme. It was known that this had not progressed far, certainly in comparison with the Manhattan Project, but it was still considered important to capture the elite group of German scientists – the so-called 'Uranium Club' – and any associated equipment, machinery or raw materials. Alsos' scientists and intelligence personnel were all given military ranks and uniforms, and attempted to blend in with their armed forces colleagues. As they approached Germany, following leads about where the German scientists had hidden their supplies of uranium, a similar party from the Soviet Union was focused on the same objectives. In the end the honours were shared: the Anglo-American Alsos Mission recruited the best scientists, and the Soviet Union found the most raw materials.[2]

The race for the German atomic expertise and materials was replicated in the hunt for those involved in the chemical, biological, aeronautical and, perhaps above all, the ballistic missile fields. Indeed, all sides went to great lengths to acquire the best scientific minds, devising special operations to capture them and deny them to the other side. Both the UK and France participated in this hunt, though it was predominantly an American and Soviet effort.[3] The numbers 'rescued' were surprisingly large: from the British Zone alone over 1,500 German scientists and technicians were removed, partly to satisfy British needs, and partly to stop them falling into Soviet hands.[4]

Much of the organisation for the new agencies designed to collect and amass technical intelligence in Germany was co-ordinated through the JIC.[5] Unquestionably the best scientific brains had been captured by the Americans, so discussion centred on ways to prevent the Soviet Union enticing and coercing German scientists to join it. In mid-1945 the JIC had approved the creation of two subordinate bodies: the Joint Scientific Intelligence Committee (JSIC) and the Joint Technical Intelligence Committee (JTIC). Differing in subject matter but similar in scope and membership, both Committees were amalgamated shortly afterwards into the Joint Scientific and Technical Intelligence Committee (JSTIC).[6] Indeed, as the DMI reported, 'although two separate Committees exist in theory, they have hitherto functioned jointly and are likely to continue to do so for a while'.[7]

The Soviet effort to capture German scientists was first brought to the JIC's attention through a report submitted by Naval Intelligence to the JSIC. Although something was known of this, the report questioned whether the JIC knew its full extent and asked what might be done to stop it.[8] The figures quoted were remarkable: it was reported and subsequently accepted that the Soviet Union had removed 800,000 engineers and specialist workers, albeit 'mainly of low grade technicians and industrial operatives'. Furthermore, as the JSIC informed the JIC, if Soviet plans to remove German scientists were successful, then 'this would very materially strengthen Russia's industrial potential'.[9] This would have serious repercussions.

In December 1945 another sub-committee, this time the Joint Intelligence Committee (Control Commission for Germany) or JIC (CCG), complained to the JIC that something ought to be done.[10] The JIC discussed the matter in January 1945, following the receipt of advice and recommendations from the COS and the Prime Minister himself. Of equal concern was the fact that the removal of Germans to the USSR was taking place not just from the Soviet Zone of Germany, but from the British Zone too. In considering the impact of this, the JIS declared that it needed the conclusions of the JIC's paper on Soviet intentions (which had not yet been approved by the COS) in order to comment on the effects this might have on Soviet capabilities. On the second point – what ought to be done – the JIC concluded that it would be difficult to stop the widespread enticement of low-grade technicians, but that efforts should be undertaken to stop senior scientists with knowledge of 'military developments' being taken by the Soviet Union.[11]

Despite the severity of the situation, decisions were slow to materialise. Following further evidence from JIC (Germany), in London the JIC finally approved an assessment in August 1946. In the JIC's opinion, 'every effort should be made to prevent the pool of scientists from becoming available to the Russians'. To address this the JIC asked the Control Commission for Germany, together with the Dominions Office, the Colonial Office and the Ministry of Supply, to try to pre-empt Soviet efforts and persuade the leading scientists to come to Britain.[12]

A more active pursuit of German specialists presented an opportunity to collect some much-needed intelligence on Soviet military programmes. Many Germans approached the Western occupying powers to volunteer their services. To the JIC this was a gift that could not be turned down: 'we are convinced that there is the opportunity now to obtain high grade Intelligence from these men . . . and so make it possible to forecast more accurately than we can at present, the progress of Russian development in modern weapons during future years'.[13] As a result, the impetus and responsibility for the collection of intelligence in Germany passed to the Scientific and Technical Intelligence Branch (STIB) of the Control Commission for Germany, who were regularly provided with lists of information needed by the JIC in London.[14] These efforts, despite their tardiness, would prove to be invaluable in filling the black holes in intelligence coverage of the Soviet weapons programmes.

An Atomic Conundrum

Topping the list of scientific priorities was the acquisition of knowledge about the atomic bomb; indeed, the JIC concluded in October 1945 that this represented the 'paramount potentiality of the future'.[15] Reinforcing this was a realisation that Soviet possession of an atomic arsenal would fundamentally alter the strategic balance, particularly given the UK's vulnerabilities to air attack from Soviet bases and the uncertainty in 1945 over future US commitments to Europe. The destructive ferocity of atomic weapons was brought home, vividly, through the findings of the British Mission to survey the damage in Hiroshima and Nagasaki, and the production of diagrams about the level of damage to be expected if Trafalgar Square was ground zero for an atomic attack. This had a two-fold effect: to convince the COS of the UK's need to create its own indigenous atomic weapons programme; and for the JIC to raise atomic intelligence to a 'priority one' target for the collection agencies.[16]

There was, however, a problem. Despite the sensitive nature of its work and its role in the war effort, the JIC had been deliberately excluded from any atomic-related discussions during the Second World War (see chapter 5). Furthermore, atomic intelligence had remained separate from the rest of scientific intelligence, a division that had resulted in much strife between departments and their respective heads. The reason for the partition was to appease US concerns about the security of the Manhattan Project, the overriding general need for atomic information to be kept secret and the consequent demand for strict compartmentalisation. After the war the JIC initially sought to redress this by amalgamating atomic and scientific intelligence, and by bringing atomic intelligence squarely back within its purview. This was opposed by Sir John Anderson (Viscount Waverley), chairman of the Tube Alloys Consultative Committee (the oversight body for atomic matters), who was instrumental in ensuring good post-war Anglo-American intelligence exchange in the atomic sphere.[17]

The JIC was initially sceptical about the continuing need to keep atomic and scientific intelligence separate, but was persuaded by Anderson that the wartime practice should continue.[18] Thus, it accepted that 'the necessity of continuing the close co-operation with the USA both technically and as regards intelligence' was such that 'we have not taken the initiative in proposing any alteration in the existing arrangements for the handling of this intelligence'.[19] A specialist atomic intelligence unit was allowed to continue its work with responsibility for co-ordinating collection efforts, analysis and the preparation of assessments. These, in turn, would then be passed to the JIC and, as was often the case, either adopted and rebadged as a JIC paper or incorporated into broader studies of Soviet capabilities. This remained the situation even after a series of reforms in the mid-1950s led to the creation of a special sub-committee of the JIC to focus exclusively on atomic weapons, as it was far more technically detailed a matter than would normally concern JIC meetings. It meant that unlike other subjects, papers on atomic matters were not to be drafted by the JIS. This does not appear to have caused any problems.[20]

Compared with the wartime effort to track the German atomic weapons programme, post-war operations against the Soviet Union were far less successful. In particular there were fewer well-placed human sources. Sigint would become important but, at least at the outset, could provide little significant information. Photographic reconnaissance was limited. Intelligence coverage therefore had to rely on more indirect sources of information which, by their nature, were difficult to evaluate. First amongst these were the oral testimonies of German scientists and technicians who were taken to the Soviet Union at the end of the war and, from the late 1940s onwards, were repatriated.[21] Evidence of the gaps in the covert coverage of the Soviet programme is provided by the JIC report of 1946 on the 'overt' aspects of atomic energy. This listed conditions from which 'it becomes possible to define provisionally the capabilities of the various nations, and to propound a series of preliminary questions, the answers to which would give a clue as to whether any real activity is being carried out or being contemplated'.[22]

Without good sources of information on what was a well-protected and rigidly compartmentalised Soviet programme, the British atomic intelligence unit had to base its assessments on a number of assumptions. These included using a comparison with programme timings of the wartime Manhattan Project as a guide for forecasting the speed with which the Soviet Union might perfect the necessary techniques. Allowance had to be made by the analysts for perceived Soviet technological inferiority and so various 'handicaps' were introduced.[23] Other assumptions included the belief that Soviet experts would not find new ways to develop the bomb that had not been discovered during the war, and that efforts would be hampered by its ability to procure the necessary raw materials.[24] These factors led the JIC to conclude that 'the most reliable estimate that can be made of Russian progress in the production of atomic weapons indicates that the limiting factor is the availability of uranium ore.'[25]

Despite the need to make these assumptions and evident gaps in coverage, the JIC still produced estimates of progress. The JIC established a universal range of criteria to be used to indicate that an atomic weapons programme had begun:

1. The establishment of a government commission or the equivalent to handle the overall problems connected with the project.
2. The allocation of large sums of money to the project.
3. An adequate supply of uranium and possibly thorium.
4. An adequate number of first-class nuclear physicists, nuclear chemists and mathematicians.
5. Specially equipped laboratories housing modern nuclear physical equipment.
6. Adequate facilities for the training of graduates in the above sciences.
7. An industrial engineering potential of a very high order.
8. An adequate supply of industrial manpower capable of working and servicing delicate and complicated machinery.[26]

For the Soviet Union, the JIC concluded that every single condition had been met. The atomic intelligence unit concluded that the Soviet programme had only begun as a full-scale enterprise following VE-day, and that the Soviet Union was striving towards the plutonium bomb. There were serious problems in getting adequate uranium, and it was unlikely that any new supplies of raw material would be discovered. Finally, it concluded that industrial factors would constrain progress.[27]

The military planners required a forecast of when the first bomb could be operational, and how quickly the Soviet Union might build up a stockpile thereafter. To this end the JIC's estimates varied from year to year, sometimes quite considerably. Thus:

Table 10.1 Assessments for first Soviet atomic bomb and annual rates of production

Year of Assessment	*Date expected for first atomic bomb*	*Number of bombs to be produced each year*
1945[28]	1952	40
1946[29]	1951	25
1947[30]	1952	Possible: 23 Probable: 5
1948[31]	Possible: January 1951 Probable: 1954	Between 2 and 10
1949[32]	Possible: July 1950 Probable: mid-1953	Between 20 and 25

It is almost impossible to penetrate the subtleties that lay behind the changes from year to year, although seemingly the alterations were down to individual scraps of information being pieced together, rather than any single, high-level source. Moreover, while the date for acquiring the first bomb was thought to remain approximately the same, views on the number of bombs that could be produced each year changed dramatically. This can largely be attributed to differing Anglo-American views on the quantities of uranium available to the Soviet Union; certainly this is why the 1948 estimate changed so markedly.[33]

The assessments of the Soviet programme were especially significant for their strategic implications. In 1947 the JIC had estimated that between 60 and 240 atomic bombs would be needed for the Soviet Union to bring about the collapse of the UK. Therefore, by extension, 'the Soviet Union would not be capable of achieving a decisive result by atomic warfare, even against the United Kingdom alone, before 1957 at the earliest.'[34] This moved even further into the future when the dates of the first bomb and subsequent stockpiling were extrapolated from the 1948 and 1949 predictions. This aspect of intelligence on Soviet capabilities was not matched by forecasts of Soviet intentions (see chapter 9), and the JIC made little attempt to reconcile them. In 1949 it was stated that until the Soviet Union achieved parity with the US and UK in terms of 'weapons of mass destruction and the means of delivery', then they would 'consider that in war their long-term aim can be best served by a defensive policy', but this degree of certainty was an exception and not the norm.[35]

On 3 September 1949 these forecasts were undermined when a US B-29 weather plane detected traces of radioactive samples in the atmosphere somewhere between the eastern seaboard of Japan and Alaska. After further collection and analysis it was concluded that these samples could only have originated from an atomic test – the Soviet Union had removed the US atomic monopoly.[36] The news was broken to the JIC by its Chairman, William Hayter, who, according to Guy Liddell, the MI5 representative at the meeting, 'cleared the room of secretaries and then said that if there was anyone present who could not keep what was going to be said to himself, would he kindly leave the room . . . it was then announced . . . that the explosion of an atomic bomb had occurred in Russia'.[37] In London it was decided that a post-mortem was needed to investigate why the Soviet Union had developed the bomb so much faster than predicted. One initial finding, by the JIC's subordinate Joint Scientific and Technical Intelligence Committee (JSTIC), was that 'in the last year or so a number of reports dealing with Soviet progress in the development of atomic weapons had been largely discounted because they were low grade. It is now assumed that many of these reports were truer than was at first thought.'[38] Other reasons included the recognition that uranium supplies might not have been such a limiting factor as had first been thought, and that espionage might have played a part.[39] This latter aspect was to be one of the areas which the JIC had completely underestimated. The JIC's conclusion was that the device had 'thrown everyone's calculations out of date' and 'would necessitate the revision of all former JIC assessments'.[40]

Policing the State – Atomic Secrets

Several aspects of the security surrounding nuclear secrets in the 1940s and 1950s are remarkable. The first is the sheer number of British scientists, civil servants and spies who provided information to the Soviet Union; the second is how unaware Whitehall was about this trend; the third is how slow the civil service was to realise that there might be future penetration; and the fourth is the peripheral role of the JIC: it did not play a role in these spy cases as it was very much an MI5 preserve. The list of senior, high-level figures who spied for the Soviet Union goes beyond just the Cambridge Five and Klaus Fuchs. Of this lengthy list, a surprisingly high number had access in one shape or form to atomic information and, whether by accident or design, these spies all served to complement each other.

Donald Maclean provided details of the political and diplomatic aspects of atomic energy policy. He was involved with several senior Anglo-American committees on atomic matters which, amongst other things, discussed worldwide stocks of uranium. He also had access to some of the Western intelligence assessments of the Soviet programme. Guy Burgess, in his role as Private Secretary to the FO Minister, Hector McNeil, would have had access to some atomic secrets, as would have John Cairncross, Lord Hankey's Private Secretary. Kim Philby would have had an even wider range of access in his position as SIS liaison with US intelligence in the late 1940s. It was also known that he was friendly with the British atomic intelligence liaison officer in Washington, Wilfrid Mann, and that all of Mann's messages to London had to be transmitted through Philby's cypher machine.[41]

In addition to these diplomatic and intelligence dimensions, was the Soviet Union's network of scientific spies. In 1946 Alan Nunn May, a lecturer at King's College London, who had worked on the wartime Manhattan Project in Canada, was arrested and imprisoned for passing information to the Soviet Union. This should have been a wake-up call, and certainly the significance was not lost at the time on the JIC which, in 1946, concluded that Nunn May's espionage might have reduced the time it would take the Soviet Union to mount a first atomic test by twelve months.[42] Yet while the JIC did look further into Nunn May's treachery, at no time did its assessments consider whether there might be further Soviet spies providing information, or if this could reduce the timescale for the development of the first Soviet atomic device. Indeed, in late 1947 the atomic intelligence unit completed a small study for the JIC on 'Russian Knowledge of the Atomic Bomb'. It concluded that 'it is clear that the Russians made definite attempts to penetrate the Atomic Bomb Project in the period between March 1943 and March 1945', but that overall 'Russian knowledge of the Atomic Bomb Project prior to August 1945 was small'. No attempt was made to re-consider these judgments, with devastating consequences.[43]

In late 1949 the long-term effort to decypher and read Soviet cables began to bear fruit. The Venona programme, as it was known, identified several different atomic scientists known to have passed information to Moscow. Always referred to by codename, some of these figures remain unknown to this day. One of those identified was Klaus Fuchs, a German-born physicist who was to do more damage than any of the British atomic spies. He had worked on the Manhattan Project during the war, and had been involved with Britain's weapons pro-grammes since returning to England in 1946. In the early 1950s he confessed to espionage and very quickly it became apparent that his knowledge would have helped the Soviet Union immeasurably.[44] There was no substantial attempt by the JIC to assess the damage done by these various spies and defectors, either to atomic warfare or more generally. The sole attempt to do so in a 1951 JIC paper is noteworthy for its lack of detail: '[Soviet] scientific intelligence has been notably successful in penetrating the defence research of the West. Russian science, is now, therefore, in a position to give considerable assistance to the Soviet war machine'.[45]

The JIC's failure to probe the strategic implications of the damage caused by Soviet espionage is even harder to understand, despite the fact that administrative responsibility for security and counter-intelligence lay with MI5. Indeed, one of the consequences of Fuchs' treachery was to usher in a new form of security checking – Positive Vetting.[46] The JIC was actively involved in the promotion and implementation of Positive Vetting, partly in the Sigint field, but particularly in the atomic weapons arena and the Deputy-Directors' JIC meeting would contain regular agenda items on security, though never on espionage.[47]

Nuclear Stockpiling

While the forecasts of the timescale of the Soviet acquisition of an atomic bomb had varied, the ability to detect and decypher the bomb's radioactive signature was an unquestionable success. The problem, as the head of the atomic intelligence unit was well aware, was, in his words, that 'long distance detection techniques supply History *not* news. Nothing is as stale as yesterday's news. What the JIC want and what the JIC *demand* is pre-knowledge of what are the enemies' intentions for tomorrow'.[48] The problem was the lack of good, high quality, reliable information and, as with other targets, penetrating the Iron Curtain was not an easy task. Thus, in 1953, the JIC could report that 'we have very little concrete information about Soviet hopes and intentions in the atomic energy field'.[49] The difficulty was to know the direction and level of scientific progress of the Soviet programme. The Anglo-American detection programme had increased in scale, scope and technical expertise. It was therefore possible to gauge, with a high degree of accuracy, the scientific composition of atomic tests.[50] Furthermore, by the mid-1950s it was possible to know in advance when Soviet tests were imminent because communications traffic greatly increased.[51] But little was known about how the Soviet Union would choose to utilise its fissile material: would it rather have a hundred small bombs or ten very big ones?[52]

By 1953, views of the Soviet atomic weapons programme had altered, as one JIC document made clear:

> It was formerly believed that a considerable proportion of the Russian success in the atomic energy field was due to the results of espionage. While it is still obvious that this has played a large part in the direction of the Russian effort, and its importance cannot be overlooked, the latest studies have clearly shown that Russian science and industrial technique were more nearly equal to the challenge presented by atomic energy than was previously thought. Their independent approach to an early solution of many atomic energy problems ... shows that they are capable of making significant progress without outside assistance.[53]

This was an admission that previous assessments had been mistaken in believing the Soviet Union to be backward and technologically inferior. The real value in the assessments prepared by the JIC was the estimate of the size of the Soviet atomic stockpile, even allowing for difficulties in judging the size and type of device held. The following assessments of the number of bombs the Soviet Union would possess by different periods were made:

Table 10.2 British Estimates of Soviet nuclear stockpile

Date of Estimate / Stockpile size by	1951	1952	1953	1954
mid-1951	35–50[54]			
end-1951	55–75[55]			
mid-1952	70–100[56]	80–120[58]		
end-1952	90–140[57]			
mid-1953	105–175[59]	105–175[60]	90–140[61]	
end-1953			150–200[62]	
mid-1954				190–265[63]

US estimates, by contrast, were much lower than those of the UK, despite often being based on the same intelligence:

Table 10.3 American Estimates of Soviet nuclear stockpile

Date of Estimate / Stockpile size by	1950[64]	1951[65]	1952	1953
mid-1950	10–20			
mid-1951	25–45	45		
mid-1952	45–90	100		
mid-1953	70–135			

The most recent estimate of the Soviet stockpile, based on a variety of archival sources, reveals that both UK and US intelligence agencies over-estimated the number of weapons available to the Soviet Union, though the US was closer than its transatlantic counterparts in the UK.[66]

Table 10.4 Actual size of Soviet nuclear stockpile

Year	Number of atomic bombs
End-1950	5
End-1951	25
End-1952	50
End-1953	120
End-1954	150

In November 1955 the Soviet Union detonated Joe-19 (all Soviet tests at this time were named and numbered in this way in the UK and US, though the UK also had a different codename for each), a high yield explosion that was its first multi-staged thermonuclear device.[67] Deciphering the nuclear fingerprint was not an easy task, and it was some months before estimates could be revised. By April 1956 however, at a joint Anglo-American meeting, new figures for the size of the Soviet arsenal were derived, based on a stockpile of 30-kiloton weapons (each double the size of the Hiroshima bomb)[68]:

Table 10.5 Anglo-American estimates of Soviet 30-KT weapons

Date	Number of 30-KT weapons
Mid-1956	650
Mid-1957	850
Mid-1958	1,100
Mid-1959	1,400–1,750
Mid-1960	1,800–2,750

By 1956 British intelligence was receiving better information about the Soviet programme. Intelligence on test preparations was now able to predict well in advance when an event might take place, including preparations at the two major test sites of Semipalatinsk in Kazakhstan, and the Arctic island of Novaya Zemlya.[69] Other information, again provided by Sigint, suggested that estimates of the Soviet uranium stockpile should be increased by 50%.[70] Central to assessments of the Soviet programme and their broader significance was the ability to gauge 'nuclear sufficiency'. This was defined by the JIC as 'when the USSR has sufficient nuclear warheads and delivery systems to allocate to the targets which she would wish to destroy in nuclear war'.[71] By early 1957 the inference was that this had now been reached, for as the JIC assessed:

> the evidence available from Soviet nuclear test explosions suggests that the Russians could make any or all of the types of weapon known to the United Kingdom, over the whole of the possible ranges of yield. We have no definite evidence on what varieties of weapons they will have decided are militarily necessary or feasible to support their strategic and tactical policies. The actual stock of weapons estimated to be available to the Russians at any date can be expressed in a variety of ways depending on what are our assumptions regarding their weapons policy.[72]

Thus, an assessment could be reached – albeit imprecise – on Soviet nuclear weapons capabilities, but knowledge of intentions remained elusive.

Bomber Gap, What Bomber Gap?

If the USSR had attained 'nuclear sufficiency' it needed an adequate means of delivery, especially in this pre-missile era, to be effective. Of absolute importance, then, was information on the nature and characteristics of the Soviet Air Force (SAF), particularly its long-range bomber fleet. US intelligence in the 1950s and early 1960s was beset by two basic errors – the bomber and missile gaps – and both, arguably, were the result of political competition rather than analytical failure. These errors were solely American and it is interesting to note how officials in London observed them, especially given the close and frank exchanges between the countries.

An important difference between the stances taken in London and Washington was the most obvious: London was geographically much closer to Soviet air bases than Washington; by the end of the war in 1945 the UK was an easily accessible target, whereas the US was out of reach, even for one-way missions. Indeed, a report produced in 1945 by Sir Henry Tizard, one of Churchill's scientific advisers, highlighted just how vulnerable Britain was to future attack, particularly a nuclear one.[73] For the US it would take some time before this feeling of vulnerability would become a central security and strategic concern. Upon being briefed by the CIA on the photographs of Soviet missiles on Cuba in 1962, for instance, Prime Minister Harold Macmillan remarked 'now the Americans will realise what we here in England have lived through for the past many years'.[74]

Although the JIC concentrated on both the Soviet bomber and fighter fleets, it becomes increasingly clear from the JIC assessments that the former was the more important: the number of bombers was intrinsically linked to the Soviet war potential on the assumption that any war would be a nuclear one.[75] Although the Soviet Union might possess sufficient nuclear weapons to launch an attack, 'this factor can only become important when the Soviet Union can deliver them effectively.'[76]

In the late 1940s a range of information was received about the Tu-4 Soviet bomber, later to be known by the NATO codename 'BULL'. It was known that it was a reverse-engineered version of the US B-29 bomber, three of which had crashed during the war and the wreckage fallen into Soviet hands.[77] The possibility that the Tu-4 bomber could reach the US mainland had certainly worried some senior US policymakers. Following the first Soviet atomic test in 1949 this became an increasing concern, albeit not widely felt among the US media and public.[78] For the UK the estimated size of the BULL inventory was more worrying. In 1950 the JIC estimated that the Soviet Union could have as many as 1,000 by 1954, by which time 'improved conventional methods' would mean that variants produced from 1954 onwards would have longer ranges.[79] These assessments were often queried by the COS, who felt they were inflated and that the Soviet aircraft industry could not maintain the production rates consistent with JIC judgments.[80] As we now know, the JIC was correct and its estimates relatively accurate: at the end of production in 1952, for example, 847 aircraft had been produced.[81]

By the spring of 1951, the JIC was confident that the Soviet Union already had a 'considerable number' of these aircraft.[82] At the same time intelligence reports indicated that the SAF was increasing not only its numbers, but also improving its training and technical abilities – areas in which they were previously thought to have been deficient.[83] Intelligence on the SAF was therefore considered critical. A 1951 review indicated that the best means of obtaining this was through aerial reconnaissance, but as yet there was little photographic coverage of bomber bases. In spite of this, the bases and weapon stores utilized became a JIC 'top priority' for photo reconnaissance.[84] Indeed, intelligence on Soviet aircraft and airfields was to continue to be a 'top priority' throughout the rest of the 1950s.

British analyses of the Soviet threat assumed that both the UK and the US would be prime targets in any future conflict; JIC studies consequently included the Soviet threat vis-à-vis the United States. While acknowledging that Soviet bombers could theoretically reach the US, the JIC believed that the practical capability for such large-scale operations did not exist.[85] Indeed, because of the distances involved it was assessed in 1954 that the 'stage when they could seriously attack the US would not occur for some 10–15 years.'[86]

The same year a JIC paper reported that although 'the Russians were rapidly reducing the Western lead in nuclear development, it was not certain that they were making the same progress in developing the means of delivering an atomic attack.'[87] By this time the UK held a fairly conservative estimate of the abilities and capabilities of the long-range Soviet bomber force. By contrast, US assessments were beginning to show the first signs of what would become the 'bomber gap' myth.[88] In the UK, the tendency of the United States Air Force (USAF) to 'skew' estimates to suit their own needs had been detected early on. The matter was discussed at the JIC itself in 1952, where it was recorded that

> for some years the United States Air Force have been keenly concerned with obtaining the funds and authority to expand . . . DDI [Deputy Director for Intelligence, RAF] who three years ago was in the USA recollects numerous occasions on which the USAF were at pains to establish the existence of the air threat to justify this expansion in the face of opposition from the Navy in particular. The USAF have worked hard on this, and the idea of this threat [of an 'aerial Pearl Harbour'] has gained wide acceptance. It is likely that this idea has now become so deeply embedded in American and in particular USAF thinking that collated intelligence upon the subject is often subjective to it; it is noteworthy that the intelligence organisation of the USAF lends itself to this sort of distortion . . . there probably [are] powerful "vested interests" at work to ensure that the "intelligence threat" against the USA is not reduced.[89]

Estimates up to mid-1954 judged that the Tu-4 BULL was the mainstay of the Soviet long-range bomber force. By 1955 a new bomber – the Tu-16 BADGER – had been developed, though this was a theatre or medium-range aircraft rather than long-range bomber. Concurrently, there were early indications of the development of a new, far superior, Soviet long-range bomber. The M-4 BISON was a turbojet bomber, giving it a greater range of 12,000km.[90] First experimental flights had been conducted in January 1953, and the BISON was observed and photographed for the first time in July of that year, but it was not until 1955 that technical details were obtained and assessed by Air Technical Intelligence at the Air Ministry.[91] By May 1956 there had been less than ten BISON sightings, yet these were sufficient for analysts to conclude that 'the Bisons are now in operational service.'[92] Further glimpses of the aircraft revealed numerous variants, each with different objectives. One modification of the original aircraft was assessed to have a 'bulge' in the bomb bay, which suggested a re-fuelling capacity which might provide a theoretical capability of reaching US shores on a one-way mission. Another variant, known in the Soviet Union as the 3M model, was correctly identified as being able to achieve an even greater range.[93] As we now know, these intelligence assessments were accurate in terms of range, but overrated other capabilities and numbers.[94]

By September 1955 the JIC concluded that the Soviet long-range bomber fleet was being upgraded and re-equipped with 'modern jet medium and long-range bombers'. Notwithstanding this, the JIC argued that even with such a capability, 'by western standards its efficiency is low and at present it lacks the technical and operational ability to mount an effective attack against the United States.'[95]

US vulnerability was increased by the appearance of yet another heavy bomber, the Tu-95 BEAR, which was a different type of advance in aeronautical engineering. The sole objective in its design was to 'create [a] bomber capable of delivering nuclear weapons to US territory.' With four turbo-prop engines the BEAR was assessed to have a maximum unrefueled range of more than 15,000km (Moscow to Washington is approximately 7900km), possibly enabling it to return to base at the limit of its range. By early 1957 it could be concluded that the 'Soviet heavy bomber programme' had been brought 'almost into line with that of the United States'.[96] This revised assessment was based on new information about the production capacity and technical expertise of the Soviet aircraft industry, and by details on the duration of trial flights.[97] Thus, the JIC could conclude correctly that 'by 1957 if our estimate of the growth of the possible Soviet heavy bomber force is correct, they will be able to mount two-way operations against all bases in North America.'[98]

Ballistic Missiles

Nuclear science and aeronautical engineering were not the only military advances that the Soviet Union tried to acquire from the wreckage of the German scientific machine. It was also anxious to obtain ballistic missile technology and, to a lesser extent, chemical and biological warfare material and expertise. On the rocketry front, German progress, epitomised by the V-2, was far in advance of any competitor.

Co-operation on ballistic missiles exemplified the closeness of the Anglo-American intelligence relationship throughout this period. Beginning in 1949 there were regular and frank exchanges of intelligence on the Soviet ballistic missiles programme.[99] As with the nuclear programme, intelligence on missile and space launcher programmes was notably incomplete but, unlike the former, both US and UK estimates concentrated on short-term predictions.[100] It was concluded in 1950 that Soviet research was beginning to move beyond simply copying the wartime German V-2 technology.[101] Intelligence only began to improve from the early 1950s with the information provided through Operation

DRAGON RETURN – the programme of interrogating returning German scientists and technicians who had been taken to the Soviet Union at the end of the war – although this was restricted in scope to those (very limited) areas in which the Germans had been involved.[102]

Analysis of Soviet progress on missiles was based on British and American experience with German technology, and extrapolation from subsequent technological advances. The 1950 assessment that the Soviet Union had moved beyond the V-2 stage was therefore significant. JIC discussions in advance of a 1954 Anglo-American conference on the Soviet ballistic missile programme revealed uncertainty about its priorities. The debate focused on resources allocated to offensive and defensive systems – an issue that would later become particularly significant in the context of the concern over anti-ballistic missile (ABM) developments.

Intelligence at this time indicated that the Soviet ballistic missile programme could be more substantial than originally thought.[103] Crucially, and as an example of how differences of opinion could arise, the JIC warned that the UK should be 'wary' of US forecasts, particularly given their tendency to over-emphasise the Soviet threat.[104] Also the first evidence of what would become the 'missile gap' began to emerge in US estimates. Much like the earlier 'bomber gap', this would turn out to be a purely American fallacy.

As with the atomic weapons programme, gathering intelligence on Soviet ballistic missile development was two-fold. Information on actual deployed capabilities was often lacking; by contrast, Soviet progress with the development of individual programmes could be deduced with a high degree of accuracy through evidence gained from the monitoring of weapons tests. RAF missions beginning in 1954, initially codenamed Operation ROBIN, were tasked with overflying the Soviet missile range at Kapustin Yar.[105] Locating the Soviet missile test sites was important primarily to obtain telemetric data from tests themselves. Electronic intelligence (Elint) stations detected the Soviet monitoring of the missile's performance. The moment the test vehicle left its launch pad Soviet technicians received data from it through the emission of electrical signals that were automatically radioed back to them. Throughout its flight, from launch to impact, ground stations received the signals and were intercepted by western Elint units, and used to analyse performance.[106] As good as Elint coverage was, it could only provide limited information, for as a 1955 JIC paper explained: 'interception of signals traffic on what we believe to be the Russian ballistic rocket firing range ... has enabled us to deduce a great deal about their firing pro- gramme and the probable ranges to which they are firing. Yet we have never seen one of their weapons, we do not know how big it is, nor the war-head weight, nor the system of guidance, if any.'[107]

While intelligence on Soviet ballistic missile advances was of obvious concern to strategic planners, only in the mid-1950s did such anxieties become interlinked with nuclear developments. The apprehension was growing within the JIC that the Soviet nuclear weapons programme might be directed towards developing a warhead capable of being attached to a missile.[108] The JIC concluded in 1956 that the Soviet atomic and missile programmes might be merging, and that intermediate-range ballistic missiles would soon be able to reach the UK.[109] Yet it was felt that the Soviet Union would not reach the stage where it could test a ballistic missile with a nuclear warhead until 1960,[110] even though monitoring of launches from the Soviet test site at Kapustin Yar by the UK, led the JIC to conclude that Soviet spending on its own ballistic missile programme now exceeded that of the UK.[111]

In January 1957 a body of evidence, gathered on both sides of the Atlantic indicated that the Soviet Union had tested a nuclear payload for mounting on a launch vehicle, with a nominal yield, at one of the missile test sites.[112] JIC estimates of April 1957 stated that a 'marriage' between the Soviet missile and nuclear programmes had to be assumed. These tests so far had only involved low-yield devices and the Soviet Union's ability to construct larger yield devices small enough to be launched from a missile was an intelligence gap.[113] By May the JIC was confident enough to assert that, once operational, Soviet ballistic missiles would, without question, be equipped with nuclear warheads.[114] Consequently, by late 1957, the scientific intelligence community was in agreement that everything must be done to 'detect the tie-up that must exist between the Soviet nuclear weapons programme and the Soviet ballistic missile programme.'[115]

On 4 October 1957 Sputnik became the first man-made projectile to be put into earth-orbit. This was a huge Soviet propaganda success but of more long term significance were the advances in launcher technology and operational knowledge that had made Sputnik possible. Sputnik clearly demonstrated that the Soviet Union had taken a major step towards developing a launcher capable of delivering a nuclear payload. Its success was far in excess of previous UK/US estimates. The US, perhaps inevitably, drew the conclusion that the Soviet programme was more advanced than its own.

The event marked a major shift from the previous intelligence analysis of the Soviet war potential for, as Dr Ray Cline (a future Deputy Director of the CIA) commented, 'Sputnik in the fall of 1957 made us all aware that a new missile age, a new weapons age, had come about.'[116] In the UK the news was received with less alarm than in Washington. Intelligence estimates were adjusted: it was now assessed that Soviet nuclear armed missiles could attack British targets and that previous judgments of the Soviet missile programme had been incorrect.[117] Revised intelligence estimates now forecast that the first Soviet ICBMs could be operational by 1959.[118] By December 1957, in response to questions put by the Prime Minister, the JIC replied that the UK could now be in range of Soviet missiles, but only if launched from Eastern Europe, not the USSR itself.[119]

Soviet Chemical, Biological and Conventional Military Capabilities

Ultimately the JIC was able to provide realistic assessments on the status of the Soviet nuclear and bomber programmes. Although the UK was vulnerable to

Soviet air attack there was no indication that the Soviet Union was preparing to initiate hostilities. In addition, it was consistently argued that a nuclear war, or indeed any large-scale military conflict, was not in the Soviet Union's best interests. Why, then, did it maintain such enormous numbers of conventional forces on the European mainland, and what were its plans for use of chemical and biological weapons (CBW)?

In absorbing the remnants of Nazi science and scientists towards the end of hostilities, a further key area of Soviet interest was the acquisition of CBW capabilities, particularly in Asia. With the ending of hostilities in the Far East, the importance the Japanese had attached to successful CBW programmes became increasingly evident. Japanese army units had created and run an extensive programme that used large numbers of humans as guinea pigs. It was known that the Soviet Union had managed to capture some of the Japanese scientists before the US had scooped up the majority; and had tried to gather information from German wartime experiments. Yet the JIC's knowledge of Soviet CBW development had not progressed much since the war; in 1947 it still could not confirm the accuracy of reports received about progress since then. However, the JIC did offer the conclusion that both stocks of weapons and significant dispersal systems were in development.[120] The JIC would continue to monitor Soviet progress on CBW, with some marginal successes in increasing intelligence coverage, although in general terms the output remained patchy and many gaps were evident. Certainly though, the Soviet CBW threat was never seen as comparable to that posed by nuclear weapons.

Of more immediate concern was the growing body of reporting about the development of Soviet conventional forces. The JIC produced regular assessments of Soviet capabilities and capacity to wage war. Over time, estimates of the scale, nature and effectiveness of conventional forces varied. Increasingly the JIC assumed that in a war between the major powers, with the possible exception of small-scale proxy wars, any conflict was likely to escalate beyond the use of conventional forces, with nuclear weapons certain to be used. It followed, therefore, that the threat posed by conventional armies and air forces alone was of less significance. Thus, as one 1947 JIC paper stated, while 'the Soviet land forces . . . are sufficiently strong . . . to achieve rapid and far-reaching successes against any likely combination of opposing land forces', it was unlikely that the Soviet leadership would choose to initiate hostilities in this way.[121]

The Scale and Nature of the Threat

The JIC was justified in seeing the Soviet Union as posing a threat to UK interests in the period 1945–57, but the difficulty it faced lay in gauging its precise nature and assessing its severity. What was needed to underpin all forecasts and estimates of both Soviet intentions and capabilities was good, accurate and verifiable intelligence. But for the most part this was lacking. Sources tended to be low level. As a result, analysts had to rely heavily on underpinning their assessments with assumptions believed to be valid.

Former JIC Chairman Sir Percy Cradock has suggested that JIC assessments on the scale of the Soviet armed forces might have been fundamentally flawed because of the different UK and Soviet usage of the term 'division'. A British army division was larger than a Soviet one, so a simple comparison of numbers of divisions implied incorrect assessments.[122] In early 1947 the JIC considered this very problem. The issue of 'mirror-imaging' (though such a term was not used) was discussed, and as the SIS representative on the JIC stated: 'referring to the calculations for Russian forces, the onus of assessing [was on] how far data, based on British estimates, could be applied to Russian forces'.[123]. Meeting with members of the JIS, the Committee also discussed problems of drafting when intelligence was lacking. Captain Wynne, one of the Admiralty officers on the JIS, outlined the problem clearly: 'a further difficulty had been encountered when the assumptions and conditions on which the appreciations were to be based had not been agreed, with the originators of the requirement, at the outset.' Given the frequent gaps in coverage, agreeing assumptions at the start would have been essential if assessments were to be relevant.

Directly linked to these problems was the use of caveats and the need to ensure that the readership, at this time principally the Directorate of Plans and the COS, understood the nature of the intelligence on which the assessments had been formulated. The vast majority of the JIC papers on Soviet capabilities contained the caveat that 'we do not have any good sources of information'. But the assessments would then proceed to itemise the number of nuclear weapons the Soviet Union might possess, types of anti-aircraft equipment, or the precise size of its air force. Thus, the JIC readership might well have had grounds to question any firm conclusions reached. This was a problem to which members of the JIC were alive. For instance, in the words of one of the JIB representatives, who 'suggested that in order to avoid expressing any definite estimates which, in spite of every caveat that might be attached to them, could be taken as a firm base for planning purposes, answers should be given broad limits on either side of the mean estimate'.[124] Another proposal was to provide parentheses around any tentative figures quoted in assessments.[125]

The nature of the assumptions underlying estimates was particularly significant and led to differences between UK and US assessments. Following the detonation of the first Soviet atomic device in August 1949, a key question was how this event, some two to three years earlier than predicted, might affect subsequent assessments of the Soviet atomic weapons programme. The issue, as JIC Chairman William Hayter informed the COS Committee in late 1949, was that:

> the Division of Atomic Energy [UK] believed that it was a test explosion and did not indicate the beginning of a full scale production. The United States, however, believed that it was the first bomb off the production line and they therefore wished to increase estimates of production rates accordingly.[126]

So the US and UK, despite regular contact and using essentially the same evidence, appear to have reached quite different conclusions.

In another, later example from 1957 concerning the Soviet ballistic missile programme, the UK assessed that a delay was likely once there had been a successful test of an ICBM, prior to it coming into service. The US, by contrast, thought that deployment would follow immediately after a test. As the JIC noted in its review of the joint 1957 UK/US/Canada conference on guided weapons:

> there was very general agreement on the dates by which the USSR could bring the various equipment into service; the differences in the forecast dates were greatest in fields where intelligence was most lacking. In some cases the US forecast dates were more optimistic from the Soviet point of view than ours, as the US considered that the Soviet Union might bring missiles into operational use before field trials had been completed. Our estimates have been based on the contrary view.[127]

At one level this difference in interpretation is harder to understand because the extent of co-operation in the ballistic missiles field was greater than for nuclear intelligence, with annual high-level conferences to discuss and interpret Soviet progress. One explanation lay in the tendency to extrapolate from differing national experiences to determine how the Soviet Union, considered somewhat technologically inferior, might progress. The UK view, that there would be a time lag between trials and operational deployment of ballistic missiles, was based on the British experience. Undermining the US position, as the JIC was only too well aware, were institutional biases, bureaucratic in-fighting, and a desire to inflate the Soviet threat.

For the most part the JIC assessments were neither alarmist nor dismissive. The language of the assessments was balanced and dispassionate; the routinely equivocal style would have done little to galvanise policy planners to action. At no stage in the period from the end of the war to the launch of Sputnik does it appear that the JIC considered that there was a significant possibility of a Soviet attack. Quite clearly the Soviet Union had the capability to strike at the UK but, in the view of the JIC, it did not intend to do so.

In many respects therefore, despite the gaps in coverage and the tremendous difficulties in penetrating the Soviet war machine, the JIC provided a balanced view, being neither exaggerated nor complacent (notwithstanding persistent perceptions of Soviet technical limitations), and the military planners were never brought into the debate. Only on rare occasions did the COS Committee question the basis of assessments or suggest re-drafting.[128] On the other hand, the failure of the JIC, and indeed Whitehall as a whole, to take the threat of Soviet espionage seriously was clearly an error that would not be re-examined until it was too late. Likewise the view, held by many, that the Soviet Union was technologically backward when compared to its Western counterparts, was frequently shown to be wrong.

In relations with the US, with the exception of nuclear matters, where a US Act of Congress barred complete exchange of technical information, intelligence liaison on Soviet capabilities was extremely close. That did not prevent differences in opinion and interpretation from arising and, where self-interest was involved, US and UK analysts often reached different conclusions on the basis of much the same information.

The JIC's role, in terms of assessing Soviet capabilities, changed during this period. Initially the priority was essentially to predict when the Soviet Union would acquire the bomb, how quickly it could be mass produced, and how well and how far it would progress technologically. By the early 1950s, the main effort was built on the interpretation of telemetric data, observations of aircraft and analysis of bomb test debris. Supported by the scientific staffs and research establishments, and the economic and industry analysts of the JIB, the JIC was able to monitor and understand these indicators, but unable to offer predictions for the future.[129] The JIC's sources were not good enough to provide definitive answers. As there was no way of obtaining clear insight into Soviet intentions, the JIC concentrated on producing sound assessments of Soviet military capabilities. While revealing some biases and shortcomings in its analytical framework, the JIC generally succeeded in providing a balanced perspective on the growth of Soviet military capabilities and, despite the difficulties, made credible judgements on intentions. It never once 'cried wolf'.

Notes

1 For instance, consider the case of the US rush to capture the components of the wartime Japanese biological warfare programme. S Harris, *Factories of Death: Japanese Biological Warfare, 1932–1945, and the American Cover-Up* (London: Routledge, 1995).

2 For more information see S A Goudsmit, *Alsos: The Failure in German Science* (New York: Schuman, 1947); B T Pash, *The Alsos Mission* (New York: Charter, 1969); and P V Oleynikov, 'German Scientists in the Soviet Atomic Project', *The Nonproliferation Review* (Summer 2000), pp.1–30.

3 For instance, see L Hunt, *Secret Agenda: The United States Government, Nazi Scientists, and Project Paperclip, 1945–1990* (London: St Martin's Press, 1991); also, J Farquharson, 'Governed or Exploited? The British Acquisition of German Technology, 1945–48', *Journal of Contemporary History* 32:1 (January 1997), pp.23–42.

4 Details can be found in AVIA 54/1403 & AVIA 54/1406.

5 Various papers on this can be found in CAB 81/130.

6 Their terms of reference can be found in CAB 81/131.

7 JIC/1883/45, 'Chairmanship of the Joint Scientific Intelligence Committee', 18 December 1945. CAB 176/8.

8 JIC/1736/45, 'Interrogation of 3 German Scientists', 20 November 1945. CAB 176/8.

9 JIC/1852/45, 'Interrogation of Three German Scientists', 11 December 1945. CAB 176/8.

10 JIC/1907/45, 'Interrogation of Three German Scientists', 23rd December 1945. CAB 176/8.

11 JIC(46)8(0)(Final), 'Disposal of German Scientists and Russian Activities Connected Therewith', 29 January 1946. CAB 81/132.

12 JIC(46)79(0)(FINAL),'Russian Enticement of German Scientists and Technicians', 21 August 1946. CAB 81/134.

13 JIC(46)102(0)(Final),'Recruitment of Low Grade Scientists in Germany For Intelligence Purposes', 16 November 1946. CAB 81/134.

14 JIC(46)109(0), 'Brief for the Scientific and Technical Intelligence Branch, Control Commission for Germany', 14 December 1946. CAB 81/134.

15 JIC/1468/45, 'Intelligence on Atomic Energy', 11 October 1945. CAB 176/8.

16 On the top priority status see JIC(47)64th Meeting (0), 24 September 1947. CAB 159/2.

17 JIC/1275/45, 'Intelligence on Tube Alloys', 5 September 1945. CAB 176/7.

18 Fuller details can be found in FO 1093/192.

19 JIC(45)311(0), 'Intelligence on Atomic Energy', 6 November 1945. CAB 81/131.

20 Further details of the atomic intelligence unit and the 1950s reforms can be found in Goodman, *Spying on the Nuclear Bear*.

21 Details of these intelligence operations can be found in 'The Organisation and Functions of STIB', November 1950. DEFE 21/24.

22 JIC/995/46, 'Overt Intelligence on Atomic Energy', 26 July 1946. CAB 176/12.

23 JIC(46)1(0)Final(Revise), 'Russians Strategic Interests and Intentions', 1 March 1946. CAB 81/132.

24 'Estimate of Russian Atomic Weapons Programme and Timetable', 28 January 1949. DEFE 21/45.

25 JIC(48)9(0)FINAL, 'Russian Interests, Intentions and Capabilities', 23 July 1948. CAB 158/3.

26 JIC/995/46, 'Overt Intelligence on Atomic Energy', 26 July 1946. CAB 176/12.

27 'Estimate of Russian Atomic Weapons Programme and Timetable', 28 January 1949. DEFE 21/45.

28 COS(45)651(0), 'Atomic Energy – Immediate Policy for Great Britain', 10 November 1945. CAB 80/98.

29 JIC(46)95(0)(Final), 'Future Scale of Attack on the United Kingdom', 12 November 1946. CAB 81/134.

30 JIC(47)7/2(Final), 'Soviet Interests, Intentions and Capabilities', 6 August 1947. CAB 158/1.

31 JIC(47)42(0)(Final), 'Forecast of the World Situation in 1957', 12 June 1948. CAB 158/1. Also, JIC(48)9(0)FINAL, 'Russian Interests, Intentions and Capabilities', 23 July 1948. CAB 158/3.

32 'Estimate of Russian Atomic Weapons Programme and Timetable', 28 January 1949. DEFE 21/45.

33 JIC(48)13(0)FINAL, 'Soviet Interests, Intentions and Capabilities', 6 February 1948. CAB 158/3.

34 JIC(47)7/2(Final), 'Soviet Interests, Intentions and Capabilities', 6 August 1947. CAB 158/1. The JIC were also asked to provide reports on offensive nuclear war plans, such as the 'best method of using the atom bomb against Russia'. Confidential Annex to COS(50)162nd Meeting, 5 October 1950. DEFE 32/1.

35 JIC/732/49, 'Soviet Interests and Intentions', 22 April 1949. CAB 176/22.

36 For a background to the monitoring effort and the successful detection, see Goodman, *Spying on the Nuclear Bear*. pp.43–9.

37 Cited in Andrew, *Defence of the Realm*. pp.385–6. Liddell was Deputy Director-General at this time.

38 JS/JTIC(49)32nd Meeting, 28 September 1949. DEFE 41/73.

39 JIC/2124/49, 'Implications of Soviet Atomic Development', 26 November 1949. CAB 176/24.

40 The JIC's views were recorded in the diary of Guy Liddell. Cited in Andrew, *Defence of the Realm*. p.390.

41 For more see Goodman, *Spying on the Nuclear Bear*. pp.69–85.

42 JIC/683/46, 'Leakages of Information on Atomic Energy', 17 May 1946. CAB 176/11.

43 JIC/1455/47, 'Russian Knowledge of the Atomic Bomb', 8 December 1947. CAB 176/16.

44 The COS were extremely anxious, not solely for the advantage given to the Soviet Union, but also that the US might suspend plans for greater collaboration, though in their discussions they did not request a fresh JIC review. See Confidential Annex to COS(50)26th Meeting, 13 February 1950 and Confidential Annex to COS(50)29th Meeting, 20 February 1950. DEFE 32/1. For more see M S Goodman, 'Grandfather of the Hydrogen Bomb? Klaus Fuchs and Anglo-American Intelligence', *Historical Studies in the Physical and Biological Sciences* 34:1 (2004), pp.1–22.

45 JIC(51)79(FINAL), 'Appreciation of Soviet Capabilities and Intelligence 1951 to 1954 for NATO Standing Group', 28 September 1951. CAB 158/13.

46 See Andrew, *Defence of the Realm*. pp.382–95.

47 For instance, on Sigint see JIC/1546/52, 'Positive Vetting', 7 July 1952. CAB 158/75.

48 Eric Welsh, 'Atomic Energy Intelligence', DEFE 41/126. Emphasis in original.

49 JIC(53)14(Final), 'Soviet and Satellite War Potential', 10 April 1953. CAB 158/15.

50 For more see Goodman, *Spying on the Nuclear Bear*. pp.86–117.

51 'Sigint Pointers to the Size of Soviet Nuclear Explosions', 7 June 1955. CAB 158/79. See also 'State of Readiness for Possible Soviet Nuclear Tests', 22 July 1955. DEFE 19/69.

52 For instance, see the results of a week-long UK-US conference on atomic intelligence: JIC/1461/50, 'Intelligence on Atomic Energy', 11 August 1950. CAB 176/27.

53 JIC/2225/53, 'Russian Atomic Energy Developments', 18 September 1953. CAB 158/78.

54 JIC(51)18(Final-Revise), 'Scale and Nature of Air Attack Against the United Kingdom', 31 May 1951. CAB 158/12.

55 JIC(51)117(Final), 'Soviet and Satellite War Potential', 22 April 1951. CAB 158/13.

56 JIC(51)117(Final), 'Soviet and Satellite War Potential', 22 April 1951. CAB 158/13.

57 JIC(51)117(Final), 'Soviet and Satellite War Potential', 22 April 1951. CAB 158/13.

58 JIC(52)63(Final), 'Military and Economic Strength of the Soviet Union', 8 October 1952. CAB 158/14.

59 JIC(51)117(Final), 'Soviet and Satellite War Potential', 22 April 1951. CAB 158/13.

60 'MoD to BJSM', 8 April 1952. DEFE 21/62.

61 JIC(53)14(Final), 'Soviet and Satellite War Potential, 1953–1957', 10 April 1953. CAB 158/15.

62 JIC(53)79(Final), 'Likelihood of General War with the Soviet Union up to the End of 1955', 10 September 1953. CAB 158/16.

63 JIC(54)36, 'Russian research and Development', 6 April 1954. CAB 158/17.

64 'The Effect of the Soviet Possession of the Atomic Bombs on the Security of the United States', CIA ORE 32–50, 9 June 1950. Harry S. Truman Presidential Library, Independence, MO (hereafter HST): PSF: Intelligence File, Box 257.

65 'Soviet Capabilities for a Military Attack on the United States Before July 1952', CIA SE-14, 23 October 1951. HST: PSF: Intelligence File, Box 258.

66 R S Norris & W M Arkin, 'NRDC Nuclear Notebook: Global Nuclear Stockpiles, 1945–2000', *The Bulletin of the Atomic Scientists* 56:2 (March/April 2000), p.79.

67 From this point the term 'nuclear' is used to describe the Soviet programme.

68 JIC(56)53(Final), 'Soviet Bloc Strengths and Capabilities, 1956–1960', 13 April 1956. CAB 158/24.

69 'Possible Soviet Test Preparation', 2 August 1956. CAB 158/80.

70 'Minutes of Atomic Energy Intelligence Committee Meeting', 1 October 1956. CAB 158/81.

71 'Nuclear Sufficiency', Note by Chief of the Air Staff, September 1958. AIR 8/1942.

72 JIC(56)113(Final), 'Military and Economic Strength of the Soviet Union', 25 January 1957. CAB 158/26.

73 'Report on Future Developments in Weapons and Methods of War', 19 June 1945. CAB 137/19.

74 Cited in Chester L Cooper Oral History, Part 2, John F. Kennedy Presidential Library, Boston, MA. Available at: www.jfklibrary.org

75 Parts of the following paragraphs have appeared, albeit in an earlier form, in Goodman, *Spying on the Nuclear Bear.*

76 JIC(50)77(Revise), 'The Likelihood of War with the Soviet Union and the Date by which the Soviet Leaders Might Be Prepared to Risk It', 18 August 1950. CAB 158/11.

77 See Goodman, *Spying on the Nuclear Bear.* pp.32–3.

78 J Prados, *The Soviet Estimate: US Intelligence Analysis and Soviet Strategic Forces* (Princeton: Princeton University Press, 1989). pp.39–40.

79 JIC(50)98(Final), 'Soviet Capabilities and Intentions 1951 and 1954 – Brief for Western European Regional Planning Group', 27 November 1950. CAB 158/11.

80 For instance, see COS(49)64th Meeting, 4 May 1949. DEFE 4/21.

81 T Kadyshev, 'Strategic Aviation' In P Podvig (ed), *Russian Strategic Nuclear Forces* (London: MIT Press, 2001). pp.340–341. Note that this figure represented the total reported production run; the number in service at any one time would have been less.

82 JIC(51)4/1(Final), 'Soviet Long Term Preparations for War – Review of Major Development During the Year Ending 31st December 1950', 4 April 1951. CAB 158/12.

83 JIC(51)6(Final), 'The Soviet Threat', 19 January 1951. CAB 158/12.

84 JIC(52)72, 'Strategic Air Photographic Intelligence', 21 November 1952. CAB 158/14.

85 JIC(54)3(Final), 'Soviet and Satellite War Potential, 1954–1958 – Report by the JIC', 15 February 1954. CAB 158/17.

86 COS 221/25/2/52, 'United States Strategic Policy', 25 February 1954. DEFE 32/4.

87 GEN 465 1st Meeting, 12 March 1954. CAB 130/101.

88 L Freedman, *United States Intelligence and the Soviet Strategic Threat* (London: Palgrave, 1986).

89 JIC/2150/52, 'Likelihood of War', 22 September 1952. CAB 176/38.

90 Kadyshev, 'Strategic Aviation', pp.375–9.

91 DDI(Tech) [Air Ministry], Paper 2/57, 'Soviet Heavy Bomber Bison', June 1957. AIR 40/2724.

92 'Air Ministry Secret Intelligence Summary', Vol.11, No.5 (May 1956), p.15. AIR 22/94.

93 DDI(Tech) [Air Ministry], Paper 2/57, 'Soviet Heavy Bomber Bison', June 1957. AIR 40/2724.

94 Kadyshev, 'Strategic Aviation', pp.375–9.

95 JIC(55)58(Final)(Revise), 'Likely Soviet Courses of Action up to 1st January, 1957', 30 September 1955. CAB 158/21.

96 JIC/319/57, 'Soviet Heavy Bomber Production', 5 February 1957. CAB 158/82.

97 JIC(57)119(Final), 'Soviet Heavy Bomber Strength and Production', 28 February 1957. CAB 158/82.

98 JIC(56)7(Final), 'The Soviet Strategic Air Plan in the Early Stages of a Global War, 1956–1960', 20 February 1956. CAB 158/23.

99 'Joint Anglo-American Conference: A Study of the Soviet Guided Missile Programme', March 1949. DEFE 44/99.

100 J Stocker, *Britain and Ballistic Missile Defence, 1942–2002* (London: Frank Cass, 2004). p.43.

101 'Evans [Director, STIB] to Chief, BAOR', 4 December 1950. DEFE 41/91.

102 B Cole, 'British Technical Intelligence and the Soviet Intermediate Range Ballistic Missile Threat, 1952–1960', *Intelligence and National Security* 14:2 (Summer 1999), p.72.

103 JIC(54)36, 'Russian Research and Development', 6 April 1954. CAB 158/17.

104 JIC(54)104th Meeting, 18 November 1954. CAB 159/17. At this meeting they also discussed whether the Russians might be working on a 'flying saucer' – something it

was known that the Germans had worked on and which the Canadians were actively pursuing. It is never revealed quite what the 'flying saucer' was.

105 'Vice-Chief of the Air Staff to the Secretary of State for Air', 17 August 1955. AIR 19/1106. See also C Pocock, 'Operation 'Robin' and the British Overflight of Kapustin Yar: A Historiographical Note', *Intelligence and National Security* 17:4 (Winter 2002), pp.185–92.

106 D S Brandwein, 'Telemetry Analysis', *CIA Studies in Intelligence* (Fall 1964), p.21.

107 JIC(55)29(Final), 'State of Our Intelligence on the Sino Soviet Bloc and Measures to Improve It', 13 July 1955. CAB 158/79.

108 JIC(54)42, 'Russian Capacity to Deliver Thermo-nuclear Weapons', 22 April 1954. CAB 158/17.

109 JIC(56)23(Final), 'US/UK Guided Weapons Intelligence Conference', 2 February 1956. CAB 158/24.

110 JIC(56)53(Final), 'Soviet Bloc Strength and Capabilities, 1956–1960. Comments on Standing Group Estimate SG 161/9', 13 April 1956. CAB 158/24.

111 JIC(56)34, 'Russian Ballistic Rocket Development', 6 March 1956. CAB 158/24.

112 JIC(57)53(Final), 'Military and Economic Strength of the Soviet Union', 8 July 1957. CAB 158/29. This was in fact the second such test, the first being in February 1956.

113 JIC(57)28(Final), 'Soviet Capabilities and Probable Programme in the Field of Guided Weapons', 11 April 1957. CAB 158/26.

114 JIC(57)41(Final)(Revise), 'Soviet Ground-Ground Guided Missiles Threat to the United Kingdom', 10 May 1957. CAB 158/26.

115 E.C.Williams [scientific intelligence adviser to the MoD] to H.S.Young [Deputy-Director Scientific Intelligence, JIB], 12 November 1957. DEFE 21/62.

116 LHCMA: Nuclear Age: 11/31, Interview with Dr R.Cline, 1989.

117 Cole, 'British Intelligence', p.81.

118 JIC/2291/57, 'Comments on Various Military Factors Affecting Soviet Capabilities and Intentions over the next Five Years', CIA Memorandum, Annex, 22 October 1957. DEFE 13/342.

119 'Replies to Questions Asked by the Prime Minister of the JIC in the Course of His Minute to the Minister of Defence No.630/57 dated 28 December 1957'. DEFE 7/970.

120 JIC(47)22(0), 'Present Stage of Progress in Biological Warfare in Foreign Countries', 25 April 1947. CAB 158/1.

121 JIC(47)7/2 Final, 'Soviet Interests, Intentions and Capabilities – General', 6 August 1947. CAB 158/1.

122 Cradock, *Know Your Enemy*. p.52. The US encountered a similar issue with this over the size of the US and Soviet navies in the 1970s.

123 JIC(47)18th Meeting (0), 26 March 1947. CAB 159/1.

124 JIC(47)15th Meeting (0), 14 March 1947. CAB 159/1.

125 JIC(47)18th Meeting (0), 26 March 1947. CAB 159/1.

126 JIC/2124/49, 'Implications of Soviet Atomic Development', 26 November 1949. CAB 176/24.

127 JIC(57)68, 'US/UK/Canada Conference on Guided Missile Intelligence', 21 June 1957. CAB 158/82. See also H Dylan, 'Britain and the Missile Gap: British Estimates on the Soviet Ballistic Missile Threat, 1957–61', *Intelligence and National Security*, 23:6 (2009), pp.777–806.

128 This happened, for example, in 1952 with JIC estimates of the overall size of the Soviet bomb force. See H Dylan, *The Joint Intelligence Bureau: Economic, Topographic and Military Intelligence for Britain's Cold War, 1946–64* (PhD thesis, University of Aberystwyth, 2010).

129 It was the role of the FO's Russia Committee to analyse trends in policy – called the 'crystal gazer' – and to look at Soviet intentions and predict what changes might happen in the future.

11 War in the Far East

Part I – Conflict in China and Korea

In September 1944 Victor Cavendish-Bentinck chaired a meeting in the offices of the War Cabinet. As Chairman of the JIC he had so far had a good war, helping the Committee to improve its standing in Whitehall. The meeting was a high-level conference of military intelligence directors drawn from Britain and the Commonwealth, designed to co-ordinate intelligence efforts in the Far East. Although the conference was primarily focussed on winning the war, in a rather sombre speech, Major General Charles Lamplough, the Director of Intelligence for South-East Asia Command (SEAC), warned how 'there was a danger . . . that when Japan was defeated, the British Government might consider that they could economise on Intelligence in the Far East; it should be remembered that there might be other nations who would need watching'.[1] The discussions concluded with a clear agreement that there ought to be a British intelligence presence in the Far East, but there was no sense of urgency, no suggestion that a potential threat might emerge in the future, and certainly no consideration of the possibility that British forces might be needed within a few short years. Whilst most of the JIC's post-war attention was focussed on Europe, the communist presence in the Far East steadily grew, threatening not just British colonial possessions, but also raising broader questions about the future battle lines of the Cold War and the global nature of the 'threat'.

A series of events, starting with the Malayan Emergency in 1948 (see chapter 12), quickly caught the JIC's attention, but it would be a matter of too little too late. Certainly the JIC's efforts in the immediate post-war period were Euro-centric, stemming from an assumption that Europe would be the Cold War battleground. The Far East, for so long the domain of colonial powers, would remain just that. At stake was the ability of the JIC to forecast long-term political developments, which was always a more difficult task. As a result, the rise of Asian nationalism was never seriously examined.

Underpinning everything was the much vaunted Anglo-American special relationship, yet, as events revealed, in the case of the Far East this was not quite so 'special' as elsewhere. There were disagreements over China, Korea, and assistance to Formosa (later Taiwan). The British were alarmed by the actions of General MacArthur in Korea, and were anxious that concerns over Hong Kong were not shared in Washington. These political differences filtered down to influence intelligence contacts, with a serious and alarming effect on collaboration and confidence. In short, events in the Far East unsettled and were in stark contrast with the friendly and mutually beneficial intelligence relationship between the UK and the US that had characterised European affairs. This divergence of opinion continued until the growing communist presence in the Far East reached a point where both sides once more understood the value of cooperation in the face of common problems and potential adversaries.

A Storm Brewing

In the latter stages of the Second World War the primary focus for Britain's intelligence services had been almost exclusively in Europe (see chapter 6). This had made strategic sense at the time and was not seriously questioned in the immediate post-war period. The conference on the 'Co-ordination of Intelligence in the Far East', held in late 1944, certainly suggested that there was a consensus amongst military intelligence officers of the Commonwealth that the Far East was still important and should not be ignored. Yet despite this, given the emerging Soviet threat, Europe remained the central focus of the JIC and British intelligence. The discussions between the military and the FO as to the Soviet Union's intentions tended to obscure other developments. Thus, when intelligence requirements were first reconsidered for the post-war world, in July 1945, it was agreed that only in those regions where Soviet influence could clearly be detected should the Far East be considered for priority treatment. Only with Soviet support could a significant threat to British interests exist, and China was cited as a typical example.[2]

Whilst the overwhelming focus was Europe, the Far East certainly was not neglected. Throughout the second half of 1945 the JIC produced a steady trickle of papers on the Far East. These tended to examine two broad areas: the evolving situation in China with the revival of the civil war between the Nationalists and the communists, and the status of the other major European powers in the region and the control of their colonies (see chapter 12). But despite the variety of papers, the conviction persisted that there could be no threat in the region without a serious commitment from Moscow.[3] For instance, one of the first post-war assessments of China concluded that 'China has emerged from the war so weak as to be negligible by herself'.[4] In late 1946 the JIC began to take a more serious look at the region, prompted by the dismantling of SEAC and the need to provide more intelligence. The JIC proposed to the COS the creation of a regional JIC supported by a regional JIS to draft the papers,[5] arrangements which would mirror its own structure and role. These proposals were subsequently accepted and JIC(FE) began work in Singapore in February 1947.[6]

One of JIC(FE)'s first tasks was to cease the issue of a weekly summary of intelligence reports from the region which had been a JIC(SEAC) practice. Instead, it would only issue reports to London as and when the situation demanded.[7] Its first substantive output comprised two papers, transmitted to London in August 1947. One was a study of defence problems in the Far East;

the other on how the region might descend into war. London's comments on the two papers provide a first glimpse into how the post-war JIC saw the region and assessed the level of Soviet involvement in the event of war. The JIC considered that any Soviet offensive would be limited to subversion, and that therefore communist activities should be 'more closely analysed'. Connected to this was the question as to whether China, as a nation, would disintegrate under the weight of the civil war. On consideration of the same intelligence, JIC(FE) was more convinced that this would be the case than was the JIC in London. JIC(FE) assessed that substantial areas would fall under the influence of Moscow exerting control through local Chinese communist regime. In this context the JIC was still firmly convinced that the Soviet Union would avoid war for the foreseeable future.[8]

The key to security lay with China, where the Soviet Union saw its best opportunity to obtain a foothold in the Far East. Since the late 1920s a civil war had been underway on the Chinese mainland, the outcome of which would not ultimately be clear until the communist victory in 1949. Initially the Nationalists, under Sun Yat-Sen, had collaborated with the communists, but following the rise of Chiang Kai-Shek as leader of the Kuomintang nationalist party in 1926, ties with Moscow were broken. From that point a bitter and deadly rivalry emerged between Chiang's movement and that of the Chinese communists, soon to be led by Mao Zedong. During the war both sides had presented a united front against the Japanese invaders, and although actual fighting between them would not resume until mid-1946, in practice by the end of the Second World War China was a divided nation: Chiang controlled large areas of the south while Mao was in charge of parts of the north. Both Britain and America had contributed to the Chinese effort to remove Japanese forces from the mainland but by late 1945, as elsewhere, the UK was forced to rethink its position for budgetary reasons: as the JIC made clear, 'she [Britain] now waits to see what America will do'. Of greatest importance then, was the issue of Chinese communist links to Moscow, particularly as, in the JIC's words, Britain was 'liable to bear the brunt of China's xenophobia'.[9]

SIS reports hinted at Soviet assistance to the Chinese but found little 'concrete evidence'.[10] The JIC's first assessments of China following the end of the war in the Pacific concluded that 'Russia is giving covert encouragement', for the very specific purpose of breaking up China and ensuring that those provinces not in the control of the nationalist Kuomintang could be turned communist. Despite apparent Chinese willingness to take up offers of Soviet assistance, it was recognised that there were differences between aspirations of the Chinese and Soviet communists, and that crucially they 'do not see eye to eye'.[11] Two things are clear from the JIC's assessment of the situation in China in November 1945: firstly, evidence indicated preparations for a major civil war as both Mao and Chiang were intent on achieving complete control of a unified China; secondly the JIC was completely unaware of American planning. This was a serious omission given that there was some evidence of proxy involvement in China by the US supporting Chiang and the Soviet Union assisting Mao, although the detail was not clear cut.[12]

A Storm across the Atlantic

Although the uprising in Malaya would be the first warning sign, events in China would reinforce the now heightened priority of the Far East. While not ignoring China, the JIC had not given it much prominence. A number of reports had looked, to a greater or lesser extent, at various topics; these included the strengths of the two factions, whether China posed a military threat to Hong Kong, and the precise level of Soviet interest and involvement. In early 1948 the JIC returned to the subject. In the most detailed assessment so far, the JIS utilised reporting from a wide array of sources, including FO reporting, Service attachés, the Colonial Office and JIC(FE), though it is not clear whether any good covert sources were available.

The 1948 assessment judged that the civil war in China was 'definitely' going the way of the communists, and that the status of the Nationalist forces would continue to deteriorate, although this was 'unlikely' to lead to 'political collapse'. The JIC concluded, accurately as events transpired, that communist forces would be concentrated around the Yangtze River, and that, despite hundreds of millions of dollars flowing from the US to the Nationalists, 'it would not prove effective' in stemming the communist tide.[13] By December the continued successes of the Chinese communists were, in the JIC's view, beginning to extend beyond national boundaries: 'there are indications that the Chinese Communist Party welcomes the leading role among communists in the Far East. The large and increasing Chinese communities in the Far East are and will continue to be influenced by the sweeping successes of the Chinese Communists against the Nationalist Government'.[14] The COS unanimously approved the report, asking for it to be revisited in three month's time, particularly as there had been disagreement between the Air Ministry and War Office about the impact of communist rule in China on other nations in the region.[15]

In January 1949 the JIC approved and circulated an assessment prepared by JIC(FE) on the 'likely effects' of a communist victory in China. The 'major assumption' of this paper, which served to narrow its focus, was that the aims of the Chinese Communist Party were 'identical' with those of the Soviet Union. The assessment made clear that it was not a question of whether the whole of China would become communist, but of when. As with the December 1948 assessment, this report concluded that the effects of a communist victory would be felt far beyond China, and would serve to increase support for the communists in the neighbouring regions of Malaya and Indochina.[16]

The JIC's quarterly update on the region, approved in April 1949, opened with the statement that a 'militant communist front throughout the Far East' was now evident. This 'front' had been strengthened greatly by the continued communist successes in China and, while it had inspired communist parties in other countries, in equal measure it had 'roused' many governments to a 'realisation of the communist threat'. Once in power – again, a question of when, not if – the Chinese communist leadership would try to increase its support and control over communism in the whole of the Far East.[17] Reflecting the change in the focus of attention, the three Services' Directors of Plans emphasised that the increased focus on China was diverting much-needed resources away from Europe. The JIC suspected that events were being orchestrated in Moscow as part of a global strategy to distract the West from concentrating on Europe.[18]

One difficulty which plagued assessments was the availability and speed by which information was analysed and transmitted. This was summed up by the Vice CIGS, Lieutenant General Sir Gerald Templer, who stated that:

> the Chiefs of Staff Committee were not at present in a position to give an immediate and co-ordinated appreciation of the situation in the Far East if it were required by His Majesty's Government . . . although factual information was available in Whitehall [albeit limited], the situation was constantly developing and changing and it would at any time be difficult to assemble all the available information into a composite appreciation at short notice.[19]

Despite these caveats, there was a great demand for up to date information. On 9 May 1949 the Cabinet discussed the situation in China and, as a direct result, the JIS was instructed to maintain a map in the 'Prime Minister's Map Room', where it could be easily accessed.[20] At the same time the JIC continued to issue a series of reports on China for which the COS seemed content, despite accepting that there was 'very little information available on which to base these reports'.[21] In briefing the COS Committee in June 1949, William Hayter, Chairman of the JIC, informed the chiefs that one of the problems of collecting intelligence was that the Hong Kong police, especially the Commissioner, had rejected calls for a local JIC.[22]

By 1949, with the JIC producing a fortnightly assessment on the threat to Hong Kong, politicians and diplomats discussed whether or not His Majesty's Government should formally recognise the Chinese communist government. For the UK the region was vitally important, not only because of the strategic significance of Hong Kong, but also given its financial links in the area. As the introduction to the document-based FO history of Britain and China makes clear, 'it was still in Britain's interests to maintain trade with China, the UK should not be squeamish about "reddening hands" and doing business with the Communists.'[23]

The position taken by the US complicated matters. As Foreign Secretary Ernest Bevin informed the Cabinet in August 1949, the UK had held a series of discussions with the US about seeking a common position in the event of a communist takeover of China. Since late 1948 the State Department had said that the US would maintain a presence in China but, as Bevin informed his colleagues, the decision had now been taken that all US government nationals would be withdrawn from China. Bevin succinctly summed up the situation: 'we are faced with the dilemma that unless we can persuade the United States authorities to agree with us we must either agree to differ and pursue our own policy of keeping a foot in the door, or abandon the whole of our interests in China in order to follow in the American wake.'[24] If HMG recognised the Chinese communist government it would risk alienating the Americans. It is known that JIC(FE) produced a report on the impact of a British recognition of the Chinese government, but unfortunately no record of the report itself, or its conclusions, has survived.[25]

In late September 1949 Mao Zedong announced the creation of a Chinese communist government in Peking. Following further discussions with his American and French counterparts, Bevin made the decision that Britain would maintain a consular presence in China, thereby offering de facto recognition of the communist government. There was a delay in this official notification reaching Washington and President Truman complained that the British had not informed him in advance of what had been planned. UK-US relations over the question of diplomatic recognition of the new Chinese communist government continued to affect Ministers and FO officials, which worsened with the UK de jure recognition of Mao's government in early 1950.[26]

Against this backdrop of diplomatic wrangling, mistrust and disagreement, the JIC focused on the military capabilities of the Chinese forces, the regime's relationship with the Soviet Union and the threat to Hong Kong and the greater Far East region. At the end of September 1949, at precisely the time that Mao proclaimed victory, the JIC produced its report (which had been four months in preparation) on the 'Implications of a Communist Success in China'. Of the various conclusions, perhaps the most significant was the assessment that 'there will be no important divergence between the policy of the Chinese leaders and the policy of the Soviet leaders.' This judgment was more nuanced than earlier assessments, which had argued that China would continue to be a Soviet puppet, despite not seeing eye to eye on all matters. A greater concern was the possibility that Mao's victory would accelerate the spread of communism in the region. Therefore, 'unless preventive action is taken and substantial material support given by the Western Powers to indigenous Governments, the countries of S.E.Asia, in their turn, may fall under Communist control'.[27] The report was greeted enthusiastically by the COS who authorised it to be passed to the Minister of Defence.[28]

To many of the senior FO officials involved, all of whom were privy to JIC assessments, Anglo-American solidarity was central to the containment of communism in the Far East.[29] Answering to the PUS, Sir William Strang, the newly created 'Permanent Under Secretary's Committee' (PUSC) was tasked with producing forward-looking policy papers. It argued that unless Britain acted to stop the spread of communism, the whole Far East would come under Soviet influence.[30] Such papers were almost certainly passed to Moscow by Guy Burgess, who at that time was based in the FO's Far Eastern Department. Burgess was also a recipient of JIC papers and contributed to many analyses of communist China.[31] Versions of the PUSC reports were passed to the United States, omitting any negative mention of US policy.

Earlier in 1949, as a result of the increased interest in China, the JIC had compiled a long list of intelligence requirements that was transmitted to the US. It was assumed that the latter had better sources of information on China.[32] At around the same time, the US requested a review by JIC(FE) of the threat posed by the Soviet Union to the region.[33] By August 1949, however, the first significant signs of rifts began to appear. In a discussion about the JIC(FE) Charter, specifically over which regions were to be included within its purview, the JIC in London agreed that it no longer made sense to differentiate between British and American 'spheres of strategic interest' and the limitations imposed as a result. Instead it was agreed that JIC(FE) should focus on any 'special requirements which might arise', regardless of region or of US interest.[34] One of the factors behind this decision was a desire not to 'overload' existing intelligence liaison channels between the UK and US in the Far East.[35]

This did not ease the problem. Towards the end of August 1949, the JIC, once more, discussed the subject of intelligence liaison in the region. The Naval Intelligence representative informed the Committee that 'at present the official flow of information from the Americans, even in London and Washington, was far from complete . . . the problem was extremely delicate and therefore required careful handling'. The JIC decided that attempts to redress the situation should be made at the local level in the Far East rather than in Washington or London.[36]

In September 1949 a high level British group, headed by Bevin, visited the United States to discuss Anglo-American policy towards the Far East. At the same time the JIC sent an 'Intelligence Team' to Washington, together with a 'Planning Team', unconnected with Bevin's visit. The 'Intelligence Team' comprised members of the Services' intelligence directorates, the JIB, FO, and the JSIC, and was headed by the Deputy Director for Military Intelligence, Brigadier Valentine Boucher.[37] Frustratingly, no record of what transpired during the week-long discussions in September 1949 exists, apart from a few references in JPS papers.[38] However, some indication that all did not go well is apparent from a later record of a JIC meeting.

The US JCS had decreed that no military assistance should be offered to the British in the case of an attack on Hong Kong because, put bluntly, its loss would not materially affect the spread of communism in the region and therefore it was not an American concern.[39] This difference of opinion, and the disunity over the recognition of Mao's government, were not the only areas of Anglo-American disagreement. There were other areas of concern. On Formosa, the US showed a commitment to assist the Nationalist forces. In the UK both the FO and the COS had agreed that 'strong representations' should be made to the US to stop this support.[40] Furthermore, as the Military Intelligence representative informed the JIC in December 1949, the US had been underhand in managing to obtain from the UK a significant number of tanks which had been sent to Formosa via the United States.[41]

There were similar concerns over Korea, where US forces had occupied the south of the country after the end of the Second World War, but had then started to withdraw in 1948 following elections. Some British reports claimed these had been rigged. Many British officials complained in the late 1940s about the inconsistent policies that the Truman administration adopted towards Asia. For instance, in the FO Strang declared that 'US policy in the Far East – or lack of policy – is a gift to the Russians'.[42]

In late December 1949 the US passed NSC-48, which called for a stronger US stance on communism in the Far East. Nevertheless problems in the Anglo-American special relationship persisted, principally over information exchange. One contentious issue was the question of releasing British or American intelligence to other countries – the so-called third party arrangement. Some of these issues were addressed by the 1950 Burns-Templer Agreement on defence intelligence cooperation (see chapter 7).[43]

To put US policy into context it is necessary to appreciate the central role of Japan in US thinking. Japan was a significant pillar of US strategy, in terms of its strategic position and industrial potential. Despite an overwhelming concentration on Japan, the fate of Korea, given its proximity to Japan, would be of huge interest to Washington. For Britain, Korea was a lesser concern than the perceived increase in the threat to Hong Kong and the pace of the emergency in Malaya.

These diplomatic wrangles had a powerful impact on intelligence relations. Referring to the September 1949 Anglo-American meetings, the Directors of Intelligence subsequently briefed the COS committee on the situation:

> When the JIC Team visited Washington last year [i.e. September 1949] the Americans had been asked for information on Korea which had been refused . . . In discussion on sources of intelligence, the Directors of Intelligence confirmed that the Americans did not consider that Korea or Formosa could be covered as regards intelligence by the Burns/Templer agreement in view of the political difference between us over China. Thus, no intelligence had been received from the Americans on either of these countries. Somewhat illogically, however, the Americans expected us to provide them with any such intelligence available, which, within limits, was being done.[44]

Anglo-American differences continued to affect intelligence sharing adversely in the Far East at all levels, from the exchange of intelligence assessments, to SIS/CIA planning for 'special operations'. By 1953 the imbalance had clearly not been resolved; in a discussion in the JIC in April, the Chairman Patrick Reilly informed members that 'whilst we were giving the Americans all the intelligence we possessed, the Americans were less forthcoming'. The difficulty, as the DMI reported, 'was that we did not know how much intelligence the Americans possessed.'[45] Later in April the FO convened a high level meeting of officials, including the JIC Chairman, policy department heads and representatives from SIS, to discuss how intelligence collaboration could be improved. The central issue was summed up in an FO memorandum written by Paul Falla of the Overseas Planning Section: 'there is at present a vicious circle in that the Americans are reluctant to make a wide range of intelligence available to us because of the divergence in policy between the two Governments, whereas on our side the improvement of intelligence is a pre-requisite of any review of policy.'[46] For the JIC these instances of communication failure would have a direct impact on its ability to gauge developments in the Far East.

Battleground Korea

Following the Japanese surrender in 1945, Korea had been divided between the victors: North Korea was in the Soviet sphere of influence, with the South going to the United States. The leaders of both North and South were united in their aims of unifying Korea, but differed as to who should control it; either the communists under Kim Il Sung or Syngman Rhee, leader of the South. Although this was a potentially explosive issue, the JIC showed little interest in Korea prior to the summer of 1950, because it was perceived as primarily a US concern. Consequently, intelligence collection in Korea was accorded the lowest priority by the JIC for SIS.[47] Thus, prior to the Korean War no papers were written specifically on the threat posed by the communists and, even when Korea was mentioned in broader reviews of the region, it was dismissed in a few lines. Further political differences over China, however, had resulted in the termination of the steady pattern of intelligence exchange across the Atlantic on Far East topics. Hence, as a 1951 JIC study made explicit: 'before the attack on South Korea the Americans had reports about military activity in North Korea which were not available to us. Had the JIC received these reports they might well have given some warning of the impending attack'.[48]

Despite this significant lacuna, did the JIC have any inkling at all of what was afoot? In February 1950 the Committee had agreed to a COS suggestion that its fortnightly assessment on the communist threat to Hong Kong should be widened to cover the Far East as a whole – in recognition of the 'development of the "Cold War" offensive' in the region.[49] By March 1950, perhaps in acknowledgment that the threat was not as serious as at first thought, the JIC decided that it would continue to brief the COS weekly on developments in Asia, but would discontinue the fortnightly series and instead produce quarterly reports, as and when the situation called for it.[50] Michael Creswell, a diplomat based in Singapore and Chairman of JIC(FE), underlined the importance of the quarterly reviews when he informed the JIC in May that 'the situation was now clearer, and although it could not be said to have greatly improved, the pace of deterioration had slackened'.[51]

Creswell also submitted a written note to the Committee, describing a recent visit he had paid to Korea as the guest of the American Mission. Since the partition in 1945 a regular series of border skirmishes had taken place. Despite the involvement of North Koreans, who were frequently referred to as 'guerrilla fighters', they were never perceived to be part of a larger force with a potential to invade the South. Consequently, Creswell could inform the JIC of the number of guerrillas caught and wounded, and how the situation was 'extremely satisfactory' at present. Creswell concluded by commenting that

> the Americans did not anticipate any actual frontier invasion from North
> Korea in the foreseeable future, though the North Korean forces are deployed
> in a fashion which is equally suitable for offence or defence . . . all the above
> information makes it clear . . . that no direct invasion is at present contemplated

but that assistance will continue to be rendered, especially in the form of arms and the training of guerrilla bands outside South Korea in order to keep the pot boiling.

This view, that North Korea could potentially launch a large-scale military offensive but would favour support for small incursions instead, was echoed by the Assistant Military Adviser at the British Embassy in Tokyo, the closest British diplomatic official to Korea.[52]

All of these forecasts and assessments were proved to be completely wrong when, in the early hours of 24 June 1950 (London time, 25 June in Korea), the North Korean Army crossed the 38th Parallel, supposedly to repel an earlier cross-border raid by the South Koreans. The invasion was immediately condemned by the United Nations (UN), with the first assessment produced by the JIS on 26 June. Despite once more citing the difficulties and reliance on the US for information on Korea, it was conceded that 'we had no intimation that this attack was about to take place'.[53] As Air Marshal Sir William Elliot, the Chief Staff Officer to the Minister of Defence, confessed 'most of our information on the situation in Korea comes from the UK Liaison Mission in Tokyo as a result of an unofficial arrangement with G2 (military intelligence). Without this we should virtually know little more than appears in the press.'[54] Despite this, the JIS's first summary of the situation proved to be remarkably accurate: 'there is no evidence that the North Korean action was Soviet inspired or that Soviet forces or Chinese communists are participating but . . . it would appear unlikely that this invasion could have been undertaken without the approval of Soviet leaders'.[55] This conclusion has now been confirmed by documents released from North Korea, China and the former Soviet Union.[56]

The US was also quick to identify the hand of Moscow in the attack, and within a few days President Truman placed Korea within America's defensive perimeter in the Far East. In addition, he authorised US forces to help stabilise and support South Korea. This confirmed the view of the JIS, that 'the North Korean forces are strong enough to defeat those of South Korea'.[57] Once more the JIS was called into action, and tasked by the COS to prepare a daily summary on events in Korea to be sent to, amongst others, the King and the Prime Minister.[58] Just as important was the preparation of a fresh study on how the invasion might impact on UK interests in the region.[59] To the JIC and the JPS, the invasion of South Korea was a two edged sword: on the one hand the JIC felt that the whole of Korea, without any serious external assistance, would be overrun by the communists; yet at the same time welcomed a more serious and greater US commitment to the region.[60]

More broadly the JIC made several observations on the impact of the Korean War. It considered that the strong and instant reaction by the US and the UK, exemplified in the discussions and condemnation by the UN, would have surprised the Soviet leadership, which might have expected a less robust response. Further, events in Korea were not the first moves of a larger communist-inspired world war.[61] Militarily Britain's options were limited because of the implications of continued unrest in Malaya, the perceived Chinese threat to Hong Kong, and major military commitments in Europe. These concerns meant that there was little left in reserve. Yet despite this, the British Cabinet authorised, from the outset, a limited naval deployment to the Korean theatre. This would subsequently become a much larger military contribution.[62] The logic for this is revealed in COS papers: a British commitment had to be tied to the US response to ensure 'that we can demonstrate to the world, and to the Russians and Eastern peoples in particular, our solidarity of purpose'.[63] To support the British position the JIC produced a lengthy and very detailed study on 'basic information on Korea', including airfields, roads, ports, railways, terrain, climate and armed forces.[64]

In July 1950 teams of British and US officials met to forge a common policy with regard to Korea. Background discussion in London before the talks included how the COS might redefine their 1948 '"stop line", beyond which the spread of communism must be resisted'.[65] The basis for planning lay in a JIC paper which concluded that despite events in Korea, there was no change to the Soviet policy that everything should be done to avoid open conflict with the West.[66]

One benefit of the North Korean attack was to bring British and American intelligence organisations closer together once more. By July, for instance, the JIC reported that with the exception of Formosa (where there remained Anglo-American differences), intelligence exchange in the Far East had improved.[67] This was important because most indigenous British information came from overt sources.[68] In late August 1950 a JIC team set forth for another bilateral intelligence meeting in Washington, with the object of discussing Soviet intentions and capabilities.[69] It was also designed to pave the way for talks later in the year between the COS and the US JCS.[70] The timing of the meeting was opportune, given the evolving military situation despite being initially postponed by the US side. As Major General Arthur Shortt, the mission leader and DMI, informed the JIC, the meeting was a success: the Americans had initially been agitated, believing that the Soviet Union was about to use Korea as a springboard to launch a world war, yet by the end of proceedings their views had mellowed, adopting the British view that a major war was unlikely.[71] The outbreak of the Korean War therefore had, at the very least, served to reinforce the advantages of a close Anglo-American intelligence relationship.

The PRC Emboldened

The failure to predict that the North Koreans would invade was not the only problem. Despite the assessment that hostilities would be relatively limited and did not signal a major communist-inspired offensive, the COS remained concerned. In late September 1950 they discussed the latest developments in the war effort. By this time the UN had committed a large army to restoring peace in Korea, yet there was disagreement over how far north UN forces should proceed.[72] The question focused on the objective: should the UN forces simply drive the North Koreans back to the 38th Parallel, or should they go beyond and invade

North Korea? For the COS the answer was clear: the advance should stop at the border. The logic was relatively straightforward: 'subsequent to the defeat of their army the North Koreans should not have sufficient strength to make possible any further attacks by them on South Korea; accordingly any such further attack could only be carried out by Russia or the Chinese Communists.' Thus, stability should be restored and nothing done to provoke Soviet or Chinese involvement. It would be necessary to leave 'sufficient forces behind in South Korea', thereby providing 'a sufficient deterrent so that any attack by Russia would only be undertaken at the risk of provoking a major war'.[73] The problem facing the Chiefs was that General Douglas MacArthur, the American military commander in Korea, and Syngman Rhee, the South Korean leader, were both vehemently urging that the UN forces continue north of the 38th Parallel.

In London, in the autumn of 1950, the likely course of events was not obvious. On 3 October a worried COS convened a meeting to discuss developments. Writing to his colleagues beforehand, Chief of the Air Staff Sir John Slessor confessed that he was 'nervous about the present situation'.[74] In attendance were the members of the JIC, along with Robert Scott, an Assistant Under Secretary in the FO. Scott notified the COS that the Chinese had informed the Indian Ambassador that, if the 38th Parallel was crossed, then China would use force to defend North Korea. Alarmingly, the British military commanders had no reliable information as to whether or not UN forces had actually crossed by this stage. This emerging situation highlighted a clear predicament: how to gauge the intentions of your adversary when the actions of your own side are not known. As Scott informed the COS: 'in his personal view the Chinese were fully conscious of the ability of the Americans to destroy all their communications and cities but this would not deter them from helping North Korea'.[75]

In preparing a report for the COS, the JIS were reminded by the FO Chairman (in this instance Archibald Ross as it was a Deputy-Director's meeting) on 4 October of the severity of the situation and the integral role that it played: 'The Joint Intelligence Staff should consider such evidence as there might be to show whether the Chinese Communists would send troops across the frontier to participate in the defence of North Korea if United Nations armed forces crossed the 38th Parallel.'[76] By 5 October there still seems to have been uncertainty in London whether or not MacArthur's UN forces had crossed the 38th Parallel. The questions preoccupying the COS were: should this line be crossed and, if MacArthur's forces did proceed, should British troops follow? There was concern over what the Chinese might do and, probably in equal measure, concern over what the reaction of the US might be if the UK decided to halt its forces at the border. These dilemmas were further complicated by conflicting assessments: the JIC believed that the Chinese would not intervene, whereas intelligence reports received via Burma by Field Marshal Slim, the CIGS, suggested 'that the Chinese Communists would march into North Korea if United Nations Forces crossed the 38th Parallel'. To Slim, therefore, 'there now seemed to be sufficient evidence to show that there was a real likelihood and danger of the Chinese taking this action'.[77]

On 7 October the UN forces finally made their move, crossing the 38th Parallel and advancing into North Korea. Concern within the FO led to a series of telegrams to the State Department urging caution and restraint, whilst officials also worked on various schemes to bring about a ceasefire before any possible Chinese advance.[78] With reluctance, Britain opted to support the UN forces. The issue for the JIC concerned the likelihood of Chinese retaliation. The Committee concluded that the Chinese would not 'embark upon operations'. The reasoning behind this, based not on intelligence but rather a reading of the character of the leadership, was that the Chinese would not risk war with the UN because it would, in effect, lead to a major war with the West, something, it was assumed, the Chinese would want to avoid. Far more likely, in the JIC's view, was that China would continue a 'political and propaganda campaign' designed to deter any further Western advances.[79] Despite what, in hindsight, was an overly optimistic assessment, the JIC's report was subsequently accepted by the COS, who used it as a briefing document for discussions with the US JCS.[80]

In mid-October President Truman met General MacArthur who personally assured him that China would not enter the war and that American forces would be home by Christmas. Up to this point MacArthur had obeyed the instructions laid down by the US JCS on how far UN and South Korean forces could advance (the latter being farther north). Following his meeting MacArthur, to the dismay of the American military hierarchy, reversed these directives, firstly by pushing the line closer to the Chinese border and then removing the restrictions on the movement of non-Korean forces. In London the COS Committee was kept apprised of developments by its personal representative to General MacArthur, Air Vice-Marshal Sir Cecil Bouchier. Bouchier, significantly, does not seem to have mentioned MacArthur's change of instructions.[81] One of Bouchier's tasks was to try and improve the exchange of information between the UK and US.[82] Reading a series of reports sent by Bouchier from Tokyo the COS would, no doubt, have been buoyed by the pace of developments. MacArthur was quick to discount any suggestion of a Chinese military build-up, even when seemingly incontrovertible evidence was presented to him. Bouchier was equally firm in his convictions. In late October he sent a cable to the COS (copied to Patrick Reilly, the JIC Chairman) to inform them that

> there is no (repeat no) evidence whatever that any Chinese Communist troops have crossed over South of Yalu River and are in conflict with our forces advancing Northwards to Manchurian border ... the Chinese Communists stated a little while back that if the United Nations Forces crossed the 38th Parallel they would send their troops to the aid of the North Korean Army. The Chinese have so far not (repeat not) done this. Informed circles here who are obviously watching the situation closely consider it is utterly unlikely that the Chinese will now intervene in force ... the opinion here is that it is altogether too improbable and fanciful for even the Chinese to think of coming into this war openly now ... if the

Chinese came in now they would have to fight virtually alone. It is therefore an impossible situation for them and I am quite certain they will keep well out of it.[83]

The JIC had no other informed sources of information, with Sigint, Humint and aerial reconnaissance coverage limited to specific regions.[84] Indeed, it confessed to be 'seriously concerned about the inadequacy of intelligence'. A JIC assessment in early November 1950 stated that intelligence on the Chinese army was considered 'negligible'; on the air force 'almost totally lacking'; and 'very little' was known about the navy.[85] Thus, it appears to have concluded that the reissue of Bouchier's conclusions in the Daily Situation Report was the best option, though the Committee was astute enough to credit him as the source for its information and to question whether it really needed to produce any reports given that Bouchier's accounts were more 'vivid' than the JIC's.

Despite the lack of any formal assessment at this point, it is clear that the feeling within the JIC was one of relative confidence over the pace of developments in the Korean peninsula, for as the Committee's Assistant Secretary made clear: 'the war in Korea has developed even more rapidly than expected and it looks as if the real fighting will be over very shortly.'[86] Almost simultaneously, however, messages began to be received indicating a large concentration of Chinese troops, even if their intent was initially unknown. However 'utterly unlikely', 'improbable' or 'fanciful' it may have seemed to Bouchier, in late October the Chinese began to engage with UN forces.

On 1 November the People's Liberation Army advanced in strength, pushing the UN forces back towards the 38th Parallel. The initial JIC reaction was one of uncertainty: it was not known whether Chinese support was officially sanctioned, whether it was merely an intensification of Chinese effort, or whether it was the start of something altogether new.[87] In 1951 the FO reviewed past SIS reporting on China, in the main questioning its authenticity and reliability. It concluded that whilst there had been some intelligence on the Chinese offensive in Korea, 'It was not circulated to the Foreign Office, since by the time the report reached London the Chinese offensive had already begun'.[88]

Whilst it was clear that the Chinese were supporting North Korea, there was still uncertainty over the level of involvement. Would China actually declare war in its support of the North Korean effort? Or would its assistance remain relatively covert?[89] On 9 November the JIC, in its monthly China update, stated that there were now 30,000 Chinese troops 'in support' of North Korea. It continued: 'we are unable to determine Chinese intentions but we do not consider China wishes to become involved in a major war with the United Nations'. Much of the information, including the troop numbers cited, was derived from US sources and although the JIC had some doubts there were simply no alternative sources of information.[90] Indeed, in a discussion on 8 November it was conceded by the Military Intelligence representative that 'he doubted whether an assessment could now be made of the way the Chinese were thinking due to the almost complete lack of evidence on the subject'.[91]

Within a few weeks the situation had clarified. The JIC's earlier predictions had been proved incorrect and, for the first time, the intentions of the Chinese leadership became apparent: 'The scale of Chinese intervention in Korea leaves no doubt that the Chinese Communist Government is intent on defeating the main aim of the United Nations forces.' More alarming was what this move signified:

> This intention may be interpreted as a desire to drive back these forces beyond the 38th Parallel or even out of Korea altogether, but we must now face the possibility that China is prepared, with Soviet support and approval, to accept the increase of existing risks of open war in an attempt to drive the United Nations forces from Korea.[92]

In a separate study, commissioned by the COS, the JIC considered China's vulnerability if it came to a major war. It concluded that not only would China manage to withstand huge casualties and loss of resources, but that 'intensive air attack' was also unlikely to work.[93] The COS reading of the situation was even more bleak, declaring that 'it is hardly an exaggeration to say that . . . they are virtually invulnerable to Western attack.'[94] The paper was shown to the US JCS who disagreed, arguing that there were strategic weaknesses. It was also seen by MacArthur who was vitriolic in his scorn. In contrast, the CIA approved of it, stating that its conclusions were broadly similar.[95] As a result the COS asked the JIC to revisit the subject in January 1951 but in discussion, perhaps as a sign of its self-assuredness, the JIC decided not to do so given that it would need to be based on operational planning assumptions and that, therefore, it made more sense for it to be prepared by the Planners.[96]

An interesting aside to the JIC's role in Anglo-American military discussions in Korea was provided by the fate of the study requested by the COS on Chinese vulnerability. Despite its reluctance to redraft the earlier report, the JIC did agree to produce a related study on China's military, political and economic strengths and weaknesses. This study, strong on facts but with limited conclusions, did none-theless identify several 'vulnerabilities'. The report was subsequently approved and transmitted to the British Embassy in Washington.[97] Here, however, the report was cancelled, specifically at the request of the Ambassador and Minister at the Embassy. The reason, as the Minister, Sir Christopher Steel, informed the JIC, was simple:

> The general argument and the conclusions of this paper as they stand are so confirmatory of all that MacArthur has been saying to Congress and to the Senate Committee that its communication to the Americans would place us in an extremely false position . . . [it is] frankly at variance with arguments we have been deploying here ever since I arrived . . . I have to put the above arguments perhaps in rather black and white but that is, of course, the American way with which we have to reckon.[98]

This blatant suppression of an intelligence report on the basis of its possible political effect did not prompt any recorded reaction from either the JIC or Reilly, to whom Steel's missive was addressed.

Up to this point matters relating to Korea, and indeed to the Far East as a whole, had been dealt with at the JIC's weekly Deputy Directors' meeting, suggesting that Korea was perceived to be of lesser importance than events in Europe, which were always discussed at the full JIC rather than the Deputy level. With the Korean War intensifying, discussion was elevated to the senior JIC committee. Consideration of the communist threat in the Far East was amalgamated with that of the Soviet threat. It was a sign that the Cold War was now a global issue which could no longer be addressed on geographical lines.[99]

Throughout late November and December of 1950 the communist forces in Korea continued to push the UN forces southwards, beyond the 38th Parallel. The US military urged action against the Chinese themselves; by contrast, in London, at a greater distance, the COS and the FO continued to press for restraint. Many even argued for a ceasefire, though they were branded as 'appeasers' by the US, for as MacArthur told Bouchier, 'you cannot appease a wild beast'.[100] The situation was summed up in a communiqué from the COS to Lord Tedder, the Chairman of the British Joint Services Mission (BJSM) in Washington: 'a war between the US and China would be the old story of the fight between the whale and the elephant – neither can directly do the other any real harm. On the other hand the unfortunate fact is that, indirectly, China could do the US and UN – especially Britain and France – far more harm than vice versa.'[101]

Chinese involvement in the Korean War, though limited to the Korean peninsula itself, was a portent of a greater presence in the region than the JIC had originally assessed. Suddenly not only was the threat to Hong Kong of greater concern (see chapter 12), but so were wider questions over the security of the whole region. On this matter the COS and the FO were in agreement, with Albert Franklin (of the FO's Far Eastern Department) commenting on the JIC's conclusions that 'we consider that Chinese policy ought not to be considered in isolation from the intentions of world communist strategy and that in the realisation of ultimate communist ambitions, Mao Tse-Tung has already played and will almost certainly continue to play an important part.'[102] For the COS the lessons from the unanticipated Chinese aggression were clear: if China wanted to, it would be able to overrun the French in Indochina and then Siam and Burma would 'crumble'; it would be knocking on the doors of India and Pakistan; Ceylon and Malaya would fall; and even Japan would be vulnerable. Thus, before long the 'rice bowl of Asia would be in Communist hands'.[103]

The JIC was in full agreement. By early 1951 fresh evidence of Soviet support and assistance to the Chinese led the JIC to conclude that China was now prepared to 'risk war' in pursuit of its aims. Much like the Soviet Union's goals in Europe, China's aspirations were thought to be aimed at splitting the Western powers and driving a wedge between Asia and the West. Although the JIC felt that the threat to Hong Kong was minimal given the lack of 'seasoned' troops in the region, Chinese intervention in Indochina was considered imminent (see chapter 12). To support this, the JIC reported rumours of six Soviet divisions assigned to Manchuria, cited as evidence of the 'visible assurance of Soviet support to the Chinese in the pursuit of their present policy'.[104]

In the annals of intelligence history there are several events routinely cited as classic examples of the failure of intelligence. Hitler's invasion of the Soviet Union is one of them; another is the invasion of South Korea by the North Koreans in June 1950. Intelligence 'failure' is an often applied but frequently misunderstood concept, and certainly it could be argued that Operation Barbarossa was not a clear example of intelligence, as opposed to policy, failure. For the JIC, however, the failure to predict the outbreak of the Korean War was certainly an intelligence fault of the highest order. In 1951 the JIC undertook a review of its past assessments of communist intentions produced since 1947. The rationale behind the study was made clear in its introduction: 'in order to determine to what extent they have been proved correct by subsequent events and, in cases where their conclusions have been proved wrong, to discover why false conclusions were drawn.'[105] In the period 1947–51, the study concluded that thirty-three different assessments had either proved to be correct, or at least not yet proven to be incorrect. In comparison only three had proved to be wrong, prompting the JIC to consider what had caused the error.

Despite the favourable statistics, in a frank statement, it was conceded that 'our assessment of Communist intentions has not, however, been as good as the small number of our miscalculations suggests. In the first place we failed altogether to forecast . . . the attack on South Korea in 1950.' Furthermore, comment was also made on the nature and tone of the assessments themselves: 'We have also, in many cases, drafted our conclusions somewhat equivocally and so allowed ourselves a fairly wide margin of error. The present tendency is to make the conclusions more definite'. The report was approved by the JIC in December 1951, and the Secretary of the Committee was tasked with circulating it 'for examination in Departments, in order that study should be made of the lessons to be learnt from previous intelligence appreciations and of measures to improve future estimates'.[106] It does not appear that any further use was ever made of it.

The JIC had got it wrong up to this point. It had not foreseen an attack by North Korea on the South, and had certainly (and completely) misread the Chinese reaction to the crossing of the 38th Parallel by the UN. A subsequent analysis by Percy Cradock argues that the JIC's conclusions were weak, based on what the Chinese would do 'if they were sensible [and] ought to do, rather than what they were likely to do'.[107] In its 1951 review of past assessments the JIC identified two factors that had undermined assessments:

(c) That our intelligence about Communist intentions in the Far East is even less adequate than our intelligence about the Soviet Union, largely due to the fact that we obtain less Sigint on China; and

(d) That we do not yet understand the mind of the Chinese Communist leaders.[108]

Probably the JIC was not surprised by the identification of these two shortcomings. The second point was a difficult one, but one, at least, of which the JIC had already been made aware. At one meeting in November 1950 the Colonial Office representative had warned about the difficulty of trying to read the Chinese mind, pointing out 'the dangers of appreciating [the] Chinese mentality with Western minds. He also noted that the psychological and political factors would predominate in any appreciation.'[109]

Underpinning the difficulties in producing good assessments was the dearth of high quality intelligence. At various points the JIC had referred to the gaps in intelligence on China. Furthermore, and perhaps as an afterthought, it was noted that more attention should be paid to open source reporting, specifically Chinese broadcasts, and that this was an area that had been largely ignored.[110] The JIC had turned its attention to addressing these matters in early 1951. One move, instigated by the Chairman Patrick Reilly, was to ask the British officials in India and Pakistan if it might be possible to forge links with their intelligence counterparts and to try and set-up a system of intelligence exchange. A problem, as Reilly admitted, was that in both countries security was 'unreliable' and the amount of information the UK might release would be limited. Certainly nothing of a sensitive nature could be transmitted. Yet collaboration could be invaluable, simply because desperate times called for desperate measures: 'the present state of affairs is far from satisfactory and is, if anything, deteriorating. The Committee, are therefore, most anxious to tap every possible source of intelligence.'[111] Positive, if wary, replies were received from diplomatic missions in both countries, but following in-depth discussion, the JIC decided that official liaison would not be sensible. Alternatively 'personal and unofficial contacts' should be stepped up, although no results are apparent from the record.[112]

Another measure was to utilise Hong Kong far more for the collection of intelligence. Hong Kong offered a unique location from which to gather intelligence. but a problem arose with the Colonial Office. The Governor of Hong Kong had forbidden the intelligence agencies to interrogate Chinese deserters. In 1952 this decision was overturned and a number of processing centres were set up, operated by the intelligence community. Although high hopes were entertained for these centres, particularly in the early years, they produced nothing of significant value.[113] On the Chinese mainland itself there was some progress and by June 1951 the JIC could comment that the volume and value of intelligence had increased.[114]

It is interesting to note here one of the many roles played by the regional JICs. Following the communist victory in China SIS had experienced great difficulty in maintaining its independent Chinese networks and had been obliged to co-operate with Nationalist Chinese sources.[115] Operating from bases in Hong Kong and Singapore, it had steadily accrued a number of different sources and sub-sources. By the spring of 1951 the volume of material acquired had made it possible, for the first time, to cross-reference and verify incoming information. Although much of this was undertaken by SIS, JIC(FE) in Singapore was asked to help. It emerged that the Royal Navy had been fed information that was known to be incorrect. More important was a general observation and a warning for the future: 'the mercenary tendencies of agents have undoubtedly increased in the last few years in China, as they did in early post-war Germany as a result of the deep American pocket'.[116] Following the review, however, the Chairman of JIC(FE) could report to London that 'MI6 are now providing considerably less material, but of a higher standard of reliability'.[117]

Following the third phase of the Korean War in late 1950 with the US response to the retreat of the UN forces South of the 38th parallel, and prolonged discussions in the UN over a ceasefire, the war became a protracted stalemate. Throughout the war the JIC supplied the military with broad based assessments on the Korean situation. In addition, each week JIC(FE) provided a summary of intelligence on the region. The JIC was also heavily involved at the conclusion of the war, providing a series of assessments on whether military action would bring hostilities to a close, whether 'special operations' could be used, and whether the armistice (once signed) would hold.[118]

An armistice to the Korean War was signed on 27 July 1953. Two million people had died, including a thousand British service personnel.[119] Anthony Farrar-Hockley, in his Official History, described the outcome as 'peace without victory'.[120] For the JIC the lesson was not so much about the conflict itself, but what it had revealed about the Chinese mentality and capacity for war. No immediate post-mortems were conducted and, aside from several assessments on whether the ceasefire would hold, the JIC reverted to its former practice of producing large bi-annual reports on communist intentions and capacities to wage war, but with much more attention given to China than had hitherto been the case. The JIC assessed that the forceful Western response to China's participation had come as a surprise to Mao, and that therefore the Korean War had impressed upon the Chinese the need for caution.[121] As with assessments of the Soviet Union, the JIC remained convinced that China was unlikely to risk a major war with the West, and certainly would not do so without the approval and support of Moscow.

By late 1954 the JIC noted, for the first time, that there was growing concern over the Middle East (see chapter 13). The JIC still assessed that in the Far East overt Chinese aggression was unlikely, with one very notable exception. Trouble had flared in the former French colony of Indochina. The JIC considered it had become the one place in the Far East 'where an all out drive to extend Communist control over the whole country is developing'.[122]

An Asian Cold War

From a UK perspective, the Far East region, in the context of the Cold War, had become the most volatile for three primary reasons: it was seen as providing a 'nexus between the pressures of anti-colonial nationalism and wider Cold War tensions, given British commitments elsewhere it was the focus of questions of 'overstretch'; and finally, the fates of countries within the region were tied to one another. Given these factors it is remarkable that for so long the Far East was ranked low in importance in the hierarchy of British concerns.[123]

It took a series of significant events for the JIC to acknowledge that the Far East was every bit as important as Europe for the protection of global British interests. Thus, in this period, the region came to be seen as a major centre of the growing communist threat. The JIC no longer distinguished between Europe and the Far East, and it was no longer a subject relegated to discussion in the less important Deputy Director's meetings of the JIC. The comparatively faster pace of events in Europe following the end of the war explains this to some extent, yet the JIC was slow to appreciate the need to think ahead, to focus attention and plan for future intelligence requirements on the Far East as a whole. As a result, as with the JIC's reporting on Europe in the late 1940s, by the time major potential adversaries were identified, intelligence coverage was insufficient and steps to rectify this would take years to become effective.

While Communist China became a strategic target of its own, the JIC continued to look for links with Moscow. In the Far East this was never clearly visible. The assumption remained that communist doctrine, ideology and aspirations were different in South-East Asia and in Europe, but views on their interdependence began to change. The significance of the Korean War was to reveal the extent of Soviet and Chinese capabilities and their preparedness to utilise them. Here, for the first time, was an internal conflict that had been internationalised, arrayed along Cold War battle lines and fought out in part by the use of proxy forces.

Undermining all efforts in the region were two intractable and recurring themes. The first was the paucity of intelligence. Whilst coverage in the European theatre might be described as weak, in the Far East it was derisory. Many of the SIS networks had been wound up following the victory of the Chinese communists; and while Sigint offered the best intelligence, it took time to develop and only began to prove its worth as the 1950s wore on. Compounding matters was the inability to gauge Chinese intentions or to understand the Chinese leadership, challenges which were never satisfactorily met. As a result, the JIC had little warning of major events, particularly the invasion of South Korea and the onset of Chinese involvement.

The second problem concerned the state of the Anglo-American special relationship. The twin principles of collective intelligence and collective defence were both, at times, seriously threatened. President Truman originally saw the Far East as the playground of the European imperial powers and was therefore reluctant to oppose nationalist movements. Only once it became clear that many of these elements were supported by the communists, however indirectly, did the US position begin to shift. Yet problems remained: arguments at the political level over Formosa, the diplomatic recognition of Mao's government, the security of Hong Kong, and the actions of Douglas MacArthur led to restrictions on the exchange of information at the intelligence level. A further fissure in the transatlantic relationship arose through trying to equate UK responses to US expectations. This was particularly the case over the involvement of British troops. For the UK this was always a delicate question involving a balancing act between various and disparate worldwide commitments. Frequently the JIC's intelligence reports on the 'threat' were unlikely to generate a credible British military commitment. Korea was the turning point, convincing both London and Washington of the need to work together and provide a united front.

The JIC itself was quick to recognise its own limitations, and it certainly cannot be blamed for the monumental difficulty of the task, the impenetrability of the Chinese mind-set, or the way in which the intelligence relationship with the US was affected by political decisions. At the tactical level the JIC clearly had an important role to play in providing assessments, sometimes producing them in London, but often acting as the conduit for regionally produced reports. The problems lay at the strategic level, particularly in providing warning of impending events. The JIC never managed to achieve a clear understanding of the Chinese psyche or an ability to read Chinese intentions. Questions over whether the Chinese would risk intervention in regional events, the extent to which Moscow's hand was present in Mao's leadership, and whether different national events were isolated or inter-connected were never satisfactorily addressed. The succession of events in the Far East, beginning with Malaya, including the Chinese civil war and the Korean war, and culminating with the onset of the Vietnam war, ensured that by the late 1950s, the Cold War was as much an Asian phenomenon as it was a European one.

Notes

1 JIC(44)404(0), 'Conference on Co-ordination of Intelligence in the Far East', 16 September 1944. CAB 81/125.
2 JIC(45)224, 'Requirements from SIS', 18 July 1945. CAB 81/130.
3 JIC(46)57, 'Requirements from SIS', 15 June 1946. CAB 81/133.
4 JIC(46)1(0)Final(Revise), 'Russia's Strategic Interests and Intentions', 1 March 1946. CAB 81/132.
5 JIC(46)105(0)(Final), 'Organisation of Intelligence in South East Asia', 9 December 1946. CAB 81/134.
6 JIC/758/47, 'Interchange of Information between JIC London and JIC(FE)', 2 August 1947. CAB 176/15.
7 JIC/758/47, 'Interchange of Information between JIC London and JIC(FE)', 2 August 1947. CAB 176/15.
8 JIC(47)50(Final), 'Reports by Joint Intelligence Committee (Far East)', 15 September 1947. CAB 158/1.
9 JIC(45)314(FINAL), 'Internal Situation in China', 10 November 1945. CAB 81/131.
10 See C Baxter, 'A Closed Book? British Intelligence and East Asia, 1945–1950', *Diplomacy and Statecraft* 22:4 (2011), p.9. On the SIS reports see WO 208/4403.
11 JIC(45)303(0)FINAL, 'Situation in Mukden', 20 October 1945. CAB 81/131.
12 JIC(45)314(FINAL), 'Internal Situation in China', 10 November 1945. CAB 81/131. The US, for instance, had issued public statements and had helped the Nationalists and, through the Marshall Mission in 1945–6, had unsuccessfully tried to mediate in the civil war. Soviet assistance was less overt, and Stalin at this time still maintained formal diplomatic recognition of the Nationalist government.
13 JIC(48)30(0)Final, 'China Military Situation', 13 May 1948. CAB 158/3.
14 JIC(48)113(Final), 'Communist Influence in the Far East', 17 December 1948. CAB 158/5.

15 COS(49)8th Meeting, 15 January 1949. DEFE 4/19.
16 JIC(48)133(Revise), 'Effects of Communist Successes in China', 6 January 1949. CAB 158/5.
17 JIC(49)33(Final), 'Communist Influence in the Far East', 29 April 1949. CAB 158/6.
18 COS(49)62nd Meeting, 29 April 1949. DEFE 4/21.
19 COS(49)67th Meeting, 9 May 1949. DEFE 4/21.
20 COS(49)67th Meeting, 9 May 1949. DEFE 4/21. Details of the Cabinet discussion are in CAB 128/15.
21 COS(49)74th Meeting, 20 May 1949. DEFE 4/21.
22 COS(49)92nd Meeting, 22 June 1949. DEFE 32/1. No further details have been found about this.
23 S R Ashton (ed), *Documents on British Policy Overseas* [hereafter *DBPO*], *Series I, Volume VIII: Britain and China, 1945–1950* (London: Frank Cass, 2002). p.xiii.
24 CP(49)180, 'Memorandum by Mr Bevin on China', 23 August 1949. CAB 129/36.
25 Reference to it is made in JIC(49)121st Meeting, 23 November 1949. CAB 159/6.
26 For more see *DBPO: 1: VIII.*
27 JIC(49)48 (Final), 'The Implications of a Communist Success in China', 30 September 1949. CAB 158/7.
28 C.R.Price [COS Secretariat] to Minister of Defence, 19 October 1949. CAB 21/3269.
29 W5573/3/500G, PUSC 51 (Final) Second Revise, 'Anglo-Americans Relations: Present and Future', 9 November 1949. FO 371/76386. See also R Ovendale, 'Britain, the United States and the Cold War in South-East Asia, 1949–1950', *International Affairs* 58:3 (Summer 1982), pp.447–64.
30 W5572/3/500G, PUSC 32 (Final), 'The United Kingdom in South East Asia and the Far East', 30 August 1949. FO 371/76386.
31 R Ovendale, 'Britain, the United States, and the Recognition of Communist China', *The Historical Journal* 26:1 (1983), p.140.
32 JIC/863/49, 'Intelligence Requirements from United States Sources on China', 12 May 1949. CAB 176/22.
33 JIC(49)69th Meeting, 13 July 1949. CAB 159/6.
34 JIC(49)77th Meeting, 10 August 1949. CAB 159/6.
35 JIC/1418/49, 'Intelligence Requirements from United States Sources on China', 10 August 1949. CAB 176/23.
36 JIC(49)82nd Meeting, 24 August 1949. CAB 159/6.
37 JIC(49)81st Meeting, 19 August 1949. CAB 159/6. Also, JIC(49)72, 'Meeting Between British and United States Planners and Intelligence Teams', 20 August 1949. CAB 158/8.
38 JP(49)133(FINAL), 'Visit of the United Kingdom Joint Planning Staff to Washington – September-October 1949', 14 October 1949. DEFE 6/11.
39 Memorandum by Mr Troy L. Perkins, of the Office of Chinese Affairs, 5 November 1949. *Foreign Relations of the United States* [hereafter *FRUS*], *1949: The Far East: China, Volume IX* (Washington, DC: USGPO, 1974).
40 COS(49)171st Meeting, 16 November 1949. DEFE 4/26.
41 JIC(49)126th Meeting, 7 December 1949. CAB 159/6.
42 Cited in M L Dockrill, 'The Foreign Office, Anglo-American Relations and the Korean War, June 1950-June 1951', *International Affairs* 62:3 (1986), p.459.
43 JIC(49)49 (Final), 'Disclosure of Anglo-American Information to Third Parties', 10 June 1949. CAB 158/7. See also CAB 163/14.
44 COS(50)107th Meeting, 11 July 1950, Confidential Annex. DEFE 11/349.
45 Confidential Annex to JIC(53)39th Meeting, 16 April 1953. PUSD Papers, FCO.
46 'S.O. and Propaganda in the Far East', 1 April 1953. PUSD Papers, FCO. This file includes details of the FO meeting. See also, Confidential Annex to COS(53)40th Meeting, 24 March 1953. PUSD Papers, FCO.

47 JIC(50)38, 'Priorities for Collection of Intelligence by SIS', 6 April 1950. CAB 158/10. An interesting footnote was that the newly created SIS station in Seoul (1948) was headed by the Soviet spy George Blake.

48 JIC(51)87(Final), 'Review of Assessments Made of Communist Intentions Since January, 1947 by the Joint Intelligence Committee', 12 December 1951. CAB 158/13.

49 JIC(50)14th Meeting, 8 February 1950. CAB 159/7.

50 JIC(50)32nd Meeting, 22 March 1950. CAB 159/7.

51 JIC(50)48th Meeting, 11 May 1950. CAB 159/7.

52 JIC/778/50, 'Visits by the Chairman, JIC(FE) to Tokyo and Korea', 5 May 1950. CAB 176/26.

53 JIC/1099/50, 'Situation in Korea', 26 June 1950. CAB 176/26.

54 Elliot to Tedder [Chairman, BJSM Washington], 27 June 1950. DEFE 11/193.

55 JIC/1099/50, 'Situation in Korea', 26 June 1950. CAB 176/26.

56 For example, see K Weathersby, 'Soviet Aims in Korea and the Origins of the Korean War, 1945–1950: New Evidence from Russian Archives', *Cold War International History Project Working Paper No. 8* (1993).

57 JIC/1099/50, 'Situation in Korea', 26 June 1950. CAB 176/26.

58 The majority of these have been preserved. See DEFE 11/193 – DEFE 11/213.

59 JIC(50)66th Meeting, 28 June 1950. CAB 159/7.

60 JIC(50)67th Meeting, 29 June 1950. CAB 159/7.

61 JIC/1146/50, 'Implications of the War in Korea on Our Defence Policy in Other Parts of the World', 3 July 1950. CAB 176/26.

62 A Farrar-Hockley, *The Official History of the British Part in the Korean War, Volume I: A Distant Obligation* (London; HMSO, 1990). pp.46–8.

63 W.Elliot [Chief Staff Officer to the Minister of Defence] to Prime Minister, 28 June 1950. DEFE 11/193.

64 JIC(50)62, 'Basic Information on Korea', 7 July 1950 CAB 158/10.

65 COS(50)103rd Meeting, 6 July 1950, Confidential Annex. DEFE 4/33.

66 COS(50)107th Meeting, 11 July 1950, Confidential Annex. DEFE 11/349.

67 JIC(50)69th Meeting, 6 July 1950. CAB 159/8.

68 JIC(50)83rd Meeting, 10 August 1950. CAB 159/8.

69 A list of papers to be discussed is in JIC/1532/50, 'Visit of United Kingdom Intelligence Team to Washington August/September 1950 – Revised Administrative Arrangements', 18 August 1950. DEFE 11/292. This file contains further background detail to the meeting.

70 COS(50)124th Meeting, 10 August 1950, Confidential Annex. DEFE 11/292.

71 JIC(50)103rd Meeting, 27 September and 28 September 1950. CAB 159/8. The combined 93pp. UK/US report is JIC(50)92, 'Soviet Intentions and Capabilities ABI-14', 28 September 1950. CAB 158/11.

72 The reason that it was a UN operation was that it followed two UN Security Resolutions, the first requesting that the North Koreans cease fire, the second to provide assistance to South Koreans to repel the attack. Although fighting and operating under the rubric of the UN, in reality this was largely a US military effort, including a small yet significant British contingent.

73 COS(50)152nd Meeting, 20 September 1950, Confidential Annex. DEFE 4/33.

74 CAS to First Sea Lord, CIGS, and Air Marshal Elliott, 2 October 1950. DEFE 11/201.

75 COS(50)160th Meeting, 3 October 1950. DEFE 4/33.

76 JIC(50)105th Meeting, 4 October 1950. CAB 159/8.

77 COS(50)162nd Meeting, Confidential Annex, 5 October 1950. DEFE 4/33. It is not obvious from the minutes what the intelligence reports were that Slim received.

78 Dockrill, 'The Foreign Office, Anglo-American Relations and the Korean War', p.463.

79 JIC(50)88 (Final – Revise), 'Chinese Communist Intentions and Capabilities – 1950/51', 11 October 1950. CAB 158/11.

80 COS(50)169th Meeting, 16 October 1950. DEFE 4/36.
81 Farrar-Hockley, *The Official History of the British Part in the Korean War, Volume I.* p.269.
82 COS(50)126th Meeting, 11 August 1950. DEFE 11/292.
83 FK1015/267/G. Bouchier to COS, 27 October 1950. FO 371/84070.
84 For instance, see JIC/884/51, 'Anti-Communist Elements in China', 26 April 1951. Also JIC/1281/51, 'Chinese Nationalist Intentions', 8 June 1951. CAB 158/73.
85 JIC(50)81(Final), 'Present State of Intelligence and Measures to Improve It', 3 November 1950. CAB 158/72.
86 JIC/2095/50, 'SITREPS', 25 October 1950. DEFE 11/202.
87 JIC/2162/50, 'Korea – Situation Report Number 90', 1 November 1950. DEFE 11/202.
88 J.O.May [FO] to D.P.Reilly, 29 March 1951. PUSD Papers, FCO.
89 JIC(50)117th Meeting, 1 November 1950. CAB 159/8.
90 JIC(50)1/16(Final), 'The Chinese Communist Threat in the Far East and South-East Asia on 7th November 1950', 8 November 1950. CAB 158/9.
91 JIC(50)120th Meeting, 8 November 1950. CAB 159/8.
92 JIC(50)1/17(Final), 'The Chinese Communist Threat in the Far East and South-East Asia on 29th November 1950', 30 November 1950. CAB 158/9.
93 JIC(50)105(Final), 'Vulnerability of China', 7 December 1950. CAB 158/11.
94 COS to Lord Tedder, BJSM, 29 December 1950. CAB 21/3269.
95 JIC/301/51, 'Vulnerability of China', 7 February 1951. CAB 176/29.
96 JIC(51)10 (Supplementary Terms of Reference), 'Vulnerability of China', 3 March 1951. CAB 158/12. Also, JIC(51)9th Meeting, 24 January 1951. CAB 159/9.
97 JIC(51)10(Final), 'The Military, Political and Economic Strength and Weaknesses of Communist China in 1951', 25 April 1951. CAB 158/12.
98 JIC/1173/51, 'The Military, Political and Economic Strength and Weaknesses of Communist China in 1951', 28 May 1951. CAB 176/30.
99 JIC(50)130th Meeting, 30 November 1950. CAB 159/8.
100 Bouchier to COS, 18 January 1951. Contained within JIC(51)10, 'Vulnerability of China', 24 January 1951. CAB 158/12.
101 COS to Lord Tedder, BJSM, 29 December 1950. CAB 21/3269.
102 FC1027/13. Note by A.A.E.Franklin, 9 February 1951. FO 371/92233.
103 COS to Lord Tedder, BJSM, 29 December 1950. CAB 21/3269.
104 JIC(51)1/1(Final), 'Chinese Communist Threat in the Far East and South-East Asia on 30th January 1951', 1 February 1951. CAB 158/12.
105 JIC(51)87(Terms of Reference), 'Review of Assessments Made Since January 1947 by the Joint Intelligence Committee on Communist Intentions', 20 September 1951. CAB 158/13.
106 JIC(51)87(Final), 'Review of Assessments Made of Communist Intentions Since January, 1947 by the Joint Intelligence Committee', 12 December 1951. CAB 158/13.
107 Cradock, *Know Your Enemy.* p.99.
108 JIC(51)87(Final), 'Review of Assessments Made of Communist Intentions Since January, 1947 by the Joint Intelligence Committee', 12 December 1951. CAB 158/13.
109 JIC(50)120th Meeting, 8 November 1950. CAB 159/8.
110 JIC(50)123rd Meeting, 15 November 1950. CAB 159/8.
111 JIC/529/51, 'Measures to Improve the State of Our Intelligence About Soviet and Chinese Intentions', 8 March 1951. CAB 176/30.
112 JIC/748/51, 'Measures to Improve the State of Our Intelligence About Soviet and Chinese Intentions', 9 April 1951. CAB 176/30. Also, JIC(51)47th Meeting, 2 May 1951. CAB 159/9.
113 JIC/52/1325, 'Intelligence in Hong Kong', 11 June 1952. CAB 176/36.
114 JIC(51)45(Preliminary Draft), 'Review of Our Present State of Intelligence', 22 June 1951. CAB 158/73.
115 Jeffery, *MI6.* p.700.

116 'Intelligence on China', 14 February 1952. CAB 158/74. This paper, produced by SIS, was distributed for discussion at the JIC in March 1952. For further background on the JIC's attempts to assess CX reporting from the Far East, see 'Reliability of CX Reports – Far East'. PUSD Papers, FCO.

117 'Organisation of Intelligence in the Far East – Report by the Chairman of JIC(FE) for the Period August 1951 to February 1952', 10 March 1952. PUSD Papers, FCO.

118 On this latter question the JIC and JIS were greatly assisted by Willard Matthias, a US representative in London. For more see 'Probable Results of a Breakdown of the Armistice in Korea'. PUSD Papers, FCO.

119 A Farrar-Hockley, *The Official History of the British Part in the Korean War, Volume II: An Honourable Discharge* (London; HMSO, 1995). p.491.

120 Farrar-Hockley, *The Official History of the British Part in the Korean War, Volume II*. p.387.

121 JIC(54)37(Revise), 'The Likelihood of War', 14 April 1954. CAB 158/17.

122 JIC(54)69(Final), 'Likely Communist Courses of Action Up To Mid-1955', 18 September 1954. CAB 158/18.

123 M Thomas, 'Processing Decolonization: British Strategic Analysis of Conflict in Vietnam and Indonesia, 1945–1950', In C E Goscha & C F Ostermann (eds), *Connecting Histories: Decolonization and the Cold War in Southeast Asia, 1945–1962* (Stanford: Stanford University Press, 2009). pp.85–6.

12 War in the Far East

Part II – Problems in the Colonies

One of the defining aspects of the UK's post-war history was its retreat from Empire. Economically crippled by the war and with a desperate need to reduce worldwide military commitments, Britain began a slow process of withdrawing from and granting independence to former colonies. Removing the last vestiges of British control was, however, by no means straightforward, and often civil unrest required small military contingents to remain. There was much concern as to the nature of the regimes that would replace the British presence, and increasingly it was feared that the void would be filled by governments owing allegiance to Moscow. Not only were British dependencies at stake, but so were those of the other European colonial powers.

The initial concern, following the end of the war, was the fate of the European colonies in the Far East, many of which had been occupied by the Japanese. There were some key concerns: whether colonial territories would return to European control; whether nationalist movements would emerge; or would communist elements try to assume control. From the outset it was assumed by the JIC that Moscow's policy towards the Far East was much the same as towards Europe: to drive a wedge between the Western powers and use all measures, however subversive, short of war.

Unfortunately, gaps in the West's intelligence coverage undermined efforts to understand the threat. Undoubtedly part of the explanation for this lay in the nature of the target. The Soviet Union, and later Mao's China, were closed societies which posed unparalleled difficulties as targets for Western intelligence agencies. Compartmentalisation and absolute secrecy were the norm, but the authoritarian nature of communist rule, particularly in the decision making processes, ensured that power was concentrated in the hands of very few. The Far East was a relatively low priority for the UK. Lagging behind Europe in importance, collection efforts were accorded minimal resources and it was only following the outbreak of the Malayan Emergency that Britain began to appreciate the scale of the threat posed in the Far East; it would take Mao's success in the Chinese civil war before the stark realities were recognised.

Despite the lack of a substantial intelligence effort in the region, the Far East, and the European colonies in particular, were of great interest and concern to the JIC, such that in 1948 the Colonial Office was made a permanent member of the Committee. In addition, the regional off-shoot JIC(FE) provided a stream of reporting, repeatedly warning about the dangers of letting intelligence resources dwindle. As it was, the lack of a specific threat ensured that the priority was not changed until it became almost too late.

The Japanese Vacuum

Immediately following the Second World War the JIC began to examine a number of countries in the Far East, particularly those under the control of European colonial powers. The picture was not promising. The Japanese, who had occupied Indonesia (then the Dutch East Indies), had promoted nationalist policies and, following the Japanese withdrawal, a modest British military commitment had been made, intended to ease the passage of the returning European powers. Despite the JIC's conviction that nationalist forces would still tolerate some level of European 'tutelage', the judgment was that independence would eventually be sought. Importantly, from a British perspective, there was no evidence of a communist or Soviet presence.[1] The key was to ensure that a settlement could be reached between the Indonesian leadership and the Dutch, thereby easing pressure on the interim British military forces there.[2]

Another area of concern was French Indochina which had also been occupied by the Japanese during the war. The 'Vietnam Republic', a self-proclaimed political entity, was led by Ho Chi Minh, termed by the JIC a 'communist agitator'. As with the Dutch East Indies, the main issue was whether the European colonial power, in this case the French, would be allowed to return. After the Japanese surrender, British forces had occupied southern Indochina, with Chinese forces taking the north. The role of the Chinese complicated matters and the JIC concluded that a significant number of troops were planning to 'live off the country'. Given Indochina's natural resources, it was clear to the JIC that the French wanted to regain power, but that they were 'afraid of Chinese intentions in this matter'.[3] More alarming for London were the evident signs of mistrust and dislike of the British, with numerous reports being received of the distribution of anti-British propaganda. The US angle was a further complication: it was known that President Roosevelt had been opposed to the return of the French and that the OSS had supported some of the rival political movements covertly. Thus, in the JIC's words: 'a situation appears to be arising in which Americans, Chinese and Japanese in Northern French Indochina are finding themselves on common ground in resisting the return of the French'.[4]

In January 1946 the intelligence directorate of SEAC, the wartime body created to control Allied operations in the Far East, informed the JIC that it appeared that the Chinese were preparing to withdraw from Indochina because the Viet Minh resistance movement was becoming increasingly regarded as communist, which was an 'embarrassment' to Chiang Kai Shek's Nationalist regime. This assessment, as we now know, was correct: Chinese Nationalist forces left the region to join the civil war at home. In the meantime the French, backed by British units in the south, were extending their rule.[5] The French regained some semblance of control relatively quickly, yet they were bitterly opposed by the Viet Minh, with frequent battles and skirmishes between the two sides. These would eventually reach a climax with the decisive battle of Dien Bien Phu in early 1954.

Britain had its own colonial problems. Malaya had also been overrun by the Japanese during the war. With their defeat and removal, it was suggested in London that a new state be created in the Malayan Peninsula. This would become the Malayan Union in April 1946. In the interim though, it had become clear that the Malayan Communist Party (MCP), whose military wing had received some funding from SOE during the war, was gaining popularity and orchestrating attacks and fomenting trouble within Malaya. According to SEAC's own intelligence, the MCP had strong links to China and had 'considerable influence over all communities'.[6]

For the JIC, developments in the Far East posed unique problems. In Marxist terms, communism operated in a different context given the largely peasant population and, in the JIC's words, 'backward political development of the Far East peoples'. This meant that colonial powers were the prime enemy, and that it would be perfectly acceptable to communists to unite with nationalists in attacking them. The Far East also posed a problem for the Soviet Union in wanting to support communist movements without being seen as imperialists. Identifying the hand of Moscow would be a much more difficult task for Western intelligence agencies than elsewhere. It was assumed by the JIC that the Chinese and Korean communists had links to Moscow, but that those in Indochina did not.[7] More broadly, Soviet policy in the region was assessed to be much the same as in Europe: namely, that all measures, short of war, would be employed to undermine and weaken Western states whilst at the same time improving its own position.[8] The Soviet Union therefore remained a threat to British interests in the region, but this was far more nebulous than in Europe.

Emergency in Malaya

For the JIC, the suspected presence of the Soviet Union in the Far East posed far less of a threat than in Europe and, consequently, was a lower priority for intelligence collection efforts. Even by early 1949, the JIC Chairman William Hayter could still advise the COS that the Far East 'had been accorded low priority'.[9]

Central to Britain's intelligence efforts in the region was JIC(FE). Although it had been created in early 1947, a year later discussions continued between officials in JIC(FE) in Singapore and the JIC in London over its precise terms of reference and geographical areas of responsibility, and whether or not it should be responsible for intelligence collection and collation.[10] In a paper circulated to London, JIC(FE) pointed out that intelligence was lacking and that the consequences were potentially disastrous:

> A democratic country, which cannot afford to maintain armed forces at war strength in peacetime, must take out an insurance policy in the form of a

strong and efficient intelligence organisation covering all the forms of activity met in modern warfare. If this policy is to pay an adequate dividend at the outset of a war, the premium in peacetime, in the form of money and man-power, must also be adequate . . . we consider that some of the weaknesses in the Far East intelligence organisation as exposed by the last war, still exist. These weaknesses are due basically to insufficient importance being attached to intelligence in all its fields.[11]

To remedy these perceived deficiencies, JIC(FE) was given a new Charter setting out, for the first time, its role and functions.[12] Working under JIC(FE) were Local Intelligence Committees (LICs) in Malaya, Singapore and Hong Kong, whose job it was to co-ordinate intelligence in their specific regions, to advise the local Defence Committees, and to send reports to JIC(FE).[13] The addition of the Colonial Office to JIC membership in London in late 1948 was a further improvement. The rationale was clear: in a minute to Hayter the Colonial Office stated that 'the Colonial territories are likely to be one of the principal objectives of Communist attack in the near future'.[14] In seeking approval from the Prime Minister, the COS committee noted that the

> object of this proposal is to ensure that we have the best possible intelligence about Communist activity in the Colonies so that we may not be taken unawares . . . we must have good intelligence services on the spot so that communist activities can be apprehended right from the start, and not after they have secured a firm foothold.

Attlee approved, although the move had come as a reaction to events rather than in anticipation of them.[15]

In April 1948 the JIC received a paper on Malaya prepared by the Colonial Office. At the outset this stated that 'the most noticeable feature of the Malayan scene at the moment is the relative calm which has descended on it.' The paper also predicted that this calm could be shattered at any moment: 'there is, however, no reason to suppose that this calm represents a real, lasting easing of the situation; on the contrary, all the evidence indicates that such a view would be danger-ously complacent, and that the disruptive forces are merely reorganising in readiness for some new line of attack.' At first glance these might seem to have been prophetic words, but the report continued, 'communist penetration . . . will probably not work through open conflict, but through the patient, pliant tactics in which international Communism has so much experience (i.e. subversion and infiltration) . . . it would be unwise to paint too dark a picture'[16].

The Colonial Office report does not seem to have been discussed by the JIC, even though it was circulated to each of its members. Such briefings may suggest a lack of urgency on the part of the JIC because there was no evidence of an immediate threat.[17] In addition, a series of rivalries undermined intelligence efforts in the Far East. For instance, the Director of the Malayan Security Service was refused permission to join JIC(FE), a decision supported by Hayter who warned that inclusion would result in undue attention to 'parochial affairs'.[18] Later, in the mid-1950s, a number of question marks surrounded the performance of JIC(FE). In a note to Patrick Dean, the JIC Chairman in London, Andrew Gilchrist, the FO JIC(FE) Chairman, confided that one of his biggest challenges was fighting against 'the twisting of factual intelligence to fit a preconceived picture', particularly in the case of assessments on Indochina.[19]

There had been sporadic protests against British rule, but from the middle of 1948 Malaya witnessed an escalation in violence and rioting, including the murder of a number of Europeans. The protagonists were an army of Chinese guerrillas, orchestrated by the MCP. By June 1948 the British High Commissioner, Sir Edward Gent, was forced to declare a State of Emergency, marking the start of the 'Malayan Emergency'.[20] During late 1948 the situation deteriorated. The British introduced several measures which, amongst other things, made the communist party illegal. As a result the MCP retreated into rural areas and began a vigorous guerrilla campaign to sabotage and undermine colonial rule.

In Singapore and London events were monitored regularly. In September 1948 the Admiralty complained, using the JIC as a forum, about the 'non-existence' of an adequate combined structure of intelligence to deal with Malaya.[21] Criticism also came from Sir Percy Sillitoe, the Director-General of MI5, that assessments issued by JIC(FE) were based on single sources and that, 'therefore, [not] much credence should be placed in them'.[22] Another problem, identified by the Chairman of JIC(FE), was that his team were under-staffed, particularly as his drafters were only part-time.[23] Indeed, by 1950 there was only one full-time drafter, the diplomat Robert Mackworth-Young (later the librarian to the Queen).[24]

The outbreak of the Emergency in Malaya in mid-1948 marked a turning point for British intelligence in the Far East. Most of the initial attention was focussed on self criticism as to why events had not been accurately predicted. Following a visit to JIC(FE) in Singapore, Hayter reported back to the JIC in London that two major factors contributed to the failing: intelligence in the Far East had been accorded a low priority; and the Malayan Security Service had not communicated information effectively and efficiently to JIC(FE). He subsequently reiterated both points in a briefing for the COS.[25] In Hayter's opinion the JIC(FE) could not be blamed. He had left Singapore satisfied with the organisation of JIC(FE). However the two responsible military entities in the region – the British Defence Co-ordination Committee and the Commanders-in-Chief Committee – did not share his confidence.[26] The former was conducting its own inquiry into how to create 'an efficient intelligence organisation'.[27] The perceived remedy, apart from improving communication between the regional players, was to appoint a full-time Chairman of JIC(FE), which happened after much acrimonious and protracted discussion.[28]

Intelligence played a crucial part in the eventual British victory in Malaya. The overwhelming majority of these intelligence successes were at the tactical and operational level, and although the JIC was involved, it did not participate in day to day deliberations and, as such, it rarely appears in the secondary literature on Malaya.[29] Collaboration between the Malayan theatre and JIC(FE) improved, as did intelligence collection.[30] For the JIC, the significance of the Malayan Emergency was to awaken concern over the Far East. In a discussion in the JIC in March 1949 it was agreed that the COS and the Planning Staff needed to be reminded of the danger of concentrating resources and attention too heavily on Europe to the detriment of events elsewhere.[31]

Almost from the outset events in Malaya were perceived as part of a broader, regional picture. In a lengthy paper on communist influence in the Far East in December 1948, the JIC took a fresh look at the situation. It was now clear, it argued, that 'the end of the war in 1945 found the Far East more vulnerable to communist influence than ever before'. This was evident in several ways: general political instability; increased nationalism; a more positive image of the Soviet Union with its increasing diplomatic representation, coupled with the declining prestige of the European colonial powers following the Japanese military successes in the war; and finally, economic disruption. Together these factors led to an increased Soviet interest in the region which, it was perceived, could only continue to grow.[32] Such views gained acceptance, for by February 1950 the JIC began to refer to a 'Cold War in south east Asia'.[33] Similarly, evidence from various JIC assessments reveal support for the domino theory: that if the communists gained control of Indochina, then Siam, Burma and Malaya could fall. The Commissioner General for South-East Asia, Malcolm MacDonald, had warned of this the previous year.[34] However, Malaya was not the only trouble spot in the Far East and whilst the Emergency ignited greater interest in the region, events in China would become the focus of the JIC's attention.

The Threat to Hong Kong

From a British perspective one of the most important reasons for monitoring the vicissitudes of the Chinese civil war was concern over the safety of Hong Kong. By 1946 Hong Kong was again becoming an important outpost for intelligence gathering, quite separate from its importance as a centre for trade and commerce. The JIC reasoned that China was the only state that could, and potentially would, 'undertake aggressive measures' against Hong Kong. Rather more seriously it also believed that the Soviet Union and the US would support Chinese attempts to diplomatically re-absorb Hong Kong.[35] British fears were not unwarranted: the Chinese Nationalists had a stated policy to reclaim Hong Kong, albeit exclusively by diplomatic means. Yet should diplomatic moves fail, the JIC assessment also considered the military means China had at its disposal. Its conclusion was that Nationalist China could not pose a serious military threat because, explicitly, 'the Chinese are singularly inept at mounting an attack'. Consequently, in line with views of the most likely course of Soviet actions, any Chinese 'threat' to Hong Kong would be subversive in nature. In reaction to this the JIC report suggested that military numbers in Hong Kong be increased and that a local JIC be created on the island.[36]

The JIC retained a keen interest in developments. An assessment of March 1948 pointed out that as the civil war in China was 'definitely' going the way of the communists, the pressing concern was whether or not the military threat to Hong Kong had altered. The JIC judged that an attack was more likely during the transitional phase of a communist take over, although the probability of an attack materialising was low.[37] JIC(FE) was also monitoring events and in early 1949 it concluded that a communist victory would 'threaten' the 'stability' of Hong Kong, and that 'in the long run we must expect a Communist demand for the rendition of the Colony'.[38] By April 1949, with communist success in China looking increasingly inevitable, the JIC still maintained that although the Chinese leadership would want to absorb it, there was still little chance of a military conflict to secure control.[39]

The threat to Hong Kong remained at the forefront of COS thinking. The view of Field Marshal Sir William Slim, the CIGS, provides a sense of the importance attached to the defence of Hong Kong:

> Our policy should be to hold Hong Kong against any threat other than a Russian attack, or an attack by Chinese communists so strongly supported by the Russians that it amounted in fact to a Russian attack. He [Slim] felt that we should be ready to defend Hong Kong against an attack by communist China even if this entailed a declaration of war against the Chinese communist authorities.[40]

As the Chinese civil war progressed, the pressure from Whitehall on the JIC to provide regular assessments on the evolving situation increased. Following a Cabinet decision in May 1949 the JIC was instructed to produce fortnightly assessments on the 'Situation in South China', with a 'particular reference' to the threat posed to Hong Kong.[41] By late August, at the time of a renewed Chinese push towards the south, the JIC concluded that while an invasion was still unlikely, for the first time fifth column 'disorders' in Hong Kong were raised as a possibility.[42] This view strengthened and a month later the JIC would report that whilst 'internal disorders' were less likely until late October, 'it must be remembered that these could take place at any time'.[43]

The JIC concluded that any serious Chinese threat to Hong Kong could only emerge once the communists had progressed far enough southwards to be able to amass large numbers on the 'Sino-British border'. Despite producing detailed statistics, the date by which a threat towards Hong Kong would be credible was constantly pushed into the future, always between one and two months hence. But the JIC at no point suggested that the communists *would* take over Hong Kong.

The problem with all the judgments on communist China and the threat to Hong Kong, particularly from mid-1949 onwards, is the JIC's relatively cautious approach. Most papers discuss what 'might' happen, what 'could' be achieved, and what the potential might be. Although the reports appear to have been of some value – certainly the COS did not complain about their frequent lack of precision – it is hard to see how they could have been of much use. A range of statistical data was provided on the number and size of the military and equipment, and observations on the movement of the communist forces. Yet little was provided in the way of hard firm predictions: not simply whether the Chinese had the potential to attack but whether they would actually do so. JIC papers from this period are almost entirely devoid of any assessment of intent, concentrating instead on an analysis of capability.

By November 1949 the JIC was more prepared to venture the belief that 'the Chinese Communists do not intend to attack Hong Kong in the near future.' At the same time, however, the LIC (Hong Kong), a local body based in theatre, warned that once any decision had been made to do so, the Chinese would only need a month to launch an attack.[44] This was based not on a fresh interpretation of the Chinese leadership's thinking, but instead on a recognition that there were 'no indications of Communist military intentions towards Hong Kong'. In other words, monitoring of Chinese military capabilities was used to infer intentions. Although this is to some extent a criticism of the JIC, there were immense difficulties in penetrating the Chinese target. Very little in the way of good, reliable intelligence was available and, as with assessments of the Soviet Union, the JIC had to rely on a variety of assumptions on which to base its forecasts.[45]

Indochina

Hong Kong and Malaya were not the only colonial concerns affecting British security. Parts of Indochina, comprising Vietnam, Cambodia and Laos, first became French concerns in the nineteenth-century. During the war Indochina fell from French rule to Japanese control. When the Imperial Army surrendered in the summer of 1945 the French attempted to regain control. However, by August the Vietminh, a communist/nationalist group, led by the charismatic Ho Chi Minh, had become far more popular in the search for independence. The Vietminh had opposed both Vichy French and Japanese rule and, in so doing, were supported the US OSS, through whom they had received training, ammunition and weapons, three factors that would become vital in their struggle against the French.

After the war the JIC surveyed a number of countries under colonial rule in the Far East. In October 1945 it published an assessment on Indochina, though in fact it had been prepared and written by JIC(SEAC).[46] Partly a historical and geographical survey of Indochina, the report noted that 'French policy in general has been rather in the interests of France than of the native population', and that, as a consequence, 'there exists a widespread movement against allowing the French to return'.

Assessments of the situation, like so much else in the early Cold War years, was frustrated by the lack of any detailed intelligence. Despite some low-level SIS reporting, considered 'useful', there was a certain degree of reliance, initially at least, on overt military sources.[47] As a result, in the JIC's words: 'it is again difficult to make an accurate assessment' on the level of resistance to the French.

The situation was delicately poised: a colonial power that 'naturally' had 'no wish to abandon' the country despite facing a rising nationalistic movement. In JIC(SEAC)'s opinion, France would have to be cautious in any use of force to overthrow the Vietminh resistance because 'they are afraid of Chinese intentions in this matter'. What of the Vietminh itself? The SEAC portrayed it solely as a nationalist movement, with no references to any links that it may have had with the communist world. The JIC was not overly impressed by Vietminh abilities, declaring it 'vociferous', and concluding that its use of radio broadcasts to garner support was 'probably a sign of weakness rather than strength'.[48]

At the same time as the report was distributed under the JIC's auspices, British troops, led by Major General Douglas Gracey, entered and occupied parts of Saigon with the specific aim of re-installing French rule. The fate of Indochina then, was not just of academic interest to the British government, and this may have been the reason why the JIC paid it close attention.[49] The decision to support the French once more put the UK in conflict with the US, which opposed European colonial rule in the region. The JIC concluded in its assessment of Indochina:

> To sum up, a situation appears to be arising in which Americans, Chinese and Japanese in Northern French Indochina are finding themselves on common ground in resisting the return of the French. It seems likely, therefore, that the French will be faced in Northern FIC [French Indochina] with an armed and vigorous Annamite [as the people of the region were known] movement which feels that it has at least tactical American support and, in its anti-French activities, will be helped rather than hindered by the Chinese.

The COS had difficulty in gauging whether Britain should continue to support the French in Indochina,[50] and were left in an unenviable position: support for the French had the potential to risk upsetting the US, but failure to do so would not only alienate the French but, far more importantly, send a signal to nationalist movements in British colonies.

The JIC issued a further report on Indochina prepared by JIC(SEAC) in January 1946. In the south and with the assistance of British troops, the French, it was reported, were beginning to gain control. Thus, the situation was 'improving', thanks largely to the increased concentration of 'Allied Forces'. In the north, by contrast, the French presence was less pronounced. Despite being described as 'singularly inefficient', the Vietminh remained in control, though it was noted that in rural areas its tenure was 'precarious'. Furthermore, the Vietminh 'army' was considered to be poor: 'the bulk of the forces of the Vietminh are almost untrained, their equipment is often improvised and of poor quality, and there is an almost total lack of technical and administrative services'.[51]

Within a few months of the January assessment French forces had reoccupied parts of Indochina, and the British forces had begun a phased withdrawal. Thereafter Indochina ceased to be of major concern to the JIC – it was mentioned in broad surveys of the Far East but no specific, substantial papers were produced. That began to change in 1949, fuelled not by concern over the communist advances in China, but rather by a French request to set up a system of intelligence exchange in the Far East. The JIC, clearly not enamoured of the idea, discussed it at several different junctures in late 1949. Finally it decided, after consultation with the COS, that the French could have a limited supply of intelligence material up to the 'Secret' classification.[52]

One of the difficulties in trying to capture how the JIC, and its subordinate regional offshoots, surveyed a situation is that whilst much of the JIC's output has been preserved, the majority of the records of JIC(FE), and indeed the relevant LICs, have long since been destroyed or lost.[53] It is clear from JIC papers that JIC(FE) produced a steady and regular stream of reports on Indochina, on the possible effects of a French withdrawal and external threats, but with few exceptions none have survived. Partial reconstruction of these assessments is possible though, as it is clear that the JIC took into account and incorporated these regional reports when preparing its own studies.

An assessment in March 1950, following the communist victory in China but before any evidence of trouble in Korea had emerged, shows that the fate of Indochina was considered to be intimately connected to the rest of the region. It was unlikely that the Chinese would attack the French forces, but it was assessed that they would provide 'moral and material support' to the Vietminh. Furthermore, this was happening at a delicate time, with the outcome in the balance and significant doubts emerging over future French policy. The implications of either a French withdrawal or a French military defeat were clear: it 'would gravely prejudice the defence of western interests throughout South-East Asia'. This view was echoed in Cabinet discussions in the 'China and South East Asia Committee'.[54] The only way to prevent this lay with the provision of external assistance to the French.[55] As with earlier discussions about British involvement and assistance to the French in 1945, this was not a straightforward decision. The JIC's assessments of the threat to French forces, within the framework of the wider threat to the region, were central to planning. A JPS report, using the JIC's study as background, agreed: given the severity of the threat, 'everything possible, therefore, should be done to support the French in Indochina'. The problem, as the JPS report continued, was that there was an 'inability' of the UK to contribute forces, and so 'military discussions' were advocated.[56]

Whatever these 'discussions' might have entailed, their impact was evidently limited. In London the JIC continued to monitor the situation through its regular assessments on the communist threat to the Far East and South-East Asia. The JIC reporting on events in Indochina shows that at no point did the intelligence received indicate an imminent French withdrawal or defeat, despite frequent reports of Chinese and Soviet supplies of arms to the Vietminh.[57]

In August 1950 the JIC reported 'indications' that the Vietminh was preparing for a large-scale offensive. Whilst the French were 'confident' that they could withstand such an attack, the JIC was not convinced, describing the French assertion as 'optimistic'. Underpinning French confidence may have been the announcement in May 1950 of US military aid, though by August it still had not materialised.[58] Within a month the JIC had reversed its assessment, now judging that an offensive was unlikely for two reasons: the Vietminh lacked technical 'know-how' for an attack; and was incapable of making tactical plans and coping with a fluid military conflict. Thus, any offensive was only conceivable with the tacit support and approval of the Chinese government.[59]

Within a month the situation had changed again. In early October, the JIC assessed that the situation had deteriorated and that the French would not be able to achieve their aspiration of uniting the country under their control. The Vietminh forces were greatly improving their military skills and numbers.[60] This trend continued throughout late 1950, with the Vietminh army gaining in capability as the resistance of the French forces weakened. The surprise of Chinese involvement in Korea further underlined the fragility of Indochina. The JIC, for the first time, now considered it a real likelihood that China would become involved militarily there too.[61] The political impact of events in Korea led to Soviet and Chinese official recognition of the Vietminh government in early 1950, and this had been followed by the provision of US aid to the French. This was a major change: 'what had begun in 1946 as an attempt by France to recover its former colonial position in the face of indigenous nationalist-communist resistance had been transformed by 1951 into a catalyst for war between the major powers'.[62]

The situation in Indochina continued to concern the JIC. In early 1951 it re-iterated an earlier conclusion that the fall of Indochina to the communists would be a major setback for the survival of a Western presence in South-East Asia.[63] Chinese involvement in Korea, and the subsequent UN military response clearly had influenced the JIC's analysis of wider Chinese intentions. Given the Chinese commitment to Korea the JIC queried an earlier assessment, subsequently concluding that the Chinese would not now intervene in Indochina.[64] And there the balance lay. Senior military figures and politicians debated long and hard about the British commitment to Indochina, particularly what should be done either in the event of a French withdrawal or a communist seizure of control. What had begun as a colonial war was now becoming a much wider conflict: supporting the French was the US, who had altered its position given that the issue had become an anti-communist as well as a colonial struggle. In the sidelines, providing assistance to the Vietminh, were the Chinese. The balancing of British concerns with US expectations was a further complicating factor. In addition to providing material assistance to the French in Indochina, the US had held discussions about a possible military commitment. If a wider war did break out in Indochina, the COS considered that UK military involvement would be almost inevitable. Hong Kong would be one of the first targets of Chinese forces. Militarily, UK resources were limited because of commitments in Europe, the Middle East, and Malaya, and so significant involvement in Indochina would mean the redeployment of forces from other key operational theatres.[65]

Against the background of this potentially explosive situation JIC assessments were central to policy and, from late 1952, a regular series of reports and updates on the situation in Indochina were issued. Throughout the second half of 1952 the FO was critical of the French commanders' tactics to preserve the status quo rather than press for the offensive. Writing in late 1952 the JIC confirmed that little had changed over the past year, with the French ensconced in the south and the Vietminh in control of the north. Indeed, the best the Committee thought the French could achieve was to 'maintain their position'.[66] This view was supported by the COS, who urged politicians to encourage a continuation of the French commitment to Indochina, especially as reports had emerged of discussions in Paris about a possible surrender and withdrawal.[67]

Indochina was considered to be central to containing the spread of communism in the Far East, and the British appreciated the need to reinforce the French commitment. Senior policymakers and the COS believed the loyal Vietnamese could not hold out against the Vietminh without external assistance; and that a military response was the only realistic option, a view supported by a fresh JIC assessment in early 1953.[68] Here, then, was a clear example of how JIC assessments were influencing the policymaking process.

Despite these developments, the Churchill government thought that it would be, in the words of Foreign Secretary Anthony Eden, 'politically undesirable' to approach the French and ask for a further commitment,[69] the rationale being that to introduce more French forces into the Far East would mean reducing their military commitment to Europe. French acquiescence might mean that they would expect a compensating gesture by the UK, such as transferring scarce British troops from either NATO or other European defence commitments, to the detriment of British national interests. Fortunately the French themselves settled the matter: in early 1953 the minister responsible for Indochina declared that it was 'improbable that the French would be able to pull out entirely in the foreseeable future'.[70]

The perceived importance of the fate of Indochina for British commitments in the region meant the JIC inevitably continued to spend a significant amount of time producing assessments of the situation. These were regularly used by the Official Cabinet Committee on Communism (Overseas) which, in turn, offered its own reports as a basis for policy recommendations. The middle of 1953 was, however, a difficult period for British foreign policy: Eden was ill and absent from duty for several months, Churchill suffered a stroke, and the stand-in Foreign Secretary, Lord Salisbury, declared himself 'out of touch' with international affairs.[71] In June, an FO brief was prepared for the Prime Minister which stated, unequivocally, that 'with their present policy the French are drifting towards an eventual collapse'.[72] This advice, however, was questioned by the JIC conclusion in July that 'there is no immediate danger to the French position in Indochina'.[73]

For the JIC, writing in mid-1953, Laos was in an important strategic position. Lying to the north-west of and bordering Vietnam, it was central to the fate of the French forces. It was an autonomous region but governed, occupied and then relinquished by the French. Laos had been overrun at several points by Vietminh forces, whose policy up to this point had been to avoid major conflict with the French, preferring instead to build up popular support in other regions. Now, however, the JIC concluded that this strategy might change, and that one option might be for the Vietminh to attack targets in north and south Laos.[74] The rainy season in mid-1953 had hampered any large military operations and, towards the end of 1953, the French settled themselves at Dien Bien Phu, in a valley in north-western Vietnam, with the aim of interdicting lines of communication into and out of Laos.

A conference was convened in Geneva in late April 1954, to be attended by the French, British, Americans, Chinese and other 'interested' powers. The purpose was to try to find a solution to Indochina (amongst other issues). At approximately the same time, news reached London that the Chairman of the JCS, Admiral Arthur Radford, had been advocating using air strikes to shore up the French position. Furthermore, it was clear that the Americans were displeased at being asked to attend a conference with the Chinese. In Washington, the British Ambassador, Sir Roger Makins, cabled back to the FO asking what HMG's position would be if the US were to become involved in supporting the French. The UK view was that whilst US assistance would surely strengthen the anti-communist position, it also had the potential to turn a regional colonial conflict into an international war, much as had happened in Korea.[75]

In seeking a political answer to the issue of US involvement, the JIC was instructed to produce a new report on the war in Indochina, concentrating on the conflict itself and the implications for the region relative to the UK's position. It was to focus on two questions, firstly what would happen if the war continued on its present course for a further one or two years; and secondly, what would be the impact of greater US involvement. A further question, seemingly added as an afterthought given the discussions going on behind the scenes, was to consider the necessary conditions for a ceasefire.[76]

While work began on addressing these issues and producing its report, events in the Far East were rapidly unfolding. On 13 March 1954 the French plan to use Dien Bien Phu to draw out the Vietminh and achieve a quick victory backfired spectacularly. The Vietminh attacked, effectively encircling the French forces and preventing reinforcements and supplies getting through. Very quickly the drafters of the report were forced to focus instead on the immediate effects of the fighting.[77]

Although the report avoided any explicit policy advice, it is hard to see how policy options could not have been drawn from it. Even if the French were successful, the report argued, it was unlikely that a victory at Dien Bien Phu would lead to a decisive result. An increase in US support, albeit not the physical presence of troops, would have 'beneficial but gradual results'. More worryingly, the JIC concluded, probably reflecting the experience of the Korean War, that 'any direct intervention by the armed forces of any external nation would probably lead to Chinese intervention, and there is a danger that it might ultimately lead to a global war.' In effect, the only practical way for the French to extricate themselves from the war was a ceasefire. In the JIC's opinion the Vietminh 'might' accept a partition of the country.[78] At its meeting a few days later the COS

Committee endorsed the report, confirming that it was 'in line with their views'. The COS also concluded that although a French military victory was the ideal option, it was the least likely. Hence, although it would imply a 'victory for Communism', the best course open would be to agree to the partition of Indochina.[79]

In the FO there remained huge concern over the US position. This was intensified when, in early April, separate minutes were received from Makins and from President Eisenhower. Both confirmed the US interest in becoming involved in Indochina and a desire for Britain to come in alongside them.[80] This was no trivial matter for, as Makins informed the FO, the decisions reached over Indochina would have far reaching consequences:

> Hitherto we have agreed pretty well with the Americans on the day-to-day handling of policy in the Far East in spite of longer range differences of political appreciation. But though we may continue for a time to agree on tactics, a decision to range ourselves with the fundamental American decision or dissociate ourselves from it cannot be long delayed and will have a profound effect over the whole field of Anglo-Americans relations.[81]

At the same time Eisenhower wrote personally to Churchill, urging him not to play into the communists' hands and to avoid allowing them to 'drive a wedge between us'.[82]

The US would not intervene without allied support but the British refused to back American plans for a strike around Dien Bien Phu. At the same time, fears of the potential domino effect permeated all thoughts about the Far East – with China gone and Korea at a stalemate, if Indochina were also to fall then there would be no significant anti-communist bastion left in the region. Discussion, both internally and with US representatives, continued but little agreement could be reached. In late April delegates at the Geneva Conference discussed a possible settlement for Indochina. On the eve of the conference, the French commander in Indochina cabled to the effect that without US military intervention, all hope was lost. A confrontation between British and American representatives, most notably with Admiral Radford and John Foster Dulles, the Secretary of State, prompted Evelyn Shuckburgh, Eden's Principal Private Secretary, later to record in his diary, Radford 'was obviously raring for a scrap' and the only option was for the US and UK to co-operate and command the war effort.[83]

Whilst discussions continued in Geneva, on 7 May 1954 the French capitulated at Dien Bien Phu. Although the conference concluded that there was no hope for the re-unification of Korea, the general consensus was that a solution to the problems in Indochina was possible. So it was that on 21 July 1954, after three gruelling months of dialogue and debate, the French and Vietminh parties agreed to a ceasefire.[84] In parallel the JIC Chairman, Patrick Dean, attempted to patch up relations with the US. He had visited Washington and held talks with Allen Dulles, the Director of Central Intelligence, to 'improve our intelligence cooperation in the Far East'. His proposal was for the US to attach an officer to JIC(FE). Dulles' reply is not recorded, though it is apparent that relations did begin to improve.[85]

The Geneva Conference had formalised a partition of Vietnam along the 17th Parallel. It had also paved the way for national elections, to be held in 1956, with the intention of unifying Vietnam through a democratic process. On the surface, therefore, the conference was a success – the anti-colonial war against the French had ended and any risk of a major war averted. In practice though, little had changed: the partition ensured that the communists continued to prosper in the north, strengthening their support base and military efficiency. In the south the anti-communist leadership was struggling. In October 1954 the JIC produced its first assessment of the region since the Geneva Accords. The report highlighted the stark contrast between the plight of the North and South Vietnamese governments: 'the Communists will retain unrestricted control of all North Vietnam up to the elections . . . [in South Vietnam] the Government is unstable and ineffective and is losing such popular support as it had.' To the JIC the implications were alarming:

> The settlement reached at Geneva has thrown the political situation in Indochina into the melting pot . . . the initiative rests with the Communists throughout the country. They already possess an efficient administration in the North and a well-established propaganda and subversive organisation in the South. Furthermore, any attempt at this stage, to predict the future policy of the Communists in Indochina must be speculative since there are so many possible courses of action open to them. In the first place, there is obviously a choice between execution and evasion of the Geneva settlement . . . a second and analogous choice facing the Communists is whether to accept the present division of Indochina as permanent or whether to seek to extend their domination over the whole country in spite of the risks this will entail.[86]

Despite providing a cogent summary of the situation, in its assessment the JIC failed to voice its own concerns. Travelling around the region in late October 1954, Andrew Gilchrist, the Chairman of JIC(FE), recorded how 'it seems to me most important and urgent to make a further effort to achieve Anglo-American co-operation in this area, partly with a view to bolstering up the remains of Indochina'.[87]

At around the same time as the Geneva Accords, another significant pact was signed. The Manila Treaty resulted in the creation of the Southeast Asia Treaty Organisation (SEATO), envisaged as a similar institution to NATO, designed to provide military assistance to the area. South Vietnam was not a member of SEATO but it could, if required, request military support. By the end of 1954 the war in Korea had ended, a diplomatic solution had been found for the war in Indochina; confrontation with China had been avoided; and the US was committed to the defence of the region. Yet behind this fragile façade, as the British were soon to realise, little had actually changed.

An Impasse

The future course of events in South-East Asia now seemed to rest on the balance of power in Indochina.[88] The JIC felt that China would concentrate on increasing its own economic and industrial capacity, but that communist 'penetration' would expand in Indochina. A substantial part of the problem, as the JIC pointed out, was the different styles of government in North and South Vietnam. In the North the new communist government had 'imparted a good impression by a show of sweet reasonableness and of unity, discipline, efficiency and freedom from corruption'. This was in stark contrast to the capitalist government in the South, 'where petty squabbling, lack of unity, inefficiency and corruption were all too apparent'.[89] The problem, once again, was UK relations with the US, who had installed and were supporting the new Diem regime, despite its many failings. As a result the JIC was very careful in deciding which papers could be shared and discussed with the Americans.[90]

In early 1955 the JIC considered that the agreement reached in Geneva for full elections in Indochina in 1956 would proceed smoothly. It was neither inclined to nor asked to predict the outcome of the elections but argued that if the communists failed to win, they would try to achieve dominance by 'pressure, persuasion and propaganda, infiltration and subversion'.[91] As part of the plans for the 1956 election the North Vietnamese were supposed to start discussions by July 1955 to decide on an electoral process. But it was also clear to the JIC, the FO, and indeed the French, that for his part Diem had little stomach for such talks and was not planning to participate. In the JIC's opinion, the implications of his reluctance were stark: without an election 'the prospects of South Vietnam preserving itself against communism are bad'.[92] This particular paper was a clear example of how US/UK differences were being played out, for as Patrick Dean informed the JIC Secretary,

> We are still opposed to giving this [JIC(55)38, 'The Situation in Indochina'] to the Americans. It would teach them nothing new, but would revive old controversies and give them the impression that we are more critical of their policies and more defeatist than we really are. At the present moment when we are trying to work out a common approach to the Vietnam elections we need to concentrate upon what is common to US and UK thinking and not upon the differences.[93]

To try and persuade Diem to take the initiative he was warned that 'if fighting recommenced as a result of his failure to comply with the Geneva Settlement it would be impossible for HMG to give any support to the South Vietnamese Government.' In commenting on this, the JIC mentioned the possible consequences of not holding elections, the results of which would be catastrophic.[94] There were two related problems: the first was that the Diem regime was, as the JIC had previously noted, unpopular; and the implications of this led to the second problem: whereas the British and French saw Diem as a serious liability to peace in Indochina, the US were providing vital assistance and were unwilling to replace him. A JIC(FE) assessment (which has survived), noted the Franco-American differences were obvious to the Vietminh, and was using the 'bitter antagonism' to 'establish political bases'.[95] Diem's position was further complicated by the way he had demolished religious opposition in South Vietnam and created a power vacuum that only he could fill.[96] To prepare for the worst, the JIC drew up very extensive threat scenarios based on different ways in which a communist victory in Indochina might materialise, be it through the electoral process or through subversion.[97]

By late 1955, with the July deadline for talks having long since passed, the JIC produced an assessment on prospects for the region. This paper, based on a mixture of JIC(FE) reporting, US National Intelligence Estimates, and (apparently) British intelligence, identified three possible outcomes: a North Vietnamese invasion of the South; an overthrow of Diem; or 'temporary acquiescence' in the partition. Of the three the last was seen as most likely, largely because the first two were not considered possible. The JIC assumed that a military invasion would be avoided at all costs given the danger that it could turn into a major conflict; and that it would not be feasible to overthrow Diem without some degree of foreign intervention.[98] The JIC retained this conclusion in a further assessment in February 1956, observing that Diem was strengthening his control in the South, and that unless there was some level of communist intervention before mid-1956, any chance of removing Diem would be seriously hampered.[99] Although the COS approved and endorsed the report's contents, they did insist on one small revision: the original report stated that 'actual invasion is unlikely', but this was changed to 'while the possibility of military invasion cannot be ruled out, this is unlikely', a surviving example of an explicit conclusion by the JIC being made more ambiguous![100]

To the JIC, events in the South East Asia were, initially, seen as self-contained. Colonial skirmishes and battles between opposing nationalist forces were viewed as internal and isolated problems. The first evidence of a shifting attitude came with the onset of the Emergency in Malaya in 1948. Here was a direct threat to British interests that had not been foreseen: the response was to strengthen the role of JIC(FE) in an attempt to improve the intelligence effort in the region. Whilst events in Malaya demanded attention, it took the success of Mao's communists in China to confirm the importance of the Far East as a global issue. However the onset of the Korean War had the greatest impact.[101] What had appeared to be relatively slow paced, contained and regional, suddenly took on a rapid, enlarged and significant perspective.

The continuing dispute between the US-backed Republic of China (Chiang Kai Shek's forces) on Formosa (Taiwan) and the Chinese communists by 1956 had re-focussed the JIC's attention on China. Events in China had continued to be monitored, but following the US Congress's approval of the use of force to defend Formosa there was a potential, however improbable, for further conflict. The JIC concluded that the US would probably resort to military means to defend the island, even if it did not regard a Chinese attack as likely.[102] On China itself, the JIC produced a series of lengthy reports, detailing the growth of its military and economic power. One factor, however, weighed heavily in the balance in favour of the West: the possession of an atomic weapon. To the JIC this meant that China would be wary of any confrontation.[103] The JIC did recognise significant differences between communist aspirations in Europe and in the Far East. Establishing communist regimes in Europe was seen as a goal of both Soviet and Chinese policy. But the chance of success by covert means was limited, whereas in comparison 'many parts of Asia are favourable to a policy of propaganda and subversion'. Thus, although open conflict could be ruled out, subversive tactics were to be expected.[104]

By the end of 1956 in the Far East, much as in Europe, a struggle between the major powers seemed to have reached an impasse. Problems with sources and the collection of intelligence persisted. In March, Patrick Dean had visited the Far East to review the intelligence organisation. In reporting back to the JIC he re-iterated long held views on the poor status of intelligence coverage, though he also recognised the realities of the situation: 'it is true that all types of intelligence on China are lacking, but the target is exceedingly hard and it seems doubtful whether any greatly increased effort at the present time would lead to much improved results.'[105]

In Vietnam, the JIC assessments had been proved largely correct; elections never materialised and Diem's position, despite the inadequacies of his rule, was strengthened. North and South Vietnam had reached 'a continuing stalemate', but the JIC concluded that 'the situation will inevitably be subject to Cold War developments generally'.[106] For China the intelligence assessment was bleak: its economy would continue to grow; it would start, over the next ten years, to develop more advanced weapons, including nuclear weapons; and the communists would strengthen their internal support. It was judged that in time, as the Chinese became more confident, they would start to distance themselves from the Soviet Union, albeit not to the extent that the communist 'bloc' would disintegrate. Overriding all of this would be a desire to spread communism while averting war.[107]

By 1956 the UK's withdrawal from its colonies was well underway. Although this had proceeded at differing speeds around the world, it had been far from straightforward. The often exaggerated fear of Soviet influence, together with under-estimates of support for nationalist movements, meant that the political climate was mis-read time and again. Part of the difficulty lay in collecting sufficiently high grade intelligence. A greater and far more subtle problem was the difficulty of understanding the culture and mindset of the peoples of the Far East. This was clearly the case with assessments of the Chinese threat towards Hong Kong, where capabilities were used to infer intentions. The JIC repeatedly resorted to using prior assumptions to gauge future events so, when the Chinese surprised the Committee by becoming embroiled in Korea, it meant a revision to all other assessments of potential Chinese actions.

The US position was staunchly anti-imperialist until the communist dimension superseded it, and the US was often at odds with Britain. With its military and financial capabilities stretched to breaking point, Britain was unable to deploy more troops to troublespots in the region, regardless of how pressing or important the need. Consequently a US desire to repel communism and to recruit like-minded allies to support it often left the UK in a difficult position. As a succession of events – Malaya, China, Korea, Indochina – revealed that the extent of support for communist presence in the region was substantial, US and British policy began to converge, which in turn improved intelligence relations. No longer did the Far East appear in London to be a series of isolated national skirmishes; rather it was being seen as part of a broader Cold War battleground. Thus the scene was set for the dramatic escalation of hostilities in Vietnam which charac-terised the following decade. Communism was firmly entrenched in the Far East and the JIC was only too aware of the threat it posed to local British interests and to the region more broadly.

Notes

1 JIC(45)294(0), 'Situation in Netherlands East Indies', 10 October 1945. CAB 81/131.
2 JIC(45)329(0), 'Situation in Netherlands East Indies', 12 December 1945. CAB 81/131.
3 JIC(45)287(0), 'Situation in French Indochina', 3 October 1945. CAB 81/131.
4 JIC(45)295(0)FINAL, 'French Indochina', 13 October 1945. CAB 81/131.
5 JIC(46)4(0), 'Situation in French Indochina', 6 January 1946. CAB 81/132.
6 JIC(46)2(0), 'The Future Situation in Malaya', 4 January 1946. CAB 81/132. In fact it was not actual attacks being organised but rather labour unrest.
7 JIC(46)70(0)(Final), 'The Spread of Communism Throughout the World and the Extent of its Direction from Moscow', 23 September 1946. CAB 81/133. This was not entirely true, as we now know, as Ho Chi Minh had spent time in Moscow in the 1920s.
8 JIC(46)72(0)(Final), 'Appreciation of the Future Strategy Policy of South East Asia', 23 August 1946. CAB 81/133. Also, JIC(46)75(0)(FINAL), 'Russia's Strategic Interests and Intentions in the Far East', 5 October 1946. CAB 81/133.
9 COS(49)53rd Meeting, 8 April 1949. DEFE 4/21.
10 JIC/948/48, 'Functions of the Joint Intelligence Committee, Far East', 21 May 1948. CAB 176/18.
11 JIC/1461/48, 'Lessons on the Organisation of Intelligence in the Far East', 5 August 1948. Enclosing JIC(FE)(48)7(Final), 'JIC(FE) Study of Despatches on Campaigns in the Far East 1941–1945 to Extract Lessons on Organisation of Intelligence in the Far East', 15 July 1948. CAB 176/19.
12 JIC(48)10 Final, 'Review of Intelligence Organisation in the Far East', 15 June 1948. CAB 158/3.
13 JIC/1567/48, 'Draft Charter for Local Intelligence Committees – Far East', 18 August 1948. CAB 176/19.
14 T.I.K.Lloyd [Colonial Office] to W.G.Hayter, 28 September 1948. DEFE 11/349.
15 L.C.Hollis to Prime Minister, 23 September 1948. DEFE 11/349.
16 JIC/810/48, 'Communist Influence in Malaya', 29 April 1948. CAB 176/18.
17 R Cormac, *The Joint Intelligence Committee and Colonial Counterinsurgency* (Unpublished PhD Thesis, King's College London, 2011). pp.56–7.
18 Aldrich, *The Hidden Hand*. p.497. On Hayter's comments see JIC(48)58th Meeting, 11 June 1948. CAB 159/3.
19 A.G.Gilchrist to P.H.Dean, 29 September 1955. PUSD Papers, FCO.
20 Prior to this Gent had been Governor of the Malayan Union.
21 JIC(48)96th Meeting (0), 3 September 1948. CAB 159/4.
22 JIC(48)87th Meeting (0), 13 August 1948. CAB 159/4.

23 JIC(48)103rd Meeting (0), 22 September 1948. CAB 159/4.

24 F.B.A.Rundall [FO] to G.H.Middleton [FO], 3 June 1950. PUSD Papers, FCO.

25 COS(49)53rd Meeting, 8 April 1949. DEFE 4/21.

26 JIC(49)36th Meeting, 1 April 1949. CAB 159/5.

27 F928/1691/61, British Defence Co-ordination Committee, Far East to Chiefs of Staff, 19 January 1949. FO 371/76084.

28 For detail see DEFE 11/349.

29 For further information on the JIC's role in Malaya, see Cormac, *The Joint Intelligence Committee and Colonial Counterinsurgency*. More broadly on intelligence in Malaya see Andrew, *Defence of the Realm*. pp.442–51.

30 Note by V.W.Street [Secretary, COS Committee], 7 May 1951. DEFE 11/350.

31 JIC(49)27th Meeting, 11 March 1949. CAB 159/5.

32 JIC(48)113(Final), 'Communist Influence in the Far East', 17 December 1948. CAB 158/5.

33 JIC(50)13th Meeting, 3 February 1950. CAB 159/7.

34 For instance, JIC(50)1/19, 'The Chinese Communist Threat in the Far East and South-East Asia on 4th January 1951', 5 January 1951. CAB 158/9.

35 This American angle needs to be understood within a wider US governmental policy towards the European colonial powers in the Far East – it was not strictly an anti-British or pro-Chinese measure. For more see C Fraser, 'Understanding American Policy Towards the Decolonisation of European Empires, 1945–64', *Diplomacy and Statecraft* 3:1 (March 1992), pp.105–25.

36 JIC(46)7(0)(Revised Final), 'Hong Kong Defence Plan', 7 February 1946. CAB 81/132.

37 JIC(48)30(0)Final, 'China Military Situation', 13 May 1948. CAB 158/3.

38 JIC(48)133(Revise), 'Effects of Communist Successes in China', 6 January 1949. CAB 158/5.

39 JIC(49)33(Final), 'Communist Influence in the Far East', 29 April 1949. CAB 158/6.

40 COS(49)62nd Meeting, 29 April 1949. DEFE 4/21.

41 For these see CAB 158/7. Details of the Cabinet discussion are in CAB 128/15.

42 JIC(49)44/8(Final), 'Situation in South China as at 23rd August 1949', 24 August 1949. CAB 158/7.

43 JIC(49)44/10(Final), 'A Review of the Threat to Hong Kong as at 19th September 1949', 21 September 1949. CAB 158/7.

44 JIC/2157/49, enclosing HK LIC(49)4(Final), 'The Threat to Hong Kong', 27 October 1949. CAB 176/24.

45 JIC(49)44/13(Final), 'A Review of the Threat to Hong Kong as at 1st November 1949', 2 November 1949. CAB 158/7.

46 JIC(45)287(0), 'Situation in French Indochina', 3 October 1945. CAB 81/131. For a subsequent JIC(SEAC) paper see JIC 14(45), 'Situation in French Indo China', 17 December 1945. WO 203/5563.

47 JIC(FE)(52)8(Final), 'Review of Organisation of Intelligence in the Far East', 1 May 1952. CAB 158/75.

48 JIC(45)287(0), 'Situation in French Indochina', 3 October 1945. CAB 81/131.

49 J Springhall, '"Kicking Out the Vietminh": How Britain Allowed France to Reoccupy South Indochina, 1945–46', *Journal of Contemporary History* 40:1 (2005), pp.115–30.

50 JIC(45)295(0)FINAL, 'French Indochina', 13 October 1945. CAB 81/131.

51 JIC(46)4(0), 'Situation in French Indochina', 6 January 1946. CAB 81/132.

52 JIC(49)119th Meeting, 17 November 1949. CAB 159/6.

53 The best repository for JIC(FE) papers in this period is the files of PUSD.

54 For instance, SAC(49)17, December 1949. CAB 134/669.

55 JIC(50)26(Final), 'Threat to Indochina', 15 March 1950. CAB 158/9.

56 JP(49)162(Final), 'Discussions between Commanders-in-Chief, Far East and French Authorities in Indochina – Scope and Limitations', 17 March 1950. DEFE 6/11.

57 For instance, see JIC(50)1/9(Final), 'The Chinese Communist Threat in the Far East and South-East Asia on 23rd May, 1950', 25 May 1950. CAB 158/9.

58 JIC(50)1/12(Final), 'The Chinese Communist Threat in the Far East and South-East Asia on 15th August, 1950', 16 August 1950. CAB 158/9.

59 JIC(50)1/13(Final), 'The Chinese Communist Threat in the Far East and South-East Asia on 12th September, 1950', 13 September 1950. CAB 158/9.

60 JIC(50)1/14(Final), 'The Chinese Communist Threat in the Far East and South-East Asia on 11th October, 1950', 11 October 1950. CAB 158/9.

61 JIC(50)1/17(Final), 'The Chinese Communist Threat in the Far East and South-East Asia on 29th November, 1950', 30 November 1950. CAB 158/9.

62 K Ruane, 'Refusing to Pay the Price: British Foreign Policy and the Pursuit of Victory in Vietnam, 1952–4', *English Historical Review* CX: 435 (February 1995), p.72.

63 JIC(50)1/19(Final), 'The Chinese Communist Threat in the Far East and South-East Asia on 4th January, 1951', 5 January 1951. CAB 158/9.

64 JIC(51)22(Final), 'Chinese Communist Intentions During the Next Six Months in the Light of Operations in Korea', 20 April 1951. CAB 158/12.

65 Ruane, 'Refusing to Pay the Price', pp.70–92.

66 JIC(52)76(Final), 'Situation in Indochina', 8 December 1952. CAB 158/14.

67 Ruane, 'Refusing to Pay the Price', pp.78–9.

68 JIC(53)18(Final), 'Possible French Military Policy in Indochina', 19 February 1953. CAB 158/15. For more on this see 'Possible French Military Policy in Indochina'. PUSD Papers, FCO.

69 Cited in Ruane, 'Refusing to Pay the Price', p.81.

70 Cited in Ruane, 'Refusing to Pay the Price', p.84.

71 Cited in Ruane, 'Refusing to Pay the Price', p.84.

72 S.Lloyd [Foreign Secretary] to PM, 25 June 1953. PREM 11/645.

73 JIC(53)45(Final), 'Future Military Developments in Indochina and their Political Consequences', 9 July 1953. CAB 158/15.

74 JIC(53)45(Final), 'Future Military Developments in Indochina and their Political Consequences', 9 July 1953. CAB 158/15.

75 See the correspondence in FO 371/112049.

76 JIC(54)26(Terms of Reference), 'The Future of the War in Indochina', 11 March 1954. CAB 158/17.

77 Details are in CAB 158/76.

78 JIC(54)26(Final), 'The Future of the War in Indochina', 26 March 1954. CAB 158/17.

79 COS(54)36th Meeting, 31 March 1954. DEFE 4/69.

80 G Warner, 'The Settlement of the Indochina War', In J W Young (ed), *The Foreign Policy of Churchill's Peacetime Administration, 1951–1955* (Leicester: Leicester University Press, 1988). pp.242–3.

81 DF1071/122/G. Makins to FO, 4 April 1954. FO 371/112050.

82 DF1071/140/G. Eisenhower to Churchill, 4 April 1954. FO 371/112050.

83 Cited in Warner, 'The Settlement of the Indochina War', p.248.

84 For more information on the Conference and Britain's role, see K Ruane, 'Anthony Eden, British Diplomacy and the Origins of the Geneva Conference of 1954', *The Historical Journal* 37:1 (March 1994), pp.153–72.

85 JIC/1663/54, 'US/UK Intelligence Co-operation in the Far East', 14 July 1954. CAB 176/49.

86 JIC(54)75(Final), 'The Political Situation in Burma, Indochina, Siam and Indonesia', 23 October 1954. CAB 158/18.

87 Q1697/3/54G. Note by A.G.Gilchrist, 28 October 1954. FO 1091/38.

88 JIC(55)3(Final), 'Soviet Bloc War Potential, 1955–59', 24 March 1955. CAB 158/19.

89 JIC(55)10(Final), 'Survey of World Communism in 1954', 24 March 1955. CAB 158/19.

90 JIC/2274/55, 'Viet Minh Policy Towards South Vietnam', 19 August 1955. PUSD Papers, FCO.

91 JIC(55)17(Final), 'Likely Courses of Communist Action in S.E.Asia in Cold War After 1956 Under Certain Assumptions', 15 February 1955. CAB 158/20.

92 JIC(55)38(Final), 'The Situation in Indochina', 9 June 1955. CAB 158/20.

93 P.Dean to Secretary, JIC, 21 June 1955. PUSD Papers, FCO.

94 JIC/1917/55, 'The Situation in South Vietnam', 4 July 1955. CAB 176/54.

95 Annex to JIC(FE)(55)28(Final), 'Vietminh Policy Towards and Penetration of South Vietnam', 26 July 1955. PUSD Papers, FCO.

96 For more detail see P Hughes, 'Division and Discord: British Policy, Indochina, and the Origins of the Vietnam War, 1954–56', *The Journal of Imperial and Commonwealth History* 28:3 (2000), pp.94–112.

97 JIC(55)18(Final), 'The Threat to South East Asia in the Event of War 1957–1960', 17 November 1955. CAB 158/20.

98 JIC(55)60(Final), 'The Situation and Outlook in South Vietnam, Cambodia and Laos', 21 October 1955. CAB 158/21. Although broadly the same, as a rare exercise in drafting it is interesting to compare the final version with three earlier drafts, both preserved in 'The Situation in Indochina'. PUSD Papers, FCO. The paper was re-issued following comments by the DMI, Major General Boucher, that it contained 'typing and spelling errors, its punctuation is appalling and, in its military paragraphs, the staff duties are slipshod.' Boucher to Dean, 28 October 1955. PUSD Papers, FCO.

99 JIC(55)82(Final), 'Probable Developments in South Vietnam in the Event of a Breakdown of the Geneva Settlement on Elections', 15 February 1956. CAB 158/22.

100 COS(56)37th Meeting, 29 March 1956. DEFE 4/85.

101 Even by mid-1949 the JIC Chairman could brief the COS Committee that 'in the past this theatre [China] had ranked low in priority for intelligence purposes in the same way as, for strategic purposes, it was not of first or second priority. Even in the light of present events, he believed this was right'. COS(49)92nd Meeting, 22 June 1949. DEFE 32/1.

102 JIC(56)66(Final)(Revise), 'The Likely Course of Events in the Formosa Straits Short of Communist Attack up to the End of 1957', 4 July 1956. CAB 158/25.

103 For instance, JIC(56)64(Final), 'The Military and Economic Strength of Communist China', 16 July 1956. CAB 158/25.

104 JIC(56)99(FINAL), 'The Probable Nature and Scale of the Communist Chinese Threat in the Far East in Conditions Short of Global War up to 1961', 1 November 1956. CAB 158/25.

105 JIC/660/56, 'Intelligence Organisation in the Far East', 9 March 1956. CAB 176/57.

106 JIC(57)35(Final), 'The Situation and Likely Developments Over the Next Eighteen Months in North and South Vietnam, Laos and Cambodia', 29 July 1957. CAB 158/28.

107 JIC(57)43(Final), 'The Outlook for China Over the Next Five and Ten Years', 6 December 1957. CAB 158/29. Also, JIC(57)90(Final), 'The Probable Nature and Scale of the Communist Chinese Threat in the Far East in Conditions Short of Global War up to 1962', 18 November 1957. CAB 158/29.

13 Adventures in the Middle East

Part I – The Rise of Nationalism

In a memorandum circulated to his Cabinet colleagues in August 1949, Foreign Secretary Ernest Bevin wrote that 'in peace and war the Middle East is an area of cardinal importance to the United Kingdom, second only to the United Kingdom itself. Strategically the Middle East is a focal point of communications, a source of oil, a shield to Africa and the Indian Ocean, and an irreplaceable base.' For Bevin the implications were clear: '. . . it is essential that we should maintain our special position and carry out our special responsibilities.'[1] Yet within less than a decade Bevin's hopes and aspirations for the Middle East had crumbled.[2]

Historically, the Middle East had been far more important to the UK than the Far East. Outside of Europe, nowhere was more crucial to British security in the immediate post-war period. Despite this, intelligence resources were rarely focussed on the Middle East. Although the Soviet interest in the region prior to the Second World War had been negligible, this quickly changed in 1945 as the victors vied for post-war influence. The refusal by the Soviet Union to withdraw its troops from Persia (Iran) in early 1946 (see chapter 8) was just the first instance of increasing Soviet involvement in the area.[3] For the British, however, there were other major issues to confront.

Principal amongst these, at least initially, was the undertaking to create a Jewish state in Palestine. Another was the UK's gradual retreat from Empire, with a host of nations – some new, some established – gaining independence. For the UK, withdrawal from these countries was not always peaceful or bloodless, and was complicated by the growing role played by the US in post-war deliberations on the Middle East as well as in Europe and the Far East. Politically the UK had to take account of US interests and differences of opinion over colonial possessions, (where the UK still held territory in Cyprus and Aden), the future of Palestine, and military action in Egypt (see chapter 14). The intelligence relationship fluctuated in response to each of these issues.

British policy in this period was based principally upon the defence of the UK and control of sea lines of communications, which underpinned JIC assumptions.[4] The Middle East was a central strategic issue which dictated a need to hold a firm line against any Soviet advance. For the JIC, the growing signs of discontent with the British in the Middle East were not simply reactions to increased communist presence in the region, but symptoms of the wider Cold

War confrontation playing out on a new front. Although this was not part of a grand communist conspiracy, the resurgence of nationalism was a consequence of a deeply felt impulse amongst formerly occupied or administered countries.

Xenophobia towards the UK and the desire for self rule and control of indigenous industries and resources, particularly oil, were taken out of context and misinterpreted, not just by the JIC, but also by some senior policymakers. Nowhere was this more evident than over Palestine and Iran. Although these were two very different issues, they were treated in similar ways. At the heart of both, for the JIC, lay suspicion of communist meddling. The Soviet presence was limited; but in the rise of both Arab and Jewish nationalism the JIC perceived a Soviet subversive influence. Similarly, the Soviet Union was thought to be behind Iran's nationalistic motives to preserve and control its oil reserves. In the case of Palestine, the UK eventually disengaged. In Iran, whilst the UK was forced to withdraw temporarily, it regained influence by ensuring that pro-British elements could take over. These issues occupied a great deal of the JIC effort and were reflected in its output.

Formulation of a Middle East Policy

As a military base during the Second World War, the Middle East had proved vital to the Allied cause; it had also been invaluable as a centre for intelligence collection. The UK had a long association with the region and, in the latter stages of the war, the JIC was instructed to start thinking about post-war issues. After the war, Soviet interest was confined to Northern Iran with little involvement elsewhere in the Middle East. Within a few months of the end of the war, however, the JIC reported to the COS that this had changed substantially. The growth of Soviet interest and influence in Iran could 'constitute a potential source of danger to the Middle East as a whole'.[5]

Exercising its management function, the JIC also undertook a review of intelligence collection requirements for the immediate post-war period. This focussed specifically on the potential contribution of SIS, as other sources of information were judged likely to be less fruitful. It was recognised that in the Middle East, the major priority would be those areas in which it was thought the Soviet Union might have an interest, principally Iran. Countries that were of lesser strategic importance to the UK but where evidence of anti-British unrest had been detected, including Egypt, Palestine and the Levant States, were accorded lower priority for SIS.[6] Hence the perceived presence and scale of a Soviet threat had a direct impact on the priority given to the allocation of intelligence resources.

The British planners faced a problem: on the one hand the Middle East was as significant for trade and economic reasons as it was for military and defence imperatives. From a purely strategic perspective, the Middle East was important for:

i) control of the Suez Canal;
ii) security of oil supplies and sources;
iii) use of airfields for transit to India, the Far East and Southern Africa;

iv) security of sea communications;
v) a base for imperial reserves.[7]

On the other hand, the war had increased the drive for nationalism in the region, and by late 1945 there were clear signs of unrest in several British colonies, dependencies and protectorates. One suggestion by General Sir Bernard Paget, the Commander-in-Chief of Middle East Command, was to create a 'Middle East Confederacy' to bring countries together, under British 'hegemony', for the defence of British interests. The JIC was called upon to consider the implications of such a proposal.[8] Ultimately Paget's ideas were not taken up, largely due to opposition from the FO, but his proposals were the genesis for the Baghdad Pact almost a decade later,

In the Middle East a major concern was the security of oil supplies. The exploitation of Soviet reserves in the Caucasus was important, but any Soviet attempt to gain access to supplies in Iranian oilfields would be a paramount concern. Apart from seeking access to oil reserves, the JIC concluded in early 1946 that the Soviet Union had wider strategic ambitions and would try to expand its influence in the region. This was likely to be limited to Iran and, to a lesser extent, Turkey. These assessments aside, the JIC conceded that 'we have no intelligence indicating further Russian objectives in the Middle East area.'[9]

Several factors influenced JIC forecasting on the Middle East by early 1946. First, the lack of intelligence on Soviet intentions meant that reliable projections of the Soviet Union's aspirations were not possible. It was assumed that the Soviet Union would become embroiled in the region. The Middle East as a whole was seen as more significant for UK interests than developing influence in individual countries, with the possible exception of the Suez Canal. Oil was a crucial commodity for both East and West. Finally, while there was some evidence of unrest over British rule, no suggestion was made by the JIC that Soviet aims might include exploitation of such feelings to undermine Western influence.

Within a few months, the course of events meant that some of these assumptions had to be revised. The Soviet Union failed to abide by the agreement to remove its troops from Iran. By June 1946 the JIC had revised its judgement and now concluded that 'the Soviet Union will take every opportunity to foment anti-British feeling and to reduce British influence throughout the Arab world, and will ultimately hope to supplant it.' More broadly the JIC now saw the Middle East as an important strategic buffer zone against the Soviet Union's southern border. This was defined as the region between the Black Sea and India and described by the JIC as its 'most vulnerable flank', implying that the Soviet Union would attach increased importance to it.[10] Concurrently the JIC decided that assessments of the Middle East should be reviewed on a monthly basis.[11]

Trouble in Palestine

One of the primary post-war issues in the region concerned the future of Palestine. After the First World War, the League of Nations formally decreed that on its behalf the UK would administer Palestine, which became the British Mandate. From the outset the territory was beset by dispute and conflict, with frequent bloody skirmishes. Populated by both Jews and Arabs the Mandate was particularly affected by violence in the years immediately preceding the Second World War. The Mandate itself had only ever been seen as temporary. By the end of the war, therefore, Britain was set on a course to disengage from Palestine.

In the immediate aftermath of the war the COS set a requirement for the JIC to consider the implications of five different courses of action for dealing with Palestine:

i)   the partition of the country and the creation of a Jewish State in part of it;
ii) a bi-national Palestinian state;
iii) keep the status quo but allow no further Jewish immigration once the quota had been reached;
iv) keep the status quo but allow further Jewish immigration once the quota had been reached following consultation with the Arabs;
v)   keep the status quo but allow further Jewish immigration once the quota had been reached but without consultation with the Arabs.

The JIC's conclusion was unremarkable, judging that regardless of which course of action was chosen, there would be varying degrees of unrest, possibly involving the Arab States and possibly the Jewish population, or even both. But it gave no indication of the scale or likely timeframe for such unrest.[12] The problem facing the JIC, as outlined in a December 1945 assessment, was that without any knowledge of the government's courses of action for the Middle East, the outcomes would be 'difficult to assess accurately' and reliable forecasts would not be possible. A joint 'Anglo-American Committee of Enquiry' on future Jewish immigration policy produced its findings in April 1946. The JIC circulated a paper assessing the likely response to the report. The conclusions were probably unwelcome to policymakers as not only did the JIC expect the likely Jewish reaction to be a 'fresh outbreak of violence', but that the Arabs would mount 'strikes and demonstrations'.[13]

This JIC assessment proved to be accurate as within a short time the level of violence in Palestine increased, with a number of attacks, killings, and kidnappings of British officials. Given the failure of the Anglo-American committee, the British government turned to the UN to help resolve the situation. The response, a plan for the partition of Palestine into Arab and Jewish territories, was subsequently rejected by the British. The unrest in Palestine continued to grow throughout 1946 and 1947. The JIC assessed that whilst the Soviet Union would ultimately side with the Arabs, in order to cause 'the British authorities as much difficulty as possible', it was likely that 'in the short run it will doubtless suit them [the Soviet Union] to promise support both to the Arabs and to the Jews'.[14]

By mid-1946, whilst offering tacit support to both sides in the Palestine conflict, Soviet interest was increasing. As a result, in July 1946 the JIC was asked by the JPS to help prepare a defence plan for the Middle East. The JIC report made various assumptions, revealing the wider intelligence concerns at the time. Above all the Soviet threat was held to be the most serious, and although a war with the Soviet Union was not seen as inevitable, 'it represents the greatest, and the only menace which is apparent at the present time'.[15]

Unlike the other regions of the world, the JIC perceived that the Soviet Union's likely course of action in the Middle East would be to adapt its message to make it more palatable. Although it enjoyed a strong support base amongst students and the 'labouring classes', given that the majority of people in the Middle East had little 'political consciousness', the JIC felt that communist support could only thrive on 'national or racial feeling'. To achieve this, the Soviet Union needed to be subtle, skilfully 'obscuring the points where it is in conflict with Islamic beliefs' and emphasising, through propaganda, 'the advantages enjoyed by Moslem communities in the USSR as compared with their brethren in the Middle East'.[16] The question facing the JIC, was what could be done to counteract the Soviet message.

On 23 August 1946 the COS met to discuss the latest JIC report on Soviet intentions in the Middle East. For the Chiefs it was not enough simply to monitor events, particularly as the situation appeared to be deteriorating. Instead, they instructed both the JIC and the planners to propose 'some positive action' to counter Soviet subversion in the region.[17] The message to be conveyed was unequivocal: 'we are greatly concerned with the increasing Russian subversive activities in the Middle East.'[18] One factor behind the JIC's assessment was the nature of the Anglo-American relationship in the Middle East. Here, as the JIC was quick to recognise, the Soviet Union could 'expect to find a less solidly united Anglo-United States front than in other parts of the world'.[19] The Committee emphasised the importance of American assistance and requested that its reports on the Soviet Union and the Middle East be passed to the US JCS.

The 'positive action' proposal was for a multi-level response, including a propaganda war to be fought along both overt and covert lines (for details see chapter 8). The JIC was to be responsible for controlling this[20] and warned that it would take a year before any results could be ascertained.[21] This proved correct. Reporting to the COS Committee the following July, the JIC described: 'in Persia an almost complete cessation of attacks on Britain and a marked tendency to prefer British methods of industry and social welfare . . . British publicity has had a considerable impact in Persia, where its rather aggressive tone is evidence that we mean business.' Admitting that results in Egypt and Palestine were not as encouraging, the JIC commissioned a further review in six month's time.[22]

The key trouble spot continued to be Palestine where discussions revolved around a partition to create a homeland for the Jews. In September 1947 the JIC produced an analysis of the possible implications of the acceptance or rejection of the United Nations Special Commission on Palestine.[23] Of greater concern was the possibility of military conflict over Palestine, specifically whether it would escalate and affect British interests more broadly. In October, a month before any decision was reached, the JIC produced another assessment, this time focussing on the possibility of an intervention by Arab states. The JIC considered this was unlikely to occur before British troops had managed to withdraw from Palestine, and any subsequent attack would have 'no effect' on other military commitments in the region. On the other hand, if there was an attack before this could be completed, then British interests would be 'severely damaged'.[24]

Such an inconclusive assessment was only too common in the post-war period. When producing a report the JIS was frequently given very specific parameters within which to work. These often involved the starting assumptions for the report, as well as the questions that were to be addressed. When tackling the threat of Arab intervention, the JIC therefore provided a summary of possible outcomes, and while considering whether the Arabs would wait for a total British withdrawal it did not assess the factors driving Arab actions. Although the JIC, since Churchill's 1940 edict, was allowed to commission its own papers, as a general rule it became too reliant on questions set by its military masters. A similarly imprecise set of predictions was offered in November on the likely reactions to any one of three possible scenarios:

i) that a settlement was reached between the Jews and the Arabs;
ii) that the UN approves a plan which does not satisfy HMG's standards of justice, in which case the UK would play no part in its settlement;
iii) that the UN approves a plan, while not acceptable to the Jews or Arabs, appears to HMG to be sufficiently just to warrant their playing a minor part in its implementation, by the contribution of armed forces of assistance with civilian administration (including police) or both.

It would have been more useful to rank these scenarios in order of probability, but this does not appear to have been requested by the COS.[25]

In discussions at the UN the Soviet Union supported the Palestinian position. For the JIC, a newly defined Palestinian state was an attractive proposition for the Soviet Union, partly because it would be open to communist exploitation but also (and possibly more importantly) that it would create an opportunity to 'embarrass' the West. It was also assumed that the Soviet Union would be equally keen to embrace a Jewish state as it would provide an opportunity to 'increase her influence'. Hence the Soviet Union would be content to exploit the situation however it might evolve, not least because the main goal would be the 'fomentation of political disorder throughout the Middle East, by the encouragement of any and every subversive agency.'[26] Yet intelligence collection on this specific topic remained a relatively low priority because requirements on Europe took precedence.[27]

The British Mandate in Palestine was set to expire on 14 May 1948. In New York discussions were underway at the UN concerning a proposal to partition Palestine and create a separate Jewish state. Within weeks of the end of the British Mandate, it was announced that all troops would leave by 1 August 1948. In London and New York there were recriminations, unease and unhappiness at the UN decisions, while in the Middle East the plans for partition were unravelling rapidly. A UN mediator, despatched to the region to soothe the warring Arab and Jewish factions, was murdered. In New York, the Soviet Union proposed a new partition plan but this was rejected by the United States. Out of this chaos, on 15 May 1948, the new State of Israel came into being.

Back in London the JIC's focus was principally to assess the future course of events in the region and how British interests might be affected. A key concern was the extent to which the Soviet Union might be involved in fomenting trouble to extend the influence of communism. On this latter point, in late July 1948, the JIC concluded that neither the Arabs nor the Jews were particularly 'influenced' by communism, stating that the creation of Israel, and the resultant influx of Jewish immigrants into the region from Europe, would create a situation that the Soviet Union could exploit.[28]

Detailed descriptions and assessments of the size, scale and quality of the fighting forces of various Middle Eastern countries were produced by the JIC, with specific reference to the ways in which the Arab-Israeli dispute might threaten Britain's interests, either inadvertently or directly. The JIC also considered related factors, including the size of communist party memberships in the various Middle East countries and the likely rates and patterns of mobilisation if an Arab-Israeli war were to occur.[29] This long paper, produced at the request of the JPS as the basis for talks with the US, did not come to any firm conclusions on the likelihood of war. It does, though, reveal an often overlooked aspect of the JIC's work. Producing forward-looking assessments occupied most of the JIC's workload, but papers such as this, designed not to predict or comment on the likelihood of conflict but rather give the military planners the information necessary to scope a future conflict, were arguably far more useful and important.

Producing intelligence assessments, however, remained the mainstream of the JIC's effort. To continue to satisfy both requirements the JIC approved a long list of intelligence requirements for the region, encompassing both political and military targets.[30] The lead responsibility for monitoring the evolving situation was given to JIC(ME). Created during the war to look after the UK's intelligence concerns, JIC(ME) was based in Egypt (see chapter 7). Comprising intelligence, military and diplomatic personnel, JIC(ME) monitored Middle Eastern countries, as well as Sub-Saharan Africa, Greece and Cyprus. Like JIC(FE), JIC(ME) was responsible for coordinating collection and collation efforts, essentially 'coordinating all intelligence activities'. It had its own team of drafters, JIS(ME), and so produced independent assessments, which were often either reissued by the JIC in London or else incorporated and redrafted in its own reports.[31]

A review of priorities for British intelligence collection in the region in 1949 raised the coverage of military matters in Palestine.[32] The effect was to emphasise that the focus would continue primarily to be on the Soviet Union and Europe, with a small, but increasingly important, nod towards the Far East. This meant that little additional effort was devoted to the Middle East, despite the desire to improve collection capabilities.

The JIC continued to issue a series of reports for the military planners, not on the likelihood of war, but rather providing necessary background material for what might be expected if there was war with the Soviet Union.[33] Other papers considered the evolving Arab-Israeli confrontation[34], and the likely reaction across the Middle East if American and British troops were to intervene in Palestine.[35] By the spring of 1949 it was clear that despite its short existence, Israel was becoming the dominant military force in the Arab-Jewish conflict. A March 1949 JIC assessment argued that Israel aimed to expand and 'acquire' the former lands of the British Mandate of Palestine.[36]

For Prime Minister Clement Attlee, Foreign Secretary Ernest Bevin and the Cabinet, the policy options lay in whether to support Israel, to resist her territorial ambitions, or stand on the sidelines. Beginning in January 1949 a series of cease fire agreements resulted in the 'Tripartite Declaration' of May 1950, an agreement signed by the UK, the United States and France. This imposed an obligation to preserve the Arab-Israeli truce, which was overturned eventually by the 1967 Arab-Israeli war. Thus the UK pledged to respect Israel's territorial position and, by so doing, abandoned its formerly pro-Arab position. This would have serious consequences as the decade drew to a close.

The Rise of Nationalist Iran

One of the determinants of Middle Eastern politics is the extent of the region's reserves of raw commodities. Oil was a major factor affecting Soviet policy in the region. As the JIC wrote in early 1949: 'we consider that the Russian aim of a campaign in the Middle East will be to deny the Middle East oilfields and the Suez Canal area to the Western Powers, and to add depth to the air defences of Southern Russia'.[37] The largest oil refinery in the world was at Abadan and Iran provided 9% of global supplies; it also ensured employment for 37,000 Iranian workers and was Britain's 'single largest overseas asset'.[38]

Soviet policy had to be flexible for the simple reason that, in the Middle East, with the exception of Israel, communism was illegal. There could be no overt political representation. Yet, as in Europe, a policy of covert subversion, of fomenting opposition to Anglo-American interests, and of promoting nationalist pride, was judged to be constant. The strategy was encapsulated by the JIC in the spring of 1950: 'Communist organisations do not appear obvious on the surface of the Middle East social structure but are for the most part clandestinely at work seeking to undermine'.[39] Nowhere was this more apparent than in Iran.

Communism in Iran had had a chequered past. Beginning in the 1920s Persian communists had succeeded, with the help of the Soviet Union, in establishing the Soviet Republic of Gilan – a short-lived communist state whose demise was brought about with British assistance.[40] The banished communists subsequently reappeared as the Tudeh Party, a communist movement that survives to this day. Following an attempt on the life of the Shah, the Tudeh Party was declared illegal in February 1949, yet it continued to attract support. In the JIC's view it was associated with Soviet Union, which had trained its leaders and continued to provide finance. This was in a country which, for the JIC, was 'autocratic ... backward, poor and abounding in discontent', therefore perfect fertile ground for communism. By early 1950, the JIC considered the Tudeh Party, despite its expulsion, 'strong enough to provide the Soviet Union with an effective Fifth Column'.[41]

The Pahlavi dynasty had ruled in Iran since 1925 and Mohammad-Reza Shah Pahlavi had been in power since 1941, having succeeded his father. Under the Shah, Iran was governed by a succession of Prime Ministers, generally being in power for less than twelve months. By March 1951 the cumulative effect of these short-lived governments, considered to be 'ineffective' in the JIC's opinion, was clear: 'the internal situation in Persia was deteriorating . . . public confidence in the regime was waning; and the influence of the Communist-controlled Tudeh party was increasing'. Events worsened even while the JIC's report was being prepared, when the then Prime Minister and Chief of the General Staff, General Razmara, was assassinated by Islamist extremists. This came as a blow to the British, and according to George Middleton, the Charge d'Affaires at the British Embassy in Tehran, this single event 'marked a turning point' in 'Persian history'.[42] Razmara's successor was an Iranian diplomat and a former Ambassador to the UK and the US, Hossein Ala. The JIC judged that Ala was a weak figure, in place only as interim Prime Minister whilst the Shah was away and who, on his return, would be replaced by a 'stronger' candidate.[43] The prediction was accurate, for on 28 April 1951 Dr Mohammad Mossadeq was appointed Prime Minister of Iran.[44]

Mossadeq was a charismatic figure. Born to landed gentry, he had completed a PhD in Islamic law in Switzerland and was, by 1951, a veteran of Iranian politics. According to one author he was 'authoritative, distrustful, inflexible and secretive'. He was also said to be 'incorruptible and fiercely nationalistic'.[45] This latter trait would prove to be his downfall. In 1908 a large oilfield had been discovered in a western province of Iran, and the British were the first to exploit it. The Anglo-Persian Oil Company was founded to manage the oil reserves and ensure that the country was suitably recompensed. This was the beginning of what would become one of the world's biggest corporations. Re-named in the 1930s as the Anglo-Iranian Oil Company (AIOC), it would later become the British Petroleum Company, or BP.

In 1933, and again in 1949, the Iranian government and the AIOC had signed agreements guaranteeing an annual payment in exchange for allowing the export of oil to the UK. At the time of signing, the fiscal arrangements in the agreement were thought to favour the Iranians; however, over time it looked increasingly less positive, not only financially but also because the agreements ensured that the AIOC could choose the best sites to drill. Successive Iranian Prime Ministers, apprehensive about public reactions, had declined to put the matter to the Majles, the Iranian Parliament, for ratification. This was reversed by General Razmara, who undertook to do so in October 1950, partly in an attempt to steer the Majles away from full nationalisation of the oilfields, which would have been disastrous for the UK. As feared, the deal was rejected, despite the promise of a large cash injection by the AIOC.

In March 1951 Razmara was assassinated. Eight days later the Majles took the unprecedented step of unanimously voting to nationalise the whole of the Iranian oil industry. The JIC's assessment, recorded in the minutes of its meeting of 15 March 1951 is almost comical in its understatement: 'the situation in Persia has taken an unfortunate turn'.[46] The British government reacted by protesting to the Iranian government, but to little avail. For the UK the situation was serious for both financial and practical reasons, and also, as the JIC made clear, because 'any Persian success in "nationalising" British oil interests will encourage nationalist extremists elsewhere in the Middle East to press on with their aims to eradicate foreign influence.' Of particular concern was the possible reaction in Iraq, where 'the British managed Iraq Petroleum Company has for some time been in dispute with the Iraqi Government.'; and in Egypt, where 'it is significant that the Egyptian press has already begun to talk about the nationalisation of the Suez Canal.'[47] Whilst the JIC's concerns were, to an extent, based on political anxieties, for the FO and many of the British politicians involved, this was primarily an economic matter, and it would take some time before the two aspects would converge.[48]

Three days after his appointment to the Premiership, Mossadeq signed and approved the Majles' nationalisation of Iranian oil. Thereafter, a bitter dispute erupted between the UK and Iran. After failing to get the UN to act, the British government issued a direct warning that Iran would face 'most serious consequences' and, to support this, British troops were moved to neighbouring bases. The United States also closely monitored events. Although considered to be solely a British problem, the Truman Administration also recognised that if the Iranian government was left floundering, particularly if there was British military involvement, then this would provide an opportunity for the Soviet Union to exploit. It could also have implications for other oil exploitation arrangements in the region.[49] Throughout 1951, as a resolution to the problem appeared less and less likely, the UK's financial position, already in a parlous state, worsened. The choice facing Washington was clearly set out by Secretary of State Dean Acheson, who wrote bluntly that it was a question of whether 'Iran goes commie or Brit goes bankrupt'.[50] For the US, therefore, a satisfactory resolution to the problem in Iran was clearly a priority.[51] In November 1951 a joint Anglo-American policy was formulated: 'we assume immediate, mutual and overriding United States-United Kingdom objective in Persia is to prevent that country from falling into Communist hands ... [if this] objective is to be achieved, it is essential that there should be an honest and efficient Government in Persia with a positive programme of reform which would weaken the appeal of Tudeh.'[52]

In London the JIC was also increasingly concerned about the course of events in Iran. Its assessment, in November 1951, was unambiguous. The JIC considered that Mossadeq would remain resolute over the oil crisis to ensure his grip on power. Moreover, it concluded that 'if the Mussadiq [sic] Government fell, and if there were no agreed Anglo/United States policy of support for an acceptable successor, the Tudeh Party would probably gain power ... this would be a most serious threat to our political and strategic position in the Middle East'. This statement highlighted the difficulties facing the UK. To ensure the communists did not take control, Mossadeq had to remain in power; yet his power-base was predicated on his tough line towards the oil crisis and the UK. The JIC concluded that the key lay in finding an 'acceptable successor'.[53]

For the UK, although the oil crisis was in many ways an imperial and financial problem, it was increasingly perceived as a Cold War problem too, and a positive outcome would be beneficial to the UK on both counts. For the United States, less concerned about Britain's financial plight or colonial concerns, sustaining a strong bulwark against communism was vital. Throughout the crisis the possibility that Mossadeq was a committed nationalist and not at all sympathetic towards communism was consistently overlooked.

Events continued to deteriorate. In November the AIOC had withdrawn the last of its staff, leaving empty the recently constructed £100 million refinery at Abadan.[54] To gain more information Monty Woodhouse, an SIS officer, was despatched to Tehran.[55] Not long after his arrival Woodhouse reported that 'any effort to forestall a Soviet coup in Iran would require a joint Anglo-American effort'. Also temporarily in the British Embassy was Robin Zaehner, a colourful character who was an Oxford don and an expert in eastern religions.[56] As Woodhouse recalled in his memoir, the idea of toppling Mossadeq was first aired by the FO, not SIS, something he considered to be an 'anomaly'.[57]

Zaehner's mission to Tehran, and his sole purpose for being there, was to foster regime change. Woodhouse subsequently recalled that 'our objectives were clear: to forestall a Soviet-backed take-over by the Communists, to remove Musaddiq from power, to establish a pro-western government, and to undo so far as possible the damage done to the UK's oil interests'.[58] In fact, it was not the FO who had dreamt up the plot to remove Mossadeq but, rather, a small circle of senior British politicians: the Prime Minister, Clement Attlee; the Foreign Secretary, Herbert Morrison; and the Lord Privy Seal, Richard Stokes. The specific aims of Zaehner's mission were clear, as he himself wrote: to overthrow Mossadeq and bring Sayyid Zia to power.[59] In London, the FO and the Foreign Secretary were kept regularly informed of developments, and made aware of the views of the Shah that 'Dr Musaddiq must be got rid of as soon as possible'.[60] Zia, an Iranian politician, had led the earlier 1921 coup, and been made Prime Minister. He was overtly pro-British and therefore an obvious candidate for Britain to support. However, by the time that Woodhouse reached Tehran, Zaehner was starting to become disillusioned with his mission. In August 1951 Stokes had travelled to Tehran to attempt to negotiate a settlement of the oil crisis. Although he ultimately failed, he did succeed, rather ironically, in becoming close to Mossadeq, with whom he instantly 'hit it off', much to Zaehner's chagrin.[61]

With the personal support of Attlee and Sir Francis Shepherd, the British Ambassador to Iran, Zaehner stayed on until the middle of 1952. Although the results were considered 'disappointing', he continued to use money appropriated from the Secret Vote (which Herbert Morrison hoped would be reimbursed by AIOC if the efforts were successful) to finance opposition to Mossadeq.[62] His main source was Ernest Perron, a Swiss national who was the Shah's Private Secretary and former tutor, and who acted on his behalf as a liaison with foreign embassies.[63] Ultimately, however, a disenchanted Zaehner returned to Oxford in 1952, with Woodhouse taking over his activities in Iran.[64]

It is not immediately clear, from the surviving records, whether the JIC Chairman was involved in approving initial plans. The Chairman at the start of operations, Patrick Reilly, was at the centre of discussions about creating a small stay-behind network in Iran, to be activated in the event of war. Reilly was also at the heart of contingency plans to save the oilfields should the necessity arise.[65]

The stalemate continued into 1952 but, by the start of the summer, it was becoming clear that support for a resurgent Tudeh Party was growing, as was nationalist sentiment. At the same time, Iranian politics were imploding. With the new legislative period the Iranian Prime Minister, traditionally, resigned and was then formally re-appointed. On this occasion in July 1952, Mossadeq presented his Cabinet to the Shah, including his own promotion to Minister of War, an appointment that the Shah had previously always controlled. The Shah's response was to reject the proposals and to sack Mossadeq as Prime Minister, appointing Ahmad Qavam in his place. Behind the scenes the Shah had been encouraged by members of the British Embassy in Iran, particularly Zaehner.[66] This move was welcomed by the UK as the US had been opposed to the former British favourite, Zia, and it was known that Qavam's views were also pro-British. Indeed, Qavam had met various British government representatives, including Conservative MP Julian Amery, from late December 1951 onwards. It is clear from FO records that both SIS and JIC Chairman Patrick Reilly were involved.[67] Within a few hours of his appointment, Qavam announced his decision to resume talks with the UK with a view to ending the oil dispute. This provoked strikes and protests, resulting in scores of deaths. After less than a week out of office, the Shah reappointed Mossadeq. Coincidentally, that same week, the Middle East was rocked by another major development as King Farouk of Egypt was overthrown in a military rebellion (see chapter 14).

In London the JIC viewed events with alarm. The reversals in Iranian politics were of concern but an even greater worry was the level of civil unrest, particularly the evidence about its instigators: 'the Tudeh Party has been mainly responsible for the demonstrations of the last few days, which have had a strong anti-monarchic character, and their influence must be expected to increase.'[68] By the end of July Mossadeq's triumphal return to power was complete and the JIC reported that recent events had revealed the 'impotence' of the Shah. For the JIC, communism in Iran was a much graver concern than nationalism. Reports suggested an increased Tudeh influence both inside and outside Mossadeq's government. The Cold War mentality was pervasive, the communist threat eclipsed all else.[69] The crisis of July 1952 ensured that this belief was widespread within the British government, a factor which served to bring the UK and US positions closer together.[70]

The JIC produced a fresh assessment of the situation in Iran in August 1952. Once more it highlighted a contradiction: Mossadeq needed to resolve the oil crisis and start operating the refineries again so that money could start to flow back into the country yet, in the JIC's opinion, so long as Mossadeq 'remains in power there is little prospect of reaching a settlement of the oil dispute satisfactory to British interests'. Concerns were also expressed about how 'effective' Mossadeq would be in resisting communist advances, something that the UK was less convinced about than the US.[71] For several reasons, therefore, it was judged that, by the middle of 1952, Mossadeq's continuation as Prime Minister was not in the UK's interest. For the JIC, the most effective means of resisting the Tudeh Party's advances was a strong Shah and a powerful Iranian army.[72]

Throughout the second half of 1952 a series of Anglo-American-Iranian discussions to resolve the oil dispute amounted to little. By October, following a further failure to reach an agreement, Mossadeq decided to break off relations with the UK. By this point the US, too, had become convinced of the need to remove Mossadeq.[73] According to the JIC, which kept a close watch on current events in its weekly 'Perimeter Review', Mossadeq was clearly trying to drive a wedge between the UK and the US.[74] The mood was summed up by George Middleton, the Charge d'Affaires at the British Embassy in Tehran: 'I am now inclined to think that the only immediate hope is a coup d'état with or without the knowledge or the consent of the Shah.'[75]

In October 1952 the JIC approved an assessment of the consequences of a communist regime in Iran. Although the paper did not try to deal with the likelihood of this happening, it did address Soviet aspirations and how they might be achieved. The conclusion, in line with previous JIC reports, was that the Soviet Union had three primary aims: preventing Iran becoming an 'Allied' military base; gaining access to Iranian oil and thereby denying it to the West; and using Iran as a platform for the 'political penetration of the Middle East'. To achieve these aims the JIC concluded the Soviet Union 'would not need to occupy Persia in peace'. In other words, through support for the Tudeh Party, it would be possible for the Soviet Union to succeed without any direct intervention. Indeed, the JIC considered it extremely unlikely that the Soviet Union would consider either 'occupying' or 'openly dominating' Iran. According to the JIC, this was because of the adverse reaction in region. An invasion or occupation of Iran would 'handicap them in their efforts to convert the rest of the Middle East to their cause', largely because any such intervention would be seen as 'provocation'.[76] This belief, based on the assumption that the Soviet Union was acutely aware of its own public image and would take this into account in deciding policy, was not based on any specific intelligence; instead it was based on a perception of how the UK would act in a similar position, another flawed analysis based on mirror imaging.

By early November the UK had vacated its Embassy in Tehran and withdrawn from the country. At no point in the JIC's discussions of the evolving oil crisis did it attribute Mossadeq's actions to any sort of nationalistic tendency or a strong desire to eliminate or at least weaken British influence in Iran. While Mossadeq's xenophobic attitude is implicit in JIC assessments, there is no hint that he was engaged in an anti-imperialist crusade. The bigger issue for Britain continued to be fear of a communist presence.[77]

Despite continuing discussions between British, American and Iranian officials, the dispute over oil remained unresolved. The JIC became a passive observer, providing commentary on events through its weekly 'Perimeter Review'. There were no fresh assessments and, judging from the detail in the weekly reporting, little secret intelligence to utilise due in part, no doubt, to the closure of the British Embassy. The JIC reported on the significant events, for example the clash between the Shah and Mossadeq in late February 1953[78], but it was not in a position to disentangle the central issues, acknowledging a week later that its reporting on Iran was based 'largely on press and agency reports'. Readers were warned that conclusions 'must necessarily be tentative'.[79]

Although the oil crisis had serious economic and political consequences for the UK it was critical for Iran itself. By late March 1953, and with no prospect of a deal in sight, Mossadeq appealed for external assistance, including to the Soviet Union and the United States. Rather than examining the desperate economic conditions in Iran or Mossadeq's need to find oil markets and to deal with any potential customer, the JIC re-visited its report of October 1952. This had concentrated on the likely consequences of a communist regime in Iran, and had argued that the Soviet Union would not openly intervene publicly, but would certainly support the communists covertly. By re-issuing that report the JIC reaffirmed its belief that communism continued to be the pre-eminent threat in Iran.[80]

Throughout the spring and early summer of 1953 the JIC continued to monitor developments. It was hampered by a dearth of reliable, first hand intelligence, largely because of the continuing absence of any UK diplomatic presence. Much of the reporting seems to have drawn on the views of the US Ambassador in Tehran. This revealed that Mossadeq's grip on power was not as strong as hitherto. A commentary in mid-May 1953, based on the views of the US Ambassador, noted that although opposition had increased, it was not strong enough to 'constitute a serious threat'.[81] Further reports from the same well-placed source, based on conversations with Mossadeq himself, suggested that unless the US provided financial assistance to Iran, the 'government would eventually fall and be replaced by a Communist-dominated Government'.[82]

In its mid-August 1953 'Perimeter Review', the JIC reported on anti-Mossadeq demonstrations in the streets of Tehran, stating that the Tudeh Party had been the main force behind the unrest.[83] On 15 August, the Shah issued a written royal decree that officially discharged Mossadeq, who refused to accept the dismissal notice, declaring it a forgery. Rioting continued to intensify in the capital while the Tudeh Party, encouraged by the protests, declared the need to end the rule of the monarchy, urging followers to tear down statues of the Shah. Much of this, though by no means all, had been carefully orchestrated. Behind the scenes Iranians, paid by the CIA and designed to look like Tudeh sympathisers, created havoc, fomenting unrest and extending the size and scale of the demonstrations.[84]

On 18 August, Mossadeq ordered a clampdown on demonstrators, with Tudeh members dealt with particularly harshly. By now, however, the armed forces were no longer fully under Mossadeq's control, and many deserted to join the protests. Large numbers joined the pro-Shah campaigners. This group grew rapidly and, with US assistance, managed to take control of the main media outlets in Tehran. Mossadeq himself was a focus for attack and his compound was surrounded by an angry mob calling for his removal. At 5pm on 19 August 1953, Mossadeq issued a brief statement, declaring that he was still in charge. By this time it no longer mattered: the security forces had ceased to be loyal to him and the pro-Shah faction had grown to such an extent that the outcome was inevitable.

The following day, on 20 August, the JIC reported that whilst 'the sequence of events which led up to Mossadeq's overthrow is still very obscure', it could be stated with certainty that Mossadeq was no longer in power. The JIC's account of what had transpired gives the impression of confusion. It could not easily explain how 'one day mobs in Tehran were dragging statues of the Shah and his father through the streets; the next day mobs were tearing Fatemi, Mussadiq's [sic] Minister for Foreign Affairs, to pieces and acclaiming the Shah'.[85] A week later Mossadeq and his Cabinet were under house arrest, the Tudeh Party was 'lying surprisingly low', and the Shah and a new Prime Minister were in control. In his first discussions with the Shah after this success, the US Ambassador reported that he had reminded the Shah that 'he had agreed that a common Anglo-US front was essential if Iran was to be saved. The Shah did not dissent'.[86] The US involvement had been critical, but at the same time British interests had suffered for despite the re-introduction into Iran of the AIOC, the US-controlled Aramco increased its stake in the oil business while the British share dwindled from its 1951 level prior to the withdrawal from Abadan. Nonetheless, the lesson of Mossadeq's removal was clear, particularly to the Foreign Secretary, Anthony Eden, who noted 'that individuals and political parties could still be manipulated to advantage'. This attitude would underpin British policy in Egypt within a few years.[87]

A Middle Eastern Cold War

In 1945 the Middle East had been seen principally as a significant military location. The Soviet stalling of its troop withdrawal from Persia in March 1946 clearly affected all subsequent thinking about the region. Now events were seen as predominantly influenced by external factors rather than by indigenous nationalism. In 1949, the JIC reiterated judgements that the Middle East was crucial to the UK for three reasons: oil supplies; the need for friendly regimes; and to ensure that the Soviet Union did not gain a foothold. As such, in the aftermath of the Second World War, the vital military significance of the region was well understood, but as the Cold War gained momentum, fear of communism began to pervade all judgments. Perhaps this is why apparently localised events like the Buraimi Crisis and the assassination of King Abdullah of Jordan were seen in a strategic context rather than warranting individual attention by the JIC.

The Soviet threat was seen as omnipresent, whether there was any direct evidence or not. The JIC could not disentangle purely nationalistic movements from those that were communist-inspired. Indeed, even when there was clear and direct evidence of nationalist tendencies these were either ignored or downplayed in the face of the greater communist threat. In this context, the events in Palestine, despite the long tradition of violence and anti-British sentiments, were immediately interpreted as either classic examples of Soviet subversion, or attributable to successful Soviet clandestine activities, or both.

The lessons of Palestine would have been useful if they had been learnt but there were no attempts to draw parallels between events there and in Iran. From the outset, with only a brief mention of nationalism, Iran was never seen as an anti-colonial, anti-British, or driven by specifically Iranian national interest. Instead, it was viewed almost exclusively through a Cold War prism, as if the Iranians themselves were incapable of challenging the status quo without the help of the Soviet Union. Similarly, whenever events adversely affected the UK or Western interests, Soviet interference was identified, regardless of whether any intelligence material supported such a contention. In hindsight, the strength of the Tudeh Party was never as serious as the JIC suspected. Whilst gaps in intelligence coverage may have contributed to the promulgation of inaccurate assumptions, the Cold War lens distorted a more balanced judgment on the actual role that the Soviet Union had played.

The JIC's coverage of events in Iran throughout 1953 was relatively shallow and hampered by a lack of diplomatic presence in the country; it reported events, offered little interpretation, and certainly avoided any attempt to predict what might happen. Yet, at the same time, the JIC was convinced (before other elements of the British government realised) that Iran was as much a Cold War battleground, as an economic crisis. The JIC also had a raft of other preoccupations at the same time: Stalin was on the verge of death, raising questions over the future course and conduct of Soviet policy; Britain and the UN were attempting to negotiate a way out of the Korean War; there was a new President in the White House; and, in the Middle East, Egypt was proclaiming itself a republic. Taken individually these were significant developments, taken as a whole they were momentous. This explains, at least in part, why the JIC spent so little time and energy on assessments of Mossadeq and Iran even though vital British political and economic interests were at stake.

The culmination of the crisis in Iran and the overthrow of Mossadeq reveals much about British policy and intelligence. Here was a classic example of a coup, organised from outside but with the assistance of those within. It was originally British in design, though largely American in execution. The coup details would have remained very closely guarded, and only two members of the JIC would have known about them. In his role as Chairman of the JIC, as well as being the leading figure within the FO for liaising with SIS on covert action, Reilly was responsible for the analytical output of the British intelligence community. Operational security and the 'need to know' principle were, and are, paramount, but this dual responsibility demonstrates the extent of compartmentalisation at the top levels of British intelligence, and underlines the delicate balance and sometimes tension between intelligence and policy.

Notes

1 CP(49)183, 'Middle East Policy', 25 August 1949. CAB 129/36.
2 A description of what the JIC took 'Middle East' to mean is in JIC/429/46, 'Use of the term "Middle East"', 5 April 1946. CAB 176/10.
3 Hereafter, unless in quotations, 'Persia' is referred to as 'Iran'.
4 JIC(48)39(0), 'Basic Assumptions for Planning', 8 April 1948. CAB 158/3.
5 JIC(45)307(Final), 'Intelligence Affecting Future Commitments in Europe and the Middle East', 4 December 1945. CAB 81/131.
6 JIC(45)268(0)(Final), 'Requirements from SIS', 5 October 1945. CAB 81/130. At this point GC&CS was still part of SIS, and the report drew no distinction between whether SIS's requirements were specifically focussed on Humint or whether it combined both Humint and Sigint. The inference is that it was based on Humint requirements alone.
7 These are taken from a Post-Hostilities Planning paper of January 1943. Cited in H Rahman, 'British Post-Second World War Military Planning for the Middle East', *Journal of Strategic Studies* 5:4 (1982), p.512.
8 JIC(45)328(0)(Final), 'Defence of the Middle East on a Confederacy Basis', 12 January 1946. CAB 81/131.
9 JIC(46)1(0)Final(Revise), 'Russia's Strategic Interests and Intentions', 1 March 1946. CAB 81/132.
10 JIC(46)38(0)(Final)(Revise), 'Russia's Strategic Interests and Intentions in the Middle East', 14 June 1946. CAB 81/132.
11 JIC/655/46, 'General Review of Intelligence Concerning Russian Military Activities in Europe and the Middle East', 14 May 1946. CAB 176/11.
12 JIC(45)228(0)(Revised Final), 'Middle East Policy', 31 July 1945. CAB 81/130.
13 JIC(46)45(0)(Final), 'The Anglo-American Committee of Enquiry into Palestine and the Condition of Jews in Europe', 1 May 1946. CAB 81/133.
14 JIC(46)64(0)(Final), 'Russia's Strategic Interests and Intentions in the Middle East', 6 July 1946. CAB 81/133.
15 JIC(46)68(0)(T. of R.), 'Defence of the Middle East', 20 July 1946. CAB 81/133.
16 JIC(46)70(0)(FINAL), 'The Spread of Communism Throughout the World and the Extent of its Direction from Moscow', 23 September 1946. CAB 81/133.
17 COS(46)129th Meeting, 23 August 1946. CAB 79/51.
18 JIC(46)87(0)(Final), 'Russian Strategic Interests and Intentions – Middle East', 12 September 1946. CAB 81/134.
19 JIC(46)38(0)(Final)(Revise), 'Russia's Strategic Interests and Intentions in the Middle East', 14 June 1946. CAB 81/132.
20 JIC/406/46, 'SOE Operational Planning', 1 April 1946. FO 1093/360.
21 JIC(46)100(0), 'Anti-British Subversive Activities – Middle East', 18 November 1946. CAB 81/134.
22 JIC(47)39(0), 'Anti-British Subversive Activities – Middle East', 10 July 1947. CAB 158/1.
23 JIC(47)52(0)Final, 'Possible Future of Palestine', 9 September 1947. CAB 158/2.
24 JIC(47)60(0)Final, 'Threat of Arab Intervention in Palestine', 18 October 1947. CAB 158/2.
25 JIC(47)67(0)(Final), 'Repercussions of the Implementation of Proposals for the Future of Palestine', 1 December 1947. CAB 158/2.
26 JIC(48)3(0)Final, 'Short Term Intentions of the Soviet Union in Palestine', 13 February 1948. CAB 158/3.
27 JIC(48)19(0)Final, 'Sigint Intelligence Requirements – 1948', 20 May 1948. CAB 158/3.
28 JIC(48)45(0)Final, 'Communist Influence in Palestine', 21 July 1948. CAB 158/4.

29 JIC(48)12/1(0)Final, 'Middle East Defence Policy – Potentialities and Scale and Direction of Attack – 1950', 7 June 1948. CAB 158/3. For the background to the commissioning of the report see JIC/163/48, 'Middle East Planning with the Americans', 27 January 1948. CAB 176/7.

30 JIC(48)80(0), 'Intelligence Requirements in Palestine', 24 July 1948. CAB 158/4.

31 JIC(48)60(Revised Final), 'Review of the Intelligence Organisation in the Middle East', 12 November 1948. CAB 158/4. Also, JIC(49)31(Final), 'Review of Intelligence Organisation in the Middle East', 13 May 1949. CAB 158/6.

32 JIC(48)129, 12 January 1949. CAB 158/5. Also, JIC(49)21, 26 March 1949. CAB 158/6.

33 JIC(48)128(Final)Revise, 'Intelligence on the Middle East for Commonwealth Countries', 11 January 1949. CAB 158/5.

34 These were relatively sporadic and seem to have been undertaken by JIC(ME), very few therefore survive. As an example see JIC/2162/48, 'Future Situation in Palestine', 9 November 1948. CAB 176/20. The JIC(ME) review of JIC(48)88(0)(Final), 'Future Situation in Palestine', 11 September 1948 is interesting: 'The Committee [JIC(ME)] are of the opinion that parts of the paper appear to be based on information which is open to dispute and that other parts, notably those on which information is most difficult to obtain, carry an emphasis which would not appear to be justified'.

35 JIC(49)6(Final), 'Reactions in Israel and the Remainder of Palestine to the Entry of British or Anglo-American Forces', 17 March 1949. CAB 158/6.

36 JIC(49)30(Final), 'Israeli Intentions in the Near Future', 26 March 1949. CAB 158/6.

37 JIC(48)128(Final)Revise, 'Intelligence on the Middle East for Commonwealth Countries', 11 January 1949. CAB 158/5. These conclusions were re-iterated six months later. See JIC(49)14(Final Revise), 'Scale and Nature of Russian Attacks on the Middle East and Turkey – 1957', 13 July 1949. CAB 158/6.

38 Wm. Roger Louis, 'Musaddiq and the Dilemmas of British Imperialism', In J A Bill and Wm. Roger Louis (eds), *Musaddiq, Iranian Nationalism and Oil* (London: IB Tauris & Co, 1988). p.229

39 JIC(50)20(Final), 'Communist Influence in the Middle East', 21 April 1950. CAB 158/9.

40 For more detail see C Chaqueri, *The Soviet Socialist Republic of Iran, 1920–1921: Birth of the Trauma* (London: University of Pittsburgh Press, 1995).

41 JIC(50)20(Final), 'Communist Influence in the Middle East', 21 April 1950. CAB 158/9.

42 G.Middleton to A.Eden, 24 March 1952. FO 317/98593.

43 JIC(51)31, 'Situation in Persia', 21 March 1951. CAB 158/12.

44 Mossadeq's name has been transliterated into English in a variety of ways. The original spelling in quotations and extracts has been retained.

45 D Bayandor, *Iran and the CIA: The Fall of Mossadeq Revisited* (Basingstoke: Palgrave Macmillan, 2010). pp.31–2.

46 JIC(51)28th Meeting, 15 March 1951. CAB 159/9.

47 JIC(51)31, 'Situation in Persia', 21 March 1951. CAB 158/12.

48 Roger Louis, 'Musaddiq and the Dilemmas of British Imperialism'.

49 For more see S Marsh, 'The United States, Iran and Operation "Ajax": Inverting Interpretative Orthodoxy', *Middle Eastern Studies* 39:3 (July 2003), pp.1–38.

50 Cited in Bayandor, *Iran and the CIA*. p.46.

51 For background details see Wm. Roger Louis, *British Empire in the Middle East, 1941–1951: Arab Nationalism, The United States and Post-War Imperialism* (Oxford: Oxford University Press, 1984).

52 EP1024/6. British Embassy, Tehran to Foreign Office, 6 November 1951. FO 371/91472.

53 JIC(51)98(Final), 'Future Developments in Persia', 7 November 1951. CAB 158/13.

54 For the background to this see R Butler, 'British Policy in the Relinquishment of Abadan in 1951', *Foreign Office History*, September 1962. FO 370/2694.

55 Woodhouse's admission that he was 'still working for C' is in a 'Confidential' note, dated 2 December 1954, he left in his private papers. C M Woodhouse Papers, LHCMA, King's College London: Woodhouse 8/1.

56 M Woodhouse, *Something Ventured* (London: Granada, 1982). p.110. Wm Roger Louis describes Zaehner as an 'Oxford don, bon vivant, erudite philosopher and linguist, he relished the lighter sides of his duties. He drank heavily. To those who wished to learn about Iranian politics, he recommended *Alice Through the Looking Glass*. He introduced other members of the embassy to the pleasures of opium'. Roger Louis, 'Musaddiq and the Dilemmas of British Imperialism', pp.235–6.

57 Woodhouse, *Something Ventured*. p.111.

58 'Iran 1950–53', C.M.Woodhouse, 16 August 1976. LHCMA: Woodhouse 8/1. This short summary was the prequel to Woodhouse's memoir. The decision to put 'my own account . . . on record' was prompted by the letter to *The Times* by Lord Greenhill, which is quoted in the introduction to this book, and the concession that an account of Mossadeq's overthrow is preserved in the FCO archive but which Woodhouse had not been invited to contribute.

59 R.C.Zaehner to R.J.Bowker [FO], 27 August 1951. PREM 8/1501.

60 G10101/230/51, F.Shepherd to H.Morrison, 16 July 1951. FO 248/1514.

61 G R Afkhami, *The Life and Times of the Shah* (London: University of California Press, 2009). p.126. There is a series of fascinating correspondence regarding the background to Stokes' mission and it is remarkable how many people, all very senior, were against him going. See FO 800/653 for more.

62 Morrison to Attlee, 19 October 1951. PREM 8/1501.

63 Details are in FO 800/653 and FO 248/1531.

64 Roger Louis, 'Musaddiq and the Dilemmas of British Imperialism', p.250.

65 Details can be found in PUSD Papers, FCO.

66 See Zaehner's flow of memos to the FO from Persia in FO 248/1531.

67 Fuller details can be found in FO 371/98683. On Reilly and his 'friends' see the note by A.D.M.Ross [FO], 22 February 1952. EP15313/3/G. FO 371/98683.

68 JIC(52)81st Meeting, Perimeter Review, 24 July 1952. CAB 159/12.

69 JIC(52)84th Meeting, Perimeter Review, 31 July 1952. CAB 159/12.

70 Wm Roger Louis, *Ends of British Imperialism: The Scramble for Empire, Suez and Decolonisation*. (London: IB Tauris, 2007). p.757.

71 'The American Proposals', Note by S.Falle, 4 August 1952. FO 248/1531. There was still a hope in the FO that Zia would assume power, something they were reluctant to discuss with the Americans. See Falle's note for more.

72 JIC(52)53(Final), 'Situation in Persia', 18 August 1952. CAB 158/14.

73 Roger Louis, 'Musaddiq and the Dilemmas of British Imperialism', p.248.

74 Details are in the Perimeter Reviews for October 1952. CAB 159/12.

75 EP15314/189. Middleton to FO, London, 28 July 1952. FO 371/98691.

76 JIC(52)58(Final), 'Effects and Consequences of the Establishment of a Communist Regime in Persia', 1 October 1952. CAB 158/14.

77 For instance see JIC(52)135th Meeting, Perimeter Review, 4 December 1952. CAB 159/12.

78 JIC(53)2nd Meeting, Perimeter Review, 26 February 1953. CAB 159/13.

79 JIC(53)25th Meeting, Perimeter Review, 5 March 1953. CAB 159/13.

80 JIC(53)22, 'Effects and Consequences of the Establishment of a Communist Regime in Persia', 23 February 1953. CAB 158/15. Also, JIC(53)27th Meeting, 11 March 1953. CAB 159/13.

81 JIC(53)50th Meeting, Perimeter Review, 14 May 1953. CAB 159/13.

82 JIC(53)57th Meeting, Perimeter Review, 10 June 1953. CAB 159/13.

83 JIC(53)87th Meeting, Perimeter Review, 13 August 1953. CAB 159/14.
84 D N Wilber, *CIA Clandestine Service History: Overthrow of Premier Mossadeq of Iran, November 1952-August 1953* (March 1954). This internal history was only declassified in 2000. Full details can be found on the National Security Archive's website, Georgetown University: www.gwu.edu See also Bayandor, *Iran and the CIA*.
85 JIC(53)91st Meeting, Perimeter Review, 20 August 1953. CAB 159/14. Hossein Fatemi was subsequently convicted of treason against the Shah and executed by firing squad.
86 JIC(53)93rd Meeting, Perimeter Review, 27 August 1953. CAB 159/14.
87 Roger Louis, 'Musaddiq and the Dilemmas of British Imperialism', p.228.

14 Adventures in the Middle East

Part II – The Suez Crisis

The Suez crisis of 1956 was the culmination of a long and drawn out dispute, which had a disastrous impact on the UK's world profile, power and reputation. At its heart were several, related factors: the UK's role in the Middle East; the rising tide of nationalism and anti-colonial sentiment; the perception of a growing Soviet influence; and, inevitably, preoccupation with supplies of oil. Of these four factors, the first was in decline, the second was in the ascendant, the third exaggerated and the final one always a concern. All of these were of varying importance in Eden's thinking during the Suez crisis. More has probably been written on Suez than on any other episode of British foreign policy. There may well be more government files on this than any other Cold War crisis. For instance, on the original transfer of files at the thirty-year point in 1986, one archivist noted that in the FCO alone there were ninety linear feet of papers, weighing almost one ton.[1] Nonetheless, significant gaps remain in our understanding of the intelligence dimension.

Given the nature of the Suez crisis, the JIC should have played an integral part. The episode had, at its heart, a military operation mounted after normal diplomacy had failed. As a committee of the COS, the JIC was involved in matters ranging from the detailed, reference material on Egyptian capabilities, through the production and security of codewords, to tactical military appreciations. It was intimately involved in the preparations and conduct of the Suez operation itself. And yet, whilst the JIC's assessments might have been integral to COS planning, they had little impact on the deliberations of senior politicians. Threats to UK interests from Arab nationalism and questions over the potential level of Soviet involvement were key factors. The JIC's role as the government's principal provider of informed assessments on the capabilities of potential adversaries, as well as the likely drivers of intentions, should have been indispensable elements in the UK's decision making process. The sober JIC assessments should also have alerted the Cabinet to the misjudgements being made. But none of this happened. The JIC issued clear and balanced reports, warning of the impact of military action, yet its advice was not heeded. There was a notable contrast between the use of its appreciations of capabilities by the military, and its assessments of intentions which were ignored by policymakers.

During the run up to the crisis, the JIC's regular reports and updates, and its involvement with military preparations, reveal an effective performance, even if its advice was not always taken on-board. The JIC's assessment role clashed with political deliberations and Eden's preferred course of action, so its warnings were discounted. Nevertheless, during the run up to war its Chairman, Patrick Dean, had access to a wide range of military planning activities and played a central role as the Prime Minister's de facto 'special representative', though he was by no means privy to all deliberations and, crucially, was not made aware of Anglo-French collusion with Israel until late in the day.[2] Dean's multiple roles included Chairmanship of the JIC; Supervising Under Secretary in the FO for security and intelligence matters; attending the COS Committee meetings and thus the lynchpin between the military and intelligence worlds, as well as being Eden's envoy. The great problems facing Dean were his conflicting responsibilities: in addition to his intelligence position he became increasingly central to policy formulation. For Dean, in 1956, there could be no clear separation.

Finally, the Anglo-American dimension was controversial. The crisis had its roots squarely in the competition for Anglo-American influence in the Middle East and in the UK's colonial past. British military preparations and eventual intervention were not kept secret from the US, even if the ultimate collusion plans with Israel and France were hidden. Although the US did not want to be publicly involved, there is clear evidence that, behind the scenes, certain elements of the US Administration supported UK policy. Different US policies were being pursued covertly from the stated, overt ones. Natural sympathies for the UK, the importance of the Suez Canal, and the need to deal with Nasser were in constant tension with US domestic political calculations, political ambitions of individuals, and anti-colonial instincts. Unfortunately for the UK, US policymakers were unable to define the relative merits of each of these impulses or adhere to a coherent policy. The result was calamitous.

Miscalculating Nasser

On resuming the Premiership in 1951, Winston Churchill had been faced with reports of guerrilla-style attacks on British forces based in the Suez Canal Zone. At his first Cabinet meeting he informed colleagues that 'policy should now be based on the principle that it was the duty of the United Kingdom Government to keep the Suez Canal open to the shipping of the world, using such force as might be necessary for that purpose.'[3] The Middle East had long been of central importance to UK interests, with the Suez Canal a vital link for the UK's economic well-being. The Canal, completed in the middle of the nineteenth century, was a narrow, one hundred mile long waterway. Transit times from Europe to the Indian Ocean were significantly shortened and shipping costs thereby reduced. Although the British government initially opposed construction, its importance had been quickly realised and, in 1875, Prime Minister Benjamin Disraeli purchased Egypt's share of the Canal. The 1888 Convention of Constantinople granted the UK control of the Canal and, in several subsequent wars, it was successfully defended.

In 1936 a treaty had been signed with Egypt promising that, if requested, Britain would remove all its forces from Egypt with the exception, crucially, of the Suez Canal. For its part, the British government agreed to help train the Egyptian army and ensure Egypt's defence in the event of war. The treaty was set to last twenty years, to be re-negotiated in 1956. For the UK, Egypt was central to the defence of the Middle East which, itself, was a fundamental element of British defence policy.

The 1936 treaty committed the UK to supply arms to Egypt. In December 1950 this decision had been overturned, and reports were received by the intelligence community and assessed by the JIC in mid-1951 that Egypt had begun to procure arms elsewhere.[4] In October 1951 the Egyptian government declared that it was renouncing the 1936 treaty, a significant decision given its timing. With fears of a communist-overrun Europe fresh in the mind, UK policymakers had decided upon an anti-Soviet defence alliance for the Middle East and, whilst there was support from countries like Iraq and Turkey, the thorn in Britain's side was Egypt, which refused to participate. While there is some evidence that the then JIC Chairman, Patrick Reilly, briefed the Committee orally on developments in Egypt based entirely on FO reporting, the JIC did not report on this.[5] Its weekly 'Perimeter Review', for instance, did not issue any items on the Middle East until December 1951, when it began to report regularly on events.

In its first major assessment on Egypt, in early December 1951, the JIC revealed the complexities involved in interpreting Egyptian motives. The suggestion of close military relations between British and Egyptian armed services was seen as 'embarrassing' for Egypt, particularly given the government's 'nationalist aspirations'. But threats to break off diplomatic relations with the UK over the proposed construction of a new road near the Suez Canal (which would have prompted the destruction of several houses) were dismissed. The impression conveyed by the report and its discussion is a lack of concern, and the JIC's discussion made no mention of any communist influence or subversion.[6]

Despite a general unease over the nature of Soviet involvement in the Middle East, communism was not seen by the JIC, initially at least, to be a significant factor in Egyptian politics. In early 1952 Cairo was rocked by a series of riots. In Whitehall there was particular concern because most were directed against UK targets. Writing about the events shortly afterwards Patrick Reilly, in a letter to Hugh Stephenson, a diplomat based in the Political Office of the British forces in the Middle East and the Chairman of JIC(ME), explained the Committee's thinking. Recognising that the unrest had not been communist inspired, equally he failed to appreciate the strength of nationalistic and anti-British sentiment. The letter made clear that the JIC in London wanted advance warning of any change in communist intentions in the region so that 'my friends', a commonly used cover name for SIS, could 'exploit their local contacts' in time.[7]

Heated discussions took place within Churchill's government. Anthony Eden, then Foreign Secretary, argued vociferously for a new agreement with Egypt principally to safeguard the Suez Canal, not least because the 1936 treaty was due to end within a few years; Churchill was less convinced.[8] Whilst such deliberations were underway, in July 1952 King Farouk of Egypt was ousted following a military coup. Surveying this change of government, the JIC's Perimeter Review reported the fact without attributing it to the influence of the Soviet government or communism.[9] A subsequent memorandum by Sir Ralph Stevenson, the Ambassador in Cairo and a pre-war JIC Chairman, revealed that there were differences between the US and UK approaches to the new government, particularly on the US side which saw greater potential for goodwill.[10]

The JIC, in this instance, played down the role of communism in Egypt, even though its influence had been identified elsewhere. It based its conclusions on a quarterly report by JIC(ME), which focussed on communism in the region. Only a handful of these papers have been preserved, but it is possible to identify several factors which influenced the JIC. In the opinion of JIC(ME), the fact that no 'organised' communist party existed in Egypt meant 'there is little direct action which the Soviet Union can profitably take'.[11] At the same time, many of the reports attached significance to other elements within Egypt, most notably the opposition political Wafd Party and the religious extremist 'Moslem Brotherhood'. Both were known to be nationalistic and therefore anti-British, though not necessarily pro-Soviet.

The JIC set out to question why the overthrow of King Farouk by military officers had not been predicted. There had been significant evidence of unrest amongst junior officers, but despite several intelligence reports about this, neither JIC(ME) or the JIC in London had attached much weight to them, primarily because the unrest was not thought to have been widespread and there was no 'capable leader' to organise matters.[12] The JIC concluded, though never stated explicitly, that this had been an analytical failure, which may explain why 'C' had written to the JIC chairman to ask him to defend SIS to his JIC colleagues.[13]

Throughout the summer of 1952 the JIC, in its weekly Perimeter Review, reported on events in Egypt. Despite the production of important papers elsewhere in government[14], and by JIC(ME)[15], no major reviews of Egyptian policy were issued by the JIC. This may be explained by an FO summary circulated to JIC members in September 1952, which argued that the new Egyptian government had done everything possible to avoid antagonising the British for fear of a military response.[16] Through his position as the lead in the FO for liaising with the military, Reilly was routinely kept informed of developments.[17] Although contingency plans had been drafted for 'escape and rescue in the Middle and Far Eastern Theatres', there is no evidence that it raised the prospect of an emergency evacuation.[18] By late 1952, however, the JIC could report two significant developments: the military government led by General Neguib was now firmly established and developing a more 'nationalist policy'[19]; and the economic situation in the country was deteriorating. Consequently, the government was becoming unpopular leading it to resort to a harder line in dealing with the UK.[20] JIC(ME) expanded upon these points, concluding that there was definite evidence of a widespread anti-British policy unprecedented in scale. As a consequence, the possibility of an evacuation of the zone around the Suez Canal was raised, a major operation given the 80,000 British troops based there.[21]

One of the officers known to be involved in the initial military coup was a Colonel in the Egyptian infantry, Gamal Abdel Nasser, at that time believed to be 'one of General Neguib's personal staff'.[22] By December 1952 the JIC reported, correctly, that Nasser was 'believed to be leading a faction which opposes General Neguib'. This was considered somewhat surprising given that Neguib himself was building up Nasser as his 'right-hand man'. The root of the disagreement between the two men, according to the JIC, lay in their differing attitude towards the UK, with Nasser objecting to Neguib's more conciliatory stance.[23]

In January 1953 a new administration took office in Washington. For the first time in twenty years the Republicans were back in power. President Eisenhower, along with Secretary of State John Foster Dulles, and his brother Allen, the Director of Central Intelligence, would all be significant figures in the ensuing crisis. In the UK in 1953 the Chairman of the JIC, Patrick Reilly, left to become Minister in Paris and was replaced by Patrick Dean, another FO diplomat.

By early 1953, with Nasser becoming increasingly prominent in the Egyptian government, and with Churchill's wartime ally in power across the Atlantic, fresh initiatives were made in London and Washington to establish a defence dialogue with Cairo. The UK and US positions were not particularly close, despite the strong personal ties of those involved. Further heated debate took place within Churchill's inner circle about the UK's stance should the US fail to agree a common course of action. An additional complication was Eden's illness in the spring of 1953, followed by Churchill succumbing to a stroke. Churchill had taken on the role of Foreign Secretary when Eden became ill, in addition to his Prime Ministerial duties. By mid-May 1953, talks faltered and then were suspended without a deal to safeguard the British base in the Canal Zone, though the decision had been taken by the UK to reinforce British forces with a naval contingent and a Commando brigade.

For JIC(ME), now producing fairly regular monthly assessments on Egypt, these reinforcements had 'dampened' Egyptian 'military ardour', bringing about the redeployment of Egyptian forces. On the whole, JIC(ME) concluded, 'the regime is becoming increasingly conscious of its insecurity and still hesitates to take the plunge' which, in this context, meant military action against British forces in the Canal Zone. Whilst this was considered unlikely, 'incidents of terrorism and sabotage', which had become the norm by this point, were expected to continue.[24] This report was warmly received and Sir William Strang, the PUS in the FO, recommended that the Prime Minister's 'attention' be 'drawn' to the conclusions.[25] Churchill's response, typically, was 'they [the Egyptians] are not enjoying themselves at all. We stand firm and calm'.[26]

As a fresh round of Anglo-Egyptian talks began, behind the scenes, according to one former officer, the CIA were grooming Nasser to assume power.[27] It is uncertain whether the British knew about this, though there were certainly some in the FO who now saw Nasser as increasingly amenable to British interests. Nasser even claimed that, once an agreement had been reached with the UK,

Egypt would welcome broader talks about a collective pact for the defence of the Middle East, which remained one of the UK's primary goals for the region. Despite these reassuring messages, other elements in the FO questioned Nasser's intentions.[28] The JIC remained silent on the issue.

Talks continued into 1954, with the American Ambassador in Egypt appearing to support the UK position. In early March, in circumstances which the JIC described as 'confusing', General Neguib was sidelined, and over the ensuing weeks Nasser increased his grip on power.[29] In April 1954, this culminated in the dismissal of Neguib with Nasser taking over as the Prime Minister of Egypt. Writing from the British Embassy in Washington, the Ambassador, Sir Roger Makins, informed the FO of the US view that Nasser wished to negotiate a new deal with the UK to resolve matters once and for all.[30] The JIC reported a similar message from Washington, and another via Cairo.[31] These views were confirmed by the signing, in October 1954, of a new agreement with the UK. British troops would withdraw from the Suez Canal Zone within eighteen months, though the workshops and stores on the base would remain. In the event of an attack on Egypt or neighbouring Arab countries (including Turkey) British forces would be permitted to return though, significantly, not if the attack was instigated by Israel.

With this improvement in Anglo-Egyptian relations, British plans for a Middle East defence agreement were resurrected. US support was regarded as crucial if any future deal was to succeed. Whilst US political opinion was divided on the UK position, at a military level there was a consensus. The implication for the COS was that defence and the diplomatic representatives in Washington were not communicating effectively.[32]

A further difficulty was the deterioration in Arab-Israeli relations. The 'Tripartite Declaration' of May 1950, which had been signed by the UK, the US and France, created an obligation to preserve the Arab-Israeli truce. Discussions in Washington in the early 1950s helped to ensure a relatively consistent Anglo-American approach towards the issue, resulting in the mid-1950s in the attempts to broker peace with Operation Alpha. This was a daring initiative originally conceived by Evelyn Shuckburgh, the diplomat in charge of Middle Eastern policy in the FO. Its overall intention was simple: to create a bulwark in the Middle East by putting a stop to the 'penetration of the Arab world by the Communists' that would, as a by-product, settle Arab-Israeli differences.[33] Maintaining Egyptian support was essential to the plan but achieving this proved to be far from straightforward and it would eventually fail.

The Soviet Union Makes a Move

In mid-1954 there were grounds for optimism over Anglo-Egyptian relations, but prospects deteriorated dramatically, leading to war less than two years later. Several connected factors were responsible, and had been identified by the JIC, but were never brought together in a single assessment. Such factors included the issue of arms supplies to Egypt and the increasing Soviet presence in the

Middle East. Nasser's subsequent apparent embrace of Moscow, his progression from Colonel to powerful dictator, and his growing awareness of how to manipulate the great powers were matched by Eden's increasingly mistrustful views of Nasser's actions.[34] The backdrop to all of these was the ambivalent attitude of the US.

One of the UK's main goals in the Middle East had been to create a multilateral defence agreement. In February 1955 this began to be realised through the creation of the Baghdad Pact. Broadly analogous to NATO this treaty, signed by the UK, Pakistan, Iraq, Iran and Turkey, was designed to guarantee the defence of the region. Egypt was not a signatory and neither was the US, a shortcoming which would cause unease in London.[35] At the same time, the Anglo-American Alpha plan, which had been progressing well, stalled when John Foster Dulles made reference to it in a public speech in August 1955. This disclosure particularly irked Eden, by now Prime Minister, and Sir Ivone Kirkpatrick, the PUS in the FO: 'there is something in Mr Dulles which particularly irritates the Prime Minister. So you will not be surprised to hear that he is more than annoyed at Mr Dulles's latest antics'.[36] This antipathy towards Dulles would not abate.[37]

The events that set in motion the Suez crisis can be traced to the end of February 1955 when Israeli and Egyptian forces clashed.[38] This would signal the start of a more serious phase of Arab-Israeli military conflict. For the JIC, this was unexceptional as such clashes had occurred regularly since the 1948 ceasefire. It was clear that Israel had initiated the incident, and the question was how the UN's Security Council would deal with it.[39] The JIC reported developments at regular intervals, suggesting that despite a clear and deliberate act of aggression by Israel, this was, to some extent, a reaction to provocation.[40]

A further indication that the established order in the Middle East was changing came in September 1955. The abrogation of the 1936 treaty had meant that the UK no longer provided arms to Egypt. Accordingly the JIC monitored Egyptian efforts to obtain arms and equipment from other suppliers. It established an ad hoc committee with representatives from policy departments, the intelligence agencies, and the COS Committee. The JIC concluded that following the 1951 embargo Egypt might have looked for arms in a number of places, expecting that only a few would have proved fruitful. The reasons for this were twofold: firstly, Egypt's aspiration to become the arsenal for the Arab League, a supranational body which aimed to look after the independence and sovereignty of Arab states; and, secondly, because it felt threatened by Israel.[41]

For the JIC, although Egypt had some arms production capability, the prospect of developing this into a comprehensive indigenous defence production capability was slim, given the size, scale and nature of its relevant industrial base. Weapons and equipment transfers from foreign sources were therefore far more likely.[42] The ad hoc committee's first report in May 1954 listed an array of countries that had provided arms to Egypt: some had stopped following UK pressure but others, most notably Italy, had provided significant quantities despite the protestations. Of the Eastern bloc countries, the report concluded, correctly, that whilst 'we know that the Egyptians are considering the purchase of arms from the Soviet Bloc, no firm reports of deliveries have been received.'[43] With concern at the potential acquisition and quality of arms, in late 1954 the embargo was lifted, and the ad hoc committee dissolved.[44] But the matter did not end there.

In January 1955, the JIC examined how the Soviet Union might conduct a full-scale war in the Middle East: this study, in effect a contingency plan, had been written for the military JPS and did not attempt to question whether there might be a war or in what circumstances, but rather what form it would take.[45] A more detailed study was issued in September, but it was confined to a discussion of possible allies in the Middle East. It conceded that although the Western Powers were a more natural ally for Egypt and the Arab States, the Soviet Union was seeking a satisfactory outcome to the Arab-Israeli conflict. This implied that if the Soviet Union could assist the Arabs they would win its support.[46]

By the time of the JIC meeting on Thursday 29 September 1955, the balance of influence in the Middle East had altered irrevocably. The JIC, in discussing its weekly summary of events, now known as the 'Review of Current Intelligence', reported on an arms deal that had just been struck between Egypt and Czechoslovakia. For both the JIC and the US representative present at the meeting, the only outcome would be an Israeli request to the West for assistance against the new communist presence in the region.[47] To the US representative present at the meeting the following week, the implication was clear: the Czechs were 'fronting' for the Soviet Union.[48] The deal came as a shock to the JIC and, in the words of the JIB member, it had 'taken us by surprise. It was strange that we had apparently had no previous inklings of it'. Although there had been limited intelligence beforehand, the first concrete details on the deal came from a public statement by Nasser himself.[49] The FO saw the move in equally stark terms, concluding that the Soviet Union

> have chosen the most powerful and one of the most anti-Communist of the Middle East dictators to be the recipient of their support and favour; and with unerring instinct they have selected the one form of inducement which must prove irresistible to such a man, and tempting to all other Arab states. The supply of arms means for any neighbour of Israel one thing only – increased strength against Israel . . . it is a master stroke, and upon our reaction to it may depend the future of this country and of Western Europe . . . there seems to be no doubt whatever that we are witnessing the major attempt by the Russians to undermine our position in the Middle East.[50]

Whether or not this assessment reached the JIC is not clear. The Chairman, Patrick Dean, would have received a copy in his FO capacity. But its importance was evident: Egypt's global and strategic importance had unquestionably increased.

The JIC subsequently concluded that, in addition to Egypt, Syria, Saudi Arabia and Yemen had also received offers of assistance from the Soviet Union and, of these, only Saudi Arabia was thought to have rejected the advances.[51] Throughout October more details emerged of the scale of the Czech arms deal.[52] By November a comprehensive summary had been produced, revealing the extent of Egypt's foreign procurement patterns: not only were large quantities of arms coming from the Eastern bloc, but weapons were also being supplied by some European countries. These ranged from guns, ammunition and technicians, to landing craft, fighter and bomber aircraft, tanks and rockets.[53] In total it was estimated that Egypt had struck deals worth £120 million which, in 2014 value, would equate to approximately £2.7 billion. At the same time, it was reported that 'Israeli arms buying continues with unabated vigour'.[54]

In the aftermath of the Czech arms deal the JIC, at the insistence of Patrick Dean, commissioned a post-mortem into why no advance notice had been received.[55] SIS was to take the lead and it examined all sources, from intelligence to diplomatic reporting and open source analysis. In total there had been sixteen separate reports on Soviet-Egyptian arms discussions. Taken together, the SIS report concluded, 'each of the items of information indicated that something was afoot and that, assessed in conjunction with one another, at any stage from early 1955 onwards, they amounted to a clear warning'.[56] In a separate note sent to Dean, 'C' correctly concluded that 'personally, I feel that the surprise which the announcement of the arms deal caused was not due to any lack of information, but to a lack of proper collation and assessment'.[57]

There are several further aspects to the Czech arms deal. On the basis of 'operational efficiency', the JIS concluded in December 1955 that it would take a year before the Egyptians would be able to master and effectively use the new arms at their disposal.[58] Of greater importance is a seemingly obvious question, but one that the JIC never seem to have discussed, which is why had Nasser decided to deal with the Soviet Union? One of the reports passed to the JIC during the post-mortem suggests that the first overtures by Nasser were 'designed merely to frighten the West into being reasonable about Egyptian demands.'[59] Another question that the JIC did not directly address was whether Nasser had sought Czech arms as a counter or a deterrent to increased Israeli aggression. The JIC had regularly produced papers not only on likely Israeli actions but also how a future Arab-Israeli war might be conducted.[60] Certainly, the JIC confidently concluded, the arms deal had strengthened arguments in Israel for pre-emptive action.[61] The US representative informed the Committee that his colleagues concurred with this analysis.[62]

At the same time as evidence was accumulating on the Czech arms deal, Eden's government was reconsidering its position. Although the Suez Canal had always been central to UK thinking, perceptions of Nasser's attitude were changing. Encouraged by FO reporting, Eden informed his Cabinet colleagues that the need for oil meant that it was vitally important for Britain to remain on cordial terms with Egypt, and try to appease Nasser through support for his plans for the Aswan High Dam: an ambitious attempt to provide resources to the Nile Valley. The UK lacked the fiscal means to make a significant contribution, but attempts were made to bring the US authorities onboard. Intelligence reports that reached the JIC described rumours of 'the concessions' the Soviet Union was seeking from the Egyptians in exchange for financing for the Aswan Dam project. One was the 'socialisation of the Egyptian economy'. In discussion, the JIC did not address directly whether or not Egypt might accept the offer.[63]

The JIC did, however, commission a paper on communist penetration of Middle Eastern and Asian economies, which was approved in early January 1956. On the face of it the paper's conclusions were reassuring: there would be no 'severe' economic competition over the next five years and Soviet penetration would be gradual. The JIC saw the graver danger as political, not economic. The potential for trouble here lay not only in fomenting anti-Western opinion but, increasingly, by supplying greater quantities of arms and equipment.[64] Taken together, as a separate JIC paper surveying world communism concluded, the threat posed to the Middle East by communism had risen significantly in the latter half of 1955 and, it was assumed, would continue to rise as national communist parties grew in strength, particularly with their renewed focus and rhetoric on nationalist and anti-imperialist issues. For the JIC, then, distinguishing between nationalistic, anti-imperialistic and communist aspirations had become immaterial.[65]

Toppling Nasser

By the start of 1956 the conclusions drawn by the intelligence and policy community were increasingly diverging. Intelligence was just one source of information feeding into decision making, but it would appear that the assessments produced were being consulted less and less. With the new Soviet presence in the Middle East, questions remained over the scale of Nasser's support and commitment to communist advances. Related to this, discussions in London had begun in late 1955 about finding a replacement to Nasser. As talk of deposing him grew the JIC Chairman became the link between intelligence and policy decisions.

In late November 1955 Sir Roger Makins, the British Ambassador in Washington, informed the FO of a recent discussion he had had with Herbert Hoover, who was deputy to John Foster Dulles in the State Department and son of the former President. Hoover had said that 'an analysis of reports from secret source [sic] received over the last few months tended to show that Nasser had been going willingly down the Communist line'. Hoover continued, 'had we thought of finding an alternative to Nasser somewhere?' In writing to London, Makins requested a clarification of the position before replying officially.[66]

The FO's response, presumably made with political clearance, was unequivocal:

> We are afraid that Nasser, whether innocently or deliberately, is dangerously committed to the Communists. Consequently, we believe that it would be advantageous in any event to overthrow him if possible. We suggest that this problem should be subjected to joint Anglo-American examination as soon as possible.[67]

Makins subsequently replied that 'I said I presumed that he [Hoover] would wish this matter to be handled on the other side of the House (i.e. in CIA) and he said "yes" . . . in brief, the CIA have already been considering this matter; they are not optimistic about the results; and they would very much welcome the chance of comparing notes with us on the service level.'[68] At the same time, the FO also received similar telegrams from the Embassy in Cairo. By December it was decided that a special codeword cover was needed for the discussion on toppling Nasser, with the need to know kept to an absolute minimum. Those privy included the Prime Minster, Foreign Secretary, the PUS, and four other senior members of the FO, including Patrick Dean. The contents of these deliberations were to be kept in a special 'Top Secret' folder in the PUS's safe and, importantly for the historian, were not to be entered into the FO registry.[69] They would have been known to Dean and 'C' individually but not to the JIC as a body.

By late 1955 Eden was arguing that Nasser needed to be encouraged and nurtured to be useful to the West, whilst high-level discussions were being held about the need to remove him and find a replacement. Attempts were also being made to resolve the Aswan Dam issue, with a series of discussions in London and in Washington held while Ambassador Makins' communiqués were crossing the Atlantic. As a result, an Anglo-American offer was made in mid-December 1955 to provide grants, under the auspices of the World Bank, to finance Nasser's Aswan Dam project. Although the JIC remained pessimistic over the growth of communism in Egypt, its reports were still realistic about the speed by which this would progress and, far more importantly, about precisely how Nasser felt towards the Soviet Union, yet no fresh analysis of Nasser's intentions was made.

Serious attempts to promote the removal of Nasser seem to date from December 1955. Once this idea had gained momentum, it proved exceptionally difficult to stop. The outgoing Foreign Secretary, Harold Macmillan, made an effort to slow plans down, arguing that while it was still necessary to 'consider what cards we would have to play if such a decision were to become necessary', it was not yet time to take action. He cited reports about a new 'revolutionary group which might conceivably be made use of'. In response Eden expressed agreement, encouraging discussion of this 'group' with the US in order to 'see what alternative possibilities to Nasser there may be and what we could do about it'.[70]

UK policy was evolving along several simultaneous lines: Operation Alpha was still, in theory at least, proceeding; the UK financial commitment to the Aswan Dam, were it to be built, would run into millions; and yet Eden was becoming increasingly fixated on removing Nasser. In February 1956 Nasser had presented an alternative plan to the UK and the US for the Aswan Dam, which did not reject their loan proposal, but it caused consternation in the US. Partly as a result, Congress delayed any further deliberation of it.[71]

A more significant event, certainly for the UK, was the Jordanian dismissal in early March of General Sir John Glubb, which prompted a debate in the House of Commons and a hostile reaction towards Eden from the British press.[72] Glubb, a British military officer had, since 1939, been commander of the Jordanian army.

Britain and Jordan had a signed a treaty in 1948 which allowed the UK to retain a military presence in the country. Despite trying to persuade the King of Jordan to re-think, Glubb was made to leave the country within twenty-four hours. The JIC commented that the 'removal of Glubb's restraining influence' would leave Jordan 'increasingly less amenable to counsels of reason in any future periods of heightened tension'.[73]

Whatever the King's actual reasoning, Eden saw the influence of Nasser behind the action. Here was definitive evidence of Nasser's intent which could not be allowed to continue unchecked. Selwyn Lloyd, the new Foreign Secretary, met Nasser in Cairo. Although their discussion was amiable and went well, Lloyd's lasting impression was that Nasser 'did not exactly condescend but he gave the impression that . . . he could do more harm to us than we could do to him'.[74] This view was unquestionably biased by the fact that Lloyd had learnt of Glubb's dismissal whilst in Egypt.[75]

Eden was receiving mixed messages from the US. Makins informed London of a conversation with Hoover, commenting that there 'might be a slight difference of approach since we [the UK] seemed to be thinking of replacing Nasser whereas they [the US] were thinking more on the lines of undermining him and creating difficulties for him without actually trying to remove him'.[76] As Makins informed the FO, plans were proceeding smoothly, with definite assurances that Allen Dulles had political support for what was being proposed. For Makins, this dichotomy of views was deliberate.[77] Perhaps sensing the reaction in certain quarters of London, he offered some words of warning: 'we must be rather careful about seeming to want to deal with policy through the CIA'.[78] Indeed, as Eden's Private Secretary, Sir Guy Millard, has recalled, amongst senior FO officials it was only Sir Roger Makins who warned that the US was not entirely committed.[79]

While Eden was driving policy from Downing Street, he had found a like-minded ally in the FO in the PUS, Sir Ivone Kirkpatrick. Both men had matured in the European politics of the 1930s, having been intimately involved with the rise of fascism, the spectre of appeasement, and Chamberlain's fated mission to Munich. For Eden, Mussolini had been the foe, the architect of the 1935 Abyssinian Crisis. For Kirkpatrick, having personally delivered the declaration of war to the German Embassy in September 1939, appeasement was to be avoided at all cost. As Eden became more incensed, Kirkpatrick spent more and more time at 10 Downing Street, much to the dismay of his colleagues in the FO.[80]

The JIC continued issuing assessments but it is far less clear to what extent Eden or Kirkpatrick were interested in it or read its reports. John Cloake, Kirkpatrick's Private Secretary, for instance, does not recall his looking at a single JIC paper during the ensuing crisis.[81] Writing in the aftermath of Glubb's removal, Kirkpatrick informed Makins that 'we are, as you know, being driven to the conclusion that Nasser has become irretrievably hostile to our interests and involved with the Russians'. The problem was the US perspective, and in particular Kirkpatrick's 'concern at the way our minds are moving ahead of the Americans on this'. Thus, Makins was asked to convey the 'disturbing facts' to the State Department.[82] His response was to try to moderate the opinion of his PUS, by saying that 'you are a little unfair to the Americans', but also by warning: 'we may find the Americans far from reluctant to change their views about Nasser.'[83]

The US continued to be more concerned than the UK about Nasser's communist associations. Kirkpatrick appears to have concluded that Nasser was both hostile to the UK and influenced by the Soviet Union; yet, as the JIC was subsequently to report, the former did not imply the latter. JIC assessments, even if he had read them, would not have led Kirkpatrick to reach such conclusions; rather he was driven by his inbuilt prejudices, the goading Anthony Eden, and reporting coming from Egypt itself.

The JIC was facing a range of demands from its customers. In March it was asked, on behalf of the COS Committee, to produce a paper on how the closure of the Suez Canal might affect the US economy.[84] At the same time an assessment was in preparation on 'factors affecting Egypt's policy'. This report, approved by the COS Committee in mid-April 1956, was one of the best JIC papers of the time. Its conclusions stand in stark contrast to the opinion being disseminated by Kirkpatrick, and have been subsequently proven correct.

The April assessment was a subtle attempt to discern the driving forces behind Nasser's actions, and to distinguish between an anti-British policy and a pro-Soviet one. In terms of both arms and economic matters, the Committee concluded, 'Egypt is already in a position of increasing dependence on Russia'. It was observed that 'the Egyptians are developing habits of collaboration with Russia', and that, ominously, Nasser had 'begun to use [his] influence to facilitate Soviet penetration into Libya and perhaps also Syria, Yemen, Saudi Arabia and the Sudan, and to market communist arms in the Middle East'. An important question was asked about Nasser's motivation:

> this does not mean that Nasser has consciously resigned himself to becoming an instrument of Soviet policy. He probably still believes he can steer a middle course, not beholden to either side . . . the question is how long this balancing act can last. It is not yet clear that Nasser has reached a point at which he cannot call a halt to his involvement with Russia. But the Russians are ready to feed the Egyptian appetite until dependence upon them is irreversible; and we must conclude that Nasser will probably soon reach the point of no return.

In reaching this conclusion, the JIC had examined examples of past behaviour in an attempt to understand Soviet designs in the Middle East from a Soviet perspective. A detailed explanation and rationale was provided for the conclusions on Nasser's thinking and likely actions. It was based less on intelligence and more on an attempt to understand the foreign actors involved. While intelligence was lacking the assessment was explicit and clear in its conclusions, yet it went unheeded and would not be used as a basis for planning.[85]

The internal machinations of the JIC system is apparent from a note prepared by an American attender at both JIS and JIC meetings. Despite the conclusions of the paper, that Nasser had not yet reached 'the point of no return', it was written that 'the weight of opinions expressed at this [where it was discussed] by several of the Deputies was that Nasser had already passed the point of salvage.'[86] The JIC minutes of the meeting do not reveal who supported which argument, though they do disclose that the report was subsequently amended by both the FO and SIS.[87]

The US representative thought it would be 'interesting' to ask for US views on the paper, which he then communicated to Patrick Dean. In general the US agreed with the conclusions drawn, though they were less pessimistic about Nasser, arguing that the single factor that would propel Nasser further towards the communists would be the actions of the West, specifically if they decided to 'write him off.' In replying, Dean accepted that Nasser was trying to 'keep the door open', but added that 'what worries us is that he seems to be drifting towards deeper and deeper entanglement with the communist bloc'. However, as Dean conceded, 'one cannot be certain in these matters; and with so much at stake one must not underestimate the dangers'.[88] Providing supporting evidence of Egypt's stance was a more highly classified 'supplement' to the assessment. This made it clear that Egypt was becoming something of an 'entrepot' for arms en route from the Soviet Union to other Middle Eastern countries.[89]

A new FO committee had been created in January 1956. At the JIC discussion there had been talk of whether the conclusions of the paper were 'different' from or 'complementary' to those contained in the FO's 'Political Intelligence Group' assessment.[90] The 'PIG', as it quickly became known, was set up under Sir Ivone Kirkpatrick's guidance, initially to develop 'a major counter-subversive campaign against communist-occupied countries.'[91] Amongst its members were Patrick Dean and Geoffrey McDermott, both FO officials involved with intelligence and the Chairmen, respectively, of the Director and Deputy-Director level JIC meetings. This 'arrangement' helped to ensure that there was a suitable mechanism within the FO for collating intelligence and producing suggestions for counter-action.[92] The PIG was to have access to all sources of intelligence, from raw Sigint and Humint, through JIC assessments and open sources, to information from the deliberations of several Cabinet Committees.[93]

The PIG paper of March 1956 stated that 'While Nasser may not be irrevocably hostile to the West it is clear that he is already deeply committed to the Communists (. . . the process may have gone further than is generally realised)'. Yet despite this, a pragmatic approach was necessary: 'because of the hurt she can do us, and in the hope of long term improvements, we must continue to give Egypt economic aid'.[94] The report was circulated to JIC members and it is clear from a separate note by Dean that the Foreign Secretary took a keen interest in it and directed the FO to continue reviewing its key points.[95]

From March 1956 onwards, the JIC produced three regular series of updates on the Middle East, all issued at regular weekly or fortnightly intervals to a wide range of Whitehall customers. The first was the Weekly Summary of Current Intelligence, monitoring developments in the region and adding a brief commentary.[96] The second was a codeword assessment – the Weekly Survey of

Intelligence.[97] Drafted and approved by the members of the JIC, it included reports on, amongst other things, arms traffic. The third product was a 'Current Intelligence Report on the Situation in the Middle East', issued by the JIC but prepared by the Heads of the Middle Eastern Sections within the JIS.[98] Whilst it was useful to the staffs to have such products, their real value has to be judged by how far anyone in authority read them and heeded their content.

Whither Intervention?

By April 1956 the JIC was advancing a steady line, conveying the Committee's apprehension; Eden was increasingly fixated on removing Nasser with covert plans under development; yet questions remained over the true nature of Egypt's relationship with the Soviet Union. Discussions on the other side of the Atlantic hindered rather than helped achieve clarity: the Americans were hesitant over whether to fund the Aswan Dam project; and mixed messages were being transmitted from the two organisations headed by the Dulles brothers, State Department and CIA, about the level of US assistance and support for UK policies. Nasser's decision in mid-May to officially recognise communist China (something the US still had not done, though the UK had) contributed to the US decision not to fund the Aswan Dam project. Final confirmation of this came at the beginning of June, when Kirkpatrick was officially informed by the US Embassy.[99]

Without US support the UK was financially unable to support the Dam project alone. Within Whitehall some were relieved by this, given the parlous state of Britain's own finances. However Michael Johnston, the official in the Treasury dealing with the project, noted: 'Nasser will undoubtedly be appalled by the apparent breach of faith by the two Governments and will seek to revenge himself. There is not much he can do against the United States but a lot he can do against us. Obvious examples are renewed pressure on the Suez Canal Company or stirring up trouble in the Gulf'.[100]

Elsewhere significant events were taking place. In April, Soviet Premier Nikolai Bulganin and First Secretary Nikita Khrushchev visited London on a goodwill visit, which ended on a sour note with the discovery of an ill-fated underwater espionage operation; this was to become known as the Buster Crabb affair (see Volume II).[101] Concurrently, UK forces were planning the final withdrawal of their forces from Suez, as approved in the 1954 agreement with Egypt. The last man left on the morning of 13 June 1956 and the troops' departure, after seventy four years of continued presence, was followed by three days of partying in Cairo. The guest of honour was the former editor of *Pravda* and the new Soviet Foreign Minister, Dmitri Shepilov. The JIC's reaction to this was far more muted than that of the senior US attender. For the JIC, the visit was simply something that had been arranged whilst Shepilov had been *Pravda* editor; for the US, as its representative informed the Committee, it could only imply one thing: 'a prime opportunity for the Russians to exert renewed pressure to accept their offers for financing the high dam . . . there appeared to be a feeling that the visit would be accompanied by a major policy pronouncement from the Soviet Union with respect to the Middle East'.[102]

The JIC regularly assessed the likelihood of an Arab-Israeli war with weekly mentions in the Red Book, and in the more strategic JIC summaries. In early July the Committee approved a report which re-affirmed earlier conclusions on the likelihood of war in light of recent events. While identifying the risk of 'inflammatory statements, frontier incidents and commando raids bringing about a major clash', there remained 'very little likelihood of either Israel or the Arab States deliberately initiating war before the end of 1956'.[103] Referring to the paper's terms of reference, which emphasised the need to differentiate between intentions and capabilities, an American attender said that

> in assessing capabilities, he thought it important to distinguish between our (i.e. US and UK) judgment of Arab capabilities and responsible Arab assessments of their own capabilities. Then it was necessary to be aware of a further difference, which was the opinion of hot-headed, irresponsible factions within the armed forces, whose assessment of their capabilities might be dangerously optimistic, and might upset the stability of more sober elements both in their own and neighbouring regimes. In arriving at the assessment of the likelihood, it was necessary to take into account all these differing assessments.

Furthermore, as he continued,

> a difference had persisted in the weekly JIC and [US] assessment of the likelihood of hostilities . . . . whereas the [Americans] had come down firmly with a statement that hostilities were unlikely, the JIC had said that hostilities could break out but refrained from saying whether, in fact, they would.

The Committee agreed to 'take note' of these points and 'invited the Joint Intelligence Staff to re-cast their report in the light of the points agreed in discussion above.'[104]

The turning point came on 26 July 1956. At dinner that evening in 10 Downing Street, Prime Minister Anthony Eden was hosting an event in honour of the King and Prime Minister of Iraq. His Private Secretary dealing with foreign affairs, Guy Millard, recalled what happened next: 'When the news came through . . . I was on duty at Number 10 and had to summon a meeting . . . I had to ring up the Chiefs of Staff and the Foreign Secretary and get them to Number 10 to discuss the situation'.[105] The 'news' was Nasser's announcement that he had nationalised the Suez Canal Company.

A week earlier the US Secretary of State, John Foster Dulles, had held a meeting with the Egyptian Ambassador in Washington. Dulles had been asked bluntly whether or not the US would fund the Dam project and had stated clearly that it would not. The following day, the UK, too, announced that it would not be providing any funds. The JIC considered the likely Egyptian reaction and was equivocal about whether or not Nasser would turn to the Soviet Union for support.[106] Whilst Nasser's decision to nationalise the Canal may have come as a surprise to the JIC, there had been indications that pointed towards a crisis over the issue. The JIC had been aware that Nasser had been considering different methods of blocking the Suez Canal, including the use of sunken ships.[107] At a meeting a week later, Egyptian naval commanders were told by Nasser that they should prepare themselves for an attack on the Canal at any time.[108] One direct result was that the scientific staff who had been at the recent atomic trials in Australia and who would have returned to the UK via the Canal, were diverted in order to ensure that 'no ships . . . might serve as hostages'.[109]

For the JIC, the information provided, together with the public knowledge of Nasser's privatisation of the Canal, was extremely worrying. The Committee's initial reaction was to describe the move as an implicit declaration by Nasser that he was now the leader of the Arab world and a 'political retort' to the West. The JIC also reported that Nasser had received messages of encouragement from the Soviet Union, though with a warning that it would not get involved in a regional conflict. These assessments implied that the decision to nationalise had 'not been prompted by the USSR'. A more practical question troubled the JIC: whether or not the Egyptians would block traffic passing through the Canal and, if so, what might prevent them from doing so. In the JIC's opinion, 'it is by no means certain that measures short of force are likely to upset the Egyptian Government's decision in the short term'.[110]

At the same time the JIC undertook to produce a more detailed assessment of Nasser's actions. The paper, approved in early August, is one of the few examples where it is possible to compare the final version with an earlier draft. The differences are substantial, even though it is not at all obvious what prompted the changes.[111] In the original, several quite important sections on the assessment of the implications of Nasser's actions for the West are missing from the final version, including the sentence: 'Hitherto he has had the skill to deny the West a casus belli; but by interference with shipping he might well provide the occasion for Western occupation of the Canal Zone and ensurance of transit rights by force'. Similarly, the following section in the original:

> Nasser's regime has served the Soviet government's interests well and they will probably wish to keep him in power. It seems likely therefore that they will be prepared to give financial support to Egypt . . . the possibility cannot be ruled out that to maintain his position with the Soviet government's support he may be forced to go much further than hitherto to subject himself to Russian infiltration and domination.[112]

Was amended to read:

> Nasser's regime has served the Soviet Government's interests well but, until the reactions of the Western Powers become clearer, the Soviet Government may well have some misgivings about his latest action. Their present interest

is that Egypt's relations with the West should be as bad as possible without Egypt becoming so completely dependent on the Soviet Union that the concept of neutrality is discredited.[113]

The revised view emphasised that the actions of the West would have a direct bearing on Soviet decision making; it was less emphatic on the Soviet influence over Nasser, suggesting that there was still some independence in Egypt's position. The Committee also produced a fresh review of Nasser's character, which not only recognised Nasser's strengths but also his weaknesses:

> There is a considerable element of emotion in Nasser's actions. As a demagogue he is liable to be carried away by the violence of the passions he himself has whipped up. As a dictator, his actions over the past three years show subtlety and calculation and have so far all resulted in gain to Egypt. We should be prepared for any action that may enhance his prestige and maintain him in power.[114]

Whilst discussions continued among policy and intelligence staff, military preparations for a possible conflict were advancing rapidly. The plan was based upon two objectives: to remove Nasser and to ensure that international control of the Suez Canal could be maintained. Originally these two goals had been separate. The COS had worked towards achieving the latter, suggesting an assault on Port Said, whereas Eden, obsessed with the former, favoured attacking Alexandria. After discussion, the COS finally submitted their plan to the Egypt Committee of the Cabinet on 10 August 1956. It was codenamed 'Operation MUSKETEER' and although the prime objective was to seize the Canal, an unstated but integral element was to ensure the overthrow of Nasser. As such it called for an aerial bombardment followed by an assault on Alexandria, which was more heavily defended than Port Said but, crucially, was closer to Malta (from where operations would be launched) and was therefore judged to be an easier militarily target.[115]

A JIC assessment of 7 August 1956 considered the efficiency and capabilities of the Egyptian armed forces, its conclusions were mixed. Morale amongst the three armed forces was assessed to be high, not least as there had been an influx of young officers. At the same time, though, capabilities were thought to be extremely limited with, for instance, 'aircraft serviceability for sustained operations unlikely to exceed 50%', and that 'proficiency' with the new Soviet weapons would not be sufficient until the end of 1956. Additionally, the assessment addressed Egyptian thinking:

> since the declared British intention is to secure the Canal Zone, she [Egypt] will probably assume that landings are likely to take place in areas adjacent to it supported by naval and air action. At the same time, she will be watching for a build-up of British forces in Libya. Egypt will assume that adequate British naval, land and air forces are being made available for this operation.

She will also realise that British air forces can be operated against her bases and lines of communication from bases beyond the normal radius of action of her own force.[116]

A vital component of the plan was maintaining secrecy. The JIC was asked to assess Egypt's Sigint capabilities and the measures needed to safeguard the UK's communication links and military plans.[117] British military planning was given a specially restricted codename – TERRAPIN – and the JIC was made responsible for administering it. In addition, the Committee became heavily involved with the provision of tactical intelligence to military planners. Nasser's nationalisation of the Suez Canal Company had brought about a new sense of urgency, particularly in the minds of Eden and Kirkpatrick. The two issues of reclaiming the Canal and removing Nasser had become inseparable and, by the start of August 1956, it was becoming increasingly apparent to the Cabinet that the only realistic solution appeared to be the use of force.[118]

Man in the Middle – Patrick Dean and the Suez Crisis

The Canal Company's nationalisation brought the JIC into much closer contact and involvement with the military. By August Patrick Dean had started to attend a wide variety of meetings which familiarised him not only with the highly secret planning for military action against Egypt, but also the plans to remove Nasser. As a senior FO official Dean was integral to the 'overt' policy and planning and, as the Chairman of the JIC, to providing intelligence assessment, but he was excluded from the really important circle of those around Eden who had decided on a covert policy of collusion with France.

A barrister by training, Dean had joined the FO in the early stages of the Second World War, acting as an Assistant Legal Adviser. He had then headed the FO's German Political Department, before becoming Minister at the Embassy in Rome. In April 1953 he was promoted to Assistant Under Secretary of State with responsibility for intelligence and security and, at the same time, became Chairman of the JIC.

The JIC first became involved in providing the strategic level intelligence context for military planning in May 1956, when the head of PUSD and Chairman of the Deputy-Director meetings, Geoffrey McDermott, agreed to attend JPS sessions.[119] Following the news of Nasser's nationalisation of the Suez Canal Company, Guy Millard gathered together the Prime Minister, Foreign Secretary and the COS, in a hastily convened meeting of the Cabinet held on the morning of Friday 27 July 1956. According to the minutes, the Cabinet 'agreed that Her Majesty's Government should seek to secure, by the use of force if necessary, the reversal of the decision of the Egyptian Government to nationalise the Suez Canal Company'.[120]

In France, too, the news of Nasser's actions had been greeted with alarm and senior officials travelled to London for urgent talks, at which the US was represented by Herbert Hoover, Dulles' deputy in the State Department.[121] In contrast to the differing UK and US approaches to the use of force, there was closer agreement between the UK and France, and on 1 August a further 'restricted' session was held.[122] At this the French Minister of Defence promised to provide military support for an attack on Egypt. The news of this highly secret discussion was transmitted to a small number of officials in the FO, one of whom was Patrick Dean.[123] That same day Dean attended a meeting of the COS Committee at which Anglo-French military plans were discussed. It concluded that Ministerial approval would be needed for any official joint planning.[124]

A 'special meeting' of the JIC was convened and the conclusions given a more limited circulation than normal. The meeting, at Deputy-Director level, was only attended by military representatives, the JIB and the FO, with no-one from the collection agencies present; Dean was also absent. Two days later the full JIC, with Dean at the helm, met in the morning with Dean and the military members attending the COS Committee meeting later the same day.[125]

At the 'special meeting' on 7 August security measures were discussed, and a small staff created within the JIB to provide tactical intelligence to Force Commanders. A JIC report on the likely implications of a military conflict with Egypt for other nations was also discussed.[126] This assessment, produced at the explicit request of the planners, was short.[127] It mostly concerned Egypt's military capabilities, but included a limited discussion on how other nations might see a conflict and how this could affect Egyptian thinking. The conclusion was that the Soviet Union would remain neutral; that the Arab States would support Egypt but would not provide military assistance; and that Israel would support any involvement and would possibly also intervene militarily.[128]

Events at the political, military, and intelligence levels were proceeding separately, at different paces and along different paths. The first international conference to discuss Suez was convened in London for August. From this a picture had begun to emerge. Whilst the US was, if pressed, prepared to accept Nasser's removal, in an election year it did not favour the use of force. At the military level, plans for 'Operation MUSKETEER' were continuing. Providing intelligence support, the JIC continued to work with the planners, at both the tactical and strategic level, from which discussions the US representatives were excluded.

While the JIC provided tactical intelligence to military planners, proposals were being made for the overthrow of Nasser. These included plans to foment internal opposition, to identify and train a suitable replacement, and to find a means of toppling Nasser. Both Roger Makins and Patrick Dean were involved in these deliberations. Initially, Patrick Reilly, Dean's predecessor as JIC Chairman and currently the Minister in Paris was also included. The plans were formulated in December 1955 and considered different ways of removing Nasser. Nothing recorded in the open or closed papers indicate that assassination was ever considered as an option. Plans centred on the prospects and implications of a military coup, or a military intervention by the West, resulting in a change of regime. Senior politicians were privy to the detail, including the Prime Minister.

Planning for Nasser's removal was providing a very different picture from that emerging at the political level. Dean and Makins were informed on 13 August

1956 that John Foster Dulles had been warned that 'Nasser's reaction would be very violent' to the withdrawal of funding from the Dam project. According to one official, this meant that the Americans were 'firmly against the use of armed force to settle the Suez problem'. Despite this warning, planning to remove Nasser went ahead.

At the start of August John Foster Dulles was in London for the first conference on resolving the Suez situation. Also in London was Kermit Roosevelt, and Dean took the opportunity to discuss some of the plans with him. From Dean's submission to Selwyn Lloyd, the Foreign Secretary, it is evident that no details were included for fear that Dulles would find out about them. Plans were tightly focussed on mounting a coup.[129]

Dean, through his responsibility for intelligence as Chairman of the JIC as well as in his position in the FO, was privy to all discussions. At the same time he was being increasingly drawn into military planning. Historically, the FO representative on the JIC has also supervised FO input into defence policy, and Dean was regularly the senior contact point for military matters, even though military representatives (albeit more junior) were attached to PUSD. For this reason, Dean often attended COS Committee meetings and although this was frequently to discuss intelligence, he was also responsible for FO liaison with the military.[130] He was intimately involved with Anglo-French staff talks, for which he travelled to Paris in mid-August 1956. A related aspect of this visit was to discuss security arrangements with the French, and in particular the vulnerabilities of their cypher system, something the JIC had earlier urged politicians to address.[131] Before his departure to Paris, Dean had attended a specially convened meeting at Chequers, the Prime Minister's country residence, to discuss Suez. The Prime Minister personally instructed Dean, as the Chairman of the JIC, to broach these security matters with the French Prime Minister, Guy Mollet.[132]

Knowledge of the detail of the talks was so tightly protected that Reilly, although aware that Dean was visiting Paris, was told nothing.[133] The Ambassador, Sir Gladwyn Jebb, personally wrote to Eden asking him for information on Dean's forthcoming visit.[134] Similarly, Denis Greenhill, then a middle ranking diplomat but a future JIC Chairman and PUS in the FO, who was also in Paris at this time as a member of the delegation to the NATO talks, later recalled: 'I came into the office early one day and to my amazement I heard talking going on in Kit's [Sir Christopher Steel, the UK's Permanent Representative to NATO] room . . . I went in and there was Pat Dean from London. Kit said to come in later; and when Pat Dean had gone Kit came in and said "under no circumstances are you to say to anybody whatsoever that Pat Dean was here this morning".'[135] Dean himself, in the only interview he later conducted, said that he did not 'remember going to any such discussions' with the French, despite composing an account of his visit.[136]

On the same day that Jebb and Dean were meeting the French Prime Minister in Paris, Sir Norman Brook, the Cabinet Secretary, had approved his 'Forecast of Time-Table' for Suez. This detailed a sequence in which the international conferences would open and close, Parliament would meet and adjourn, Egypt would discuss and reject international proposals, and air bombardment and the assault on Egypt would begin.[137]

On his return to London, Dean noted in his visit report, that one of the underlying rationales had been to 'bring out more clearly the intention of the French Government and Her Majesty's Government to reach a solution, if possible, at the forthcoming conference of the present dispute without resort to force.'[138] Nothing relating to the later collusion plans with Israel was mentioned in his report for, even if it had been discussed (which is unlikely), Dean would not have risked including such detail. Following this visit, the Prime Minister advised colleagues on the Egypt Committee, the senior ministerial body set-up to co-ordinate plans, that the meeting had been a 'success'.[139] Jebb, whose personal plea to Eden for more information must have been successful as he accompanied Dean to see Mollet in Paris, wrote afterwards to the Prime Minister to inform him that 'everything went very well', adding that 'may I just say in conclusion how splendidly your special representative conducted himself.'[140] It would not be the last time that Dean would be involved.

Throughout all of Dean's involvement with Suez and with the myriad paperwork that he initialled, nothing reveals his personal opinion. His position and different roles must have been difficult to balance, particularly where his responsibilities for intelligence overlapped with his involvement in policy. Whilst chairing the JIC and providing impartial, objective intelligence assessments, he also represented the wider intelligence community in discussions with the military Planners, and the FO in defence-related discussions with the COS. Yet, at the same time, he was also intimately involved with the plans to topple Nasser, was the Prime Minister's 'special representative', and involved in conducting liaison discussions with the French: roles that are impossible to disentangle.

One request passed to the JIC reveals what Dean thought its remit should be, and his concern to limit it, and is an example of the strength of Dean's position. At a COS Committee meeting Lord Mountbatten, the First Sea Lord, had suggested an assessment to examine the extent to which a post-conflict Egyptian government would back British policies and gain the support of the Egyptian population. Dean's objection, expressed in the minutes, was that the Egyptian population were so 'solidly behind Nasser that it might be impossible to find such a Government'. The JIC was asked to provide a forecast.[141] Dean's response was that 'he had doubts as to whether the JIC was the appropriate body to prepare a report of this nature, which was almost entirely a political question',[142] without revealing that he knew that plans for the emergence of a post-conflict Egyptian government were being developed with US support.

Dean was also on several other committees relating to Suez. The JIC had previously assessed Egyptian efforts to broadcast propaganda directed against the UK. In late August Dean, along with other FO colleagues, attended a meeting of 'Mr Dodds-Parker's Advisory Committee'. This oddly-named body was chaired by Douglas Dodds-Parker, the SOE veteran and Conservative politician who was the Joint Parliamentary Under Secretary of State for Foreign Affairs. Its role was to conduct 'political warfare and propaganda in connexion with the

Suez dispute'.[143] Dean attended other related inter-departmental committees too: the 'Official Committee on Radio Policy and Plans (War)',[144] the 'Home Defence Committee – Advisory Group',[145] and the 'Defence (Transition) Committee'.[146] A further committee, which Dean sometimes attended and occasionally chaired, was the 'Official Committee on the Middle East'.[147] Dean was included in these committees through his JIC Chairmanship as much as his FO membership. The 'Home Defence Committee – Advisory Group', for instance, was designed to look at changes in 'intelligence assumptions' and to ensure that they were incorporated into preparations for war.[148] For the 'Official Committee on Radio Policy and Plans (War)' Dean was included principally because of his position as JIC Chairman, noting that he also represented the Foreign Office.[149] It is hard to imagine someone who had more extensive knowledge of all aspects of the Suez operation.

Meanwhile the JIC was continuing to produce and approve a number of fresh assessments. It discussed Suez-related issues at most meetings, ranging from the processing of requests from the Air Ministry for more information on the Egyptian air force, to the preparation of codewords for military operations.[150] Of more potential strategic value were those discussions, beginning in August and gradually increasing in frequency, on how a potential military conflict with Egypt would affect surrounding areas, particularly where British interests were involved.[151] One paper discussed a JIC(ME) report on the political and military effects of war. Its conclusions were both explicit and optimistic and were probably well received by the pro-war elements of the Cabinet and Whitehall. It argued in favour of a military intervention, concluding that:

A.   If we are forced to go to war to achieve our aim:

    (i)   the Soviet Union will not risk starting a global war;

    (ii)   operations against Egypt will be short and decisive;

    (iii)   military action may be needed elsewhere in the Middle East to restore the position in certain areas (e.g. Jordan);

    (iv)   the Western position in the Middle East and that of our Arab friends will be greatly strengthened;

    (v)   Soviet penetration will receive a severe setback;

    (vi)   militarily we shall have a continuing commitment in Egypt for some years;

    (vii)   Arab xenophobia in the longer term will become stronger if we fail to forge a new basis of relations with the Arab world;

    (viii)   favourable conditions will exist for a settlement of the Arab/Israel dispute provided Israel exercises restraint.

B.   If we achieve our aim by diplomatic means:

    (i)   the Western position and that of Iraq will be greatly strengthened;

    (ii)   if Nasser however remains in power, the improvement may only be short-lived; in the longer term he will resort again to his policy of exploiting Arab nationalism to achieve his ambitions.

C. If we have to accept a bad compromise, our whole position in the Middle East may very soon be in complete jeopardy.[152]

This intelligence assessment contrasts with a policy paper prepared two weeks later. Written by the FO's PUS, Kirkpatrick, for the Foreign Secretary, it was designed to set forth the main factors to consider:

(i) if we use force the Americans will not support us and will probably be openly critical.
(ii) We shall get very little support from any other quarter.
(iii) The effect in the Arab States and in the Far East will be bad.
(iv) The economic consequences will be, at the very least, an intolerable burden to our economy.
(v) On the other hand, we cannot possibly risk allowing Nasser to get away with it.[153]

Kirkpatrick's summary of the situation was far more balanced than that of JIC(ME). On the basis of the JIC(ME) paper, and other material, the JIC revised its earlier assessment on how a military conflict – given the assumption that there would be war – would affect other nations' views of the UK and whether or not they would intervene militarily. This subject was examined at all levels of the central intelligence machinery, from the JIC, through the two regional committees, particularly JIC(ME), down to the LICs.[154] Although the JIC assessed that a number of Middle Eastern countries would provide Egypt with military facilities, it considered that only Syria and Jordan might offer military assistance, but that this would be 'insignificant'.[155] In discussion with the COS, Dean accepted that 'perhaps certain parts of the paper were unduly pessimistic' and agreed to make a 'number of small amendments'.[156]

From the last week of August, for about four weeks, Dean was absent from work, having a much needed break. He was also promoted and appointed a Deputy Under Secretary of State (DUS), one level down from the PUS. Dean's FO deputy in all matters related to intelligence was Geoffrey McDermott, the head of PUSD. In his memoirs McDermott recalls his surprise that Dean was promoted over so many colleagues, calling it 'sensational'. Indeed, as McDermott claims, it was 'unprecedented' for he was now more senior than the other members of the JIC. The justification for Dean's promotion has been lost since his personnel file, in accordance with the normal practice, has been destroyed.[157] The implications were clear for, as Archibald Ross, AUS and the person responsible for 'keeping in touch' with PUSD on the 'planning aspects' of Suez, has recalled: Dean 'was promoted to Deputy [Under Secretary], which made him senior to all Assistant Undersecretaries [sic] and gave him rights of access, rights of overruling and so on. Some saw Eden's hand in this.'[158]

In his absence, Patrick Reilly, Dean's predecessor as JIC Chairman, was recalled from Paris to take charge of intelligence and security. The four weeks for which Dean was on leave were, in Reilly's words, 'miserable'.[159] As Reilly wrote in his memoirs, 'I soon found my way around, having done the same job for three years, but with one essential difference. I was not to take the chair of the JIC. I did not go to its meetings.' His position was not helped as Dean had already left for holiday and Kirkpatrick gave him no instructions.[160] By this time, as his Private Secretary has noted, Kirkpatrick was spending almost all day every day at 10 Downing Street.[161] This fact did not go unnoticed by Reilly, who observed, more broadly, that military planning was proceeding at a rapid pace with little or no FO involvement. As he recalled, 'I did what was required of me as best I could, but deprived of the chief power element in Dean's job, the Chairmanship of the JIC, I had little opportunity to intervene effectively'.[162] Furthermore, as he noted in a later interview, 'with my previous experience of the Chiefs of Staff machine and the handling of the political-military affairs generally in the Foreign Office and in Whitehall, it took me no time at all to realise that things were not being handled in the proper traditional way'.[163]

Unknown to Reilly, both Dean and McDermott had been in regular contact with the military and were aware of how plans were advancing. In a personal letter to McDermott, Dean asked that in his absence a specific matter be resolved, that once more shows the confidence Dean felt in his own position:

> There is one tiresome matter, namely a demand by the Chiefs of Staff for an assessment about a year ahead of possible military commitments in the Middle East. This involves the JIC, or really the Foreign Office, in crystal-gazing about the political situation in the main areas in the Middle East . . . I think that either you or Patrick [Reilly] should attend the Chiefs . . . and see that the Chiefs do not try and cast their net too wide.[164]

Dean returned from leave on Monday 17 September 1956. There was no handover from Reilly, who had departed the previous Friday.[165] Whilst he had been away there had been discussions, both formally at the JIC and informally between members, about the impact of war on surrounding nations and their likely views of the UK. For the large part these focussed on the Middle East, with no consideration of how the United States might react.[166]

Intelligence, military and political planning continued to proceed independently of each other. Within the JIC, Dean would have known that planning for Nasser's removal continued unabated. The first London Conference had ended on 23 August, culminating in a resolution calling for the creation of an international board to run the Sue Canal. The Australian premier Robert Menzies tried to get support for this, and flew to Cairo to persuade Nasser to agree.

Throughout August the plans for Operation MUSKETEER began to unravel. General Sir Charles Keightley, the Commander in Chief of Middle East Land Forces, had been appointed in mid-August to oversee the intervention plan. However Keightley had always had misgivings. The original planning date for 'D-Day' had been repeatedly pushed back, but with a significant number of personnel and equipment ready and poised in the region, the hiatus could not last indefinitely. In addition, weather considerations meant that unless it was launched by 6 October, implantation of the plans would have to be suspended until the spring. Keightley's solution was 'MUSKETEER REVISE', a plan that could be delayed until late October. A fresh interpretation had revised upward the estimated number of British casualties likely in an attack on Alexandria. Keightley's new plan envisaged a three stage operation. An initial aerial attack would be followed by a propaganda campaign designed to persuade Egyptians to turn on Nasser, resulting in a coup or his resignation. The third stage would be a military assault on Port Said, some days later, to secure the Canal.[167] The JIC was involved in this tangentially through the provision of tactical intelligence to the military planners.[168] This work was important, valuable, and part of the normal JIC workload yet, as Alexander Craig has argued, 'political factors were becoming decisive in determining the form which military action would take.'[169]

Planning was also proceeding on the basis that Nasser would be toppled either by a coup d'etat or as a result of foreign military intervention. Plans that, incidentally, Ministers had ruled should not be conveyed to the COS.[170] Nasser's influence was growing and the early efforts to find a credible opposition to support were faltering.[171] A bigger issue, as Dean was informed upon his return from holiday, concerned the impact of military intervention. Secretary of State Dulles had stated earlier that he did not want to be kept abreast of UK military plans. This dovetailed with some concern, expressed within Whitehall, about keeping the US fully informed. This was because of the possibility that Nasser's removal would be achieved through an invasion in which the US would not participate and which it might oppose.[172]

For the JIC, too, there was anxiety about ensuring that the British and American communities worked together. To help satisfy this, at their 1030 meeting on 27 September 1956 the JIC welcomed a large contingent of Americans. Opening the meeting, Patrick Dean outlined how the JIC 'were concerned with the likely factors which the Russians would take into account in deciding their further action if there were an incident or if force were used'. The Americans, starting with the caveat that the opinions expressed were 'personal and not official', expressed the view that the Soviet Union would be unlikely to use force and would certainly advocate a cautious line. Summarising the discussion, Dean highlighted the common agreement between both sides, concluding that possible Soviet assistance would be political rather than military.[173]

Unusually for the JIC a further meeting was held that afternoon, this time without any US participants. It focussed on discussing the paper on which the JIC had expressed 'concerns' that morning, on the nature of Soviet assistance to Egypt. In discussion, the Committee agreed certain assumptions, one of which was that 'the United States would not be hostile to our resort to force'.[174] The minutes do not explain how this judgment was reached, nor is there any reference to US comments expressed in the report of the morning meeting.

The JIC found it particularly difficult to judge intentions. In a section on the Israeli attitude towards the Suez dispute in the Weekly Review of Current Intelligence, the DNI informed the JIC that he understood that the report 'represented a compromise between conflicting viewpoints.' Instead, the JIC recommended the preparation of a note 'setting out the arguments on either side', and if still unable to reach a consensus, then the JIC itself would decide. Another development concerned the draft of a JIC assessment, which would become JIC(56)98: 'Possible Soviet Assistance to Egypt's Military Effort in Certain Circumstances'.[175] In discussion, the Committee felt that not only was the original title misleading ('Possible Soviet Assistance to Egypt in Certain Conditions'), but that the report was 'unduly pessimistic' and needed additional work, primarily to justify its conclusions and add more detail on Soviet motives.[176] This reveals that the JIC was as much concerned with strategic topics as with points of detail. It also underlines the principle that assessments were the product of consensus, and that all members had to agree to the conclusions for reports disseminated in the JIC's name.

While military and covert planning continued, a diplomatic solution was sought. Robert Menzies, in his attempt to persuade Nasser to agree to an international board to supervise the Suez Canal, was rejected by a stern and unyielding Egyptian president and the mission ended in failure. At Dulles' instigation, a further conference was convened in mid-September in London which, after much acrimonious discussion, resulted in the formation of the Suez Canal Users' Association (SCUA), to deal with the Canal's financial and administrative matters. Ultimately SCUA, too, would fail to resolve matters. In late September, the UK and France took the dispute to the UN's Security Council, where agreement was reached in early October on 'six principles', which, it was hoped, would ensure that any potential dispute would be resolved and the Canal stay open. Yet despite most sides agreeing to the detail of the 'six principles', efforts stalled because there was no consensus on how they would be administered or implemented.

In the US, President Eisenhower was preoccupied with campaigning for re-election in November. Throughout the summer of 1956, in a series of personal letters to Eden, he had maintained that he would not support the use of force to remove Nasser. Dulles' position was less clear and was regarded by the UK as inconsistent. Whilst at one point making it explicit to his British counterparts that he would not entertain military intervention, at the same time Dulles frequently hinted that Nasser was a menace who needed to be removed and, if force was the only option, then it would have to be the employed.[177]

The JIC was operating in relative isolation from the core decision-making process. In addition to its tactical input into military planning, it continued to produce and approve relevant strategic assessments on Suez. One of these, a hypothetical exercise, considered Nasser's options for future action if the Suez crisis turned out 'satisfactorily' for him. The impetus had come from the JIC itself; a revealing example of where the Committee tried to cover any possible eventuality by producing assessments examining alternative scenarios.[178] The conclusions, however, were not encouraging and provided the bleakest assessment to date: Nasser would increasingly have to rely on Soviet economic aid. This assistance would become intertwined with political interference and Nasser would have to remove the last remaining foreign involvement in Egypt, underpinned by nationalising the oil industry. He would encourage other Middle Eastern states to terminate contracts with Western powers and, finally, attempt 'by subversion' to 'remove or reduce British influence'.[179] The implication of this depressing scenario was that Nasser had to be replaced to prevent it becoming fact.

Another JIC paper, considering possible Soviet assistance, was finally approved after numerous revisions in late October 1956. The JIC's earlier assumption in late September, that the US 'would not be hostile to our resort to force', was now amended. In a handwritten correction it now read: 'the United States will adopt a strictly neutral attitude towards the operation'. At the instigation of the Committee as a whole, in late October, the wording was altered 'to make the assumption more realistic'.[180] Briefing the COS Committee, Geoffrey McDermott explained that 'admittedly the report had taken some time to prepare and the attitude of the United States had altered somewhat during that time'.[181] Despite the amended assumption on the US position the JIC's broader conclusions were explicit: the Soviet Union would wish to avoid direct conflict, though it would help 'as much as possible' in order to prove its 'dependability as an ally' to the rest of the world, and to cause as much embarrassment to the West as might be achieved.[182] What had caused the shift in the hypothesis about the US position between late September and late October?

Allies in Crisis

In late September the UK received a fillip, both in political and intelligence terms, brought about by indications from Washington that the US was now more supportive of, or at least less opposed to, a military conflict. Selwyn Lloyd had travelled to New York to discuss Suez at the UN and, while there, he met Dulles. Once more, discussion turned to the possible use of force. Commenting on Lloyd's reports, Eden summarised his feelings: 'we have been misled so often by Dulles' ideas that we cannot afford to risk another misunderstanding.'[183]

At this time Harold Macmillan, now Chancellor of the Exchequer, was in the US. He wrote to Eden to inform him about very private and personal talks he had had separately with Eisenhower and Dulles. 'Ike', Macmillan wrote, 'is really determined, somehow or another, to bring Nasser down'.[184] Similarly Dulles, who had sat down alone with Macmillan without his personal advisers, 'went on to talk about different methods of getting rid of Nasser . . . Dulles then observed that he quite realised that we might have to act by force'.[185] Macmillan's impression was that this was a positive and supportive private message from Washington, even if the public presentation was more ambivalent.[186]

In both letters Macmillan emphasised the importance of the Republican campaigning and how 'Dulles said that at present Suez was not playing much part in the election . . . but if anything happened it might have a disastrous effect'.[187] Crucially, neither Eisenhower nor Dulles was advocating imminent action, with the implication that the election needed to be over before anything should take place. But this obvious proviso was seemingly overlooked by Eden and his

advisers. The outgoing British Ambassador, Sir Roger Makins, informed the
Foreign Secretary that:

> Our relationship with the Americans in this crisis is following the pattern
> which has appeared on previous occasions and which is becoming more and
> more marked. We agree about the substance of the policy, but differ on
> method and timing. We press for immediate action while the Americans are
> inclined to move with greater phlegm and deliberations. This is the opposite
> of what our natural temperaments are supposed to be.[188]

At the same time as Dean was guiding the JIC production process at a particularly
busy time, he was being asked to give policy advice on what should be done as a
result of the assessments. Thus, on 25 September he attended a meeting at the
FO, together with representatives from other sections of the FO and SIS, to
discuss a forthcoming visit to the United States to create a special 'Working
Group'. The idea for such a meeting had been approved by both Dulles and Lloyd
during their talks in New York, but its significance has been underplayed by
historians.[189]

The visit took place against the backdrop of yet another of Dulles' contradictory
statements, where he had argued that Nasser should be removed within six
months, citing a desire to 'take advantage of it [i.e. Nasser's removal]'. The UK
contingent was to comprise Dean, William Armstrong (Treasury) and Francis
Murray (FO), as well as George Kennedy Young, the deputy chief of SIS.[190] The
objective of the visit – to the CIA and the State Department – was clear: 'the talks
should concentrate on getting rid of Nasser and should not get side-tracked into
discussion of reducing his influence, which although important is for this purpose
subsidiary'. Related to this was to try and get 'an open American denunciation of
Nasser'.[191]

Whilst discussions were therefore to focus on removing Nasser, the use of force
was to be barely mentioned. Instead, as Dean confirmed in a preparatory note to
Selwyn Lloyd, the 'best hope' lay in political or economic measures, with a coup
being the preferred option.[192] Having discussed his intentions with Lloyd, Dean
added a further note to the effect that 'it was agreed that some of the issues',
specifically a possible use of force, 'raised very difficult problems'. At the end of
the discussion Dean, together with 'C', went to see Field Marshal Sir Gerald
Templer, the CIGS, to speak to him 'very privately' and explain 'the present
situation'. Templer, who would have known all about the military plans and
discussions for intervention, suggested that a 'diversion – whether British, Israel or
other' might be useful to draw the Egyptian army away from Cairo to leave the
path open for the coup plotters to topple Nasser.[193] Meanwhile British military
forces could not be kept waiting for long.

The UK contingent flew to Washington, to be joined by two members of the
Embassy staff, John Coulson and Willie Morris.[194] At the outset of their first
meeting with the US on 1 October, the head of the US delegation, William
Rountree, the Assistant Secretary of State for Near East Affairs, described 'the

objective as creating a situation which would lead to the unseating of Nasser as soon as possible through actions of an economic and political character rather than by force'. Dean, the head of the UK delegation, '. . . agreed. He described the objective as to "disembarrass" ourselves of Nasser'. The talks themselves were 'ad referendum', conclusions needing political approval. An exchange part-way through the first meeting clarified the essence and difficulties of the British position:

> Mr Dean replied that he assumed it was not possible to negotiate with Nasser. He stated he could not conceive of the United Kingdom relaxing its various restrictions until an agreement was cut and dried. Mr Rountree inquired whether the United Kingdom objective was (1) to get rid of Nasser or (2) to bring about a situation where it was possible to get a settlement of the Suez Canal question. Mr Dean said that the mission of the present group was to devise means of getting rid of Nasser. Mr Rountree asked whether this was another way of saying that the British were not really seeking a negotiated settlement with Egypt. After consulting with Mr Coulson, Mr Dean replied that if it looked as if real negotiations were possible, it would be up to "our masters" to decide whether they wished to proceed with the programme being developed by the present group.[195]

The two teams met again on 2 October and the following day, and both leaders, Rountree and Dean, expressed satisfaction with the agreed proposals. As Selwyn Lloyd was still in New York for the UN Security Council discussions on Suez, Dean was able to inform him that both sides agreed on the principle of removing Nasser, yet at the same time conceded that 'at present [the Americans] were unwilling to commit themselves too far about ways, means and timing'. Crucially, though, there was no mention of the use of force as a possible method.[196] Lloyd himself was also happy with the report, cabling back to Sir Norman Brook in London that 'the report seems satisfactory' and that Dean's 'party did very well in the short time they were in Washington'.[197]

Brook, as instructed by Lloyd, passed the report to Eden, who was not impressed. One of his Private Secretaries informed Brook's Private Secretary that 'he did not have time to do more than glance at the enclosure and at first sight it did not seem to him likely that much would result'.[198] Dean informed Kirkpatrick in a remarkably accurate and candid assessment, that the report 'will probably be thought by the Prime Minister to be too slow moving. The truth is that, although Nasser's collapse may be brought about quite suddenly, it is far more likely that it will take a long time'.[199]

In Washington, the report was passed to Dulles for approval. His response, typically, was contradictory. He immediately asked for the first two paragraphs of the report – outlining the importance of the removal of Nasser – be expunged, not because they were incorrect or that the US disagreed, but rather because 'they are too explosive to have on paper'.[200] Dulles' objection was raised in more detail by Coulson, who informed the FO that Dulles 'had, of course, fully recognised the dangerous effects of Nasser's policy and the need to get rid of him, but the statement of our objectives in these terms might be held to commit the United States Government to Nasser's removal by any means, e.g. assassination. He did not think that the President would agree to this'.[201] In commenting on these discussions to Lloyd, Dean accepted that whilst 'Dulles' reply is satisfactory', it suggested that 'Dulles is beginning to hedge a bit on this'. Furthermore, given that 'Dulles himself in this case suggested a Working Party and a full report, he now seems to jib at being asked to stand by his own words. In the circumstances it seems better not to withdraw the request but to allow it to go forward to the President. It will be interesting to see what his reaction is.'[202]

In Washington, too, Lloyd tried to argue for keeping the two paragraphs intact. 'To delete these paragraphs', Dulles was informed, 'leaves the paper without any statement of our aim'.[203] In response, Dulles wrote that the two paragraphs should not be adopted because they 'constitute a political decision' and were, therefore 'incomplete'.[204] Along with this failure to reach agreement on a form of words, a further issue arose over whether the document constituted an agreed UK-US position as an alternative to the use of force. Once more Dulles objected. He communicated this through Rountree to Coulson arguing that, as it currently stood, the wording did not satisfactorily explain the US position. For Coulson, as he told Dean, the US stance was clear:

(a)   they agree that Nasser must go
(b)   they agree to the programme for his removal by peaceful means
(c)   they are not prepared to be <u>committed</u> to his removal by forcible means.

For these reasons any document formally recording (a) must be qualified by (c).[205]

A final telegram came from Dean. Writing to Lloyd on 22 October 1956, Dean advocated that the two offending paragraphs now be removed in their entirety. Off the record talks with the US had confirmed to him that 'the Americans are ready to work for the removal of Nasser but are terrified of saying so on paper . . . there is sufficient confirmation in the subsequent conversations to prevent any serious back-sliding later on by the Americans'.[206] By this point, however, planning in Europe had started to run away.

Re-Enter the French

In London the JIC, unaware of Dean's activities abroad, continued to study Suez on a broad front.[207] Between late September and mid-October papers were issued on: Nasser's possible future courses of action if the Suez dispute was settled on terms favourable to him; the Israeli attitude towards Arab States; and a larger study on the threats to UK interests worldwide.[208] By mid-October the pace of events was beginning to outstrip the speed of response. The US, the UN and some parts of the Commonwealth were urging restraint; at the same time the French and a sizeable number of politicians at home were demanding action.

Large sections of the British public, too, felt aggrieved over Egypt's actions. Despite the practical difficulties and financial cost of maintaining military personnel at a state of readiness in the region, the Prime Minister remained committed to destroying Nasser. As Macmillan wrote in his diary, 'the Suez situation is beginning to slip out of our hands'.[209] The JIC's assessments were almost certainly being ignored by the politicians. The military, however, continued to rely upon them.[210] A JIC paper in early October concluded that 'Nasser will probably not feel strong enough to attack Israel' in the short term, and that 'Soviet influence will probably attempt to restrain Nasser from such an attack'.[211] A further report prepared at the same time, concluded that 'the Russians would stop short of any action which might precipitate American intervention'.[212]

A crucial JIC assessment was issued in mid-October on the threat to UK interests overseas, geared towards a more political than military audience, despite having been authorised by the COS Committee.[213] This report, written at the height of the escalating crisis, examined how an unsuccessful resolution would affect a range of countries and regions of the world. In the Middle East it would have a direct impact but, further afield in Asia and Africa, the consequences would be felt no less severely. The JIC's conclusion was unequivocal:

> it should be emphasised that any concessions made by the United Kingdom under pressure are likely to have repercussions throughout the world, encouraging further claims and exacerbating potential points of friction. Conversely, a successful demonstration of resolution and firmness by the United Kingdom would have the effect of discouraging similar pressure throughout the world.[214]

There is no evidence that this assessment had any impact on decision making.

France had offered military assistance in the aftermath of Nasser's nationalisation of the Suez Canal, and Mollet, as Prime Minister, had asked to be involved with planning. On Sunday 14 October 1956, Eden had been joined at Chequers by two French visitors: Albert Gazier (the acting Foreign Minister) and General Maurice Challe (Deputy Chief of the Air Staff). One of the major points of attention was the role of Israel. Israel was not directly involved in negotiations, but its attitudes had been a cause of concern throughout.

The UK had maintained a constant interest in Arab-Israeli affairs through the 1948 Anglo-Jordanian treaty, under which the UK had promised to come to Jordan's aid in the event of an attack. The State of Israel had also been created in 1948. In mid-1953 the JIC had reported that 'we could rely on Israel's moral support for any measures we took to maintain our position in Egypt. Although she would like to exploit the opportunity of expanding at Egypt's expense we doubt whether she would in fact decide to do so'.[215] A similar conclusion was reached by Geoffrey McDermott in late September 1956: 'although she would like nothing better than to be invited to assist us in military operations against Egypt, we doubt if Israel will force her assistance upon us'.[216] A JIC assessment the previous day had concluded that 'of all the Arab countries Egypt is potentially the most dangerous to Israel . . . Israel would like to associate herself with the Western Powers in any action against Egypt'.[217] While this might be read as JIC support for joint action with Israel, the issue in mid-October had been the increasing raids by Israel on Jordan which, as noted, the UK was obligated to defend.

The two Frenchmen at Chequers that weekend warned Eden that the Israelis needed to be brought under control. At the meeting Challe proposed an outline of a solution. If Israel was encouraged to attack Egypt, then the UK and France could advise both sides to withdraw, offering to send in a security force to keep the peace. The Suez Canal area could then be re-taken and occupied. An aggrieved Egypt would attack and the UK would have a legitimate reason to respond in kind. Eden was clearly attracted to the idea, though he was non-committal. A few days later the Israelis were invited to Paris to discuss the concept in more detail with British and French representatives.

Patrick Dean knew nothing about the talks at the time and did not find out about them for another week.[218] Nonetheless, Selwyn Lloyd returned home quickly from the UN in New York to have a meeting with the French. On 18 October, the date of the JIC report on the benefits of a successful resolution of matters with Egypt, Eden informed Cabinet colleagues that 'there were signs that Israel might be preparing to make some military move' and that this would be directed towards Egypt. 'The Cabinet', Eden continued,

> should therefore be aware that, while we continued to seek an agreed settlement of the Suez dispute in pursuance of a resolution of the Security Council, it was possible that the issue might be brought more rapidly to a head as a result of military action by Israel against Egypt.[219]

There was no information on what the 'signs' were (certainly not from JIC assessments) or how Eden was so attuned to Israeli intentions. The UK's plans for Egypt were crystallising and collusion between the UK, Israel and France to engineer a war with Egypt was underway.

Discussions held in a villa in Sèvres, a suburb of Paris, were at the centre of the planning process. Following Eden's statement to the Cabinet on 18 October there had been a flurry of behind the scenes visits to discuss the Anglo-French-Israeli plans for action. Officially no minutes were taken or records kept of the meetings in France but details were recorded, which eventually became public knowledge. The first meeting in Sèvres was held on Monday 22 October 1956 and was attended by Lloyd and Donald Logan, Lloyd's Assistant Private Secretary. On the way to the meeting from the airport, Lloyd and Logan's car narrowly missed another car at a cross-road, an event which, according to Logan, set 'me thinking how the secrecy of our mission could be preserved if at the next turning we were less lucky'.[220]

Meeting the two-man UK contingent were a number of senior figures from France and Israel, including their Prime Ministers and Defence Ministers. Talks on tactics for action started at 1600 and continued until midnight when the UK delegation left for London. Lloyd refused to approve any plans without the agreement of the Cabinet and by mid-morning the following day, Logan was once more despatched to Paris to inform the French and Israelis that no decision would be reached that day. The same morning, Eden informed his Cabinet colleagues that since his last reference to Suez, six days earlier, 'secret conversations had been held in Paris with representatives of the Israeli Government', and that given that the Israelis were unlikely to act alone, the UK was faced with 'the choice between an early military operation or a relatively prolonged negotiation'.[221] The Cabinet agreed to meet the following day to resume discussions.

Dean did not produce any memoirs and kept no private papers or diaries.[222] The Dean family were, however, close friends with Chester Cooper's family, and Cooper did keep records. On the evening of 24 October Dean was to host a dinner party at his central London mansion flat. Those invited were Cooper; Frank Wisner, the head of the CIA's Directorate of Plans; and Admiral Harvey Overesch, from the US Embassy in London. On arrival, as Cooper recorded, 'the guests were greeted by Mrs Dean – sans husband. "Pat has been called away suddenly", she said. She was a charming substitute for the absent host, but was unable to dispel the air of mystery that surrounded her husband's whereabouts'.[223]

The 'absent host' had, in the small hours of that morning, been called by Sir Norman Brook, the Cabinet Secretary, to see the Prime Minister urgently. Brook stressed the secrecy of his call and the reason. Dean was to go to Paris, avoiding using the FO's travel section. At 0830 on the morning of 24 October Dean arrived at 10 Downing Street and was ushered into Eden's bedroom where, for the next twenty minutes, from the comfort of his bed, Eden informed him of the continuing secret discussions.[224] There are no official documents to confirm that this was the first that Dean heard of the Anglo-Israeli-French plans, but this thesis is supported by Logan and Dean's wife.

Dean was to be despatched immediately to Paris by private military aircraft. He had time to see the PUS at the FO, whom he described as 'very depressed and in a bad temper'. Dean told Kirkpatrick about his mission, but 'he displayed very little interest and it became clear to me that he was not enthusiastic about Sir A.Eden's ideas'. Dean's wife has recalled just how unhappy he was about being asked to go to Paris. Before visiting Kirkpatrick, she reminisced, Dean complained bitterly, saying that he did not want to go. Kirkpatrick's instruction, as Dean later recalled, was 'that as the Prime Minister had charged me with undertaking this mission I must carry it out'. Dean's unease over the assignment would only intensify as his role became more widely known.[225]

Accompanying Dean to the meeting in Paris that afternoon was, once more, Donald Logan. Dean received no written instructions from Eden, only the advice that he should emphasise the UK point of view and ensure that he and Logan were content with the outcome. On the short flight to Paris Logan informed Dean, for the first time, that this group had already met two days earlier. Joining the French and Israeli parties at 1600, it was obvious to Dean that considerable time had been spent already discussing the subject, the meeting concentrated on detailed military planning of the operation. 'After a brief suspension', Dean wrote, 'a paper was suddenly produced from the next room where it had apparently been very recently typed'. The short document, subsequently known as the Sèvres Protocol, contained the plan of action.

Logan and Dean had thought, as had been the case two days earlier, that all discussions were to be oral with nothing put in writing. They were, therefore, somewhat surprised to see the document, especially when they were asked to sign it, though Logan has recalled that its 'contents caused us no surprise'.[226] Dean, as the senior of the two man British party, put his signature on the paper and initialled each page. Importantly, as both Dean and Logan subsequently emphasised, the signature did not represent approval of the paper, but rather confirmed that it was an accurate record of what had been discussed at the meeting; thus it was signed ad referendum. This is a crucial point, yet its significance would be lost on Eden.

Leaving Paris, Dean and Logan flew back to London that night. 'In the air', as Logan recalled, 'the stars shone as brightly as I have ever seen them. It seemed wholly incongruous.'[227] They arrived in Downing Street at about 2230. Some secondary accounts have stated that Eden flew into a rage at the news that Dean had signed the protocol, instructing both diplomats to return immediately to Paris and destroy all copies of the document. By contrast, Dean's recollection was that although Eden was not happy at such a record being signed, he apologised for having put Dean in such an awkward position. Yet, the next morning, 25 October, Dean and Logan were instructed to return to Paris and obtain and destroy all copies. But the Israelis had already departed, safely clutching their copy; Dean and Logan were locked in a room in the Quai D'Orsay for four hours while the French discussed what to do, and eventually decided to keep their version.[228]

Dean and Logan were in an unenviable position. By following Eden's instructions, confirmed by the PUS, both knew that the UK was committed to a deception plan to draw Egypt into war, but neither could inform their colleagues or change what had now been agreed. The JIC, for instance, was never asked to provide relevant intelligence for planning, despite Dean's foreknowledge. Dean, in particular, has taken the brunt of the criticism for his participation in Sèvres. His wife has said that he remained 'upset', 'distressed', and 'unhappy' about his role. He was particularly distraught because some FO colleagues never quite trusted him again.[229]

By signing the document Dean was simply following Eden's instructions yet, as Sir Guy Millard has said, although he had been put in a 'difficult position' it was 'naïve' of a seasoned diplomat and former barrister to have put his signature to it.[230] Both Dean and Logan have recorded the suspicious mood that characterised the proceedings, noting particularly that the French and Israelis did not entirely trust the UK, so Dean's signature could be seen as a gesture of reassurance and support.

In the UK no copy of the Sèvres protocol existed, even though France and Israel held versions.[231] In the late 1970s the then Cabinet Secretary Sir John Hunt, who had been Sir Norman Brook's Private Secretary during Suez, asked

Patrick Dean to produce his own account of what had happened at Sèvres, including the circumstances surrounding the protocol itself. Commenting on it, Hunt noted that 'my understanding was that he had behaved entirely honourably and properly over Suez, but a hostile reader of the note could derive a different impression'. The issue, as Hunt continued, was why, 'if the document was innocent', was Dean instructed to go back and destroy it?[232]

War and a Storm Cloud over the Atlantic

On the day that Patrick Dean and Donald Logan flew back to Paris in their doomed attempt to round up all the copies of the Sèvres Protocol, the Cabinet met, once more, to discuss Suez. Introducing the topic, the Prime Minister outlined how it now appeared likely that Israel would attack Egypt, and suggested that if Israel did so, both sides would be given twelve hours to cease fire and withdraw to a distance of ten miles from the Canal. Failing that, UK and French forces would 'intervene in order to enforce compliance'. After some discussion the Cabinet agreed. Crucially, however, no mention was made of the discussions in Paris, and the decision already taken behind the scenes was not revealed.[233]

Unaware of these developments, the JIC met that same morning, albeit in the absence of its normal chairman. Although there is no record in the minutes to explain this, we now know that he had returned to France. Geoffrey McDermott was in attendance but, as Dean later made clear, he had not informed him why he would be away.[234] Although Suez was not specifically addressed at the JIC meeting, it was raised in the discussion of the Weekly Survey of Intelligence. The conclusion was made in ignorance of events elsewhere: 'tension over the Suez Canal crisis has somewhat diminished . . . there have been no further reports of Israeli mobilisation or other military preparations'.[235]

The JIC also discussed other pressing topics. In late September, the Committee had instructed the JIS: 'inviting the Heads of Sections to note that, although the Suez crisis was dominating the world scene at the present time, the fact should not be overlooked that serious trouble could break out in other parts of the world'.[236] While the Cabinet was deciding to go to war, and while military commanders geared up for conflict, the JIC was also heavily involved with monitoring the continuing protests in Poland and the violent suppression of demonstrations in Hungary (see chapter 9).

The JIC was not neglecting Suez, but it also had to deal with events elsewhere. On Monday 29 October when Israel attacked Egypt, the JIC was immediately involved. It began to produce daily summaries on events in Egypt, issuing a 'situation report' five times daily and a specially produced daily précis for the Queen and Prime Minister.[237] The JIC also installed and maintained, around the clock, a 'Joint Intelligence Room', with the Directors of Intelligence meeting daily, including at weekends.[238] In addition, JIC(ME) produced detailed, tactical summaries which were issued daily,[239] and a bi-weekly, more operationally-focussed review.[240] The JIC did not produce any strategic papers, concentrating on providing the tactical intelligence picture instead.

On 30 October, the day after the Israeli attack, the Cabinet formally authorised its plan to act as 'peacemaker'; the French government did likewise. That same day the US formally admonished the UK and, encouraged by the news, the Egyptians rejected the Anglo-French plan. Despite protests from Washington, overnight on 31 October/1 November, UK and French aircraft began bombing targets in Egypt. Further criticism ensued. The US weighed in and, during a speech at the UN on 2 November, Dulles reprimanded the UK. The Leader of the Opposition, Hugh Gaitskell, informed Eden that the Labour Party unequivocally condemned the military intervention.

By 4 November, in addition to the growing international condemnation, the military operations were not going well. Despite the combined air attack, Nasser's military position had not weakened, and the Suez Canal itself had been blocked by ships that had been deliberately scuttled. Domestically, some of Eden's colleagues were also expressing misgivings about the enterprise, particularly the imminent start of airborne landings. By 5 November British and French paratroopers had seized approximately a third of the length of the Canal but, by midnight, Eden and senior colleagues decided that a ceasefire was now in order and so, at midnight on 6 November, the invasion was halted.

Even if the US had maintained a relatively consistent stance against the use of force, there had been vacillating views, at the Executive level, about the removal of Nasser. At the UN, the UK was castigated for its actions. Eden and Lloyd were criticised personally by their US counterparts and an ultimatum issued, which if ignored, would inflict serious economic damage on the UK. Despite all efforts to keep collusion plans secret, the US had found out. As Admiral Sir Michael Denny, the Chairman of the UK Joint Services Mission in Washington, told the Minister of Defence, Antony Head, following a discussion with a senior US Representative to NATO, 'Leon Johnson then stated that US Government was in possession of a piece of intelligence of highest possible reliability and factual exactness which established that the Anglo-French move was done in concert with and in accord with Israeli Government'.[241] As a consequence, the US had informed the Chancellor, Harold Macmillan, that unless a ceasefire was signed, it would call a halt to economic assistance to the UK.

A major concern arising from the intervention in Egypt was the reaction of the Soviet Union, and its impact on Anglo-American relations. Soviet support and assistance for Egypt had become a second order issue, although the JIC had continued to monitor it. It had judged that the Soviet Union would try to drive a wedge between the Western allies whilst exploiting local political opportunities. With Soviet intervention in Hungary now underway, the Soviet leaders, Khrushchev and Bulganin, turned their attention to Suez. On the morning of 6 November, the day of the US Presidential election, Eden received a message from Bulganin, chilling in its tone, which stated that:

> ... there is no justification for the fact that the armed forces of Britain and France, two Great Powers that are permanent members of the Security Council, have attacked a country which only recently acquired national

independence and which does not possess adequate means for self-defence. In what situation would Britain find herself if she were attacked by stronger states, possessing all types of modern destructive weapons? . . . Were rocket weapons used against Britain and France you would, most probably, call this a barbarous action. But how does the inhuman attack launched by the armed forces of Britain and France against a practically defenceless Egypt differ from this? . . . We are fully determined to crush the aggressors by the use of force and to restore peace in the East.[242]

Similar letters were delivered to the French and Israeli leaders, with a note to President Eisenhower requesting that the Soviet Union and US act together as arbiters. Eisenhower's response was swift and sharp. He rejected Soviet overtures as an attempt to detract attention from the violence in Hungary. The French appeared to be worried by the Soviet note whereas Eden was seemingly unconcerned.[243]

Despite what was, in effect, a threat from Moscow, there is no evidence that the JIC was asked to consider it specifically, or that it did so on its own initiative. The Committee did, however, address what Patrick Dean described as a 'concerning' number of 'unconfirmed reports' of Soviet military reinforcements in the region. Dean's aim was to prevent 'unconfirmed and inaccurate intelligence reports' being widely circulated, thus ensuring that they 'should not give rise to undue alarm'.[244]

JIC(ME) concluded that the Soviet aim of improving its position in the Middle East would involve sustaining Nasser, providing him with increased arms, and encouraging neighbouring countries to unite against Israel and the West.[245] The JIC's Heads of Sections initially agreed,[246] as did the JIC itself, which called it 'part of the "Trojan Horse" technique'.[247] The JIC did not think that the Soviet Union would take any 'drastic action single handed' on the grounds that it would wish to avoid war.[248] JIC(ME) revised its view over the likelihood of Soviet assistance, a judgment adopted by the JIC in London.[249]

As reports of Soviet military movement continued to be received, the JIC convened a special meeting on a Sunday morning in mid-November specifically to address them.[250] Other reports suggested that the 'Arabs' expected 'unspecified' large-scale attacks on Anglo-French 'interests' in mid-November.[251] General Keightley, the commander of British forces, was given instructions on how to respond if such an attack materialised.[252] The JIC discounted these reports, correctly as it transpired.[253]

In seeking to identify signs of Soviet assistance to Nasser, the JIC saw a potential route to repair strained relations with the US. Patrick Dean told the Committee that 'he thought it was important that every effort should be made to find evidence to give to the United States that proved Nasser was a tool of the Soviets.' In turn, 'the Committee agreed and invited Departments to see what fresh evidence they could find'.[254] The impetus for this was contained in a top secret note from Dean to senior members of the FO circulated the same day. Dean noted that a US contact had told him 'last night in great confidence that he thought we should be doing all we could to produce evidence to show that Nasser was a Russian tool and that support for Nasser meant support for the Communists'. The problem, though, was the lack of any such intelligence: 'I think this should be looked at urgently. I do not think that intelligence sources can produce much more than they already have done, but we will certainly see what can be done on that side.'[255]

The JIC's assessment of Soviet designs in the Middle East took just two days to prepare and approve, such was the priority and importance accorded to it. The JIC had concluded that whilst Nasser would 'remain the principal instrument of Soviet policy in the Middle East', the Soviet Union would also try to 'win Arab sympathies' in a number of other countries.[256] To help convince both the US and opinion in the Middle East of the gravity of the situation, a public campaign was instigated. A message from PUSD to UK embassies in the Middle East reported that: 'the London press is devoting much attention to the Soviet supplies of arms to the Middle East. For your own information, this is the result of information supplied by us.' Diplomats were to attempt to convince Middle Eastern governments that Nasser was merely 'an instrument in the achievement of their [Soviet] ends in the Middle East'.[257] To achieve further support, as Dean informed the COS Committee, the contents of the JIC's assessment on 'Soviet designs in the Middle East' had been deliberately leaked to the press,[258] with the intention that it should receive 'wide publicity'.[259]

Behind the scenes however, senior figures were less convinced about the existence of aggressive Soviet plans for the region. Sir Ivone Kirkpatrick, for instance, informed his Ambassador in Paris that 'there is an appreciable element of bluff in the Russian attitude', and that they would 'do nothing serious without United Nations cover'.[260] Similarly, the specialists in the Soviet Section of the FO Research Department, concluded that 'Nasser is not irrevocably committed to the Russians'.[261]

In some quarters these British efforts were seen as a propaganda ploy.[262] But more positive messages were emerging from the CIA. The new British Ambassador in Washington and former JIC Chairman, Sir Harold Caccia, informed Dean that a recent meeting at which CIA head 'Allen Dulles could not have been more cordial . . . Dulles' willingness to continue to cooperate with us on the intelligence side is the first indication of its kind that there has been in day to day business here so far'.[263]

Post-Mortem

By December Anglo-American intelligence relations were as strong as they had been before the crisis. In many ways business continued as if nothing had happened and the plot to unseat Nasser was back up and running. One US official informed the FO that 'it still remained the policy of the US Government to get rid of Nasser'.[264] Furthermore, JIC(W) reported to London that 'collaboration' with US intelligence had been 'in no way adversely affected . . . . there has, on the contrary, been considerable evidence that the American intelligence community as a whole are anxious to reassure the UK representatives that from their standpoint the value of cooperation with the United Kingdom is permanent, whereas the recent political divergence is essentially temporary.'[265]

Henry Hainworth, the outgoing Chairman of JIC(ME), which had moved to Nicosia in Cyprus, had tried to conduct a post-mortem into intelligence and Operation MUSKETEER, with the objective of learning lessons for the future. The biggest error, in his opinion, was that the intelligence effort was isolated from the military and planning personnel, with the effect that current and forward-looking assessments were produced without any knowledge of UK plans. Furthermore, given the scale and breadth of MUSKETEER, the size of the Middle Eastern intelligence staff was far too small. Hainworth's report was despatched to London but there is no record of a reaction.[266] JIC(ME) also produced a review of its performance during the crisis, which identified flaws in the links between intelligence and policy, and in the analysis of tactical intelligence.[267]

The correspondence shows that Patrick Dean took a keen interest in such reviews, and he was certainly enthusiastic about conducting one in London. His rationale was clear: 'there is no reason why we should not profit from mistakes so we do things better next time'. Ultimately, though, this did not happen as MUSKETEER was considered to have been conducted under 'peculiar circumstances' and, as the JIC Secretary informed Dean, an inquest 'would be profitless, the more so since . . . the official reports are to be suppressed'.[268] Instead the JIC's operational procedures were tightened up, focussing on the 'machinery for converting the peacetime intelligence organisation into the wartime organisation'.[269]

A more immediate problem was the enforced removal, in the wake of the invasion, of a number of diplomatic missions in the region. The impact on defence attachés was of particular concern, as was the shortage of military attachés, as they had been responsible for undertaking valuable intelligence collection activities, and their withdrawal was therefore viewed with some regret. The JIC was instructed to review what might be done to remedy this new deficiency.[270] The solution was to make more use of defence sections in neighbouring countries and to ask 'friendly foreign countries' to help.[271]

On 22 December 1956 the last of the British and French troops withdrew from Egypt. British military involvement in the Middle East was, however, far from over: covert planning had already begun for operations in Syria, codenamed Operation STRAGGLE.[272] The JIC continued to monitor the situation in Egypt, particularly the strength and stability of Nasser and, more widely, the scale and nature of Soviet interest in the Middle East. For Eden, Suez marked the beginning of the end. His health problems grew worse and there was widespread criticism of his leadership. He resigned in January 1957. His successor, Harold Macmillan, accelerated the process of de-colonisation. Internationally reactions were varied. The crisis led to the deterioration of the UK's relations with France whilst, at the same time, the special relationship with the US was rebuilt.

Long after the event, in 1978, the prominent journalist and former Director-General of the BBC, Sir Hugh Greene, wrote a letter to *The Times* newspaper, reflecting a conversation he had had with a former Cabinet Secretary about Suez: 'I remarked that one day presumably the whole truth would emerge. "Damned good care" replied Lord Normanbrook, "has been taken to see that the whole truth never does emerge".'[273] Certainly there remain significant gaps in the records kept of the Suez crisis, notably on the timing of when, and how much, senior individuals were made aware of the collusion plans.

Historically, Patrick Dean has been singled out for criticism of his role during Suez, particularly his involvement in the discussions and signing of the Sèvres protocol, though one analysis of his role rightly concludes, 'this memory of Dean is misleading'.[274] Whilst he enjoyed a successful FO career, culminating as Ambassador to the US, Dean forever regretted his involvement with the Sèvres meeting and thought that it had prevented his promotion to PUS, the top seat in the FO.[275] Dean had been involved in operational planning as well as intelligence and assessment. Yet he remained ignorant of Eden's real plans until the final moment when he had no option but to follow the instructions of the Prime Minister, to which he was seemingly privately opposed. Dean's role reveals the multi-faceted aspect of his position as JIC Chairman and how he had to cope with the tasks undertaken for the FO and the Prime Minister at the same time. It illustrates the difficulty of combining the roles of policy advice and intelligence assessment, something that future JIC Chairmen would also be expected to do.

For the JIC, Suez was an example of how the Committee could produce good strategic forecasts yet be widely ignored by key customers. Its tactical role – providing up to date military assessment and security arrangements – was fulfilled admirably but barely acknowledged. The JIC recognised that military action against Nasser was highly likely, but the potential Israeli involvement was hidden from the Committee as a whole. Although Dean and 'C' would have known about the covert plans, most JIC members would have remained ignorant of the wider political imperatives. Even when operational intelligence was obtained it often circumvented the JIC en route to the Prime Minister. The Committee was never intended to be the sole channel through which intelligence reports reached policy-makers, but it was important that the Chairman was aware of what reporting reached Ministers.

At the outset, events in Egypt were correctly interpreted as driven by anti-British and pro-nationalist, rather than communist-inspired. The Czech arms deal altered this perception as it instantly brought together several crucial themes: Egypt's need for arms; Nasser's acceptance of the Soviet Union as an ally; and hence an increased Soviet role in the region. But the relationship between Nasser and Moscow fluctuated, as did the JIC's assessment of it. By 1956, Egypt had come to be regarded, incorrectly, as yet another aspect of the global Cold War but, as we now know, Nasser was never a pawn of Moscow.

Suez also marked a difficult point in Anglo-American relations. In the US the CIA, State Department, and White House were more often than not at odds and, while there was more general agreement on rejecting the use of force to resolve the crisis, the message reaching London and the JIC was often confused and frequently misinterpreted. Assurances given by Dean on the nature of US support for removing Nasser were often taken as broader political endorsements, despite warnings from the British Ambassador, Roger Makins. Perhaps one of the biggest mistakes was to assume that, in a pre-election period, a US president would be prepared to stand aside and allow its closest ally to become involved in a war in such a key region. Yet despite political differences, Anglo-American relations, particularly between intelligence communities, recovered rapidly. Long term relationships were largely unaffected and, if anything, were to become closer.

The role of the JIC cannot be put accurately into context without consideration of the political, military and intelligence aspects of the Suez crisis. These provide clear evidence that senior politicians were intent on implementing a particular course of action, with the necessity to keep many senior individuals, including the JIC as a body, in the dark. There was a disconnect between the military, political and JIC's advice, with the JIC's accurate assessments based on intelligence reporting being disregarded. Finally, policymakers and intelligence analysts alike were unable to grasp fully the real motives and intentions of close allies, specifically the US. Taken together these points constitute an indictment of the working of the whole government machine. Taken together they proved to be catastrophic.

Notes

1 'Release of Records of the Suez Operation', 27 February 1986. FCO 12/180.
2 The description of Dean as Eden's 'special representative' comes from G.Jebb to A.Eden, 14 August 1956. PREM 11/1126.
3 CC(51)1, 30 October 1951. CAB 128/23.
4 JIC/2751/51, 'Purchase of Armaments by Egypt', 14 December 1951. CAB 158/74. The report stated that 'the trade and financial agreement signed with Czechoslovakia on 24 October 1951, incorporates a secret protocol which provides for the despatch of arms to Egypt. The Egyptian Minister of War has sent technical experts to Prague in connexion with the types of weapons to be supplied.'
5 See the JIC minutes for the second half of 1951. CAB 159/10.
6 JIC(51)135th Meeting, Perimeter Review, 13 December 1951. CAB 159/10.
7 JIC/911/52, 'Communism in Egypt', 4 April 1952. CAB 176/35.
8 R Ovendale, 'Egypt and the Suez Base Agreement', In J W Young (ed), *The Foreign Policy of Churchill's Peacetime Administration, 1951–1955* (Leicester: University of Leicester Press, 1988), pp.135–58.
9 JIC(52)81st Meeting, Perimeter Review, 24 July 1952. CAB 159/12.
10 Cairo to FO, 12 September 1952. PUSD Papers, FCO. Stevenson had dropped the 'Skrine' part of his name by this point.
11 JIC(ME)(52)-22(Final), 'Likely Political Development in Egypt in the Short Term', 20 May 1952. PUSD Papers, FCO.
12 JIC(52)83rd Meeting, 30 July 1952. CAB 159/12. The contribution by JIC(ME) to this enquiry can be found in JIC(ME)(52)-46(Final), 'The Egyptian Military Coup of 23rd July 1952', 6 September 1952. PUSD Papers, FCO.
13 C/2351, 'C' to Reilly, 19 August 1952. PUSD Papers, FCO.
14 For instance, see Anthony Eden's memorandum on how British interests might be affected: C(52)267, 'Suez Canal', 28 July 1952. CAB 129/54.
15 The paper, JIC(ME)(52)47(Final), is referred to in the JIC's minutes but has not been preserved. See JIC(52)101st Meeting, 17 September 1952. CAB 159/12.
16 JIC/2072/52, 'Situation in Egypt', 12 September 1952. PUSD Papers, FCO.

17 For instance, see the correspondence between the Prime Minister, Foreign Secretary and the military, to which Reilly was an addressee, in PREM 11/632.

18 The relevant report by the JIC's 'Evasion and Escape Sub-Committee' has not been preserved. It is referred to in JIC(52)120th Meeting, 31 October 1952. CAB 159/12. 'Evasion and Escape' in this context referred to downed aircraft, not the evacuation of British garrisons.

19 JIC/2171/52, 'Situation in Egypt: Future Developments', 24 September 1952. CAB 176/38.

20 JIC(52)132nd Meeting, Perimeter Review, 27 November 1952. CAB 159/12.

21 JIC(ME)(52)-63(Final), 'Assessment of the Situation in Egypt As At 30th November 1952', 30 November 1952. PUSD Papers, FCO.

22 JIC(ME)(52)-46(Final), 'The Egyptian Military Coup of 23rd July 1952', 6 September 1952. PUSD Papers, FCO.

23 JIC(52)139th Meeting, Perimeter Review, 11 December 1952. CAB 159/12.

24 JE1192/345/G. JIC(ME)(53)-38(Final), 'The Egyptian Situation', 18 May 1953. FO 371/102810.

25 JE1192/345/G. Note by W.Strang, 27 May 1953. FO 371/102810.

26 JE1192/345/G. Handwritten note by W.S.Churchill on the letter from W.Strang to the Prime Minister, 30 May 1953. FO 371/102810.

27 M Copeland, *The Game Player: Confessions of the CIA's Original Political Operative* (London: Aurum Press, 1989).

28 K Kyle, *Suez: Britain's End of Empire in the Middle East* (London: IB Tauris, 2003). pp.50–2.

29 JIC(54)19th Meeting, Perimeter Review, 4 March 1954. CAB 159/15.

30 JE1192/67. Makins to FO, 9 March 1954. FO 371/108415.

31 JIC(54)24th Meeting, Perimeter Review, 18 March 1954. CAB 159/15.

32 Chiefs of Staff to Air Chief Marshal Sir William Elliot, 27 January 1954. Cabinet Office papers.

33 'Notes on the Arab-Israel Dispute', 15 December 1954. FO 371/111095. The more detailed Alpha plan is in FO 371/115866. For an overview see N Caplan, *Futile Diplomacy, Volume Four: Operation Alpha and the Failure of Anglo-American Coercive Diplomacy in the Arab-Israeli Conflict, 1954–1956* (London: Frank Cass, 1997).

34 Eden's biographer is particularly good on this latter point: R R James, *Anthony Eden* (London: Weidenfeld & Nicolson, 1986).

35 N R Ashton, 'The Hijacking of a Pact: The Formation of the Baghdad Pact and Anglo-American Tensions in the Middle East, 1955–1958', *Review of International Studies* 19 (1993), pp.123–37.

36 H Macmillan, *The Tides of Fortune, 1945–1955* (London: Macmillan, 1969). p.634.

37 James, *Eden*. p.618.

38 This is Kyle's view, *Suez*. p.62.

39 JIC(55)20th Meeting, Review of Current Intelligence, 3 March 1955. CAB 159/18.

40 JIC(55)22nd Meeting, Review of Current Intelligence, 10 March 1955. CAB 159/18. However, this should not be read as meaning that the JIC held sympathetic views towards Israel.

41 JIC(54)57, 'Egyptian Arms Imports', 19 June 1954. CAB 158/17.

42 JIC(54)21st Meeting, Perimeter Review, 11 March 1954. CAB 159/15.

43 JIC/1253/54, 'Arms and Equipment Reported to Have Been Imported into Egypt', 26 May 1954. CAB 176/48.

44 JIC/2305/54, 'Egyptian Arms Imports', 15 September 1954. CAB 176/50.

45 JIC(54)64(Final)(Revise), 'Soviet Threat to the Middle East in a General War up to the End of 1959', 14 January 1955. CAB 158/18.

46 JIC(55)42(Final), 'Soviet Threat to the Middle East in a General War up to the End of 1959', 15 September 1955. CAB 158/21.

47 JIC(55)79th Meeting, 29 September 1955. CAB 159/21. For detail of the Israeli perspective, see O Leslau, 'Israeli Intelligence and the Czech-Egyptian Arms Deal', *Intelligence and National Security* 27: 3 (June 2012), pp.327–48.

48 JIC(55)80th Meeting, 6 October 1955. CAB 159/21.

49 JIC(55)80th Meeting, 6 October 1955. CAB 159/21.

50 'Policy in the Middle East', C.A.E.Shuckburgh [AUS in charge of the Middle East, FO], 14 October 1955. FO 800/669.

51 JIC/2758/55, 'Middle East Arms Purchases from the Soviet Bloc', 17 October 1955. CAB 158/79.

52 For instance, see JIC/2913/55, 'Arms Traffic in the Middle East', 3 November 1955. CAB 158/79.

53 JIC/3014/55, 'Arms Traffic in the Middle East', 16 November 1955. CAB 158/79. Subsequently, Switzerland decided not to supply any further arms. JIC/3142/55, 'Arms Traffic in the Middle East', 30 November 1955. CAB 158/79.

54 JIC/3302/55, 'Arms Traffic in the Middle East', 19 December 1955. CAB 158/79.

55 JIC(55)82nd Meeting, 13 October 1955. CAB 159/21.

56 JIC/3358/55, 'Egypt-Soviet Arms Deal', 29 December 1955. CAB 158/79.

57 C/3520. 'C' to P.H.Dean, 21 December 1955. PUSD Papers, FCO. In writing to Dean, 'C' provided three different CX reports, including, crucially, the comments by different departments upon their receipt – in hindsight the CX reporting was good, and the error was with the analysis by receiving departments.

58 JIC/3342/55, 'Egyptian Proficiency with New Soviet Arms', 21 December 1955. CAB 176/55.

59 'The Egyptian Arms Deal and Soviet Bloc Economic Penetration of the Middle East'. PUSD Papers, FCO.

60 For instance, see JIC(55)68(Final), 'Likely Israeli Course of Action and Scale of Attack in War with the Arab States in the Near Future', 9 November 1955. CAB 158/22.

61 JIC/2942/55, 'Review of Current Intelligence – Israel', 7 November 1955. CAB 176/55.

62 JIC/3006/55, 'The Likelihood of War Between Israel and the Arab States in the Near Future', 15th November 1955. CAB 176/55.

63 JIC(55)93rd Meeting, 1 December 1955. CAB 159/21.

64 JIC(56)9(Final)(Revise), 'The Economic Policy of the Sino Soviet Bloc in the Middle East and South and South East Asia in 1956–60 and its Impact on Western Interests', 12 January 1956. CAB 158/23. At the same time, discussion was also underway in Whitehall as to the relative importance of the economic, strategic and political elements of competing influences in the Middle East. See Kyle, *Suez*. pp.125–6.

65 JIC(56)10, 'Survey of World Communism in 1955', 20 April 1956. CAB 158/23.

66 JE1423/252. Makins to FO, 27 November 1955. FO 371/113738.

67 FO to Washington, 28 November 1955. PREM 11/2287.

68 Makins to FO, 30 November 1955. PREM 11/2287.

69 Note by A.M.Palliser [Kirkpatrick's Private Secretary], 1 December 1955. PREM 11/2287. The other FO members aside from Dean and Kirkpatrick were Evelyn Shuckburgh; Adam Watson (head of the African Department, FO), and a 'Mr Williams'. In an interview with Scott Lucas, Reilly states that, in addition to these codeword papers, 'Patrick Dean used to get every morning a small bunch of hyper-secret telegrams which were kept out of the normal Foreign Office distribution'. LHCMA: Suez Oral History Project: 'Interview with Sir Patrick Reilly conducted by W Scott Lucas'.

70 H.Macmillan to Prime Minister, 12 December 1955. PREM 11/2287.

71 Kyle, *Suez*. p.124.

72 Glubb's dismissal was portrayed by the press as a failing of the FO and the Foreign Secretary, Eden, in particular. See Kyle, *Suez*. pp.94–5.

73 JIC(56)24th Meeting, Review of Current Intelligence, 8 March 1956. CAB 159/22.

74 Lloyd to Eden, 2 March 1956. FO 371/121243.

75 Kyle, *Suez*. pp.93–4.

76 Makins to FO, 24 March 1956. PREM 11/1285.

77 Makins to FO, 25 March 1956. PUSD Papers, FCO.

78 Makins to FO, 29 March 1956. PUSD Papers, FCO.

79 Interview with Sir G.Millard, 29 September 2010.

80 Interview with J.Cloake, 11 November 2010.

81 Interview with J.Cloake, 11 November 2010.

82 JE1041/1. I.Kirkpatrick to R.Makins, 19 March 1956. FO 371/118869.

83 JE1041/1. R.Makins to I.Kirkpatrick, 23 March 1956. FO 371/118869.

84 JIC/827/56, 'Effect on US Economy of Closing Suez Canal', 27 March 1956. DEFE 11/134.

85 JIC(56)20(Final), 'Factors Affecting Egypt's Policy in the Middle East and North Africa', 4 April 1956. CAB 158/23.

86 Note to P.H.Dean, 26 March 1956. PUSD Papers, FCO.

87 JIC(56)26th Meeting, 14 March 1956. CAB 159/22.

88 Note to P.H.Dean, 26 March 1956; Dean to Cooper, 28 March 1956. PUSD Papers, FCO.

89 JIC(56)20(Final)(Supplement), 'Factors Affecting Egypt's Policy in the Middle East and North Africa', 4 April 1956. CAB 158/80.

90 JIC(56)26th Meeting, 14 March 1956. CAB 159/22. See also 'Organisation of Intelligence in the Foreign Office'. PUSD Papers, FCO.

91 ZP2/7/G. SC(58)6, 'Overseas Planning Committee and Political Intelligence Group', 10 June 1958. FO 371/135610.

92 'Record of a Meeting', 19 January 1956. PUSD Papers, FCO.

93 PIG/1, 'Political Intelligence Group – First Meeting, January 24, 1956'. PUSD Papers, FCO.

94 'Report of the Political Intelligence Group', [n.d. but mid-March 1956]. PUSD Papers, FCO.

95 JIC/872/56, 'Communist Policy 1956–57: Report of the Political Intelligence Group', 4 April 1956. Also, Dean to JIC Secretary, 29 March 1956. PUSD Papers, FCO.

96 See CAB 158/23. This subsequently became the Weekly Review of Current Intelligence.

97 To start with in 1956 these are appended to the Committee's minutes. From May they were issued in two forms, the 'Weekly Review of Current Intelligence' (or Grey Book), and the more classified codeword version the 'Weekly Survey of Intelligence' (or Red Book). For 1956 the former can be found at CAB 179/1; the latter at CAB 179/13.

98 An extract from one of these can be found at JIC(56)51/1, 'Current Intelligence Report on the Situation in the Middle East', 9 April 1956. CAB 158/24. It had been agreed that the Heads should meet and discuss the situation three times per week. JIC(56)33rd Meeting, 5 April 1956. CAB 159/23.

99 See correspondence in FO 371/119055.

100 Cited in Kyle, *Suez*. pp.125–6.

101 For detail on this see M S Goodman, 'A Cold War Cover Up: British Intelligence, Whitehall and the Buster Crabb Affair', *International History Review* XXX:4 (December 2008), pp.768–84.

102 The JIC's reaction is in the 'Weekly Survey of Intelligence', 8–14 June 1956. CAB 179/13. The American response is in JIC(56)52nd Meeting, 14 June 1956. CAB 159/23.

103 JIC(56)73(Final), 'The Likelihood of War Between Israel and the Arab States', 5 July 1956. CAB 158/25.

104 JIC(56)55th Meeting, 27 June 1956. CAB 159/23.

105 LHCMA: Suez Oral History Project: Interview with Sir Guy Millard conducted by Anthony Gorst.

106 'Weekly Survey of Intelligence', 19 – 26 July 1956. CAB 179/13.

107 N.Brook [Cabinet Secretary] to H.Macmillan, 30 July 1957. PREM 11/1130.
108 'Weekly Survey of Intelligence', 26 July – 2 August 1956. CAB 179/13. There is also a naval intelligence version of this information in a note from the DNI to the First Sea Lord, 30 July 1956. ADM 205/120.
109 EC(56)2nd Meeting, 28 July 1956. PREM 11/1098.
110 'Weekly Survey of Intelligence', 26 July – 2 August 1956. CAB 179/13.
111 It would appear that the alterations were suggested by Patrick Dean, as the draft copy was personally addressed to him; the handwriting also looks to be consistent with notes made by Dean on other documents.
112 JIC(56)80(Draft), 'The Implications of Egyptian Nationalisation of the Suez Canal', 31 July 1956. PUSD Papers, FCO. Emphasis in original.
113 JIC(56)80(Final)(Revise), 'Egyptian Nationalisation of the Suez Canal Company', 3 August 1956. CAB 158/25.
114 JIC(56)80(Final)(Revise), 'Egyptian Nationalisation of the Suez Canal Company', 3 August 1956. CAB 158/25.
115 For more details see Kyle, *Suez.* pp.167–79.
116 JIC(56)84(Final), 'Considerations Affecting Action by Egypt in the Event of Armed Intervention', 7 August 1956. CAB 158/25.
117 On the former see JIC/2212/56, 'Egyptian Sigint Capabilities', 4 September 1956. CAB 158/80. On the latter see JIC(56)82, 'Security of Planning for Action Against Egypt', 1 August 1956. CAB 158/25.
118 Although not quite as straightforward as this, it is clear that the risk of war was to be seriously entertained and that Egypt had to be convinced that it would be pursued if other means failed. From the minutes it would appear that this was seen as the most likely option. See CM(56)54th Conclusions, 27 July 1956. CAB 128/30.
119 JIC(56)42nd Meeting, 3 May 1956. CAB 159/23.
120 CM(56)54, 27 July 1956. CAB 128/30.
121 For instance, see M Vaisse, 'France and the Suez Crisis', In Wm Roger Louis and R Owen (eds), *Suez 1956: The Crisis and its Consequences* (Oxford: Clarendon Press, 1989), pp.131–44.
122 Kyle, *Suez.* pp.143–8.
123 JE11924. 'Anglo-French Talks: Suez Canal', Note by A.D.M.Ross, 1 August 1956. FO 371/118996.
124 This description of the meeting is from a handwritten note, though its author's signature is illegible. JE11924. FO 371/118996. The minutes of the meeting can be found in DEFE 4/89.
125 JIC(56)67th Meeting, 9 August 1956. CAB 159/24. For the COS Committee see COS(56)78th Meeting, 9 August 1956. DEFE 4/89.
126 JIC(56)66th Meeting, 7 August 1956. CAB 159/24.
127 This is clear from a note recommending the conclusions of the report, sent from the DNI to the First Sea Lord, 9 August 1956. ADM 116/6137.
128 JIC(56)84(Final), 'Considerations Affecting Action by Egypt in the Event of Armed Intervention', 7 August 1956. CAB 158/25.
129 The preceding detail is taken from PUSD Papers, FCO.
130 For instance, at a COS Committee meeting at the start of August on military plans Dean was responsible for liaising with the FO on several matters, including some specific intelligence aspects. COS(56)76th Meeting, 1 August 1956. DEFE 4/89.
131 EC(56)14th Meeting, 10 August 1956. CAB 134/1216.
132 'Minutes of a Staff Conference Held at Chequers on Saturday, 11th August at 3.30pm'. PREM 11/1099.
133 JE11924. D.P.Reilly to P.H.Dean, 10 August 1956. FO 371/118996. The rest of the JIC structure was seemingly also in the dark. For a fascinating account by one of the Naval members of the JIS at that time see C C Anderson, 'Suez – 1956', *The Naval Review* 79: 4 (October 1991), pp.356–61.

134 G.Jebb to A.Eden, 11 August 1956. PREM 11/1126.
135 Interview with Lord Greenhill of Harrow. Churchill College Cambridge: British Diplomatic Oral History Programme.
136 Interview with Sir Patrick Dean conducted by Anthony Gorst and W.S.Lucas. LHCMA: Suez Oral History Project.
137 EC(56)19, 'Forecast of Time-Table', 14 August 1956. CAB 134/1217.
138 'Security for Planning', Report by P.H.Dean, 14 August 1956. PREM 11/1139. Dean's brief, which he was given beforehand and which he 'amended to make somewhat clearer', is in 'Anglo-French Discussions on Security of Planning for Action Against Egypt'. PUSD Papers, FCO.
139 EC(56)16th Meeting, 16 August 1956. CAB 134/1216.
140 G.Jebb to A.Eden, 14 August 1956. PREM 11/1126.
141 COS(56)80th Meeting, 14 August 1956. DEFE 4/89.
142 Confidential Annex to JIC(56)72nd Meeting, 16 August 1956. CAB 159/24.
143 'Record of Meeting of Mr Dodds-Parker's Advisory Committee at 1030am August 24, 1956.' DO 35/6227.
144 A collection of minutes and papers are in CAB 134/1211.
145 See CAB 134/940.
146 Minutes of this, at which Dean was present, can be found in CAB 134/815.
147 For instance ME(0)(56)23rd Meeting, 24 September 1956. PREM 11/1102. Other papers can be found in CAB 134/1297.
148 DTC(55)2, 'War Planning: Committee Structure', 17 May 1955. CAB 134/815.
149 CRRP(56)1, 'Composition and Terms of Reference', 12 July 1956. CAB 134/1211.
150 For instance, in mid-August the Committee was asked by the COS Committee to look into whether the codeword 'Operation MUSKETEER' had been 'compromised by being mentioned over the open telephone'. COS(56)80th Meeting, 14 August 1956. DEFE 4/89.
151 These examples are taken from JIC(56)72nd Meeting, 16 August 1956. CAB 159/24. See also, JIC(FE)(56)23(Final), 'Implications of the Suez Canal Dispute in South East Asia and the Far East', 15 August 1956. PUSD Papers, FCO.
152 JIC(ME)(56)-39(Final), 'Political and Military Effects in the Middle East of Certain Developments in the Suez Canal Situation', 17 August 1956. CO 1035/24.
153 JE14211/2127. I.Kirkpatrick to Secretary of State, 4 September 1956. FO 371/119154.
154 For instance, for the views of LIC(Aden) see Governor, Aden to Secretary of State for the Colonies, 13 August 1956. CO 1035/24.
155 JIC(56)93(Final)(Revise), 'The Situation Which Might Arise in the Middle East at the Conclusion of the Suez Conference', 25 August 1956. CAB 158/25.
156 COS(56)83rd Meeting, Confidential Annex, 23 August 1956. DEFE 4/89. The amendments included: that it was now considered unlikely (as opposed to likely in the draft) that 'the position [of the local authorities] in the Persian Gulf Sheikhdoms would get out of control'; that the Ethiopians would be 'unlikely to cause trouble'; and that the 'appreciation that the Iranian Government would be forced to suspend deliveries of oil, painted too gloomy a picture'. Various drafts of the resulting paper, JIC(56)93, 'The Situation Which Might Arise in the Middle East at the Conclusion of the Suez Conference', can be found in PUSD Papers, FCO.
157 G McDermott, *The Eden Legacy and the Decline of British Diplomacy* (London: Leslie Frewin, 1969). p.137.
158 Interview with Sir Archibald Ross conducted by Anthony Gorst and W Scott Lucas, 25 July 1989. LHCMA: Suez Oral History Project.
159 P.Reilly to P.Wright [PUS, FCO], 31 October 1986. FCO 12/179.
160 Bodleian Library, University of Oxford: Patrick Reilly Papers, c.6921, folios 317–48, 'Suez 1956'. p.5.
161 Interview with Sir G.Millard, 29 September 2010.

162 Bodleian Library, University of Oxford: Patrick Reilly Papers, c.6921, folios 317–48, 'Suez 1956'. p.9.

163 Interview with Sir Patrick Reilly conducted by W Scott Lucas. LHCMA: Suez Oral History Project.

164 Note by G.L.McDermott, 28 August 1956. PUSD Papers, FCO.

165 Interview with Sir Patrick Reilly conducted by W Scott Lucas. LHCMA: Suez Oral History Project.

166 For an example of these, see various correspondences in ADM 116/6137.

167 Further details are in PREM 11/1104.

168 Some examples of this can be found in 'Egypt: Tactical Intelligence Operation MUSKETEER'. PUSD Papers, FCO.

169 Craig, 'The Joint Intelligence Committee and British Intelligence Assessment', p.234.

170 PUSD Papers, FCO.

171 PUSD Papers, FCO.

172 P.L.Carter [PUSD, FO] to P.H.Dean, 24 September 1956. PUSD Papers, FCO.

173 JIC(56)86th Meeting, 27 September 1956. CAB 159/24.

174 JIC(56)87th Meeting, 27 September 1956. CAB 159/24.

175 JIC(56)98(Final), 'Possible Soviet Assistance to Egypt's Military Effort in Certain Circumstances', 4 October 1956. CAB 158/25.

176 Both points are detailed in JIC(56)83rd Meeting, 20 September 1956. CAB 159/24. The original cannot be found but this title comes from the terms of reference. The approved version of the 'conflicting viewpoints' is in the 'Weekly Review of Current Intelligence', Period ending 20 September 1956. CAB 179/1.

177 For more detail see Kyle, *Suez*.

178 JIC(56)79th Meeting, 6 September 1956. CAB 159/24. Upon completion of the preliminary draft the JIC discussed whether the paper should be expanded to look at the impact on other countries in the region but decided against it, largely because 'it would be too speculative' and because the relevant departments of the FO who would write it were 'already swamped with work'. JIC(56)85th Meeting, 26 September 1956. CAB 159/24.

179 JIC(56)97(Final), 'Probable Actions by Nasser in Certain Circumstances', 11 October 1956. CAB 158/25. Earlier drafts of the same report can be found in CO 1035/25.

180 Note from D.J.P.Lee [Secretary, COS Committee] to the Chiefs of Staff, 30 October 1956. CAB 158/25.

181 COS(56)104th Meeting, Confidential Annex, 24 October 1956. ADM 116/6138.

182 JIC(56)98(Final), 'Possible Soviet Assistance to Egypt's Military Effort in Certain Circumstances', 4 October 1956. CAB 158/25.

183 Prime Minister to the Foreign Secretary, n.d. but early October 1956. PREM 11/1102.

184 H.Macmillan to A.Eden, 26 September 1956. PREM 11/1102.

185 H.Macmillan to A.Eden, 26 September 1956. PREM 11/1102.

186 Makins, who attended some of these meetings, later wrote that he felt that Macmillan had 'misinterpreted' Eisenhower's 'cautious remarks'. R Makins, *The Suez Crisis – The Makins Experience* (Unpublished Memoir). p.21. Bodleian Library, University of Oxford: MS.Sherfield 959, Lord Sherfield Papers. Makins did concede, however, that he did not accompany Macmillan to the specific meeting with Dulles referred to above.

187 H.Macmillan to A.Eden, 26 September 1956. PREM 11/1102.

188 Makins to FO, 10 September 1956. WO 32/16709.

189 For instance, see Kyle, *Suez*. p.150; and W S Lucas, *Divided We Stand: Britain, the US and the Suez Crisis* (London: Hodder & Stoughton, 1991). p.218.

190 The members of the British Mission are disclosed in a declassified American archival file. US NARA, College Park, Maryland: RG59, Lot 59D 518, Box 36, 'Mask US-UK Bilateral'.

191 'Egypt'. PUSD Papers, FCO. This is a record of the meeting held to discuss the visit.

192 Dean to Secretary of State, 27 September 1956. PUSD Papers, FCO.

193 Note by Dean, 28 September 1956. PUSD Papers, FCO.

194 As Minister Coulson would become the de facto Ambassador during Suez as the previous incumbent, Sir Roger Makins, had returned to London to become Permanent Secretary to the Treasury. Rather ironically, Morris would later become the British Ambassador to Egypt, 1975–9.

195 'US-UK Bilateral, Department of State, Oct 1, 2.30pm.' US NARA: RG59, Lot 59D 518, Box 36, 'Mask US-UK Bilateral'. Interestingly, this aspect of the meeting is not mentioned in the British version of the discussions. See 'Record of a Meeting in State Department at 2.30pm, October 1, 1956.' PUSD Papers, FCO.

196 Dean to Lloyd, 3 October 1956. PUSD Papers, FCO.

197 Lloyd to Brook, 4 October 1956. CAB 21/4114.

198 N.Cairncross to J.J.B.Hunt, 8 October 1956. CAB 21/4114.

199 Dean to Kirkpatrick, 8 October 1956. PUSD Papers, FCO.

200 J.E.Coulson to Dean, 6 October 1956. PUSD Papers, FCO.

201 Washington to London, 18 October 1956. PUSD Papers, FCO.

202 Dean to Lloyd, 19 October 1956. PUSD Papers, FCO.

203 Lloyd to Dulles, 17 October, 1956. US NARA: RG59, Lot 59D 518, Box 36, 'Mask US-UK Bilateral'.

204 Dulles to Lloyd, 19 October, 1956. US NARA: RG59, Lot 59D 518, Box 36, 'Mask US-UK Bilateral'.

205 Coulson to Dean, 20 October 1956. PUSD Papers, FCO. Emphasis in original.

206 Dean to Lloyd, 22 October 1956. PUSD Papers, FCO.

207 In his memoir McDermott writes: 'While we continued in the JIC to collaborate with our US friends we had to take great care that no whiff of our planning activities reached them. Although we had all the hard intelligence at our disposal we did not know all that was going on behind the scenes at the highest level. Or rather, only two [Dean and McDermott] of us knew.' McDermott, *The Eden Legacy*. p.137,

208 JIC(56)97(Final), 'Probable Actions by Nasser in Certain Circumstances', 11 October 1956. CAB 158/25; JIC(56)102, 'Israel Attitude Towards Arab States in the Context of the Suez Canal Crisis', 28 September 1956. CAB 158/26; JIC(56)104(Final), 'The Threat to United Kingdom Interests Overseas', 18 October 1956. CAB 158/26.

209 P Catterall (ed), *The Macmillan Diaries: The Cabinet Years, 1950–1957* (London: Pan, 2004). p.607.

210 For instance, the minutes of the COS Committee meetings for this period are full of references to JIC papers. See DEFE 4/90 and DEFE 4/91.

211 JIC(56)97(Final), 'Probable Actions by Nasser in Certain Circumstances', 11 October 1956. CAB 158/25.

212 JIC(56)98(Final), 'Possible Russian Assistance to Egypt's Military Effort in Certain Circumstances', 4 October 1956. CAB 158/25.

213 COS(56)97th Meeting, 9 October 1956. DEFE 4/90.

214 JIC(56)104(Final), 'The Threat to United Kingdom Interests Overseas', 18 October 1956. CAB 158/26. For further detail and a copy of the document itself see G Bennett, 'Suez and the Threat to UK Interests Overseas', In R Dover & M S Goodman (eds), *Learning from the Secret Past: Cases in British Intelligence History* (Washington, DC: Georgetown University Press, 2011). pp.211–38.

215 JIC(53)60(Final), 'Possible Consequences of an Outbreak of Hostilities with Egypt', 10 August 1953. CAB 158/15.

216 G.L.McDermott to H.C.Hainworth [Political Officer Middle East Forces], 29 September 1956. PUSD Papers, FCO.

217 JIC(56)102, 'Israel Attitude Towards Arab States in the Context of the Suez Canal Crisis', 28 September 1956. CAB 158/26

218 Keith Kyle states that in King Charles Street, only two FO officials were told of the ideas: the PUS, Sir Ivone Kirkpatrick, and Archibald Ross, the Assistant Under Secretary of State responsible for the Middle East. Furthermore, Kyle cites Ross as saying that no official paperwork was prepared, only an informal summary which was subsequently destroyed. Kyle, *Suez*. p.297, 301 and 623.

219 CM(56)71st Conclusions, 18 October 1956. CAB 128/30.

220 Interview with Sir Donald Logan. Churchill College Cambridge: British Diplomatic Oral History Programme.

221 CM(56)72nd Conclusions, Confidential Annex, 23 October 1956. CAB 128/30.

222 Letter from Lady Patricia Dean, 12 August 2009.

223 C L Cooper, *The Lion's Last Roar: Suez, 1956* (London: Harper and Row, 1978). p.158. The list of guests is from Interview with Lady Patricia Dean, 19 October 2009.

224 'Dean Memorandum'. FCO 73/205. The background to this paper, written by Dean in 1978, is contained in the file. Essentially he was called into the FO to discuss his role at Sèvres, because the archival documents were shortly to be released to the Public Record Office. As far as can be ascertained, it is the only primary source document written by Dean on Suez. For more background see also CAB 164/1356.

225 This paragraph draws on the Dean Memorandum and the interview with Lady Dean.

226 D.Logan to P.Reilly, 16 October 1983. Patrick Reilly papers, Bodleian Library, University of Oxford: MS. Eng c.6890.

227 Interview with Sir Donald Logan. Churchill College Cambridge: British Diplomatic Oral History Programme.

228 Interview with Sir Donald Logan conducted by Anthony Gorst and W.S.Lucas. LHCMA: Suez Oral History Project. See also D Logan, 'Collusion at Suez', *The Financial Times* (8 January 1986).

229 Interview with Lady Patricia Dean, 19 October 2009.

230 Interview with Sir Guy Millard, 29 September 2010.

231 See, for instance, a French version (the language of the original) in FCO 12/183.

232 'Note for Record', J.Hunt, 9 June 1978. FCO 73/205.

233 CM(56)74th Conclusions, 25 October 1956. CAB 128/30.

234 See the handwritten notes on the draft of the 'Dean Memorandum' in CAB 164/1356.

235 'Weekly Survey of Intelligence', 19–25 June 1956. CAB 179/13.

236 JIC(56)79th Meeting, 6 September 1956. CAB 159/24.

237 Details are in CAB 21/4114. Unfortunately none of the summaries seem to have survived.

238 JIC/2691/56, 'Co-Ordination of Intelligence During Present Middle East Emergency', 2 November 1956. CAB 176/59.

239 These can be found in ADM 116/6138 and also AIR 20/9679.

240 These can be found in CAB 158/81.

241 Denny to Minister of Defence, 2 November 1956. DEFE 13/12. A similar quote can be found in Coulson to FO, 31 October 1956. Cabinet Office, FOI release 240080.

242 Cited in Kyle, *Suez*. pp.456–7.

243 Kyle, *Suez*. pp.457–60.

244 JIC(56)101st Meeting, 8 November 1956. CAB 159/25.

245 63056/JIC, 'JIC(ME) Appreciation of Possible Nature of Soviet Intervention in Middle East', 8 November 1956. AIR 20/9680.

246 JIC/2780/56, 'Possibility of Russian Intervention in the Middle East in the Immediate Future', 13 November 1956. PUSD Papers, FCO.

247 JIC(56)117(Terms of Reference), 'Russian Designs in the Middle East', 9 November 1956. CAB 158/26.

248 JIC(56)111, 'Soviet Threat of Intervention in Middle East', 6 November 1956. CAB 158/81.

249 JIC(ME) to Secretary, JIC, 10 November 1956. PUSD Papers, FCO.

250 JIC(56)103rd Meeting, 11 November 1956. CAB 159/25.

251 JIC/2780/56, 'Possibility of Russian Intervention in the Middle East in the Immediate Future', 13 November 1956. PUSD Papers, FCO.

252 Ministry of Defence to Allied Forces Head Quarters, 8 November 1956. DEFE 11/111.

253 JIC(56)122, 'Possibility of Russian Intervention in the Middle East in the Immediate Future', 15 November 1956. CAB 158/81. See also JIC/2780/56, 'Possibility of Russian Intervention in the Middle East in the Immediate Future', 13 November 1956. PUSD Papers, FCO.

254 JIC(56)109th Meeting, 16 November 1956. CAB 159/25.

255 JE10338/1/G. P.Dean to J.H.A.Watson [Head of African Department, FO], 16 November 1956. FO 371/118853.

256 JIC(56)117(Final), 'Soviet Designs in the Middle East', 11 November 1956. CAB 158/26.

257 FO to Her Majesty's Representatives, 13 November 1956. PUSD Papers, FCO.

258 COS(56)117th Meeting, Confidential Annex, 14 November 1956. DEFE 4/92.

259 JIC(56)103rd Meeting, 11 November 1956. CAB 159/25.

260 I.Kirkpatrick to G.Jebb, 17 November 1956. PUSD Papers, FCO.

261 JE10338/1/G. 'Soviet Influence in Egypt', FO Research Department, 20 November 1956. FO 371/118853.

262 J.H.A.Watson to P.Dean, 21 November 1956; handwritten note by Dean, 22 November 1956. PUSD Papers, FCO.

263 JE1074/10/G. Washington to FO, 18 November 1956. FO 371/118873.

264 Note by P.L.Carter [PUSD, FO], 19 December 1956. PUSD Papers, FCO.

265 Secretary, JIC(W) to Secretary, JIC, 14 December 1956. PUSD Papers, FCO. For more on JIC(W) see chapter 7.

266 JIC/3017/56, 'Intelligence in Operation "MUSKETEER"', 12 December 1956. CAB 176/59.

267 JIC(ME)(56)-52(Final), 'Role of JIC(ME) in Operation MUSKETEER', 28 January 1957. PUSD Papers, FCO.

268 JIC/534/57, 'Intelligence in Operation "MUSKETEER"', 26 February 1957. Also JIC/1792/57, 'Lessons from "MUSKETEER"', 22 August 1957. PUSD Papers, FCO. By 'official reports' he referred to the redactions made to General Keightley's account of Suez.

269 For more details see JIC(57)76(Final), 'Notes on JIC Operational Procedure', 18 November 1957. CAB 158/29.

270 For some background see CO 1035/27.

271 'Post "MUSKETEER" Intelligence', Note by D.J.P.Lee [Secretary, COS], 13 December 1956. ADM 116/6138.

272 For the earlier plans see A Gorst & W S Lucas, 'The Other Collusion: Operation Straggle and Anglo-American Intervention in Syria, 1955–56', *Intelligence and National Security* 4:3 (July 1989), pp.576–95. For post-1956 activities see DEFE 32/5.

273 H Greene, 'The Suez Story', *The Times* (27 June 1978).

274 W S Lucas, 'The Missing Link? Patrick Dean, Chairman of the Joint Intelligence Committee', In S.Kelly & A.Gorst. (eds). *Whitehall and the Suez Crisis* (London: Frank Cass, 2000). p.117.

275 See Dean's obituary in *The Times* (9 November 1994).

Conclusion

> *. . . looking back can be a salutary exercise. If we could spare the time or the staff we should probably derive great benefit from examining in retrospect the accuracy of the information on which policy was based and the correctness of the conclusions drawn from it.*
>
> R.W.J.Hooper, Head of PUSD[1]

Intelligence in a Changing World

This volume covers a twenty-year period from the JIC's creation in 1936 to its involvement in the Suez crisis of 1956. The JIC was born out of the anxieties over the military rise of Nazi Germany. It matured dealing with the very different concerns of the Cold War and the threat of nuclear annihilation. As it developed its own personality, the JIC became a key contributor to British and allied politico-military debates. It was responsible for the invention of all-source intelligence assessment as we know it in Britain today, and the development of intelligence analysis as a function supporting government as a whole and not just the naval, military and air staffs. It made a major contribution to bringing military planners to a greater appreciation of the potential of intelligence, including the work of the civilian agencies. Later, similar close links were forged between Whitehall's foreign and defence policymakers and the intelligence chiefs, not least because of the institutionalised requirement that they should debate their disagreements to reach a consensus on JIC papers. Finally, the JIC was the first example of the development of a governing body for a national intelligence community, overseeing the interactions between individual agencies and departments, liaising with overseas services, establishing requirements for intelligence and assessing performance.

The birth of the JIC was not easy, nor did it progress according to any preconceived plan, but it evolved to meet the needs of national survival and global war. It helped that, in its early years, the JIC had the advantage of access to perhaps the most comprehensive intelligence on the enemy ever known, through the work of Bletchley Park on ULTRA. After the Second World War such success in reading enemy communications was difficult to emulate and, through the formative years of the Cold War, as described in this volume, the British intelligence community struggled to reach the levels of performance and insight against its principal adversaries achieved during 1939–45.

Throughout this period the JIC had some notable successes but also serious failings. Almost inevitably, perhaps, the major factors leading to the JIC's achievements were mirrored by the factors contributing to its shortcomings. Its performance reflects a natural consequence of a committee based on consensus, inter-departmental working, operating at the interface between the worlds of intelligence and policy. Further, the JIC's core outputs were invariably required to forecast the likely course of events, usually based on information that was far from comprehensive. Variable performance along a continuum between 'success' and 'failure' was inevitable.

At the time of the creation of the JIC in 1936 Britain controlled territories around the globe and occupied a position of international authority. Across Europe this power balance was beginning to shift as the growing influence of Nazi Germany, Fascist Italy, and Soviet Russia increased. Despite these political developments, 'Intelligence' was very much military in focus and scope and was concerned primarily with gauging capabilities. The three Services each had dedicated intelligence branches and it was problems in their working relationship and disagreements about their analyses that ultimately led to the formation of the JIC.

The stimulus for its creation lay was provided by Major General John Dill, the DMO&I (Director of Military Operations and Intelligence), yet it would be the great Whitehall 'man of secrets', Sir Maurice Hankey, the Secretary to the Committee of Imperial Defence, who would turn Dill's vision into reality. Dill had wished to create a body that would avoid the duplication of effort among the three Services' intelligence branches and would be charged, specifically, with ensuring that the best possible intelligence was used for defence planning. Hankey's practical solution was to create a sub-committee of the COS Committee thereby ensuring that, from the outset, intelligence and planning were closely aligned. The JIC was not the first inter-service committee on intelligence but it was different from its predecessors because it was taken seriously (as borne out by the senior attendance it attracted), with a specific but loosely defined remit. Instantly it had a serious policy-related matter with which to grapple: the implications for British military equipment and tactics of the conduct of the Spanish Civil War.

The original JIC concept in 1936 had focussed on the function of military intelligence co-ordination. Yet the changing nature of the 'threat' and the evolution of intelligence had meant that, by 1939, it was considered necessary to include the FO to ensure that intelligence was fed into policymaking and that the foreign political context, albeit rarely discussed, could be covered. The FO began to chair the meetings which helped ensure that, by the outbreak of war in September 1939, the JIC had become as much a strategic assessment body as a producer of tactical military intelligence reports for the Planners. Despite this trend, the JIC's activities continued to reflect its tasking as a sub-committee of the COS, whose focus had to be geared towards military matters. Even though the FO chaired meetings, diplomatic and internal political developments in Germany and Italy continued to be of secondary importance to military concerns.

The advent of war brought about several other changes to the JIC's tasking. Whilst the Committee maintained focus on military assessments required for operational planning, it increasingly addressed wider issues involving operational matters and Fifth Column activities. It was, however, only in 1940 that the intelligence agencies, the Security Service and SIS (incorporating GC&CS) would became permanent members. By the last years of conflict the JIC had also begun to produce a number of assessments, albeit few and limited in scope, on wider strategic issues, particularly on such topics as German morale or the conditions required for an unconditional Japanese surrender.

The wartime JIC was undoubtedly a success. It grew from a small and specialised gathering of military intelligence officers on the fringes of government into a fully-fledged and integral component of the government's war machine. The role of individuals was highly significant here. The real opportunity for the JIC came with the failure to foresee the German invasion of Norway in 1940, combined with Churchill's accession to power. Churchill believed in the value of intelligence and gave the Committee freedom to operate independently. Despite insisting on reading much single-source reporting, he also valued the all-source assessed product of the JIC. The contributions of Cavendish-Bentinck, the JIC Chairman, and his colleague Denis Capel-Dunn, who was JIC Secretary for the first part of the war, were highly significant.

From the dry records of the proceedings of the JIC it is difficult to single out the contributions of an individual to the workings of a Committee, but there are tangible glimpses of the quality of administration and diplomatic skill that Cavendish-Bentinck brought to his task. He described his role as Chairman as being akin to 'a sort of conductor'.[2] He was clearly adept at dealing with senior figures in the military, almost all of whom outranked him. He chaired the Committee skilfully, ensuring that any disagreements were resolved. Handling the sometimes fraught relationship between the military and the FO was a particular challenge.[3] Most crucially, he was able to represent the JIC effectively at meetings of both the COS Committee and other senior fora in Whitehall, finessing the inevitable bureaucratic wrangling to ensure that the JIC was influential at senior levels of government. Together with Capel-Dunn, who was promoted to become Secretary to the Joint Planning and Intelligence Staffs, Cavendish-Bentinck created a vision for the future machinery of British intelligence with the JIC firmly at its centre.

Although the personalities of the Chairman and Secretary undoubtedly helped, the JIC would still not have been able to establish itself so firmly and so quickly, without success in terms of both the accuracy and timeliness of its own assessments. This in turn was a reflection of the quality of the underlying intelligence. As the stature of the JIC increased so, too, did its involvement in the war effort. From 1941 onwards the JIC was briefing the COS Committee weekly and all planning papers began, routinely, to have an intelligence input. This ensured that the military planning process included both strategic and tactical assessments. The creation, that same year, of a dedicated drafting team, the Joint Intelligence Staff, meant that the JIC members themselves could concentrate on the highest priorities. That did not mean that JIC reports were always read or that its judgments were accepted but, by and large, intelligence was seen as an essential component of policy and perceived as fundamental to the war effort.

As the war progressed assessing enemy strategic intentions became as vital a task for the JIC as were the details of German military deployments. By 1945 the JIC had been involved, in one way or another, in supporting Allied decision making in all aspects of war planning. It had coped with, and adapted to, the requirements of world war in various theatres of conflict and responded to the changing demands that modern warfare made on the intelligence community. Its output ranged from broad assessments of the strategic threat; monthly reports on the signs of German collapse; weekly papers, based on ULTRA, on what the enemy knew and might expect of Allied plans; to multiple daily operational products on the developing nature and conduct of the war. As already noted, the Committee's stature in Whitehall and the military commands benefitted significantly from having access to ULTRA in the production of intelligence assessments, allowing the JIC to generate for its wider audience who were not indoctrinated into the ULTRA secret an unparalleled regular and much valued series of tactical and strategic reports concerning the conduct of the war. Although few of the daily operational and tactical reports have been preserved, it is quite clear that this was the hidden JIC success story of the war. As a result the JIC achieved perhaps the best result to which an intelligence organisation can aspire: it had gained a reputation for sound judgements and a growing and important audience for its assessments.

In a report on the post-war 'Intelligence Machine', written for the JIC in January 1945 in the final few months of the conflict, Cavendish-Bentinck and Capel-Dunn characterised the Committee as fundamental to the future of British intelligence. Service budgets and the size of the armed forces were correctly assumed to decline in the inevitable austerity of the post-war world. They argued perceptively, therefore, that this would increase the future reliance of British forces on having a steady and reliable stream of intelligence. Provision of strategic warning of the emergence of new threats was to be the vision for the future. The guarantor that this requirement would be met was to be the JIC, through its co-ordinating role and the continuation of its interdepartmental, consensus-based approach to assessments, involving policymakers as well as intelligence chiefs.

After the end of the Second World War, as the threat from Soviet and later Chinese communism emerged, along with the rise of anti-colonial movements, one of the great difficulties facing the British intelligence community was that it had to adjust to operating against targets on which it had little current knowledge. The intelligence dominance achieved over the German and other Axis military forces would not be repeated. The intelligence community had to try to assess the intentions and the future military capabilities of the Soviet Union with initially very little conclusive evidence from intelligence sources to go on. The demand was for a much more strategic level of analysis than had been the staple diet of the Committee during the military operations of the war. Yet it still had a tactical, current focus, which was apparent in the weekly survey of intelligence, particularly evident at times of crisis. At the same time, the JIC's coordinating functions in relation to the development of the intelligence community and relationships with intelligence allies increased in significance.

The JIC's first major post-war challenge was to determine the future direction of Soviet policy. Here it was hampered by the lack of intelligence resulting from the restrictions that had been imposed by the FO on intelligence gathering against the Soviet target, and the continuing post-war disagreement between the FO and the COS over attitudes to the Soviet expansion of influence in Eastern Europe. A consensus on policy towards the Soviet bloc was not reached until several years after the end of the war. By the early 1950s the intelligence community had been able to make up some of this lost time and effort on the Soviet target and Anglo-American intelligence cooperation was bearing fruit. But, the wide diversification of the Cold War brought new challenges.

A succession of crises ensured that the JIC's position within government as an authoritative source of assessment of the international situation was secure, even though it was not able to predict accurately several important events, including the Berlin Blockade, the invasion of South Korea by the North, and the intervention of the Chinese in the Korean War. Nevertheless, the Committee's performance in steadying the Whitehall ship in rough water was effective. Whilst its strategic forecasting sometimes failed, its operational analysis of the resulting situation was generally accurate, if sometimes coloured by perceiving the influence of Moscow in the Middle East and Far East as greater than it probably was. The Suez crisis concluded a turbulent first twenty years for the JIC and tested to the limits its formula of bringing intelligence chiefs together with policymakers to reach key judgments to inform Government decisions.

The Machinery for Joint Intelligence

The JIC's original construction as an inter-departmental forum between the three Service Departments continued to bring considerable benefits in this period. It encouraged closer collaboration as the key to sounder and more valuable assessment, presaging the centralisation that would come with the defence reforms of the 1960s. The existing evidence shows that despite its disparate membership – the three services, intelligence, and diplomatic – meetings were cordial, sober, serious, and driven by a desire to achieve consensus. The JIC performed more than an assessment role, important though that was. It formed a motor for the central intelligence machinery: an organisation that linked the intelligence world with the policy and military worlds through numerous sub-committees and subordinate regional offshoots. In essence, the JIC in the 1950s had four main functions:

i) producing joint, inter-departmental assessments;
ii) guiding the national intelligence effort by considering and issuing guidance on the annual requirements for intelligence and overseeing intelligence liaisons and other community issues;

iii)   helping to bring together the resource requirements of the intelligence agencies and lobbying on their behalf for necessary funds; and

iv)   exercising a responsibility for the security of sensitive material.

These specific functions established a unique culture. Beyond this, however, was the broader value increasingly derived by the UK (uniquely, since there were no exact foreign comparators) from having such a variety of senior people from the worlds of policy and intelligence sit down around a table once every week, argue their way to consensus and have to 'dip their hands in the blood of the assessments'. Percy Cradock has said:

> as we look back over these first twenty to twenty-five years of the post-war era, the record of the JIC shows it as an important part of central government, intimately involved in the main crises of the period and exerting a powerful influence on foreign policy in Britain . . . it looks at the world coolly and realistically, with few illusions . . . its main merit, however, may lie less in individual assessments of greater or lesser accuracy than in the fact of its existence as a responsible and increasingly influential organisation bringing together at manageable and less than Cabinet level the chief sources of knowledge on international affairs and engaging them in a continuous and forward-looking discussion and evaluation of the evolving scene. Thereby it contributed substantially to the ideal of efficient and prescient policy-making.[4]

An earlier recognition of the value of this is provided in a 1944 note by Capel-Dunn, who wrote that:

> . . . the JIC has . . . become a forum for discussion of many matters affecting SIS. 'C' discusses his needs at JIC meetings and agreement is then reached as to the best means of meeting them. Similarly, it is at meetings of the JIC that the Service consumers and MEW [Ministry of Economic Warfare] bring their needs to the attention of 'C'. Much duplication of effort is thus avoided and coordination of requests is achieved . . . the JIC today provides machinery for integrating political and military demands on SIS and political and military views on priorities. This should continue.[5]

Undoubtedly other branches of government came to benefit from such close proximity to the intelligence world. Confirmation of this can be sought in the statistics for just how often the JIC members themselves came to the meetings, not their deputies.

The ability of JIC members to work together and take collective responsibility for the product was an essential pre-requisite for its influence, reflecting Hankey's original insight in creating it as part of the Whitehall system of collective decision making. The pre-war JIC had been involved, peripherally, with disagreements over German rearmament, and the immediately post-war JIC by the disagreement between the FO and the COS on the threat posed by the Soviet Union. But the JIC was able to work effectively despite differing departmental positions. The explanation may lie in the recognition by its members of the increased trust and confidence which Ministers and Service Chiefs had in it; possibly it was a reflection of the personalities present. Consensus may have had its price, but it is striking that the JIC rarely offered an explicit opinion in the bitter strategic debates of 1944–1947 over the Soviet threat. This was at a time when a JIC judgment might have helped clarify British thinking on policy and strategy in this area.

Positive perceptions of the JIC were assisted, undoubtedly, by a succession of very able, very successful, high-flying FO Chairmen. In one respect their task was a simple one, for as the COS put it: 'the Chairman should inspire initiative and drive in the conduct of intelligence work.'[6] Chairing the JIC was not a full-time job, and all the post-war incumbents were also either head of PUSD or the DUS responsible for intelligence within the FO. This ensured that a clear and unequivocal link existed between intelligence assessment, community management, operational planning, and the formulation of foreign policy. The events surrounding Suez in 1956 tested the practice of placing the FO policymaking and the intelligence role of the JIC Chairman in the hands of the same official. The nature of the Suez crisis generated fissures between the political, military and intelligence planning machineries, with the JIC Chairman intimately involved in all three but unable to use his role to build a coordinated approach.

Consensus lay at the heart of the JIC deliberations and output: any assessment distributed with a JIC appellation was understood to have been agreed by all constituent members. It was here that the disparate membership of the Committee was, in many ways, invaluable: the mix of policy, military and intelligence departments ensured that senior figures, in this period primarily the COS, received the collective opinion of those whose job it was to produce intelligence and those who had to act upon it. Yet producing consensus could be problematic.

The first difficulty lay in actually reaching a consensus in the first place. JIC papers in this period were drafted by individual members of the JIS, who were effectively not divorced from their parent departments, and whilst they were supposed to be free from any departmental biases, they were also responsible for liaising with them to gather information. Quite what expertise each drafter brought to bear on individual papers is not obvious from the files, but it is clear that JIC assessments were often redrafted a number of times before they were distributed. Committee members frequently commented on drafts, as did the Chairman. The nature of the JIC minutes for this period rarely reveal arguments or serious discussions, but as R.V. Jones, the head of scientific intelligence in the early 1950s recalled,

> Only a minority of the members of the JIC had been selected on their past achievements as intelligence officers. Had they been, they might have recognised that much of the time spent arguing around the table about the interpretation of evidence was due to there being too little information, so allowing for too many hypotheses to explain it. Two members could therefore have

two differing interpretations with neither being able to dispose effectively of the other. In such circumstances the remedy should have been to save time in argument and instead press for more intelligence.[7]

Prior to the introduction of the permanent staff of the JIS in 1941, the JIC system was too slow to meet customer requirements for papers. The creation of the JIS enriched matters and ensured that, as the wartime demand for informed assessments grew, the ability to respond was improved. In an attempt to ensure consistency and consensus the JIS was regularly given very specific parameters within which to work. These often involved the starting assumptions for the report, as well as the questions that were to be addressed. It would not be an exaggeration to say that although the JIC was, from its early days, permitted to propose its own papers, in attempting to satisfy its readership it became too reliant on questions set by its military masters.

The JIC was not averse to re-writing a paper if the COS Committee was not happy with it. Sometimes, even if the paper was accepted, the COS could limit or even prevent its distribution. A few examples of both of these cases exist. These instances were not considered to be particularly problematic. After all, the JIC was a sub-committee of the COS Committee and therefore if the senior customers were not content, then the report would have to be revised. That this had the potential to cause trouble was a concern of Victor Cavendish-Bentinck, the Committee's wartime Chairman, who later said: 'I trust that the JIC is successfully performing the task – which I regarded as its most important duty – of preventing the Intelligence Directorates of the various services from providing intelligence which fits in with the pre-conceived views or suits the policy of their superiors.'[8]

An associated problem was the question of the matters to be studied. Although the JIC wrote mainly on topics chosen by the COS, it was entitled to commission its own assessments, occasionally producing papers that were of no interest to the COS. There is no evidence that, during the period up to 1956, the JIC investigated whether its reports were read by consumers or that it attempted to establish what its customers might find of most value.

Achieving a consensus was the main imperative, which meant that the JIC readership knew nothing of any alternative interpretations that had been discussed and discounted. Moreover, the FO Chairman would sometimes brief the FO based on his own individual view, without reference to the Committee's joint view to which he had agreed. It does not appear that such comments were shared more widely. Presumably other JIC members would also express individual views to their Ministers or other officials in their departments when relevant, but few examples survive.

Another result of seeking consensus was the tendency to draft assessments in an equivocal manner, presumably to satisfy all concerned but running the risk of pleasing no-one. A further issue lay in the way in which JIC assessments were sometimes used by the Service staffs. For instance, the COS used a JIC paper on Soviet capabilities and intentions as the basis for discussions with the French and the US, resulting in an assessment drafted for NATO. Difficulties then arose when the JIC's judgments altered over time but the assessment for NATO was not revised. The JIC's Secretary warned Committee members that 'the situation may thus arise of there being both in Whitehall and in UK Command Headquarters two estimates of probable Soviet campaigns, both endorsed by the JIC yet not entirely agreeing with each other'.[9]

The intention was always to have language that was clear and concise, yet at times those interacting with the JIC must have been left bewildered. Consider the following point on future Soviet actions which the JIC wanted the COS Committee to note: '. . . the JIC thought that we could always count on a congenital inability on the part of the Russians to resist any temptation to resort to opportunist overt tactics incompatible with the conduct of a genuine Calming Campaign'.[10]

Assessments were rarely less than four pages long, and more often seven or eight pages, with several annual surveys of Soviet military capabilities running to over one-hundred pages. It is hard to imagine that the majority of the reports were read, let alone digested. One astute Secretary to the COS Committee in the early 1950s recognised this, commenting:

> I should be grateful if you would ensure that from now on all JIC Reports which have even the remotest chance of being seen by a Minister have a Cover Note of, at the very most, two sheets. This Cover Note or Summary should be not merely a repetition of the Conclusions of the paper, but a true Summary which can go before a Minister on its own account.[11]

The JIC's most important and widely recognised task was the production of intelligence assessments. To maximise their value to decision makers, these should satisfy four conditions:

a) they have to be timely;
b) delivered in the right way to the right people;
c) be relevant to the work and interests of the target audience; and
d) be sufficiently accurate or, at least, provide better information than that found elsewhere.

In 1941, the creation of the JIS ensured that assessments could be produced rapidly, on a variety of topics and in a variety of formats, and distributed securely and quickly. Thus, the JIC was able to produce operational and tactical summaries, as well as longer, strategic assessments. Much the same can be said for aspects of the post-war period, when it was intimately involved with the military planning needed for Korea, Indochina, and Egypt.

Although, as noted, the JIC did not consult its customers, a 1951 retrospective study concluded that, on the whole, it had performed well in monitoring Soviet actions, though with some notable failures in predicting Soviet moves. Several assumptions underlay its assessments of the Soviet Union, ranging from the conclusion in the early 1950s that Germany was the key to the Cold War, to the belief that Moscow's reach was global even if its underlying characteristic was to be cautious. The JIC developed with the military intelligence staffs a huge list of indicators which, if activated, would suggest that the Soviet Union was preparing for war. In addition to set-piece assessments it provided a weekly summary of worldwide current events. The nature of its work encompassed what we would now call the functions of horizon scanning, prediction, early-warning, explanation, anticipating surprise, and situational awareness. This last function was important because the JIC was much more than a 'crystal ball gazer', and in its routine monitoring function, particularly once a crisis was underway, it provided a measured account of what was happening. The JIC also maintained an organisational structure that could be mobilised and expanded when the need arose.

The increasingly global nature of the Cold War from the late 1940s onwards posed a major challenge. The intelligence community found it difficult to penetrate the Soviet system and understanding the Chinese psyche was even harder. The eventual victory for the communists in the Chinese civil war and the conflict in Korea, together with the increasing signs of unrest in places like Malaya and Iran, extended the JIC's horizons. As in Eastern Europe, there were gaps in intelligence coverage underpinning assessments on both the Far East and Middle East. All-source analyses and the assumptions on which they were based therefore became even more important.

Understanding of the mentality of the Soviet leadership, particularly after the harrowing experiences of the war with Germany, was hard. The JIC struggled to comprehend whether Stalin's actions in the early Cold War period were examples of defensive paranoia or offensive expansionism. The JIC took the view that the key to solving this dilemma was to understand how quickly the Soviet Union would be able to recover and reconstruct after the Second World War. The JIC soon concluded that overtly the Soviets would be cautious and that war would be a final resort, whilst deceit and deception would be deployed where Soviet aims required it. This assumption, immensely difficult to prove or disprove, was soon applied to other theatres. In the Far East, at least initially, the JIC correctly did not detect the hand of Moscow, though it did accept that any indigenous action by client states would need Soviet approval. In the Middle East, by contrast, the strength of nationalism and communism became conflated in the JIC's view, and the Committee tended to identify underhand tactics on the part of the Soviet Union, even if there was no explicit evidence to support such a judgment. In the case of Nasser, for example, the JIC was inclined to equate his anti-British stance with a pro-Soviet one.

The difficulty in all of these instances, as Cradock has observed, was 'in attributing rational motivation to the other side.'[12] The general lack of high level, reliable and verifiable intelligence had an impact on the quality of analysis. There is an obvious point here: that intelligence assessment tends to be as strong, or as weak, as the intelligence collection which feeds it. Given the pre-war difficulties in penetrating enemy intentions, the JIC had been alert to the need to plan for the future, culminating in the 'Intelligence Machine' model advocated by Cavendish-Bentinck and Capel-Dunn in early 1945. But the intelligence community was faced with the immense task of gathering valuable intelligence in the face of extensive and near impenetrable protective security surrounding the Soviet leadership. The JIC certainly recognised the scale of the challenge faced, not just in the case of the Soviet Union but more broadly, commenting in a 1954 paper that 'there has never been so hard a task as the penetration of the Communist bloc'.[13]

To its credit the JIC frequently began assessments by highlighting the difficulties in gathering intelligence, including gaps in its knowledge. A typical example was the opening phrase 'we do not have any good sources of information'. There is no record of the readership's reaction to such candour, but exposing the problem in this way is certainly an example of good practice. The JIC, as the voice of the intelligence community, was able to secure greater funds and, slowly but surely, by the early 1950s intelligence coverage began to improve. It also began to establish priorities for intelligence collection and to coordinate demands placed on the agencies for intelligence.

Issues with intelligence collection underlined the importance of another aspect of the JIC's work – liaison. This was conducted at a strategic level and its role and importance can be best demonstrated by the turbulent relationship with the US intelligence community. The war effort ensured that British and American intelligence agencies needed to collaborate and, from the outset, the UK assumed the role of senior partner. This assumption, at least on the British part, continued into the immediate post-war period whilst President Truman established a US intelligence community. However, British intelligence increasingly had to rely upon US sources to make up for gaps in its own coverage. Rapidly the balance of power shifted across the Atlantic and the Americans, with their far greater resources, became the dominant partner. On the whole the JIC worked well with its US counterparts, but initial difficulties in comprehending the shifting nature of the relationship, together with the impact of US political rulings (particularly over colonial conflicts) on intelligence collaboration, created tensions. Nonetheless, the JIC – and the British intelligence community – saw itself as an essential partner for the US in assessing intelligence, as well as contributing to areas of collection where the US lacked geographical sites and analytical expertise.

The inherent difficulties of trying to avoid surprise, of producing predictive assessments, of attempting to impose a rational explanation of events only dimly perceived, pose epistemological problems of the highest order. The performance of the JIC cannot solely be judged by how often it was surprised by dramatic events. It is also important to recognise that the JIC made an important contribution to day to day planning and policy.

The intelligence successes of the Second World War set a precedent that was impossible to repeat and post-war performances of the JIC should not be judged against this standard. A 1952 minute perfectly summarised the JIC's own view on the system:

> The British Intelligence machine in the UK is required to deal with a welter of miscellaneous subjects at top speed. It might, in fact, be said without

exaggeration that the machine is propelled by a succession of panics, due to insufficient time being available to deal with questions of the highest importance . . . one cause is undoubtedly the difficulty of sorting out the mass of detailed intelligence available into the form of reasoned appreciations.[14]

The production of regular assessments at both strategic and tactical levels; the weekly forum for discussions between the most senior figures in intelligence, defence and foreign policy; the compilation of almost encyclopaedic references and orders of battle for different countries; and the capability to spring into action in crisis, ensured that the JIC had a unique contribution to make and was an indispensable component in defence, foreign and security policymaking. Despite the Suez setback, by 1957 the JIC's position was secure. Maurice Hankey's 1935 belief that 'there is a good deal which could be done to put our intelligence on a better footing' had been vindicated.[15]

Notes

1   ZP2/15/G. SC(58)20, 'Sir N. Brook's Letter of December 5, 1957', Note by R.W.J.Hooper. FO 371/135611.
2   Cavendish-Bentinck to P Beesly, 10 January 1978. Churchill College, Cambridge: MLBE 3/24.
3   On this he helped steer a particularly difficult moment when his JIC colleagues complained about Godfrey's 'somewhat over-bearing attitude towards them and the fact that he was not temperamentally a "team-worker".' Cavendish-Bentinck to P Beesly, 28 March 1978. Churchill College, Cambridge: MLBE 3/24. The result was that following a request from Cavendish-Bentinck, the Vice Chief of the Naval Staff conducted a review which led to Godfrey's removal as DNI, a move approved by the First Lord of the Admiralty. Details are in ADM 205/20 and letters from Cavendish-Bentinck in Churchill College, Cambridge: MLBE 3/24.
4   Cradock, *Know Your Enemy.* p.296.
5   Capel-Dunn to P.Loxley [FO], 27 September 1944. FO 1093/188.
6   COS to Middle Eastern Land Forces, 22 January 1952. DEFE 11/350.
7   R V Jones, *Reflections on Intelligence* (London: William Heinemann, 1989). p.28.
8   V.Cavendish-Bentinck to W.Hayter, 7 December 1946. PUSD Papers, FCO.
9   JIC/1200/55, 'The Relation between JIC and International Estimates', 28 April 1955. CAB 176/53.
10 Confidential Annex to COS(51)140th Meeting, 5 September 1951. DEFE 11/350. The Calming Campaign referred to the idea that the Russians would try to deliberately relax tensions.
11 R.W.Ewbank [Secretary, COS Committee] to JIC Secretary, 6 November 1951. DEFE 11/350.
12 Cradock, *Know Your Enemy.* p.294
13 'The State of Our Intelligence', draft JIC paper, n.d. 1954. PUSD Papers, FCO.
14 JIC/2221/52, 'World-Wide Intelligence Organisation', 30 September 1952. CAB 176/38.
15 M.P.A.Hankey to W.M.James, 31 October 1935. CAB 21/2651.

Appendix I – JIC Chairmen

Brigadier Desmond F. Anderson [Army]	July 1936 – December 1937
Brigadier Roger Evans [Army]	February 1938 – July 1938
Brigadier Frederick G. Beaumont-Nesbitt [Army]	November 1938 – July 1939
Ralph C. Skrine Stevenson [FO]	August 1939 – December 1939
Victor F. W. Cavendish-Bentinck [FO]	December 1939 – August 1945
Harold A. Caccia [FO]	November 1945 – August 1946
William G. Hayter [FO]	October 1946 – November 1950
D. Patrick Reilly [FO]	November 1950 – April 1953
Patrick H. Dean [FO]	May 1953 – July 1960

Appendix II – JIC Secretaries

Major L. C. Hollis, [Royal Marines]	July 1936 – March 1939
Major A. T. Cornwall-Jones [Army]	April 1939 – June 1939
Major A. N. Barnard [Army]	June 1939 – April 1940
Major R. White Cooper [Army]	May 1940 – May 1940
Lt. Colonel C. T. Edwards [Army]	May 1940 – February 1941
Lt. Colonel S. N. Shoosmith [Army]	March 1941 – November 1941
Major D. C. Capel-Dunn [Army]	November 1941 – June 1943
Lt. Colonel E. J. C. King-Salter [Army]	July 1943 – October 1945
Lt. Colonel T. Haddon [Army]	October 1945 – May 1946
Lt. Colonel P. Gleadell [Army]	August 1946 – September 1948
Lt. Colonel J. K. Gardiner [Royal Marines]	October 1948 – July 1951
Colonel E. E. G. L. Searight [Army]	August 1951 – February 1956
Colonel J. G. Atkinson [Army]	February 1956 – November 1957

Appendix III – JIC Meeting Rooms

July 1936–July 1938	No. 2 Whitehall Gardens
November 1938–	Richmond Terrace
January 1942–	Secretary's Room, Great George Street
January 1945–	Secretary's Room, Offices of the War Cabinet
1946–November 1947	Joint Staff Conference Room, Offices of the Cabinet and Minister of Defence, Great George Street
November 1947–*	Conference Room 'G', Ministry of Defence, Great George Street

---

* From January 1954 the location of the meetings was not recorded in the minutes. The practice resumed with the move to the Cabinet Office in 1957.

Appendix IV – Annual JIC Meetings and Reports

Year	Meetings	Papers
1936	5	17
1937	7	30
1938	8	32
1939 Jan-Aug	14	60
Sept-Dec	18	7
1939 total	32	67
1940	75	65
1941	40	92
1942	63	51
1943	65	188
1944	75	233
1945[1]	83 (55)	121 (93)
1946	77	110
1947	92	85
1948	142	138
1949	133	118
1950	135	114
1951	139	131
1952	137	79
1953	133	122
1954	118	102
1955	102	85
1956	124	141
1957	104	132

Note: For September 1939 to December 1945, the number of JIC reports has been extracted from the total number of memoranda listed, which also includes JIC secretarial notes and other memoranda from individual JIC members.

Note

1 The numbers in brackets represent the total by VJ Day, 15 August 1945.

Appendix V – JIC Sub-Committees

The dates listed do not necessarily represent the start of these committees; rather, they are representative of the period in which they existed.

1937

April   Proposal to set up a sub committee to consider 'Air Warfare on Spain'.[1]

1938

April   Proposal to extend the scope of the 'Air Warfare Committee on Spain' to cover all Air Warfare.[2]

June   Reference to a sub-committee on 'Bombing and Anti-Aircraft Gunfire Experiments'.[3]

July   Terms of reference for 'Air Warfare Sub-Committee'.[4]

1939

March   Dissolution of 'Air Warfare Sub-Committee'.[5]

June   Reference to Air Warfare Sub-Committee on 'Active Air Defence and Passive Air Defence in the Field'.[6]

1943

August   'Inter-Services Security Board'.[7]

1945

April   'Ad Hoc Committee on the Joint Intelligence Bureau'.[8]

May   'Ad Hoc Committee for Co-ordination of Scientific and Technical Intelligence'.[9]

July   'Advisory Committee on the Intelligence Exploitation of German Science and Industry'.[10]

August   Directive to the 'Joint Photographic Reconnaissance Committee'.[11]

September   'Ad Hoc Committee on the Middle East'.[12]

November   'Interservice Topographical Department'.[13]

November   Proposals for the dissolution of the 'W/T Security Committee'.[14]

1946

April	'Ad Hoc Committee on Carrier Pigeons'.[15]
August	Dissolution of the 'Interservice Topographical Department'.[16]
September	'Documents Panel'.[17]

1947

| August | Future of the 'Inter-Service Language Committee'.[18] |
| September | Composition and functions of 'JIC (Far East)'.[19] |

The various ad hoc and sub-committees subsequently became formal sub-committees of the JIC and are first listed in a 1948 review.

1948
Review of JIC Organisation and Procedures[20]
Security Sub-Committee
Service Attachés Sub-Committee
Inter Services Languages Sub-Committee
Carrier Pigeon Sub-Committee
Joint Air and Photographic Intelligence Board
Intelligence Mobilisation Plans

1949
Intelligence Organisation[21]
Joint Scientific Intelligence Sub-Committee
Joint Technical Intelligence Sub-Committee
Exchange of Military Information Sub-Committee
Security Sub-Committee
Metric Security Sub-Committee
Inter-Service Languages Sub-Committee
Intelligence Mobilisation Plans Sub-Committee
BBC Monitoring Requirements Sub-Committee
Service Attachés Sub-Committee
Joint Air Photographic Intelligence Board
Carrier Pigeon Sub-Committee
Evasion and Escape Sub-Committee

1955
History of the Joint Intelligence Organisation[22]
Joint Scientific and Technical Intelligence Sub-Committee
Service Attachés Sub-Committee
Intelligence Mobilisation Plans Sub-Committee
BBC Monitoring Requirements Sub-Committee
Inter-Service Languages Sub-Committee
Air Reconnaissance and Photographic Intelligence Sub-Committee

1957
History of the Joint Intelligence Organisation [23]
Scientific and Technical Intelligence Sub-Committee
Intelligence and Nuclear Weapons Sub-Committee
Intelligence Mobilisation Plans Sub-Committee
Defectors Sub-Committee
BBC Monitoring Sub-Committee
Joint Air Reconnaissance Intelligence Board

Notes

1 JIC(1937)8th Meeting, 26 April 1937. CAB 56/1.
2 JIC(1938)15th Meeting, 25 April 1938. CAB 56/1.
3 JIC(1938)17th Meeting, 15 June 1938. CAB 56/1.
4 JIC(1938)19th Meeting, 21 July 1938. CAB 56/1.
5 JIC(1939)24th Meeting, 22 March 1939. CAB 56/1.
6 JIC(1939)28th Meeting, 13 June 1939. CAB 56/1.
7 JIC/1282/43, 'Inter-Services Security Board', 26 August 1943. CAB 176/1.
8 JIC/557/45, 'Ad Hoc Committee on the Joint Intelligence Bureau', 26 April 1945. CAB 176/5.
9 JIC/579/45, 'Ad Hoc Committee for Co-ordination of Scientific and Technical Intelligence', 2 May 1945. CAB 176/5.
10 JIC/901/45, 'Advisory Committee on the Intelligence Exploitation of German Science and Industry', 1 July 1945. CAB 176/5.
11 JIC/1133/45, 'Directive to the Joint Photographic Reconnaissance Committee', 13 August 1945. CAB 176/7.
12 JIC/1301/45, 'Meeting of the Ad Hoc Committee on the Middle East', 10 September 1945. CAB 176/7.
13 JIC/1681/45, "Interservice Topographical Department', 16 November 1945. CAB 176/8.
14 JIC/1755/45, 'The Work of the W/T Security Committee and Proposals for Its Dissolution', 27 November 1945. CAB 176/8.
15 JIC/418/46, 'Ad Hoc Committee on Carrier Pigeons', 2 April 1946. CAB 176/10.
16 JIC/1036/46, 'Closing Down of the ISTD', 2 August 1946. CAB 176/12.
17 JIC/1270/46, 'Documents Panel', 17 September 1946. CAB 176/12.
18 JIC/796/47, 'Future of the Inter-Service Language Committee', 13 August 1947. CAB 176/15.
19 JIC/904/47, 'Composition and functions of the Joint Intelligence Committee, Far East', 5 September 1947. CAB 176/15.
20 JIC(48)14th Meeting, CAB 159/3.
21 JIC/1416/49, 'Intelligence Organisation', 10 August 1949. CAB 176/23.
22 JIC/1009/55, 'History of the Joint Intelligence Organisation', 22 April 1955. CAB 163/8.
23 JIC(57)123, 'History of the Joint Intelligence Organisation', 29 November 1957. CAB 158/30.

Appendix VI – Terms of Reference for the Ad Hoc Committee on Carrier Pigeons

JIC/418/46   CAB 176/10

Joint Intelligence Sub-Committee

<u>Ad Hoc Committee on Carrier Pigeons</u>

Minutes of the first meeting of the Ad Hoc Committee on Carrier Pigeons held in the Joint Staff Conference Room, Offices of the Cabinet and Minister of Defence, on <u>Tuesday 2nd April 1946 at 1100am</u>

<u>Present</u>

Brigadier E.K.Page
War Office (In the Chair)

Colonel J.M.Phillips,   Wing Commander W.D.L.Rayner
R.M. Admiralty   Air Ministry

Squadron Leader R.L.Matthews   Flight Lieutenant R.M.Walker
Security Service

Captain J. Caiger

<u>Secretary</u>

Major J.K.Gardiner, R.M.

Terms of Reference of the Committee

- To ensure that the valuable experience gained by the use of carrier pigeons during the war is not lost.
- To be responsible for considering matters concerning research and development in connection with carrier pigeons.
- To maintain liaison between Departments and to collect and collate information on developments in the Civilian Pigeon Fancy.
- To instigate Service research into special equipment.
- To consider and collate information and data on foreign pigeon racing and to collate information on developments in the use of pigeons by Foreign Powers.
- To report progress at appropriate intervals to the Joint Intelligence Sub-Committee.

Appendix VII – JIC Records for 1936–56

Though it changes slightly over time, generally speaking the material is organised in a regular way[1]:

- CAB 56   JIC Minutes and Memoranda, 1936–9 (**complete**)
- CAB 81   JIC Minutes and Memoranda, 1939–46 (**largely complete**)
- CAB 158   JIC Memoranda, 1947–68 (**largely complete**)[2]
- CAB 159   JIC Minutes, 1947–68 (**largely complete**)
- CAB 163   JIC Secretariat files, 1939 onwards (**large gaps**)[3]
- CAB 176   JIC Secretariat minutes, 1942–68 (**large gaps**)[4]
- CAB 179   JIC Weekly Reviews, Surveys and Summaries, 1956 onwards (**largely complete**)[5]
- CAB 182   JIC Sub-Committees, Working Parties etc, 1957 onwards (**varied**)[6]
- CAB 191   JIC regional and local Committees, 1947 onwards (**largely missing**)[7]

Notes

1 A more detailed summary, including a longer time period, can be found at www.cabinetoffice.gov.uk 'Notes on the Central Intelligence Machinery division of Cabinet Office records'.

2 The preservation policy was to keep only the final, disseminated version of papers. In only a few instances has an earlier draft been found, and there is virtually no information about the JIS drafting process or meetings. This is a shame as there were at least three iterative stages before the final draft (Preliminary Draft; Draft; Revised Draft). CAB 158 also includes volumes of sensitive Confidential Annexes to Committee minutes, essentially the material that is too secret for the mainstream minutes, often with codewords (**largely complete**).

3 This is a fantastic series, containing JIC papers and correspondence on specific subjects. Originally these were known as J-Series files. In a 1976 review of pre-1957 material, it was discovered that of 1200 original files, only 12 had been preserved. This was considered to be a 'rather ruthless destruction of records'! Note by M.E.Green, 'JIC Records', 5 August 1976. Cabinet Office papers.

4 Until 1964 only a representative selection for each year were preserved. From the file references it is clear that several thousand Secretariat minutes were produced each year, but only a small selection has been preserved.
5 This includes the 'Weekly Review of Current Intelligence' (the Grey Book) and the Weekly Survey of Intelligence' (the Red Book). The Grey Book was intended for a fairly wide distribution, whereas the Red Book expanded on selected items of current intelligence at higher levels of classification and had a much more limited distribution.
6 Until 1957 these papers were disseminated as Secretariat Minutes and as such the record is quite patchy.
7 The difficulty is that these were never, technically speaking, Cabinet Office committees, so it was the responsibility of parent departments to maintain and preserve the files. JIC(G), for instance, was an MoD committee, while the regional LICs were subordinate to local governors – for this reason some of the relevant papers are amongst the India Office files at the British Library and the Colonial Office records at the TNA.

Appendix VIII – Suez Chronology

A Comparison of Events and JIC Products

	1952
	11 Dec - JIC(52)13(meeting) Report on Nasser's opposition
	1953
	18 May - JIC ME(53)38 Final, Report on insecurity of the Egyptian regime; passed to the PM (Churchill)
	1953
	10 Aug - JIC (53)60 Final Possible Consequences of an outbreak of hostilities with Egypt
1954	**1954**
	26 May - JIC/1253/54 reports on possible arms shipments to Egypt, warning of Soviet involvement
October - Britain signs Suez base evacuation agreement with Nasser	
1955	**1955**
18 May - Nasser initiates Czech arms deal	
27 September - Egyptian Czechoslovak arms deal announced	29 September - JIC(55)42Final, Soviet threat to the Middle East (reporting the Czech arms deal with Egypt).
	16 November - JIC/3014/55 Arms traffic to the Middle East (report on the scale of the purchases)
21 November - start of talks with UK/US on financing the Aswan High Dam	
	12 December - JIC/3942/55 report on Egyptian proficiency with the new arms equipment

1956	1956
	4 April - JIC(56)20 Final, 'Factors affecting Egypt's Policy in the Middle East and North Africa'
13 June - UK completes evacuation from Suez base	5 July - JIC (56)73 Final, The Likelihood of war between Israel and the Arab states (judged likely before the end of 1956)
19 July - US government announces it will not finance the Aswan high dam	19–26 July - JIC (WSI) Nasser's reaction to UK/US refusal to fund the Aswan Dam
26 July - Nasser's speech on nationalisation of the Suez Canal	26 July – 2 August - JIC (WSI), Nasser discussions with his naval chiefs and the possible attack on the Suez Canal
27 July - Cabinet decision taken to prepare for war in the last resort	
29 July - Egypt committee set up (PM and Ministers)	
31 July - Dulles arrives in London for talks with UK and France	1 August - JIC(56)82 Security of planning for action against Egypt
2 August - Speech by the PM on need for an international authority to control the Suez Canal (and hence to reverse Nasser's coup)	3 August - JIC(56)80 Final, The implications of Egyptian nationalisation of the Canal
5 August - PM visit to the US President (to discuss dual objectives – to reverse the ownership of the Canal and to bring down Nasser)	7 August - JIC(56)66th meeting Likely implications of a conflict with Egypt
	7 August - JIC(56)84 Final, Considerations affecting Egypt in the event of armed intervention (including possible Israeli intervention)
10 August - Chiefs of Staff present plan "MUSKETEER" to the Egypt Committee of the Cabinet	
	15 August - JIC(FE)(56)23 Final Implications of the Suez Canal dispute in SE Asia and the FE
16 August - Suez conference in London, Menzies mission to Nasser agreed	
August - UK forces called up	17 August - JIC(ME)(56)39 Final, Political and Military effects in the ME of certain developments in the Suez Canal situation

1956	1956
19 August - PM message to Dulles, cannot maintain preparations indefinitely – Dulles rejects the use of force	
	25 August - JIC(56)93 Final(Revise) The situation which might arise in the ME at the conclusion of the Suez Conference
3 September - Nasser rejects Menzies mission	
4 September - Dulles proposes Suez Canal Users Association	
7 September - Chiefs of Staff change invasion plan to MUSKETEER Revise	
10 September - Cabinet endorses SCUA	
19 September - Second international conference opens	
21 September - approves SCUA	
	27 September - JIC(56)86th meeting Discussions in London with US representatives
	28 September - JIC(56) 102 Israel attitude towards Arab States in the context of the Suez Canal crisis
	4 October - JIC(56) 98 Final, Possible Soviet assistance to Egypt's military effort in certain circumstances
	11 October - JIC(56)97 Final, Probable actions by Nasser in certain circumstances
16 October - PM and FO Sec to Paris talks, reported to Cabinet on 18 Oct	18 October - JIC(56)104(Final) The threat to UK Interests overseas
23 October - UK and France refer dispute to the UN	
24 October – Sèvres Protocol agreed and signed by UK France and Israel	
29 October - Israel attacks Egyptian army in Sinai	29 October - JIC situation reports - 5 times a day following Israel's attack on Egypt
31 October - Anglo French attack on Egyptian airfields	
2 November - UN calls for ceasefire	
4 November - Egypt blocks the Canal	
4 November - Russian troops enter Budapest	
5/6 November - UK–French landings at Suez Canal	

1956	1956
6 November - Eisenhower elected US president	
6 November - JIC(56)111 Soviet Threat of Intervention in the Middle East	
	8 November - JIC(ME)63056 Appreciation of possible nature of Soviet intervention in the Middle East
	11 November - JIC(56)117 Final Soviet Designs in the Middle East
	13 November - JIC/ 2780 Possibility of Russian intervention in the Middle East in the immediate future
15 November - US refuse financial assistance until withdrawal from the Canal	15 November - JIC(56)122 Possibility of Russian Intervention in the Middle East in the immediate future
30 November - Cabinet accepts that unconditional withdrawal from Egypt inevitable	
20 December - Eden tells House of Commons no foreknowledge of Israel attack	
22 December - Evacuation of UK/French troops completed	

1957	
9 January - Eden resigns	
1 March - Israel announces to UN plan to withdraw	
10 April - Suez Canal reopens	
	22 August - JIC 1792 Lessons from "MUSKETEER"
	12 December - JIC/3017 Intelligence in Operation "MUSKETEER"

Appendix IX – JIC Terms of Reference: 1936a

JIC 1   'Note by Secretary, Joint Planning Sub-Committee', 30 June 1936.[1]

The Sub-Committee agreed:

To approve the proposals put forward to enlarge the functions of the Joint Intelligence Committee, the effect of which would be:

a. to extend its functions to include work in connection with papers under preparation by the Joint Planning Committee;
b. that the Joint Planning Committee would, as necessary, give terms of reference to the Joint Intelligence Committee asking for information required for the preparation of Joint Planning Reports;
c. that the Joint Intelligence Committee was empowered to co-opt the services of Major Morton in any enquiries which they undertook in this connection;
d. that the Secretary to the Joint Planning Committee would assist the Joint Intelligence Committee in an organising and liaison capacity only, his duties with the Joint Planning Committee not being interfered with.

Note

1 CAB 56/2.

Appendix X – JIC Terms of Reference: 1936b

JIC 3   'Revised Functions and Working Arrangements', 14 July 1936.[1]

. . . such subjects as the following appear suitable for co-ordination in order to prevent overlapping:

a. Preparation of Intelligence Reports and provision of maps and plans for such publications.
b. Joint appreciations on possible enemy operations from the Intelligence point of view, e.g. Japanese operations against Hong Kong and Singapore.
c. Press liaison and security in combined exercises.
d. A.A. [anti-aircraft] defences of foreign countries.
e. Coastal defences of foreign countries.
f. Intelligence from Procedure Y. [signals intelligence]
g. Signal communications and developments.
h. Co-ordination of the work of the Intelligence Staffs of the three Services in special circumstances.
i. Questions involving the Defence Security Service where the three Defence Departments are concerned.

Note

1 CAB 56/2.

Appendix XI – JIC Terms of Reference: 1948

'Charter for the Joint Intelligence Committee', 24 February 1948[1]

The Joint Intelligence Committee is given the following responsibilities:

a. Under the Chiefs of Staff to plan, and to give higher direction to, operations of defence intelligence and security, to keep them under review in all fields and to report progress.
b. To assemble and appreciate available intelligence for presentation as required to the Chiefs of Staff and to initiate other reports as the Committee may deem necessary.
c. To keep under review the organisation of intelligence as a whole and in particular the relations of its component parts so as to ensure efficiency, economy and a rapid adaptation to changing requirements, and to advise the Chiefs of Staff of what changes are deemed necessary.
d. To co-ordinate the general policy of Joint Intelligence Committees under United Kingdom Commands overseas and to maintain an exchange of intelligence with them, and to maintain liaison with appropriate Commonwealth intelligence agencies.

Note

1 DO(48)21, 'Charter for the Joint Intelligence Committee', 24 February 1948. CAB 131/6.

Appendix XII – JIC Terms of Reference: 1955

JIC(55)74   'Charter for the Joint Intelligence Committee', 7 November 1955.[1]

a. To give higher direction to, and to keep under review, intelligence operations and defence security matters.
b. To assemble, appreciate and present intelligence as required by the Chiefs of Staff and to initiate such other reports as may be required or as the Committee may deem necessary.
c. To keep under review the organisation and working of intelligence and defence security as a whole at home and overseas so as to ensure efficiency, economy, and a rapid adaptation to changing requirements, and to advise what changes are deemed necessary.
d. To co-ordinate the activities of Joint Intelligence Committees under United Kingdom commands overseas and to maintain an exchange of intelligence with them.
e. To maintain liaison with appropriate intelligence and defence security agencies in the self-governing Commonwealth countries and the United States and other foreign countries, and with the intelligence authorities of international defence organisations of which the United Kingdom is a member.

Note

1 CAB 158/22.

Bibliography

a) Public archives

i) The National Archives, London

ADM 1   Admiralty, and Ministry of Defence, Navy Department: Correspondence and Papers
ADM 116 Admiralty: Record Office: Cases
ADM 199 Admiralty: War History Cases and Papers, Second World War
ADM 205 Admiralty: Office of the First Sea Lord, later First Sea Lord and Chief of the Naval Staff: Correspondence and Papers
ADM 223 Admiralty: Naval Intelligence Division and Operational Intelligence Centre: Intelligence Reports and Papers
AIR 2   Air Ministry and Ministry of Defence: Registered Files
AIR 8   Air Ministry and Ministry of Defence: Department of the Chief of the Air Staff: Registered Files
AIR 9   Air Ministry: Directorate of Operations and Intelligence and Directorate of Plans: Registered Files
AIR 19   Air Ministry, and Ministry of Defence, Air Department: Private Office Papers
AIR 20   Air Ministry, and Ministry of Defence: Papers accumulated by the Air Historical Branch
AIR 22   Air Ministry: Periodical Returns, Intelligence Summaries and Bulletins
AIR 40   Air Ministry, Directorate of Intelligence and related bodies: Intelligence Reports and Papers
AVIA 54 Ministry of Supply and predecessor and successors: Research, Registered Files (Series 7), Reports and Specifications
CAB 2   Committee of Imperial Defence and Standing Defence Sub-committee: Minutes
CAB 4   Committee of Imperial Defence: Miscellaneous Memoranda (B Series)
CAB 16   Committee of Imperial Defence, Ad Hoc Sub-Committees: Minutes, Memoranda and Reports
CAB 18   Committee of Imperial Defence: Miscellaneous Reports and Papers
CAB 21   Cabinet Office and predecessors: Registered Files (1916 to 1965)
CAB 27   War Cabinet and Cabinet: Miscellaneous Committees: Records (General Series)
CAB 37   Cabinet Office: Photographic Copies of Cabinet Papers

CAB 48	Committee of Imperial Defence: Sub-Committee on Industrial Intelligence in Foreign Countries: Minutes and Memoranda (IFC and FCI Series)
CAB 53	Committee of Imperial Defence: Chiefs of Staff Committee: Minutes and Memoranda
CAB 54	Committee of Imperial Defence: Deputy Chiefs of Staff Committee: Minutes and Memoranda
CAB 55	Committee of Imperial Defence: Joint Planning Committee: Minutes and Memoranda
CAB 56	Committee of Imperial Defence: Joint Intelligence Sub-Committee: Minutes and Memoranda (JIC, JIC(S), JIC(A))
CAB 79	War Cabinet and Cabinet: Chiefs of Staff Committee: Minutes
CAB 80	War Cabinet and Cabinet: Chiefs of Staff Committee: Memoranda
CAB 81	War Cabinet and Cabinet: Committees and Sub-Committees of the Chiefs of Staff Committee: Minutes and Papers
CAB 84	War Cabinet and Cabinet: Joint Planning Committee, later Joint Planning Staff, and Sub-Committees: Minutes and Memoranda (JP, JAP and other Series)
CAB 102	War Cabinet and Cabinet Office: Historical Section: War Histories (Second World War), Civil
CAB 104	Cabinet Office and predecessors: Supplementary Registered Files (1923–1951)
CAB 119	War Cabinet and Cabinet Office: Joint Planning Staff: Correspondence and Papers
CAB 120	Cabinet Office: Minister of Defence Secretariat: Records
CAB 121	Cabinet Office: Special Secret Information Centre: Files
CAB 122	War Cabinet and Cabinet Office: British Joint Staff Mission and British Joint Services Mission: Washington Office Records
CAB 127	Cabinet Office: Private Collections of Ministers' and Officials' Papers
CAB 128	Cabinet: Minutes (CM and CC Series)
CAB 129	Cabinet: Memoranda (CP and C Series)
CAB 130	Cabinet: Miscellaneous Committees: Minutes and Papers (GEN, MISC and REF Series
CAB 131	Cabinet: Defence Committee: Minutes and Papers (DO, D and DC Series
CAB 134	Cabinet: Miscellaneous Committees: Minutes and Papers (General Series
CAB 137	War Cabinet and Cabinet: Joint Technical Warfare Committee: Correspondence and Papers
CAB 154	War Cabinet and Cabinet Office: London Controlling Section Correspondence and Papers
CAB 158	Ministry of Defence and Cabinet Office: Central Intelligence Machinery: Joint Intelligence Sub-Committee later Committee: Memoranda (JIC Series)
CAB 159	Ministry of Defence and Cabinet Office: Central Intelligence Machinery: Joint Intelligence Sub-Committee later Committee: Minutes (JIC Series)
CAB 163	War Cabinet, Ministry of Defence, and Cabinet Office: Central Intelligence Machinery: Joint Intelligence Sub-Committee, later Committee: Secretariat: Files
CAB 164	Cabinet Office: Subject (Theme Series) Files
CAB 176	War Cabinet, Ministry of Defence and Cabinet Office: Joint Intelligence Sub-Committee, later Committee: Secretariat: Minutes (JIC(SEC))
CO 1022	Colonial Office: South East Asia Department: Original Correspondence

CO 1030   Colonial Office and Commonwealth Office: Far Eastern Department and successors: Registered Files (FED Series)

CO 1035   Colonial Office: Intelligence and Security Departments: Registered Files (ISD Series)

DEFE 4   Ministry of Defence: Chiefs of Staff Committee: Minutes

DEFE 5   Ministry of Defence: Chiefs of Staff Committee: Memoranda

DEFE 6   Ministry of Defence: Chiefs of Staff Committee: Reports of the Joint Planning Staff and successors

DEFE 7   Ministry of Defence prior to 1964: Registered Files (General Series)

DEFE 11   Ministry of Defence: Chiefs of Staff Committee: Registered Files

DEFE 13   Ministry of Defence: Private Office: Registered Files (all Ministers)

DEFE 19   Ministry of Defence: Central Defence Scientific Staff and predecessors: Registered Files (CSA, AE 1 and A Series) and Papers

DEFE 21   Ministry of Defence: Directorate of Scientific Intelligence: Joint Intelligence Bureau: Division of Scientific Intelligence and Division of Atomic Energy Intelligence and Directorate of Scientific and Technical Intelligence: Registered Files

DEFE 32   Ministry of Defence: Chiefs of Staff Committee: Secretary's Standard Files

DEFE 41   Foreign Office and Ministry of Defence: STIB and Overseas Liaison Branch: Registered Files

DEFE 44   Ministry of Defence – Directorate of Scientific Intelligence: Joint Intelligence Bureau; Division of Scientific Intelligence and Division of Atomic Energy Intelligence; Defence Intelligence Staff: Directorate of Scientific and Technical Intelligence: Reports, Notes and Memoranda

DO 35   Dominion Office and Commonwealth Relations Office: Original Correspondence

FCO 12   Foreign and Commonwealth Office and predecessors: Library and Records Department and predecessors: Registered Files (CL, L and LR Series)

FCO 73   Foreign Office and Foreign and Commonwealth Office: Private Offices: Various Ministers' and Officials' Papers

FO 248   Foreign Office and Foreign and Commonwealth Office: Embassy and Consulates, Iran (formerly Persia): General Correspondence

FO 366   Foreign Office and Diplomatic Service Administration Office: Chief Clerk's Department and successors: Records

FO 370   Foreign Office: Library and the Research Department: General Correspondence from 1906

FO 371   Foreign Office: Political Departments: General Correspondence from 1906–1966

FO 372   Foreign Office: Treaty Department and successors: General Correspondence from 1906

FO 800   Foreign Office, Private Offices: Various Ministers' and Officials' Papers

FO 1005   Foreign Office and Predecessors: Control Commission for Germany (British Element): Records Library: Files

FO 1020   Foreign Office and Predecessors: Allied Commission for Austria (British Element): Headquarters and Regional Files (ACA Series)

FO 1032   Economic and Industrial Planning Staff and Control Office for Germany and Austria and Successor: Control Commission for Germany (British Element), Military Sections and Headquarters Secretariat: Registered Files (HQ and other series)

FO 1050 Control Office for Germany and Austria and Foreign Office: Control Commission for Germany (British Element), Internal Affairs and Communications Division: Files

FO 1091 Commissioner General for the United Kingdom in South East Asia, and United Kingdom Commissioner for Singapore and South East Asia: Registered Files

FO 1093 Foreign Office: Permanent Under-Secretary's Department: Miscellaneous Unregistered Papers

HO 144 Home Office: Registered Papers, Supplementary

HW 1 Government Code and Cypher School: Signals Intelligence Passed to the Prime Minister, Messages and Correspondence

HW 3 Government Code and Cypher School and predecessors: Personal Papers, Unofficial Histories, Foreign Office X Files and Miscellaneous Records

HW 4 Government Code and Cypher School: Far East Combined Bureau, Signals Intelligence Centre in the Far East (HMS Anderson): Records

HW 14 Government Code and Cypher School: Directorate: Second World War Policy Paper

HW 42 Government Code and Cypher School: Sigint Board and Related Committees and Sub-Committees: Minutes, Papers and Correspondence

PREM 1 Prime Minister's Office: Correspondence and Papers, 1916–1940

PREM 3 Prime Minister's Office: Operational Correspondence and Papers, 1937–1946

PREM 4 Prime Minister's Office: Confidential Correspondence and Papers, 1934–1946

PREM 8 Prime Minister's Office: Correspondence and Papers, 1945–1951

PREM 11 Prime Minister's Office: Correspondence and Papers, 1951–1964

T 220 Treasury: Imperial and Foreign Division: Registered Files (IF series)

WO 32 War Office and successors: Registered Files (General Series)

WO 106 War Office: Directorate of Military Operations and Military Intelligence, and predecessors: Correspondence and Papers

WO 190 War Office: Directorate of Military Operations and Intelligence: German and adjacent Countries Military Situation Reports (Appreciation Files)

WO 193 War Office: Directorate of Military Operations and Plans, later Directorate of Military Operations: Files concerning Military Planning, Intelligence and Statistics (Collation Files)

WO 201 War Office: Middle East Forces; Military Headquarters Papers, Second World War

WO 203 War Office: South East Asia Command: Military Headquarters Papers, Second World War

WO 208 War Office: Directorate of Military Operations and Intelligence, and Directorate of Military Intelligence; Ministry of Defence, Defence Intelligence Staff : Files

WO 219 War Office: Supreme Headquarters Allied Expeditionary Force: Military Headquarters Papers, Second World War

ii) American National Archives, College Park, Maryland

RG 59 General Records of the Department of State

RG 263 CIA History Source Collection

RG 319 Records of the Army Staff

iii) US Presidential Libraries

Harry S. Truman Library, Independence, MO.
John F. Kennedy Library, Boston, MA.

iv) Canadian National Archives, Ottawa

RG24   Records of the Department of National Defence

b) Private papers

Annan, Lord N, (King's College, University of Cambridge)
Beaumont-Nesbitt, Major General F G, (LHCMA, King's College London)
British Diplomatic Oral History Programme (Churchill College, University of Cambridge)
British Naval Intelligence Papers, (Churchill College, University of Cambridge)
Capel-Dunn, Colonel D (Privately Held)
Chamberlain, N (Birmingham University)
Crick, A J P (LHCMA, King's College London)
Davidson, Major General F H (LHCMA, King's College London)
Dixon, Sir P (Privately Held)
Fitzgerald, E (Imperial War Museum)
Goddard, Air Marshal Sir V (LHCMA, King's College London)
Godfrey, Admiral J (National Maritime Museum)
Haddon, Brigadier T (Imperial War Museum)
Hankey, Lord M (Churchill College, University of Cambridge)
Hart, Sir B L (LHCMA, King's College London)
Kennedy, Major General Sir J (LHCMA, King's College London)
Lewin, R (Churchill College, University of Cambridge)
Lewis, J (Privately Held)
Nuclear Age Interview Transcripts (LHCMA, King's College London)
Reilly, Sir D P (Bodleian Library, University of Oxford)
Ridsdale, Sir J (Churchill College, University of Cambridge)
Sherfield, Lord (Bodleian Library, University of Oxford)
Shortt, Major General A C (Defence Intelligence and Security Centre, Chicksands)
Skrine Stevenson, Sir R C (Manx National Heritage Library, Isle of Man)
Suez Oral History Project (LHCMA, King's College London)
Troubridge, Vice Admiral Sir T (Churchill College, University of Cambridge)
Terrington (Woodhouse), Lord C M (LHCMA, King's College London)

c) Interviews

Alldis, Wing Commander C, 21 September 2009.
Cavendish-Bentinck, V, BBC Radio 4 Series 'The Profession of Intelligence', broadcast 16
   August 1981.
Cloake, J, 11 November 2010.
Millard, Sir G, 29 September 2010
Norman, E, 8 June 2009.
Ricketts, Sir P, 18 May 2009.
Walker-Sloan, K, 24 March 2010.

d) Printed primary sources

Ashton, S R (ed), *Documents on British Policy Overseas, Series I, Volume VIII: Britain and China, 1945–1950* (London: Frank Cass, 2002).

Benson, R L, 'The Origin of US-British Communications Intelligence Cooperation (1940–41)'. Available on the National Security Agency's website: www.nsa.gov

Cmd.6351, *The Organisation for Joint Planning* (London: HMSO, 1942).

Cmnd.8787, *Falkland Islands Review* (London: HMSO, 1983).

'Dulles Survey'. Available at: www.foia.cia.gov/helms/pdf/dulles_correa.pdf

Foreign Relations of the United States: The Conference at Washington, 1941–2 and Casablanca, 1943 (Washington, US Department of State, 1968).

Foreign Relations of the United States: The Far East: China, Volume IX, 1949 (Washington, DC: USGPO, 1974).

'Notes on the Central Intelligence Machinery division of Cabinet Office records'. Available at: www.cabinetoffice.gov.uk

'The Law and Custom of the National Intelligence Estimate'. Available at: www.cia.gov

The UK Government's Official History Programme (Cabinet Office booklet, 2010).

Troy, T F, *Donovan and the CIA: A History of the Establishment of the Central Intelligence Agency* (Washington, DC: CIA Center for the Study of Intelligence, 1981).

Warner, M, *The Office of Strategic Services: America's First Intelligence Agency* (CIA, 2000). Available at www.cia.gov

Warner, M, (ed.), *Central Intelligence: Origin and Evolution* (CIA History Staff, 2001). Available at www.cia.gov

Wilber, D N, *CIA Clandestine Service History: Overthrow of Premier Mossadeq of Iran, November 1952-August 1953* (March 1954). Available at www.gwu.edu

e) Published memoirs

Anderson, C C, 'Suez – 1956', *The Naval Review*, 79:4 (October 1991).

Annan, N, *Changing Enemies: The Defeat and Regeneration of Germany* (New York: Cornell University Press, 1995).

Burrows, B, *Diplomat in a Changing World* (County Durham: The Memoir Club, 2001).

Cline, R S, *Secrets, Spies and Scholars: The Essential CIA* (Washington, DC: Acropolis, 1976).

Colville, J, *Strange Inheritance* (London: Michael Russell, 1983).

Cooper, C L, *The Lion's Last Roar: Suez, 1956* (London: Harper and Row, 1978).

Cooper, C L, *In the Shadows of History: 50 Years Behind the Scenes of Cold War Diplomacy* (New York: Prometheus Books, 2005).

Copeland, M, *The Game Player: Confessions of the CIA's Original Political Operative* (London: Aurum Press, 1989).

Cradock, P, *In Pursuit of British Interests: Reflections on Foreign Policy under Margaret Thatcher and John Major* (London: John Murray, 1997).

Goddard, V, *Skies to Dunkirk: A Personal Memoir* (London: William Kimber, 1982).

Goudsmit, S A, *Alsos: The Failure in German Science* (New York: Schuman, 1947).

Greenhill, D, *More by Accident* (York: Wilton, 1992).

Hayter, W G, *A Double Life: The Memoirs of Sir William Hayter* (London: Penguin, 1974).

Kennedy, J, *The Business of War* (London: Hutchinson, 1957).

Jones, R V, *Reflections on Intelligence* (London: William Heinemann, 1989).

Lee, R E, *The London Observer: The Journal of General Raymond E. Lee, 1940–1941* (London: Hutchinson, 1971).

Macmillan, H, *The Tides of Fortune, 1945–1955* (London: Macmillan, 1969).

Matthias, W C, *America's Strategic Blunders: Intelligence Analysis and National Security Policy, 1936–1991* (Pennsylvania: Penn State Press, 2003).

McDermott, G, *The Eden Legacy and the Decline of British Diplomacy* (London: Leslie Frewin, 1969).

Pash, B T, *The Alsos Mission* (New York: Charter, 1969).

Peck, E H, *Recollections, 1915–2005* (New Delhi: Paul's Press, 2005).

Stewart, B, *Scrapbook of a Roving Highlander: 80 Years Round Asia and Back* (Newark: Acorn Publications, 2002).

Winterbotham, F W, *The Nazi Connection* (New York: Dell, 1978).

Woodhouse, C M, *Something Ventured* (London: Granada, 1982).

f) Newspaper articles

'A Liberator Missing, British Officials on Board, San Francisco Staff', *The Times* (7 July 1945).

'Awful Widmerpool is Unmasked At Last', *The Daily Telegraph* (30 December 1991).

'Caccia, Harold Anthony', *Oxford Dictionary of National Biography*.

'Col D.C.Capel-Dunn: An Appreciation', *The Times* (25 July 1945).

'Dean, Sir Patrick Henry', *Oxford Dictionary of National Biography*.

'Eton v. Old Etonians', *The Times* (19 March 1923).

'Hayter, Sir William Goodenough', *Oxford Dictionary of National Biography*.

'Law Report, March 27', *The Times* (28 March 1947).

'Law Report, November 6', *The Times* (7 November 1947).

'Letter to the Editor', *The Daily Telegraph* (3 January 1992).

'Mrs V.F.W.Cavendish-Bentinck, Appeal to House of Lords Withdrawn', *The Times* (6 July 1948).

'Obituary: Col. D.C.Capel-Dunn', *The Times* (19 July 1945).

'Obituary: John Colvin', *The Daily Telegraph* (17 October 2003).

'Obituary: Sir Patrick Dean', *The Times* (9 November 1994)

'Smear Technique', *TIME Magazine* (10 February 1947).

Greene, H, 'The Suez Story', *The Times*, (27 June 1978).

Greenhill, D, Letter to the Editor, *The Times* (7 May 1977).

Logan, D, 'Collusion at Suez', *The Financial Times* (8 January 1986).

Trevor-Roper, H, 'Hitler: Does History Offer a Defence?', *Sunday Times* (12 June 1977).

g) PhD theses

Case, S, *The Joint Intelligence Committee and the German Question, 1947–61* (PhD: Queen Mary, University of London, 2009).

Cormac, R, *The Joint Intelligence Committee and Colonial Counterinsurgency* (PhD: King's College London, 2011).

Craig, A J, *The Joint Intelligence Committee and British Intelligence Assessment, 1945–1956* (PhD: University of Cambridge, 1999).

Dylan, H, *The Joint Intelligence Bureau: Economic, Topographic and Military Intelligence for Britain's Cold War, 1946–64* (PhD: University of Aberystwyth, 2010).

h) Published works

Adamthwaite, A, 'Britain and the World, 1945–9: The View from the Foreign Office', *International Affairs,* 61:2 (Spring 1985).

Afkhami, G R, *The Life and Times of the Shah* (London: University of California Press, 2009).

Aldrich, R J, 'Never-Never Land and Wonderland? British and American Policy on Intelligence Archives', *Contemporary Record,* 8:1 (1994).

Aldrich, R J, *Intelligence and the War Against Japan: Britain, America and the Politics of Secret Service* (Cambridge: Cambridge University Press, 2000).

Aldrich, R J, *The Hidden Hand: Britain, America and Cold War Secret Intelligence* (London: John Murray, 2001).

Aldrich, R, & Coleman, M, 'The Cold War, the JIC and British Signals Intelligence, 1948', *Intelligence and National Security,* 4:3 (1989).

Alexander, M S, 'Perceptions by US Officials in Washington DC and London of Britain's Readiness for War in 1939', *Contemporary British History,* 25:1 (March 2011).

Anderson, S, 'The Evolution of the Canadian Intelligence Establishment, 1945–1950', *Intelligence and National Security,* 9: 3 (1994).

Andrew, C, *Her Majesty's Secret Service: The Making of the British Intelligence Community* (London: Heinemann, 1985).

Andrew, C, *The Defence of the Realm: The Authorized History of MI5* (London: Allen Lane, 2009).

Armstrong, B, 'Through a Glass Darkly; The Royal Air Force and the Lessons of the Spanish Civil War, 1936–1939', *Air Power Review,* 12:1 (Spring 2009).

Ashton, N R, 'The Hijacking of a Pact: The Formation of the Baghdad Pact and Anglo-American Tensions in the Middle East, 1955–1958', *Review of International Studies,* 19 (1993).

Athanassopoulou, E, *Turkey: Anglo-American Security Interests, 1945–1952* (London: Frank Cass, 1999).

Barenblatt, R, *A Plague Upon Humanity: The Secret Genocide of Axis Japan's Secret Germ Warfare Operation* (London: HarperCollins, 2004).

Baxter, C, 'Forgeries and Spies: The Foreign Office and the "Cicero" Case', *Intelligence and National Security,* 23:6 (December 2008).

Baxter, C, 'A Closed Book? British Intelligence and East Asia, 1945–1950', *Diplomacy and Statecraft,* 22:4 (2011).

Bayandor, D, *Iran and the CIA: The Fall of Mossadeq Revisited* (Basingstoke: Palgrave Macmillan, 2010).

Beevor, A, *The Battle for Spain: The Spanish Civil War 1936–1939* (London: Weidenfeld & Nicolson, 2006).

Bekes, C, 'The 1956 Hungarian Revolution and World Politics', *Cold War International History Project,* Working Paper #16 (1996).

Bekes, C, 'The 1956 Hungarian Revolution and World Politics', *Cold War International History Project,* Working Paper No.16 (September 1996).

Bekes, C, 'Soviet Plans to Establish the COMINFORM in Early 1946: New Evidence from the Hungarian Archives', *Cold War International History Project,* Bulletin 10 (1998).

Bennett, G, *Churchill's Man of Mystery: Desmond Morton and the World of Intelligence* (London: Routledge, 2007).

Bennett, G, 'Suez and the Threat to UK Interests Overseas' In Dover, R, & Goodman, M S, (eds.), *Learning from the Secret Past: Cases in British Intelligence History* (Washington, DC: Georgetown University Press, 2011).

Bennett, R, 'Intelligence and Strategy: Some Observations on the War in the Mediterranean 1941–45', *Intelligence and National Security*, 5:2 (1990).

Best, A, 'Constructing an Image: British Intelligence and Whitehall's Perception of Japan, 1931–1939', *Intelligence and National Security*, 11:3 (July 1996)

Best, A, '"This Probably Over Valued Military Power": British Intelligence and Whitehall's Perception of Japan, 1939–41', *Intelligence and National Security*, 12:3 (1997).

Best, A, *British Intelligence and the Japanese Challenge in Asia, 1914–1941* (London: Palgrave, 2002).

Borg, D, & Okamoto, S, (eds.), *Pearl Harbor as History: Japanese-American Relations, 1931–1941* (Columbia: Columbia University Press, 1973).

Brandwein, D S, 'Telemetry Analysis', *CIA Studies in Intelligence* (Fall 1964).

Brent, J, & Naumov, J, *Stalin's Last Crime: The Plot Against the Jewish Doctors, 1948–1953* (London: HarperCollins, 2004).

Buchanan, T, *Britain and the Spanish Civil War* (Cambridge: Cambridge University Press, 1997).

Butterfield, H, 'Official History: Its Pitfalls and Criteria', *Studies: An Irish Quarterly Review*, 38:150 (1949).

Caplan, N, *Futile Diplomacy, Volume Four: Operation Alpha and the Failure of Anglo-American Coercive Diplomacy in the Arab-Israeli Conflict, 1954–1956* (London: Frank Cass, 1997).

Carew Hunt, R N, *The Theory and Practice of Communism* (London: Pelican, 1969).

Catterall, P, (ed.), *The Macmillan Diaries: The Cabinet Years, 1950–1957* (London: Pan, 2004).

Cerda, N, 'The Road to Dunkirk: British Intelligence and the Spanish Civil War', *War in History*, 13 (2006).

Chadwick, O, *Acton and History* (Cambridge: Cambridge University Press, 1998).

Chaqueri, C, *The Soviet Socialist Republic of Iran, 1920–1921: Birth of the Trauma* (London: University of Pittsburgh Press, 1995).

Charles, D M, '"Before the Colonel Arrived": Hoover, Donovan, Roosevelt and the Origins of American Central Intelligence, 1940–41', *Intelligence and National Security*, 20:2 (June 2005).

Churchill, W S, *The Second World War, Volume I: The Gathering Storm* (London: Cassell, 1948).

Churchill, W S, *The Second World War: Volume III, The Grand Alliance* (London: Cassell, 1964).

Cole, B, 'British Technical Intelligence and the Soviet Intermediate Range Ballistic Missile Threat, 1952–1960', *Intelligence and National Security*, 14:2 (Summer 1999).

Cormac, R, 'Organising Intelligence: An Introduction to the 1955 Report on Colonial Security', *Intelligence and National Security*, 25:6 (2010).

Cradock, P, *Know Your Enemy: How the Joint Intelligence Committee Saw the World* (London: John Murray, 2002).

Cubbage, T L, 'The German Misapprehensions Regarding Overlord', *Intelligence and National Security*, 2:3 (July 1987).

Cubbage, T L, 'The Success of Operation Fortitude: Hesketh's History of Strategic Deception', *Intelligence and National Security*, 2:3 (July 1987).

Delaney, D E, 'Churchill and the Mediterranean Strategy: December 1941 to January 1943, *Defence Studies*, 2:3 (2002).

Dockrill, M L, 'The Foreign Office, Anglo-American Relations and the Korean War, June 1950-June 1951', *International Affairs*, 62:3 (1986).

Doughty, R A, 'The Illusion of Security: France, 1919–1940' In Murray, W, et al, (eds.), *The Making of Strategy: Rulers, States and War* (Cambridge: Cambridge University Press, 1994).

Dylan, H, 'Britain and the Missile Gap: British Estimates on the Soviet Ballistic Missile Threat, 1957–61', *Intelligence and National Security*, 23:6 (2009).

Ehrman, J, *Grand Strategy: Vol. V, August 1943-September 1944* (London, HMSO: 1956).

Erskine, R, 'From the Archives: A Bletchley Park Assessment of German Intelligence on Torch', *Cryptologia*, 13:2 (1989).

Erskine, R, 'The Holden Agreement on Naval Sigint: The First BRUSA?', *Intelligence and National Security*, 14:2 (1999).

Farquharson, J, 'Governed or Exploited? The British Acquisition of German Technology, 1945–48', *Journal of Contemporary History*, 32:1 (January 1997).

Farrar-Hockley, A, *The Official History of the British Part in the Korean War, Volume I: A Distant Obligation* (London; HMSO, 1990).

Farrar-Hockley, A, *The Official History of the British Part in the Korean War, Volume II: An Honourable Discharge* (London; HMSO, 1995).

Ferris, J, '"Indulged in all Too Little"? Vansittart, Intelligence and Appeasement', In his *Intelligence and Security* (London: Routledge, 2005).

Fitzgibbon, C, *Secret Intelligence in the Twentieth Century* (London: Hart-Davis, 1976).

Folly, M, *Churchill, Whitehall and the Soviet Union, 1940–45* (London: Macmillan, 2000).

Ford, D, B*ritain's Secret War Against Japan, 1937–1945* (London: Routledge, 2006).

Fraser, C, 'Understanding American Policy Towards the Decolonisation of European Empires, 1945–64', *Diplomacy and Statecraft*, 3:1 (March 1992).

Frazier, R, 'Did Britain Start the Cold War? Bevin and the Truman Doctrine', *The Historical Journal*, 27:3 (1984).

Freedman, L, *United States Intelligence and the Soviet Strategic Threat* (London: Palgrave, 1986).

French, D, 'Spy Fever in Britain 1900–1915', *Historical Journal*, 21 (1978).

Gilbert, M, *Winston S. Churchill, Vol. V, Companion Part 3, Documents: The Coming of War, 1936–1939* (London: Heinemann, 1982).

Gilbert, M, *Continue to Pester, Nag and Bite: Churchill's War Leadership* (London: Pimlico, 2004).

Goldstein, E, 'Neville Chamberlain, The British Official Mind and the Munich Crisis' In Lukes, I, & Goldstein, E, (eds.), *The Munich Crisis, 1938: Prelude to World War II* (London: Frank Cass, 1999).

Goodman, M S, 'Grandfather of the Hydrogen Bomb? Klaus Fuchs and Anglo-American Intelligence', *Historical Studies in the Physical and Biological Sciences* 34:1 (2004).

Goodman, M S, *Spying on the Nuclear Bear: Anglo-American Intelligence and the Soviet Bomb* (Stanford: Stanford University Press, 2008).

Goodman, M S, 'A Cold War Cover Up: British Intelligence, Whitehall and the Buster Crabb Affair', *International History Review*, XXX:4 (December 2008).

Goodman, M S, 'British Intelligence and the British Broadcasting Corporation: A Snapshot of a Happy Marriage'. In Dover, R, & Goodman, M S, (eds.), *Spinning Intelligence: Why Intelligence Needs the Media, Why the Media Needs Intelligence* (London: Hurst, 2009).

Gorst, A & Lucas, W S, 'The Other Collusion: Operation Straggle and Anglo-American Intervention in Syria, 1955–56', *Intelligence and National Security*, 4:3 (July 1989),

Greenwood, S, 'Frank Roberts and the 'Other' Long Telegram: The View from the British Embassy in Moscow, March 1946', *The Journal of Contemporary History*,25 (1990).

Harris, S, *Factories of Death: Japanese Biological Warfare, 1932–1945, and the American Cover-Up* (London: Routledge, 1995).

Hartcup, G, *The Effect of Science on the Second World War* (London: Macmillan, 2003).

Hennessy, P, *Secret State: Whitehall and the Cold War* (London: Penguin, 2003).

Herman, M, 'The Post-War Organization of Intelligence: The January 1945 Report to the Joint Intelligence Committee on "The Intelligence Machine"', In Dover, R, &

Goodman, M S, (eds.), *Learning from the Secret Past: Cases in British Intelligence History* (Washington: Georgetown University Press, 2011).

Hinsley, F H, et al, *British Intelligence in the Second World War: Five Volumes* (London, 1979–91).

Howard, M, *Grand Strategy: History of the Second World War: Volume IV, August 1942-September 1943* (London: HMSO, 1972).

Howard, M, *British Intelligence in the Second World War: Volume 5 – Strategic Deception* (London: HMSO, 1990).

Howarth, P, *Intelligence Chief Extraordinary: The Life of the Ninth Duke of Portland* (London: The Bodley Head, 1986).

Hughes, P, 'Division and Discord: British Policy, Indochina, and the Origins of the Vietnam War, 1954–56', *The Journal of Imperial and Commonwealth History*, 28:3 (2000).

Hunt, L, *Secret Agenda: The United States Government, Nazi Scientists, and Project Paperclip, 1945–1990* (London: St Martin's Press, 1991)

Jackson, P, 'French Military Intelligence and Czechoslovakia, 1938', *Diplomacy and Statecraft*, 5:1 (March 1994).

Jackson, P, & Maiolo, J A, 'Strategic Intelligence, Counterintelligence and Alliance Diplomacy in Anglo-French Relations before the Second World War', *Militärgeschichtliche Zeitschrift*, 65:2 (2006).

James, R R, *Anthony Eden* (London: Weidenfeld & Nicolson, 1986).

Jeffery, K, *MI6: The History of the Secret Intelligence Service, 1909–1949* (London: Bloomsbury, 2010).

Jones, M, *Britain, the United States and the Mediterranean War, 1942–44* (London: Macmillan, 1996).

Jones, R V, *Most Secret War: British Scientific Intelligence, 1939–1945* (London: Hamish Hamilton, 1978).

Kennedy, G, 'The Royal Navy, Intelligence and the Spanish Civil War: Lessons in Air Power, 1936–39', *Intelligence and National Security*, 20:2 (June 2005).

Kyle, K, *Suez: Britain's End of Empire in the Middle East* (London: IB Tauris, 2003).

Leslau, O, 'Israeli Intelligence and the Czech-Egyptian Arms Deal', *Intelligence and National Security*, 27:3 (June 2012).

Lewin, R, *ULTRA Goes to War* (London: Grafton Books, 1978).

Lewis, J, *Changing Direction: British Military Planning for Post-War Strategic Defence, 1952–1947* (London: Frank Cass, 2003).

Louis, Wm Roger, *British Empire in the Middle East, 1941–1951: Arab Nationalism, The United States and Post-War Imperialism* (Oxford: Oxford University Press, 1984).

Louis, Wm Roger, 'Musaddiq and the Dilemmas of British Imperialism' In Bill, J A, and Louis, Wm Roger, (eds.), *Musaddiq, Iranian Nationalism and Oil* (London: IB Tauris & Co, 1988).

Louis, Wm Roger, *Ends of British Imperialism: The Scramble for Empire, Suez and Decolonisation* (London: IB Tauris, 2007).

Lucas, W S, *Divided We Stand: Britain, the US and the Suez Crisis* (London: Hodder & Stoughton, 1991).

Lucas, W S, 'The Missing Link? Patrick Dean, Chairman of the Joint Intelligence Committee' In Kelly, S, & Gorst, A, (eds.), *Whitehall and the Suez Crisis* (London: Frank Cass, 2000).

Macklin, G D, 'Major Hugh Pollard, MI6, and the Spanish Civil War', *The Historical Journal*, 49:1 (2006).

Madeira, V, '"No Wishful Thinking Allowed": Secret Service Committee and Intelligence Reform in Great Britain, 1919–1923', *Intelligence and National Security*, 18:1 (Spring 2003).

Maiolo, J A, *The Royal Navy and Nazi Germany, 1933–39: A Study in Appeasement and the Origins of the Second World War* (London: Palgrave, 1998).

Marsh, S, 'The United States, Iran and Operation "Ajax": Inverting Interpretative Orthodoxy', *Middle Eastern Studies*, 39:3 (July 2003).

McKercher, B J C, 'The Foreign Office, 1930–39: Strategy, Permanent Interests and National Security', *Contemporary British History*, 18:3 (Autumn 2004).

McLachlan, D, *Room 39, Wherein Took Place the Exciting Story of British Naval Intelligence During World War II* (New York: Atheneum, 1969).

McMurdo, T L, 'The United States, Britain, and the Hidden Justification of Operation TRAJAX', *CIA Studies in Intelligence*, 56:2 (June 2012).

Melman, Y, & Raviv, D, 'The Journalist's Connections: How Israel Got Russia's Biggest Pre-Glasnost Secret', *International Journal of Intelligence and Counterintelligence*, 4:2 (1990).

Merrick, R, 'The Russia Committee of the British Foreign Office and the Cold War, 1946–47', *Journal of Contemporary History*, 20 (1985).

Middlebrook, M, *The Peenemunde Raid: The Night of 17–18 August 1943* (London: Cassell, 2000).

Miller, R, 'Britain and the Rhineland Crisis, 7 March 1936: Retreat from Responsibility or Accepting the Inevitable?', *Australian Journal of Politics and History*, 33:1 (1987).

Millman, B, *The Ill-Made Alliance: Anglo-Turkish Relations, 1934–40* (Montreal: McGill-Queens University Press, 1999).

Moneypenny, W F, *The Life of Benjamin Disraeli, Earl of Beaconsfield* (London: John Murray, 1920).

Montague, L L, 'The Origins of National Intelligence Estimating', *CIA Studies in Intelligence*, 16:2 (Spring 1972).

Murray, W, 'The Luftwaffe before the Second World War: A Mission, A Strategy?', *The Journal of Strategic Studies*, 4:3 (September 1981).

Myers, D P, 'Publication and Declassification of Records', *The American Journal of International Law*, 56:1 (1962).

Neilson, K, 'The Defence Requirements Sub-Committee, British Strategic Foreign Policy, Neville Chamberlain and the Path to Appeasement', *English Historical Review*, 477 (June 2003).

Neville, P, 'Rival Foreign Office Perceptions of Germany, 1936–9', *Diplomacy and Statecraft*, 13:3 (September 2002).

Norris, R S, & Arkin, W M, 'NRDC Nuclear Notebook: Global Nuclear Stockpiles, 1945–2000', *The Bulletin of the Atomic Scientists*, 56:2 (March/April 2000).

Oleynikov, P V, 'German Scientists in the Soviet Atomic Project', *The Nonproliferation Review*, (Summer 2000).

Ovendale, R, 'Britain, the United States and the Cold War in South-East Asia, 1949–1950', *International Affairs*, 58:3 (Summer 1982).

Ovendale, R, 'Britain, the United States, and the Recognition of Communist China', *The Historical Journal*, 26:1 (1983).

Ovendale, R, 'Egypt and the Suez Base Agreement' In Young, J W, (ed.), *The Foreign Policy of Churchill's Peacetime Administration, 1951–1955* (Leicester: University of Leicester Press, 1988).

Pocock, C, 'Operation 'Robin' and the British Overflight of Kapustin Yar: A Historiographical Note', *Intelligence and National Security*, 17:4 (Winter 2002).

Podvig, P, (ed.), *Russian Strategic Nuclear Forces* (London: MIT Press, 2001).

Prados, J, *The Soviet Estimate: US Intelligence Analysis and Soviet Strategic Forces* (Princeton: Princeton University Press, 1989).

Puri, S, 'The Role of Intelligence in Deciding the Battle of Britain', *Intelligence and National Security*, 21:3 (June 2006).

Rahman, H, 'British Post-Second World War Military Planning for the Middle East', *Journal of Strategic Studies*, 5:4 (1982).

Reynolds, D, *The Creation of the Anglo-American Alliance, 1937–41: A Study in Competitive Cooperation* (London: Europa Publications, 1981).

Riste, O, 'Intelligence and the 'Mindset': The German Invasion of Norway in 1940', *Intelligence and National Security*, 22:4 (August 2007).

Roskill, S, *Hankey: Man of Secrets: 3 Volumes* (London: Collins, 1970).

Ross, G, 'Foreign Office Attitudes to the Soviet Union 1941–45', *Journal of Contemporary History*, 16 (1981).

Ruane, K, 'Anthony Eden, British Diplomacy and the Origins of the Geneva Conference of 1954', *The Historical Journal*, 37:1 (March 1994).

Ruane, K, 'Refusing to Pay the Price: British Foreign Policy and the Pursuit of Victory in Vietnam, 1952–4', *English Historical Review*, CX: 435 (February 1995).

Seaman, M, '"A New Instrument of War" The Origins of the Special Operations Executive' In Seaman, M, (ed.), *Special Operations Executive: A New Instrument of War* (London: Routledge, 2005).

Sims, J C, 'The BRUSA Agreement of May 17, 1943', *Cryptologia*, 21:1 (1997).

Sissons, D C S, 'More on Pearl Harbor', *Intelligence and National Security*, 9:2 (1994).

Smart, N, 'Four Days in May: The Norway Debate and the Downfall of Neville Chamberlain', *Parliamentary History*, 17:2 (1998).

Smith, B F, *The ULTRA-Magic Deals and the Most Secret Special Relationship, 1940–1946* (Shrewsbury: Airlife, 1993).

Smith, R, 'A Climate of Opinion: British Officials and the Development of British Soviet Policy, 1945–7', *International Affairs*, 64:4 (Autumn 1988).

Spencer, C O, 'Intelligence Analysis Under Pressure of Rapid Change: The Canadian Challenge', *The Journal of Conflict Studies*, XVI: 1 (Spring 1996).

Springhall, J, '"Kicking Out the Vietminh": How Britain Allowed France to Reoccupy South Indochina, 1945–46', *Journal of Contemporary History*, 40:1 (2005).

Stafford, D, *Churchill and Secret Service* (London: Abacus, 1997).

Stocker, J, *Britain and Ballistic Missile Defence, 1942–2002* (London: Frank Cass, 2004).

Stone, G, 'Britain, Non-Intervention and the Spanish Civil War', *European Studies Review*, 9 (1979).

Strong, K, *Men of Intelligence: A Study of the Roles and Decisions of Chiefs of Intelligence from World War I to the Present Day* (London: Cassell, 1970).

Thomas, E, 'The Evolution of the JIC System Up to and During World War II' In Andrew, C, & Noakes, J, (eds.), *Intelligence and International Relations, 1900–1945* (Exeter: University of Exeter, 1987).

Thomas, M, *Britain, France and Appeasement: Anglo-French Relations in the Popular Front Era* (New York: Berg, 1996).

Thomas, M, 'Processing Decolonization: British Strategic Analysis of Conflict in Vietnam and Indonesia, 1945–1950' In Goscha, C E, & Ostermann, C F, (eds.), *Connecting Histories: Decolonization and the Cold War in Southeast Asia, 1945–1962* (Stanford: Stanford University Press, 2009).

Till, G, *Air Power and the Royal Navy, 1914–1945: A Historical Survey* (London: Jane's, 1979).

Ulunian, A A, 'Soviet Cold War Perceptions of Turkey and Greece, 1945–58', *Cold War History*, 3:2 (2003).

Vaisse, M, 'France and the Suez Crisis'. In Louis, Wm Roger, and Owen, R, (eds.), *Suez 1956: The Crisis and its Consequences* (Oxford: Clarendon Press, 1989).

Valero, L A, 'The American Joint Intelligence Committee and Estimates of the Soviet Union, 1945–1947', *CIA Studies in Intelligence,* (Summer 2000).

Wark, W K, *The Ultimate Enemy: British Intelligence and Nazi Germany, 1933–1939* (Oxford: Oxford University Press, 1986).

Wark, W K, 'British Intelligence and Small Wars in the 1930s', *Intelligence and National Security,* 2:4 (1987).

Wark, W K, 'The Evolution of Military Intelligence in Canada', *Armed Forces and Society,* 16:1 (Fall 1989).

Warner, G, 'The Settlement of the Indochina War' In Young, J W, (ed.), *The Foreign Policy of Churchill's Peacetime Administration, 1951–1955* (Leicester: Leicester University Press, 1988).

Watt, D C, 'Foreign Affairs, the Public Interest and the Right to Know', *Political Quarterly,* 34 (1963).

Watt, D C, 'British Intelligence and the Coming of the Second World War in Europe' In May, E R, (ed.), *Knowing One's Enemies: Intelligence Assessment Before the Two World Wars* (Princeton: Princeton University Press, 1986).

Watt, D C, 'An Intelligence Surprise: The Failure of the Foreign Office to Anticipate the Nazi-Soviet Pact', *Intelligence and National Security,* 4:3 (1989).

Weathersby, K, 'Soviet Aims in Korea and the Origins of the Korean War, 1945–1950: New Evidence from Russian Archives', *Cold War International History Project, Working Paper No. 8* (1993).

Wells, Jnr, S F, 'Sounding the Tocsin: NSC 68 and the Soviet Threat', *International Security,* 4:2 (1979).

West, N (ed), *British Security Coordination: The Secret History of British Intelligence in the Americas, 1940–1945* (London: Fromm International, 1999).

Whaley, B, *Codeword Barbarossa* (Cambridge, MA: MIT Press, 1973).

Woodward, G, 'Enigmatic Variations: The Development of National Intelligence Assessment in Australia', *Intelligence and National Security,* 16: 1 (2001).

Young, J W, *Britain, France and the Unity of Europe, 1945–51* (Leicester: Leicester University Press, 1984).

Young, R, 'Spokesmen for Economic Warfare: The Industrial Intelligence Centre in the 1930s', *European Studies Review,* 6 (October 1976).

Index